INTRODUCTION TO SOCIAL WORK AND SOCIAL WELFARE

CRITICAL THINKING PERSPECTIVES

SECOND EDITION

Karen K. Kirst-Ashman
University of Wisconsin–Whitewater

THOMSON

BROOKS/COLE

Australia • Brazil • Canada • Mexico • Singapore • Spain
United Kingdom • United States

THOMSON

BROOKS/COLE

Introduction to Social Work and Social Welfare:
Critical Thinking Perspectives, **Second Edition**
Karen K. Kirst-Ashman

Executive Editor: Lisa Gebo

Assistant Editor: Alma Dea Michelena

Editorial Assistant: Sheila Walsh

Executive Marketing Manager: Caroline Concilla

Marketing Assistant: Rebecca Weisman

Senior Marketing Communications Manager: Tami Strang

Project Manager, Editorial Production: Christine Sosa

Creative Director: Rob Hugel

Art Director: Vernon Boes

Print Buyer: Barbara Britton

Permissions Editor: Kiely Sisk

Production Service: Ben Kolstad, International Typesetting and Composition

Text Designer: Roy Neuhaus

Photo Researcher: Terri Wright

Copy Editor: Meg McDonald

Cover Designer: Denise Davidson

Cover Image: © Left Lane Productions/CORBIS

Cover Printer: Coral Graphic Services, Inc.

Compositor: International Typesetting and Composition

Printer: R.R. Donnelley/Crawfordsville

ExamView® and ExamView Pro® are registered trademarks of FSCreations, Inc. Windows is a registered trademark of the Microsoft Corporation used herein under license. Macintosh and Power Macintosh are registered trademarks of Apple Computer, Inc. Used herein under license.

Library of Congress Control Number: 2005932706

Student Edition: ISBN 0-495-00244-5

Thomson Higher Education
10 Davis Drive
Belmont, CA 94002-3098
USA

For more information about our products, contact us at:
Thomson Learning Academic Resource Center
1-800-423-0563

For permission to use material from this text or product, submit a request online at **http://www.thomsonrights.com**. Any additional questions about permissions can be submitted by e-mail to **thomsonrights@thomson.com**.

To
Andrea Lee Drollinger,
Lucas James Spielman,
Daniel Mark Kirst,
Brittany Michelle Spielman,
Laura Anne Kirst,
Rebecca Lynn Kirst, and
Margaret Patricia Kirst

KAREN K. KIRST-ASHMAN is a full professor and former chairperson in the Social Work Department at the University of Wisconsin–Whitewater. She earned her BSW degree in 1972 and MSSW in 1973 at the University of Wisconsin–Madison, and her Ph.D. in Social Work at the University of Illinois at Urbana–Champaign. She is the author of five social work textbooks and numerous publications, articles, and reviews social work and women's issues, and has served as a consulting editor for many social work journals. She has been a board member of CSWE from 1998 through 2001, and has served as a member of several CSWE accreditation site teams. She is also certified as a License Clinical Social Worker in the State of Wisconsin.

BRIEF CONTENTS

CONTENTS

PART ☖ ONE

THE PROFESSION OF SOCIAL WORK 1

PART 🐢 TWO

SOCIAL WORK PRACTICE   101

PART 🐢 THREE

SOCIAL WELFARE POLICY   157

PART 🐢 FOUR

CLIENT POPULATIONS AND CONTEXTS   267

Chapter 11   SOCIAL WORK AND SERVICES FOR PEOPLE
             WITH DISABILITIES   343

PREFACE

Given limited time and massive volumes of content, what vital information should be conveyed to students in an introductory course about social welfare and social work? What student learning outcomes should instructors strive to attain? This text focuses on the most significant elements of social work. Content complies with the new Council on Social Work Education's Educational Policy and Accreditation Standards (EPAS). The text's style is intended to be clear, readable, interesting, and engaging. The goal is to enhance students' ability to grasp the essence and spirit of generalist social work and the issues in social welfare that social workers address every day. Critical thinking perspectives are emphasized throughout by encouraging identification of values and evaluation of serious issues.

Themes integrated throughout the text include these:

- The pursuit of social and economic justice for populations-at-risk.
- Client empowerment.
- Dimensions of human diversity ("related to clients' age, class, color, culture, disability, ethnicity, family structure, gender, marital status, national origin, race, religion, sex, and sexual orientation")[1].
- The significance of professional values and ethics.
- A generalist approach interrelating micro, mezzo, and macro levels of social work practice.
- Numerous case examples dramatizing various aspects of social work.
- Various global and international perspectives.

A key word describing this text is *integration:* These themes are infused throughout the book instead of being isolated in independent chapters. For example, values, ethics, aspects of diversity, and client empowerment are defined early on and then addressed throughout the text in various contexts including fields of practice. Boxed features appear regularly to emphasize important concepts and cases, to spark students' interest, and to stimulate critical thinking.

Organization

The book is organized into four major parts: (1) the profession, (2) social work practice, (3) social welfare policy, and (4) client populations and contexts. A fifth section, the epilogue, focuses on personal values and consideration of a social work career. The intent is to give students a broad look at what social work is all about. Social welfare policy is stressed as the foundation of social welfare programs and social work practice.

[1]These are the categories reflecting diversity as stated by the Educational Policy and Accreditation Standards passed by the Council on Social Work Education board of directors in June 2001 (Educational Policy I.C and III.A.3).

Students are encouraged to explore issues based on theoretical orientations to social welfare policy development and the resulting program implementation.

Students are provided with thought-provoking information about social welfare and social work within a broad range of circumstances and fields of practice. Settings range from those focusing on child maltreatment, to health care, to work with the elderly, to corrections. Social issues are raised in a way to encourage new insights and examination of personal values. This book stresses *what* social workers do, not *how* they do it. Abundant case examples give insights into who clients are and what issues they face in the macro social environment.

Concepts incorporated in the new Council on Social Work Education Educational Policy and Accreditation Standards (EPAS) including newly articulated aspects of diversity—national origin, family structure, marital status, and color—are discussed. Macro aspects of generalist practice, in addition to micro and mezzo aspects, are frequently highlighted.

This book gives students contemplating a social work major a solid orientation to the profession. The text should help students determine whether social work is really the field for them. For nonmajors, the text is designed to provide a sound introduction to social welfare, social work, available services, social welfare policy development and implementation, and social workers' involvement in the helping process. The emphasis is on those issues and fields of practice in which social workers are most likely to be employed. For example, significant attention is given to child and family services, mental health, and health care.

Part I, "The Profession of Social Work," includes three chapters. Chapter 1 defines social welfare and social work, discusses political values and views about social welfare, reviews content areas in the social work curriculum, introduces the various fields of practice, and reviews the social work career continuum. Critical thinking is defined and its importance throughout the text stressed. Chapter 2 focuses on the importance of social work values and ethics, thus providing a framework for remaining chapters. This chapter introduces the concept of ethical dilemmas, summarizes the NASW Code of Ethics and gives examples of practice applications, and helps students explore personal values.

Chapter 3 defines and discusses various dimensions of human diversity, empowerment, and cultural competence, paving the way for integration of this content throughout the book.

Part II, "Social Work Practice," includes two chapters that focus on what social workers *do*. Chapter 4 defines generalist social work practice, introduces the wide range of social work roles, and describes the planned-change process. Emphases include the importance of client empowerment, appreciation of cultural differences, and intervention with macro systems. Chapter 5 focuses on the settings in which social workers practice. It describes what micro, mezzo, and macro practice involve in terms of social workers' functions and practice settings. Finally, it explores social work licensure, employment, and salaries.

Part III, "Social Welfare Policy," includes three chapters. Chapter 6 explains the historical development of social welfare and social work, thereby providing a context for the next chapter, which focuses on social welfare policy and policy practice. Chapter 7 defines policy, discusses its significance, and describes how it is developed and structured. The significance of social welfare policy as the basis upon which social programs are developed is stressed. Chapter 8 discusses the infrastructure of policies and programs designed to combat poverty and provide financial assistance to those in need. It also describes social insurance (including the new Medicare Prescription Drug Program) and public assistance programs, and explores students' values about various aspects of social welfare.

Part IV, "Client Populations and Contexts," includes seven chapters that focus on specific social work settings. Chapter 9 introduces service provision for children and families. It describes supportive services for children and families, including those involving child maltreatment, intensive family preservation, and child day care. It stresses the importance of addressing macro issues. This chapter also reviews substitute services for children and families including kinship care, foster family care, residential settings, and adoption. Alcohol and other substance abuse and the effects of alcoholism on families are addressed.

Chapter 10 discusses social work with the elderly. Issues include common problems facing elderly people, critical thinking about Social Security, the global context for aging, contexts of social work practice with the elderly, and empowerment for diverse populations of elderly people.

Chapter 11 explores social work with people who have disabilities. Ethical implications for social work practice are discussed. Empowerment through policy practice and advocacy, legislative advocacy, and community support are stressed.

Chapter 12 explains social work roles in healthcare, healthcare problems in the macro environment, issues involving healthcare policy, managed care, and international perspectives on the global crisis of AIDS. Sensitivity to populations-at-risk and macro issues in practice are emphasized.

Chapter 13 addresses social work and mental health. Employment settings in mental health for social workers are identified, social work functions explained, and clients' conditions described. Managed care in mental health is critiqued, and cultural competence in the field is discussed.

Chapter 14 focuses on social work with youths and in the schools. Positive social programming in macro practice, violence in the schools, and teenage sexual activity and pregnancy are examined. Social work roles with respect to each are discussed.

Chapter 15 explores social work and corrections. Questions requiring critical thinking are posed regarding the complexity of the crime rate, the issue of punishment versus empowerment, and health care for prisoners. Practice settings and gang membership are also discussed.

The epilogue, "Your Values and Your Future: Applying Critical Thinking Skills," serves as a capstone for the book. Students are urged to come to conclusions about various issues in social welfare policy and programming. Finally, they are encouraged to evaluate their personal characteristics and values and their potential for a career in social work, responding to many questions initiated in Chapter 1.

New additions to the book include the following:

- Updated references throughout

Chapter 1

- The social work career continuum.
- Deciding what career to pursue.

Chapter 2

- Conflicts of interest and dual relationships.

Chapter 3

- Expanded content on Hispanic, First Nations, African American, and Asian American people, including spirituality.
- Islam and Muslims, a population-at-risk of prejudice and discrimination.
- The concept of resilience as strength.

Chapter 4

- Greater emphasis on empowerment when defining generalist practice.
- Updated and expanded content on nonverbal and verbal behavior from a multicultural perspective.

Chapter 5

- Rural social work and urban social work.
- Expanded content on social work with families and on the importance of social networks.
- Case example of a multipronged treatment group for adolescents illustrating the complex nature of groups.
- Extensive, updated information on social work licensure, employment, and salaries.

Chapter 6

- Enhanced content on diversity, including discussion of the Cherokee Trail of Tears, the Treaty of Guadalupe Hidalgo, Chinese and Japanese immigration, and the history of Puerto Rico.
- Profiles of Jane Addams and Mary Richmond.
- Expanded content on the Clinton era and the conservatism of George W. Bush.

Chapter 7

- Social workers in politics.

Chapter 8

- The Medicare Modernization Act of 2003.
- Critical thinking about the Medicare Prescription Drug program.
- Significant updates on Temporary Assistance to Needy Families (TANF).
- Expanded content on Supplemental Security Income, Medicaid, food stamps, and housing assistance.

Chapter 9

- Updated content on day care.
- New content on alcohol and other substance abuse, the effects of alcoholism on families, and treatment approaches.

Chapter 10

• Critical thinking about saving Social Security.

Chapter 11

• Updated content on nursing homes, autism (including a definition of Asperger's syndrome), and federal government employment of people having severe disabilities.

Chapter 12

• Updated content on HIV and AIDS.

Chapter 13

• New content on personality disorders.
• Suggestions for learning more about a career in mental health.

Chapter 14

• Social workers' role in the prevention of school violence.

Chapter 15

• Updated and new content on crime
• Critical thinking about health care costs for prisoners.

 # Ancillaries

Additional resources are available, including a *Student Manual* filled with classroom exercises and assignments. These are designed to coincide directly with text content and can be used to help students integrate reading material. The *Student Manual* also contains detailed outlines of each chapter. The intent is to help students organize the material and take notes if they so choose. An *Instructor's Manual* includes a copy of the *Student Manual* in addition to numerous multiple-choice, true/false and essay test questions for each chapter.

A free, four-month subscription to InfoTrac® College Edition, an extensive online library, can be included with each book. (Please make sure to order the correct ISBN that includes this component.) This resource features hundreds of top journals and other popular information sources. At the corresponding Book Companion Website at **www.socialwork.wadsworth.com/kirstashman_intro2e,** relevant articles in InfoTrac InfoMarks® have been chosen so that students may explore primary topics in greater depth.

Also at the Book Companion Website, relevant websites are listed and hyperlinked for further exploration. Tutorial quizzes for students are also available at the site, as are Microsoft® PowerPoint® slides for instructors.

My sincere hope is that students will find this text interesting and informative, and that instructors will find it an easy one from which to teach. The intent is to provide a sound foundation on which to build professional expertise and commitment.

Acknowledgments

This book is possible due to the dedication and hard work of many people. I express my sincere appreciation to Lisa Gebo, executive editor, whose brilliant suggestions and genius, boundless enthusiasm, and consistently strong support made this book possible. Also playing a key role was Sheila Walsh, editorial assistant, whose conscientious work and resourceful assistance greatly facilitated the writing process. Many thanks go to Caroline Concilla, marketing manager, who provided abundant imaginative ideas for marketing the book, and marketing assistant Rebecca Weisman. Earnest thanks also to Tami Strang, senior marketing communications manager, and Barbara Britton, print buyer. Heartfelt appreciation is extended to Vicki Vogel, who creatively developed all the ancillary materials and provided me with help and constructive feedback whenever I requested it (which was often). Thanks also to Karen Thomson who assisted her. Much appreciation goes to Alma Dea Michelena, assistant editor, and Dennis Cogswell, Radford University, who worked diligently to produce an innovative WebTutor product. Many thanks are extended to Ben Kolstad, who did an amazing job of coordinating the day-to-day editing and production process. Much gratitude goes to Christine Sosa, production editor, who oversaw the production process and made certain it progressed smoothly and efficiently. Sincere appreciation is extended to Vernon Boes, creative director; Roy Neuhaus, designer of the book's interior; and Denise Davidson, cover designer, whose creative brilliance resulted in a vivid and exceptionally attractive product. Thanks also to Kiely Sisk, permissions editor, for her conscientious work. I also want to thank the following reviewers of this book for their help and input: Sally Alonzo Bell, Azusa Pacific University; Nancy Chavkin, Southwest Texas State University; Sharon Eisen, Mott Community College; Robert Jackson, Colorado State University; Gerald Landsberg, New York University; Joan M. Lewis, Alvernia College; Donna McIntosh, Siena College; Jean Nuernberger, Central Missouri State University; Gerri Outlaw, Governors State University; Paul G. Shane, Rutgers University; and Kim Womack, Jacksonville State University. Much appreciation is extended to Tim Reutebuch, University of Wisconsin–Whitewater, who, at my request, provided useful feedback concerning Chapters 6 and 7.

My most sincere thanks go to Gary A. Kirst, MSW, who read the draft cover to cover and provided me with excellent feedback. Genuine thanks also go to Ruth Kirst, who provided me with ongoing support and encouragement. I also want to thank Gary S. Kirst for his input concerning the Turkana Tribe in Northern Kenya. Thankful recognition is also extended to my delightful nieces and nephews who bring so much joy and inspiration to my life. Finally, I express my sincere gratitude and appreciation to Nick Ashman, who provided incredible support and encouragement throughout the 15-year process since this book's inception.

PART ☙ ONE

THE PROFESSION
OF SOCIAL WORK

What is social work? How does it differ from sociology, psychology, or other types of counseling? What types of people choose it as a career? This book answers these and many other questions you might have about what social workers do, what rules and policies they must follow, and whom they serve.
   This book has four parts:

1. The Profession of Social Work
2. Social Work Practice
3. Social Welfare Policy
4. Client Populations and Contexts

   Part 1 contains three chapters that emphasize key aspects of social work and provide a general introduction to the field. Chapter 1 defines social work and social welfare and discusses various theoretical perspectives you can use to think about how to help people. It introduces you to the concept of critical thinking, which will be emphasized throughout the book. It also describes the content areas in the social work curriculum.
   Chapter 2 focuses on social work values and ethics. It summarizes social work's ethical principles and practitioners' ethical responsibilities to clients. It also challenges you to examine your own personal values and how they relate to social work values. Finally, it examines a range of ethical dilemmas potentially facing social workers.
   Chapter 3 explores human diversity and the ways in which people might be empowered to enhance their well-being and reach their full potential. It stresses

social work's quest for social and economic justice, especially for populations-at-risk of deprivation and oppression. Populations-at-risk include groups characterized by diverse aspects of race, ethnicity, culture, national origin, class, gender, sexual orientation, family structure, marital status, age, disability, and religion.

I hope you will enjoy this book and gain a much better understanding of social work and social welfare. Let's begin.

CHAPTER ONE

INTRODUCTION TO SOCIAL WORK AND SOCIAL WELFARE

© JLP/Sylvia Torres/CORBIS

Case A: The couple is ecstatic. In their early 30s, they have been struggling with infertility for almost a decade and have been languishing on a waiting list to adopt a baby for almost five years. The moment has finally almost come: They will soon meet their new baby, Juliette. Alani, their social worker in the adoptions unit at a family services agency, is assisting them in completing the paperwork and helping them launch their new family life.

Case B: Cassius, a social worker at a community mental health center, is about to start the weekly support group session. His seven clients all are dealing with spouses who have Lou Gehrig's disease, which is characterized by deterioration of neurons in the brain stem and spinal cord. It involves loss of muscle function, paralysis, and finally death. The purpose of the group is to provide mutual emotional support and share information about coping with the disease. Cassius facilitates the group to keep things moving along and, when necessary, gives information about the disease. He notices that Erica, one of his clients, seems to be struggling to hold back a flood of tears. He knows that her husband, Tom, is deteriorating rapidly, so she must have had a rough week. This may be a difficult session.

Case C: Lolita is exhilarated. Several hundred people have shown up for and are eagerly participating in this "Take Back the Night" march against sexual assault. Lolita, a social worker at a rape crisis center, was one of the primary organizers of the event. The march's intent is to raise people's consciousness about this serious issue, promote education about sexual assault, and increase funding for crisis centers.

These vignettes portray brief moments in the actual lives of social workers. Some moments may be tremendously difficult, and others enormously satisfying.

When you think of social work, what comes to mind? Helping people? Being on welfare? Facing bureaucratic red tape? Solving problems? Saving children? What do social workers actually do?

I once visited a quaint little crafts shop in Bar Harbor, Maine. It had little shadow boxes, about five inches square, filled with tacks. On these tacks, someone had painted little symbols to reflect the tools, tasks, and people involved in various professions. For example, one shadow box reflecting dentistry had tacks painted with tiny teeth, big toothy smiles, and toothbrushes (which is probably no surprise). I managed to find a box for social work. What do you think was painted on those tacks?

There were tiny images of the following: a Kleenex® box, a pencil, a compact car, a smiling face, a watch, and a heart. What do you think each of these are supposed to mean?

Here are some ideas. The *Kleenex box* reflects how social workers help people deal with tough, and frequently very sad, issues. Sometimes clients are hurting badly, and sometimes they cry. The *pencil* signifies record keeping and paperwork, a mainstay of what social workers do. It probably should have been a computer, but the artist most likely couldn't fit one on that little tack. The *compact car* symbolizes travel because social workers often must visit clients' homes and other agencies. The *smiling face* signifies how social workers aim to help people solve their problems, to seek social justice on their behalf, and to make their lives a little bit better. (*Social justice* involves the concept that all citizens should be treated equally and have equal access to resources.) The *watch* reflects scheduling—there's always a lot to do and limited time in which to do it. Finally, the *heart* symbolizes caring about the welfare of others: That's the core of what the social work profession is all about.

This chapter will

- Define social work and social welfare.
- Explain critical thinking and provide a framework for examining a wide range of concepts and issues.
- Discuss residual, institutional, and developmental perspectives on social welfare.
- Explain the conservative–liberal continuum with respect to viewing the social welfare system.
- Examine your personal attitudes about some social welfare issues.
- Explore the process of choosing a career.
- Address how social work builds on other disciplines.
- Discuss the uniqueness of social work.
- Identify some basic concepts in systems theories and the ecological perspective that are important for understanding social work.
- Identify the main content areas in the social work curriculum.
- Explain social work's fields of practice.

 ## What Is Social Work?

The National Association of Social Work (NASW) defines *social work* as follows:

> Social work is the professional activity of helping individuals, groups, or communities enhance or restore their capacity for social functioning and creating societal conditions favorable to this goal. Social work practice consists of the professional application of social work values, principles, and techniques to one or more of the following ends:
>
> - Helping people obtain tangible services (e.g., those involving provision of food, housing, or income).
> - Providing counseling and psychotherapy with individuals, families, and groups.
> - Helping communities or groups provide or improve social and health services.
> - Participating in relevant legislative processes. (NASW, 1973, pp. 4–5)

What does this really mean? Imagine the vast range of human problems and issues. Because social workers can be in positions to help people deal with almost anything, it is difficult to define the field adequately in a few words. Highlighted here are some of the important concepts inherent in the definition just cited. Because of its breadth, the foundation of social work practice is referred to as *generalist practice,* described more thoroughly in Chapter 4.

Five themes permeate social work practice in virtually any setting (e.g., child welfare agencies, nursing homes, schools, or corrections facilities). First, social work concerns helping individuals, groups, or communities. Social workers provide counseling when necessary to help clients address problems. In addition to counseling an individual or family, much social work involves collaborating with organizations and communities to improve social and health services. Second, social work entails a solid foundation of values and principles that guide what practitioners should and should not do. Third, a firm basis of techniques and skills provides directions for *how* social workers should provide treatment and accomplish goals. Fourth, social workers help people get the services they need by linking them to available resources. If the right resources are not available, social workers may advocate for service development on their clients' behalf. Fifth, social workers participate in legislative processes to promote positive social change. Such participation might include urging lawmakers to pass laws that improve social services and conditions. Social workers can also serve as expert witnesses to educate legislators about social issues and client needs, write or phone legislators to share socially responsible opinions, and run for elected office themselves.

NASW reports how Representative Bob Etheridge (D–N.C.) paid homage to social workers during Social Work Month (March 2001). He shared with the speaker of the U.S. House of Representatives the following remarks:

> Social workers affect our lives in so many ways. . . . Their work touches all of us as individuals and as whole communities. They are educated, highly trained, and committed professionals. They work in family service and community mental health agencies, schools, hospitals, nursing homes, and many other private and public agencies. They listen, they care. And most importantly, they help those in need. (Vallianatos, 2001, May, p. 1)

What Is Social Welfare?

What does the term *social welfare* mean? And exactly whose welfare are we talking about? Answers to these questions require critical thinking because, as a citizen and voter, your opinions are vital. You have the opportunity to help determine and shape how you and others are treated, how your own and their welfare is respected and nurtured.

A central theme of this book is encouraging you to think critically about problems, issues, and policies affecting people's lives and welfare. Highlight 1.1 defines critical thinking and provides a basic framework for analysis.

Social welfare is "a nation's system of programs, benefits, and services that help people meet those social, economic, educational, and health needs that are fundamental to the maintenance of society" (Barker, 2003, p. 408). *Social welfare,* then, is a broad concept related to the general well-being of all people in a society. Inherent in the definition are two basic dimensions: (1) what people get from society (in terms of programs, benefits, and services) and (2) how well their needs (including social, economic, educational, and health) are being met.

Reid (1995) describes social welfare as "an idea, that idea being one of a decent society that provides opportunities for work and human meaning, provides reasonable security from want and assault, promotes fairness and evaluation based on individual merit, and is economically productive and stable" (p. 2206).

How are social welfare and social work related? Simply put, *social work* serves to improve people's social and economic welfare. It does so in the many fields or settings discussed in this book, including health, mental health, and financial assistance, among many others. Populations served include the elderly, children and families, people with disabilities, and people involved with the legal system.

HIGHLIGHT 1.1

What Is Critical Thinking?

Critical thinking is (1) the careful scrutiny of what is stated as true or what appears to be true and the resulting expression of an opinion or conclusion based on that scrutiny, and (2) the creative formulation of an opinion or conclusion when presented with a question, problem, or issue. Critical thinking concentrates on "the process of reasoning" (Gibbs & Gambrill, 1999, p. 3). It stresses *how* individuals think about the truth inherent in a statement or *how* they analyze an issue to formulate their own conclusions. As Gibbs and Gambrill (1999) so aptly state, "Critical thinkers question what others take for granted" (p. 13).

Two dimensions in the definition of critical thinking are significant. First, critical thinking focuses on the questioning of beliefs, statements, assumptions, lines of reasoning, actions, and experiences. Suppose you read a "fact" in a book or hear about it from a friend or an instructor. Critical thinking focuses on *not* taking this "fact" at face value. Rather, it entails the following "Triple-A" approach to examining and evaluating its validity:

1. *Ask* questions.
2. *Assess* the established facts and issues involved.
3. *Assert* a concluding opinion.

For example, a friend and fellow student might tell you, "It's impossible to get financial aid at our school." To what extent is this statement really true? To find out, you first *ask* questions about what the statement is really saying. What does "impossible" mean? Some people must be eligible for financial aid. What are the criteria for receiving aid? What experiences has your friend had to come to such a conclusion?

Second, you *assess* the established facts and issues involved by seeking relevant information. What does the financial aid policy state? To what

extent does eligibility depend on students' and their parents' earnings? To what extent is grade point average or full-time student status involved? How many students are actually receiving aid at any time? What percentage of the student population does this number reflect?

Third, you *assert* a concluding opinion. To what extent do you agree with your friend's statement? If you find out that only two people on your campus are receiving aid, you might agree that such aid is almost impossible to get. However, if you find out that about a third of the student population is receiving aid, you might heartily conclude that your friend's statement is false.

Critical thinking can be applied to virtually any belief, statement, assumption, line of reasoning, action, or experience claimed as true. Consider the following statements of proposed "facts":

- Rich people are selfish.
- Taxes are unfair.
- A crocodile cannot stick its tongue out.
- Most lipstick contains fish scales.
- It is physically impossible for a person to lick his or her elbow.
- Over 75% of people who read this will try to lick their elbow.

These statements may seem silly (although some may also be true), but the point is that critical thinking can be applied to an infinite array of thoughts and ideas. For each of the statements, (1) what questions would you *ask*, (2) how would you *assess* the established facts and issues involved, and (3) what concluding opinion would you finally *assert*?

The second facet of the definition of critical thinking is the creative formulation of an opinion or conclusion when presented with a question, problem, or issue. Instead of being told a proposed "fact" to be scrutinized for its validity, you

(continued)

HIGHLIGHT 1.1 *(continued)*

are asked your *opinion* about an issue, assumption, or action. Examples include the following:

- Should prisoners who commit violent crimes be ineligible for parole? (In other words, should they be required to serve their full sentences?)
- Should all interstate highways have toll booths to finance them and their repairs, so that only the people who use them pay for them (instead of general tax revenues paying for highway construction and repair)?
- What is the best way to eliminate poverty in this nation?

Consider answering the last question, which could be posed as a term paper or exam topic in one of your courses. First, what questions about it would you ask? What are the reasons for poverty in a rich industrialized country? What social welfare programs are currently available to address poverty? What innovative ideas for programs might be tried? Where might funding for such programs be found? How much money would it take to eliminate poverty, and who would pay for this?

Second, what facts and issues would you seek to address and assess? You probably would first try to define poverty—what income level or lack of income makes a person or family "poor"? You then might research statistics, costs, and studies concerning the effectiveness of various programs intending to reduce poverty. You might also investigate innovative ideas. Perhaps there are proposals for programs that look promising. You might explore what various programs cost and how they are funded. Note that these suggestions only scratch the surface of how you might examine the issue.

Third, what opinion or conclusion would you assert? To what extent do you think it is possible to eliminate poverty? What kinds of resources and programs do you think it would take? What do you feel citizens and their government should do about poverty?

Gibbs and Gambrill (1999) stress that critical thinking enhances self-awareness and the ability to detect various modes of distorted thinking

(continued)

Note that social work is not the only field concerned with people's social welfare. Others include those providing health, educational, recreational, and public safety services (Johnson, 1998a). Physicians, nurses, other health care personnel, teachers, park recreational counselors, police, firefighters, and many others work to enhance people's well-being and quality of life.

Social welfare can be quite controversial on two counts. One involves individuals' responsibility to take care of themselves independently of government, which reflects the old saying "You get what you deserve." The other concerns society's responsibility to take care of all its members, especially those belonging to oppressed groups. There is constant political debate about what social services should and should not provide, and about who should receive them and who should not.

The following section explores various perspectives that structure how you might think about social welfare. Each addresses the following questions: What should be the most important focus and goals of social welfare? Who should assume responsibility for people's social welfare?

HIGHLIGHT 1.1 *(continued)*

that can trick people into assuming truth. Critical thinking can help you do the following:

1. *Identify propaganda* ("ideas, facts, or allegations spread deliberately to further one's cause or to damage an opposing cause" [Mish, 1995, p. 935]). Propaganda may be true or untrue. It often sensationalizes a point of view by blowing it out of proportion. For example, a law firm with the slogan "Our Way Is the Only and Best Way" emphasizes its own prowess while demeaning the effectiveness of other firms. Critical thinking would prompt you to assess upon what basis this law firm is making its claim of superiority.

2. *Distinguish intentionally deceptive claims.* For instance, an advertiser might boast, "This mir-acle drug has been scientifically proven to make you lose a pound a day—without exer-cising or changing your eating habits!" when, in actuality, little or no meticulous research has been done. Critical thinking would lead you to question how the drug has been scientifically proven to be effective.

3. *Focus on and choose words carefully.* Critical thinking helps you focus your attention on the meaning of each word used to convey an idea or concept. For example, consider the state-ment "Schools produce a bunch of real losers these days." What does each word really mean or imply? Which schools produce "losers"? What is a "loser"? What does "a bunch" mean? To what are "these days" compared?

4. *Be wary of emotional ploys and appeals.* They play on your emotions and urge you to concur with their intent by using as little logical thinking as possible. For instance, a sales representative on a televised marketing program might urge you to "buy this genuine fake leather jacket now and we'll send a pair of matching gloves—and a pair of matching boots. This is the only time you'll get this additional value. Aren't they lovely? But you have to act now—we have only two jackets left!" The intent here is to pressure you to make a decision quickly based on desire rather than on logical thinking about what the jacket costs and how you will make the payments.

Residual, Institutional, and Developmental Perspectives on Social Welfare

We can look at social welfare and the ways its programs are developed from three different perspectives—residual, institutional, and developmental (Dobelstein, 2003; Gilbert & Terrell, 2002; Segal & Brzuzy, 1998; Wilensky & Lebeaux, 1965). The *residual* perspective conceives of social welfare as focusing on problems and gaps. Social welfare benefits and services should be supplied only when people fail to provide adequately for themselves and problems arise. The implication is that it's people's own fault if they require outside help. Society, then, must aid them until they can once again assume responsibility for meeting their own needs. Blaming women and children for being "on welfare," for example, reflects a residual view. The focus is on their supposed failures and faults; they are viewed in a demeaning and critical manner.

The *institutional* perspective of social welfare, in contrast, views people's needs as a normal part of life. Society has a responsibility to support its members and provide needed benefits and services. It's not people's fault that they require such services, but rather an expected part of the human condition. People have a right to receive benefits and services on an ongoing basis. In many ways, this is a more humane and supportive approach to helping people. Public education available to all is an example of an institutional form of social welfare; similarly, fire and police protection are available to all (McInnis-Dittrich, 1994).

Prior to the Great Depression in the 1930s, the residual approach to social welfare dominated. Since then, however, both approaches have been apparent, depending on the program at issue. Temporary Assistance to Needy Families (TANF), described in a later chapter, is an example of a residually oriented program. Families in need receive temporary, limited financial assistance until they can get back on their feet.

The newest view on social welfare is the *developmental* perspective. This approach "seeks to identify social interventions that have a positive impact on economic development" (Midgley & Livermore, 1997, p. 574). It originated after World War II in Third World countries seeking to design social welfare programs that would also enhance their economic development. This perspective gained impetus in the United States in the 1970s because "it justifies social programs in terms of economic efficiency criteria" (Lowe, 1995; Midgley & Livermore, 1997, p. 575).

Midgley and Livermore (1997) cite three major ways that economic development can occur in a developmental context. First, "investments in [services to people such as] education, nutrition, and health care" can be evaluated so that people get the most for their money (p. 577). For example, investments in education may result in a more skilled labor force that, in turn, generates a stronger economy. Second, investment in physical facilities involving "the creation of economic and social infrastructure, such as roads, bridges, irrigation and drinking water systems, clinics, [and] schools . . . provide[s] the economic and social bases on which development efforts depend" (pp. 577–578). Workers must have a transportation system to get to work and a building in which to work to get anything done. Therefore, resources expended on developing such things are economically productive. Third, developing "programs that help needy people engage in productive employment and self-employment" is more economically viable than giving people public assistance payments over years and even decades (p. 578). It is an efficient economic investment to educate and train people in need so that they can get jobs and eventually support themselves.

The developmental perspective is relatively new and requires a more extensive grasp of social welfare issues and policies than can be described in an introductory book such as this. It involves both in-depth analysis of current social programs and the ability to creatively propose new ones. Therefore, it will not be a primary focus in this book.

What are your views about social welfare? Focus on Critical Thinking 1.1 poses some questions.

FOCUS ON CRITICAL THINKING 1.1

What Are Your Views About Social Welfare?

We have established that a consistent theme in social work is the importance of thinking critically and formulating opinions about what is right and wrong. A key question here concerns your own views about social welfare. What ensuing questions might you ask? What facts would you need to seek out and assess? What opinions and conclusions would you finally assert?

A related question concerns the extent to which your opinions reflect residual or institutional views about social welfare programs, benefits, and services. What are your opinions about the following concerns posed? (The issues are more complicated than you might think.) Does your thinking lean more toward a residual or institutional perspective?

- Should single mothers of young children be required to work, or should they be entitled to public assistance while they care for their children at home?
- Should public housing be routinely provided to homeless people at public expense?
- Should national health insurance automatically be provided to all Americans, or should they be expected to obtain health insurance through employment or by purchasing it themselves?
- Should homeless people who have mental illnesses be institutionalized, or should they be allowed to roam at will in the community?
- Should children in families suspected of child abuse be placed elsewhere, or should treatment focus on strengthening the family so that children remain in their own homes?

The Conservative–Liberal Continuum

Another way of thinking about how people should be served by social welfare programs involves the conservative–liberal continuum (Dolgoff, Feldstein, & Skolnik, 1997; Jansson, 2003; McInnis-Dittrich, 1994). In some ways, this continuum reflects concepts similar to those of the residual and institutional perspectives of social welfare program development. However, the continuum focuses more on values related to social responsibility for human welfare.

Conservatism

Conservatism is the philosophy that individuals are responsible for themselves, government should provide minimal interference in people's lives, and change is generally unnecessary.

Three concepts tend to characterize conservatives (Popple & Leighninger, 2002). First, conservatives usually oppose change and thrive on tradition. They generally feel that change results in more trouble than it's worth, so it's best to leave things the way they are. In other words, if it ain't broke, don't fix it. Second, conservatives tend to have a "basically pessimistic view of human nature"; they believe people in general are "corrupt, self-centered, lazy, and incapable of true charity" (p. 7). If they can get "welfare," they'll take it, and society is foolish for giving it to them. Third, conservatives usually conceive of people as perfectly capable of taking care of themselves. This implies that if people would work hard and take responsibility for their actions, they wouldn't need any help. People "on welfare" don't deserve such resources, but rather should be taking care of themselves. Karger and Stoesz (1998) describe the conservative approach in which "government should have a minimal role, as a safety net," providing resources only to those who really need them (p. 8).

Liberalism

Liberalism is the philosophy that government should be involved in the social, political, and economic structure so that all people's rights and privileges are protected in the name of social justice.

Three concepts tend to characterize liberals, more or less reflecting the opposite of a conservative perspective (Popple & Leighninger, 2002). First, liberals like change and tend to think there's always a better way to get things done. They "view history as progress, and they believe that continuing change will bring continuing progress" (p. 6). Second, liberals are "much more optimistic" about "human nature" (p. 7). They tend to believe that "people are born with infinite possibilities for being shaped for the good, . . . and, if not corrupted, are naturally social, curious, and loving" (p. 7). If people have enough resources to get their needs met, they will do well. Third, liberals believe that people are significantly affected by things in their environment. It's not that people lack free will, but rather that their free will is limited by environmental impediments such as "racism, poverty, and sexism, among others" (Karger & Stoesz, 1998, p. 8). Liberals believe that it's the government's job to protect people from these impediments and provide a nurturing environment in which they can thrive.

Radicalism

A more extreme approach is *radicalism,* the philosophy that the social and political system as it stands is not structurally capable of truly providing social justice. Rather, drastic, fundamental changes are necessary in the basic social and political structure to achieve truly fair and equal treatment.

According to a radical philosophy, for example, poverty, defined as "the result of exploitation by the ruling or dominant class," exists for at least two reasons (Karger & Stoesz, 2002, pp. 115–116). First, having a multitude of poor people as workers enables higher classes to keep wages low because of the numerous replacement workers. If low-paid workers complain, they can simply be fired, with someone else eagerly waiting to take their place to avoid poverty. The working class thus serves to labor for the wealthy and keep them rich. Second, keeping a class of people in poverty enhances the "prestige" and status of the middle class. To remedy this state of affairs, an entirely new social structure would have to be developed.

A radical perspective requires the ability to propose a new social structure. It is far beyond the scope of this book to discuss how to plan new policies and promote broad social change. Therefore, from here on, when the term *radical* is used, it will be in the context of soliciting any *very general* ideas you might have about changing social welfare service provision.

How Do You Fare on the Conservative–Liberal Continuum?

Return to the preceding box and review the answers you gave to those questions. Do they lean toward a liberal or conservative point of view? Focus on Critical Thinking 1.2 contains a series of statements geared to assessing further your liberal or conservative views.

Note that this discussion of conservatism and liberalism is overly simplified. Many people, and perhaps most, have a complex mixture of views depending on their perceptions and personal experiences. (That last sentence probably reflects a liberal perspective.)

Social Work and Social Welfare History

Social work has been a developing field since the late 19th century. The profession is intimately intertwined with historical events and trends in social welfare. Social work emphasizes the importance of the social environment as it affects the quality of people's lives. Therefore, the way people are treated by laws that govern them and services and resources provided them is an integral part of the social work perspective.

Chapter 6 reviews the history of social welfare beginning in European medieval times, continuing throughout U.S. history, and culminating with today's programs and services. It elaborates on the effects of history on the social work profession's development. The chapter is placed immediately before Chapter 7 (which addresses policy, policy analysis, and policy advocacy) because today's programs, all based on current social welfare policies, are products of historical events concerning social welfare. Chapter 8 then discusses the policies and programs developed to combat poverty.

Fields of Practice in Social Work

The reminder of the book focuses on *fields of practice* in social work. These are the various practice contexts that address certain types of populations and needs and require a special knowledge and skill base for effective work. Each field of practice involves a labyrinth of typical human problems and the services attempting to address them. Current fields of practice include children and families, aging, disabilities, health, mental health, schools, and corrections. Other contexts for practice are occupational social work (focusing on work in employee assistance programs or directed toward organizational change), rural social work (addressing the unique problems of people living in rural areas), police social work (emphasizing work within police, courthouse, and jail settings to provide services to crime

FOCUS ON CRITICAL THINKING 1.2

Where Do You Stand on the Conservative–Liberal Continuum?

Rate how much you agree with statements 1–6 by assigning a number for each. The scale is as follows:

Strongly agree	Somewhat agree	Somewhat disagree	Strongly disagree
1	2	3	4

1. I don't like change very much.
2. The old tried-and-true way of getting things done is usually the best way.
3. People will do whatever they can to get things for themselves.
4. If they're sure they can get away with it, students will inevitably cheat on exams.
5. People should be independent, take care of themselves, and not rely on the charity of others.
6. People who commit crimes should be punished with severity to match the severity of their crimes.

Now rate how much you agree with statements 7–12 by assigning a number for each. The scale is as follows:

Strongly agree	Somewhat agree	Somewhat disagree	Strongly disagree
1	2	3	4

7. I like to see and do new things because it makes life more interesting.
8. Trying some new way to get things done often results in a better, more effective approach.
9. People are generally good at heart.
10. It's often the bad things that happen to people that make them "go wrong."
11. With a little help and support, people who are less privileged than the rest can usually pull themselves together and do pretty well.
12. It's better to try to rehabilitate people who commit crimes than to throw them in jail.

Now add up your total score for all 12 items and divide by 12. A score of 1 means that you probably are quite conservative, a 2 that you're somewhat conservative, a 3 that you're somewhat liberal, and a 4 that you're quite liberal.

This little exercise in no way defines your political orientation or labels you as a conservative or liberal for life. Its intent is to give you some food for thought about your own values.

Social work values tend to be more liberal than conservative, as is demonstrated by the NASW Code of Ethics and NASW's usual support of Democratic political candidates, who traditionally are more liberal than Republicans.

However, people's values and belief systems often are much more complex than that. For example, you may be conservative in that you don't want to pay a high percentage of taxes for social welfare programs. But you may also be liberal in that you believe in a woman's right to choice when it comes to having an abortion. Or you might feel just the opposite.

Social workers must continuously examine their personal values, on the one hand, and respect the values of their clients, on the other. They must constantly strive not to impose personal values on clients. It's a difficult but interesting task.

victims), and forensic social work (dealing with the law, educating lawyers, and serving as expert witnesses) (Barker, 2003).

Social workers require information about people who need help in each of these areas. They also must be knowledgeable about the services available to meet needs and the major issues related to each area. A social worker may be called upon to work with a problem that clearly falls within one field of practice or a problem that involves several of these fields.

For example, the Wullbinkle family comes to a social worker's attention when a neighbor reports that Rocky, their 5-year-old son, is frequently seen with odd-looking bruises on his arms and legs. The neighbor suspects child abuse. Upon investigation, the social worker finds that the parents are indeed abusive. They often grab the child violently by a limb and throw him against the wall. This problem initially falls under the umbrella of family and children's services.

However, the social worker also finds a number of other problems operating within the family. The mother, Natasia, is seriously depressed and frequently suicidal, so she needs mental health services. And the father, Boris, is struggling with a drinking problem that is beginning to affect his performance at work. A program is available at his place of employment, where an occupational social worker helps employees deal with such problems. Thus occupational social work may also be involved.

In addition, the maternal grandmother, Emma, is living with the Wullbinkle family. Emma's physical health is failing. Although her daughter dreads the idea of nursing home placement, the issue must be addressed. Emma, who is also overweight, finds it increasingly difficult to move around by herself. She is demanding more and more physical help and support from Natasia. Natasia, who has back problems, is finding it increasingly burdensome to help her mother. Finally, Vernite, Boris and Natasia's 12-year-old daughter, is falling behind in school, and truancy is becoming a problem. This last issue falls under the school's umbrella.

Most of the problems that social workers face are complex. They may involve a variety of practice fields all at one time. To understand clients' needs, social workers must know something about a wide range of problems and services.

The Continuum of Social Work Careers

There are various ways to look at advancement through a social work career. Some workers progress through a series of levels, while others remain at an earlier point of entry. Degrees in social work include the baccalaureate, master's, and doctorate.

Baccalaureate Social Workers (BSWs)

Baccalaureate social workers (BSWs) complete an accredited course of study, with required content described later in the chapter, to prepare for entry-level social work. They are also required to complete at least 400 hours of field experience supervised by a social work practitioner. Job settings involve many fields of practice and include child welfare agencies (e.g., those involving protective services, foster care, or adoption), residential treatment centers (e.g., serving adolescents with behavioral or emotional problems), services for people with various disabilities (including cognitive), settings serving the elderly, correctional institutions, public welfare agencies, schools, health centers and hospitals, substance abuse treatment centers, shelters for the homeless, shelters for domestic violence survivors, and family planning organizations.

At the preprofessional or paraprofessional level involving people who assist social workers in their practice are social service technicians and social service aides (Suppes & Wells, 2000). *Social service technicians* typically hold an associate's degree (e.g., in human services) or a baccalaureate degree in a non–social work discipline and serve as a paraprofessional (a person trained to assist the social worker under the social worker's supervision in designated tasks such as conducting basic interviews, making referrals, and completing paperwork). *Social service aides* are people, often with relevant life experience or strong connections to the community, who perform clerical and scheduling tasks. Aides may or may not have an associate's degree.

Master's Social Workers (MSWs)

Master's social workers (MSWs) receive more specialized training built on the same foundation as the BSW curriculum and integrated with field internships. Most master's programs require two years of study. However, many give *advanced standing* to BSWs (as opposed to people entering the program with non–social work undergraduate majors) where up to one year of study is waived because they've already completed the foundation curriculum.

Both BSWs and MSWs can find employment in a wide range of settings. However, there are some differences in the types of jobs for which each is qualified. MSWs are considered more specialized than BSWs. The implication is that MSWs are competent to address more difficult problems than BSWs and have the potential to assume greater responsibility. In reality, this distinction is not always so clear-cut. Performance expectations and job availability vary significantly depending on the area of the country and state.

The realm of psychotherapy is generally limited to MSWs instead of BSWs. *Psychotherapy,* sometimes referred to simply as *therapy,* is a skilled treatment process whereby a therapist works with an individual, couple, family, or group to address a mental disorder or alleviate other problems the client(s) may be having in the social environment. Another difference between MSWs and BSWs is that higher-level supervisory and administrative positions in any field of practice often require an MSW or other master's-level degree. Such positions usually offer higher salaries. MSWs generally earn significantly more than BSWs, although years of experience enhance salaries for both groups.

Licensure or certification of some level of social work practice exists in all 50 states. Chapter 5 discusses this more thoroughly.

Doctorates in Social Work

A small percentage of social workers hold doctorate degrees, either a Ph.D. (Doctor of Philosophy) or DSW (Doctor of Social Work). Either degree qualifies the holder to teach at the college level or conduct research. Some Ph.D.s or DSWs assume administrative positions or enter private practice in psychotherapy. These degrees involve advanced and specialized study, a focus on research, and completion of a dissertation.

This section has reviewed the continuum of social work careers according to the college and university degrees attained. Focus on Critical Thinking 1.3 suggests how you might start thinking about the career that's right for you in whatever field you choose.

FOCUS ON CRITICAL THINKING 1.3
Thinking About Your Career

As a student, you may have some career goals clearly in mind. Or you may still be wondering what the best career path is. The following is a discussion of how you might think about determining a career course. You might be a student of traditional age or an older student returning to school. Note that not all career ideas and possibilities are mentioned because they are countless. Although this career consideration process is oriented toward social work, the purpose here is to stimulate your thinking, not to tell you what to do. Each person must decide for herself or himself how to spend time and life.

1. General orientation toward the future (conducting a self-assessment)
What values are important to you? Achieving personal satisfaction? Becoming famous? Earning money? Being respected? Building a family life? Finding security? Having adventures? Leading others? Finding excitement? Developing personal relationships? Having fun? Being loved? Helping others? Getting ahead? Being successful? Being happy? Being popular? Fitting into a work environment? Feeling important?

Having free time? Traveling? Having a good reputation?

What work have you done or thought about doing in life?

What dimensions of work appeal to you most? Liking the people you work with? Communicating with others? Working alone? Working with others? Giving attention to detail? Solving problems creatively? Using specific skills? Being successful? Having flexibility? Having structured work expectations? Maintaining predictability? Helping others? Having opportunities to get ahead? Being productive? Making lots of money? Being a leader? Fitting in? Being challenged?

What jobs or careers come to mind? Which, if any, have you given any thought to?

Your answers may be vague or specific at this point, depending on where you are in your decision-making process. You may know more about what jobs you don't want (e.g., fast-food restaurant worker, waitress/waiter, pizza delivery person, factory worker, or cashier) because of prior experience in minimum-wage or close to minimum-wage jobs that you know you don't want to do for the rest of your working life.

(continued)

FOCUS ON CRITICAL THINKING 1.3 (*continued*)

Why are you taking the course that requires this book? Is it to fulfill some general education requirement? Is it because you're mildly interested in the topic? Or is it because you think this might be the major for you?

2. People-oriented versus non-people-oriented careers (exploring your options)

What types of things tend to interest you?

Do you enjoy being with others? Or do you prefer being by yourself?

Are you interested in human relationships, issues such as mental health, health, and women's concerns, and problems such as substance abuse, child maltreatment, and crime?

Do people tend to come to you to talk about their problems? Do you enjoy "helping" people?

If you say yes to these questions, then you might consider occupations that deal with people and continue the career consideration process addressed here. Non-people-oriented career courses might include those such as engineering, accounting, biology, chemistry, or computer science. Of course, it's not that you don't have to work with people in those jobs. Relating to and communicating with others in the work environment is always important. However, in non-people-oriented careers, the focus and goal are accomplishing specific tasks using specific skills, not interpersonal interaction and problem solving.

3. Ways of working with people

In what capacities do you think you'd like to work with people? Are you more interested in physical, business, legal, educational, spiritual, or psychosocial aspects?

Examples of hands-on work with people include being a medical doctor, nursing, occupational therapy (treatment that uses creative activity to improve psychological or physical rehabilitation), and physical therapy ("the treatment or management of physical disability, malfunction, or pain by physical techniques such as exercise, massage, hydrotherapy, etc." [Nichols, 1999, p. 996]). These fields also have varying requirements in science, so you probably should have some interest in this area.

Many business careers also focus on developing relationships, but, of course, with the ultimate goal of making a monetary profit instead of helping people improve their life conditions. To what extent is your ultimate goal to earn large amounts of money instead of having impacts on the human condition? This is a significant issue. One family comes to mind in which almost all members have various types of business degrees. They can't understand why I might be interested in how to address human problems such as child maltreatment, sexual assault, or mental illness. They cringe when I talk about watching movies about such issues. They think of these issues as someone else's problem and focus their energies on their own families, finances, and lives. Social work would not be their preferred field. Each of us must follow our own calling.

Law or teaching provides other career options. Law, of course, requires a serious interest in the legal process and more years of study beyond the bachelor's degree. In my school we see many students deciding between social work and teaching. They must determine whether they're more interested in helping children learn information and skills, or in working with clients and their families to help them deal with psychological, behavioral, and economic issues. Students more interested in pursuing a spiritual career such as rabbi, priest, or minister might seek education preparing them for such religious callings. One person comes to mind

(*continued*)

FOCUS ON CRITICAL THINKING 1.3 *(continued)*

who, after receiving his master's degree in meteorology, decided that he really wanted to be a minister and attained a degree in divinity four years later.

If you're primarily interested in psychosocial aspects of human functioning and improving the human condition, continue reading the next section.

4. Selection of a major

To what extent do you understand the differences among fields addressing psychosocial issues such as social work, psychology, sociology, psychiatry, criminal justice, or counseling? How can you determine which field is for you?

If you decide you want to work with people concerning psychosocial issues, it's best to talk with advisers in the various majors available to you at your school. Think about what aspects of a major appeal to you most. Find out what kind of jobs its graduates tend to get. Explore what courses make up the curriculum, and determine the extent to which the major will give you the values, knowledge, and skills necessary for you to "hit the ground running" when you get your first job after graduating. Does it prepare you with skills such as interviewing, running groups and meetings, and working within organizations? Does the major provide a significant field internship to help prepare you for work with clients? To what extent does each major you're considering match your values, interests, and goals?

Understanding the primary focus of various majors can be confusing. Just a few alternatives will be mentioned here. Generally speaking, *psychology* emphasizes the study of behavior and cognitive processing (Barker, 2003). Work is often associated with treatment of mental disorders or testing people for intelligence or aptitude. A master's or Ph.D. degree is required to provide

psychotherapy. *Sociology* is the study of human society, how various groups interact with each other, and how social institutions structure the social environment in which we live. *Social work* uses a significant amount of the knowledge produced both by sociology and psychology, and applies it to helping situations. Figure 1.1 illustrates the broad range of foundation knowledge contributing to social work practice. *Psychiatry* is the branch of medicine that specializes in the diagnosis and treatment of mental disorders. Psychiatrists must have advanced training beyond a medical degree and assume responsibility for diagnosing mental illness and prescribing psychotropic drugs. *Criminal justice* is the configuration of programs, policies, and agencies dealing with crime, incarceration, legal processes, and the rehabilitation of criminal offenders. Social workers can assume a wide range of positions in the criminal justice system. *Counseling* is a field overlapping various other fields, including social work, that focuses on problem solving and providing help to individuals, families, or groups. Often it involves additional education and expertise such as that in marriage and family therapy. Many social workers in clinical practice also are licensed marriage and family therapists. Generally, counseling focuses on providing some kind of psychotherapy, whereas social work also emphasizes the importance of the social environment concerning human behavior and advocacy to improve people's quality of life.

An issue related to choice of major involves the extent to which you're interested in attending graduate school. Some career paths require graduate education. Graduate school raises more questions. To what extent do you think you'll be tired of school by the time you graduate? So many seniors tell me they can't wait "to get

(continued)

FOCUS ON CRITICAL THINKING 1.3 *(continued)*

out" and "work to make money" instead of doing schoolwork and spending money on tuition. To what extent is graduate school financially feasible? Do you have access to funding or loans? To what extent are you already financially burdened? What, if any, is your motivation to attend graduate school? Is your grade point average sufficient to be accepted?

If you decide to consider social work as a major or have already declared this major, the next section addresses some choices within the realm of social work.

5. Considering or choosing a social work major

Because social workers practice in so many different settings and work with so many kinds of people, it can be daunting trying to decide what field of practice is right for you. Such struggle makes sense when you still know little about all the types of social work settings available. How can you make an informed choice without adequate information? Many students, even as they complete their major, have difficulty deciding what they prefer even as they enter a supervised field practicum within an agency setting. Usually, however, by that time students have narrowed their preferences considerably. It takes time to

think things through as you acquire more information about the field and gain broader experiences.

The following list should at least give you an idea of the social work career options available. At this point, what interests you the most? What settings are most attractive to you? What client populations, problems, and issues concern you most? What are your reactions to considering work in the following settings, which are just a sampling of those available?

- Mental health settings such as inpatient hospitals, where people experience and seek treatment for various mental health problems.
- Health settings such as hospitals, where people need help understanding complex information and getting the appropriate resources.
- Settings aimed at enhancing the welfare of children, including protective services, adoption, foster care, school social work, and treatment for behavioral and emotional difficulties in outpatient, group home, or residential facilities.
- Settings for the elderly, such as health care facilities where elderly people who require physical and medical support live, or supportive services aimed at keeping people in their own homes as long as possible.

(continued)

Social Work Builds on Many Disciplines

The foundation of professional social work is a body of knowledge, skills, and values. Knowledge originates not only from social workers but also from a range of disciplines that focus on understanding people's needs and behavior. These include psychology, sociology, political science, economics, biology, psychiatry, and cultural anthropology (Zastrow, 2004). Figure 1.1 illustrates how social work knowledge builds on both other disciplines and its own firm and growing body of research. It summarizes the primary focus and core concepts involved in each discipline. Social

FOCUS ON CRITICAL THINKING 1.3 *(continued)*

- Agencies providing services to people with physical disabilities, including linking them to appropriate services and advocating for services when necessary.
- Correctional settings for adults or juvenile delinquents, such as prisons where social workers help inmates by providing counseling and assisting in inmates' adjustment to the correctional environment or preparing for release, and probation or parole offices where they monitor the behavior of people released into the community.
- Domestic violence hotlines and programs addressing the needs of women who have been physically and emotionally abused.
- Counseling programs for alcohol and other substance abuse.
- Services for people with cognitive disabilities, such as those aimed at linking them to needed services, supervising noninstitutional living settings such as group homes, helping them gain employment, and advocating for resources that are unavailable.
- Crisis hotlines, where a wide range of crises including threats of suicide or violence toward others, mental health and substance abuse issues, or physical abuse are addressed and referrals to appropriate services made.

- Family planning agencies that help people make choices about contraception.
- Homeless shelters that provide temporary shelter, counseling, and training for people on the street.

Another facet of thinking about your career involves the types of responsibilities characterizing a work setting and the skills needed to practice effectively in it. What are your thoughts about undertaking the following?

- Counseling.
- Running groups.
- Working with families.
- Linking people with needed resources.
- Coordinating service provision for people receiving multiple services through case management.
- Supervising staff or administering agencies.
- Supervising volunteers.
- Community organizing.
- Running meetings.
- Writing grants.
- Policy development.
- Advocacy.
- Lobbying.

There are lots of things to consider. Choosing a career is not easy.

workers use knowledge drawn from each field, in conjunction with social work skills and values, to help individuals, families, groups, organizations, and communities solve problems and improve their quality of life.

The Uniqueness of Social Work

We have established that social work builds on the knowledge base of other professions in addition to its own. Other fields perform some of the same functions as social work. For instance, mental health clinicians in psychology, psychiatry, and counseling

Foundation of knowledge

Psychology: The scientific study of mind and behavior

Sociology: The organized study of how groups develop, interact, behave, and function within the larger society

Political science: The study of political and governmental structures and functioning

Economics: The study of the production, distribution, and consumption of goods and services

Biology: The study of living organisms and their physical functions

Psychiatry: The branch of medicine that deals with the diagnosis and treatment of mental, emotional, and behavioral disorders

Cultural anthropology: The branch of anthropology that deals with human culture, especially its history, social structures, language, and technology

Social work: The practical application of knowledge, skills, and values to enhance the well-being of individuals, families, groups, organizations, and communities

Input

Social work profession

Intervention applications

Micro practice (individuals)

Micro/mezzo practice (families)

Mezzo practice (groups)

Macro practice (organizations and communities)

Figure 1.1   The social work knowledge base

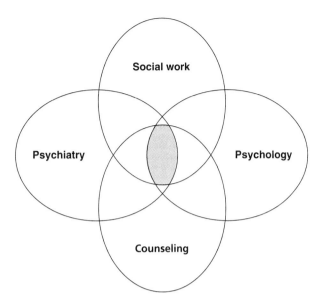

The shaded area in the center reflects a common core of interviewing and counseling skills used by the helping professions.

Figure 1.2   Social work and other helping professions

use interviewing skills, and some also use a planned-change approach. Figure 1.2 illustrates how social work overlaps, to some extent, with other helping professions. All, for example, have a common core of interviewing and counseling skills.

However, social work involves much more than simply sitting down with an individual, group, or family and solving some problem. (This is not to imply that this is all other helping professions do. Their own unique thrusts and emphases are beyond the scope of what can be included here.) Social work has at least five major dimensions that make it unique.

First, social workers may focus on any problems or clusters of problems that are complex and difficult. Social workers don't refuse to work with clients or refer them elsewhere because those clients have unappealing characteristics. For instance, there may be a family in which sexual abuse is occurring, and that abuse must be stopped. Likewise, there may be a community in which the juvenile crime rate is skyrocketing, and something must be done.

Not every problem can be solved, but some can be—or at least alleviated. Social work practitioners are equipped with a repertoire of skills to help them identify and examine problems. They then make choices about where their efforts can be best directed.

The second dimension that makes social work unique is that it often targets the environment encompassing clients, and not the clients themselves, for change. Sometimes services are unavailable or difficult to obtain, policies are unfair, or

HIGHLIGHT 1.2
Theoretical Ways of Viewing Social Work: A Focus on Systems in the Environment

Theoretical approaches provide ways of organizing information and looking at the world. For example, the medical model is a theoretical approach characterized by four major features (Barker, 2003). First, the focus of attention is the individual, who is seen as having something wrong such as an illness. Therefore, treatment focuses on curing or helping the individual. Second, little attention is paid to factors outside the individual in his or her environment. The individual, not the environment, is the target of change. Third, the problem or illness is identified or diagnosed and categorized by placing a label on it. Fourth, the individual is the target of treatment that usually involves a series of clinical treatments.

In contrast, a common theoretical approach to social work focuses on the interactions between individuals and various systems in the environment. The focus on the individual and the environment is important because the latter is where social workers direct their efforts at change.

This system- and environment-oriented approach, called *ecosystems theory,* is particularly relevant to social work (Beckett & Johnson, 1995). It combines some of the major concepts from two different theoretical perspectives: the ecological approach and systems theories.

Important Concepts in Systems Theories

Systems theories focus on the dynamics among and interactions of people in their environment. A *system* is a set of elements that are orderly and interrelated to make a function whole. Social work refers primarily to social systems composed of people (as opposed to, say, an industrial manufacturing system or an ant colony system). An individual, a family, a social services agency, and a neighborhood are all examples of systems.

Social workers work with and on the behalf of various sized systems. A *micro system* is an individual, and a *mezzo system* a group. Families, because of their intimate nature, arbitrarily lie somewhere between micro and mezzo systems. A *macro system* includes organizations and communities. This terminology is important . because it's used throughout social work and this book.

(continued)

people are oppressed by other people. Administrators and people in power don't always have the motivation or insight to initiate needed change. Social workers must look at where change is essential outside the individual and work with the environment to effect that change. Highlight 1.2 discusses some of the theoretical concepts underlying social work practice.

Consider an example of targeting the environment for change involving a midwestern city of about half a million people. Several dozen teenagers in the city had been expelled from various schools. They all had lengthy delinquency records and serious emotional problems. These young people had been attending a private day treatment program that provided them with special education and counseling at the individual, group, and family levels. The day treatment approach allowed them to

HIGHLIGHT 1.2 *(continued)*

Target Systems and Client Systems

It's helpful to conceptualize social workers and clients in terms of systems. A *target system* or *target of change* is the system that social workers need "to change or influence in order to accomplish (their) goals" (Pincus & Minahan, 1973, p. 58). Targets of change may be individual clients, families, formal groups, administrators, or policymakers. At the micro level, a 5-year-old child with behavioral problems might be the target of change, the goal being to improve behavior. At the mezzo level, a support group of people with eating disorders might be the target of change in an attempt to control their eating behavior.[1] Finally, at the macro level, an agency director might be the target of change when the social worker's aim is to improve some agency policy and the director is the primary decision maker capable of implementing that change.

Another system critical to the planned-change process is the *client system*—any individual, family, group, organization, or community that will ultimately benefit from social work intervention (Pincus & Minahan, 1973; Resnick, 1980a; Resnick, 1980b). For example, individual clients are client systems when the social worker's goal is to get them needed resources. Families are client systems when the practitioner is working on behalf of the entire family. Similarly, a community is the client system when a social worker is trying to help residents open a new community center to improve their quality of life.

Important Ecological Concepts

Two important concepts taken from the ecological approach are the social environment and coping. The *social environment* includes the conditions, circumstances, and interactions that encompass human beings. Individuals must have effective interactions with their environment to survive and thrive. The social environment involves the type of home a person lives in, the type of work a person does, the amount of money that is available, and the laws and social rules people live by. The social environment also includes the individuals, groups, organizations, and systems with which a person comes into contact, such as family, friends, work groups, and governments.

Coping is the struggle to adjust to environmental conditions and overcome problems. This is significant because social workers often help people cope with problems in their environments.

---

[1]Eating disorders, extremely serious disturbances in eating patterns, are considered mental disorders by the American Psychiatric Association (APA) (APA, 2000). Examples include anorexia and bulimia.

remain living at home in the community but still receive special treatment. The program had been paid for by public funds, with the county department of social services purchasing treatment services from the private agency.[2] The public schools had no special resources to help these teens. Therefore, purchasing such services from a private agency was more cost-effective for the county than developing its

---

[2]Public agencies are those run by a designated unit of government and are usually regulated by laws that directly affect policy. The county department of social services is a public agency. Private agencies, of course, are privately owned and run by people not employed by government. Chapter 5 describes social service agencies in greater detail.

own program from scratch. Suddenly, however, money became scarce, and community leaders decided they could no longer afford a day treatment program. Now these teenagers had nowhere to go.

This problem involved many children and their families, and the social environment was no longer responding to their desperate needs. A social worker addressing this problem might look at it from several perspectives. First, the city's various communities might need to be made acutely aware both of the existence of these teens and of the sudden cuts in funding. The media may need to be contacted as well. Second, the public school system may need to develop its own program to meet these children's and their families' needs. Third, the parents of these children may need to band together and lobby for attention and services.

In this case, social workers involved in the agency whose funding had been cut off mobilized immediately. They contacted the parents of their clients and told them about the situation. Outraged, the parents demanded that the community provide education for their children as it did for all the other children. Several parents became outspoken leaders of the group. Assisted by social workers, they filed a class action suit. The court determined that until the situation had been evaluated, funding for services must continue. Eventually, the public school system (also with the help of social workers) developed its own programs to meet the needs of such teenagers, and the private program was phased out.

The third dimension that makes social work unique is related to targeting the environment: namely, social workers often find it necessary to advocate for their clients. *Advocacy* involves actively intervening to help clients get what they need. Most frequently, this intervention focuses on "the relationship between the client and an unresponsive 'system'" (Epstein, 1981, p. 8). Clients have specified needs, and social agencies, organizations, or communities may not be meeting these needs. These unresponsive systems must be pressured to make changes so needs can be met.

The fourth dimension that makes social work unique is its emphasis on and adherence to a core of professional values. The NASW Code of Ethics focuses on the right of the individual to make free choices and have a quality life (NASW, 1999). Social workers do not force people into specific ways of thinking or acting. Rather, they help people make their own decisions about how to think or act.

The fifth dimension making social work unique is related to the core of social work values and how important it is for clients to make their own decisions. Social workers do not track people into specific ways of thinking or acting. Rather, they practice in a *partnership* with clients, making and implementing plans together. Most other professions emphasize the authority and expertise of the professional, on the one hand, and the subordinate status of the client as recipient of services, on the other.

 ## Content Areas in the Social Work Curriculum

One way of looking at what social work is all about is to review the required content areas in an accredited social work curriculum. The Council on Social Work Education (CSWE) is the organization that accredits social work programs throughout the country and specifies required content for a social work major. Considered the foundation of social work's knowledge base, the eight major required areas of content currently include values and ethics, diversity, populations-at-risk and social and economic justice, human behavior and the social environment, social welfare policy and services, social work practice, research, and field education (CSWE, 2001).

1. Social Work Values and Ethics

From the many times they've been mentioned already, you probably have noticed that social work values and ethics are critical to social work practice. They make up the first curriculum content area for accredited social work programs. They help practitioners assess what's important or right in any situation and provide guidelines for making ethical decisions and good judgment calls.

The NASW Code of Ethics mentioned earlier provides some basic guidelines for social work practitioners. Chapter 2 reviews values, ethics, and some of the issues involved more thoroughly.

2. Diversity

Diversity, the second curriculum area in social work's knowledge base, refers to the wide variety of differences characterizing people. People meriting special attention from the social work profession include, but are not limited to, groups distinguished by "age, class, color, culture, disability, ethnicity, family structure, gender, marital

Social welfare concerns all people—both rich and poor.

status, national origin, race, religion, sex, and sexual orientation" (CSWE, 2001, III.A.3). Any time a person can be identified as belonging to a group that differs in some respect from the majority of others in society, that person is subject to the effects of human diversity.

Because social workers have a wide variety of clients, demonstrating almost every type of need and problem, they must be familiar with the concept of human diversity. Two facets are especially significant. First, social workers must appreciate the differences and focus on strengths. Second, they must be sensitive to and address any hardships and negative treatment clients may face because they belong to some diverse group.

3. Populations-at-Risk and Social and Economic Justice

The concepts of populations-at-risk and social and economic justice are clearly related to the concept of human diversity. *Populations-at-risk* are groups of people with some identified characteristics who are at greater risk of social and economic deprivation than those in the mainstream. Because social work practice involves getting people resources and helping them solve problems, social workers frequently work with populations-at-risk of such deprivations. It follows that social workers need information and insight concerning these populations' special issues and needs. Therefore, social workers require both theoretical and practice content concerning the dynamics and results of differential, unfair treatment.

The second dimension of this curriculum area is the promotion of social and economic justice. *Social justice* involves the idea that in a perfect world all citizens would have identical "rights, protection, opportunities, obligations, and social benefits" (Barker, 2003, p. 405). Similarly, *economic justice* concerns the distribution of resources in a fair and equitable manner. Social work education programs are required to "provide content related to implementing strategies to combat discrimination, oppression, and economic deprivation and to promote social and economic justice"; additionally, social workers must be prepared "to advocate for nondiscriminatory social and economic systems" (CSWE, 2001, IV.C).

One especially important social work values is *empowerment*—the "process of increasing personal, interpersonal, or political power so that individuals can take action to improve their life situations" (Gutierrez, 2001, p. 210). Some groups of people suffer from stereotypes, discrimination, and oppression. It is social work's task to empower clients in general and members of oppressed groups in particular.

4. Human Behavior and the Social Environment

Knowledge about human behavior and the social environment is the fourth foundation curriculum area. We have established that focusing on people's functioning within the environmental context is an important thrust of social work. Only after assessing and understanding that functioning can social workers proceed with an intervention plan.

People are constantly and dynamically involved in ongoing activity and communication with others in the environment. *Assessment* is the identification of the "nature and extent of client needs and concerns, as well as critical information about client resources and supports and other environment factors" so that a helping plan can be devised and implemented (Blythe & Reithoffer, 2000, p. 551). Social work assessment seeks to discover what in any particular situation causes a problem to continue despite the client's expressed wish to change it. Focusing on the environment means looking not only at individuals themselves but also at their involvement with family members, neighbors, work colleagues, the political system, and agencies providing services within the community. This means that clients' problems are not viewed solely as their own fault. The forces surrounding the client frequently cause or contribute to problems, so social workers must focus their assessment on many levels. How the client and the problem fit into the larger scheme of things is critical. Poverty, discrimination, social pressures, and the effects of social welfare policies are all aspects of people's lives that can fall under scrutiny. Focus on Critical Thinking 1.4 provides an example of how social workers might focus on the environmental context of a problem.

5. Social Welfare Policy and Services

The fifth curriculum content area is social welfare policy and services. Policy, in its simplest form, can be thought of as *rules.* Our lives and those of social workers' clients are governed by rules—about how we drive our cars, when we go to school, how we talk or write sentences, and so on.

Policies, in essence, are rules that tell us which actions among a multitude of actions we may take and which we may not. Policies guide our work and our decisions. For the purpose of understanding social welfare and the provision of social welfare services, policy might be divided into two major categories: social welfare policy and agency policy. *Social welfare policies* are the laws and regulations that govern which social welfare programs exist, what categories of clients are served, and who qualifies for a given program. They also set standards regarding the type of services to be provided and the qualifications of the service provider.

In addition to the broader realm of social welfare policies, *agency policies* are standards adopted by individual organizations and programs that provide services (e.g., a family service agency, a Department of Human Services, or a nursing home). Such standards may specify the agency's structure, the qualifications of supervisors and workers, the rules governing what workers can do, and the proper procedures for completing a family assessment.

Knowledge of policy is vital for social workers. An organization's policy can dictate how much vacation an employee can have and how raises are earned. An adoption agency's policy can determine who is eligible to adopt a child. A social program's policies determine who gets needed services and resources.

One more thing should be said concerning social workers and social welfare policy. Iatridis (1995) maintains that social workers must become actively involved in establishing and changing social welfare policies for the benefit of their clients; policies determine how money is budgeted and spent, and where resources are made available for clients. Sometimes, for whatever reason, social welfare policies are unfair or oppressive to clients. Ironically, although such policies are intended to enhance people's welfare, sometimes they do not. A social worker may decide that a policy is ethically or morally intolerable and advocate on the behalf of clients to try to change it. Practitioners can work to change policy "to improve social justice, fairness, and equality," potentially affecting "well-being for the overwhelming majority of citizens" (p. 1865).

FOCUS ON CRITICAL THINKING 1.4

Focusing on the Environmental Context of Problems

Trevor is a 15-year-old gang member in an inner city. The gang is involved in drug dealing, which, of course, is illegal. However, when assessing the situation and potential actions, a broader perspective is necessary. Looking at how the environment encourages and even supports the illegal activity is critical in understanding how to solve the problem. Trevor's father is no longer involved with Trevor's family. Now it's only Trevor, his mother, and three younger brothers. Trevor's mother works a 6-day-per-week, 9-hour-per-day second-shift job at Harry's Hole, a local all-night diner, where she slings burgers. Although she loves her children dearly, she can barely make ends meet and has little time to supervise them.

All of the neighborhood kids belong to one gang or another. It gives them a sense of identity and importance, and it provides social support that often is lacking in their families. Easy access to drugs offers an opportunity to escape from impoverished, depressing, and apparently hopeless conditions. Finally, gang membership gives these young people a source of income. In fact, they can get relatively large amounts of money in a hurry.

The gang members' alternatives appear grim. There are few, if any, positive role models to show them other ways of existence. They don't see their peers or adults close to them becoming corporate lawyers, surgeons, or nuclear physicists. They don't even see anyone who's going or has gone to college. In fact, finishing high school is considered quite a feat. Neighborhood unemployment runs at more than 50 percent. A few part-time, minimum-wage jobs are available—cleaning washrooms at Bugger's Burger Bungalow or unloading freight at Shirley's Shop-Right. But these are unappealing alternatives to the immediate sources of gratification and income provided by gang membership and drug dealing. Even if another minimal source of income could be found, the other rewarding aspects of gang membership would be lost. Also, there's the all-consuming problem of having no positive future to look forward to, so the excitement of the present remains seductive.

This is not to say that it's right for people like Trevor to join vicious gangs and participate in illegal activities. Nor does it mean that Trevor's

(continued)

Because social welfare policy sets the stage for what social workers can do in practice, Chapter 7 explores the topic more thoroughly. Other chapters discuss many types of social welfare policies that affect various client populations and social work practices.

6. Social Work Practice

Practice skills are the sixth curriculum content area in social work's broad knowledge base. Practice is the *doing* of social work: forming relationships with clients, defining issues, collecting and assessing data, identifying alternatives for action, making and implementing plans, evaluating progress, and terminating the client–worker

FOCUS ON CRITICAL THINKING 1.4 *(continued)*

plight is hopeless. Going beyond a focus on the individual to assess the many environmental impacts and interactions gives the social worker a better understanding of the whole situation. The answer might not be to send Trevor to the state juvenile correctional facility for a year or two and then return him to the same community with the same friends and same problems. Such a "remedy" focuses on the individual in a very limited manner.

A social work perspective views Trevor as a person who's acting as part of a family and a community. Trevor is affected, influenced, supported, and limited by his immediate environment. Continuing along this line of thought, other questions can be raised: How might Trevor's environment be changed? What other alternatives could be made available to him?

Many alternatives would involve major changes in the larger systems around him. Neighborhood youth centers with staff serving as positive role models could be developed as an alternative to gang membership. Trevor's school system could be evaluated. Does it have enough resources to give him a good education? Is there a teacher who could serve as his

mentor and enthusiastic supporter? Can a mentorship system be established within the school? Are scholarships and loans available to offer him a viable alternative of college or trade school? Can positive role models demonstrate to Trevor and his peers that other ways of life may be open to them? Where might the resources for implementation of any of these ideas come from?

Concerning Trevor's family environment, can additional resources be provided? These might include food and housing assistance, quality day care for his younger brothers, and even educational opportunities for Trevor's mother so that she, too, could see a brighter future. Is there a Big Brother organization to provide support for Trevor and his siblings? Can the neighborhood be made a better place to live? Can crime be curbed and housing conditions improved?

There obviously are no easy answers. Scarcity of resources remains a fundamental problem. However, this illustration is intended to show how a social worker would look at a variety of options and targets of change, and not just at Trevor.

relationship (CSWE, 2001; Kirst-Ashman & Hull, 2002). Other practice skills include "providing leadership for policies and services" and "promoting social and economic justice" (CSWE, 2001, IV.F).

Practice involves working with individuals, families, groups, organizations (large and small), and large social and governmental institutions. The acquisition of practice skills is what makes social work useful and practical. Skills provide the muscle to make social work practice effective. Chapter 4 describes the process of generalist social work practice and skills application.

The social work knowledge base includes knowledge of skills in addition to knowledge of problems and services. A social worker must know what skills will be most effective in what situations.

Consider a family whose home suddenly burns to the ground. Its members need immediate shelter. The social worker decides it's necessary to use brokering skills—that is, skills for seeking out and connecting people with the resources they need. In this situation, brokering skills take precedence over other skills. For instance, using less directive counseling techniques to explore the relationship between the spouses is inappropriate at this time because there is no current evidence of need. Such intervention may be necessary in the future, but only after the immediate crisis of a lack of shelter has been resolved.

Social workers can choose from a multitude of practice techniques and theories about these techniques. Knowledge of the effectiveness of various techniques is critical to selecting those that can accomplish the most in a given situation. Regardless of techniques chosen and used, emphasis is placed on client strengths and empowerment, ongoing client collaboration at all stages of the change process, and appreciation of diversity (Pinderhughes, 1995).

7. Research

Research is the seventh content area in the social work curriculum. Knowledge of social work research is important for two basic reasons. First, it can help social workers become more effective in their direct practice, thereby getting better and clearer results. Framing social work interventions so they can be evaluated through research provides information about which specific techniques work best with which problems. Evaluation of practice throughout the intervention process can help determine whether a worker is really helping a client.

Second, accumulated research helps build a foundation for planning effective interventions. Knowledge of what has worked best in the past provides guidelines for approaches and techniques to be used in the present and in the future. Research forms the basis for the development of programs and policies that affect many people. Such knowledge can also be used to generate new theories and ideas to further enhance the effectiveness of social work.

Evidence-Based Practice

There is currently major interest in evidence-based practice—"the conscientious, explicit, and judicious use of current best evidence in making decisions about the care of clients" (Gambrill, 2000, p. 46). Gambrill (2000) explains:

> It involves integrating individual practice expertise with the best available external evidence from systematic research as well as considering the values and expectations of clients. External research findings related to problems are drawn on if they are available and they apply to a particular client. Involving clients as informed participants in a collaborative helping relationship is a hallmark of evidence-based practice. Clients are fully informed about the risks and benefits of recommended services as well as alternatives (including the alternative of doing nothing). . . . The term *evidence-based practice* is preferable to the term *empirical practice.* The latter term now seems to be applied to material that has been published, whether or not it is evidence-based. Such use represents an appeal to authority (not evidence). (pp. 46–47)

Content of Social Work Research

The content of social work research tends to fall within four major categories (Reid, 1995). First, many studies involve the behavior of individual clients and their interactions with others close to them, including families and small groups. Second, much research focuses on how services are provided to clients, what such services involve, and how successfully they accomplish their goals. Third, some studies address social workers' attitudes and educational backgrounds, in addition to major trends in the profession. Fourth, some research involves the study of "organizations, communities, and social policy" (p. 2044). This latter category emphasizes the importance of the larger social environment and its effects on clients' behavior and conditions.

8. Field Education

Field education is the final curriculum area in social work's knowledge base. As the culmination of their social work education, most students find their field practicum a valuable and challenging experience. Field education reinforces "students' identification with the purposes, values, and ethics of the profession, fosters the integration of empirical and practice-based knowledge, and promotes the development of professional competence" (CSWE, 2001, IV.H). Baccalaureate programs require a minimum of 400 hours of fieldwork and master's programs at least 900 hours.

Looking Ahead

This chapter introduced the basic concept of social welfare and the foundations of the social work profession. It reviewed the various curriculum content areas that provide the basis for professional education. The next chapter focuses on social work values and ethics, a primary content area that underlies and guides the social work profession.

For Further Exploration on the Internet

See this text's Book Companion Website at **www.socialwork.wadsworth.com/ kirstashman_intro2e** for descriptors and hot links to URLs relevant to this chapter, selected InfoTrac articles and exercises, and tutorial quizzes.

CHAPTER 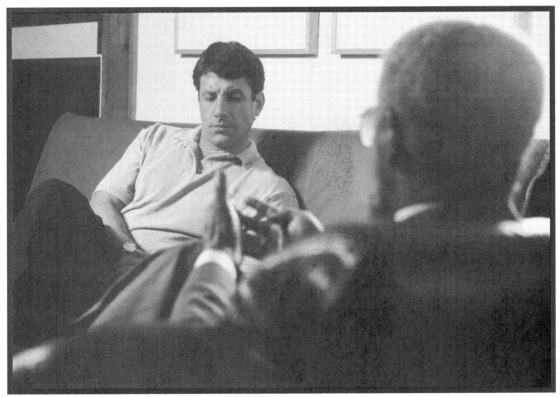 TWO

SOCIAL WORK VALUES AND ETHICS

How might you answer these questions?

- How do you determine what is right and what is wrong?
- Have you ever run into situations in which it's difficult to decide what is the right thing to do? If so, what were the circumstances?
- What personal values do you have about controversial issues such as the death penalty? Abortion? School prayer? Gun control? Affirmative action? Assisted suicide?

Social work is a values-based profession; that is, everything social workers do must be with professional values in mind. *Values* involve what you do and do not consider important and worthwhile. They also involve judgments and decisions about relative worth—that is, about what is more valuable and what is less valuable.

Ethics involve principles that specify what is good and what is bad. They clarify what should and should not be done. The National Association of Social Workers (NASW) Code of Ethics is based on professional values (NASW, 1999). Dolgoff, Loewenberg, and Harrington (2005) explain, "Ethics are deduced from values and must be in consonance with them. The difference between them is that values are concerned with what is *good* and *desirable,* while ethics deal with what is *right* and *correct*" (p. 18). Values determine what beliefs are appropriate. Ethics address what to *do* with or how to *apply* those beliefs to do the "right" thing.

Cournoyer (2005) clearly summarizes the importance of social work ethics:

> Every aspect of practice, every decision, every assessment, every intervention, and vir-tually every action you undertake as a social worker must be considered from the per-spective of your professional ethics and obligations. This dimension supersedes all others. Ethical responsibilities take precedence over theoretical knowledge, research findings, practice wisdom, agency policies, and, of course, your own personal values, preferences, and beliefs. (p. 82)

Professional judgments may seem to be a simple matter of common sense. However, in real-life decisions, values and ethical principles conflict constantly. This can result in *ethical dilemmas*—problematic situations in which one must make a difficult choice among two or more alternatives. A dilemma occurs when no one answer can conform to all the ethical principles involved.

For example, a client might inform her social worker that she plans to murder her mother-in-law because she can't take the condescending nagging anymore. On the one hand, is the social worker required to report to the authorities that this client has threatened to harm another person? On the other, how can this worker maintain confidentiality and report the threats at the same time? (*Confidentiality* is the ethical principle that workers should not share information provided by or about a client unless that worker has the client's explicit permission to do so.)

Social workers have established guidelines to ethical decision making that can help them get through the difficult decision-making process when solving an ethi-cal dilemma (Kirst-Ashman & Hull, 2002; Dolgoff, Loewenberg, & Harrington, 2005; Reamer, 1998). The NASW Code of Ethics offers a good starting point for discussing professional values and ethics. It highlights some of the field's primary values and provides suggestions for working in an ethical manner. However, it's only a beginning. The potential value conflicts and ethical dilemmas social workers may face are infinite.

It should be clear to you by now that the social work profession has a strong set of values. Some of you reading this are embracing these values and deciding whether to become a social worker. Others take this course out of some level of interest in people's welfare or simply for the credits. You may have personal opinions strongly opposed to some of the value stances. Regardless, the content of this book will provide some provocative food for thought. It seeks to challenge some of your views about the world and enhance your understanding of people and their environments, and ways they can work together to improve the welfare of all.

This chapter will

- Review the general categories in the NASW Code of Ethics.
- Provide case examples of compliance and noncompliance concerning some of the major ethical issues involved, including self-determination, privacy and confidentiality, conflict of interest and dual relationships, sexual relationships, respect for colleagues, and referral for services.
- Recognize ethical obligations at the macro level.
- Introduce the importance of social work in a global context.
- Introduce critical thinking about ethical dilemmas.
- Discuss the difference between personal and professional values.

The NASW Code of Ethics

We have established the importance of ethics in guiding professional behavior. Because of its significance, we will examine various aspects of the NASW Code of Ethics, which has four primary facets (1999). First, the preamble summarizes social work's general goals or mission and identifies its core values. The mission "is to enhance human well-being and help meet the basic human needs of all people, with particular attention to the needs and empowerment of people who are vulnerable, oppressed, and living in poverty" (NASW, 1999). The six core values include these:

1. *Service:* Providing help, resources, and benefits so people can achieve their maximum potential.
2. *Social justice:* Upholding the condition that in a perfect world all citizens would have identical "rights, protection, opportunities, obligations, and social benefits" regardless of their backgrounds and membership in diverse groups (Barker, 2003, pp. 404–405).
3. *Dignity and worth of the person:* Holding in high esteem and appreciating individual value.
4. *Importance of human relationships:* Valuing "the mutual emotional exchange; dynamic interaction; and affective, cognitive, and behavioral connections that exist between the social worker and the client to create the working and helping atmosphere" (Barker, 2003, p. 365).

5. *Integrity:* Maintaining trustworthiness and sound adherence to moral ideals.
6. *Competence:* Having the necessary skills and abilities to work effectively with clients.

The second major facet in the Code, "Purpose of the NASW Code of Ethics," identifies its six major aims:

1. Identifying primary social work values.
2. Summarizing broad ethical principles as guidelines for practice.
3. Helping determine relevant considerations when addressing an ethical dilemma.
4. Providing broad ethical standards to which the public in general may hold the profession accountable.
5. Socializing new practitioners to the mission, goals, and ethics inherent in the profession.
6. Articulating specific standards that the profession may use to judge its members' conduct.

Of particular note is the Code's emphasis on the complexity of ethical dilemmas. The Code provides no simple formula for resolution; rather, it stresses that ethical dilemmas may be viewed from a range of perspectives. Therefore, social workers must use critical thinking to resolve ethical issues with the Code as a springboard. Focus on Critical Thinking 2.1 provides examples of ethical dilemmas social workers may experience.

The Code's third facet, "Ethical Principles," is based on the six core values described previously and sets forth standards to which all practitioners should strive. For example, the ethical principle relating to the value of *social justice* states that "social workers challenge social injustice." Likewise, the principle based on *integrity* states that "social workers [should] behave in a trustworthy manner."

The final facet of the Code, the "Ethical Standards," is by far the most extensive. It encompasses 155 specific principles clustered under six major categories. These include social workers' ethical responsibilities to clients, to colleagues, in practice settings, as professionals, to the social work profession, and to the broader society. Highlight 2.1 lists the concepts involved in each, and subsequent sections discuss the major categories, providing some specific examples for each.

Social Workers' Ethical Responsibilities to Clients

The first category of ethical standards addresses how practitioners should behave with respect to clients and what aspects of worker–client interaction are most significant within an ethical context. It is beyond the scope of this book to cover all 16 areas within this category, so we will focus on only a few arbitrarily selected ones. These are self-determination, privacy and confidentiality, conflict of interest and dual relationships, and sexual relationships with clients. After each, examples of compliance and of violation are provided.

Self-Determination

Practitioners should nurture and support client *self-determination*—each individual's right to make his or her own decisions. Applied to social work, this means that

FOCUS ON CRITICAL THINKING 2.1
What Should a Social Worker Do?

The following are examples of ethical dilemmas confronting social workers. Answers are difficult because there are no perfect solutions. What would you do if you were a social worker in each of the following situations?

Scenario A[1]

Evita was a hospital social worker called in to talk with parents who had just brought their 6-week-old infant Eric to the emergency room. Eric, whose skin had turned blue and who was not breathing, was placed on a respirator in intensive care for three days. After that time, the medical staff determined that he was brain-dead, and the parents, Bill and Brenda, sorrowfully gave their permission to "pull the plug."

Evita had the opportunity to speak with Bill and Brenda as they waited steadfastly by Eric's bedside hoping he would revive. She discovered that Bill had been baby-sitting Eric while Brenda ran some errands. Eric had been sleeping on the bed when Bill lay down to take a nap next to him. Apparently Bill had fallen asleep and rolled over on Eric, accidentally smothering him. Evita thought it was odd that Bill had not awakened

when Eric, an active baby who was large for his age, must have been struggling desperately for breath. Bill admitted that he had had a couple of beers prior to his nap but insisted that he was not drunk.

Tests revealed that Eric displayed no sign of injuries or other suspicious symptoms. The physician in charge of Eric was unaware of the story's details. Therefore, she determined that Eric must have died of sudden infant death syndrome (SIDS), which she planned to cite as the cause of death. SIDS is "death from cessation of breathing in a seemingly healthy infant, almost always during sleep" (Nichols, 1999, p. 1305).

Evita knew Eric's death was not due to SIDS. Yet informing the overseeing physician about what really happened would probably do little good. Bill and Brenda were filled with sorrow and blamed themselves for the tragedy. What good would it do to raise suspicions about the cause of death? It would only put the parents through an agonizing investigation, and their two other children would likely be removed from the home if suspicions regarding parental

(continued)

[1]This case is based on one presented in Robison and Reeser (2000, pp. 2–3).

practitioners are responsible for (1) informing clients about available resources, (2) helping them define and articulate their alternatives, and (3) assisting them in evaluating the consequences of each option. The goal is to assist clients in making the best, most informed choices possible.

Example of Compliance   Gilda is a social worker in a protective services unit for the elderly in a large urban county's Department of Social Services. Her job is to visit elderly people who may be at risk of some harm (e.g., being unable to care for themselves or suffering physical abuse by others), assess the situation, and help them in whatever ways possible. Sometimes Gilda connects clients with appropriate resources like Meals-on-Wheels, an agency that delivers daily hot meals to elderly people's homes for minimal cost. Other times, Gilda helps place elderly people

FOCUS ON CRITICAL THINKING 2.1 *(continued)*

competence were raised. If you were Evita, what would you do?

Scenario B

Harry is a county Department of Social Services worker whose clients consist primarily of poor, female-headed families receiving public assistance. During one of his meetings with Dora, a single mother of three small children, she happily reveals that she is baby-sitting for several neighborhood children. She is thrilled to earn the extra income and is proud to share her news with Harry. Regulations state that people receiving public assistance must report any additional income, with benefits then decreased proportionately. But reporting her extra income would probably undermine Dora's trust and destroy Harry's relationship with her. And Dora would probably stop baby-sitting because it would no longer get her ahead. She is barely making ends meet as it is with her meager public assistance payments. Dora already is participating in a compulsory job-training program, preparing her for full-time employment. What good would it do to report this scanty income despite the fact that regulations

require such reporting? Dora likely will get a full-time job soon, at which time public assistance payments will no longer be an issue. What should Harry do?

Scenario C

Ping is a social worker at a mental health center that provides individual and group counseling for a wide range of problems and issues. One of Ping's clients is Cheyenne, age 14, who is depressed and potentially suicidal. During one of their individual counseling sessions, Cheyenne tells Ping that she is sexually active. She states that if she gets pregnant with her current boyfriend she will surely kill herself. Cheyenne asks Ping to help her get some form of contraception, possibly from Planned Parenthood. Cheyenne indicates that her boyfriend refuses to use condoms because he says he doesn't like to feel restricted. Ping knows Cheyenne's parents are very religious and are fervently against premarital sex. They would never consent to Cheyenne using contraception and would vehemently oppose Ping's interference in this matter. But what about Cheyenne's life and well-being? What should Ping do?

in more structured settings, such as nursing homes, to meet their increasingly dependent needs.

One of Gilda's clients, Desiree, age 89, tripped on a crack in the sidewalk outside her home and severely sprained her ankle. Desiree is adamant that she will not leave her home, no matter what. She feels that would destroy her independence and effectively be the first step into the grave. However, Desiree is having a terrible time getting around in her own home. She can barely walk and usually has to crawl to the bathroom when no one is around to help her.

Gilda thinks Desiree would probably be better off in a more structured setting where she could get the help she needs. However, Gilda respects Desiree's right to self-determination. So she works out a plan with Desiree that's satisfactory to the client. Desiree will temporarily reside in a nearby health care facility

HIGHLIGHT 2.1

Ethical Standards in the NASW Code of Ethics

1. Social Workers' Ethical Responsibilities to Clients
   1.01 Commitment to Clients
   1.02 Self-Determination
   1.03 Informed Consent
   1.04 Competence
   1.05 Cultural Competence and Social Diversity
   1.06 Conflicts of Interest
   1.07 Privacy and Confidentiality
   1.08 Access to Records
   1.09 Sexual Relationships
   1.10 Physical Contact
   1.11 Sexual Harassment
   1.12 Derogatory Language
   1.13 Payment for Services
   1.14 Clients Who Lack Decision-Making Capacity
   1.15 Interruption of Services
   1.16 Termination of Services

2. Social Workers' Ethical Responsibilities to Colleagues
   2.01 Respect
   2.02 Confidentiality
   2.03 Interdisciplinary Collaboration
   2.04 Disputes Involving Colleagues
   2.05 Consultation
   2.06 Referral for Services
   2.07 Sexual Relationships
   2.08 Sexual Harassment
   2.09 Impairment of Colleagues
   2.10 Incompetence of Colleagues
   2.11 Unethical Conduct of Colleagues

3. Social Workers' Ethical Responsibilities in Practice Settings
   3.01 Supervision and Consultation
   3.02 Education and Training
   3.03 Performance Evaluation
   3.04 Client Records
   3.05 Billing
   3.06 Client Transfer
   3.07 Administration
   3.08 Continuing Education and Staff Development
   3.09 Commitments to Employers
   3.10 Labor–Management Disputes

4. Social Workers' Ethical Responsibilities as Professionals
   4.01 Competence
   4.02 Discrimination
   4.03 Private Conduct
   4.04 Dishonesty, Fraud, and Deception
   4.05 Impairment
   4.06 Misrepresentation
   4.07 Solicitations
   4.08 Acknowledging Credit

5. Social Workers' Ethical Responsibilities to the Social Work Profession
   5.01 Integrity of the Profession
   5.02 Evaluation and Research

6. Social Workers' Ethical Responsibilities to the Broader Society
   6.01 Social Welfare
   6.02 Public Participation
   6.03 Public Emergencies
   6.04 Social and Political Action

for the elderly until she can once again put pressure on her ankle and walk. Gilda makes arrangements with the facility for Desiree to stay there. Gilda also helps Desiree arrange for someone to watch her home and forward her mail to her temporarily.

Example of a Violation   Jorge is a job coach for a county social services department. His job involves evaluating people's strengths, skills, and interests; linking them with appropriate employment; and helping them adjust to their work environments. Daisy, age 19, is one of Jorge's clients. Daisy emphasizes that she would like to get a job as a secretary or administrative assistant. Daisy says that she's generally shy with people and would like a job in which she could work in a more solitary manner. She also says that she has always been good at typing. Jorge knows that Daisy never graduated from high school, and he doesn't believe that her typing or writing skills are anywhere near adequate for such a position. Therefore, he decides not to inform Daisy about available clerical positions. Rather, he steers her to think about becoming a sales clerk.

Privacy and Confidentiality

Social workers must uphold client privacy and confidentiality. *Privacy* is the condition of being free from unauthorized observation or intrusion. We have established that *confidentiality* is the ethical principle that workers should not share information provided by a client or about a client unless they have the client's explicit permission to do so.

There is more to confidentiality than may be immediately apparent. Confidentiality means more than not revealing information about clients to others. It also involves not asking for more information than is necessary, as well as informing clients about the limitations of confidentiality within the agency setting. For example, will supervisors, researchers, or students have access to private information? Must statistics and other data about clients' personal lives be submitted to public regulatory agencies or funding sources for accountability (a profession's responsibility to clients and the community that workers are effectively doing what they say they are going to do)? Highlight 2.2 explores some issues involving confidentiality and the Internet.

Example of Compliance   Mackenzie is a school social worker who is just beginning a support group for sixth-grade children coping with their parents' recent divorces. Early in the first session, she explains to the children the limits of confidentiality. For example, if they share anything about wanting to hurt someone or themselves, committing a crime, or participating in sexual activity, it's her responsibility to report it. This way, group members know where they stand. If they share this kind of information, they know Mackenzie has no choice but to report it.

Example of a Violation   Peter and Piper are social work counselors at a group home for adolescent boys with emotional and behavioral problems. They and their significant others occasionally have dinner with a mutual friend, Jack, a county social services worker, along with his significant other. The three social workers regularly

Social Work, Confidentiality, and the Internet

The Internet has become "one of the major and indispensable tools for knowledge acquisition, and is increasingly being used by social work professionals as a means of both accessing and providing social work–related information" (Finn & Smith, 1997, p. 71). Marson (2000) indicates that Internet ethics (or "netiquette") in some ways corresponds with ethics in person-to-person or "hardcopy" situations and in other ways does not (p. 20). He maintains that "cyberspace remains a new culture and has unique social forces and social sanctions that have no functional equivalent in the real world" (p. 20). For example, client confidentiality is important in virtually all situations, yet the means of maintaining it electronically are unique. At least three issues are significant (Marson, 2000).

First, social workers and their agencies must be well versed in any Internet functions they undertake. It must be clear who has access to client information and how. In the real world, workers lock their offices and, sometimes, their filing cabinets when they go home. They must know how to do the same thing in the electronic environment if that's where client communications and records are kept. Some simple rules apply:

1. Keep passwords confidential.
2. Avoid calling up a password on the screen when others are in the room (this is akin to

talking loudly about clients in a crowded lunchroom).
3. Avoid writing the password down or making it readily available on some database.
4. Alter passwords every few months.

Second, any language used should be professional and socially appropriate. Many people seem to feel more comfortable using "profanity and derogatory language" on the Internet than they ever would in other situations (Marson, 2000, p. 19). Perhaps it's the anonymity or lack of physical interpersonal contact that makes people using the Internet feel more informal and, possibly, freer. It's interesting that the Supreme Court ruled against the Communications Decency Act (CDA) in 1997. The CDA was "designed to protect children by prohibiting 'indecent' speech or images from being sent through cyberspace"; however, it was struck down "because in trying to protect children it would also keep adults from getting material they have a legal right to see" (Quittner, 1997, p. 28). The right to free speech on the Internet, therefore, remains carefully guarded.

Professional ethics can provide guidelines for proper behavior. The NASW Code of Ethics states that "[s]ocial workers should not use derogatory language in their written or verbal

(continued)

compare "battle stories" about their most difficult cases. This occurs despite the fact that they have very different caseloads and their significant others are present to hear their discussion. Sometimes, after a few cocktails, voices elevate, and other diners can overhear.

Conflict of Interest and Dual Relationships

The Code of Ethics warns practitioners to be acutely aware and steer clear of any possible conflicts of interest that might obstruct professional judgment. In the

HIGHLIGHT 2.2 *(continued)*

communications to or about clients" (NASW, 1999, 1.12).

A third issue involving confidentiality concerns the ease with which information can be shared with large numbers of people such as those on a *listserv*—"a computerized system by which subscribers are able to communicate to all other subscribers by sending a transmission to one address" (Marson, 1998, p. 21). It is easy to reply to all listserv members, instead of only the person who initiated a contact or raised a question. Information conveyed in chatroom conversations (in which a number of people can communicate concurrently at a Web site) should also be carefully monitored.

Marson (1998) cites the following reasons, among others, that social workers use the Internet:

- *Networking.* This involves the establishment of communication and interpersonal interaction among people to provide support, exchange information, or achieve some designated goal. For example, social workers in one state network with each other to share information about pending social legislation and advocate for positive changes.
- *Sharing resource material to improve practice and agency service.* However, note that not all resource material is of equal value or even of any value. Marson (1998) mentions a Web

page (http://turnpike.net/mirsky/worse.html) managed by "David Mirsky, a Harvard graduate," where, among other things, one can access "a translation of Hamlet in Klingon" (p. 27).

- *Identifying referral services for specific client needs.* Marson (1998) cites a case in which "an anonymous social worker had a client who was suffering from terminal lung cancer and was receiving hospice services at her home. [A *hospice* is a place of rest or a system of services providing care for people who are terminally ill. The idea is to make people as comfortable as possible in the little time they have before they die.] The client's physical isolation made a dreadful situation worse. In an effort to assist with her last months, the social worker linked the client to UseNet's cancer support group [on the Internet], which provided her with the support vital for her morale" (p. 24).
- *Seeking out or conducting research.* It's easy to consult with colleagues and to exchange documents regarding effective practice techniques and research projects.
- *Avoiding phone tag by communicating efficiently.* Sometimes it's difficult to reach people, especially when they're busy and unavailable. When information must be conveyed quickly, e-mail provides a good alternative.

social work context, a *conflict of interest* is a clash between the responsibilities of the professional role and the potential for personal gain. An example is a hospital social worker who encourages clients to purchase health insurance policies from her spouse, who is an insurance salesman. To what extent might this practice not be in the clients' best interest? To what extent will this worker be biased to experience personal income gain? Another example involves a practitioner running for office who pressures clients to vote for her. To what extent does this interfere with her ability to work with and help these clients? What if the clients don't agree with the worker's political views? How will this alter the clients' perception of the worker–client relationship? "Similarly, a practitioner who invests money in a client's business is embedded in a conflict of interest; the professional's financial interests may clash with her duty to the client (for example, if the professional's relationship with the client becomes strained because they disagree about some aspect of their shared business venture)" (Reamer, 2001, p. 5). A client who is a used car salesman may even "offer to sell . . . [a worker] a car at a discount"; Dolgoff and his colleagues (2005) emphasize to workers, "Don't accept his offer, no matter how good it is!" (p. 142). Such a scenario may result in the client expecting something from the worker in return, such as special treatment or personal closeness.

The Code emphasizes that clients' best interests must be protected to the maximum extent possible. If these interests are jeopardized, termination of the worker–client relationship and appropriate referral elsewhere may be necessary.

One type of conflict of interest involves dual or multiple relationships. Corey, Corey, and Callanan (2003) explain:

> "*Dual* or *multiple relationships* occur when professionals assume two or more roles at the same time or sequentially with a client. This may involve assuming more than one professional role (such as instructor and . . . [counselor]) or blending a professional and nonprofessional relationship (such as counselor and friend or counselor and business partner). Other examples of dual relationships include bartering . . . [counseling] for goods or services, providing . . . [counseling] to a relative or a friend's relative, socializing with clients, attending a social event of a client, accepting gifts from clients, becoming emotionally or sexually involved with a client or former client, or combining the roles of supervisor and . . . [counselor]. (p. 246)

The Code of Ethics states that "[s]ocial workers should not engage in dual or multiple relationships with clients or former clients" where such people have any risk of being harmed (NASW, 1999, 1.06c). As in other potential conflicts of interest, social workers should always give top priority to clients' best interests. Dolgoff and his colleagues (2005) reflect:

> Must dual-role relationships necessarily interfere with professional relationships or be conflictual? In modern society, everyone fills multiple roles, and there are many opportunities for social workers and clients to participate in dual or multiple relationships. Both may be members of the same political party, church, mosque, or synagogue, or their children may attend the same schools or be classmates. There is no reason for a social worker to withdraw from these activities simply because the client also engages in them. The issue is to separate the professional relationship from other relationships [in order to avoid ethical dilemmas]. (p. 142)

However, it remains important for the worker to remember that "there is always the potential for a conflict of interest and of exploitation of the person seeking help. This makes it critical that whenever there is a possibility of a dual relationship the . . . [practitioner], who is the person who knows the difficulties that could arise in such relationships, must think about and perhaps discuss with a supervisor the potential conflicts of interest and exploitation before entering into such a relationship" (Syme, 2003, p. 8).

Example of Compliance[2]   Javon is a social worker at a substance abuse counseling center. He has just received a referral of a client, Laura Hedgehog, whose name is not familiar to him. When she arrives at his office, he is surprised to find out he knows her. He used to work with her at another social services agency several years ago and had even formed a mild friendship with her. She apparently had since married and changed her last name. Laura greets Javon enthusiastically and emphasizes how happy she is that he will be her counselor. She stresses how much she trusts his competence and knows he can help her. Javon feels uncomfortable about this dual relationship, knowing Laura both as a client and a former colleague. Javon gently thanks her for her confidence, and then explains how he feels such a dual relationship would create a serious ethical dilemma for him. He feels he cannot be objective and offer her the best help possible. He refers her to one of his colleagues, whom he candidly describes as an excellent counselor.

Example of a Violation   Huda is a Protective Services worker whose primary job is to investigate alleged cases of child maltreatment and make recommendations for treatment, sometimes involving children's removal from the home. Huda attends the first session of a yoga class where she is startled to see that the instructor, Hope, is the mother in one of the families with whom Huda is currently working. Huda participates in the whole class, after which Hope approaches her. Hope enthusiastically welcomes her and says she'd be happy to give Huda a discount in registration fees. Huda thinks to herself, "What would it hurt? I'm pretty strapped for cash this month. It certainly won't influence my decision about her family or anything like that." *Will it?*

Sexual Relationships

Another type of dual relationship involves sexual relationships, which the Code emphasizes by addressing it as a separate topic. Simply put, social workers should not have sexual relationships with current clients, clients' relatives, or others personally involved with clients. The Code of Ethics also discourages social workers from having sexual relationships with former clients. If a social worker pursues this under "extraordinary circumstances, it is social workers—not their clients—who assume the full burden of demonstrating that the former client has not been exploited, coerced, or manipulated, intentionally or unintentionally" (NASW, 1996, 1.09). Additionally, social workers should not provide clinical services to clients with whom they were formerly sexual partners.

The Code uses powerful language to emphasize that workers should not have sex with clients under any circumstances. Parsons (2001) explains that the "inappropriateness of sexual relationship between helper and client rests in the fact that the helping relationship is unbalanced in power. . . . Thus, the reciprocal nature characteristic of a healthy intimate relationship is not possible" (p. 146). Corey, Corey, and Callanan (2003) indicate that harmful effects can range

---

[2]This example is loosely based on one presented in *Ethical Decisions for Social Work Practice* (7th ed.) by Dolgoff et al. (Pacific Grove, CA: Brooks/Cole, 2005), p. 247.

"from mistrust of opposite sex relationships to hospitalization and, in some cases, suicide. Other effects of sexual intimacies on clients' emotional, social, and sexual adjustment" include "negative feelings about the experience, a negative impact on their personality, and a deterioration of their sexual relationship with their primary partner" (p. 277).

Example of Compliance   Tyrone is a social worker with a caseload of families, mostly young women, receiving public assistance. Diana, one of his clients, has worked quite hard to get through a job-training program and find stable employment. They had hit it off since the beginning and respected each other's efforts. One day, Diana casually asks Tyrone if he'd be interested in dinner and a movie the following weekend. He politely declines. They continue working together until Diana gets back on her feet and leaves Tyrone's program.

Example of a Violation   Alyssa, age 24, is a counselor at a community-based halfway house for men on parole who are also substance abusers. *Halfway houses* are transitional dwellings that provide structure, support, and guidance for persons unable to function independently in the community. They are transitional because they provide a middle ground between a full-time residential setting (e.g., an institution or prison) and the relative freedom of living in the community.[3] *Parole* is the "conditional release of a prisoner serving an indeterminate or unexpired sentence," usually for good behavior or the promise of good behavior, under the supervision of a designated parole officer (Mish, 1995, p. 846).

   Most of the clients residing in the halfway house are in their 20s and early 30s. Alyssa finds herself physically attracted to Butch, a good-looking, charming 26-year-old parolee who resides in the house. She fights her feelings but finally gives in. When he asks her for a date, she assents and begins an intimate relationship with Butch "on the sly." Agency policy clearly forbids any such relationships with current clients or anyone who has been a client within the past six months.

Social Workers' Ethical Responsibilities to Colleagues

The NASW Code of Ethics specifies 11 areas in which practitioners have ethical responsibilities to colleagues. The focus is on maintaining respect for colleagues even when differences of opinion arise and on working cooperatively for clients' benefit. Social workers should make referrals to professionals with other areas of expertise when necessary. In addition, they should address situations in which colleagues are functioning ineffectively due to personal problems or unethical conduct. They should either approach the colleague directly or go through appropriate channels (such as in the agency or through professional associations) to help alleviate the problem. Arbitrarily, two areas involving social workers' ethical responsibilities to colleagues are discussed here—respect and referral for services.

[3]Clients using halfway houses may also include people with a history of mental illness.

Respect

Social workers should respect and work cooperatively with colleagues. They should avoid unfounded criticism of colleagues, including that directed at personal characteristics unrelated to professional performance.

Example of Compliance   Bo, a social worker at a diagnostic and treatment center for children with multiple disabilities, has a different professional orientation than many of her colleagues in the other disciplines there. For example, she feels that the family environment is important and so often works with families to discuss issues and link them with needed services. She sees the entire family as the client system. However, Darwin, the agency's psychologist, does not see such family work as important. Rather, he views the child as the client and focuses on changing the child's behavior by using structured behavior modification techniques. He primarily does individual therapy with children and offers consultation to other therapists (including speech, occupational therapy,[4] and physical therapy[5]) regarding how to control and improve children's behavior.

Bo respects Darwin and strives to work together with him in a cooperative effort. Although she does not always agree with his treatment focus, she appreciates how they both bring their professional strengths to the process.

Example of a Violation   Simon, a foster care worker, intensely dislikes his colleague Joellen, a worker in the same unit. He feels that she is lazy, knows little, and fails to take her job seriously. Simon takes every opportunity to criticize Joellen behind her back to other workers by focusing on the fact that she has a high-pitched, screechy voice and a grating, cackling laugh.

Referral for Services

Social workers should refer clients to other professionals when these others have the knowledge and skills necessary for making progress with clients. Practitioners should make such referrals as smoothly as possible, conveying vital information to the new service provider. Workers should receive no personal payment or gain from such referrals.

Example of Compliance   Jacob is a housing worker for a county social services department who helps "disadvantaged populations who need assistance in obtaining quality and affordable housing in the housing market" (Gibelman, 1995, pp. 298–299). One of Jacob's clients, Kendra, has significant physical disabilities including advancing arthritis and declining eyesight. Jacob determines that only one of Kendra's needs is housing. Her health requirements are also critical. Jacob acknowledges that he knows little about the health services that Kendra needs and so refers her to another agency worker with expertise in that area. Meanwhile, Jacob continues working to fulfill her housing needs.

---

[4]*Occupational therapy* is "therapy that utilizes useful and creative activities to facilitate psychological or physical rehabilitation" (Nichols, 1999, p. 914).

[5]*Physical therapy* is "the treatment or management of physical disability, malfunction, or pain by physical techniques, such as exercise, massage, hydrotherapy, etc." (Nichols, 1999, p. 996).

Example of a Violation   Olivia is a case manager for people with cognitive disabilities (formerly referred to as mental retardation). Tyler, age 20, has just begun living in a group home for people with cognitive disabilities and working in *sheltered employment,* a program involving work in a safe, closely supervised environment for people who have trouble functioning more independently. Clients usually receive at most minimum and usually significantly less than minimum wage. Because of his relatively high level of functioning, Olivia thinks Tyler could actually do well in regular employment (e.g., doing maintenance work or stocking shelves at a grocery store). He has good job skills, such as readily complying with supervisors' instructions, being punctual, and taking his work seriously.

The problem is that Olivia has a large caseload of clients and can barely keep up with her most critical work. Referring Tyler to a job specialist, filling out all the required paperwork, and arranging whatever transportation is necessary would take a huge amount of time. On the one hand, referring Tyler would help him better live up to his potential, enhance his self-esteem because he could hold a regular job, and, frankly, earn him more money. On the other, it's not really hurting him to remain where he is, despite the fact that it's not the best work setting for him. Olivia decides that Tyler will stay working in sheltered employment. Her time is too valuable, and she simply doesn't have enough of it.

Social Workers' Ethical Responsibilities in Practice Settings

This section of the Code of Ethics focuses on appropriate behavior in practice settings. Social workers who supervise others should be competent and evaluate supervisees fairly. Any information or data social workers record should be accurate. They should advocate for increased funding both inside and outside their agencies when resources are needed for clients. They also should "act to prevent and eliminate discrimination in the employing organization's work assignments and in its employment policies and practices" (NASW, 1999, 3.9e). Finally, practitioners should make sure their employers are aware of unethical practices. The following is an example of a dilemma faced by a social worker in an agency setting.

Case Example   Lakeisha got a job as a social worker at a nursing home three weeks ago. She is just beginning to feel comfortable there and is gradually learning the agency's policies and practices. Unfortunately, twice she's observed a disturbing scenario. Papers such as wills or insurance statements must be signed by witnesses. On these two occasions, Lakeisha saw the nursing supervisor, who is really quite powerful within the agency, ask a resident with Alzheimer's disease[6] to sign the paper for another patient with the same disease. Witnesses who sign legal papers are supposed to be of sound mind, and these residents obviously were not. No one was safeguarding either of the patients' best interests. Lakeisha was new at the agency and did not want to come across as a troublemaker, yet this signing practice was clearly wrong. The Code of Ethics instructs social workers to "act on behalf of

---

[6]Alzheimer's disease is a common disease of unknown origin that is characterized by mental decline and numerous cognitive problems.

All clients, including nursing home residents, merit ethical treatment.

clients who lack the capacity to make informed decisions" and to "take reasonable steps to safeguard the interests and rights of those clients" (NASW, 1999, 1.14). Lakiesha was also responsible for making sure the agency was aware of unethical practices (NASW, 1999, 3.09c). What should Lakiesha do?

Example of Compliance   Lakeisha decides that she cannot overlook this unethical practice despite the fact that speaking up might endanger her job. She has over five months of probation to go. She resolves to speak with the nursing supervisor. If that doesn't work, she will go over the nursing supervisor's head and speak with the home's director, who is also her immediate supervisor.[7] If worst comes to worst, she'll report this to the state agency that licenses and regulates nursing homes. She knows that will make almost everyone at the home angry because it will make the entire agency and all its employees look bad to the outside world.

Example of a Violation   Lakeisha determines that she doesn't want to make waves. After all, she thinks to herself, the practice really isn't hurting anybody, is it? The papers being signed aren't all that important anyway. She decides to forget that she ever saw the signings happen and look the other way if she ever sees it again.

---

[7]Note that when a worker has a complaint it's often most useful to go directly to the people the complaint involves and give them feedback. Subsequently, if that doesn't work, it's usually best to go to a supervisor and, as needed, gradually go up the chain of command. Going over supervisors' and administrators' heads without first approaching them with complaints generally makes them mad. It implies that they can't handle the problem at their level and may make them look incompetent to those above them in the agency's power structure.

Social Workers' Ethical Responsibilities as Professionals

Social workers' ethical responsibilities as professionals include eight broad dimensions by which they should judge their behavior and responsibility. First and foremost, they should be competent to do their jobs. If they are not, they should either seek education and learn the skills they need to become competent or get another job. Next, they should not "practice, condone, facilitate, or collaborate with any form of discrimination on the basis of race, ethnicity, national origin, color, sex, sexual orientation, age, marital status, political belief, religion, or mental or physical disability" (NASW, 1999, 4.02). They should also be honest, avoid fraud, and seek help when personal problems begin to interfere with their professional effectiveness. Finally, they should represent themselves and their qualifications accurately, and never take credit for someone else's work.

Social Workers' Ethical Responsibilities to the Social Work Profession

Ethical responsibilities to the social work profession focus on two dimensions—integrity, and evaluation and research. *Integrity* refers to social workers' promotion of high practice standards. Social workers should strive to maintain and enhance professional knowledge, values, and ethics. They should participate in activities aimed at professional contributions such as "teaching, research, consultation, service, legislative testimony, presentations in the community, and participation in their professional organizations" (NASW, 1999, 5.01c). And they should contribute to the social work knowledge base.

Similarly, social workers should encourage research and evaluation of practice effectiveness, monitor practice policies and interventions to ensure effectiveness, and maintain current knowledge of evaluation approaches. Research should be done in an ethical manner. Social workers should be honest with all involved regarding what they plan to do while conducting the research, who will have access to any information and findings gained, and who deserves credit for any findings obtained.

Social Workers' Ethical Responsibilities to the Broader Society

Ethical responsibilities to the broader society include four areas that reflect the core of social work—namely, to advocate and work for people's general welfare. This responsibility surpasses those listed in most job descriptions. Social workers should promote people's general welfare on all levels, from the local to the global. They should become actively involved in the formulation of public policy and flock to provide help during emergencies (e.g., floods, tornadoes, or earthquakes).

As part of their professional responsibilities, social workers should pursue social and political action to ensure fair and equal access to resources and opportunities. They should actively support policies to improve the human condition and promote social justice for all. They should especially work to enhance opportunities for "vulnerable, disadvantaged, oppressed, and exploited people and groups" (NASW, 1999,

Social Workers' Ethical Obligations to Help People at the Macro Level

The following two scenarios reflect situations in which social workers might confront an ethical dilemma that goes beyond their own practice with individuals, families, and groups.

Scenario A

The private social service agency Jack works for does not have a formalized affirmative action policy for hiring personnel. He has overheard the agency director make several crude racial remarks and jokes about people of color. He cannot believe that a person with such authority has gotten away with that. The agency has no people of color on staff despite having numerous clients who are. Jack feels that recruiting staff who are people of color is essential to the agency's ability to perform the way it's supposed to. He also believes that current staff members, including the agency director, need feedback to work on changing their prejudicial and discriminatory behavior.

Jack determines that he must confront this ethical issue despite possible negative consequences, including being fired. He decides to talk with his colleagues to see if he can muster more support. He knows that often a cohesive group can have a greater impact on making changes in organizations and communities than can one person alone. He finds out that several other agency workers feel the same way he does. Together, they develop a plan to talk to the agency director and provide some suggestions.

Scenario B

L'Toya is a worker at a rural county social services agency. She, her colleagues, and agency administrators have identified a significant lesbian and gay population within the area. She and the other professionals would like to implement a new program providing support groups for lesbian and gay people dealing with several issues, including single parenthood and legal difficulties such as housing discrimination. Two relatively powerful members of the County Board get wind of the idea and react in an angry, negative fashion. They consider people with a sexual orientation other than heterosexuality sinful. They also contend that there are no gay or lesbian people in the area—they surely would know about it if there were.

L'Toya works with the other interested professionals to devise a plan. First, these two board members need to be educated regarding the issues and needs of lesbian and gay people. Perhaps other board members are more knowledgeable and enlightened, and would be more supportive. Maybe some advocates of a gay rights organization in another part of the state can help. And perhaps they can assess gay and lesbian people's needs by conducting some research in the area. L'Toya and the others are on their way to developing a plan.

6.04b). They should support conditions and policies that respect cultural diversity. Similarly, they should work to prevent and eliminate conditions and policies discriminating against or exploiting people, especially vulnerable populations. Highlight 2.3 presents two situations in which social workers are ethically responsible for helping people and go beyond their job of providing direct services to clients.

International Social Welfare in a Global Context

Even beyond a macro focus at the national level, international issues are of concern to social workers. *Globalization* is the "process of global integration in which diverse peoples, economies, cultures, and political processes are increasingly subjected to international influences" (Midgley, 1997, p. xi). The world is indeed getting smaller. I recently traveled to Southeast Asia, including Ho Chi Minh City in Vietnam. As we motored along a main roadway after dusk, it was amazing to see family members huddled around 12-inch television sets in tiny home after tiny home. I thought of the millions of American homes in which essentially the same thing was happening, although the television sets and homes were much bigger.

We also stayed in a huge new hotel in the cosmopolitan, modern city–state of Singapore. My roommate was going to a grocery store in a shopping center next door to pick up some deli items for an informal supper in our room. I jokingly told her to pick up some Merkt's cheese spread, a brand found all over the Midwest including Wisconsin, where we live. When she returned and showed me her bounty, she held up a plastic container of Kaukauna cheese spread, amazingly made in Wisconsin only a few miles from my home. I was astonished. We were on the other side of the world.

The world is also getting more interdependent. In a global economy, what social and economic forces impact one nation may well result in repercussions in many other nations. Hokenstad and Midgley (1997) explain:

> Social work is one of many players in the response to these realities of global interdependence. The scope of global poverty and the intensity of ethnic conflict require first political and economic responses by nations and international organizations. Global challenges require action on many levels by many actors. Nevertheless, these are problems that are directly related to social work commitment and expertise. Social workers at the local level are directly involved with the implications of international realities by working with refugees or helping displaced workers. At the national level in many countries, the profession is active in promoting economic and social justice policy. Internationally, social work organizations are increasingly active in combating human rights violations. Thus, it is essential for social workers to have an international perspective and understanding to be effective practitioners in today's world. (pp. 3–4)

Link, Ramanathan, and Asamoah (1999) assert that "through building a global perspective, [social work] students can add insights about the human condition and more adequately understand, analyze, and predict human behavior" (p. 31). They provide an example of "the 18th Street Gang members in Los Angeles," whose families originated in El Salvador and who maintain an ongoing cultural connection with that country. Link and his colleagues (1999) stress how a global perspective helps social workers

> recognize how artificial it is to see national borders as separations between micro or macro systems. . . . These disenfranchised young people are frequently rounded up and deported to El Salvador, where they pick up with another branch of their gang so that their interactions are seamless despite the structural efforts of immigration and law enforcement to disband or break them. (p. 31; DeCesare, 1993)

International social work organizations that actively engage social workers around the globe include the International Federation of Social Workers (IFSW) and the International Association of Schools of Social Work (IASSW). The IFSW is especially involved in "promoting human rights and protesting human rights violations," and the IASSW develops internationally oriented education programs and helps train educators to teach in these areas (Hokenstad & Midgley, 1997, pp. 4–5).

Personal and Professional Values

We have established that values involve what is considered important and what is not. They concern making judgments about right and wrong. We all have the right to our personal values; we all have our own ideas about how things should be. It's a wonderful thing to be able to enjoy our own opinions and have the freedom to express them. An ongoing task for social workers is to identify their own values and distinguish between those and their professional values. As you now know, clients' right to self-determination is a key principle in social work. Therefore, social workers must be careful not to impose their personal values on clients. How difficult do you think this might be?

For example, consider a social worker who strongly supports women's rights. She may work with a Hispanic family that rigidly adheres to patriarchal values. In this family, the wife and daughters are expected to be obedient and follow the rules imposed by the father. Female family members are given much less respect, are allowed less input, and generally have significantly less power than male members. In this case the social worker must work hard to respect the family's values, but she must also focus on the right of self-determination for the family's females. It is the worker's responsibility to help such women articulate their feelings and identify their alternatives as they see them within their own cultural frame of reference. Clients must evaluate the potential positive and negative consequences for each alternative within their own cultural environment. The worker must do all this and still keep her own values in check throughout the intervention process.

Another example concerns a social worker whose adult client has a life-threatening disease and desperately needs surgery to ensure survival. However, the client refuses such medical help because it conflicts with his strong religious beliefs. The social worker personally feels that this perspective is ridiculous, yet he still must respect the client's right to make his own decisions. Focus on Critical Thinking 2.2 identifies a number of potentially controversial issues involving personal values.

Looking Ahead

This chapter established the significance of social work values in all aspects of practice. Primary values include an appreciation of human diversity and respect for people's rights to self-determination, optimal health, and enhanced well-being.

FOCUS ON CRITICAL THINKING 2.2

Identifying Personal Values

Social workers must identify their own personal values so that they are careful not to impose them on clients. What are your personal values and opinions concerning the following issues? How easy or difficult would it be for you to work with people having the opposite opinions?

- Should there be a death penalty for extreme crimes? If so, for what types of crimes (e.g., terrorism, murder, or armed robbery)?
- Should women be allowed the freedom of choice regarding abortion? If not, are there any circumstances under which an abortion could be performed (e.g., rape, incest, or a threat to the life of the mother)?
- Should women change their names to those of their spouses when they marry? Why or why not?

- Should people who are critically ill and in intense pain be able to "pull their own plug"—that is, put themselves to death?
- Should teachers in elementary and secondary school be able to use corporal punishment (i.e., inflicting punishment by causing physical pain)?
- Should prayers be allowed in public schools? What if there are children of various faiths involved (e.g., Buddhist, Muslim, Roman Catholic, Methodist, Unitarian, Hindu, or atheists)?
- Should schools provide sex education to children? If so, what should be taught?
- Should oil companies be allowed to develop untouched lands in the Arctic to keep domestic gas prices down? Or should lumber companies be allowed to cut down old-growth trees such as the giant redwoods in California?

The next chapter will focus on these and related values issues in the context of human diversity.

For Further Exploration on the Internet

See this text's Book Companion Website at **www.socialwork.wadsworth.com/ kirstashman_intro2e** for descriptors and hot links to URLs relevant to this chapter, selected InfoTrac articles and exercises, and tutorial quizzes.

CHAPTER ✦ THREE

EMPOWERMENT
AND HUMAN DIVERSITY

© Robert Brenner/PhotoEdit

How many of the following sound familiar to you?

Stereotype: White males are second-rate basketball players.
Stereotype: Women are too emotional to make good supervisors.
Stereotype: All Hispanic people have Spanish as their primary language.
Stereotype: Elderly people can't think well.
Stereotype: Gay and lesbian people really want to be the opposite gender.
Stereotype: People with physical disabilities are unemployable.

Do you have stereotypes about people from other ethnic groups, races, religions, or age groups? How about people of the other gender or those with disabilities? If so, what are these stereotypes? To what extent do you think that they really characterize every person belonging to that group?

Some people are short, and others are tall. Some are pinkish white, others ebony black, and still others various shades of golden brown. Some have astonishing IQs, and others struggle to make it through early elementary grades. Some are very young, and others are very old. Some are agile athletes; others can barely hit a volleyball over a net let alone get a basketball through a hoop; and still others can't walk at all. Our society is a vast, surging concoction of many types of diversity.

This chapter explores various aspects of human diversity, with a focus on the importance of equality, justice, and empowerment, especially for people at risk of discrimination and oppression. Specifically, this chapter will

- Define *discrimination, oppression, stereotypes,* and *prejudice,* and examine their relevance to social work practice.
- Explore the concepts of populations-at-risk and social and economic justice.
- Define *empowerment* and introduce a strengths perspective to social work practice.
- Examine empowerment for women in groups.
- Describe the concept of resiliency.
- Recognize various aspects of human diversity including age, class, color, culture, disability, ethnicity, family structure, gender, marital status, national origin, race, religion, and sexual orientation.
- Discuss some of the major values characterizing Hispanic, Native American, African American, and Asian American families.
- Define *cultural competence* and explain its application to social work.
- Identify some of the basic tenets of Islam and discuss Muslims as a population-at-risk of prejudice and discrimination.

Discrimination, Oppression, Stereotypes, and Prejudice

A major social work value involves the importance of people being treated fairly and equally. Unjust treatment impairs people's ability to determine their own life paths and achieve their optimal well-being. Membership in groups that differ from the young white male heterosexual mainstream can place people at increased risk of inequitable treatment in the forms of discrimination, oppression, and economic deprivation. *Discrimination* is the act of treating people differently based on the fact that they belong to some group rather than on merit. *Oppression* involves putting extreme limitations and constraints on some person, group, or larger system. *Economic deprivation* is the condition of having inadequate or unjust access to financial resources. The latter can result from a number of circumstances including unemployment, job discrimination, insufficient work benefits, and unsatisfactory public fiscal policies (e.g., unfair tax rates or eligibility standards for financial benefits and services that make them inaccessible to those in need).

Stereotypes often contribute to discrimination, oppression, and economic deprivation. A *stereotype* is a fixed mental picture of member of some specified group based on some attribute or attributes that reflect an overly simplified view of that group, without consideration or appreciation of individual differences. Stereotypes are related to *prejudice*—an opinion or prejudgment about an individual, group, or issue that is not based on fact; although it may be positive, it is usually negative.

Stereotypes and prejudice can involve preconceived ideas based on a person's skin color, gender, age, ethnic heritage, or external appearance. What mental images and assumed expectations come to mind when you picture a 67-year-old woman, a person using a wheelchair, or a gay man? To what extent do these images reflect stereotypes instead of unique characteristics and strengths?

It's easy to envision a number of scenarios concerning potential discrimination and oppression based on stereotypes. For instance, think of an African American family moving into a small, virtually all-white midwestern town. Picture a 58-year-old woman applying for a job in a software production center where all the employees are under age 30. Or consider a gay couple expressing affection in a primarily heterosexual bar.

Membership in any diverse group provides a different set of environmental circumstances. A wealthy, middle-aged Asian American man who just immigrated to Los Angeles from Tokyo experiences a very different world from an elderly woman of Scandinavian heritage living in Michigan's economically depressed Upper Peninsula.

What stereotypes do you harbor about various groups? Focus on Critical Thinking 3.1 provides a self-awareness exercise that might give you some insights.

 ## Populations-at-Risk and Social and Economic Justice

People from various diverse groups may be *populations-at-risk*—groups of people who share some identifiable characteristic that places them at greater risk of social and economic deprivation and oppression than the general mainstream of society. Such groups include "people of color, women, and gay and lesbian persons" in addition to people "distinguished by age, ethnicity, culture, class, religion, and physical or mental disability" (CSWE, 2001, B6.6, M6.8).

To reemphasize, a major responsibility of social work practitioners is to pursue social and economic justice for populations-at-risk and people in need. Recall from

FOCUS ON CRITICAL THINKING 3.1

Racial Self-Awareness

Self-awareness is a key quality for people entering social work and other helping professions. To assess your own level of self-awareness, ask yourself these questions:

- What adjectives and concepts automatically come to mind when you think of Hispanics? Native Americans/American Indians? African Americans? Asian Americans? Caucasians?
- Do all of the adjectives for each group apply to every single person in that group?
- In what group or groups do you include yourself? Do all the adjectives and concepts you identified for that group characterize you accurately?
- When did you first become aware of your race? Did you think of yourself as being different

from people of other races? If so, in what ways?

- In what ways, if any, have you noticed people of different races being treated differently? What do you think are the reasons for such treatment?
- What experiences have you had with people of races different from your own? To what extent were they positive or negative, and why?
- While you were growing up, was your school integrated with people from other racial backgrounds? How about your neighborhood?
- Did you or your parents have friends of different races? Why or why not?
- Did you ever question why all our presidents have been white males (Schram & Mandell, 2000)?

Chapter 1 that *social justice* involves the idea that in a perfect world all citizens would have identical "rights, protection, opportunities, obligations, and social benefits" regardless of their backgrounds and membership in diverse groups (Barker, 2003, p. 405). Similarly, *economic justice* concerns the distribution of resources in a fair and equitable manner.

In real life, social and economic justice are hard goals to attain. Rarely are rights and resources fairly and equitably distributed. Even the definitions of *fair* and *equitable* are widely debated. Do they mean that all people should receive the same income regardless of what work they do, or even whether they have jobs? As you now know, social workers must constantly be on the lookout for injustice because it is their ethical responsibility to combat it whenever necessary and possible to do so.

 ## Empowerment and a Strengths Perspective

Simply put, social workers help people solve problems. However, to do this, practitioners must focus on clients' strengths. Concentrating on the problem at hand tells workers what is wrong, but not what to do about it. Focusing on clients' strengths provides social workers with clues about how to proceed by building on these strengths.

Saleebey (2002b, pp. 87–88) provides an example of emphasizing client strengths with Michael, a middle-aged man who has moderate cognitive disabilities.

A social work student working with Michael visited him in his apartment one day. Michael was capable of living alone if he had some supportive supervision, including help with getting groceries, paying bills, and organizing other necessary activities. The student noticed that Michael's walls were covered with intricately drawn maps of his town, state, and country, and was awestruck at the careful detail and attractive colors. Taking the initiative, the student worked with Michael to make the local newspaper and museum aware of his talent and his output. The paper published articles about Michael, and a local museum exhibited his work. Subsequently, a greeting card company with national distribution approached Michael and other amateur artists with cognitive or physical disabilities about initiating a whole new card line.

We have established that *empowerment* is the "process of increasing personal, interpersonal, or political power so that individuals can take action to improve their life situations" (Gutierrez, 1990, p. 149). Empowerment means increasing, emphasizing, developing, and nurturing strengths and positive attributes. It aims at enhancing individuals', groups', families', and communities' power and control over their destinies.

Cowger (1994) maintains that social work historically has focused on dysfunction, pathology, and "individual inadequacies" (p. 262). He states that "if assessment focuses on deficits, it is likely that deficits will remain the focus of both the worker and the client during remaining contacts. Concentrating on deficits or strengths can lead to self-fulfilling prophecies" (p. 264). He continues that a strengths perspective can provide "structure and content for an examination of realizable alternatives, for the mobilization of competencies that can make things different, and for the building of self-confidence that stimulates hope" (p. 265).

Saleebey (2002a) articulates a *strengths perspective* that is essentially based on empowerment. He cites five primary underlying principles (pp. 14–17):

1. "Every individual, group, family and community has strengths."
2. "Trauma and abuse, illness and struggle may be injurious but they may also be sources of challenge and opportunity."
3. Social workers should assume that they "do not know the upper limits of the capacity to grow and change and take individual, group, and community aspirations seriously."
4. Social workers "best serve clients by collaborating with them."
5. "Every environment is full of resources."

As noted previously, empowerment implies that people lack power and thereby need it increased. Several designated groups of people suffer from stereotypes, discrimination, and oppression. It is social work's task to empower clients in general and members of oppressed groups in particular. Highlight 3.1 discusses some research about effective empowerment approaches with women.

Resiliency: Seeking Strength amid Adversity

A concept related to the strengths perspective and empowerment is resiliency: the ability of an individual, family, group, community, or organization to recover from adversity and resume functioning even when suffering serious trouble, confusion, or hardship. For example, Norman (2000) provides an illustration of this notion:

HIGHLIGHT 3.1
Empowerment for Women in Groups

Parsons (2001) conducted a qualitative study of effective empowerment strategies for women. There is substantial support for the use of consciousness-raising as a strategy to empower women (GlenMaye, 1998). *Consciousness-raising* is the process of facilitating people's understanding of a social issue, with personal implications when there was little grasp of that issue before. Women often don't realize the relationship between their troubles and the world around them, thereby unjustly assuming all the blame themselves. For example, a woman in a relationship in which she is regularly battered will frequently blame herself, and not the batterer, for her problems. She might think that she shouldn't have yelled back at him because that was only asking to be punched. Or she might think that she should have ironed his collar the correct way and then he wouldn't have had to hit her in retribution.

Parsons (2001) studied two women's groups and evaluated the conditions conducive to women's empowerment. The Domestic Violence Survivors (DVS) was made up of women coping with battery who were trying to regain control of their lives. The All Families Deserve a Chance group was made up of women receiving public assistance who wished to advocate for improved policies and conditions for themselves and other women receiving aid. The two groups were chosen because they reflected two very different objectives. One involved improving

the lives of individuals by gaining personal control, a micro goal. The other concentrated on advocating for change in social policy, a macro goal.

The following themes emerged as providing successful conditions for women's empowerment within a group setting:

- *Safety:* Knowing nothing horrible will happen makes group members feel more comfortable about participating and having control.
- *Mutual interaction:* Having the ability to interact and communicate with other group members without feeling threatened is reassuring.
- *Commonality:* Finding out that they are not the only ones having these problems is empowering.
- *Acceptance:* Feeling that they belong, regardless of their problems, self-criticism, or mistakes, gives group members increased self-confidence and a sense of power.
- *Validation:* Having what they say about their experiences be "confirmed" and "heard" by others helps them learn "that they . . . [are] not crazy" (Parsons, 2001, p. 168).
- *Interdependence:* Feeling that they can rely on each other for help and support bolsters their confidence and ability to take action.

Strategies used by the social workers running the groups were also found to enhance feelings of empowerment. First, social workers provided

(continued)

When a pitched baseball hits a window, the glass usually shatters. When that same ball meets a baseball bat, the bat is rarely damaged. When a hammer strikes a ceramic vase, it too usually shatters. But when that same hammer hits a rubber automobile tire, the tire quickly returns to its original shape. The baseball bat and the automobile tire both demonstrate resiliency (p. 3).

Resiliency involves two dimensions—"risk factors" and "protective factors" (Norman, 2000, p. 3). In this context, *risk factors* involve "stressful life events or adverse environmental conditions that increase the *vulnerability* [defenselessness

HIGHLIGHT 3.1 *(continued)*

support by encouraging group members to speak, listening to what they had to say, and believing them. Group members thus felt they had the right to be listened to and to think through their issues. One group member explained:

> "[The group leader] is like a mentor. She challenges you. She won't let me get away with being afraid. She isn't going to let *me* get in the way of me. Her instincts for people have made me aware of my own feelings. She taught me that even though I am not always strong, I am not a weak person. I have high expectations, push myself. She says you are doing a good job even though you are not doing everything you want to be doing. She has more faith in me than I do in myself sometimes. I say, if she has this kind of faith in me, why can't I have it myself?" (Parsons, 2001, p. 170)

Breton and Nosko (1997) cite an interaction demonstrating worker support that occurred in another group for women who had suffered domestic violence:

Woman: I have no self-esteem.

Worker: What does self-esteem mean to you?

Woman: I don't know, really.

Worker: Well, then, maybe you have some. (p. 137)

A second effective social work strategy for empowerment involved educating group members about relevant issues. For the DVS, such education entailed talking about the cycle of violence (i.e., building up of tension, explosive battering incident, making up)—how difficult it is to break it and how perpetrators do all they can to maintain their control through violence. For All Families Deserve a Chance, the social worker taught women the steps for advocacy. Group members learned how to clarify their position, formulate recommendations for changing public assistance policy, and effectively communicate with decision makers.

Third, the social workers actively advocated on the group members' behalf. Workers demonstrated that they were ardently on their clients' side by encouraging them, spurring them on, and readily bestowing positive feedback for their achievements.

Fourth, the social workers helped group members learn how to express, deal with, and resolve conflict without anger or violence. Fifth, the social workers encouraged the women to take risks by trusting others and allowing themselves to hope that things could actually get better. Sixth, the social workers provided a role model for group members, thereby affording guidance for more effective communication and appropriate assertiveness in addition to conflict management. Finally, group members learned that taking small steps could enhance empowerment. Small successes slowly led to increased confidence and achievement of bigger goals.

or helplessness] of individuals" or other systems (p. 3). *Protective factors*, on the other hand, "buffer, moderate, and protect against those vulnerabilities" (p. 3).

For example, Watkins (2002) studied six urban girls between ages 11 and 14 who were at risk of negative influences including poverty, "poor parental education, tenuous family structure, . . . history of abuse or neglect, and the influence of negative home environments" (p. 117). The study investigated how these girls were able to survive and even thrive in the midst of adversity, demonstrating their capacity for resiliency. Two of the girls are described as follows (Watkins, 2002):

Shatika: This 12-year-old African American girl was tall and thin. She described herself as "I'm what you call light-skinned." Adolescent acne (which she called "skin bumps") was noticeable on her forehead, nose, and cheeks. Shatika's brown hair with red highlights was pulled behind her ears with a rubber band. She explained that her hair "needed to be done," but her mother was unable to afford the cost of a permanent. Shatika was very soft-spoken and hesitatingly made eye contact as the interview process was explained. . . .

Daisy: This 13-year-old Caucasian girl was petite with symmetrical fullness of hips and breasts. Her heavily permed dark blond hair was shoulder length and she wore a ribbon to keep her hair out of her small and closely set gray eyes. Daisy was dressed in "daisy dukes"—short shorts with matching gingham shirt. As she spoke in soft, hushed tones, Daisy made it clear that she was willing to help with the project only if she could be assured that no one would "find out my secrets." She said, "I ain't never got to talk about me before and it could help me. It's good to talk with someone sometimes to hear yourself." (p. 119)

The study found that these girls exhibited resiliency when they actively sought means to enhance their own well-being and protect them from harm in at least two ways (Watkins, 2002). First, the girls used their own positive relationship-building skills to seek positive, close connections with people who were or became central in their lives. Such people might include a parent or parents, members of their extended family (several girls mentioned their close relationships with their aunts), other adults such as "youth workers, coaches, clergy, neighbors, [or] teachers," and peers with whom they were "sharing activities, hanging out together, keeping secrets, and 'keeping . . . out of trouble'" (Watkins, 2002, pp. 121–122).

A second way these girls used resiliency was in developing strategies to protect themselves in an unsafe urban environment. "The girls would deliberately pre-arrange travel companions when walking to the corner store. To avoid danger, they would map out the route they would take through the streets. They developed other physical resistance strategies, such as personal safety plans or not 'hanging on the streets'" (Watkins, 2002, p. 125).

Resiliency can also characterize larger systems. An example at the organizational level is a public university experiencing budget cuts of several million dollars. That university is resilient to the extent that it responds to the risk of loss, protects its most important functions, makes plans to adapt to the shortfall of resources, and continues providing students with a quality education. Resiliency involves focusing on its strengths to maintain basic functioning.

Resiliency in a community is illustrated by a group of urban neighborhoods that addresses an increasing crime and drug use problem. These troubles put the community at risk of disorganization and destruction. Community strengths include availability of organizations that provide resources; residents' expectations for appropriate, positive behavior; and opportunities for "neighborhood youths to constructively participate in the community" (Greene & Livingston, 2002, p. 78). A resilient community might use its concerned citizens to form neighborhood organizations that oversee community conditions and upkeep, work with public services to improve conditions, and advocate for increased resources (Homan, 2004). Neighborhood Watch programs may be formed, where neighborhood residents volunteer to carefully watch each other's premises to prevent and combat crime. Community residents might work with local police and schools to establish drug education and prevention programs for young people. They might also advocate for more police to increase surveillance and apprehension of drug dealers. Many communities have successfully driven out drug vendors, reclaiming and securing their neighborhoods and parks so children can feel safe in these places. A resilient community uses its strengths to address the risks threatening it and protect its residents.

Human Diversity

Chapter 1 established that *human diversity* is the vast range of differences among groups including those related to "age, class, color, culture, disability, ethnicity, family structure, gender, marital status, national origin, race, religion, sex, and sexual orientation" (CSWE, 2001, I.C, III.A.3, Accreditation Standard [AS] 6.0). Social workers must understand human diversity for two reasons. First, many members of diverse groups are populations-at-risk of discrimination and oppression. Second, it's necessary to recognize the values and issues of diverse groups to appreciate differences and build on strengths.

Social work by nature addresses virtually any type of problem posed by any type of person from any type of background. To help people, practitioners must be open-minded, nonjudgmental, knowledgeable, and skilled. Because the range of human diversity is endless, learning about it is a continuous process.

Race and Ethnicity

Race and ethnicity are related concepts that reflect primary dimensions of human diversity. *Race* refers to a category of people who share a common descent and genetic origin, previously based on "an arbitrary selection of physical characteristics, such as skin color, facial form, or eye shape, and now frequently based on such genetic markers as blood groups" (Nichols, 1999, p. 1085). *Ethnicity* refers to the affiliation with a large group of people who have "common racial, national, tribal, religious, linguistic, or cultural origin or background" (Mish, 1995, p. 398). Race implies a greater genetic determinant, whereas ethnicity often relates to cultural or national heritage. Other terms such as *minorities* and *people of color* are also commonly used to refer to people of different racial and ethnic heritage.

People of color "is a collective term that refers to the major groups of African, Latino, Asian, and Native Americans who have been distinguished from the dominant society by color" (Lum, 2003, p. 68).[1] *Minorities* are members of "a group of people who, because of physical or cultural characteristics, are singled out from the others in the society in which they live for differential and unequal treatment, and who therefore regard themselves as objects of collective discrimination" (Sue et al., 1998, p. 11; Wirth, 1945, p. 347). It is interesting that in the past many minorities did indeed make up a smaller proportion of the total population than did Anglos (i.e., U.S. citizens of European heritage, also referred to as Caucasians or whites). However, some minority

[1]Note that not all Hispanic people are people of color. Consider, for example, a white woman born in Argentina who speaks Spanish, the national language, and whose ancestors originated in Spain.

HIGHLIGHT 3.2
Terms Used to Describe Latino/a/Hispanic People

The U.S. government's Office of Management and Budget originally coined the term *Hispanic* in 1978 for use in the census (Green, 1999). According to the original definition, a Hispanic was "a person of Mexican, Puerto Rican, Cuban, Central or South American or other Spanish culture or origin, regardless of race" (Green, 1999, p. 256). However, the concept is much more complex than this. For example, does this umbrella term include Brazilians who speak Portuguese, South American Indians whose original language is not Spanish, Filipinos who speak Spanish, or immigrants from Spain (Green, 1999)?

An alternative term is *Latino/Latina,* which makes reference both to the Latin American languages, including Spanish, and to Latin America itself. However, this term omits South Americans who speak English, such as those from Belize or the Guyanas, and "people whose family roots extend to Italy, Germany, and some areas of the Mediterranean" (Green, 1999, p. 256).

Still another term often used is *Chicano/Chicana,* which refers to U.S. citizens with a Mexican heritage. The obvious disadvantage of this term is that it focuses only on Mexico and excludes people with origins in other countries, including those that are primarily Spanish speaking.

Longres (1995) concludes that social workers "should take the lead from the individuals, families, or communities they work with" and use the terms people prefer (p. 1215). This book will use the terms *Hispanic* and *Latino/a* interchangeably unless a specific group (e.g., Puerto Rican Americans or Chicanos/as [Mexican Americans]) is discussed.

populations such as Latinos/as/Hispanics are making substantial gains and within several decades may surpass Anglos in actual numbers. Highlight 3.2 discusses the terms used to describe the Latino/a/Hispanic population in the United States.

Culture and Cultural Competence

Culture, another dimension of diversity, is "the sum total of life patterns passed on from generation to generation within a group of people and includes institutions, language, religious ideals, habits of thinking, artistic expressions, and patterns of social and interpersonal relationships" (Hodge, Struckmann, & Trost, 1975; Lum, 2003, p. 4). Aspects of culture are often related to people's ethnic, racial, and spiritual heritage.

Social workers need to attain *cultural competence*—"the set of knowledge and skills that a social worker must develop in order to be effective with multicultural clients" (Lum, 1999, p. 3). Cultural competence, strongly supported by the NASW Code of Ethics, involves the following six tasks for social workers (Arredondo et al., 1996; Lum, 2003; NASW, 1999, 1.05):

1. Develop an awareness of personal values, assumptions, and biases.
2. Establish an appreciation of other cultures and nurture attitudes that respect differences.

3. Understand how one's own cultural heritage and belief system differ from and may influence interaction with clients who have a different cultural background.
4. Recognize the existence of stereotypes about, discrimination against, and oppression of various diverse groups.
5. Commit to learning about clients' cultures.
6. Acquire effective skills for working with people from other cultures.

Focus on Critical Thinking 3.2 stresses how important it is for social workers to be aware of their clients' values, traditions, and customs.

Ethnic and Cultural Differences

We've established that understanding and appreciating diversity are essential for social workers to practice effectively with clients. Because families provide a primary arena for conveying values, much of the following discussion will focus on them.

Three points are helpful when we think about multicultural diversity. The first is that certain values tend to characterize each major racial and ethnic group. However, the second point concerns how critical it is not to overly generalize. Various individuals may embrace such cultural values to different degrees. The third point involves the importance of respect for and appreciation of the differences within large groups. For example, American Indians have been referred to as "Indians" only for the past 500 years. In reality, they make up over 500 nations including Tsististas, Lakota, Dine, Muscogee, and Ojibway that "maintain 300 separate languages and dialects" (Harjo, 1993, p. 199; Weaver, 2003).

The following section discusses some of the values, beliefs, and perspectives assumed by several cultural groups in our society: Hispanics, Native Americans, African Americans, and Asian Americans. Figure 3.1 summarizes the primary concepts.

Hispanics

We have established that the terms *Hispanic* and *Latino/a* have generally been used to refer to people originating in countries in which Spanish is spoken. However, we have also established that the terms refer to people originating in a wide range of places. Essentially, no one term is acceptable to all groups of people. The three primary Hispanic groups in the United States in terms of size are Mexican Americans (63% of all Hispanics), Puerto Ricans who live on the mainland (12%), and Cuban Americans (6%) (Goldenberg & Goldenberg, 2002). Other groups include those from the Dominican Republic and from other countries in Central and South America (Santiago-Rivera, Arredondo, & Gallardo-Cooper, 2002). However, for any particular family, Goldenberg and Goldenberg (2002) caution, "Socioeconomic, regional, and demographic characteristics vary among Hispanic American groups, making cultural generalizations risky" (p. 326). Santiago-Rivera, Arredondo, and Gallardo-Cooper (2002) reflect:

> Perhaps no other ethnic group in the United States is as heterogeneous in its ethnicity, physical appearance, cultural practices and traditions, and Spanish language dialects as the Latino population. Latinos in the United States are a diverse group of multigenerational . . . [people] from different Spanish-speaking countries as well as long-term residents in the

FOCUS ON CRITICAL THINKING 3.2
Cultural Issues to Address

Census 2002 (U.S. Census Bureau, 2003) indicates that almost 68% of the total U.S. population of 288,369 million is non-Hispanic white; over 12.7% is African American; almost 1% is American Indian and Alaskan Native; 4% is Asian; and almost .2% is Native Hawaiian and other Pacific Islander. Over 1.4% reported being a member of more than one race. Almost 13.5% are Hispanic, who may be of any race.

Two facts stand out from these figures. (1) There is significant diversity in the population, and (2) a person's race is not always clear-cut. A person's family line and genetic heritage may be quite complex.

The racial mix of the United States is rapidly changing. Currently, about 30% of U.S. residents are people of color, and it's predicted that almost half will be by the middle of the century (Neukrug, 2004). Given such a diverse world, social workers and other helping professionals must be prepared to work with people having cultural backgrounds quite different from their own.

Social workers and other helping professionals must address at least four issues to work effectively with multicultural clients. First, they should rebuff the *melting pot myth,* which implies that we're all blended together into one big pot of creamed soup, that we all become essentially the same (Neukrug, 2004, p. 200). In reality, we're more like a salad bowl filled with various types of vegetables and croutons. Although we're all in there together, we maintain our individual and cultural distinctiveness.

The second issue that social workers must address is how people from various cultures have different ideas and expectations about

what should happen during the intervention process (Neukrug, 2004, p. 200). For example, an Anglo approach "assumes that the counseling process should emphasize the individual; stress the expression of feelings; [and] encourage self-disclosure, open-mindedness, and insight" (Neukrug, 2004, p. 200). However, people from other cultures may assume very different perspectives. For example, a Hispanic man might emphasize the importance of family over what's best for himself as an individual. Similarly, he may find the blatant expression of emotions inappropriate and distasteful.

The third issue concerns *worldviews*— "one's perceptions of oneself in relation to other people, objects, institutions, and nature. It relates to one's view of the world and one's role and place in it" (Leashore, 1995, p. 112). With an *ethnocentric worldview,* people perceive their own race, ethnic background, or cultural values as being better than that of others (Neukrug, 2004, p. 201). Essentially, it's similar to the view "My way is not only the best way, it's the only way."

Sue (1992) provides an interesting example:

A white female elementary school teacher in the United States posed a math problem to her class one day. "Suppose there are four blackbirds sitting in a tree. You take a slingshot and shoot one of them. How many are left?" A white student answered quickly, "That's easy. One subtracted from four is three." An African immigrant youth then answered with equal confidence, "Zero." The teacher chuckled at the latter response and stated that the first student was right and that, perhaps, the second student should study more math. From that day forth, the African student seemed

(continued)

southwest United States. All have unique social, economic, and political histories. Latino groups vary in their ancestry, blending indigenous [people originating in an area] (e.g., Aztec and Mayan) and Spanish cultural traditions and, for some Latino groups, African traditions.

FOCUS ON CRITICAL THINKING 3.2 *(continued)*

to withdraw from class activities and seldom spoke to other students or the teacher. (pp. 7–8)

What the teacher didn't know was that the African boy viewed the problem from an entirely different perspective. He looked at the whole picture of what shooting a bird with a slingshot meant. If the teacher had sought clarification of his answer instead of making fun of him, she might have better understood. The student's answer made perfect sense to him: If you shoot a slingshot at four birds sitting in a tree and hit one, the other three will fly away immediately, of course, and none will be left. Nigerian educators frequently use this anecdote to portray how differently people in the United States and Africa view the world. The African perspective takes into account how all the parts involved in a problem work together. In contrast, an Anglo perspective tends to focus on individuals searching for isolated, specific, technical aspects of a problem to determine the one correct answer.

The fourth issue concerns the importance of family. Anglos tend to focus on the *nuclear family*—the immediate family group composed of parent[s] and children—and give less credence to the *extended family*—relatives beyond the nuclear family including at least grandparents, aunts, uncles, and cousins (Neukrug. 2000, p. 203). A related concept is *kinship,* which refers to the state of being related through a common ancestry.

For example, I once worked as a social worker at a day treatment center for children and adolescents with emotional and behavioral problems. They attended the center during the day to receive special education and therapy, and then returned to their homes in the community at night and on weekends. A number of African American clients seemed to be staying at a different relative's home each week. This was a problem because clients were bused in from all over the city, so scheduling the bus route was a nightmare. The treatment center's administration, all of whom were Anglos, identified multiple residences as a problem. However, it really was a strength and should have been viewed as such. These adolescents had a strong kinship system with their extended family. Many relatives were ready and willing to take care of these children when their nuclear family (in this case, their mothers) did not always have the resources and capabilities to do so.

Another example of the strengths demonstrated by extended families involves Navajo who live on a reservation stretching from the south central Colorado plateau to parts of Arizona, New Mexico, and Utah. The tribe opened and ran its own nursing home for tribal members (Mercer, 1996). The home's staff had to be very sensitive to the fact that residents had numerous visitors from their extended family, many of whom were quite distant from the nuclear family and some of whom would travel great distances at significant cost. This was in stark contrast to many Anglo nursing homes, in which staff are accustomed to receiving few visitors for residents, and often only immediate family. Staff there frequently view visits as cumbersome and unmanageable. Chapter 10 elaborates further on the Navajo's empowering treatment of elderly family members.

It's important not to make stereotyped assumptions about such a diverse group. Santiago-Rivera and her colleagues (2002) continue:

Although it is not often reported, Latinos may also be of Asian heritage. The Philippine islands, conquered by Spain, were populated by people of Asian heritage. Whereas the

Hispanics	Native Americans	African Americans	Asian Americans
Common language	Extended family and respect for elders	Extended family	Family vs. individuals as primary unit
Extended family	Noninterference	Role flexibility	Interdependence
Respect for elderly	Harmony with nature	Respect for elderly	Filial piety
Spirituality	Less formal and rigid concept of time	Strong religious beliefs	Investment in children
Strict division of gender roles	Spirituality		Partriarchal hierarchy

Figure 3.1   Common cultural values for four diverse groups

native language of the island is Tagalog, Spanish surnames are commonplace, and in the United States, Filipinos may claim either Asian or Latino heritage. In South America and Mexico, there are settlements of Chinese families as well. Peru is one such example. (p. 23)

Keeping in mind that more specific variations exist within the many subgroups, we will discuss some cultural themes important to Hispanic families in general. Hispanic heritage is rich and diverse, but the groups tend to share similarities in terms of values, beliefs, attitudes, culture, and self-perception. These include the significance of a common language, the importance of family relationships including extended family and other support systems, spirituality, and the traditional strictness of gender roles.

The first theme important in understanding the environment for children growing up in Hispanic families is the significance of a common language. Although everyday communication among Latinos is frequently in English (Longres, 1995b), "90% of Latinos in the United States continue to use the Spanish language"; therefore, social workers should "know that there is a growing population of bilingual Latinos who have varying degrees of language proficiencies in English and Spanish" (Santiago-Rivera et al., 2002, p. 121). For instance, recent immigrants may use little if any English, whereas people whose families have been here for centuries may be bilingual or lack any knowledge of Spanish. One strong implication of such diversity is the need for social workers to assess Latino clients' language history and use on an individual basis.

Another important note is the fact that so many cultural activities and aspects of cultural pride are associated with Spanish. Consider the events and holidays (e.g., Cinco de Mayo for Mexican Americans, which refers to the glorious day a small Mexican army defeated a French army battalion), "history and traditions, Spanish posters, and foods associated with Spanish-speaking homelands" that are so meaningful in daily cultural life (Longres, 1995, p. 1215).

A second theme reflecting a major strength in many Hispanic families is the significance placed on relationships with nuclear and extended family including "aunts, uncles, cousins, and grandparents, as well as close friends," referred to as *familismo* (Santiago-Rivera et al., 2002, pp. 42–43; Weaver, 2005). "Latino families are typically large, intergenerational, and interdependent, and offer an important source of support to their members. . . . Extended family ties are highly valued and serve as a source of pride and security. . . . This emphasis on respect and responsibility to family members often leads to elderly adults both being cared for and taking on caregiving responsibilities within the family. The elderly are often cared for within the family rather than through formal social services. When nursing homes are used, family members often continue to fulfill supportive caregiving responsibilities" (Kolb, 1999; Weaver, 2005, p. 148).

Another important related concept reflecting a cultural strength is *compadrazco* (godparentage). *Compadres* (godparents) often serve as "substitute parents" who "may be prominent leaders or older people who hold some position of authority and respect within the Latino community. Such individuals play an important role in the Latino family's life and are included in all traditional celebrations. The practice of godparentage formalizes relationships between the child's parents and the *compadres* and promotes a sense of community" (Santiago-Rivera et al., 2002, p. 44).

Other vital sources of strength involve the community support systems often available to Hispanic families. These include the following:

Botanicas: "[S]hops that sell herbs as well as records and novels in Spanish."

Bodegas: "[G]rocery stores" that "also serve as information centers for the Hispanic community, providing such information as where folk healers can be found . . . " (Mexican, Puerto Rican, and Cuban Hispanic cultures espouse folk healers who help people deal with physical, emotional, and spiritual difficulties).

Club socials: Settings that "provide recreation as well as links to community resources, including employment and housing" (Chilman, 1993, p. 160).

A third theme characterizing many Hispanic families is the importance of spirituality and religion. "Spirituality has a fundamental shaping influence on the lives of many Latinos. Catholicism is a defining force of family and gender roles for Latino people. . . . Latino Catholicism revolves around the concepts of life and death. This fatalistic belief system emphasizes that God will provide. There is a pervading sense that much of what happens is beyond an individual's personal control. Most Latinos are Roman Catholic, but many espouse beliefs and practices influenced by indigenous and African belief systems" (Santiago-Rivera et al., 2002; Weaver, 2005, p. 147). Examples of such folk beliefs are the following:

Espiritismo (among Puerto Ricans): "[T]he belief in spirits. Everyone is believed to have spirits of protection, and these can be increased by performing good deeds and decreasing evil. Latinos who ascribe to *espiritismo* believe that loved ones can be around in spirit after death and can lead one's life in times of difficulties. *Espiritistas* (spiritist healers) communicate with spirits and can be incarnated by them. Healing can take place with prescribed folk healing treatment."

Curanderismo (among Mexican Americans and other Central and South Americans): The practice of curing "physical, emotional, and folk illnesses. *Curanderos/as* are healers who use a range of treatments, such as herbal remedies, inhalation, sweating, massage, incantations, and *limpieza* (a ritual cleansing)."

Santeria (among Cuban Americans): Practices that combine "African deities with Catholic saints. The *santeros/as* are priests who function as healers, diviners, and directors of rituals" (Negroni-Rodriguez & Morales, 2001, p. 135; Santiago-Rivera et al., 2002; Weaver, 2005).

A fourth theme often characterizing Hispanic families involves a strict division of gender roles reflected in two major concepts (Weaver, 2005). *Machismo* is the idea of male "superiority" that "defines the man as provider, protector, and head of the household"; *marianismo,* on the other hand, is the idea that, "after the Virgin Mary," females are valued for their "female spiritual sensitivity and self-sacrifice for the good of husband and children. . . . The mother and wife roles offer power to exercise authority in the home. However, women are also expected to be dependent on men" (Negroni-Rodriguez & Morales, 2001, p. 135). Additionally, females are supposed to stay virgins until marriage (Santiago-Rivera et al., 2002).

Santiago-Rivera and her colleagues (2002) note that these beliefs may give mothers an important yet challenging role in the family. If a woman is self-effacing and giving at all times, she may appear to outsiders to be more like a submissive doormat. However, those who know Latinas, especially mothers, often note that women are the silent power in the family.

In *The Maria Paradox* (Gil & Vasquez, 1996), the 10 commandments for women who subscribe to the paradigm of *marianismo* are listed. These include the following:

Do not forget a woman's place;
Do not forsake tradition;
Do not be single, self-supporting, or independent-minded;
Do not forget that sex is for making babies, not for pleasure;
Do not be unhappy with your man, no matter what he does to you;
Do not ask for help;
Do not discuss personal problems outside the home; and
Do not change.

Although Latinas of varying generations may recognize the commandments, many report that as a result of . . . [becoming more absorbed into the majority culture], education, and involvement in relationships that do not reinforce the commandments, they experience less conflict about not living according to the commandments. It can be argued that many women, not just Latinas, have been socialized according to this belief system; however, *marianismo* is still considered a Latino cultural value (p. 50).[2]

Weaver (2005) indicates that "[a]lthough distinct gender roles exist, it is important to recognize that not all Latinas fit these roles to the same extent. For example, Latinas are often stereotyped as passive and submissive, but many changes have taken

---

[2]Note that in academic circles and in Latin American women's studies, the meaning of *marianismo* has been expanded over the last few decades; "[i]t has now evolved into a term used to describe the feminine spiritual superiority, moral superiority, and spiritual strength of the modern Mexican woman" (Bocchi, 2005).

place in marriages and families in the last decade. Many Latinas now work outside the home and may wield decision-making power about family finances. It is important to understand evolving gender roles within Latino families" (p. 146). Today over 58% of Hispanic women are in the workforce compared to 64% of African American women and 59% of white women (U.S. Census Bureau, 2004). From a strengths perspective, Hispanic women function as socializers, educators, and promoters of values and beliefs within family systems. Hispanic couples vary widely in terms of who assumes decision-making power and responsibility for family support, as do couples in any other ethnic or racial group. Other factors to consider that influence gender roles include educational level, income, location, history in this country, verbal communication, and family structure (Santiago-Rivera et al., 2002).

American Indians/Native Americans/First Nations Peoples

We have stressed that there are over 500 separate American Indian nations with hundreds of dialects (Weaver, 2003). Weaver (2003) comments on the terms used to refer to these indigenous peoples (that is, people who originally populated these geographic areas):

> There are many terms for the indigenous people of North America including *American Indian, Native American,* and *First Nations Peoples.* There is no consensus about which term is best, yet some Native people have strong preferences for one term over the others. These terms all include many different groups of distinct people. (p. 197)

Some people feel that the term *First Nations Peoples* emphasizes the true status of these population groups as the first inhabitants of North America who populated intact nations before Europeans arrived (Kirst-Ashman & Hull, 2006). There is also some evidence that many people in these groups prefer the term *American Indian* over *Native American* (Barker, 2003). Additionally, the term *Native American* is "a broader designation [than that referring to North American peoples] because the U.S. government includes Hawaiians and Samoans in this category" (American Psychological Association, 2001, p. 68). This book will arbitrarily use the terms *American Indian* and *First Nations Peoples* interchangeably when referring to these population groups. When quoting other sources, I sometimes use the term *Native American.*

Whenever possible, it's best to "name the participants' specific group" (American Psychological Association, 2001, p. 68; Brave Heart & Chase, 2005). Although some nations consist of fewer than 100 people (Weaver, 2003), others including the Cherokee, Chippewa, Choctaw, Navajo, and Sioux have over 100,000 members according to the U.S. Census Bureau (2003). Weaver (2003) further describes the picture:

> Extensive diversity also exists among people within nations. Some people are very knowledgeable about and grounded in their indigenous culture, while others are not. Sometimes this is based on choices an individual has made; however, it is more often the result of decades of damaging U.S. policies that tried to assimilate Native people. These policies were deliberate in their attempts to eradicate indigenous cultures. Many people lost their ability to speak their language and lost touch with their cultural traditions when they were forcibly taken away from their community and sent to government or church-run boarding schools. This sort of cultural loss impaired their ability to pass

Sexual orientation is an important facet of human diversity.

on cultural traditions to their children, and left many Native people with limited knowledge of their indigenous heritage. (p. 199)

Sensitivity to differences among American Indian nations and to individuals within nations, along with appreciation of these differences, is vital to effective social work practice. However, as with Hispanic people, several themes characterize many First Nations Peoples. These include the importance of extended family, noninterference, harmony with nature, the concept of time, and spirituality.

As with Hispanic people, *family ties* including those with extended family are very important (Brammer, 2004; Ho, 1987; Paniagua, 2005). The sense of self is secondary compared to that of the family and of the tribe (Paniagua, 2005). Baruth and Manning (1999) explain:

Family extends well beyond one's immediate relatives to extended family relatives through the second cousin, members of one's clan, members of the community, all other living creatures in this world, nature as a whole, and the universe itself. The entire universe is thought of as a family, with every one of its members serving a useful and necessary function. Native American children develop a heightened level of sensitivity for everything of which they are a part, for the cyclical motion of life, and for the customs and traditions of their people. (p. 325)

Edwards and Edwards (2002) comment:

> It is not unusual for large numbers of extended family members to participate in healing ceremonies for cousins, aunts, uncles, parents, and grandparents. It is sometimes confusing to accurately identify family members, as cousins may be affectionately referred to as brothers and sisters, and respected aunts and uncles (sometimes several times removed) may be addressed as mothers, fathers, and grandparents are. Elders are often referred to as "Grandmother" or "Grandfather" when there are no kinship ties to these people. (p. 247)

Elders typically are turned to for advice and consultation on important matters. Paniagua (2005) explains:

> American Indians emphasize the "administration" of the family by the father and older relatives. Thus, mutual respect between wife and husband, between parents and children, between immediate family members and other relatives, and between family members and the tribe is highly valued. . . . An important part of the American Indian cultural value of familism [the well-being of the family is most important and the interests of the individual secondary] is the tradition of consulting tribal leaders, elders, and medicine men or women when marital conflicts emerge. (p. 100)

Children receive supervision and instruction not only from their parents, but also from relatives of several generations; thus biological parents have "greater opportunity to engage in more fun-oriented activities with their children" and often are able to establish relationships with their children that are "less pressured and more egalitarian than that of the dominant culture" (Ho, 1992, p. 76).

A second significant concept in American Indian culture involves the emphasis on *noninterference,* "the deep respect for the rights and dignity of individuals [to make their own decisions]. . . . The highest form of respect for another person is respecting his or her natural right to self-determination. This means not interfering with another person's ability to choose, even when it means keeping a person from doing something foolish or dangerous" (Baruth & Manning, 1999, p. 328; Kirst-Ashman & Hull, 2002). Although First Nations life emphasizes collective work and common goals, it also stresses the individual's right to have opinions (Paniagua, 1998). Therefore, "American Indian children are rarely told directly what to do and are often encouraged to make their own decisions" (Paniagua, 1998, p. 81). Locke (1998) explains:

> [M]any Native American Indians use noncoercive parenting styles that encourage the child's self-determination. . . . Child-rearing practices are characterized by early training in self-sufficiency, and psychological development is in harmony with knowledge gained from the natural world. . . . [American] Indian parents are generally quite permissive in their training, and children have no fixed schedules for eating or sleeping. (pp. 68–69)

Another facet of noninterference involves how fathers or older male adults in a family do not control families. Rather, they administer or organize the family so that it may arrive at a decision regarding how to proceed (Paniagua, 1998).

A third conceptual theme that characterizes American Indian culture is that of *harmony with nature* (Baruth & Manning, 1999; Dhooper & Moore, 2001; Ho, 1987). Ho (1987) explains:

> American Indians hold nature as extremely important for they realize that they are but one part of a greater whole. There are many rituals and ceremonies among the tribes that express both their reverence for nature's forces and their observance of the balance that must be maintained between them and all other living and nonliving things. (p. 71)

A fourth concept basic to First Nations life and related to harmony with nature is the *concept of time* (Ho, 1987; Locke, 1998; Paniagua, 1998; Weaver, 2005). Time is considered an aspect of nature. Time flows along with life. It is not something that should take precedence over how you relate to others in your life. Therefore, time should not control or dictate how you live and spend your time. Hence other aspects of life, including interaction with other people, become more important than punctuality.

One other theme reflecting the perspective of many First Nations Peoples is that of *spirituality* (Weaver, 2005). Dhooper and Moore (2001) explain:

> It was not until the passage of the American Indians Religious Freedom Act of 1978 that Native Americans were permitted religious freedom in the United States. Prior to that time, they were considered heathens and were often arrested and imprisoned for practicing their religion. Religion is a universal concept among Native Americans. When they refer to the universe they include the world, god, the self, and others. Their religion embraces many gods or spirits, but there is usually one great god or Great Spirit to whom reference is made. Faith, an outgrowth of their religiosity, is a harmonizing force that gives purpose and significance to their culture, life, and land (Kasee, 1995). They believe in the reincarnation and infinite existences of their spirits and consider the elements and forces of nature such as the rain, sun, lightning, water, and fire as objects of worship. They believe that the natural world is controlled by the supernatural through spirits. From their perspective, every sphere of life is governed by religion. God and nature are inseparable, and being in disharmony with God will cause disharmony with nature, which will have a negative impact upon the self. pp. (178–179)

African Americans

There are almost 34.7 million African Americans in the United States; almost 55% live in the South, almost 19% in the Midwest, over 17% in the Northeast, and almost 9% in the West (U.S. Census Bureau, 2003). Parham and Brown (2003) continue:

> Nearly 80 percent of African Americans earn a high school diploma, and 17% attain a bachelor's or graduate degree. Despite these advances in educational achievement when compared to previous census data, African Americans continue to suffer as a people under a veil of poverty, with 22% of families being at or below the poverty line of approximately [$18,400 per year for a family of four]. . . . Poverty rates vary across the lifespan but impact children and older adults more significantly. And despite a growing number (25%) of middle-class African Americans with incomes of $50,000 and above, their median income levels continue to represent only 87% of what their white counterparts earn. (p. 81)

African Americans, like other racial, cultural, and ethnic groups, reflect great diversity. "The term African American subsumes a diverse array of peoples including

African Americans born in this country, Africans, and individuals from the West Indies and Central and South America" (Diller, 2004, p. 197).

Despite this diversity, however, four dynamics have "shaped African American experience and culture" (Black, 1996; cited in Diller, 2004, pp. 197–198):

1. The African legacy, rich in culture, custom, and achievement.
2. The history of slavery, a deliberate attempt to destroy the core and soul of the people, while keeping their bodies in enforced servitude.
3. Racism and discrimination, ongoing efforts to continue the psychological and economic subjugation started during slavery.
4. The victim system, a process by which individuals and communities are denied access to the instruments of development and advancement, and then blamed for low levels of accomplishment and achievement, while their successes are considered deviations from the norm (Black, 1996, p. 59).

Devore (2001) cautions that, on the one hand, we should "begin with the understanding that African American families are not homogeneous. One cannot point to the African American family. No composite exists. Therefore, social workers must understand that African American [families] will differ in style and composition, but will experience persistent racism" (p. 34).

On the other hand, Solomon (2002) maintains that although many groups have been effectively integrated into the dominant culture (e.g., "Dutch, German, Scandinavian, and Irish"), this has not been the case with African Americans (p. 299). She continues that "the result has been the maintenance of a distinctive culture that possesses elements of the dominant culture, elements of other subcultural groups who have been oppressed, and elements that are a consequence of the unique African American experience. This cultural distinctiveness may be observed" in a variety of ways (Solomon, 2002, p. 299). These include four general commonalities that tend to characterize African American families.

First, extended family ties are very important for African American families (Diller, 2004; Dhooper & Moore, 2001; Green, 1999). Often children are raised not only by the nuclear family consisting of parents and children but also by extended family members including grandparents, aunts and uncles, cousins, and others even further removed. This reflects a significant strength in that children often receive nurturance and support from multiple caring family members, who also provide each other with mutual aid.

A second, related dimension characterizing African American families is role flexibility (Diller, 2004; Weaver, 2005). Winkelman (1999) explains that traditional gender roles

tend to be less rigid, with few uniquely male or female characteristics. . . . Both male and female African American children are taught to be assertive and nurturing. The emphasis on interdependence, cooperation, flexibility, adaptation, and mutual respect has required an abandonment of traditional definitions of sex roles. (p. 297)

Paniagua (1998) continues:

The mother sometimes plays the role of the father and thus functions as the head of the family. In addition, older children sometimes function as parents or caretakers for younger children. In fact, older African American children may drop out from school to work and help younger children secure a good education. (p. 22)

A third characteristic of African American families is respect for the elderly. Dhooper and Moore (2001) report:

> The elderly are held in high regard in the African American family and community. This results from (a) the acknowledgment of their having a collective history of lifelong discrimination; (b) the belief that offspring should provide in-home care when the need for assistance arises; and (c) the habit of allowing relatives and nonrelatives to live with them in times of family crises. (p. 103)

A fourth theme in African American life involves strong religious beliefs and a close relationship with the church, especially an African American church (Diller, 2004; Dhooper & Moore, 2001; Paniagua, 1998). Many African American families consider the church to be a part of the extended family, providing similar nurturance and support (Paniagua, 1998). Dhooper and Moore (2001) explain:

> The African American church continues to address not only the religious and spiritual needs of the individual, family, and community, but also their social needs. It serves as a coping and survival mechanism against the effects of racial discrimination and oppression and as a place where African Americans are able to experience unconditional positive regard. (p. 101)

Frame (2003) reflects that for many African Americans,

> [S]pirituality and identity are inseparable. Religion is not compartmentalized into a set of beliefs, doctrine, or dogma. Instead, it is in the life and breath of most African Americans, whether or not they are involved in organized religion. . . . Some African Americans believe that spirit may be found in everything. Religion and spirituality are considered major strengths for African Americans, which contributed to their resilience, their survival of slavery, and their ability to overcome present struggles. For many African Americans, spirituality dominates their thinking and is integrally related to their sense of security, adjustment, identity development, behavior, and problem-solving ability. . . . When they find themselves in a crisis or particularly stressed, many African Americans seek solace and strength in their religious and spiritual practices. . . .
>
> The focus of worship in most African American churches is on God, who through Jesus Christ, enters into a personal relationship with believers, reconciles, liberates, heals, and guides. . . . There is an emphasis on God's "healing presence in life despite suffering and pain" (Wimberly, 1991, p. 16). Worship in African American churches is spirited, emotional, expressive. It often includes "involuntary acts of praise" (Mitchell & Mitchell, 1989, p. 105). In addition, clapping, dancing, and shouting are common in African American worship, which results in spiritual uplifting and an indwelling sense of hope in the worshiper. . . . There is the expectation that upon leaving a worship service, participants are empowered to manage the demands of daily life. (pp. 132–133)

Asian Americans

Asian Americans are composed of three basic groups that, in turn, consist of numerous subgroups. These include, but are not limited to, "Asian Americans (Japanese, Chinese, Filipinos, Asian Indians, and Koreans); Pacific Islanders (Hawaiians, Samoans, and Guamanians); and Southeast Asians (Vietnamese, Cambodians, and Laotians)" (Paniagua, 1998, p. 57). Obviously, there is huge variation among these groups despite the fact that they are clustered under the umbrella term *Asian Americans*.

Diller (2004) explains that "[u]nlike African Americans, Latinos/as, and Native Americans, Asian Americans have been quite successful economically and educationally, even in comparison with the White population"; this includes median income levels, rate of small business ownership, and attainment of educational degrees (p. 217). However, he maintains that this provides an overly simplistic view and urges us to consider the following facts:

> High median income doesn't take into consideration the number of wage earners, the level of poverty among certain Asian subgroups, or the discrepancy between education and income for Asian workers. Education in the Asian community is bimodal; that is, there are both highly educated and uneducated subpopulations. Asian towns in large urban areas represent ghettos with high unemployment, poverty, and widespread social problems. Underutilization of services does not necessarily mean a lack of problems, but may in fact have alternative explanations such as face saving, shame, or the family's cultural tendency to keep personal information hidden from the outside world. In short, the belief in Asian success does not mean that there is any less racism or discrimination directed toward Asian Americans or that there are not serious problems within crowded urban enclaves (Diller, 2004, p. 218; Sue & Sue, 1999).

Discussed here are five themes that tend to characterize many Asian American families. These include the significance of family, interdependence, filial piety, investment made in children, and patriarchal hierarchy.

First, like Hispanics, Asian Americans tend to consider the family as the primary unit and individual family members as secondary in importance (Slattery, 2004; Diller, 2004; Goldenberg & Goldenberg, 2002). Phillips (1996) describes a key concept:

> The welfare and the integrity of the family are of great importance. The individual is expected to submerge or to repress emotions, desires, behaviors, and individual goals to further the welfare of family and maintain its reputation. The individual is obligated to save face, so as to not bring shame onto the family. Therefore, there is incentive to keep problems within the family so that the family will not "lose face." (p. 1)

A second theme, related to the significance of the family, that is common among Asian American families involves interdependence (Green, 1999; Phillips, 1996). For example, Chinese culture emphasizes "kinship from birth to death, and it is expected that the family will serve as a major resource in providing stability, a sense of self-esteem, and satisfaction" (Goldenberg & Goldenberg, 2002, p. 341). Such respect and maintenance of responsibility is expected even when family members move to some other country and never or rarely see the rest of the family again (Goldenberg & Goldenberg, 2002).

A third theme concerns *filial piety*—"a devotion to and compliance with parental and familial authority, to the point of sacrificing individual desires and ambitions" (Kirst-Ashman & Hull, 2002, p. 422). It is expected, for instance, that children will care for elderly parents (Balgopal, 1995; Green, 1999). Goldenberg and Goldenberg (2002) comment:

> Elders are afforded unquestioned respect. In Filipino families, for example, elders are greeted in culturally defined ceremonial ways and with kinship terms that denote their special rank; failure either to carry out the ritualized greeting or to use these terms would be considered disrespectful. (p. 345)

A fourth theme characterizing many Asian American families involves the high priority of and tremendous investment in children (Goldenberg & Goldenberg, 2002; Green, 1999; Wong, 1988). Goldenberg and Goldenberg (2002) explain:

> Young children are indulged long beyond what is considered standard among traditional American families. Toilet training is often delayed, according to Berg and Jaya (1993), until the child insists on it, and older children, even up to the age of 10 or 11, frequently sleep with their parents. Adolescents are not encouraged to learn self-care skills (cleaning their rooms, doing their own laundry, cooking their own meals) and are permitted to maintain a dependent position as long as they wish. What they are expected to do, however, is to be well behaved and obedient and, above all, to bring honor to the family. School achievement is a particularly visible way to do so, but so is earning praise from others in the community for being respectful, knowing good manners, and eventually marrying into a good family. (pp. 341–342)

A fifth related theme distinguishing many Asian American families involves their patriarchal hierarchy (Diller, 2004; Goldenberg & Goldenberg, 2002; Green, 1999). Balgopal (1995) explains:

> Asian families are generally patriarchal, and in traditional Asian families, age, sex, and generational status determine the roles that members play. The father is the head of the family, and his authority is unquestioned; he is the main disciplinarian and is usually less approachable and more distant than the mother, who is the nurturer and caretaker. (p. 234)

A Note on Difference

Of course, any discussion of these general cultural themes of values and behaviors is just that—general. Actual practices vary dramatically from one ethnic group to another and from one family to another. It's important not to make mistaken assumptions about an individual's values and expectations simply because that person is a member of some group.

National Origin

National origin, another dimension of diversity, involves individuals', their parents', or their ancestors' country of birth. National origin often is an important factor in people's cultural values and expectations. How individuals are raised, what they're taught, and how they learn to perceive the world around them vary dramatically from one corner of the world to another. Understanding values and customs derived from national origin helps social workers better understand their clients' perspectives and needs. Several concepts are important, as Ahearn (1995) explains:

> Millions of people around the world are categorized as displaced people, refugees, immigrants, migrants, and illegal aliens. *Displaced people* are those people who have been uprooted within their own country. [Consider how former Yugoslav president Slobodan Milosevic led a campaign attempting to "cleanse" the Yugoslavian province of Kosovo of its almost three-quarters of a million ethnic Albanians. They were expelled from the province, their homes destroyed, and their villages obliterated. Many were massacred on the way and had their possessions and papers stolen.] *Refugees* are people who have crossed national boundaries in search of refuge. The United Nations defines refugees as people who flee to another country out of a fear of persecution because of

religion, political affiliation, race, nationality, or membership in a particular group. *Immigrants* are those individuals who have been granted legal permanent residence in a country not their own. *Migrants* are those people, usually workers, who have temporary permission to live in a country, but plan to return to their country of origin. *Illegal aliens* are people who migrate illegally to another country. (p. 771)

Many people from other countries may receive or need social services. Immigrants represent an important portion of the U.S. population. In 2000 over 31 million people, 11.1% of the total population, were foreign-born (U.S. Census Bureau, 2003). Padilla (1999) reports:

> [I]mmigration to the United States is characterized by steady growth, dramatic changes in ethnic composition, and declining socioeconomic levels. Over 7 million people immigrated during the past decade, reflecting consistent increases over previous decades . . . , and these increases are expected to continue. By 2040 one in four Americans will be an immigrant (first generation) or the child of immigrants (second generation), and by 2010 children of immigrants will account for 22 percent of the school-age population. (p. 590)

People with different national origins often find it difficult to integrate themselves into the mainstream culture, especially when language barriers exist (Gushue & Sciarra, 1995). Finding employment and adequate housing and "fitting into" the social fabric of neighborhoods and communities can be difficult. Kamya (2001) cites "social isolation, cultural shock, cultural change, and goal-striving stress as four significant experiences" newcomers often face (p. 607). They may have difficulties understanding new behavioral expectations imposed on them, interacting effectively with others in the new culture, and achieving the goals they had hoped for. Highlight 3.3 identifies some of the differences between cultural expectations in the United States and those adopted by the Turkana tribe in northern Kenya.

Increasing cultural competence is helpful in working with a population having a different national origin. Consider the following example. Thanh, a counselor at a homeless shelter, is seeing an increasing number of Haitian immigrants enter the shelter. He determines that he must enhance his knowledge of their cultural values to work with them more effectively. As he does this, he begins to understand that "the plight of Haitian immigrants is noteworthy because of its complexity and because of their flight from political and economic oppression" (Allen, 1995, p. 125). Thanh discovers that a local organization exists primarily to assist immigrants of Caribbean origin socially, economically, and politically. The organization's goals include "contributing to the economic welfare of the community through the stimulation of businesses, promoting the housing needs of their constituents, and assisting their members in securing employment" (Allen, 1995, p. 125). Obtaining this information about Haitian immigrants enhances both Thanh's understanding of their culture and his ability to communicate with his clients. It also makes him aware of a whole new set of resources potentially available to clients.

Note that when we speak about any racial, ethnic, or cultural group, it is important not to overgeneralize. Persons with other national origins may embrace traditional cultural norms to various degrees. They may also experience *acculturation*—"the adaptation of language, identity, behavior patterns, and preferences to those of the host/majority society" (Lum, 2004, p. 229). In other words, people from another

HIGHLIGHT 3.3
Appreciating Cultural Differences in National Origin

Imagine a family of the Turkana tribe in northern Kenya immigrating to the United States.[3] What difficulties would members face in terms of cultural differences and expectations? Primarily nomadic goatherds, these people are not accustomed to handling currency, as their subsistence is based on bartering (exchanging goods for other goods). Even if they enter a store, have currency, and want to make a purchase, it is unthinkable to pay the asking price without trying to negotiate a lower cost.

Another difference is the common practice of polygamy. The number of a man's wives reflects his wealth, with each wife being purchased with some negotiated number of goats. A wealthy man is one with many wives and many goats.

The Turkana tribe's conception of time reflects yet another difference. Many tribal members have never seen watches. Their time is not split into precise units such as minutes and hours. Rather, they depend on the position of the sun in the sky to determine what should be done at that time of day. They value relationships and mutual respect more than rigorous scheduling and strict punctuality. For example, the person providing this information was two days late for a meeting due to international and internal transportation difficulties. Instead of being angry, tribal members were unconcerned about the lateness and cheerfully welcomed their visitors when they finally arrived. A two-day delay most likely would not be accepted so tranquilly in the United States.

One aspect of U.S. culture Turkana tribe members would probably appreciate is the ready access to public education, as education is highly valued there. Four years of primary school and another four years of secondary are available to children, but it still costs each family an additional $100 for elementary and $300 for secondary school per year. In the United States, this may not seem like much, but in northern Kenya, a professional person holding an exceptionally good job might earn $1,000 in an entire year.

The point of this is not to make judgments about which cultural values are better or worse, but rather to emphasize that significant differences do exist based on ethnicity and national origin. Social workers, then, must listen carefully to such clients regarding their needs, work with them as they adjust to new conditions, and provide the best services possible to meet their needs.

[3]This information was gathered from a personal communication with Gary S. Kirst, who had visited the Turkana tribe within the month prior to this writing.

country may gradually blend into the larger society and adopt its values and customs. Therefore, for a given racial, ethnic, or cultural group, it is important that social workers not assume that all members comply with all cultural values or conform to the same extent. Being of German ethnic heritage does not automatically mean a person loves sauerkraut, liver sausage, and raw ground beef with onions on rye bread simply because these are traditional ethnic foods.

Gushue and Sciarra (1995) address the difference in acculturation between first-generation and later-generation immigrants:

As family members differentiate according to ability levels of the language of the dominant culture, distinct forms and levels of acculturation begin to emerge. Children, having gained a knowledge of the language and wanting to be accepted by their peers, take on the ways of the dominant culture. Parents, more isolated because of language and perhaps suspicious of the ways of the dominant culture, enter into conflict with their children. Issues of racial/cultural identity also emerge because children and parents feel differently about their cultural heritage. (p. 597)

Class

Class or *social class,* another aspect of diversity, refers to people's status or ranking in society with respect to such standards as "relative wealth, power, prestige, educational level, or family background" (Barker, 2003, p. 402). What comes to mind when you think of social class? Whom do you picture when you think of people in higher classes? In lower classes? How would you characterize yourself in terms of class membership? How do you relate to people of other classes?

Social workers must carefully scrutinize their own answers to these questions. They must strive to avoid imposing stereotypes and prejudgments. Rather, they must continue to expand their knowledge base about the environmental circumstances characterizing people's lives in other social classes.

Gender

Gender is an important dimension of diversity because of the widely different worldviews assumed by women and men. As racial, ethnic, and cultural backgrounds affect people's worldview, so does their gender. Women experience many issues, expectations, and life situations that men do not, and they perceive the world in a different way. Land (1995) reviews women's plight in the United States:

> Domestic violence is rapidly increasing: Reports of wife abuse, child abuse, and incest have never been higher. We see an aging society with limited resources for employment opportunity and health care, especially for frail elderly people. Women of color and other vulnerable groups are more represented in the changing face of acquired immune deficiency syndrome (AIDS). Increased immigration from Third World countries results in populations at risk for poverty, poor health care, and lack of educational opportunity. . . . Women are overworked, underpaid, and undersupported by our social programs. . . . [Rapidly growing] pressures on family life, . . . [for women] include fewer resources for children; greater caregiving responsibilities for aging, ill, and disabled family members; and consequent role overload and stress. (p. 3)

Some disturbing facts reflect the different life contexts of women and men in this country. Consider the following:

- Women are significantly more likely to be poor than men (Kirk & Okazawa-Rey, 2004; Shaw & Lee, 2004).
- "The two poorest groups in the United States are women raising children alone and women over 65 living alone" (Kirk & Okazawa-Rey, 2004, p. 329).
- For all races, women earn significantly less than men do at every educational level (U.S. Census Bureau, 2003).
- Non-Asian women of color are significantly more likely to be poor than white women (Kirk & Okazawa-Rey, 2004; Renzetti & Curran, 2003).

- Women earn about 77 percent of what men earn; "[f]or women of color, this drops to 64%" (Shaw & Lee, 2004, p. 337). Managerial and professional women as a group earn about 71% of what managerial and professional men earn (U.S. Census Bureau, 2003).
- Over half of all women workers "hold sales, clerical and service [e.g., waitresses, maids, and dental assistants] jobs" (National Committee for Pay Equity, 2003). Many of the rest are employed in other occupations made up mostly of women including nurses, health technicians, elementary and secondary school teachers, and apparel and textile workers (U. S. Census Bureau, 2003). Men, on the other hand, tend to work in better-paying occupations such as engineers, lawyers, dentists, and skilled laborers.
- Research conducted since 1961 reflects a significant, consistent wage differential between men and women in social work (Gibelman, 2003). Some research indicates that female social workers earn about 80 cents for every dollar earned by male social workers (Linsley, 2003).
- "Even with a college education . . . and equivalent work experience and skills, women are far less likely than men to get to the top of their professions or corporations" (Kirk & Okazawa-Rey, 2004, p. 321; Padavic & Reskin, 2004).
- 71% of single women and almost 61% of married women with children under age 6 work outside the home (U.S. Census Bureau, 2003).

Women, therefore, often are victims of oppression manifested in many ways. They are more likely than men to be poor and are more likely to be primary caregivers for children and elderly people. They are victimized by specific kinds of violence, including sexual assault and domestic violence, rarely experienced by men.

Important concepts related to these issues are sexism and sex discrimination. *Sexism* is "prejudice or discrimination based on sex, especially discrimination against women" that involves "behavior, conditions, or attitudes that foster stereotypes of social roles based on sex" (Mish, 1995, p. 1073). *Sex discrimination* is the differential and potentially unfair treatment of people based solely on their gender. Examples include paying males more than females for the same or comparable jobs, or hiring only one gender for certain jobs.

Many people are initially turned off by the concepts of sexism and sex discrimination. They find it difficult consciously to recognize and accept the possibility that this is an imperfect, sexist world. They think that things are supposed to be fair and that they shouldn't have to waste their time and energy battling such problems as sexism. For many women, it's easier to adopt an "out of sight, out of mind" philosophy. In other words, if one doesn't think about a problem, then it doesn't really exist. Why dwell on problems that are nonexistent or insignificant?

To what extent do you think sexism and sex discrimination exist today? How much do they account for the discrepancies between women and men in terms of their life circumstances and treatment? How might you begin to think about these concerns so that you could figure out the reasons for their existence? What theoretical perspective might help you organize information and your view of the world to increase your understanding?

One such theoretical framework is the *feminist perspective,* one in which women's experiences, ideas, and needs are valued in their own right. Put another way . . . [the perspective that views] man as the norm ceases to be the only recognized frame of reference for human beings. Women's experiences are seen as constituting a different view of "reality"—an entirely different . . . way of making sense of the world. (Cummerton, 1986, p. 85)

Focus on Critical Thinking 3.3 explores the meaning of feminism for women and men and raises some provocative questions.

Sexual Orientation

Sexual orientation, another significant aspect of diversity, involves sexual and romantic attraction to persons of one or both genders. People having a sexual orientation toward the same gender are generally referred to as *gay* if they are male or *lesbian* if they are female. However, many people use the term *gay* to refer to both lesbians and gay men. The older term referring to same-gender sexual orientation is *homosexual.* People having a sexual orientation toward persons of the opposite gender are *heterosexual,* or *straight.* People sexually oriented toward both genders are referred to as *bisexual.* Because lesbian, gay, and bisexual people face some of the same problems, when referring to them as a group, we will use the term *LGB* (i.e., lesbian, gay, or bisexual).

It's difficult, if not impossible, to state exactly how many people are lesbian or gay. The issue remains complex. "[H]omosexuality is stigmatized. Gay men and lesbian women are often reluctant to reveal their identities in random surveys, and large-scale national surveys have been blocked until recently because of conservative opposition" (Strong DeVault, Sayar, & Yarber, 2005, pp. 185–186). Carroll (2005) reports that "[e]stimates for homosexuality range from 2–4% to greater than 10% in males and 1–3% in females . . . , while estimates for bisexuality are approximately 3%" (p. 317). Based on Kinsey's work in the 1940s and 1950s, "many authors have used 10% as the proportion of men who are gay" (Berger & Kelly, 1995, p. 1066). And many lesbian and gay organizations maintain that they make up 10% of the population. One major lesbian and gay organization is called "The Ten Percent Society." The controversy regarding the actual number of lesbian and gay people continues. Regardless of whether lesbian and gay people make up 1% or 10% of the population, they are a sizable minority group.

Focus on Critical Thinking 3.4 explores the complexity of sexual orientation and gender.

Homophobia

A major problem gay people face is *homophobia*—the irrational "hatred, fear, or dislike" of gay, lesbian, and bisexual people (Morales, 1995, p. 1089). LGB people are one of the primary groups at risk of discrimination and oppression. Highlight 3.4 reflects the feelings of one person who faces homophobia every day.

Although not all LGB people suffer every day from homophobia in all its forms, all LGB people endure some forms at some times (Tully, 2001). To help LGB people cope with the results of homophobia, social workers must understand their life situations and environmental issues.

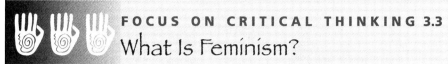

What Is Feminism?

How do you respond to these questions?

- What words and images come to mind when you hear the word *feminism?*
- What does feminism represent and suggest to you?
- How would you define feminism?
- To what extent do you feel the concept is significant or meaningless in your life?

Some people have extremely negative reactions simply to the word *feminism.* The emotional barriers they forge and the resulting resistance they foster make it difficult even to think about the concept. Others consider feminism a radical ideology that emphasizes separatism and fanaticism. In other words, they think feminism involves the philosophy adopted by women who spurn men, resent past inequities, and strive violently to overthrow male supremacists. Still others think of feminism in terms of an outmoded tradition of women seeking equality with men. They feel it is no longer relevant in contemporary times, nor does it merit their attention.

What Is a Feminist?

Both men and women can be feminists. The definition of feminism proposed here is designed to relate to basic concepts involving the daily lives of people like you. It entails readily understandable concepts. Many people have failed to develop a sensitivity to the sexist barriers surrounding them. For one thing, it's painful to acknowledge such unfairness. For another, it's easy to assume "that's the way things are" simply because people haven't thought about other, better ways of doing things.

For our purposes, *feminism* is the philosophy of equality between women and men that involves both beliefs and actions, that infiltrates virtually all aspects of life, that often necessitates providing education and advocacy on behalf of women, and that appreciates the existence of individual differences and personal accomplishments regardless of gender (Kirst-Ashman, 1992). Five major components within this definition relate directly to the values and goals of professional social work.

First, equality is the core of feminism. *Equality* does not mean identicalness or sameness. It does not mean that women are trying to shed their female identities and become clones of men. Nor does it mean that women should seek to adopt behaviors that are typically "masculine." Feminism does promote equal or identical rights to opportunities and choices. It relates to women's and men's rights not to be discriminated against and not to be denied opportunities and choices on the basis of gender.

The second major component inherent in feminism is the fact that it embodies both beliefs and actions. Beliefs concern how we look at the world and perceive other people; actions reflect expression of the beliefs. Feminism espouses a belief system that views other people objectively and fairly. It means avoiding both stereotypes and assumptions about people on the basis of gender. A person who fails to behave in accordance with expressed feminist beliefs is not a true feminist according to our definition. For example, one of your instructors might say he supports feminist principles yet frequently emphasize how women are too emotional and make sexist jokes that fixate on breast size. Feminism involves acting on one's beliefs on behalf of gender equality and fair, respectful treatment.

The third critical aspect in the definition of feminism is the idea that all aspects of life are involved. The concept of equality does not apply only to an equal chance of getting a specific job

(continued)

FOCUS ON CRITICAL THINKING 3.3 (*continued*)

or promotion. It also involves having the rights to hold personal opinions about political issues and to make decisions within personal relationships. It entails a woman's right to make a decision about what to do on a Friday night date or whether to have a sexual encounter. Essentially, this aspect includes the acknowledgment that our social, legal, and political structure is oriented toward men, not women.

The fourth important aspect of feminism is the frequent necessity of providing education and advocacy on the behalf of women, a dimension coinciding with major social work roles. This might involve giving feedback to a person behaving in a sexist fashion or speaking out on the behalf of others being treated unfairly. For example, I once went to a travel agency for vacation information. While the lone travel agent worked with another customer, I waited patiently for about 15 minutes. At that point, two men in business suits walked in. As soon as the agent was finished with her customer, she looked directly at the men—as if I were invisible — and asked them if she could help them. If I had behaved more compatibly with feminist principles, I might have assertively stated that I had been waiting for quite a while and that men should not be given precedence simply because of gender. As it was, I was furious and stomped out. I missed an opportunity to educate the agent regarding her sexist behavior so that she might treat women more equitably in the future.

The fifth major concept involved in the definition of feminism is the appreciation of individual differences. The feminist perspective lauds the concept of empowering women by emphasizing individual strengths and qualities. Feminism stresses freedom and the right to make choices about one's own life. Note that this concept applies to both women and men.

A feminist perspective refutes and challenges the idea that the potential of women and men is limited by their gender. Rather, it proposes that women should be empowered to develop their abilities and pursue activities to achieve optimal well-being.

Van Den Bergh and Cooper (1987) stress that in many ways a feminist perspective conforms with the core of traditional social work practice in terms of principles and values. Both emphasize the significance of being concerned with "human dignity and the rights of self-determination" (Van Den Bergh & Cooper, 1986, p. 3). Both stress the importance of individuals' interactions with their environments and communities.

Are You a Feminist?

In light of the preceding discussion, do you think that you are a feminist? Respond to the following questions to help come to a conclusion:

- Do you believe that women and men should have the same rights?
- Do you believe that women and men should have the same access to jobs and social status?
- Do you believe that women and men should not be discriminated against or denied opportunities and choices on the basis of their gender?
- Do you think that employers should treat women and men equally in work settings?
- Do you believe that ideally people's attitudes and behavior should reflect the equal treatment of women and men?
- Do you think that many people need to become more educated about women's issues?
- Would you be willing to advocate on behalf of women (e.g., for poor women or women who have been raped)?

(*continued*)

FOCUS ON CRITICAL THINKING 3.3 (*continued*)

- Do you believe that both women and men have the right to their own individual differences (of course, differences that don't harm other people)?
- Do you think that our society is generally structured legally, socially, and economically by and for men instead of women? (This last

question is probably the most difficult, and perhaps the most painful, to answer.)

If you answered "yes" to all or most of these questions, according to our definition, there's a good chance that you are a feminist.

LGB people may suffer from homophobia in at least three ways, one of which is *overt victimization*. Dworkin (2000) remarks,

> Anti-LGB violence is more common than most people realize. . . . All the symptoms commonly associated with posttraumatic stress[4] are likely to follow a physical or verbal attack, in varying degrees of intensity, depending on the circumstances of the attack and the vulnerability of the victim. In a four-year study of hate crimes against LGB people, Herek et al. [1997] found that stress, depression, and anger lingered for as long as five years after the attack. In addition to posttraumatic symptoms, an LGB client can experience anxiety about his or her sexual identification. . . . Often there is regression to earlier stages of the coming out process. (p. 170)

A second way LGB people encounter homophobia involves *covert victimization*—discrimination that is not obvious. For instance, Jay, a 21-year-old gay man and college student, applies for a part-time job at Hilda's Humongous Hamburgers, a local fast-food restaurant. Daryl, the manager, somehow finds out that Jay is gay. He then hires another applicant who is heterosexual (or so Daryl thinks) because that applicant is more "appropriate."

A third way LGB people suffer from homophobia involves *internalizing* it (Dworkin, 2000; Tully, 2001). If the majority of those around LGB people are homophobic, making fun of and severely criticizing them, it's fairly easy for LGB people to start believing it themselves. Results may include "low self-esteem, depression, suicidal ideation, substance abuse, isolation, self-loathing, . . . or acting out" (Tully, 2001, p. 610).

Family Structure

A *family* is "a primary group whose members assume certain obligations for each other and generally share common residences" (Barker, 2003, p. 154). This definition shows how flexible the notion of family has become. First, a family is a *primary group*—that is, "people who are intimate and have frequent face-to-face contact with

---

[4]*Posttraumatic stress disorder* is a condition in which a person continues to reexperience some traumatic event like a bloody battle or a sexual assault.

FOCUS ON CRITICAL THINKING 3.4
What Does *Gender* Really Mean?

In an overly simplistic, naive view of the world, one might think, "You're either a male or you're a female. Period." However, in reality neither gender nor sexual orientation are such simple concepts. Money (1987) proposes eight factors of gender that more fully portray some of the complexity of gender. The first six are physical variables that include chromosomal predisposition to gender; the presence of either ovaries or testes; exposure to male or female hormones prior to birth and brain differentiation resulting from hormones prior to birth; the presence of female or male internal reproductive organs; exterior genital appearance; and the production of either male or female hormones during puberty. The two psychological variables are the gender assigned at birth ("It's a boy" or "It's a girl") and the person's *gender identity* (the perception of oneself as being either "female" or "male").

About 2% of people are born with contradictions among Money's physical variables (Blackless et al., 2000). Reasons include "having an atypical combination of sex chromosomes or as a result of prenatal hormonal irregularities" (Crooks & Baur, 2005, p. 54). For example, a newborn who is a genetic female might develop an internal uterus and ovaries, but also a clitoris enlarged enough to resemble a penis, possibly even containing a urethra (the tube in a male's penis through which urine and semen are discharged); the labia (folds of tissue in the female around the vaginal entrance) may converge and resemble a scrotum (the pouch that holds the male testes) (Carroll, 2005). When this condition is diagnosed at birth, cosmetic surgery can often be performed to "feminize" the person's genitalia. Often, if her uterus and ovaries are intact, she can become pregnant.

Another example of contradiction in physical gender is a genetic male who has a syndrome where the body produces but fails to respond to male hormones (Carroll, 2005). Neither male nor normal female genitalia develop, although testes develop and are contained in the abdomen. Such people can develop breasts because genetic males do produce some female hormones. This condition is usually not diagnosed at birth and goes unnoticed until puberty when the person, who has been treated as a female her whole life, doesn't menstruate. These people can neither become pregnant nor impregnate because they don't have the necessary reproductive equipment. Most people with this condition continue to live as females.

There are many other examples of people who have some mixture of male and female predisposition and configuration of reproductive structures. Such a person is referred to as *pseudohermaphrodite* or *intersex*. A true *hermaphrodite* is a person "born with fully formed ovaries and fully formed testes, which is very, very rare" (Carroll, 2005, p. 70).

Crooks and Baur (2005) address some of the ethical issues:

> Intersex activists, who have established many advocacy organizations, such as Bodies Like Ourselves and the Intersex Society of North America (ISNA), argue that intersexed people are cases of genital variability, not genital abnormality. The ISNA advocates a noninterventionist, child-centered approach in which an intersexed child is not subjected to genital-altering surgery; he or she may choose such procedures later in life. (p. 63)

Additionally, they raise a number of ethical questions:

> Does genital-altering surgery performed on mere babies violate their rights as humans to give informed consent? Would intersexed children left with ambiguous genitals have problems functioning in schools or other settings where their condition might become known to others?

(continued)

FOCUS ON CRITICAL THINKING 3.4 *(continued)*

Might society eventually evolve beyond the two-sex model and embrace the legitimacy of a third intersexed condition located somewhere on the spectrum between male and female? (p. 63)

Another variation in the expression of gender involves *transgenderism,* including "people whose appearance and/or behaviors do not conform to traditional gender roles" (Crooks & Baur, 2005, p. 63), "who live full- or part-time in the other gender's role [that is, their nonbiological gender] and derive psychosocial comfort in doing so" (Carroll, 2005, p. 85). Among these people are *transsexuals,* people who feel they are imprisoned in the physical body of the wrong gender. Because their gender identity and sense of self are at odds with their biological inclination, they often seek to adjust their physical appearance to that of their gender identity through surgery and hormonal treatment. Many transsexual people prefer to be referred to as transgender people. The word *transsexual* emphasizes *sexual,* whereas *transgender* emphasizes *gender,* which they say is the real issue.

Several other groups of people are also often included under the transgender umbrella. *Transvestites* are people who derive sexual gratification from dressing in the clothing of the opposite gender. In our society, almost all transvestites are heterosexual males (Carroll, 2005; Docter, 1988). This might be due to the fact that women experience much greater freedom and flexibility in how they dress. *Drag queens* are gay men who dress up as women. Lesbians who dress up in traditionally masculine clothing may be referred to as *drag kings. Female impersonators* are men who dress up as women usually for the purpose of providing entertainment. They may be heterosexual or gay. A common performance involves mimicking the dress and style of famous female performers, often lip-synching

(moving their lips to a song and music without producing any sound) their greatest hits.

The Social Construction of Gender

Considering these diversities of gender expression, the concept of gender doesn't appear to be quite so clear. One theoretical approach to understanding how we view and interpret gender as a society refers to the social construction of gender. *Social construction* refers to the perspective where the social world is considered "a social creation, originating and evolving through our everyday thoughts and actions. Most of the time, we assume and act as though the world is a given, objectively predetermined outside of our existence. However, . . . we also apply subjective meanings to our existence and experience. In other words, our experiences don't just happen to us. Good, bad, positive, or negative—we also attach meanings to our reality" (Leon-Guerrero, 2005, p. 6).

The *social construction of gender* "looks at the structure of the gendered social order as a whole and at the processes that construct and maintain it" (Lorber, 2005, p. 242). It assumes that traditional gender expectations are not facts carved in stone, but rather perceptions and expectations that can be changed. Lorber (2005) reflects:

[G]ender and sexuality are performances, and . . . individuals modify their displays of masculinity and femininity to suit their own purposes. Males can masquerade as women, and females can pass for men. . . . [One might argue] that, like clothing, sexuality and gender can be put on, taken off, and transformed. Transgenders especially display the fluidities of gender and sexuality, challenging normals to prove that they aren't also making themselves up. . . . [A] focus of gay, lesbian, and transgender studies, turns the . . . [two categories of male and female] sex, sexuality and gender, inside out with 'third terms'—intersex, bisexual, transsexual, transvestite. (p. 197)

HIGHLIGHT 3.4

Reflections About Being a Lesbian in a Homophobic Society

Jackquelyn is a doctoral student in a counseling program at a prestigious eastern university. She reflects on what it's like to live as a lesbian in a homophobic world:

> I am a European American upper-middle-class student. . . . I am thoroughly embedded in a Eurocentric, achievement-oriented, individualistic way of life that I am finding to be increasingly maladaptive. . . . I seek to unify various parts of me. I am female, lesbian-identified, white, athletic, academic, emotional, and other things that my culture insists be compartmentalized from one another, from other people, and from myself as a whole person. . . . Politically, I am a lesbian, but I am also a white person who confronts racism and ethnocentrism. My labels do not describe me fully, of course; the word *lesbian* does not account for my full range of emotional, behavioral, and cognitive ways of being. . . . I have been told overtly and covertly that I don't belong. Professors, supervisors, and peers . . . [treat me like an object] in offices, . . . [make offensive gestures] in the hallways, [and] use sexualized language in professional conversations with me. (Lowe & Mascher, 2001, pp. 773–774)

one another, have norms [that is, expectations regarding how members in the group should behave] in common, and share mutually enduring and extensive influences" (Barker, 2003, p. 338). Thus family members have significant influence on each other. The second concept in the definition of family involves having obligations for each other, which means a sense of mutual commitment to and responsibility for other family members. The third concept in the definition is common residences, such that, to some extent, family members live together.

Family structure is "the nuclear family as well as those nontraditional alternatives to nuclear family which are adopted by persons in committed relationships and the people they consider to be 'family'" (Council on Social Work Education, 2002). The traditional family structure in the United States consisted of two married parents who had never been divorced living together in one household with their own birth children. Today, however, typical family structures are much more varied. *Single-parent families* are family units in which only one of the parents, usually the mother, is present in the household. *Stepfamilies* are family structures in which "members are joined as a result of second or subsequent marriages" (Barker, 2003, p. 417). "In *blended families* one or both spouses have biologically parented one or more children with someone else prior to the current marriage [or union]. In many blended families the newly joined couple gives birth to additional children. In some blended families the children are biologically a combination of 'his, hers, and theirs'" (Zastrow & Kirst-Ashman, 2004, p. 453). Blended families are also often referred to as stepfamilies. *Intergenerational families* are those in which family members include persons spanning at least three generations (e.g., grandparents living under the same roof and caring for grandchildren while the parents work).

Social workers must be sensitive to the various configurations families may take and appreciate this aspect of diversity. Open-mindedness is essential when we assess the strengths of any family group regardless of its structure. Workers should not make assumptions about how families *should be,* but should work with the family group that *is.*

Gay and Lesbian Families: A Population-at-Risk

At special risk of discrimination are families with LGB parents. Patterson (1995) explains:

> The central heterosexist [the prejudiced attitude that gay and lesbian people are inferior or immoral, often resulting in discriminatory behavior toward them] assumption that everyone is or ought to be heterosexual is nowhere more prevalent than in the area of parent–child relationships. Not only are children usually assumed to be heterosexual in their orientation, but mothers and fathers are also generally expected to exemplify heterosexuality in their attitudes, values, and behaviors. (p. 255)

Matthews and Lease (2000) describe the exceptional circumstances of LGB families:

> These special issues can include problems brought on by being members of a stigmatized group in which the relationships are disapproved of by the majority of society, lack of formal or legal recognition of lesbian and gay families, nonheterosexual lifestyles being seen as incompatible with child rearing, fear of losing custody, and the perceived need for secrecy. (p. 259)

Despite these additional stressors, children growing up in lesbian or gay homes do just as well as those raised in heterosexual homes (Laird, 1995; Woodman, 1995). Most children in LGB families "want people to understand that there's lots of love in their household . . . it's the pressure from society that makes things hard for them. . . . Their lives are as traditional and boring as anyone else's" (Carton, 1994, p. 45). "They have parents who help them with homework, worry about college choices, drive them to hockey games, and yell at them for staying out late" (Morales, 1995, p. 1091).

Marital Status

Marital status, simply put, is the condition of being legally married or single. As with family structure, prejudicial assumptions are often made about the importance and significance of marital status. For example, a single-parent family might be viewed as less effective than one in which both parents are present.

Marital status is especially problematic for LGB families. On May 17, 2004, Massachusetts "became the first state in the nation to legalize gay marriage" (American Association of Sex Educators, Counselors, and Therapists [AASECT], June 2004, p. 7). The prior November "the Massachusetts Supreme Court held that limiting civil marriage to different-sex couples violates principles 'of individual liberty and equality under the law'" (Ballman, 2004, p. 2J). On July 9, 2004, "Oregon became the second state to register same-sex marriage licenses after a state appeals court upheld a lower court order directing officials to record more than 3,000 licenses issued to gay couples" (Ballman, 2004, p. 2J).

On the international scene, "[p]arts of Canada recognize same-sex marriages, and Canada is expected to have marriage available to same-sex couples throughout the country some time" soon (Ballman, 2004, p. 2J). "Denmark and Norway allow same-sex couples to legally marry, and Sweden and Iceland recognize same-sex civil weddings, which carry most of the legal benefits of heterosexual marriage. Although Hungary does not permit same-sex marriage, a same-sex partner can inherit property or a pension from a deceased" partner (McAnulty & Burnette, 2003, p. 284).

On the other hand, Alaska, Nebraska, and Nevada have forbidden same-sex marriage by amending their state constitutions; numerous other groups are pressing for same-sex marriage bans in other states and urging state legislatures to consider constitutional changes (AASECT, June 2004, p. 7). President George W. Bush has maintained that he would do "'what is legally necessary to defend the sanctity of marriage'" (Lacayo, 2003, p. 46). Having "pushed hard" for a federal constitutional amendment outlawing same-sex marriage, he suffered "a big defeat" when it failed to pass the U.S. Senate in July 2004 (Dewar, 2004, p. 1A).

Other states are assuming more middle-of-the-road approaches. For example, Vermont has passed a "civil union measure" that stops "just short of allowing same-sex couples to marry" (AASECT, April 2000, p. 6). The law lists 24 legal arenas in which "the law would treat gay and lesbian couples the same as straight couples, including child custody, probate court, workers' compensation, and family leave benefits" (AASECT, April 2000, p. 6). California and New Jersey have established "domestic partnerships" that allow same-sex couples "some, but not all" of the advantages provided by marriage (Ballman, 2004, p. 2J). However, such rulings do not allow partner eligibility at the national level, including receipt of a partner's Social Security benefits and acceptance of such liaisons by other states if the couple should move (Ballman, 2004; Crooks & Baur, 2005).

Some people feel that the concept of marriage is clear and specific. However, Ballman (2004) cites the following facts:

- Mormons have practiced polygamy, primarily in Utah; and although this is now illegal, some still do.
- Marriages were not part of the Roman Catholic Church (the sole Christian church then existing) until the 12th century, and not until the 18th century in England. Before the church or state regulated marriage, people became "'married' through ceremonies in their community's tradition or simply by pairing up."
- People in the United States and many other nations are allowed to marry, divorce, and remarry multiple times.
- Slaves were not permitted to marry in the United States until the Emancipation Proclamation (although they often did marry during secret ceremonies, usually presided over by religious leaders who were also slaves).
- Up to 40 states forbade marriage between whites and people of color until 1967, when the U.S. Supreme Court struck down such laws as violating essential personal rights. (p. 1J)

One "gay sex-advice columnist has a unique solution for those uncomfortable with gay sex: '. . . if they really want to stop the gay sex, they should be behind gay adoption, because nothing put a stop to the sex in my house faster than adopting'" (Crooks & Baur, 2002, p. 289).

Age

The elderly population is swelling (U.S. Census Bureau, 2003). This will be even more evident as the baby boomer population reaches retirement age. As people age, they are more likely to experience increasing health problems and to require more health and other support services. Kropf and Hutchinson (2000) explain:

> Social workers are serving more elderly clients than ever before. Elderly adults are a diverse population, presenting a wide range of practice needs and social issues. Social workers encounter two general types of elderly clients. One group, older people with developmental disabilities, have used social services at earlier life stages and continue to use services into their later life. The second type of elderly client seeks a practitioner's help for conditions associated with the aging process. An example is the older person who requires assistance with household maintenance because of physical disabilities associated with aging. Both types of clients have similarities to younger clients. However, the unique aspects of aging must be understood if social work practice with older clients is to be effective. (p. 3)

Chapter 10 explores in much greater depth the misconceptions about elderly people, their needs, resources available to them, and the social work services involved.

Disability

The world population displays huge variation in physical and developmental disabilities, other dimensions of diversity. Many mistaken beliefs and misunderstandings exist concerning the abilities and prospects of people who have various types of disabilities, often minimizing these people's potential. Myths include, for example, that people with paraplegia (paralysis of both legs due to a spinal cord injury or disease) or cognitive disabilities are unable to work. Chapter 11 addresses types of disabilities, special needs, the issues involved, the emphasis on people's strengths, and social workers' involvement in service provision.

Religion and Spirituality

Religion and spirituality reflect yet another aspect of human diversity. *Religion* involves people's spiritual beliefs concerning the origin, character, and reason for being, usually based on the existence of some higher power or powers, that often involves designated rituals and provides direction for what is considered moral or right. *Spirituality,* a related concept, involves "the views and behaviors that express a sense of relatedness to something greater than the self; spirituality connotes transcendence or a level of awareness that exceeds ordinary physical and spatial boundaries" (Beckett & Johnson, 1995, p. 1393). Religion implies membership in a spiritual organization with customs, traditions, and structure. Spirituality may involve religion, or it may reflect a personal, internalized view of existence.

Social workers help people cope with very difficult issues. Consider the following:

> An elderly hospice patient spends his last days overwhelmed by depression. A young woman, estranged from family and friends, numbs her loneliness with one-night stands and alcohol. A grieving couple drift apart after the death of their child. (Miller, 2001, p. A12)

Gotterer (2001) maintains that spirituality can be a "a bastion of strength" for clients, offering "emotional consolation, inspiration, guidance, structure and security. It can foster personal responsibility, identity, respect for ethical codes, meaningful ritual, and community building" (p. 188). Gotterer (2001) suggests that

> [s]ocial workers, typically involved with vulnerable people in situations of pain or crisis, need a greater awareness of spiritual and religious issues. Tragedies such as the untimely death of a loved one force a person to confront the inexplicable. People nearing death often wonder whether there is an afterlife. Trying times may cause a person to question the meaning and purpose of life. Those subjected to serious disease or long-term oppression need some way to make sense of their experience. Spiritual concerns such as hope, meaning, inner strength, and doubt are relevant in many clients' lives. (p. 187)

O'Neill (September 1999) warns, however, that the social work community concurs that

> one overriding principle is that of self-determination: social workers should never try to impose their own beliefs on clients. "There are many people who really do need faith and we need to honor it," said [Leona] Furman [associate professor at the University of North Dakota, who undertook the first major national survey of social workers' spirituality]. "We also need to honor those who don't have" the need to seek spiritual help and guidance. (p. 3)

As already indicated, spirituality can also be expressed in ways other than those determined by formal religions. Highlight 3.5 describes Kwanzaa, which "emphasizes spiritual grounding" for many African Americans (Karenga, 2000, p. 62).

Islam and Muslims: A Population-at-Risk of Prejudice and Discrimination

Alavi (2001) cites the following scenario:

> During an annual meeting for the Catholic Archdiocese of Cincinnati, a primary agenda item concerned anti-Muslim furor in the United States during the 1979 Iranian hostage crisis. "Particular attention went to a young boy in Wilmington, Ohio, a small, closely knit farming community that was proud of its Quaker college, considered a beacon of tolerance and intellectualism. The fifth-grade boy on the meeting's agenda had an American mother and an Iranian father working at the college. Being the lone child in town with an Iranian connection made him the only target of abuse in the entire school system. The first sign of trouble, a large rock, flew through his bedroom window, shattering glass on him and landing in the crib of his baby sister. By the end of the week, things were so bad that school administrators decided to dismiss the boy 15 minutes early every day. This would enable him to run home and lock the door before the other children caught up with him and beat him up, as they had done from the beginning of the hostage crisis.
>
> That child was my son, Jason. Although he had always been a confident and popular boy, he was never again able to fit into the social scene of his school. He carried the stigma of being 'Iran Man' until graduation, and as an adult he feels little desire to see any of his school colleagues again."

Similar pictures exist today in the post-9/11 world. One survey indicated that "nearly 75% of Muslim Americans ether know someone who has or have themselves

HIGHLIGHT 3.5

Kwanzaa: A Spiritual Celebration of Life, Culture, and History

Kwanzaa, meaning "first fruits of the harvest" in Swahili, is a week-long celebration of life, culture, and history for many African Americans (Woodward & Johnson, 1995, p. 88). Developed by African American Maulana Karenga in 1966, it is celebrated annually from December 26 through January 1. It was created as a means of reaffirming community and heritage, strengthening the bonds among "African people both nationally and internationally" (Karenga, 2000, p. 57). Karenga explains:

> It was conceived as a cultural project, as a way to speak a special African truth to the world by recovering lost models and memory, reviving suppressed principles and practices of African culture, and putting them in the service of the struggle for liberation and ever higher levels of human life.

Kwanzaa is based on the following seven principles, called the Nguzo Saba (Karenga, 2000, pp. 58–59; Woodward & Johnson, 1995, p. 88). They each focus on concepts in Swahili because that is the most extensively spoken language in Africa.

1. *Unity (Umoja):* African Americans strive for harmony and a feeling of community in their families, neighborhoods, and nations.
2. *Self-determination (Kujichagulia):* African Americans "define" themselves, "name" themselves, "create" for themselves, and "speak for" themselves "instead of being defined, named for, and spoken for by others" (Karenga, 2000, p. 58).

3. *Collective work and responsibility (Ujima):* African Americans work together in their communities and help each other solve their problems.
4. *Cooperative economics (Ujamaa):* African Americans work together to establish their own economic base, taking responsibility for each other, developing businesses, and sharing wealth.
5. *Purpose (Nia):* African Americans adopt a guiding principle that they will build a world community restoring them "to their historical greatness" (Karenga, 2000, p. 58).
6. *Creativity (Kuumba):* African Americans do as much as possible to make their communities "more beautiful and beneficial" than before they inherited them (Karenga, 2000, p. 58).
7. *Faith (Imani):* African Americans believe strongly in themselves, focus on their strengths, and have faith that in the future they will blossom and stand out as a "free, proud, and productive people" (Karenga, 2000, p. 59).

Kwanzaa is a time when African Americans gather together to celebrate their culture, reach out to old friends, and forge commitments to a bright future. Each day, family members light a candle and focus on one of the Nguzo Saba's seven principles. At the end of the celebration, they exchange gifts usually having cultural significance (Woodward & Johnson, 1995). Kwanzaa is a celebration of African heritage and culture that serves as an avenue of empowerment for African American communities.

experienced an act of anti-Muslim discrimination, harassment, verbal abuse, or physical attack since September 11, 2001" (Hamilton College, 2002). Other reports corroborate the significant increase in anti-Muslim sentiment and actions since that infamous day (Abdelkarim, 2002; Fung, 2001; Info-Prod [Middle East] Ltd., 2003;

Morrison, 2002; PR Newswire Association, 2004). Muslim people are a population-at-risk of prejudice and discrimination. Because of the fear, the unfair condemnation, and the misperceived relationship between Muslims and the terrorist extremists, it is critically important for social workers to develop understanding of Muslim religion and culture.

The first thing to understand is the meaning of the terms involved. The religion of *Islam* is "derived from the Arabic word meaning peace, the inference being that one who willingly submits to the will of God is a person who has found peace" (Alavi, 2001). *Muslims* are followers of Islam (Pickett, 2002). The word *Arab* means "a member of an Arabic-speaking people or citizen of an Arabic-speaking nation" (Mish, 1995, p. 68). It is not synonymous with the word Muslim: The former reflects national origin and language and the latter involves religion (Weaver, 2005).

Sheler (2001) provides a brief description of the foundation of Islam:

Islam embraces the monotheism [the belief in one god] of Christianity and Judaism, accepts the Hebrew Bible, and . . . [reveres] Jesus as a prophet. It is centered on the Koran—the Islamic scriptures [or Qur'an], which Muslims believe were revealed to the prophet Muhammad—which command five basic devotional duties, called the "Five Pillars":

1. A declaration of belief that "there is no God but Allah [Arabic for 'the God'] and Mohammed is his prophet."
2. Prayers offered five times a day.
3. Daytime fasting during the month of Ramadan.
4. Charitable giving.
5. At least one pilgrimage to Mecca [an Arabian city near the Red Sea that is the birthplace of Muhammad]. (p. 50)

Frame (2003) explains that "Muslims believe that they are called by God (Allah) to be grateful for their blessings and to choose to serve God. For Muslims, both faith and good works are required, but faith is also considered a gift from God. . . . Muslims believe that people are essentially created good. Although they may make poor choices, persons can be forgiven if they repent and follow their repentance with ethical living" (pp. 68–69).

Many people have leapt to the conclusion that Islam encourages terrorist attacks. Alavi (2001) stresses that Muslims worldwide have reviled the 9/11 assault and that Islam forbids murdering innocent victims. "In fact, American Muslim and Arab-American organizations and leaders were among the first to react in an organized fashion to condemn the terrorist attacks on that very same day, long before it became clear that individuals calling themselves Muslims were involved in the attacks" (Abdelkarim, 2002).

Robert S. Mueller III, Director of the Federal Bureau of Investigation (FBI), reported that numerous American Muslim "leaders have generously sent educational materials to our [FBI] field offices and to our headquarters. They have taken the time to talk with our agents and support professionals to help them better understand Muslim perspectives and Muslim beliefs. Muslim Americans have cooperated with our interviews and supported our investigations. . . . The active work of many in the American Muslim community in cities nationwide has merited public thanks and praise. But perhaps the greatest act of support has been the way

Muslim and Arab Americans have responded to our urgent need for translators. Six days after September 11, I announced that the FBI was seeking Arabic and Farsi language experts. The response was extraordinary. Within hours, our switchboard was overwhelmed with calls. Those who came forward included doctors, lawyers, engineers, academics—Muslim and Arab Americans from all walks of life who were willing to quit their jobs, come to work for the FBI, and give something back to their country in the fight against terrorism" (Mueller III, 2002).

One-fifth of the world's population is Muslim, and there are an estimated 7 million Muslims in the United States (Sheler, 2001). As with other ethnic and racial groups discussed earlier, they reflect a wide diversity of backgrounds: "12.4% are Arab, 42% are African American, 24.4% are Asian, and 21% are 'other'" (Frame, 2003, p. 68; Power, 1998). The degree to which individuals practice Muslim beliefs and traditions also varies radically from "traditional—strongly practicing" to "assimilated [into the mainstream culture]—marginally practicing" or "nonpracticing" (Nadir & Dziegielewski, 2001, p. 159).

Several values characterize the life of Muslims including conception of family, selection of marriage partners, diet, and dress (Nadir & Dziegielewski, 2001). Note that traditional values often conflict with current practices and expectations in the United States. "Family is considered to be the cornerstone of Muslim society, and parents are expected to raise children who will work for social justice. Obedience to parents is a divinely ordained value" (p. 152). Muslims face the dilemma of raising children in a non-Muslim environment. For example, "Muslim children in the public schools, in general, receive negative messages about Islam from their textbooks and their teachers" (p. 154).

Western-style dating (i.e., spending time alone together doing various activities in the process of getting to know each other) is prohibited to avoid risking sexual relationships prior to marriage. Instead, "[a]rranged, not forced, marriage is the tradition in Islam. Chaperoned courtship provides opportunities to meet one's future spouse and discuss concerns and plans for the future. As individuals become more identified with mainstream U.S. culture and less religious, traditional practices meet with resistance from young people, who participate in mixed-gender activities and live in isolated communities far from other Muslims" (pp. 152–153).

Diet restrictions include being forbidden to eat pork or pork by-products. Islam also prohibits the consumption of alcohol or other mind-altering substances. "During the month of Ramadan in which the receipt of the Koran is celebrated, Muslims may not eat, drink, smoke, or have sexual intercourse between sunup and sundown" (Frame, 2003, p. 69).

Islam provides guidelines for both men's and women's dress, emphasizing modesty. "Traditionally, Muslim women show nothing but their face, hands, and feet when they are in the company of those not part of their *mahram* (close family members, those who are not eligible to marry the woman, including her father, grandfather, brothers, sons, uncles, nephews, sons-in-law, and father-in-law). The women's clothing is opaque, loose-fitting, long-sleeved, and ankle-length" (Nadir & Dziegielewski, 2001, p. 151). They also wear a veil, a *khimar*, over their head, neck, and breasts, although dress requirements become less formal when women are with close family.

Nadir and Dziegielewski (2001) reflect:

Because of media stereotypes and sensationalism, many non-Muslims perceive Islam as oppressive to women. Many Muslim women, however, do not agree, as they see Islam as a way of life that provides them with a sense of purpose, peace, and freedom not common in Western society. . . . It is important to recognize that many of the inequities Muslim women face are the result of cultural or political traditions that have nothing to do with and are not sanctioned by the teachings of Islam. (p. 154)

Muslim men must also adhere to a dress code. They are required to cover from their navel to their knees. Their garments must be loose-fitting. Traditionally Muslim men wear a shirt, which covers their private area, and loose-fitting slacks; [in addition, they] are forbidden to wear gold or silk. (p. 152)

Looking Ahead

This chapter described various aspects of human diversity and emphasized the importance of social workers being knowledgeable about these dimensions. The significance ascribed to diversity is based on the social work values discussed in Chapter 2. Part I of this book has established a foundation for understanding social welfare and social work. The two chapters in Part II will explain the process of and settings for generalist social work practice.

For Further Exploration on the Internet

See this text's Book Companion Website at **www.socialwork.wadsworth.com/ kirstashman_intro2e** for descriptors and hot links to URLs relevant to this chapter, selected InfoTrac articles and exercises, and tutorial quizzes.

Case Study for Critical Thinking: An Agency Providing Foster Family Care

Consider the following ethical dilemma involving an agency providing foster family care for children (Robison & Reeser, 2000). (*Foster family care* is the provision of substitute care with a family for a planned temporary or extended period when parents or legal guardians are unable to care for a child.) This case study illustrates how the social work profession must continuously address the issue of quality of care versus cost of care. The more intensive and extensive the services provided, the greater the cost. Similarly, social workers must frequently struggle with the issue of providing quality service to clients at minimal cost. The case study also shows how important the agency context is for how social workers can provide services.

Case study: Jose directs an agency that places children in foster family care. The state mandates that no more than six children may be placed with any one family. The intent is to make certain that the family's ability to care for the children is not overextended.

Jose's agency must make enough money to cover its own costs and pay its workers' salaries. Any "money the agency makes from the placement that is not used for the placement itself or for training the foster parents is used to support other agency activities," such as various programs serving poor people. The state pays an annual administrative fee of $8,733 per child placed in a foster home by the agency.

Being a foster parent is not always easy. Sometimes, when needed, the agency's social workers provide training in such skills as effective parenting, communication, behavior management, and anger control:

> The problems that the foster parents face with the children can be remedied if they are the result of lack of proper training, and in the worst cases, children are taken from the home. But there are always going to be marginal cases, "gray areas" [where training won't help]. . . . The agency has solved the problem of what to do with cases that fall into the "gray areas" through "benign neglect," preferring to assume that the problems are not serious enough for the child to be taken out of the home. (Robison & Reeser, 2000, p. 238)

A problem is that the agency is receiving for placement increasingly difficult children who have more extreme problems. Workers report that provision of training for the foster parents is not working because the children's behavioral and emotional problems are so extreme. All the workers can do is tell foster parents they must "deal with" the problems "somehow" (p. 238).

Jose decides to cut down the number of children placed in a foster home from six to four. This would alleviate some of the stress placed on the parents and allow them to give each child more time and attention. However, this means that both the agency and the foster parents (who are also paid by the state) make significantly less money. In fact, Jose's agency is starting to lose money instead of make it. If that doesn't stop, the agency will have to close.

Critical Thinking: How would you use the three-step Triple-A critical thinking process to establish what might be done in this case?

First, *ask* questions like these:

- What options are possible other than the one Jose chose?
- Can children somehow be screened to determine which ones are the most difficult to handle?
- Could these more difficult children be placed in special homes run by the most effective foster parents, with less difficult children placed in homes having six foster children?
- Does decreasing the number of foster children from six to four really make sense? Will this actually solve the problem of better managing difficult behavior? (Workers feel that training still will not help.)
- How possible and effective might it be to decrease the number of children per foster home to five instead of four? Would this be more financially feasible?
- Could other areas of the agency's budget be cut to make up for the decreased number of children in each home?
- What other questions could you ask when thinking about possible solutions in this case?

Second, *assess* the established facts and issues involved. How would you seek answers to the questions just posed and to others you might think up? What information do you need? Where might you find this information? Who could help you get it?

Third, *assert* a concluding opinion. The case poses a difficult problem. After carefully considering the facts, what final conclusion might you reach?

PART ⚇ TWO

SOCIAL WORK PRACTICE

Part 2 includes two chapters that introduce you to the *doing* of social work practice. Chapter 4 discusses the process of social work practice. It defines generalist practice and explains the various roles social workers can assume. It also examines the planned-change process social workers follow as they work with clients.

Chapter 5 describes the various practice settings in which social workers do their work. It explains how practitioners work with individuals, families, groups, organizations, and communities. It also introduces you to the professional organizations in social work and discusses career options.

CHAPTER ✠ FOUR

THE PROCESS
OF GENERALIST PRACTICE

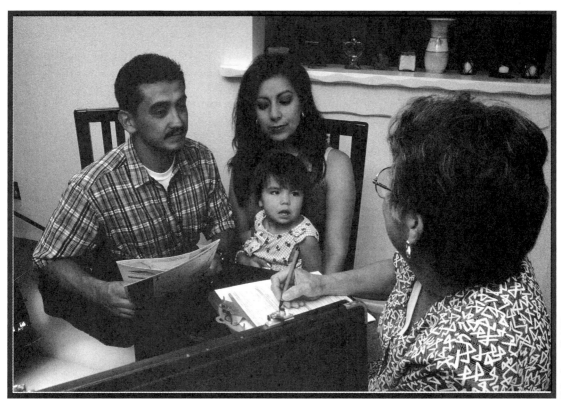

Working with individuals (micro systems), a social worker can

- Help a homeless person get medical help from a community clinic and find a place to stay at a local shelter.
- Counsel a young woman regarding what type of contraception is best for her.
- Assist an elderly man in a hospice in making his end-of-life decisions and help him rest as comfortably as possible during his final days.

Working with groups (mezzo systems), a social worker can

- Run a social skills group for adolescents with cognitive disabilities.
- Lead a support group for parents of children diagnosed with cancer.
- Be in charge of an agency meeting in which various agency staff discuss a client's progress.

Working with organizations and communities (macro systems), a social worker can

- Initiate cooperation among social service agencies to sponsor a holiday gift collection program for needy families.
- Contact legislators and advocate for increased funding for low-income housing for poor people.
- Work with residents in a neighborhood with a high crime rate to start a Neighborhood Watch Program in which neighbors, working together, watch each other's homes and report suspicious behavior to reduce crime.

These scenarios provide examples of what generalist social workers can do at various levels of practice. There are many ways to describe what social workers do. We have established that they work with individuals, families, groups, organizations, and communities to enhance people's well-being. They are prepared to help individuals with highly personal issues and with broad problems that affect whole communities. Social workers identify problems, even difficult ones, and try to help people solve them.

The foundation of social work practice is generalist practice (Landon, 1995; Sheafor & Landon, 1987). The *Encyclopedia of Social Work* (Landon, 1995, p. 1102) states that no "agreed-on definition of generalist practice" exists (p. 1102). However, it adds that there are three dimensions that most people agree should be included. First, the definition should focus on the importance of multiple-level interventions (including those with individuals, families, groups, organizations, and communities). *Intervention* is the use of "thoughtful and planned efforts to bring about a specific change" (Sheafor & Horejsi, 2003, p. 119). Second, the definition should involve a knowledge base carefully chosen from a range of theories. Third, it should maintain a focus "on both private issues and social justice concerns" (p. 1103). Generalist social workers, then, must have infinite flexibility, a solid knowledge base about many things, and a wide range of skills at their disposal.

Micro practice is intervention involving an individual client (a micro system). *Mezzo practice* involves work with small groups (mezzo systems). Social work with families combines micro and mezzo practice because it involves a small group (i.e., the family) but one with intimate ties. *Macro practice* is intervention involving organizations and communities (macro systems).

Integral links exist among micro, mezzo, and macro practice. Generalist practice skills build on each other in a progression from micro to mezzo to macro levels. Relating to individuals in groups (mezzo practice) requires basic micro skills. Likewise, macro practice requires mastery of both micro and mezzo skills for relating to and working with individuals and groups in organizational and community (macro) settings.

Note that throughout this book the terms *social worker, generalist social worker,* and *generalist practitioner* are used interchangeably. Specialized aspects of social work practice, usually referring to social workers with master's degrees, will be specified as such.

This chapter will

- Define generalist practice and explain each concept that is involved.
- Explain how to use critical thinking to review a number of fallacies that can cause people to miss the truth.
- Describe the six steps involved in the planned-change process, the procedure used to undertake social work intervention.
- Discuss some cross-cultural differences in nonverbal and verbal communication.
- Examine how the assessment process should emphasize strengths and empowerment.
- Provide examples of intervention with macro systems.

 # Defining Generalist Practice

Generalist social work practice may involve almost any helping situation you can think of. A generalist practitioner may be called on to help a homeless family, a child unable to get along with peers, a pregnant teenager, a sick elderly person unable to care for herself any longer, an alcoholic parent, a community that's trying to address its drug abuse problem, or a public assistance agency struggling to amend its policies to conform to new federal regulations. Therefore, as has been established, generalist practitioners must be well prepared to address many kinds of difficult situations.

The social work profession has struggled with the concept of generalist practice for many years. In the past, new practitioners were educated in only one skill area (e.g., work with individuals, groups, or communities) or one area of practice (e.g., children and families, or policy and administration). A generalist practitioner needs competence in a wide variety of areas instead of being limited to a single track.

For our purposes, we will define *generalist practice*[1] as the application of an eclectic knowledge base,[2] professional values, and a wide range of skills to target any size system for change within the context of four primary processes. First, generalist practice emphasizes client empowerment. Second, it involves working effectively within an organizational structure and doing so under supervision. Third, it

---

[1] Most of the concepts involved in the definition are taken directly from or based on those required by the Educational Policy and Accreditation Standards (CSWE, 2001).

[2] The term *eclectic* refers to "selecting what appears to be best in various doctrines, methods, or styles" (Mish, 1995, p. 365).

HIGHLIGHT 4.1

Concepts in the Definition
of Generalist Practice

1. Acquiring an eclectic knowledge base
   A. Systems theory
   B. Ecological perspective
   C. Curriculum content areas
      1) Values and ethics
      2) Diversity
      3) Populations-at-risk and social and
         economic justice
      4) Human behavior and the social
         environment
      5) Social welfare policy and services
      6) Social work practice
      7) Research
      8) Field education
   D. Fields of practice
2. Emphasizing client empowerment
3. Using professional values
   A. National Association of Social Workers
      Code of Ethics
   B. Application of professional values to
      solve ethical dilemmas

4. Applying a wide range of skills
   A. Micro
   B. Mezzo
   C. Macro
5. Targeting any size system
   A. Micro
   B. Mezzo
   C. Macro
6. Working in an organizational structure
7. Using supervision appropriately
8. Assuming a wide range of professional
   roles
9. Employing critical thinking skills
10. Using a planned-change process
    A. Engagement
    B. Assessment
    C. Planning
    D. Implementation
    E. Evaluation
    F. Termination
    G. Follow-up

requires the assumption of a wide range of professional roles. Fourth, it involves the application of critical thinking skills to the planned-change process. Highlight 4.1 outlines the basic concepts involved in this definition.

Figure 4.1 illustrates how the various concepts involved in the definition of generalist practice fit together. The large square in the top half of the figure portrays the organizational structure. An organization (or agency) employs social workers and provides the context for them to do their jobs. *Organizational structure* involves how lines of authority and communication operate within an agency, how the administration runs the organization, and what the agency environment is like. Social workers practice within this environment with all its constraints, requirements, and rules, similar to any other place of employment. Thus, in Figure 4.1, a social worker is represented as a smaller rectangle within this large square.

That same rectangle contains the terms *knowledge, values,* and *skills.* These illustrate how social workers bring to their job a broad knowledge base, professional values, and a wide range of skills so they can do their work effectively. Also in the

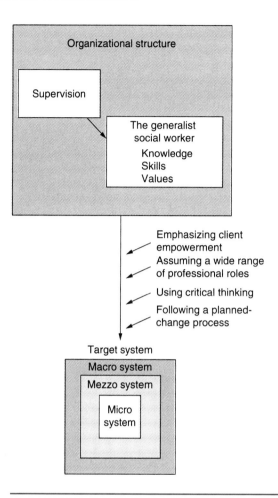

Figure 4.1 A pictorial view of generalist practice

large upper square is another rectangle representing supervision. A downward pointing arrow links the supervision rectangle to the social worker rectangle, indicating that part of working as a generalist practitioner involves receiving and using supervisory input appropriately.

The large square at the bottom of Figure 4.1 illustrates social workers' potential target system. We have established that generalist practitioners may choose to work with a micro, mezzo, or macro system as the target of their change efforts. These three systems are arbitrarily portrayed in concentric squares to reflect their respective sizes.

An arrow flows from the organizational structure square down to the target system square. This depicts how social workers apply their knowledge, skills, and values to help change a micro, mezzo, or macro system. Likewise, four smaller arrows lead from concepts listed to the right of the application arrow into the application process. This depicts how social workers use client empowerment, a wide range of professional roles, critical thinking skills, and the planned-change process as they work to solve a problem or help a system improve its functioning.

Chapter 1 discussed the eclectic knowledge base supporting social work, Chapter 2 social work values and ethics, and Chapter 3 client empowerment. The following sections review the other concepts involved in the definition of generalist practice.

Working in an Organizational Structure Under Supervision

Social workers most likely work within an organizational structure (or agency context) under supervision. As mentioned previously, organizational structure is the formal and informal manner in which tasks and responsibilities, lines of authority, channels of communication, and dimensions of power are established and coordinated within an organization. Understanding the organizational structure involves knowing how decisions are made, what chain of command is followed, what procedures regulate service provision to clients, and how the social work job expectations fit into the larger scheme of things.

Supervision is the process by which a designated supervisor watches over a worker's performance, directs activities, and provides feedback. A good supervisor can be valuable in helping social workers perform effectively within an agency setting.

A Wide Range of Roles

Assuming a wide range of professional roles is a key concept in the definition of generalist practice. We have emphasized that generalist practitioners can tackle a wide range of problems using many different methods; that is, they assume many roles. We have established that a professional role consists of the behaviors and activities involved in performing some designated function. Roles characterizing generalist practitioners include the following:

- *Counselor:* One who provides guidance to clients and assists them in a planned-change or problem-solving process. For example, a worker might help a troubled teenager make decisions about friendships and sexual activity by identifying alternatives and evaluating their potential consequences.
- *Educator:* One who gives information and teaches skills to others (Kirst-Ashman & Hull, 2002; Yessian & Broskowski, 1983). For instance, a practitioner might teach child management skills to parents.
- *Broker:* One who links client systems to needed resources (Connaway & Gentry, 1988; Kirst-Ashman & Hull, 2002). For example, a worker might refer a client to a substance abuse treatment center for inpatient treatment.
- *Case manager* (or *case coordinator*): A practitioner who, on the behalf of a specific client, coordinates needed services provided by any number of agencies,

organizations, or facilities. For instance, a worker might coordinate the many services needed by a cerebral palsy[3] patient living in a group home.

- *Mobilizer:* One who identifies and convenes community members and resources to identify "unmet community needs" and "effect changes for the better in their community" (Halley, Kopp, & Austin, 1998, p. 179). For example, a practitioner might encourage community residents to band together and start a drug education program for residents' children.
- *Mediator:* One who resolves arguments or disagreements among micro, mezzo, or macro systems in conflict (Kirst-Ashman & Hull, 2002; Yessian & Broskowski, 1983). For instance, a worker might serve as a go-between to reach an agreement between an agency that wants to start a group home for people with developmental disabilities and neighborhood residents who oppose having the facility in their neighborhood.
- *Facilitator:* One who guides a group experience. For instance, a practitioner might run a support group for young women with bulimia.[4]
- *Advocate:* One who speaks out on behalf of clients to promote fair and equitable treatment or gain needed resources. For example, a worker might meet with an administrator on behalf of a client to change an agency policy to benefit the client.

 # Critical Thinking Skills

Chapter 1 defined *critical thinking* as (1) the careful scrutiny of what is stated as true or what appears to be true and the resulting expression of an opinion or conclusion based on that scrutiny, and (2) the creative formulation of an opinion or conclusion when presented with a question, problem, or issue. The process of critical thinking involves asking questions, assessing facts, and asserting a conclusion (the Triple-A approach).

Social workers must have the ability to think critically as they work with clients to achieve goals. Gibbs and colleagues (1994) state that critical thinking in social work practice usually involves four dimensions. First, practitioners should be predisposed to ask questions about how their clients are served and treated. Second, they should investigate how interventions are supposed to work and whether they are really effective. Third, they should carefully examine any assertions presented as facts by evaluating arguments on both sides of an issue. Fourth, they should use "scientific reasoning" to analyze arguments, keeping their eyes open for inconsistencies and deviations from the truth.

In other words, don't believe everything you hear. Rather, critically evaluate for yourself whether it's true. Focus on Critical Thinking 4.1 identifies some common fallacies to watch out for.

[3] *Cerebral palsy* is a disability involving problems in muscular control and coordination resulting from damage to the brain before it has matured—that is, before or during birth.

[4] *Bulimia* is an eating disorder occurring primarily in females and characterized by uncontrolled overeating followed by purging activities such as self-initiated vomiting and the use of diuretics, as well as excessive guilt and shame over the compulsive behavior.

FOCUS ON CRITICAL THINKING 4.1
Avoiding the Fallacy Trap

Gibbs and Gambrill (1999, pp. 95–103) cite several fallacies that can trick people into false beliefs. A *fallacy* is a false or erroneous idea, often hidden behind what appears to be a sound argument or presentation. A fallacy or mistaken assumption can trick you into believing what is not true. Fallacies often appear to be true, but really are not. They include the following.

Relying on Case Examples

Just because something worked for one person doesn't mean it will work for everyone. It's important to identify what other variables might have been operating.

Example in everyday life: Ernestine lost 20 pounds in two weeks on the baked bean diet. That baked bean diet is the best thing and it really works. I think I'll try it.

Critical thinking: What proof is there that this baked bean diet really works? How nutritious is it? Does it endanger a person's health if practiced for long? Can other people readily maintain the same willpower as Ernestine, or is she exceptional? How many baked beans can other people really tolerate over that same time? What else was going on in Ernestine's life (e.g., excessive exercise) that could have contributed to her weight loss?

Example in social work practice: Harvey stopped drinking completely after seeing an alcohol and drug abuse counselor for six weeks who used guilt therapy. If you have a drinking problem, you should go to a counselor who uses guilt therapy. It's great.

Critical thinking: What is guilt therapy anyway? Did the therapy really help Harvey stop drinking, or was it something else (e.g., his

wife threatened to leave him, or he joined Alcoholics Anonymous)? How long will Harvey stay "on the wagon"?

Relying on Testimonials

This is similar to relying on case examples. However, here a person swears that something is effective based on personal experience.

Example in everyday life: Gibbs and Gambrill (1999) provide an interesting example:

> "After taking so many other medicines without being helped, you can imagine how happy and surprised I felt when I discovered that Natex was doing me a lot of good. Natex seemed to go right to the root of my trouble, helped my appetite and put an end to the indigestion, gas and shortness of breath." (Local lady took Natex year ago—had good health ever since, 1935, p. 7). This woman's testimonial appeared on the same page of a newspaper as her obituary. (p. 97)

Critical thinking: What proof is there that Natex helped? What else might have affected this woman's condition? What caused her death?

Example in social work practice: Georgia, an agency worker, insists that the most effective child management technique is to bonk the misbehaving child on the nose with a flyswatter. She swears it immediately and permanently curbs obnoxious behaviors such as swearing, hitting other children, and sticking fingers into various facial orifices.

Critical thinking: What are the theoretical underpinnings of the flyswatter approach to behavior management? How has it been proved effective, with whom, and under what conditions? What are some

(continued)

FOCUS ON CRITICAL THINKING 4.1 (*continued*)

potential negative consequences of this technique? To what extent can it cause children physical injury?

Being Vague

Making a generalized, imprecise statement about occurrences or conditions may give false impressions. Vagueness can lead to inaccuracies and potentially bogus assumptions.

Example in everyday life: Life in Salt Lake City is better.

Critical thinking: Does this mean life there is good or bad? Does "better" refer to housing conditions, social life, employment opportunities, quality of restaurants, climate, or access to the mountains for good skiing?

Example in social work practice: Working with the neighborhood group improved community conditions.

Critical thinking: What conditions? Specifically, how were they improved? What proof exists that the neighborhood group, and not some other factors, "improved" conditions?

Being Biased or Unobjective

When a person is so committed to one side of an issue that the other side hardly seems to exist, beware. One-sidedness works against objective evaluation of an idea, practice, or issue. As Gibbs and Gambrill (1999) observe, one-sidedness reflects this attitude: "In matters controversial, my perception's rather fine. I always see both points of view: the one that's wrong and mine" (p. 101).

Example in everyday life: All politicians are crooks. They don't know anything, and all they do is steal your money.

Critical thinking: How many politicians do I know? What has led me to believe they're all crooks? What exactly is a political crook? Don't politicians differ regarding their stands on issues? How logical is it to clump them all into one bunch? How do they get away with stealing your money? Aren't most politicians monitored by the public? If there weren't any politicians, who would run the government, and how? If I don't like

(continued)

The Planned-Change Process

Planned change involves the development and implementation of a strategy for improving or altering "some specified condition, pattern of behavior, or set of circumstances that affects social functioning" (Sheafor & Horejsi, 2003, p. 119). Planned change is a process whereby social workers engage a client, assess issues, identify strengths and problems, establish a plan of action, implement the plan, evaluate its effects, and finally terminate the process.

Another term often used to describe what generalist practitioners do is *problem solving*, initially introduced by social work pioneer Helen Harris Perlman in 1957. Essentially, problem solving refers to the same process as planned change, although many debate the nuances of difference. Social work's more recent emphasis on client strengths may be at odds with the more negative connotations of the

FOCUS ON CRITICAL THINKING 4.1 (*continued*)

politicians, why don't I run for office myself and fix the system?

Example in social work practice: The social services agency I work for is the only one in the state that's any good.

Critical thinking: To what extent am I biased in claiming that my organization's the best one? What proof do I have that mine is better than the others? How do I know that other agencies don't have similar strengths? How many agencies am I familiar with anyway?

Believing That if It's Written Down It Must Be Right

Stating something as a fact in a book, article, newspaper, or other medium such as radio or television doesn't mean it's accurate or true.

Example in everyday life: The book said that there have been thousands of alien sightings and abductions, so it must be true. There are even some photos of flying saucers in there.

Critical thinking: What concrete evidence is there that flying saucers have been here? Who has said they've been abducted, and what do they say about it? Are those really saucers in the pictures or some doctored-up hoax?

Example in social work practice: This textbook says that critical thinking is a necessity in social work practice.

Critical thinking: What does critical thinking mean? Does it make sense to scrutinize so carefully the things you're told? Is your ability to think as good as that of the people who write textbooks? What have you agreed with and disagreed with so far in this book? Do you tend to agree with everything you read or hear on television?

The point is that critical thinking concerns not necessarily accepting situations or stories at face value. Rather, it entails using your own judgment to seriously consider their worth and relevance.

---

word *problem.* The term *change* may have more positive implications despite the fact that most social work intervention deals with problem situations. Given some evidence that the term *planned change* is more frequently used in generalist practice, we will use it here (Hoffman & Sallee, 1993; Landon, 1995).

Social workers help people deal with problems ranging from personal relationships to lack of resources to blatant discrimination. For instance, a social worker may need to address the problem of a battered woman who is economically and emotionally dependent on her abusive husband and who also has three children to protect. Another social worker might have an adolescent client who has committed a number of serious crimes and who is heavily involved with drugs. Still another social worker may need to advocate for change in a public assistance policy that discriminates against people who don't speak English well and are unable to follow an intricate, exasperating application process to receive benefits. Regardless of the problem being addressed, the planned-change effort follows the same course of action, described shortly.

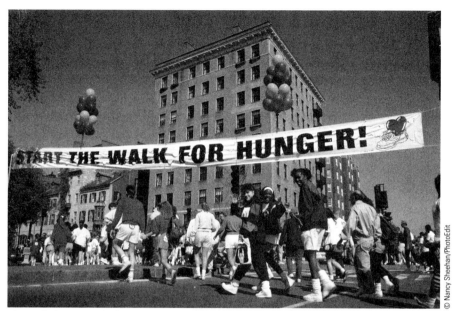

Planned change includes micro-, mezzo-, and macro-level practice. Here, marchers fight hunger in a macro event.

Case Example We have established that a key feature of a generalist social work approach is that virtually any problem may be analyzed and addressed from multiple levels of intervention (i.e., involving micro, mezzo, or macro systems). An example of the application of a generalist approach involves DeRon, a social worker for Phenomenal, Inc., a large, urban diagnostic and treatment center serving children with various disabilities including physical, speech, and psychological. Phenomenal is a private agency funded primarily by private insurance payments, medical assistance reimbursement, voluntary donations, and government grants. DeRon's job description specifies that he is responsible for providing family counseling, educating parents about behavior management techniques, and brokering resources.

DeRon receives a new case referral, Peyton, a 5-year-old boy who has severe speech and behavioral problems. He stutters and has difficulty enunciating words and formulating sentences. At home, he frequently refuses to obey his parents, often lashing out in violent temper tantrums. At school, he has very poor communication and relationship-building skills with his peers. He is unable to play with peers without acting out aggressively, such as hitting them in the stomach or poking them in the eye. Such behavior causes serious problems for him with his kindergarten teacher.

Unfortunately, his parents have indicated that their insurance will not pay for Peyton's treatment. They are not receiving any public assistance and will be hard-pressed to pay for services by themselves.

As a generalist practitioner DeRon can assess and proceed with this case on several levels, considering the possibility of micro, mezzo, or macro intervention. First, on a micro level, Peyton requires speech and behavioral assessments to determine a treatment plan. To what extent are his speech difficulties physiologically based? What speech therapy goals might be established? How do Peyton's speech problems affect his ability to interact with others? How are his parents and other family members reacting to and handling his speech and behavior problems?

On a mezzo level, Peyton is having difficulty interacting with family members, peers, and other adults. Remember that we arbitrarily consider the family as placed between the micro and mezzo levels of practice because of its interpersonal dimension and the importance of group dynamics. Peyton's parents may require family counseling and education about behavior management techniques. Mezzo-level intervention also may address Peyton's peer relationships. His teacher may need consultation regarding behavioral control in the classroom. Peyton might benefit from membership in a treatment group with other children experiencing similar difficulties. Group activities might include discussing feelings and behavior, providing role models for improved behavior, and encouraging positive interaction among group members.

Macro-level intervention investigates and promotes changes in the broader macro environment. Peyton's parents indicate that it is difficult, if not impossible, to pay for his treatment by themselves. Can agency policy be changed so that families in financial need like Peyton's receive services based on a sliding fee scale (i.e., a payment schedule that varies according to clients' income, so that people who make less pay proportionately less for the same service)? Can a special fund based on private donations be established for families in financial need? Should a fund-raising drive for such a cause be initiated? Should the school be expected to provide speech therapy and behavioral counseling in view of Peyton's inability to function in the academic environment? Potential macro-level interventions, then, might involve changes in community services or agency policies and practices to make needed resources more readily available. Figure 4.2 illustrates the generalist approach to assessing this situation and planning intervention involving micro, mezzo, and macro goals.

Figure 4.3 illustrates the six primary steps involved in planned change: engagement, assessment, planning, implementation, evaluation, and termination.

Step 1: Engagement

Engagement is the initial period when practitioners orient themselves to the problem at hand and begin to establish communication and a relationship with others also addressing the problem. Regardless of whether workers pursue micro, mezzo, or macro change, they must establish rapport with clients and target systems in order to communicate and get things done. Engagement is based on the acquisition of a range of micro skills. Both the words social workers speak (verbal communication) and their coinciding actions and expressions (nonverbal communication) can engage others in the helping process.

Nonverbal communication is body language and sounds that convey information about how a person feels without saying so in words. It includes body positions, facial expressions, vocal tone and expression (e.g., raising your voice or speaking very quietly and meekly), and vocal noises other than words (e.g., grunts, snorts, chortles, hums). Patterson and Welfel (2000) explain:

> You have been with people whose body language invites communication, and you have been with others whose body language indicates disinterest and perhaps even anxiety about communicating. The active, interested listener faces and leans toward the

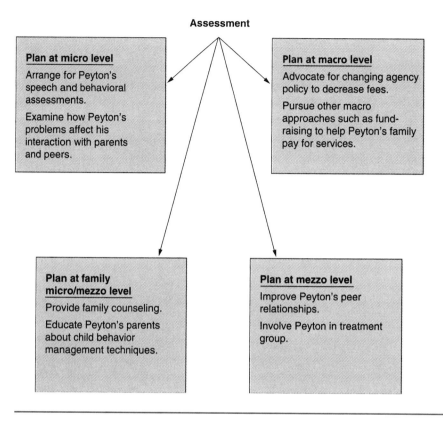

Assessment

Plan at micro level

Arrange for Peyton's speech and behavioral assessments.

Examine how Peyton's problems affect his interaction with parents and peers.

Plan at macro level

Advocate for changing agency policy to decrease fees.

Pursue other macro approaches such as fund-raising to help Peyton's family pay for services.

Plan at family micro/mezzo level

Provide family counseling.

Educate Peyton's parents about child behavior management techniques.

Plan at mezzo level

Improve Peyton's peer relationships.

Involve Peyton in treatment group.

Figure 4.2 Initiating micro-, mezzo-, or macro-level change during assessment

speaker in a posture of interest and even excitement. Eyes are focused in the general direction of the person's face. Arms are in an open mode in relation to the trunk, as if to say, "I am very interested in receiving, with all my sensory processes, what it is you want to say to me." The attentive listener maintains an interested facial expression and makes encouraging gestures (nods, smiles, hand gestures, and so forth). (pp. 41–42)

Social workers also need to pay attention to cultural variations in people's nonverbal and verbal behavior. Highlight 4.2 discusses some of the differences among cultures.

Many other dimensions are involved in engagement. Social workers' overall demeanor—including their ability to convey warmth, empathy, and genuineness, concepts related to nonverbal behavior—can enhance engagement. Conveying *warmth* involves enhancing workers' positive feelings toward another person by promoting a sense of comfort and well-being in that person. *Empathy* involves not only being in tune with how clients feel but also conveying to them in a sincere and open manner that workers understand how they feel. *Genuineness* simply means that workers continue to be themselves while working to accomplish goals in their professional role.

Likewise, how social workers introduce themselves and arrange an initial meeting's setting affects the engagement process. Other engagement skills include alleviating initial client anxiety and introducing the worker's purpose and role.

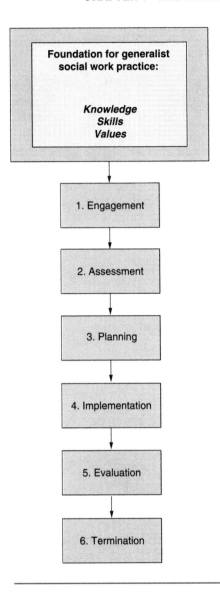

Figure 4.3   Planned-change steps in generalist social work practice

Step 2: Assessment

According to Siporin (1975), assessment is the "differential, individualized, and accurate identification and evaluation of problems, people, and situations and of their interrelations, to serve as a sound basis for differential helping intervention" (p. 224). Meyer (1995) defines *assessment* simply as "knowing, understanding, evaluating, individualizing, or figuring out" (p. 260). For our purposes, *assessment* is the investigation and determination of variables affecting an identified problem

HIGHLIGHT 4.2

Cultural Differences in Nonverbal and Verbal Communication

Cultural expectations for nonverbal communication vary widely. Anglos may stress the importance of making direct eye contact, leaning forward to express interest, and shaking hands upon meeting. However, people from other cultures do not necessarily feel the same way. For example, Corey and Corey (2003) explain some of the differences in eye contact:

> In European North American middle-class culture, direct eye contact is usually considered a sign of interest and presence, and a lack thereof is interpreted as being evasive. It is common for individuals to maintain more eye contact while listening and less while talking. Some research indicates that African Americans may reverse this pattern by looking more when talking and slightly less when listening. Among some Native American and Hispanic groups, eye contact by the young is a sign of disrespect. Some cultural groups generally avoid eye contact when talking about serious subjects. (p. 202)

In Chinese culture, when two people "talk to one another," they "use much less eye contact, especially when it is with the opposite sex"; this implies, for instance, that a male social worker's extended gaze at a female Chinese client could "be considered rude or seductive" (Zhang, 2003, p. 47).

Expectations for touching also have cultural variations. For example, one study examined "the average number of times friends of different cultural groups touch each other in an hour while talking in a coffee shop. The results showed that English friends did not touch each other at all, French friends touched 110 times, and Puerto Rican friends touched 180 times" (cited in Ivey & Ivey, 2003, p. 105).

Even smiling has variable expectations. Whereas "[s]miling is a sign of warmth in most cultures . . . in some situations in Japan, smiling may indicate discomfort" or nervousness (Ivey & Ivey, 2003, p. 105). Okun, Fried, and Okun (1999) comment:

> Imagine how a Japanese person visiting the United States might feel if everyone she or he was introduced to smiled. Even if we "know" that smile means welcome in the United States and indicates discomfort in Japan, our knowledge is formal, intellectual, and technical, and our informal, emotional knowledge inserts an element of confusion into the communication process. In short, we smile automatically. (p. 79)

Another difference between Japanese people and Anglos involves how Anglos typically nod their heads to indicate that they concur with what the

(continued)

or issue as viewed from micro, mezzo, or macro perspectives. It refers to gathering relevant information about a problem so decisions can be made about potential solutions.

The crucial task of generalist practice is to look beyond the individual and examine other impinging factors within the client's environment. In a given case, the emphases on different assessment categories may vary. However, each category must still be reviewed and considered for its potential contribution to the problem.

For instance, a couple may come to a social worker for help in their marital relationship. Thus assessment of the mezzo aspects, or relationship issues of the situation, would be emphasized. However, a generalist practitioner would also consider

HIGHLIGHT 4.2 *(continued)*

speaker is saying. Japanese people, on the other hand, may nod their heads to indicate they are paying close attention to what's being said. However, this behavior has nothing to do with agreement (Lum, 2000, p. 170).

An additional aspect of nonverbal behavior involves the amount of space people allow among themselves as they interact. Ivey and Ivey (2003) explain:

> A comfortable conversational distance for many North Americans is slightly more than arm's length, and the English prefer even greater distances. Many Latin people often prefer half that distance, and those from the Middle East may talk practically eyeball to eyeball. As a result, the slightly forward leaning we recommend for attending behavior is not going to be appropriate all the time. A natural, relaxed body style that is your own is most likely to be effective, but be prepared to adapt and flex according to the individual with whom you are talking. (p. 46)

The way clients from various cultural backgrounds respond verbally also differs considerably. "Many cultures of the world do not place as much premium on talking as do the cultures in the Western Hemisphere. Consider the following" case example cited by a counselor about his client (Berg-Cross, Craig, & Wessel, 2001):

Ms. B. was an undergraduate student from Asia. She had failed in one of her clinical rotations in an allied health field. Her failure was attributed not to her knowledge or her ability in her field but to poor judgment in her interpersonal relations. She came to see me in total frustration. One of her negative evaluations by her field supervisor had to do with her insufficient verbal participation in case conferences. Essentially her supervisors were saying that she didn't talk much and interpreted that as a lack of interest and involvement. When this . . . [counselor] explored further her lack of participation in classroom and group discussions, the client uttered in frustration, "I only speak if I have anything to say. In this country people talk even if they have nothing to say." She told me she just doesn't engage in superficial conversation. (p. 862)

How things are said also varies from culture to culture (Brave Heart & Chase, 2005):

> First Nations clients may manifest a more indirect communication style, and the social worker must listen closely for disguised requests. Content is often veiled in stories and . . . [symbolic comparisons]. First Nations clients often respond indirectly to questions, and the worker must listen closely; the response may initially appear unrelated, but the answer is usually given in a disguised manner, in a story or through recounting a personal experience or that of another individual (p. 39).

both the micro aspects such as the strengths, needs, and issues of each partner, and the macro aspects impinging upon their situation. Macro aspects might involve the fact that both spouses have been laid off from their jobs at the local bowling pin manufacturing plant. They had both held these jobs for over 10 years. The layoffs were probably due to a serious economic downturn and a decrease in the growth of recreational facilities such as bowling alleys. The social worker might not be able to do much about the economy's current condition. However, the economic impact on the couple is vital to the assessment of the couple's current conflictual situation.

The social worker also must assess the client's strengths. Highlight 4.3 discusses how a social worker assesses an individual's mental health problems and

Assessment Emphasizing Strengths and Empowerment

Traditional Versus Strengths-Based Assessments

A traditional social work assessment model for an individual seeking mental health services involves seven dimensions: (1) presenting problem, (2) problem history, (3) personal history, (4) substance abuse history, (5) family history, (6) employment and education, and (7) summary and treatment recommendations (Graybeal, 2001, p. 235). The traditional medical model described in Chapter 1 focuses on identifying what's wrong with the individual and then trying to fix it. Each dimension emphasizes the negative because the eventual goal is to cure the problem. A strengths-based perspective maintains that "individuals will do better in the long run when they are helped to identify, recognize, and use the strengths and resources available in themselves and their environment" (Graybeal, 2001, p. 234).

Graybeal (2001, p. 238) emphasizes the importance of identifying and using a client's strengths in addition to focusing on problems. For example, when assessing the presenting problem (i.e., the stated reason the client seeks treatment), traditional information solicited includes "detailed descriptions of problem(s)" and a "list of symptoms." A strengths-based assessment also explores personal strengths and available resources, and emphasizes potential solutions to the problem.

Similarly, the problem, personal, substance abuse, and family histories focus on more than all the bad things that have occurred. In addition, the social worker conducting a strengths-based assessment seeks information about what happened during the good times when the problem was not evident. What variables kept the client functioning well and staying healthy? What coping strategies were used? Who provided needed support during crises?

Traditional assessment of employment and education focuses on the facts concerning what occurred and on identification of gaps and problems. Strengths-based assessment of problems emphasizes the individual's skills, interests, and connections with other people in the community, including "spiritual and church involvement."

Finally, the traditional assessment summary and treatment recommendations focus on making a diagnosis and recommending a treatment plan. A strengths-based assessment downplays labeling the problem and instead stresses a "summary of resources, options, possibilities, exceptions, and solutions."

Graybeal (2001) indicates that significant differences exist between a traditional problem-oriented and a strengths-based assessment in cases concerning depression and suicidal thoughts. Consider Sara, who seeks help for her depression.

Traditional Assessment

Presenting problem: Sara, age 24, looking tired, haggard, and older than her years, reports a history of lethargy, depression, lack of self-confidence, low self-esteem, feelings of disheartenment, and thoughts of suicide. She also reports significant weight loss and difficulty sleeping.

Problem history: Sara indicates that these feelings of depression originated at age 16 when she was in a serious car accident in which some of her facial bones were crushed. She experienced 10 difficult and painful plastic surgeries that restored her face nearly to its original condition. She indicates that she has been helped by therapy and medication twice beginning at the time of the accident, although she has not been involved with a therapist for over a year.

(continued)

H I G H L I G H T   4.3 (*continued*)

Strengths-Based Assessment

Presenting problem: Sara, age 24, reports feelings of depression, uselessness, and loneliness. She also reports significant weight loss and difficulty sleeping. She indicates that these feelings began when her sister moved two states away. Although she has had thoughts of suicide, she is not seriously considering that now. She states that she feels best when at work and when telephoned by her sister.

Problem history: Sara indicates that her depression began at age 16 when she was in a serious car accident resulting in a series of painful facial surgeries. She indicates that members of her family and friends were very supportive of her throughout her physical and emotional trauma. She reports that her depression lifted when she first started this job but gradually crept back over the past few months. She has been involved in therapy twice in the past that she found very helpful. She is hopeful that therapy will result in improving her mood, energy level, and social life. Eventually, she hopes to have friends instead of a therapist provide her with the support she needs.

Differences Between Traditional and Strengths-Based Approaches in Sara's Assessment

Note that the traditional assessment of the presenting problem stresses the bad things about Sara's problem—how she looks, feels, and experiences difficulties. The strengths-based assessment identifies the problems but also recognizes strengths. Sara has a strong support system in her sister; although her sister has moved away, they still maintain phone contact. It's also a strength that Sara is currently not considering suicide, although she has in the past.

The traditional problem history assessment goes into more detail about Sara's car accident at age 16. It also states that Sara has not been involved in therapy for a year. In contrast, the strengths-based assessment notes the supportiveness of relatives, a significant strength, during Sara's years of surgery and recovery. It also reports that Sara's mood lifted when she first started her job, so there were some positive variables involved there. The strengths-based approach indicates that Sara has found therapy helpful in the past, that she is hopeful it will do so again, and that eventually she hopes to develop a social support system so she will no longer need therapy. In summary, focusing on strengths provides some clues for how to proceed in helping Sara fight her depression.

Mezzo and Macro Aspects of Assessment

Generalist social workers also look at potential mezzo and macro aspects of assessment when scrutinizing a problem. When assessing Sara's personal, substance abuse, and family histories, the social worker works with her to examine her relationships with family members and others. Might she need to resolve some issues with her family members? Should they be involved in treatment? Might a support group be appropriate in which she could talk with others also suffering from depression? Or might a socialization group be useful in which members strive to improve their interpersonal behavior and social skills? This may be fitting because Sara has expressed a desire to improve her social life.

Macro aspects of assessment might involve how accessible treatment is to Sara. Is agency policy such that she can receive affordable treatment? If she can't afford it, is advocacy to change policy needed on her behalf?

needs by emphasizing strengths. Chapter 13 elaborates on mental health issues and practice.

Human Diversity and Assessment

Social workers must also take aspects of diversity into consideration when conducting assessments. Chapter 3 discussed various facets of human diversity including "age, class, color, culture, disability, ethnicity, family structure, gender, marital status, national origin, race, religion, sex, and sexual orientation" (CSWE, 2001, III.A.3). For each case, social workers should ask themselves whether any aspects of diversity may be significant.

Case Example   Consider Andrew, a hospital social worker whose client, Florence, age 78, was temporarily hospitalized for complications from diabetes. (*Diabetes* is a disease of the pancreas in which the body doesn't manufacture enough insulin to process sugars adequately.) Andrew is now helping Florence arrange to stay with relatives until she is well enough to return home. In the process of helping Florence, Andrew must identify aspects of diversity that might affect the assessment process or Florence's treatment.

Andrew discovers that Florence is of Italian heritage, a relevant aspect of ethnic and cultural diversity. Florence also feels strongly about her membership in a local Roman Catholic church that many other elderly people of similar heritage also attend. For several reasons, Florence's church involvement is very important to her. Therefore, Andrew must take this into consideration when developing Florence's treatment plan with her. She needs a means of maintaining contact with her church.

Another aspect of diversity to consider is Florence's age. Is Florence being treated differently or in a discriminatory manner because of ageism? *Ageism* refers to discrimination based on preconceived notions about older people, regardless of their individual qualities and capabilities. Andrew closely evaluates his own attitudes here. For instance, is he tempted to make assumptions about Florence's mental capability because of the stereotype that older people don't think as well as when they were younger?

Likewise, Andrew must be aware of any sexist biases he might harbor. *Sexism* refers to any preconceived notions about a person based solely on gender. For instance, does Andrew feel that Florence is a dependent person who needs to be taken care of simply because she's a woman? Such a bias fails to take into account the client as a unique individual with her own strengths and weaknesses.

Step 3: Planning

Assessment sets the stage for the intervention by identifying problems and strengths. *Planning* specifies what should be done. The following aspects of planning are important:

- The social worker should work *with* the client, not dictate *to* the client, to create the treatment plan.
- The social worker, together with the client, should prioritize the problems so that the most critical ones are addressed first.

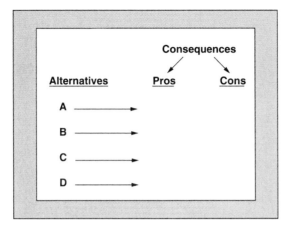

Figure 4.4   Social workers help clients identify alternatives and evaluate the pros and cons of each.

- The social worker should identify the client's strengths to provide some guidance for the planned-change process.
- The social worker should identify alternative interventions. Should micro, mezzo, or macro systems be targets of change?
- The social worker should help the client evaluate the pros and cons of each course of action to choose the best approach. Figure 4.4 depicts this process.
- With the client, the social worker should develop *goals*—the results that the client and worker seek to accomplish.
- The social worker should establish a *contract* with the client—that is, an agreement between a client and worker about the goals, time frames, and responsibilities of people involved in the intervention process.

Step 4: Implementation

Implementation is the process whereby client and worker follow their plan to achieve their goals. It is the actual *doing* of the plan. As you know, social work intervention can involve virtually any size system. Highlight 4.4 describes a series of potential social work interventions involving macro client systems.

Step 5: Evaluation

Evaluation is "a process of determining whether a given change effort was worthwhile" (Kirst-Ashman & Hull, 2001, p. 322). After engagement and assessment, a social worker makes a plan with the client, implements the plan, and then evaluates the extent to which the plan was successful. It boils down to the social worker asking, "Does it work?" and "How do we know?" (Kirst-Ashman & Hull, 2001, p. 322). Social workers need to be accountable; that is, they must prove that their interventions have

Implementation with Macro Client Systems

The concept of macro intervention concerns agency or social change that affects larger numbers of people than individuals, families, or small groups. The following are examples of interventions involving communities and organizations on the behalf of macro client systems. Social workers might initiate any of these for the benefit of their clientele, community, or organization.

Fund-Raisers

Social workers can initiate, advocate for, help organize, and implement fund-raising events for a wide range of purposes. Fund-raising might involve a door-to-door campaign. It might also entail sponsoring special events and charging fees for admission to activities such as bingo nights, turkey dinners, or community dances. Similarly, it might involve selling donated things such as baked goods, crafts, or rummage items to finance some event or activity. Sponsored activities might include a bus trip to Washington, D.C., to march in favor of gay and lesbian rights, a Thanksgiving dinner for the local homeless, or renovations for a community recreational center.

Advocacy for Agency Policy Changes

Social workers can advocate to change internal agency policies when they're inefficient, ineffective, or discriminatory. Although an agency's administration is supposed to institute such changes, it often doesn't. Sometimes administrators are too far removed in the administrative structure from direct service provision to clients to know what's really going on. Other times, they are resistant to change because it requires greater effort or more money.

You may not have any experience in social work, but think of the jobs you've had. To what extent were supervisors always aware of the issues you faced daily? Were the employers' rules and requirements always sensible and fair? Were employees and customers always treated in the most effective, efficient, and considerate way possible? Were you never disgusted with or angry at how you or others were treated? If you can answer "yes" to these four questions, you're lucky. In some ways, agencies, businesses, and other organizations can have similar problems. For whatever reason, agency social workers might be in the position of having to advocate with their own agency on the behalf of clients.

For instance, one worker advocated to initiate a policy to reserve the agency's best parking spaces for clients. Historically, staff would park in the best spots in the parking lot each morning because they always got there first. Clients thus regularly got the very worst parking spots—if there were any spots left at all.

Social workers can also advocate for change when an agency policy gets in the way of their doing their jobs. The policy might state that social workers should visit their clients' homes only when absolutely necessary to hold down transportation costs. The workers might strongly feel that it's essential to visit clients in their home environments to assess accurately what's going on in the family. Therefore, it's their responsibility to advocate for positive policy change.

A Volunteer Dental Program

Social workers can initiate and help organize programs for dentists to volunteer to help people with chronic illnesses, developmental disabilities, or other problems prohibiting them from working and having dental insurance. The program can

(continued)

also be made available to people working in low-paying jobs that don't provide dental insurance. Social workers can contact potential volunteers, help coordinate efforts, work with social service agencies to publicize the service, and link clients with the resource when they need dental help.

For instance, Harry, age 60, has severe heart disease and serious, painful gum disease. Because of numerous health expenses, he was financially strapped. He did have upper dentures made several years earlier. His coverage as a veteran at a Veteran's Administration hospital allowed for him to have his lower teeth removed but prohibited coverage for any further work. Harry's mouth was in appalling shape, and he had extreme difficulty eating and talking. A social worker helped initiate and organize a Tri-County Troubled Teeth Treatment program in which dentists were systematically recruited to volunteer some of their time. One dentist in the program worked carefully with Harry during a half dozen appointments. At the end of the process, Harry couldn't believe he had brand-new porcelain lower dentures. He beamed at the dentist in appreciation.

Murals

Large pictures painted or drawn on walls or ceilings, known as murals, can provide an important means of self-expression and cultural pride. For example, concerning Chicanos and their pride in their history, Treguer (1992) comments about murals:

> Pre-Columbian themes, intended to remind Chicanos of their noble origins, are common. There are motifs from the [ancient] Aztec . . . [manuscripts], gods from the Aztec . . . [temples], allusions to the Spanish conquest and images of the Virgin of Guadalupe, a cherished Mexican icon. (p. 23)

Additionally, such murals can reflect religious and spiritual symbols, and issues related to social justice. Delgado and Barton (1999) remark,

> In some Latino communities, scenes of police brutality, arson, alcohol and other drug abuse, prison, U.S. imperialism (particularly related to government-sponsored terrorism in the Caribbean and Latin America), and infant mortality are commonplace. . . . In essence, mural scenes are based on historical events and are a daily reminder of the trials and tribulations of being Latino in this country and of the search for social justice. (p. 233)

Delgado and Barton (1999) describe a case in Holyoke, Massachusetts, where a large Puerto Rican population lives. They note how "El Arco Iris (the Rainbow), an after-school program" under the auspices of "a local community-based organization, received funds to create a mural" (p. 241). Having obtained authorization from the owner of a deserted building, 20 Puerto Rican young people painted a mural of a nature panorama on one of the building's large, blank walls. The youths incorporated the U.S. and Puerto Rican flags into the landscape. They positioned the Puerto Rican flag above the U.S. flag, with the latter depicted upside down. Although the youths' intent was to demonstrate the harmony between the two countries, several other community residents were offended by the upside-down U.S. flag. The incident caused serious debate among community residents with different cultural heritages. On the positive side, it stimulated discussion and consciousness-raising among groups throughout the community. It also brought together Puerto Rican community members, including adults and young people, "to fight for their beliefs and to strengthen their

(continued)

HIGHLIGHT 4.4 *(continued)*

voice within the community" (Delgado & Barton, 1999, p. 241). Eventually, the Puerto Rican youths decided to end the controversy by enlarging the Puerto Rican flag to cover the U.S.flag.
Delgado and Barton (1999) conclude,

Social workers can play an instrumental role in helping communities negotiate with government authorities and private parties for the painting of murals using their spaces. Murals in prime locations can serve to empower communities to organize to seek services and other resources to help them develop their capacities to help themselves. (p. 236)

been effective. Each goal must be evaluated in terms of the extent to which it has been achieved.

For example, consider Yvonne, a parole[5] officer for adults. George had been imprisoned for six years for armed robbery. He had been drunk when he committed the offenses. As a result, George's goals include attending biweekly Alcoholics Anonymous meetings, avoiding drinking altogether, seeking work from at least four sources weekly, checking in to the halfway house[6] where he resides by 8:00 PM every evening, and faithfully attending his weekly meetings with Yvonne on time. If George goes out drinking and gets a ticket for driving under the influence, he and Yvonne must evaluate the extent to which his rehabilitation plan is working. Does George require more intensive inpatient treatment instead? Is his parole unsuccessful, and so he should return to prison? What appropriate research-based knowledge is available for Yvonne and George to reconsider these goals and develop alternative ones?

Note that evaluation is also essential in mezzo and macro practice. For example, social workers must determine whether intervention involving agency functioning and service provision is successful. *Program evaluation* is the systematic examination of the success, effectiveness, and efficiency of an ongoing program (i.e., a structured plan and procedures for providing designated services to a sizable number of clients or a community).

Step 6: Termination

Termination is "the end of the professional social worker–client relationship" (Kirst-Ashman & Hull, 1999, p. 324). The worker–client relationship eventually must come to an end. It is not a good ending for a worker to get up one day and, out of

[5] *Parole* is "the conditional release of a person from prison prior to the end of the sentence imposed" (Nichols, 1999, p. 961).

[6] *Halfway houses* are transitional dwellings that provide structure, support, and guidance for persons unable to function independently in the community. They are transitional because they provide a middle ground between a full-time residential setting (e.g., an institution or prison) and the relative freedom of living in the community. Persons requiring halfway houses include those on probation, substance abusers, and those with a history of mental illness.

the blue, say, "Well, good-bye." Termination in generalist practice involves specific skills and techniques, regardless of the level of intervention.

Appropriate timing of the termination is important. Hellenbrand (1987) cites at least three basic types of termination (p. 765). First, some terminations are "natural"; that is, goals have been achieved, and it is time for clients to take what they have learned and go out on their own. Other terminations are "forced." For example, a worker might leave the agency, or a client might leave an institution for some reason or lose eligibility to receive services. Finally, there are "unplanned" terminations. Perhaps the client simply fails to come back, or the family moves, or the client is no longer motivated to return. Or maybe other aspects of the client's life takes precedence over the problem he or she originally came to the social worker to help solve.

The most effective terminations follow a thoughtful, planned process so that clients are prepared for the relationship to end. Social workers need to acknowledge that endings are near before they abruptly occur. They need to encourage clients to share feelings about the termination and, in turn, to share their own. Additionally, practitioners need to identify clearly whatever progress has been made. This increases the chance that the client will use what has been learned during this intervention to help solve other problems in the future.

The client may be an individual, group, or large agency. Regardless, each needs help in the transition from depending on the worker for support or guidance to making decisions and functioning independently.

Looking Ahead

This chapter discussed the process of generalist social work practice. The next will explain the various practice settings in which this process is implemented.

For Further Exploration on the Internet

See this text's Book Companion Website at **www.socialwork.wadsworth.com/ kirstashman_intro2e** for descriptors and hot links to URLs relevant to this chapter, selected InfoTrac articles and exercises, and tutorial quizzes.

CHAPTER ✤ FIVE

PRACTICE SETTINGS

© Bruce Ayres/Getty Images

Consider these questions:

- Why are social welfare programs the way they are today?
- What social welfare problems and issues do we foresee in the future?
- What kinds of treatment groups do social workers run?
- What fields of practice do most social workers go into?

This chapter addresses these and many other questions and issues concerning social welfare and social work in the past, present, and future. Chapter 4 discussed generalist social work practice. This chapter focuses on the contexts in which social work has been, is, and will be practiced. Specifically, this chapter will

- Identify the context of social work practice today in organizations and communities.
- Explain the core treatment approaches in micro, mezzo, and macro practice.
- Identify some of the major professional associations in social work.
- Discuss employment settings for social workers in terms of fields of practice.
- Propose questions to stimulate critical thinking about career goals.

Social Work Practice Today

Chapter 4 discussed the process of generalist social work practice. The following sections continue the exploration of the current context of practice, including social work's organizational and community settings; primary treatment approaches used in micro, mezzo, and macro practice; key professional social work organizations; and social workers' most common employment settings according to fields of practice.

Settings in Social Work Practice: Organizations and Communities

Social work practice generally takes place within the context of organizations and communities. *Organizations* are entities made up of people that have rules and structure to achieve specified goals. Social workers practice under the auspices of organizations providing social services.

Social Services in the Context of Social Agencies

Social services include the tasks that social work practitioners and other helping professionals perform with the goal of improving people's health, enhancing their quality of life, increasing autonomy and independence, supporting families, and helping people and larger systems improve their functioning in the social environment (Barker, 2003). That is quite a mouthful. In essence, social services include the wide range of activities that social workers perform to help people solve problems and improve their personal well-being.

A *social agency* or *social services agency* is an organization providing social services that typically employs a range of helping professionals including social workers in addition to office staff, paraprofessionals (persons trained to assist professionals), and sometimes volunteers (Barker, 2003). Social agencies generally serve some designated client population experiencing some defined need. Services are provided according to a prescribed set of policies regarding how the agency staff should accomplish their service provision goals.

Social agencies come in many forms. For example, they can be either public or private. *Public* social agencies are run by some designated unit of government and are usually regulated by laws impacting policy. For instance, a county board committee oversees a public welfare department and is responsible for establishing its major policies. (Of course, such a committee must function in accordance with the wishes of the state or federal governments that often provide at least some of the money for the agency's programs.)

Private social agencies, in contrast, are privately owned and run by people not employed by government. The services they provide include individual and group counseling, family planning, and other services for children and the elderly (Barker, 2003). Note that services sometimes resemble those furnished by public social agencies such as corrections, protective services for children, and job preparation and training for public assistance recipients.

Private social agencies may be either nonprofit or proprietary. *Nonprofit* social agencies seek to accomplish some service provision goal, not to make a profit for private owners. Sources of funding for services can include taxes, private donations, grants, and service fees. A board of directors presides over a private nonprofit agency, formulating policy and making certain that agency staff run the agency appropriately.

Proprietary or *for-profit* private social agencies also provide some designated social services, often quite similar to those provided by nonprofit private social agencies. However, a primary purpose for the existence of a proprietary social agency is to earn a profit for its owners.

Sometimes public agencies buy services from private agencies through a *purchase-of-service contract* or agreement. In a typical scenario, a public agency needs specialized services that it does not normally provide. It may be more cost-effective for the public agency to purchase the service from a private agency. The private agency then assumes responsibility for developing and overseeing service provision.

Social Work Practice in the Context of Communities

A *community* is "a number of people who have something in common with one another that connects them in some way and that distinguishes them from others" (Homan, 2004, p. 9). A key feature of a community is the fact that participants share some mutual characteristic, such as "location, interest, identification, culture, and/or activities" (Fellin, 1995, p. 3).

Thus communities can be of two primary types—those based on geographic proximity and those based on common ideas, interests, loyalty, and "a sense of belonging" (Martinez-Brawley, 1995, p. 539). Locality-based communities include smaller towns such as Crouch, Idaho; Eggemoggin, Maine; and Necessity, Louisiana. Larger communities include mammoth urban environments such as the greater Los Angeles Metropolitan Area or New York City. Still other locality-based communities include smaller portions of larger cities such as a struggling inner-city ghetto or a posh suburban neighborhood.

Nongeographic communities are based on some commonality other than location. For example, African Americans might form a community based on racial identification and a shared history and culture. Similarly, a community of professional social workers shares common values, beliefs, and generalist practice skills. Additionally, there are "gay communities and military communities that have discernible structures and functions and that share many cultural and psychological characteristics" (Harrison, 1995, p. 560). Even scuba divers make up a community based on common interests, activities, and experiences.

In the social work perspective, communities are entities in which citizens can organize or be organized to address mutual concerns and improve their overall quality of life. Social workers have the responsibility to examine the community environment in which their clients reside. Although social workers are surely focused on how specific clients function as individuals, they are also concerned about the environment in which clients live and whether adequate resources are available.

Highlight 5.1 discusses the special circumstances concerning social work practice in rural communities and Highlight 5.2 those involved in urban social work.

Micro Practice: Social Work with Individuals

Micro practice is intervention involving an individual client (a micro system). It may include counseling, educating, brokering, or case management, all roles described in Chapter 4. In a *counselor* role, social workers follow the planned-change process described in Chapter 4 and help clients develop solutions to problems. For example, a social worker in corrections might work out with a client on parole a plan for

Social workers perform many roles. Here they link survivors of Hurricane Katrina with needed services.

© AP/Wide World Photos

HIGHLIGHT 5.1
The Special Circumstances of Social Work Practice in Rural Communities

Social work practice in rural communities merits special attention. What do you picture when you think of a rural environment? A farmer wearing a straw hat and chewing on a blade of grass? Cows grazing? Endless, lonesome prairie? Barren desert? Some things you probably *don't* think of are skyscrapers, chaotic traffic jams, and thousands of people swarming on crowded streets.

Defining the concept of a rural community is not an easy task. An increasing population, spreading suburban sprawl, and decreasing numbers of farmers complicate the issue of what *rural* means. Yet you may have a sense that life in rural America is quite different than that in urban enclaves.

One definition of a rural community involves three major facets—having a low population density (i.e., number of residents per square mile), being located a significant distance from large urban hubs, and concentrating its activity in some specialized area like lumbering, farming, ranching, or mining (Davenport & Davenport, 1995). Some definitions indicate that to be "rural," a community must be unincorporated and have fewer than 2,500 inhabitants (Carlton-LaNey, Edwards, & Reid, 1999).

Carlton-LaNey and her colleagues (1999) comment on the special problems of rural communities:

> Rural communities experience many of the same social problems as their urban counterparts. Nevertheless, some problems are specific to rural communities. Although the problems themselves may not differ greatly from those in urban centers, they are magnified by the rural communities' inability to target the needed resources in ways that alleviate suffering and ultimately eliminate the problems.
>
> The list of problems with which rural and small town residents must cope includes poverty, lack of transportation, inadequate child care, unemployment, substandard housing, and insufficient health care. Problems of access and adequacy, for example, remain critical issues that must be addressed in rural social work practice. Krout (1994) noted that access problems add time and expense to service delivery efforts, ultimately discouraging both the development of new services and the expansion of existing services into rural areas. For example, rural homebound individuals who could benefit from home-delivered meals and thereby maintain independence are denied this service because it is too expensive. The cost of delivering meals to remote areas can significantly limit the amount of money available for the service itself.
>
> Health care is another significant problem. Rural areas, particularly low-income areas, are underserved because of a lack of physicians and other health care providers. The South especially suffers from a maldistribution of health care professionals and facilities. (p. 7)

Social workers practicing in rural communities must address at least four special issues. First, they must be true generalists who are prepared to work with individuals, families, groups, local organizations, and the community, using a wide range of skills to meet clients' diverse needs (Daley & Avant, 2004; Davenport & Davenport, 1995; Carlton-LeNay et al., 1999). Urban areas with large populations and a larger tax base can better afford to specialize in service provision. For example, public and private social service agencies might provide specific services such as substance abuse counseling, elderly protective services, services for people with cognitive disabilities, crisis counseling for victims of sexual assault, shelter for victims of domestic violence, and so on. A rural community, on the other hand, probably does not have the resources or enough

(continued)

population to support such specific services (Davenport & Davenport, 1995). Therefore, rural practitioners typically must be more flexible and willing to address a broader range of people with a varied assortment of problems.

A second special issue involves interagency cooperation (Carlton-LeNay et al., 1999, p. 10). Because fewer, more general services are usually provided by public agencies, it's critical for agencies and their staffs to work more closely together than in many urban communities. It's common for practitioners and agency administrations "to know each other and to reach out to each other regularly" to meet clients' diverse needs (Carlton-LeNay et al., 1999, p. 10). In urban areas with hundreds of available services, this may not be the case.

A third issue involving rural social work is the importance placed on understanding the community, knowing its values, and developing relationships with rural residents (Daley & Avant, 2004). People living in rural communities have different life experiences than those living in bustling cities. Because there are fewer people, social interaction and relationships tend to be much more informal. Rural social workers and their family members might attend the same church or school, participate in the same civic clubs and organizations, and shop at the same grocery store as clients. Therefore, a rural practitioner must be careful to portray an image that reflects positively on his or her agency (Daley & Avant, 2004). Private lives might be more public—some say as if "living in a fishbowl" (Davenport & Davenport, 1995). For example, it would not be impressive for a social worker counseling a client with an alcohol problem to be cited

in the local newspaper for driving under the influence (DUI).

Because of the close interpersonal nature of rural communities, there is a strong likelihood that dual relationships exist. As described in Chapter 2, "*dual* or *multiple relationships* occur when professionals assume two or more roles at the same time or sequentially with a client" (e.g., both social worker and neighbor or member of the same church, temple, mosque, or synagogue) (Corey et al., 2003). Especially in rural communities, dual and multiple relationships may be unavoidable. Watkins (2004) suggests that rural social workers in such situations "above all, do no harm; practice only with competence; do not exploit; treat people with respect for their dignity as human beings; protect confidentiality; act, except in the more extreme instances, only after obtaining informal consent; [and] practice, insofar as possible, within the framework of social equity and justice" (p. 70).

The fourth issue important for rural social work practice involves emphasizing the strengths inherent in rural communities. Because of the informal nature of relationships, rural clients are often integrally involved with informal support systems or social networks of other people willing to help them out—sometimes referred to as *natural helping networks* (Tracy, 2002; Watkins, 2004). Such networks can include family members, neighbors, coworkers, fellow church members, community benefactors, and others not providing formal agency services who are willing to volunteer assistance. (Social networks are discussed in more detail later in the chapter with respect to working with families.)

HIGHLIGHT 5.2
Urban Social Work[1]

Urban social work is practice within the context of large cities, with their vast array of social problems, exceptional diversity, and potential range of resources. Phillips and Straussner (2002) stress how urban social workers "need to be sensitive to the situations commonly found in the cities and to be knowledgeable about the nature of urban life and the range of impact that the urban environment can have on people" (p. 20). Work in the urban context is important in view of how both the national and global population has been shifting from rural to urban settings. People often flock to cities in search of new opportunities, higher-paying jobs, and greater access to activities and services. Many times, although hopes are high, actual opportunities are scarce or nonexistent, which results in a "disproportionate number of the poor" in the "country's largest cities" (p. 107).

Urban areas are characterized by a number of conditions (Marsella, 1998). First, population is denser and often contains diverse population subgroups (for example, ethnic, racial, cultural, age, sexual orientation). Second, urban economic conditions involve a range of industries, businesses, rent levels, and transportation availability and costs. Third, the urban environment is often a bustling tangle of concrete, traffic, noise, and questions about air quality—in sharp contrast to the more natural rural environment. Fourth, an urban lifestyle entails more condensed interaction and contact with many people. Fifth, the political situation may be intense with many layers of bureaucracy and numerous people in "the system" who have various amounts of power. Sometimes crime, corruption, and social injustice are evident. Conditions in urban environments are often very different than those addressed by rural social workers (described in Highlight 5.1).

Watkins (2004) explains:

Urbanization brought dramatic changes in the way people interacted with each other. Individuals moved away from extended family and other primary relationships to cities where primary relationships were replaced by more role-based interactions [for example, employee, renter, customer, student]. Population density and crowding were accompanied by emotional distancing to preserve a sense of privacy and individuality. In low-income neighborhoods, needs overwhelmed the resources of neighbors. Many persons in need were new to the cities and had no support networks. Formalized or institutionalized social services were a rational response to the peculiar social patterns and needs of these urban residents. . . . However, when federal, state, and local governments increased their role in providing services, the programs were no longer tailored to a specific community. In efforts to increase efficiency and fairness, services became more bureaucratic and standardized. The new model of service delivery that developed preferred secondary, "professional" relationships and interactions that were rule- and role-based rather than more personal. Needy individuals were depersonalized into "clients." . . . Personal relationships between client and social workers were not only unlikely in the urban environment, they were actively discouraged. (p. 67)

At least five problems tend to characterize urban areas more than rural areas (Phillips & Straussner, 2002). For one thing, "[p]roblems such as poverty, discrimination, overcrowded housing, crime and violence, homelessness, high rates of school dropouts, substance abuse, and HIV/AIDS exist in communities of all sizes. However, they occur with greater frequency and therefore are more visible in the cities" (p. 25).

A second problem is the widespread occurrence of discriminatory behavior because of the

(continued)

[1] Note that many of the ideas in this highlight are taken from *Urban Social Work: An Introduction to Policy and Practice in the Cities* by N. K. Phillips and S. L. A. Straussner (Boston: Allyn & Bacon, 2002), unless otherwise indicated.

wide variety of ethnic, racial, religious, and cultural groups living in cities. Groups may be in conflict and fighting for power and resources. Often public schools are disadvantaged because of inadequate funding, resulting in poorer buildings, libraries, laboratory equipment, and technology, as well as underpaid staff.

"Migration of people unprepared" for the pressures and demands of urban living is a third problem characterizing cities. Phillips and Straussner (2002) explain:

> With their promise of freedom and opportunity, the cities have always been magnets for both the adventurous and the desperate. Most people move to urban areas in search of better opportunities for work or for education, either for themselves or their families, and for many, the cities have served and continue to serve as gateways to success.
>
> However, some who migrate to urban areas, whether from other parts of the United States or from other countries, are faced with unemployment, underemployment, discrimination, poor housing, and language barriers. Those without families or social supports to help them make the transition to the new culture and to city life are at greater risk for poverty, social isolation, and personal and family problems. (p. 27)

Financial shortfalls or unavailability of resources make up a fourth problem characterizing urban areas. "Some cities do not have the financial resources to provide services that would assist people in maximizing their potential, while other cities may have the resources, but do not choose to provide services, particularly for the poor. Consequently, there may be a lack of affordable, good-quality housing, or a lack of adequate police protection, schools, or recreational facilities. For example, preschool children and their parents are underserved in many urban communities" (Phillips and Straussner, 2002, p. 28). Because of

cities' dense population, service gaps can affect huge numbers of people.

The fifth problem characterizing cities involves greater amounts of psychological stress. Stressors including "noise, dirty streets," "abandoned buildings," overcrowded housing, lack of geographic mobility, and substance abuse can impose psychological pressure and increase general anxieties (Phillips and Straussner, 2002, p. 29).

As in other types of social work, urban social workers use micro practice skills in their work with clients, including establishing and working toward goals, using effective communication and interviewing techniques, respecting client values and perspectives, emphasizing strengths, expressing empathy, and "developing self-awareness" to combat biases and effectively understand clients' perspectives (Phillips and Straussner, 2002, p. 201). Additionally, urban social workers must focus on using skills in at least four major arenas (Phillips and Straussner, 2002):

1. *Paying close attention to human diversity:* Because urban environments more likely have a wider variety of ethnic, racial, and religious backgrounds, urban social workers must be sensitive to the wide range of cultural differences, become knowledgeable about their various clients' cultures, and focus on the identification and use of clients' respective cultural and personal strengths. Urban practitioners must also be attuned to the potential discrimination experienced by people "based on race, ethnicity, culture, age, gender, religion, sexual orientation, disability, poverty, or language spoken. While historically various immigrant groups such as the Irish, the Jews,

(continued)

the Italians, the Chinese, and the Japanese have experienced discrimination in the United States, the most persistent discrimination today is experienced by Native Americans; blacks, including African Americans, people from the Caribbean, and people from Africa; Latinos; Asians; and people of Middle Eastern backgrounds" (Phillips & Straussner, 2002, p. 26).

2. *Understanding their agency environment:* Urban agencies may be large and complex, or may serve large client populations. Urban workers must understand the intricacy of their agency's power structure, who has decision-making power about what they can and can't do, and where resources are located. Large bureaucracies are often highly impersonal. They tend to emphasize following rules and regulations to coordinate their complex maze of service provision. Often workers are called on to work with other personnel they don't know. Workers must then be sensitive to other staff's roles and use good communication skills to work effectively in collaboration with other service providers. Even smaller agencies in urban settings must work within a complex interplay of numerous organizations also addressing client needs. Urban social workers must understand the functioning of other agencies serving the same clients and work carefully with other staff to coordinate service provision.

3. *Seeking resources in the external urban environment:* Urban social workers often function in a complex labyrinth of many public and private agencies, each providing specialized services in one of a broad range of areas (for example, mental health counseling, administration of public assistance, domestic violence shelter, sexual assault hotline, or adolescent pregnancy prevention). This differs from rural agencies that often provide a broader range of services to a smaller population; in other words, they are less likely to specialize to the degree that urban agencies can. In their broker role, urban social workers must often seek resources in a confusing tangle of red tape and available services.

4. *Using advocacy:* Note that just because urban areas tend to have larger and more services, this does not mean that there are no significant gaps in service due to limited or lacking resources. Such gaps may involve massive numbers of people. At the agency level, an urban practitioner may need to develop a coalition with colleagues and approach decision-making administrators with suggestions for positive changes. On another level, public policy may not serve clients' best interests. Therefore, strategies to change legislation may include the use of letter-writing or e-mail campaigns to lawmakers, lobbying (seeking direct contact with legislators to influence their opinions), or using the mass media to publicize clients' needs and issues to gain public support for positive change.

finding housing and employment. Or a social worker who does alcohol abuse counseling might explore with a client her reasons for using alcohol and establish plans to maintain sobriety.

In an *educator* role, a social worker might teach an abusive parent effective child management techniques. Similarly, a hospital social worker might inform a person receiving kidney dialysis about the disease's progression and the dialysis process. (*Kidney dialysis* is a process by which a machine removes uric acid and urea from the blood, thereby substituting for the function of normal kidneys.)

Social workers in the *broker* role link clients to needed resources and services. For instance, a social worker might refer a homeless person to a shelter and to agencies providing financial assistance and job training. Social workers performing *case management* functions coordinate services provided by a number of agencies or services on a client's behalf. For example, a client with quadriplegia (i.e., paralysis of all four limbs due to spinal cord injury or disease) might be receiving resources from a variety of agencies including housing, transportation, financial assistance, personal care, and job training. A *case manager* or *case coordinator* synchronizes and oversees services to make sure the client gets what he or she needs.

Note that frequently a social worker may assume a range of roles with the same clients. For example, consider a family including two parents and children ages 2, 4, and 7 that has been referred to a Protection Services worker to assess possible child maltreatment and develop a service plan if necessary. After conducting the assessment, the worker may serve as counselor to help the parents learn to control their anger and behavior more effectively. The educator role might include teaching them child behavior management skills. The worker might serve as broker in linking the family to resources where they receive resources such as rental vouchers (that subsidize rent for eligible families) to ease their economic stress. The practitioner might also take on the facilitator role if these parents participate in a group she's leading of parents that have maltreated their children. Finally, the worker might become an advocate for the family to receive needed services that are not readily available.

 ## Micro/Mezzo Practice: Social Work with Families

As noted previously, social work with families combines micro and mezzo practice because it involves a small group (i.e., the family) linked by ties of an intimate nature. Working with families is a very important aspect of social work as later chapters will emphasize. Collins, Jordan, and Coleman (1999) explain:

> The primary purpose of family social work is to help families learn to function more competently while meeting the developmental and emotional needs of *all* members. . . . There are many ways in which a family social worker can provide on-the-spot, concrete assistance. For example, when a teenager and a parent become involved in a conflict, the FSW [family social worker] has an opportunity to identify the problem and intervene. A FSW can help the parent and child discover what led up to the argument and identify ongoing repetitive and problematic interaction patterns that keep arguments going. Once these tasks have been achieved, the FSW can work with the parent and teenager to replace dysfunctional behavior with more rewarding behavior. When a young child throws a temper tantrum, the FSW can teach the parent more effective methods of dealing with problematic behavior on the spot. (p. 2)

Maluccio, Pine, and Tracy (2002) stress that when working with families, social workers should

- Be responsive to the styles and values of families from communities of color, immigrants, and other special populations [e.g., leaning forward toward the client and maintaining eye contact to demonstrate attentiveness are considered rude and intrusive by many First Nations Peoples].

- Break complex tasks into smaller specific steps [e.g., how to look for housing; how to talk with your child's teacher].
- Assess the key skills needed for less stressful family interactions [e.g., accepting "no," giving direct commands, handling anger].
- Explain and model appropriate skills, using techniques such as role play, modeling, or videotaped practice.
- Assess individual learning styles and ways to teach adults and children [e.g., children learn differently as they age with increasing ability for complex thought; an adult may learn more effectively by observing a modeled behavior than being given verbal instructions or vice versa].
- Establish homework and other means of ensuring generalization of skills from one setting to another [e.g., asking family members to practice new communication techniques when in their own home setting].
- Promote and reward skill acquisition [e.g., praise family members when they follow through on homework or reach goals].
- Emphasize strategies that help develop the strengths of family members [e.g., high motivation to improve or exceptional aptitude at coping with family crises].
- Motivate the family to stay involved even when faced with challenges and setbacks [e.g., an alcoholic family member falls off the wagon or a teenager runs away]. (pp. 149–150)

Social workers can also help families deal with crises and problems they encounter in the external environment. For example, if a breadwinner is laid off, a social worker can help the family cope with these new conditions, link the family with available resources, and assist in the search for new employment. Sometimes it's necessary to advocate for resources that aren't readily available or to change social policies that are not in families' best interests.

The Importance of Social Networks for Families

An important concept concerning social work with families and other systems is the *social network,* "the structure and number of people and groups with whom you have contact or consider yourself to be in contact" (Tracy, 2002, p. 402). Social workers can help families get connected with social networks that provide three types of social support (Tracy, 2002). First, *emotional support* is "having someone listen to your feelings, comfort you, or offer encouragement" (p. 402). Second, *informational support* is "having someone teach you something, give you information or advice, or help you make a major decision" (p. 402). Finally, *concrete support* is "having someone help in tangible ways, loaning you something, . . . helping with a chore, or taking you on an errand" (p. 402).

Maluccio and his colleagues (2002) explain:

Social support [including emotional, informational, and concrete] can occur spontaneously, as in one neighbor bringing meals to another, or it can occur in professionally arranged helping networks, such as Meals on Wheels. [*Formal*] social services staffed by paid human service professionals . . . often provide social support as either the sole or partial focus of their service; for example, a social worker facilitating a parent education group may provide information, resource referrals, skills training, and emotional support for the participants. [*Informal*] support . . . can be delivered by kinship networks, volunteers, or local community groups. . . . In many cases social workers can be the catalysts that mobilize and enhance various forms of informal helping to benefit individual clients, family members, and communities. (p. 175)

A social worker can identify potential participants in a social network that might be available to provide various types of support to a family, link the family with network participants, and facilitate how the network can help the family. For example, a worker could link a family with needed child care resources including relatives, friends, neighbors, or a day care center. Another example of enhancing social network support involves more formal family support programs that "address family self-sufficiency by offering services such as job training, English as a second language, and literacy classes" (Maluccio et al., 2002, p. 151). Still another example concerns "support groups for children experiencing life transitions or losses as in children of divorce, teenage parents, or children of battered women" (Maluccio et al., 2002, p. 184). Community programs such as neighborhood or cultural centers can also provide programming (e.g., recreational or educational) to help once struggling families prosper.

An example of how social networks can serve a family involves Gene Yuss, age 13, who lived with his mother and younger brother Perry, age 8, in a federal low-income housing project for people whose family incomes are not high enough to pay for regular housing (adapted from Maluccio et al., 2002). Gene, a husky young 5'5" young man with bright red hair, already had a long history of truancy and delinquent behavior including illegal drug use and petty shoplifting. His problematic behavior and connections with delinquent peers were linked to inadequate parental support and supervision.

The family's social worker, Bertha Day, helped Gene's mother, Ms. Yuss, identify more effective means of addressing Gene's behavior. One idea involved having Gene, who was athletically inclined, join the school's football team. Gene, a relatively popular student, already had some mildly positive relationships with other team players who were doing well in school and had no problems with the law. Ms. Yuss agreed that joining the team might be a good idea, so she encouraged this plan of action, to which Gene agreed. Meanwhile, Bertha linked Gene with the football coach, who became part of Gene's supportive social network. Bertha and Ms. Yuss contacted Gene's uncle, who lived only a few blocks from the Yuss family, and asked whether he would transport Gene home from practice. The uncle, Ms. Yuss's brother, readily agreed because he had been quite concerned about Gene's downward spiral into trouble. Bertha and Ms. Yuss then asked the Yuss's church to contribute funding needed for required team equipment and transportation costs, which it did.

Another concern was what Gene would do on days when there was no practice. With Ms. Yuss's approval, Bertha worked with Gene to involve him in a number of other after-school activities in which he expressed some interest. Bertha also arranged for a tutor to help him in subjects with which he was having difficulty.

In addition, Bertha worked with Ms. Yuss to link both herself and Gene's younger brother Perry to a broader social network. Ms. Yuss joined a group for Parents Without Partners (who meet to provide support, discuss mutual concerns about raising children, and offer opportunities for social interaction) and became more actively involved in her church. She signed Perry up both for recreational activities at the local YMCA[2] and as a participant in a Big Brothers program so Perry could have the opportunity to form a special relationship with a supportive adult role model.

In this case, Gene's football team involvement, his linkage with the coach, the uncle's help with transportation, the church's funding contribution, other after-school activities, tutoring, Ms. Yuss's Parents Without Partners group, her church activities, and Perry's YMCA and Big Brothers program involvement all helped to expand and strengthen the Yuss family's social network.

 # Mezzo Practice: Social Work with Groups

Mezzo practice is social work intervention with groups. As with other levels of treatment, group work can involve any number of problems, goals, and types of people. The two primary types of groups in social work practice are treatment and task.

Treatment Groups

Treatment groups help individuals solve personal problems, change unwanted behaviors, cope with stress, and improve quality of life. Efforts focus on clients solving their personal problems, enhancing personal qualities, or providing each other with support. Highlight 5.3 identifies and defines the five primary types of treatment groups and provides examples of each (Toseland & Rivas, 2005, p. 21).

Task Groups

Task or *work groups* are those applying the principles of group dynamics to solve problems, develop ideas, formulate plans, and achieve goals. Task groups in the macro social environment are formed to meet the needs of individuals, families, groups, organizations, or communities. For example, an agency task group might focus on developing treatment strategies to meet the needs of Eastern European immigrants seeking agency resources. This targets both individuals and families. Another task group might include social services personnel and representatives from community groups coordinating a neighborhood watch program aimed at preventing crime. This task group works on behalf of various neighborhood groups and the entire community. Still another organizational task group might consist of representatives from various departments to review the agency's policy manual and recommend changes. This task group serves the organization.

---

[2]The YMCA (Young Men's Christian Association) is a global group of organizations that serves to enhance young men's and others' physical, mental, emotional, and interpersonal well-being, and offers a range of recreational and other services (Barker, 2003).

HIGHLIGHT 5.3

Treatment Groups in Social Work

1. *Therapy:* Groups that help members with serious psychological and emotional problems change their behavior.

Examples: Groups formed to treat "depression, sexual difficulties, anxiety, and psychosomatic disorders[3]" (Corey & Corey, 2002, p. 15).

2. *Support:* Groups whose members share common issues or problems and meet on an ongoing basis to cope with stress, give each other suggestions, provide encouragement, convey information, and furnish emotional support (Barker, 2003; Kurtz, 2004). Note that support groups differ from therapy groups in two main ways. First, support groups place greater emphasis on members supporting and helping each other—in contrast to therapy groups, in which the focus is on the leader assisting members in solving serious personal problems. Second, support groups differ from therapy groups in stressing ongoing coping and support instead of alleviating psychological difficulties.

Examples: A group of persons living with AIDS, recovering alcoholics, adult survivors of sexual abuse, and veterans experiencing posttraumatic stress disorder.[4]

3. *Educational:* Groups that provide some type of information to participants.

Examples: A group of parents learning child behavior management techniques, teens receiving sex education, a group of adults interested in finding jobs, and a group of elderly people in a nursing home requesting information about their prescribed drugs.

4. *Growth:* Groups aimed at expanding self-awareness, increasing potential, and maximizing health and well-being.

Examples: A group of heterosexual singles exploring their attitudes about the opposite gender, "a values clarification group for adolescents," and a group of gay men focusing on gay pride issues (Toseland & Rivas, 2005, p. 25).

5. *Socialization:* Groups that help participants improve interpersonal behavior, communication, and social skills so they might better fit into their social environment.

Examples: An urban neighborhood's youth activities group, a school-based group of shy teens working to improve interpersonal skills, and a Parents Without Partners group sponsoring various social activities such as parties and outings (Toseland & Rivas, 2005).

Commentary

Sometimes it's difficult to put a particular group in a specific category. What transpires in treatment groups is as complex as the people who make them up. For instance, Fiske (2002) describes an exceptionally creative treatment group program with adolescent residents from several group homes developed by Susan Ciardiello, a clinical social worker. Adolescents typically are placed in residential treatment (including group homes and larger institutions) because of behavioral and emotional problems (discussed more thoroughly in later chapters). For many reasons ranging from their normal quest for independence to having had severely negative experiences with the adults in their lives, it's difficult for these young people to trust adults. Fiske emphasizes that "adolescents in groups can provide an environment where they learn from each other and benefit from the wisdom

(continued)

---

[3]*Psychosomatic disorders* are physical symptoms (e.g., stomachaches, numbness, pain) caused by emotional problems.

[4]*Posttraumatic stress disorder* is the psychological and emotional reaction to an extremely stressful and disturbing experience such as a battle, rape, fire, or earthquake.

HIGHLIGHT 5.3 *(continued)*

and experience of those traveling the same path" (p. 16).

Ciardiello first surveyed the adolescents to determine their primary interests—not surprisingly, "hip-hop music and basketball" (p. 17). She then pursued a three-faceted group treatment program. First, she divided participants into two co-ed basketball teams that played each other twice a week. However, instead of just playing neighborhood ball, the difference was that she "arranged it so that the players would get points when they demonstrated teamwork and self-control" (p. 17).

The program's second facet involved a biweekly disc jockey program, for which Ciardiello sought funds from a major recording company and purchased equipment. The program consisted of two parts. During the first hour, the group listened to various carefully chosen hip-hop songs that addressed issues significant in the teens' lives such as drugs, poverty, child abuse, romantic relationship concerns, hope for the future, and racial pride. Participants then discussed how the lyrics affected them and related the songs to their own lives. It allowed them to share stories, empathize with each other, provide support, suggest means of coping, and develop trust. During the second hour, participants were rewarded by taking turns being the DJ and even making their own music.

The program achieved such success that a third empowering facet was added. The group

members started their own magazine titled *The Real Deal: Kids Keeping It Real.* Through it they could express themselves and their opinions and talk about things that interested them. Ciardiello indicated that this three-pronged approach to a treatment group incorporating sports, music, and writing "decreased unexcused absences from the [group] homes and improved relations among residents" (p. 18).

What type of treatment group would you label this? *Therapeutically,* throughout the three facets of the program, participants worked on identifying feelings and controlling angry outbursts. One potential result was to help them better understand themselves, improve self-esteem, and make more effective decisions to control behavior that caused them problems. Group members also provided *support* to each other by listening to each other's opinions and making suggestions about coping. *Educationally,* participants learned how to be a DJ, a potentially viable job skill, and worked on writing skills through the magazine. As a *growth* group, they worked on expanding awareness of social issues and interpersonal dynamics. Finally, the entire process involved *socialization,* through which they learned how to get along better with their peers. Hence this treatment group appears to be a combination of approaches. It provides a good illustration of how social workers can be ingeniously resourceful and imaginative in their interventions.

The main difference between task and treatment groups is that the task group's aim is to achieve a desired goal or to implement a change in the group's external environment. In contrast, a treatment group's purpose is to alter group members' behaviors or attitudes in the internal group environment (Fatout & Rose, 1995). Highlight 5.4 identifies the six major types of task groups and provides an example of each (Fatout & Rose, 1995; Toseland & Rivas, 2005).

HIGHLIGHT 5.4

Task Groups in Social Work

1. *Team:* A group of two or more people gathered together to work collaboratively and interdependently to achieve a designated purpose.

Example: A team of social workers in a Veteran's Health Administration (VHA) hospital[5] where social workers assigned to the temporary housing unit for homeless vets, a substance abuse counseling unit, and the hospital surgical unit work together on behalf of a homeless vet who is an alcoholic and has serious kidney malfunctioning.

2. *Treatment conference:* A group that meets to establish, monitor, and coordinate service plans on behalf of a client system (Fatout & Rose, 1995; Toseland & Rivas, 2005).

Example: A group of professionals (including a social worker, psychologist, psychiatrist, physician, teacher, and unit counselor) at a residential treatment center[6] for children with severe behavioral and emotional problems meeting to discuss the progress of a client residing there and to make recommendations for future treatment. (Note that teams and treatment conferences are groups formulated to meet clients' needs, whereas the following three task groups usually address organizational needs [Toseland & Rivas, 2005].)

3. *Administrative group:* A group of social service agency administrators who meet regularly to discuss issues and develop plans for running the organization.

Example: A board of directors authorized to formulate an organization's mission, objectives, and policies, and to oversee its ongoing activities.

4. *Delegate council:* A group of representatives from various agencies or from units within a single agency that meet to discuss issues of mutual concern.

Example: A group of professionals working in rape crisis centers throughout a state, with each agency designating a representative to meet in the council to discuss education and treatment issues.

5. *Committee:* A group of persons "delegated to consider, investigate, take action on, or report on some matter" (Mish, 1995, p. 231).

Example: A group of staff representatives appointed to investigate, assess, and make recommendations about the quality of food served in a nursing home.

6. *Social action group:* A group formed to engage in some planned-change effort to modify or improve aspects of their macro social or physical environment (Staples, 2004; Toseland & Rivas, 2005).

Example: A group of agency workers and clients who join forces to conduct a letter-writing campaign to legislators to place stoplights at a dangerous intersection.

---

[5] The Veteran's Health Administration "provides a comprehensive range of health and mental health care services" for the nation's veterans including "acute medical, surgical, and psychiatric inpatient and outpatient care; intermediate hospital, nursing home, and domiciliary [taking place in one's own home] care; noninstitutional extended care; and a range of special programs and professional services in outpatient settings" (Becerra & Damron-Rodriguez, 1995, p. 2433; Department of Veterans Affairs, 1994).

[6] Discussed more thoroughly in a later chapter, a *residential treatment center* is an agency that provides children with serious emotional and behavioral problems with residential round-the-clock care; education (often with an emphasis on special education); interpersonal skills training; and individual, group, and sometimes family therapy.

Macro Practice: Social Work with Organizations and Communities

Macro practice is intervention involving organizations and communities (macro systems). Historically, *community organization* has been the term used to refer to macro practice in social work. The methods and directions of social work practice have changed and evolved, just as the economic and social realities of the times have drastically changed. However, reviewing the historical perspective on community practice will help us to understand the significance of community assessment and work today.

Past methods of community organization engaged in by social workers included social action, social planning, and locality development (Rothman, 2001). *Social action* is coordinated effort to advocate for change in a social institution to benefit a specific population (e.g., homeless people), solve a social problem, correct unfairness (e.g., racism),[7] or enhance people's well-being. Social action applies macro practice skills to advocate for people in local, state, national, and global communities. Frequently social action can be used to remedy imbalances of power.

Social planning involves "a technical process of problem-solving regarding substantive social problems, such as delinquency, housing, and mental health" (Rothman, 2001, p. 31). Experts or consultants work, usually with designated community leaders, to solve specific problems. People in the general community have little, if any, participation in or input into the problem-solving process. For example, a city might call in an urban renewal expert to recommend what should be done with a deteriorating area in the community.

Locality development emphasizes "community change . . . pursued through broad participation by a wide spectrum of people at the local community level in determining goals and taking civic action" (Rothman, 2001, p. 29). The idea is to involve as many people as possible within the community in a democratic manner to define their goals and help themselves. Locality development fits extremely well with social work values because individual dignity, participation, and free choice are emphasized.

Today macro practice remains a major thrust of generalist social work. The basic concept of community is just as important as ever. Most macro practice today takes place within an organizational context.

Necessary macro skills involve at least three facets (Kirst-Ashman & Hull, 2001). First, agency or public social policies may require change. For example, social workers may advocate to change a policy that requires all persons receiving public assistance to undergo mandatory drug testing—a practice that is expensive, condescending, and invasive.

A second important macro skill entails initiating and conducting projects within agency or community contexts. An example of a project is fund-raising for homeless families in need of food and clothing. Another is initiating an in-service training program to teach agency staff a new treatment technique. (*In-service training*

[7] *Racism* is "a belief that race is the primary determinant of human traits and capacities and that racial differences produce an inherent superiority of a particular race," most often resulting in prejudice or discrimination (Mish, 1995, p. 962).

programs are educational sessions provided by an agency for its staff to develop their skills or improve their effectiveness.)

A third significant macro skill concerns planning and implementing new social service programs within an agency or community. An example is development of a program to educate students on a college campus about date rape. Another is developing a new recreation and field trip program for residents in a nursing home.

Generalist Practice: A Three-Level Process

The point of generalist social work practice is to seek change at all three levels of practice, depending on what the client system needs. Many times, a social worker will simultaneously pursue a combination of micro, mezzo, and macro practice goals.

For example, a teacher refers Ralph, age 8, to Juanita, the school social worker. The teacher reports that Ralph is consistently mounting fellow students on the playground in a manner resembling sexual intercourse (more vulgarly referred to as "humping"). Ralph also makes frequent sexual comments and uses sexual language quite inappropriate for his age. Juanita suspects the possibility of sexual abuse. (A later chapter on child welfare discusses child sexual abuse in more depth.)

At the micro level, Juanita talks with Ralph about what's occurring in his life at home. She informs the school principal, Adolf, that she intends to report the situation to Child Protective Services, which would initiate a more thorough investigation. Adolf forbids Juanita to make the referral on the basis that there is not enough evidence. Why cause trouble when you don't have to? But in her state, Juanita is required to report any *suspected* child abuse (which includes sexual abuse). Juanita knows that it is her ethical responsibility to report Ralph's behavior.

At the macro level, Juanita must address the issue with Adolf and possibly the School Board, which supervises Adolf. The school (a macro system) must change so that it becomes responsive to instances of possible abuse instead of simply ignoring them. In the event that Ralph's victimization is proved, family counseling may be called for at the micro/mezzo level and possibly group therapy for Ralph at the mezzo level.

Professional Organizations in Social Work

The National Association of Social Workers

The National Association of Social Workers (NASW) has already been mentioned several times, especially with respect to its Code of Ethics. Established in 1955, NASW is the major social work organization with the largest and broadest membership in the profession. Persons holding bachelor's or master's degrees in social work and students in accredited social work programs can join.

NASW fulfills at least five purposes. First, membership in a professional organization lends credibility (Simpson & Simpson, 1992). Most, if not all, established professions have an organization to which members can belong. Such membership bolsters members' professional identity, helps them identify with other members, and enhances the visibility of a profession.

NASW's second purpose is to provide opportunities for networking. State, regional, and national conferences and meetings enable members to talk with each other and share news and ideas. Such meetings also provide a means for finding out about new career and job opportunities.

NASW's third purpose is to provide membership services. These include *Social Work*, a quarterly journal that addresses various aspects of practice; *NASW News*, a national newspaper published almost monthly that focuses on relevant research, social welfare policy and service issues, and social workers' accomplishments around the country and the world; and newsletters published by some state chapters.

NASW's fourth purpose is to sponsor organized efforts for lobbying on behalf of socially responsible social welfare policies and services (Simpson & Simpson, 1992). NASW exerts influence in support of causes and political agendas concurrent with professional social work values. It has also helped states establish licensing or certification regulations for social workers. Highlight 5.5 discusses the importance of licensing for social workers and identifies the common levels of practice.

NASW's fifth purpose is to publish policy statements on various issues (e.g., youth suicide, health care, people with disabilities, affirmative action, and environmental policy) to help guide members in their practice (NASW, 2003).

A number of other organizations reflect more specific facets or subsets of social work. Examples include the Association of Community Organization and Social Administration (ACOSA) and the National Association of Black Social Workers (NABSW).

The Council on Social Work Education

The Council on Social Work Education (CSWE) is the body that accredits bachelor's and master's programs in social work education. A doctorate of social work and doctorate of philosophy in social work are also available, but CSWE has determined that they need not be accredited. CSWE's membership is composed primarily of social work educators but also includes practitioners. CSWE develops guidelines for the social work curriculum as explained in Chapter 1. In social work, *accreditation* is the official confirmation that a school, college, or program fulfills the necessary requirements in curricular development, program structure, resources, and academic achievement to assume that status.

It is important to make sure a social work program is accredited. To be eligible for licensure or certification, many states require graduation from an accredited program.

 # Careers in Social Work

Because social workers are employed in such varied areas of human life, it is difficult to gather accurate data on what members of the entire profession are doing. The Bureau of Labor Statistics predicts that between 1998 and 2008 the number of social workers will increase by 3.1% per year, for a 36% increase overall; this contrasts significantly with the general U.S. labor force, which will increase by only 1.2% each year (Barth, 2003; O'Neill, April 2001).

HIGHLIGHT 5.5

Social Work Licensure and Categories of Social Work Practice

Every state, the District of Columbia, Puerto Rico, the Virgin Islands, and every Canadian province have laws that define and regulate social work practice, involving some form of licensure or certification (Association of Social Work Boards [ASWB], 2002, p. 1). Social work licensure means that one has fulfilled designated requirements to practice social work in a particular state. Certification is used instead of licensure in a number of states. Some feel that *licensure* is a stronger word, implying more advanced skills than *certification*. For example, a social worker with a bachelor's degree might be certified, and one with a master's degree licensed.

Many states have several levels of licensing or certification and require an examination and possibly some work experience (at least for higher levels) to qualify for each level (Ginsberg, 2001). The "generalized minimum requirements" of the four common levels of practice include the following:

1. *Basic:* Baccalaureate social work degree (BSW) upon graduation. (In some instances, non–social work degrees are accepted at the basic level.)
2. *Intermediate:* Master's degree in social work (MSW) with no postdegree experience.
3. *Advanced generalist:* MSW with two years' postmaster's supervised experience.
4. *Clinical:* MSW with two years' postmaster's direct clinical social work experience (ASWB, 2002; Barth, 2001, pp. 27–28).

The Association of Social Work Boards [ASWB], initiated in 1979, established and sustains licensing examinations for social workers in 48 states, the District of Columbia, the U.S. Virgin Islands, and Alberta, Canada (ASWB, 2002).[8] Although some states offer licenses or certification for only one level of practice, most offer such validation at two or more levels of practice. The structure of examinations and specific requirements for each level vary from state to state, so people interested in becoming a social worker should explore the regulations in their own state, province, or jurisdiction. ASWB examinations for each level include 170 multiple-choice questions that are administered electronically and provide four hours for test completion (ASWB, 2004a). Because of the differences from one jurisdiction to another, certification or licensure does not automatically transfer from one locale to another (ASWB, 2002). Social workers with licensure or certification in one state who want similar recognition in some other state must complete the application process in that other state. A few states have special reciprocal agreements where they accept each other's validation.

Note that 33 states, the District of Columbia, Puerto Rico, the Virgin Islands, and eight Canadian provinces require some form of licensure or certification for BSWs (ASWB, 2002). For each social work program, the ASWB can report the percentages of people taking the ASWB basic examination who pass the first time and who pass when they repeat the test.

A major purpose of licensing is to protect clients from unqualified service providers and maintain the legitimacy of the profession (Licensure, October 2004). Ginsberg (2001) comments on the significance of a social work degree with respect to licensing and getting jobs:

> Although there are many professions engaged in human services work, it is becoming the law in most states that persons may not refer to themselves

(continued)

[8] More information can be obtained at www.aswb.org.

HIGHLIGHT 5.5 (*continued*)

as social workers or hold a position designated as a social work job unless they have a social work degree. State licensing and regulation laws . . . provide legal protection for the title of social worker. But even without legal regulation, many social work employers want employees with social work preparation because they understand the social services system and have developed some of the skills needed to practice social work. (p. 44)

Additional Credentials

Whereas licensing and certification represents minimal standards to protect clients as consumers of services, the National Association of Social Workers (NASW) credentials represent an even "higher level of competence" (Licensure, October 2004, p. 12). NASW "establishes and promotes additional standards and credentials required for excellence in the practice of social work. A credential certifies that a social worker has achieved competence and professionalism beyond a college degree or state license. Credentials generally require a degree, supervised experience, and a standard examination" (NASW, 2004).[9] Such advanced credentials include these:

- Academy of Certified Social Workers (ACSW), "the most widely recognized and respected social work credential" where workers are "certified for independent, self-regulated practice."
- Qualified Clinical Social Worker (QCSW), recognizing social workers "who have met national standards of knowledge, skill, and experience in clinical social work" (work in settings addressing mental health issues or private practice).
- Diplomate in Clinical Social Work (DCSW), "the highest distinction bestowed on clinical social workers."
- Specialty certifications in the following areas:
  - Certified and Certified Advanced Children, Youth, and Family Social Worker (C-CYFSW and C-ACYFSW).
  - Certified Social Worker in Health Care (C-SWHC).
  - Certified Clinical Alcohol, Tobacco, and Other Drugs Social Worker (C-CATODSW).
  - Certified and Certified Advanced Social Work Case Manager (C-SWCM and C-ASWCM).
  - Certified School Social Work Specialist (C-SSWS).

[9] For more information on specific requirements for advanced credentials, see http://www.socialworkers.org/credentials.

Highlight 5.6 summarizes the findings of two recent surveys addressing the fields of practice in which social workers are employed. Ongoing research by a group involved with the Association of Baccalaureate Social Work Program Directors (BPD) regularly collects information about BSW graduates that reflects BSW employment both at graduation and two years thereafter (hereafter referred to as *alumni*) (G. H. Hull, personal communication, November 22, 2004; Buchan et al., 2004).[10] Another survey, sponsored by the National Association of Social Workers

[10] Information is gathered by a BPD team using the Baccalaureate Educational Assessment Package [BEAP]. Current members are Vicky V. Buchan, Grafton H. Hull, Jr., Jannah Mather, Cathy K. Pike, JoAnn Ray, Roy W. Rodenhiser, John P. Rogers, and Marshall L. Smith.

H I G H L I G H T   5.6

Employment Settings for
Social Workers by Fields of Practice

	BSWs (Employment at Graduation)	BSWs (Two Years Postgraduation)	MSWs
Corrections/criminal justice	34.5%	3.0%	—%
Child welfare/child protective services	12.6	18.7	—
Child welfare/family	—	—	7
Youth services	7.1	—	—
Mental/behavioral health	6.1	14.9	37
Aging/geriatrics	5.4	11.1	4
Family services	5.3	7.9	—
Mental retardation/developmental disabilities	5.0	6.0	—
Alcohol, drug, or substance abuse	4.4	3.9	3
Crisis intervention	2.9	4.3	—
School social work	2.6	5.5	5
Health/medical care	2.5	7.3	8
Violence/victim services	2.2	2.0	1
Education/training	1.7	2.1	—
Housing	1.2	1.3	—
Public assistance/public welfare	1.0	1.5	—
Adult protective services	.7	.7	—
Community planning	.7	1.5	<1
Group services	.6	.9	—
Rehabilitation	.5	1.0	—
Grief/bereavement	.3	.7	—
Income maintenance	.2	.3	—
Occupational/EAP[11]	.1	.4	1
Adolescents	—	—	3
Disabilities	—	—	1

[11]*EAP* stands for *Employee Assistance Programs,* which are services provided by organizations that focus on the prevention and treatment of workers' mental health and adjustment problems that interfere with their work performance. Chapter 13 describes them more fully.

(NASW), reviews the major fields of practice in which MSWs (full-time) tend to be employed (O'Neill, 2003). Respondents in this study were all NASW members, the vast majority of whom have MSWs (versus BSWs as their highest degree or degrees in other fields). Note that dashes in the chart reflect lack of data due to different data-gathering techniques.

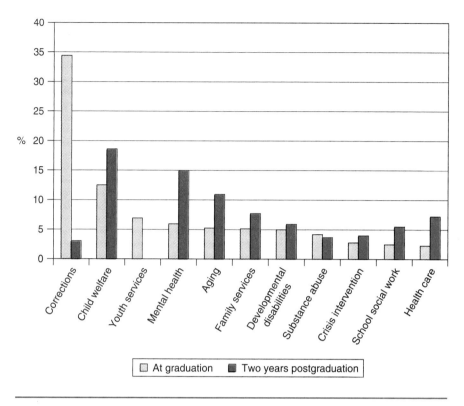

Figure 5.1   Employment of BSW graduates

Be cautious when interpreting this information, however, because a major difference between the two surveys involves social workers' years of experience. For example, BSW respondents have only two years experience at the time of the survey, whereas MSWs have a median (midpoint) of 16 years (Survey Data, 2004). There's no way to tell how results might differ if both groups had identical experience.

Note that the two surveys reflect some different categories because data were not gathered in identical ways. The categories listed here for MSWs reflect only those in which the most social workers were employed. Because of this and because some responses didn't fit clearly into defined categories, none of the columns add up to 100%.

It's interesting to note that few social workers (of BSWs, 1.2% at graduation and 1.8% two years after) are employed in public welfare and income maintenance. This refutes the stereotype of a social worker sitting in a drab office reviewing applications for welfare checks. Rather, the BSW survey reflects the wide range of practice contexts where social workers find employment.

Let's focus for a moment on the differences in employment settings experienced by BSWs who have jobs at graduation and what they're doing as alumni two years later. Figure 5.1 highlights the differences in practice areas where most BSWs find jobs. Whereas over a third of people at graduation find jobs in corrections,

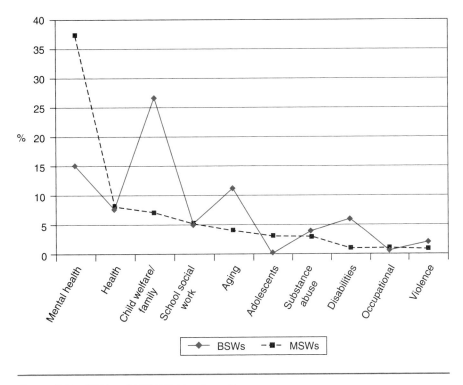

Figure 5.2   BSW and MSW fields of practice

for two-year alumni this drops to only 3%. What are the implications? Might it be that it's relatively easy to find jobs in corrections, but most people discover they don't like it and leave quickly?

The second most common job placement for BSWs at graduation is child welfare and protective services: 12.6% of BSWs start out there. Two years later this figure jumps to 18.7% of BSWs surveyed. BSW alumni also shift in greater numbers to the fields of mental health, aging, and health care. Smaller increases occur in family services, school social work, developmental disabilities, and crisis intervention.

Figure 5.2 compares BSW alumni with MSWs concerning their fields of practice. Three major trends immediately surface. First, the largest proportion of MSWs (37%) work in mental health. Second, most BSWs work in the child welfare/family arena (26.6%).[12] Third, BSWs are also somewhat more likely to work in the areas of aging and disabilities than their MSW counterparts.[13] Note that although fewer than 1% of MSWs cited "community development" as their major practice field, 4% indicated that they were engaged in this area to some extent.

[12] Note that the categories in the BSW study of *child welfare/protective services* and *family services* were combined to reflect this result. The intent is to compare this figure with the MSW study's category of *child welfare/family*.

[13] Note that the BSW study uses the term *mental retardation/developmental disabilities* whereas the MSW study simply uses the word *disabilities*.

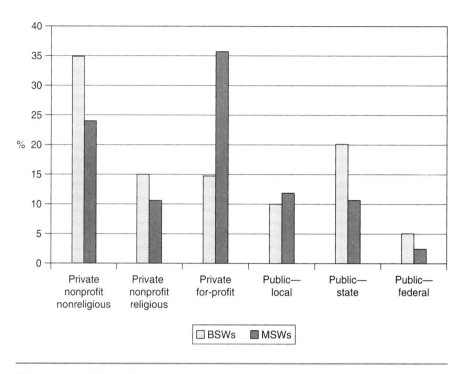

Figure 5.3   Public- and private-sector employment

An alternative approach to examining where social workers are employed involves the structure and funding sources of the agency. An earlier part of this chapter discussed public and private organizational settings. Figure 5.3 depicts where BSWs (at their first social work job) and MSWs are employed in the public and private sectors (G. H. Hull, personal communication, November 22, 2004; O'Neill, 2003). This can provide clues regarding where to seek jobs.

Most social workers at both the BSW and MSW level are employed in private social service agencies, with the rest (more than a third) working in public agencies. Over one-third of BSWs get their first social work job in private *nonprofit* nonreligious settings (e.g., family service agencies, Planned Parenthood, United Way). In contrast, over one-third of MSWs work in private *for-profit* agencies. This probably reflects the significant number of MSWs providing private therapy in agencies where a major goal is to make a profit. Note that BSWs are also more likely than MSWs to work in public *state* agencies. The smaller percentages of practitioners working for the federal government include both military and nonmilitary jobs, with military jobs being less common.

Services provided to clients by BSWs and MSWs also vary somewhat, as illustrated in Figures 5.4 and 5.5 respectively. Data were gathered differently in the two surveys, so the charts use different formats to illustrate results. BSW alumni were asked to cite their four prioritized major roles; Figure 5.4 summarizes what they felt their first major role was (G. H. Hull, personal communication, November 22, 2004).

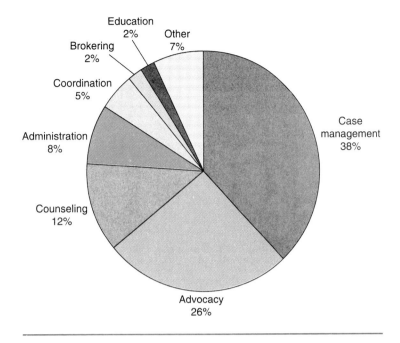

Figure 5.4 BSWs' major roles

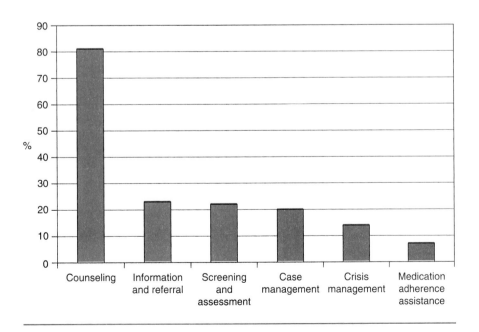

Figure 5.5 MSW services to clients

Over 38% identified case management (the coordination of needed services provided by any number of agencies, organizations, or facilities) as their primary role. Advocacy (speaking out on behalf of clients to promote fair and equitable treatment or gain needed resources) was cited by more than one-quarter of respondents. Other roles mentioned were counseling, identified by almost 12%; administration, almost 8%; coordination, almost 5%; brokering (linking client systems to needed resources), almost 2%; and providing education and training, almost 2%. Other roles (consultant, mediator, facilitator, and so on) were identified by fewer than 1% each.

The NASW survey asked MSWs what services they typically provided to their clients without prioritizing them (Survey Data, 2004). As Figure 5.5 illustrates, 81% identified counseling, 23% information and referral, 22% screening and assessment, 20% case management, 14% crisis management, and 7% medication adherence assistance services. It's notable that "[s]ocial workers in organizational settings provided more information/referral, screening/assessment, case management, and crisis interventions than those in private practice settings" (p. 8). Private practice focuses on providing some type of counseling or therapy, usually within an office context, to address some psychological issue or problem for a specified fee. Twenty-three percent of MSWs surveyed work only in private practice, 18% work both in private practice and organizational settings, and 45% work only in organizational settings (Survey Data, 2004, p. 8).

When we compare Figures 5.4 and 5.5, at least two implications are evident. Both BSWs and MSWs provide counseling and case management. However, BSWs are much more likely to view case management as a major role, whereas MSWs tend to focus on counseling. Second, over one-quarter of BSWs identify advocacy as a major function, which we have established as a critical basis of the profession.

Social Work Salaries

When looking at salary data, remember that there is tremendous variation in salary from one geographic location, field of practice, and type of job (e.g., direct service versus administration) to another. Standards of living (including rents, utilities, and taxes) vary dramatically between parts of the country. Take this into consideration when reading the salary data discussed here. The idea is to give you a general picture of what to expect as a BSW entering the field and as a seasoned MSW who has been in the field many years.

It makes sense that more education usually provides greater opportunities and potentially higher salaries. BSWs tend to work at the foundation level of practice with skills that apply to social work fields of practice across the board, whereas MSWs tend to specialize. People with MSW degrees earn significantly more than those with BSWs according to the data. However, we have identified one of the problems in comparing the BSW and MSW surveys discussed here as the vast difference in years of experience, BSWs having only about 2 years and MSWs having a median of 16.

According to a survey of 2,000 BSW graduates from 2001 to 2003, their mean (average) salary was $26,796 with a median (midpoint) of $27,500 (G. H. Hull, personal communication, July 2, 2004). Figure 5.6 breaks salary frequencies down into

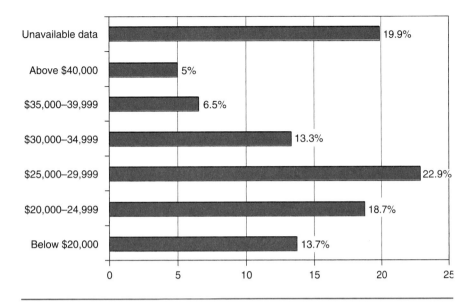

Figure 5.6 BSW two-year full-time and part-time salaries

units of $5,000 (G. H. Hull, personal communication, November 22, 2004). Almost two-thirds of BSWs earn between $20,000 and $35,000 two years after graduation.

The NASW survey of primarily MSWs indicates that the median income for full-time social workers in 2003 was $51,900, depicting a 4.8% raise from 2001 (Survey Data, 2004). Workers in private practice earned a higher median salary than people working in organizational contexts. Figure 5.7 shows the salaries for full-time and part-time MSWs. Almost two-thirds of MSWs reported earning between $40,000 and $80,000.

The picture, though, is more complex. The typical member responding to the survey is "51 years old (median age), white (87%) and of non-Hispanic origin (94%), [and] female (80%)"; they also tend to be located "proportionally more in the New England and mid-Atlantic regions and proportionally fewer in the Southern and Pacific regions" (Survey Data, 2004, pp. 1, 8). Almost three-quarters of those surveyed work for private versus public agencies (Survey Data, 2004, p. 8).

We have indicated that length of time in social work also affects salaries. Social workers who have an MSW degree and "more than 25 years of experience made 68% more than those with fewer than four years in the field. The median pay for those with 2–4 years experience was $35,000; 5–9 years, $42,400; 10–14 years, $48,300;" and "25-plus years, $60,000" (Practitioners Surveyed, 2003, pp. 1, 8).

MSW salaries also vary by field of practice. The median full-time salary for MSWs working in mental health was $52,500, school social work $49,400, child and family welfare $49,300, health care $47,900, and aging $44,000 (Practitioners Surveyed, 2003, p. 8). Subsequent chapters emphasize the fields of practice in which social workers will most likely be employed.

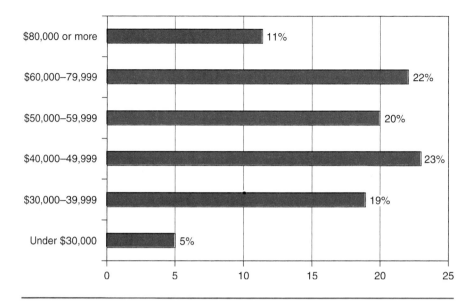

Figure 5.7 MSW full-time and part-time salaries

When looking at the social work salary picture, consider also the gender vari-able. Research conducted since 1961 reflects a significant, consistent wage differ-ential between men and women in social work (Gibelman, 2003; Practitioners Surveyed, 2003). Some research indicates that female social workers earn about 80 cents for every dollar earned by male social workers (Linsley, 2003; Lott, 1994). Other research found that in 1999 the average hourly wage for male social workers was about 14% higher than for females (Linsley, 2003). One study found that sig-nificant gender differences in salary persisted for social workers with master's degrees even "when other factors were controlled: age, years of experience, number of hours worked per week, method of practice (administrative versus direct prac-tice), and field of practice" (Huber & Orlando, 1995, p. 585).

Looking Ahead

Building on the process of social work practice discussed in the last chapter, this chapter described various settings in which social work takes place. Part III of this book includes three chapters focusing on social welfare policy. Policy establishes the parameters for what social workers can do, including how they practice and in what contexts. The next chapter lays the groundwork for understanding policy by reviewing the history of social welfare and social work.

For Further Exploration on the Internet

See this text's Book Companion Website at **www.socialwork.wadsworth.com/ kirstashman_intro2e** for descriptors and hot links to URLs relevant to this chapter, selected InfoTrac articles and exercises, and tutorial quizzes.

Case Study for Critical Thinking: An Elderly Woman with Multiple Needs

The case presented here involves an elderly woman facing various problems. Critical thinking for this case focuses on the assessment phase of the planned-change process in social work. Chapter 4 discussed how assessment in generalist practice stresses understanding the many aspects of a problem. Information is needed about the client and about those aspects of the client's environment that the worker feels are useful. The social worker might help this client by focusing on the individual (micro), family (micro/mezzo), group (mezzo), and community and organizational (macro) levels of practice. Aspects of human diversity are also important to explore.

Case study: A social services worker in a rural county receives a call about Georgia from Georgia's neighbor. Georgia, age 84, lives in an old farmhouse where she has lived for most of her life. Georgia's health is deteriorating. She is falling more and more frequently, and her eyesight is failing. The neighbor worries that Georgia may fall, break something, and lie helpless for days.

The worker visits Georgia to assess her and her situation. The worker needs information to make decisions about what he and Georgia can do. Georgia may need some supportive services or even health care center placement.

The information needed falls into four major categories. These include micro, mezzo, and macro levels of assessment in addition to consideration of elements of human diversity. In each category, problems must be defined and strengths identified.

Critical thinking: How would you use the three-step Triple-A critical thinking process to establish what might be done in this case? First, *ask* questions. On the micro level, you might ask

- What are Georgia's most critical problems?
- What things about Georgia contribute to her problems?
- What are Georgia's primary strengths upon which a treatment plan might be built?
- How does Georgia feel about herself and her situation?

   On the family (micro/mezzo) level, you might ask

- Does Georgia have any relatives in the immediate vicinity?
- Does she have children who are available to help out?
- What are her relationships with relatives who might be accessible?

   On the mezzo level, you might ask

- Does Georgia have friends she can talk to?
- Do people visit her? If so, how often?
- Does she have opportunities to get out of the house at all?

On the macro level, you might ask

- What services might be available to help Georgia with her identified problems?
- Is there a Meals on Wheels program available (through which daily hot meals are delivered to elderly people at minimal cost)?
- Is there a Visiting Friends program through which paraprofessionals (people with specialized training who perform a limited range of professional tasks under the professional's supervision) regularly visit elderly residents in their homes and help them with shopping, paying bills, making medical appointments, and so on?
- If needed services are not available for Georgia and other needy elderly residents, should you seek to get some developed?

Concerning aspects of diversity, you might ask

- Are there any significant aspects of diversity characterizing Georgia and her situation?
- What is her ethnic and racial heritage? How does this affect her life circumstances?
- Is Georgia being treated differently or in a discriminatory manner because of her age (and people's unfair, preconceived notions about older people and their abilities)?
- Is Georgia suffering any negative consequences because she is a woman and is being treated in a sexist manner?

The second step in critical thinking involves *assessing* the established facts and issues involved. Did you get as much information from Georgia as possible? Are there any other potential sources of information you can think of?

The third step in critical thinking is *asserting* a concluding opinion. What might be your final recommendations for providing Georgia with the resources and services needed to enhance her quality of life?

PART ❦ THREE

SOCIAL WELFARE POLICY

Part III of this book includes three chapters that introduce social welfare policy as the groundwork for social service provision. Policy dictates how social welfare programs may be implemented. It also structures the context in which practitioners can do their work.

Chapter 6 provides a brief overview of social welfare and social work history. History provides the necessary background to understand how people think about social welfare and develop social welfare policy.

Chapter 7 describes social welfare policy development and the structural components of policy. Because policy drives what programs can do, it must be clearly understood. The chapter explores value perspectives on social responsibility and social welfare program development. Additionally, it formulates an approach to policy analysis to evaluate how social welfare policy affects and serves clients. Finally, it defines policy practice and policy advocacy as basic responsibilities of generalist practitioners.

Chapter 8 describes the policies and programs that are designed to combat poverty in the United States. The concept of poverty is defined, and explanations for its existence discussed. Social insurance and public assistance are defined and discussed, along with specific programs under the umbrella of each.

CHAPTER SIX

AN OVERVIEW OF SOCIAL WELFARE AND SOCIAL WORK HISTORY

A Time Line of Major Events in Social Work

1898	First training course offered for "charity worker" by New York Charity Association
1918	Formation of American Association of Medical Social Workers
1919	Formation of Association of Training Schools for Professional Social Work (later becoming the American Association of Schools of Social Work [AASSW])
	Formation of National Association of School Social Workers
1920	Formation of American Association of Social Workers
1926	Formation of American Association of Psychiatric Social Workers
1927	AASSW development of educational requirements for its membership that quickly evolved into accreditation standards for MSW programs
1929	Beginning of Great Depression that opened doors for social workers in the public sector
1936	Formation of American Association of Group Workers
1942	Formation of National Association of Schools of Social Administration (NASSA)
1943	Recognition of NASSA as official accrediting body for baccalaureate programs
1946	Formation of National Council on Social Worker Education (NCSWE) to coordinate AASSW and NASSA activities
	Formation of Association for Study of Community Organization
1949	Formation of Social Worker Research Group
1952	Formation of Council on Social Work Accreditation (CSWE) reflecting the merger of AASSW and NASSA
	Writing of first CSWE Curriculum Policy Statement and Accreditation Standards
1955	Formation of National Association of Social Workers (NASW)
	Formation of National Association of Puerto Rican Hispanic Social Workers
1956	Publication of profession's primary journal, Social Work
1960	NASW approval of Code of Ethics
1960s	War on Poverty that focused attention on social change versus individual pathology
1962	CSWE development of criteria for accrediting BSW programs
1968	Formation of National Association of Black Social Workers (NABSW)
	Formation of National Association of Puerto Rican Social Service Workers (NAPRSSW)
1969	Formation of Association of American Indian Social Workers (now called National Indian Social Workers Association)
	Formation of Asian American Social Workers organization
1974	CSWE accreditation of BSW programs
1976	NASW establishes Political Action for Candidate Election (PACE)

Figure 6.1   Major events in the history of the social work profession in the United States (*continued*)

1977	Formation of Group for Advancement of Doctoral Education in social work (GADE)
1979	Incorporation of American Association of State Social Work Boards (AASSWB) to synchronize state licensing procedures
1982	Formation of Association for Advancement of Social Work with Groups (AASWG)
1984	CSWE declares common generalist practice foundation for both BSW and MSW programs
1987	NASW initiates Center for Social Policy and Practice to disseminate information about social welfare policy
1991	Formation of Academy of Certified Baccalaureate Social Workers (ACBSW)
1996	NASW approval of revisions of Code of Ethics
1998	U.S. social workers commemorate over 100 years of social work

Figure 6.1   (*continued*)

You might feel that history is boring and irrelevant in view of alarming contemporary issues, rapidly accelerating technological advances, and global political, economic, and social concerns. However, events in history have shaped our current ways of thinking. To comprehend how and why social welfare programs are the way they are today, it is critical to understand social welfare history. Current social welfare policy and programs didn't simply appear out of nowhere. Rather, a long history of ideas, values, and events has shaped the present—and paves the way for the future.

The profession's history is intertwined with the history of social welfare. Social work grew and matured in response to significant social trends, events, and needs as they occurred over time. What social workers could do in the past and what they can do now are governed by social welfare policies and programs.

It is beyond the scope of this book to provide a detailed history of social welfare and social work.[1] Therefore, our focus will be on the key trends, events, and figures. The time line at the end of this chapter summarizes some of these events.

[1]Many thorough books have been written about social welfare and social work history. This chapter can provide only a brief overview of and introduction to major concepts. For futher, more extensive information, you might refer to *From Poor Law to Welfare State* by W. I. Trattner (New York: Free Press, 1999); *A New History of Social Welfare* by P. J. Day (Boston: Allyn & Bacon, 2000); *The Faces of Social Policy: A Strengths Perspective* by C. J. Tice and K. Perkins (Pacific Grove, CA: Brooks/Cole, 2002); *Social Welfare: A History of the American Response to Need* (6th ed.) by J. Axinn and M. J. Stern (Boston: Allyn & Bacon, 2005); *Milestones* by R. L. Barker (Washington, DC: NASW Press), or to topics such as "Social Welfare History," "Social Welfare Policy," "Social Work Profession: History," "National Association of Social Workers," and "Council on Social Work Education" in R. L. Edwards (Ed.), *Encyclopedia of Social Work* (Washington, DC: NASW Press, 1995).

Note that when we talk about ideas, trends, and social movements over time, it is impossible to quantify them as abruptly halting one year and being replaced by something else the next year. Ideas and concepts change gradually, and transitions between them are indistinct. Therefore, this chapter will periodically reflect some overlap from one section or historical period to another.

Because Europe, especially England, provided the primary model for the development of current social welfare strategies in North America, we will initially focus on what occurred there. We will then concentrate on events and developments in the United States from the early years to the present. Specifically, this chapter will

- Describe some of the early European approaches to social welfare.
- Review some of the main events characterizing the history of social welfare in the United States.
- Describe some of the issues and events affecting African Americans, American Indians, and Hispanics over U.S. history.
- Focus on some of the historical issues concerning mental health, children and families, people with disabilities, and the elderly.
- Propose questions to stimulate critical thinking about various historical trends and events.
- Discuss major events involved in the history of the social work profession.
- Provide a foundation for understanding social welfare policy and policy development.

 # Early European Approaches to Social Welfare

Some of our current basic ideas about how people should or should not be treated can be traced back a millennium to medieval times. Until the mid-1300s, *feudalism* reigned in Europe as the principal type of political organization. In this system, wealthy landed gentry oversaw the labor of landless serfs who made a living by working their overseer's lands. In return, serfs received general protection and care during sickness and old age.

Other sources of aid included medieval hospitals that provided refuge and care for the elderly, the impoverished, orphans, and people with serious illnesses and disabilities, as well as charitable help from the church. These times reflected a rigid social structure with little mobility, free choice, or potential for personal growth and change. Grounded in Judeo-Christian thought, a common theme was that those who were better off should provide help to those who were poor. That some people were poor and others were rich was perceived as an unalterable fact of life. The church played a primary role in redistributing resources from the rich to the poor. It emphasized "good deeds, love of one's enemies, and entry into heaven through mercy and charity" (Trattner, 1999, p. 3).

England After Feudalism's Demise

As time passed, trade increased, technology bloomed, and the feudal system with its rigid hierarchy of power and social expectations underwent a gradual demise.

With the development of urban factories, rural people were drawn to the cities looking for work and, they hoped, better wages. Centralized government became stronger, and the church lost both political and financial power. With these changes, people gained mobility and independence but lost much of the safety and security the old feudal system had provided. Many wandered in search of work, with pain, suffering, and poverty the norm.

Political leaders decided that something must be done to control the mobile population and provide some relief for the poor. In 1348 the Black Death (bubonic plague) began its destruction of almost a third of the English population, causing a serious labor shortage. As people migrated in search of competitive wages, political leaders passed legislation to regain social control. For example, the Statute of Laborers, passed in 1349, restricted the unemployed from moving about and established maximum wages allowable. The intent was to make people stay put and take whatever work was available there instead of seeking better options.

In 1531 another statute was passed forbidding able-bodied people from begging, with violations punishable by bloody public whippings while naked. However, this legislation also provided for designated government figures to help people unable to work (referred to as the "impotent poor") by assigning them legitimate areas where they could beg. Subsequent laws addressed who should receive aid, from whom, and under what conditions, as well as what punishments should befall those who did not obey the rules.

The English Elizabethan Poor Law of 1601

The 1601 Elizabethan Poor Law is often considered the first piece of legislation establishing coherent, consistent public support for needy people through local taxes. It also was the first to establish categories of eligible recipients by identifying the following three:

1. *Dependent children* without relatives capable of supporting them were placed in service under whatever citizen placed the lowest bid for public reimbursement to provide the child's care. Boys served as apprentices, theoretically being taught a trade, until their 24th birthday, and girls provided domestic help until they were either 21 or married.
2. The *impotent poor* included those who were physically or mentally unable to work. They were given either "indoor relief" (i.e., placed *inside* institutions providing food and shelter called *almshouses* or *poorhouses*) or "outdoor relief" (i.e., offered the opportunity to live *outside* of the institution but receive material help in the form of food, clothing, and fuel).
3. The *able-bodied poor* were provided any substandard employment available and forced to work or suffer jail or other punishment, even death. Some people were forced into workhouses, special facilities in which poor people were forced to work and live. Unlike the impotent poor, these people were considered undeserving of help because they should be able to take care of themselves.

One later change in the poor laws, the 1662 Law of Settlement, established a notable new principle of social welfare service provision, the *residency requirement*. Potential aid recipients were required to establish that they had dwelled in some location for some designated time before they could receive assistance or benefits from the political body governing that location. And people who had moved and needed help were required to return to their former parish (a portion of a county coinciding with the original religious parish and serving as a unit of local government) to receive help.

The Speenhamland System

In 1795 what became known as the Speenhamland system (because it was developed in Speenhamland, England) reflected a new approach to the problems of working poor people. Bread had became so expensive that many poor people could not afford it. Speenhamland government leaders responded by initiating the policy of supplementing the income of all poor people so that everyone would have what was deemed the minimum income necessary for survival.

Unfortunately, the result was an unexpected flop for two reasons (Garvin & Tropman, 1998; Reid, 1995). First, wages fell. Why would employers pay higher wages when the government would supplement workers' wages to the minimum necessary for survival? Why shouldn't employers let the government pay the difference to have wages reach the minimum level, rather than taking it out of their own pockets? Second, unemployment soared because people didn't have to work. They would get the same amount whether they worked or not. And even if they did work, they had little chance of getting ahead. In other words, there were no *work incentives*—logical rewards or benefits that encourage people to work.

The English Poor Law Reforms of 1834

As time passed, people began to resent the Speenhamland system for two reasons (Garvin & Tropman, 1998): (1) It cost a fortune to support *everyone,* and (2) people felt it created a dependent population of people who would never get out of poverty. The Poor Law Reforms of 1834 significantly reduced all outdoor relief and brought back workhouses as the only place where able-bodied people could receive benefits.

Three important ideological trends resulted from these reforms (Garvin & Tropman, 1998). First, public attitudes toward the poor became hostile and resentful. Second, the public came to blame the poor for their poverty. Why couldn't those people pull themselves up by their bootstraps and make it on their own? Today we would refer to this as a form of *blaming the victim*—that is, ascribing fault to the people who are hurt, have problems beyond their control, have few resources, or have been victimized by some crime or unexpected circumstance. This reflects the attitude that if only poor people would expend a little more effort and put in a full day's work every day, they wouldn't be poor (Barker, 2003). The third result of these reforms was the concept of being *less eligible*

(Garvin & Tropman, 1998; Reid, 1995). This is the idea that benefits should be lower than what the poorest working people could earn. People who received public assistance, then, would always be poorer than the poorest people who worked.

U.S. Social Welfare History: Early Colonization to the Mid-1800s

Early poor laws in the American colonies closely resembled, and in some cases were identical to, those in England, although each colony remained unique in its specific legislation. The colonists maintained a strong sense of individualism and commitment to personal freedom; however, they also expressed concern for the well-being of others and respect for a sense of community (Reid, 1995). The result was an interesting and uneven blend of programs and services, such that the beneficiaries of some programs received substantial help and others received very little.

The colonists viewed the poor as a natural part of the social order and the community. In many ways, this reflected an *institutional* view of social welfare—namely, it's simply society's ongoing responsibility to provide its citizens with needed benefits and resources.

Services often reflected a mix of public and private collaboration, with services being provided in a relatively informal manner (Reid, 1995). Local government units assumed responsibility of administering aid but often called upon local churches for help (Dolgoff & Feldstein, 2003).

Early residency requirements for assistance were established. Communities tended to provide aid for their own residents, shunning strangers. Communities also made decisions about who was worthy to receive benefits and who was not. This demonstrated the concept of the *worthy* versus the *unworthy poor;* the former deserved help and the latter did not (the implication being that they were doing something wrong) (Dolgoff & Feldstein, 2003).

The worthy poor were pitied, and the community found ways to care for them. One of the easiest was for families to take turns housing the poor during the year. A second way to help the poor was to reduce their taxes. Still another way involved providing free medical attention to them, with physicians either donating such care or receiving inducements such as tax breaks.

Dependent children were frequently placed in apprenticeships. This was viewed positively for a number of reasons (Trattner, 1999). First, apprenticeship afforded them some connection with a family and the related stability. Second, it provided a context in which they might be disciplined and taught to become good citizens. Third, it saved the community the cost of caring for children. Finally, it trained children to develop a useful skill and become productive community members. And because labor was scarce in colonial America, people who had learned trades were highly valued. Highlight 6.1 discusses some of the early philosophical views about children.

By the 1820s and 1830s, ideas were changing, and people were beginning to view poverty as a "social problem" and "a potential source of crime, social unrest,

HIGHLIGHT 6.1
Early Philosophical Views About Children

Trattner (1999) presents some of the early philosophical perspectives on children. From colonial times to the 1870s, children were viewed as similar entities with little individuality—they were all thought to be innately evil and lazy. Therefore, they required supervision to keep them busy and out of trouble so that they might grow up to be "industrious, upright, godly" adults (Trattner, 1999, p. 110). By the mid-18th century, however, philosophical thinking was changing. John Locke's *tabula rasa* (clean slate) approach suggested that children were inherently pure and good. It was society and its negative influences that corrupted children as they grew up.

Effects of the environment became increasingly important from a number of perspectives. Social Darwinism, espoused by 19th-century English sociologist Herbert Spencer, highlighted the importance of genetically inherited attributes but also stressed the ability of the environment to influence these traits over time. Sigmund Freud emphasized the importance of early nurturing within the family and its effect on child development.

In general, trends in thinking reflected an increasing focus on children's welfare (Kadushin & Martin, 1988). People began to believe that children's environment and the treatment they received affected what kinds of adults they grew up to be.

and long-term dependence" (Reid, 1995, p. 2209). Therefore, interest began to turn to reform. People now believed that outdoor relief had spoiled poor people and that it resulted only in dependence (Reid, 1995). Therefore, great almshouses were built in which the poor could be housed and converted into industrious, functional citizens.

Focus on Mental Health and Mental Illness

In colonial America, people who had mental illness, often referred to as "lunatics," typically were cared for by their own families or boarded out to other families, with communities paying these families to provide care (Dembling, 1995; Fellin, 1996, p. 56). As time passed, people with mental illness increasingly were placed in almshouses, clustered together with the poor and people with other disabilities.

By the early 19th century, the *moral treatment* movement, the first of three focusing on mental health policy, had been initiated by Philippe Pinel, a French physician who worked in a Parisian hospital for the "insane." The idea was that people with mental illness "should be treated with humane, sympathetic, and personal care in a hospital or asylum setting" (Fellin, 1996, p. 57; Lin, 1995; U.S. Department of Health and Human Services [USDHHS], 1999). (Figure 6.2 summarizes the three major

Movement	Time Frame	Emphasis
Moral treatment	1770s–1900	Humane treatment in structured institutional settings
Mental hygiene	1900–1945	Specialized psychiatric units and psychotherapy
Deinstitutionalization	Early 1950s to present	Provision of care in people's own communities

Figure 6.2   Major mental health movements in the United States

mental health movements occurring in the United States during the 19th and 20th centuries. The last two will be described in greater detail later in the chapter.)

In the United States, the movement assumed "more of a moralistic flavor related to the idea that bad habits lead to tendencies toward mental disorders" (Fellin, 1996, p. 57; Rochefort, 1993). Structured, "corrective" settings providing a remedial environment were thought to help cure mental illness (Lin, 1995, p. 1705). Highlight 6.2 focuses on Dorothea Dix, an early advocate for the humane treatment of people with mental illness.

Focus on American Indian (First Nations Peoples) History: Treaties and Federal Control[2]

Most of social welfare history in the United States, including that discussed thus far, is written from a very white perspective (Lewis, 1995). In reality, American history did not begin in 1492 when Columbus "discovered" America. Rather, North America had been populated for 25,000 years or more (Day, 2000; Lewis, 1995). During initial European colonization, there were an estimated 500 different nations with a wide range of well-developed, self-sufficient societies (Weaver, 2003).

Residents of a conquered society generally remain on their own land and at least retain hope of regaining control. European victory over American Indian nations, however, usually resulted in their permanent removal from their lands, pressures to surrender their values and culture, and imposed submission to external laws and regulations.

Treaties

As whites pushed westward in exploding numbers and with an insatiable desire for land, the United States, newly formed and in its infancy, decided to deal with

[2]For greater detail and good introductory content on American Indians, see Lewis (1995, pp. 216–231), which provides an excellent beginning source for understanding some of the crucial issues experienced by First Nations Peoples.

HIGHLIGHT 6.2

Dorothea Dix: Mental Health Advocate

A notable early advocate during the 1840s for people with mental illness was Dorothea Dix (Barker, 1999a; Fellin, 1996; Trattner, 1999). A volunteer Sunday school teacher in a Massachusetts women's prison, she was appalled by the treatment of people with mental illness who were placed there. She waged a dynamic publicity campaign condemning the deplorable conditions in which these people were forced to live.

Trattner (1999) explains how Dix "described vividly how many of the unfortunate crazed were impounded in cabins, cages, closets, stalls, and other pens of one kind of another, often chained and then abandoned to filth and neglect, or else brutally beaten—a horrifying picture" (p. 65).

Beginning in Massachusetts and then focusing on other states, she insisted that it was the public's responsibility to establish hospitals providing more humane treatment and medical care for persons with mental illness.

As a result of Dix's and her followers' efforts, over 30 state mental hospitals were established (Fellin, 1996). Unfortunately, "[a]lthough well intentioned, her selling and marketing of state-run institutions were based on two dubious premises: first, that such asylums were the most cost-effective means of treatment, and second, that insanity was a highly curable phenomenon" (Gomory, 1997, p. 165).

First Nations Peoples by developing treaties. The United States viewed treaties as ways "of defining both the legal and political relationships" between the federal government and various nations (Lewis, 1995, p. 218). The first treaty to be established (of more than 600 over the next century) was with the Delaware nation in 1778. Congress finally ceased making treaties with nations in 1981 when "agreements" and legislation formally replaced the treaty process (Lewis, 1995, p. 219).

Other Early Policies

A significant early piece of legislation was the 1781 Articles of Confederation. This was related to treaties because it gave "the federal government sole and exclusive authority over Indian affairs," reinforcing the government's right to make treaties in any way it saw fit (Lewis, 1995, p. 218). Thus the federal government could develop treaties regardless of First Nations Peoples' locations in North America. The implication is that, as the government broke treaties, First Nations Peoples could be moved from place to place, usually further west.

Other significant pieces of legislation, the trade and intercourse acts passed between 1770 and 1834, reinforced two more ideas (Canby, 1981; Lewis, 1995). One was that American Indians and non–American Indians should be separated. The other was that the federal government should control all relations between

American Indians and whites. The federal Bureau of Indian Affairs, established in 1824, reflected an attempt to address issues with American Indians.

The theme during this period was "the belief that Indians were culturally inferior and that the American government had a responsibility to raise them to the level of the rest of society, which meant to 'Christianize and civilize'" them (Lewis, 1995, p. 218). White people believed that the federal government should interfere not only in political matters but also in social, economic, religious, and cultural practices.

Removal Policy

Tensions continued to mount as whites pushed westward into American Indian territory. The Indian Removal Act, passed in 1830, resulted in thousands of American Indians being removed from their own lands and relocated to distant "reservations" that were generally smaller than their homelands and had clearly defined boundaries. Morales and Sheafor (2002) explain that "[m]any negative sanctions and restrictions were imposed on American Indians living on reservations. They were often denied use of their language and participation in religious ceremonies" (p. 244).

The Cherokee Nation poses a heartrending example of the cruel removal practice. By the early 1800s, the Cherokee had called western Georgia home for almost 1,000 years (Cherokee Messenger, 1995). By this time the nation had adopted many European customs, including women wearing gowns, and had developed a system of "roads, schools, and churches" (Cherokee Messenger, 1995). Their literacy rate in their own tongue was 90 percent, they published a bilingual newspaper and a range of textbooks, and they established a "written constitution" as an independent nation (Lewis, 1995, p. 218). Most of them worked as farmers and ranchers (Golden Ink, 1997).

After gold was discovered in Georgia in 1828, the tension increased between the Cherokee and their non-Native counterparts. Although the Cherokee challenged the legality of the 1830 Indian Removal Act in the Supreme Court and at first appeared to be successful, it was determined that they could be removed if they signed a treaty to that effect (Golden Ink, 1997). Against the majority's will, in 1835 a small faction (less than 3%) of the Cherokee Nation signed such a treaty relinquishing all land east of the Mississippi in return for promised new western lands, cash, equipment, and supplies (Cherokee Messenger, 1995; Golden Ink, 1997). Three years later, 17,000 Cherokee men, women, and children were torn from their land and made to endure squalid conditions on a 1,200-mile trip to Indian Territory in the West (Cherokee Messenger, 1995). On that journey 4,000 perished "from hunger, exposure, and disease" (Cherokee Messenger, 1995). This infamous journey is aptly and sadly called "The Trail of Tears."

In all, during the 1830s between 70,000 and 100,000 American Indians were uprooted from their homes and herded to Oklahoma (Lewis, 1995).

Focus on Chicano/a History: The Treaty of Guadalupe Hidalgo

The history of the Southwest and its early inhabitants merits attention, especially in view of the large and growing U.S. Chicano/a population. Beginning in 1519 the Spanish conquistadors along with their Native allies conquered the Aztec Empire in Central Mexico; from there expansion took place in all directions, overtaking areas including Arizona, New Mexico, Texas, and California (National Park Service, undated). Colonization of these regions continued with many of the residents having a mixed heritage including Spanish and Native American ancestry (National Park Service, undated).

In view of a growing population, increasing infiltration by Anglos (whites), and budding trade with other areas, the struggle for control of land escalated. Texas declared itself an independent republic in 1836, but continued grappling with Mexico over its southern boundary (Library of Congress, 2004). When the United States decided to annex Texas in 1845, the boundary struggle with Mexico continued. Conflict intensified and war was declared in 1846, initiating the Mexican-American War. Subsequently, the United States attacked Mexico on numerous fronts, eventually capturing Mexico City in mid-1847 (Library of Congress, 2004). The result was the February 2, 1848, signing of the Treaty of Guadalupe Hidalgo, in which Mexico ceded more than half of its territory to the United States, including contemporary Arizona, New Mexico, and upper California in addition to portions of Colorado, Nevada, and Utah in exchange for $15,000,000; additionally, Mexico recognized U.S. retention of Texas with its southern boundary at the Rio Grande (U.S. National Archives and Records Administration, undated). (The remaining portions of present-day states were ceded under the 1853 Gadsden Purchase [Curiel, 1995].)

The Treaty of Guadalupe Hidalgo did address the rights of Mexicans living in the ceded regions. It provided the options of retaining their land and becoming U.S. citizens, which the vast majority chose, or moving south into Mexico (Curiel, 1995). Although the treaty guaranteed land, personal, and religious rights, Anglos generally opted to ignore these guarantees (Day, 2000). Many Anglos took Chicano landowners to court over land rights, usually winning because many Chicanos had lost proof of land titles during the conflict and could not afford to hire attorneys to defend themselves adequately (Day, 2000). As a result, Chicanos were generally disenfranchised from their property and their rights, becoming strangers in their own land (Curiel, 1995). Many were forced into hard agricultural labor that Anglos preferred not to do. Anglos commonly viewed Chicanos as a "minority" group with its own culture; although Chicanos outnumbered Anglos and were living in their own homelands, they were marginalized, discriminated against, and commonly treated as second-class citizens (Curiel, 1995). This set the stage for the discrimination and many of the issues Chicanos must deal with today.

 ## The Civil War Era

The Civil War (1861–1865) had a huge impact on the social structure of the United States. Day (2000) explains that it "affirmed federal responsibility over states' rights and laid the groundwork for the United States to become a welfare state" (p. 187).

Jansson (2005) describes how, despite the fact that the main conflict concerned "the legal status of slaves," President Abraham Lincoln (whose administration lasted from 1861 until his 1865 assassination) did not initially propose an immediate end to slavery (p. 105). Although his decisions were apparently made in the context of political concerns, such an omission might raise questions regarding the strength of Lincoln's opposition to slavery.[3] It was not until 1863 that he issued the Emancipation Proclamation, declaring freedom for all slaves in Confederate states at war with the Union. Note that this sidestepped the issue of freedom for slaves in border slave states, including Delaware, Kentucky, Maryland, Missouri, and West Virginia (Tice & Perkins, 2002).

Focus on African Americans: The Freedmen's Bureau

A major problem during this era involved the newly freed, dislocated former slaves, who had no property and few resources. Although charity groups in the North sent supplies and volunteers to help displaced people, this only scratched the surface in terms of meeting people's needs. National concern about the issues and needs resulted in Congress establishing the Bureau of Refugees, Freedmen, and Abandoned Land (more commonly known as the Freedmen's Bureau) in 1865. (Note that its formal name emphasizes how legislators sought to avoid giving African Americans preferential treatment [Jansson, 2005].) This bureau, the "first federal welfare agency" (Reid, 1995, p. 2210), established "a precedent for federal participation in social welfare during emergency periods" (Axinn & Stern, 2005, p. 96).

The Freedmen's Bureau was placed under the auspices of the War Department. This emphasized its temporary, crisis-related (postwar) purpose, as opposed to status as an institutional program designed to meet ongoing needs. Eligibility for resources was based purely on need. In its initial three years, the bureau distributed rations to 18.3 million people, over 28% of whom were white (Day, 2000; Tice & Perkins, 2002). Additionally, it provided transportation home for refugees, distributed medical supplies, built 46 hospitals, and established over 4,300 schools for African American children (Axinn & Stern, 2005). The Freedmen's Bureau was disbanded in 1872.

One of the Freedmen's Bureau's initial goals was to distribute 40 acres of abandoned or confiscated land to each male refugee. This could be accomplished only if the government took possession of such property and legally distributed it. The results of this program were modest: Only a little over 1% of eligible African Americans were allocated property (Jansson, 2005). President Andrew Johnson (whose administration lasted from 1865 to 1869) subsequently proclaimed that the African Americans had no legal right to these properties and forced recipients to return land to its former owners (Jansson, 2005).

The 1870s to 1900

Economic growth skyrocketed between the Civil War and the early 20th century (Axinn & Stern, 2005). Three broad trends emerged in the United States both economically and socially (Garvin & Cox, 1995). The first was *industrialization*. Mammoth growth in manufacturing and technology brought with it a "wide range of

---

[3]Possible reasons for Lincoln's hesitation in eradicating slavery include having as a top priority keeping the Union together, believing that the Constitution gave him no authority to free slaves, being concerned that the Confederacy would only "fight harder" and the war would last longer if slaves were freed, and fearing alienation of the border slave states (Tice & Perkins, 2002, p. 74).

social problems" including "problems of working hours and conditions, safety, and child labor" (Garvin & Cox, 1995, p. 65).

The second trend was *urbanization*. Concurrent with the centralization of industry within urban settings was the tremendous growth of urban populations. Masses of people moved from rural to urban areas in search of work and prosperity. Unfortunately, most were forced to move into the oldest, most crowded, and least sanitary portions of the cities.

The third trend was explosive *immigration*, primarily from northwestern Europe. Immigrants brought with them their own problems. Many came from poor rural environments and had little to start their lives with in this country, and many became ill during the immigration process. Immigrants usually were forced to live in some of the worst conditions and accept whatever work they could find.

Focus on Children: Early Policies

The 1870s saw the origins of child welfare policy as it has evolved today (Karger & Stoesz, 2002). Prior to this time, abandoned, unwanted, or orphaned children had been placed in almshouses along with adults suffering from poverty and disabilities. By this time, however, people were beginning to view children as special beings requiring treatment qualitatively different from that provided adults and people with disabilities. Orphanages intended solely for children began to multiply, replacing almshouses as places to house children. This practice was, however, still institutional placement.

The Reverend Charles Loring Brace, founder of New York's Children's Aid Society, became the first proponent of placing children in homes other than their own instead of in institutions. Brace gathered up thousands of juvenile paupers from the New York City streets and sent them to live with farm families in the Midwest. He believed that farmers were the ideal citizens and that farming was the ideal occupation. A staunch believer in the importance of the environment, as stressed by social Darwinism, Brace felt that placing children in such positive environments would make them better, more productive citizens.

By the early 20th century, most large cities had their own children's aid societies that placed or "farmed out" children to families instead of putting them in institutions. This movement reflected the beginnings of foster care and adoption in the United States. Highlight 6.3 discusses the early development of protective services.

Settlement Houses, Charity Organization Societies, and Generalist Social Work

In response to the rapidly growing social problems, two social and ideological movements became the foundation for social work practice in the 1880s and continued into the early 1900s (Lewis & Suarez, 1995). They were the settlement house movement and charity organization societies.

Settlement Houses

Settlement houses were "places where ministers, students, or humanitarians 'settled' (hence the name) to interact with poor slum dwellers with the purpose of alleviating the conditions of capitalism" (Smith, 1995, p. 2130). Settlement houses

The Early Development of Protective Services

The concept of *protective services* was born under some unusual circumstances in 1874. Etta Wheeler, a New York City relief worker for the poor, discovered that Mary Ellen Wilson, age 9, who had been an indentured servant since age 18 months, "was being tied to a bed, whipped, and stabbed with scissors" (Karger & Stoesz, 2002, p. 418). It was subsequently determined that Mary Ellen was the illegitimate child of her tormentor Mary Connelly's first husband.

Wheeler "sought help from the police, benevolent societies, and charitable gentlemen," but to no avail (Watkins, 1990, p. 501). Finally, in desperation, she appealed to the president of the New York Society for the Prevention of Cruelty to Animals. Interested in the case, he helped Wheeler get "a special warrant" from a New York Supreme Court judge to remove Mary Ellen from the abusive home (Watkins, 1990, p. 502).

Historical and current myths often imply that children living in the 1870s had to be categorized as animals before they could receive legal protection (Watkins, 1990). In reality, the court never treated Mary Ellen as if the same laws applied to her as to animals. However, the case received extensive publicity focusing on how Mary Ellen had been treated worse than what was legally allowed for animals. It brought to people's attention how children were sometimes in need of protective treatment.

What happened to Mary Ellen? Wheeler's own mother, and later her sister, took Mary Ellen in; Mary Ellen "was married at age 24 and had two daughters" (Watkins, 1990, p. 502). "As a punishment to herself, but more as a warning to others," Mary Connelly was sentenced to "one year in the Penitentiary at hard labor," the maximum sentence possible ("Mary Ellen," 1874, p. 8; Watkins, 1990, p. 502). As a result of Mary Ellen's case, societies for the prevention of cruelty to children were established all over the country in the late 1800s and early 1900s.

"wanted to be 'neighbors' to the poor and to help communities solve self-identified problems, such as day care, literacy, and citizenship" (Popple, 1995, p. 2282). Additionally, the people developing them "advocated for child labor laws, urban parks, women's suffrage, public housing, and public health" (Smith, 1995, p. 2130).

Settlement houses formed a strong foundation for generalist social work practice within communities in at least three ways (Smith, 1995). First, the settlement house approach addressed the problems of people in an environmental context instead of focusing on individual pathology. Environmental problems created difficulties for individuals, who were not viewed as the targets of blame, punishment, and change. Settlement houses thus focused on addressing social issues and improving living conditions, especially for the poorest and least fortunate people.

Second, an environmental focus led naturally to an emphasis on advocacy and social reform. (*Advocacy* is the act of standing up for and defending the cause of another.) This is appropriate when the macro social environment requires change to meet people's needs.

Third, settlement houses emphasized the empowerment of people. At its most basic level, *empowerment* involves providing people with authority or power.

According to the settlement house perspective, people had strengths and capabilities to effect their own change. Families and neighborhoods were seen as potential vehicles for positive change. The concepts of community organization and group work (both described in Chapter 5) developed within the settlement house context. Jane Addams and Ellen Gates Starr opened perhaps the most famous settlement house, Hull House, in Chicago in 1889. Highlight 6.4 focuses on Jane Addams, an immensely important figure in the development of social work and advocacy for social change.

Charity Organization Societies

The settlement perspective contrasted strikingly with *charity organization societies* (COS). According to Lewis and Suarez (1995), the "emphasis was not on lay communal expertise but on scientific practice and expert knowledge" (p. 1769). They continue that "the underlying assumption was that individual need was a result of moral turpitude and that moral teaching, combined with minimal assistance, would support people in taking care of themselves" (p. 1769). Initially, the societies used "friendly visitors" who tried to help people figure out how to solve their problems (Brieland, 1995, p. 2247).

As time passed, charity organization societies sought to establish a base of scientific knowledge and apply it to the helping process. The scientific emphasis in fields such as medicine and engineering inspired this orientation. The societies "wanted to study the problem of dependence, gather data, test theories, systematize administration, and develop techniques that would lead to a cure" (Popple, 1995, p. 2283). The impetus to obtain social work professionalism began when the societies recognized the fact that friendly visitors needed more education and training to perform their tasks effectively (Brieland, 1995; Popple, 1995).

Charity organization societies focused on curing individuals, not on empowering communities. Traditional social casework developed from the former approach. Additionally, because expert knowledge was emphasized, the significance of administration and supervised practice was incorporated in the casework concept. This emphasis on expertise contrasted sharply with the settlement approach, which stressed the empowerment and self-sufficiency of all. Highlight 6.5 focuses on the life and contributions of Mary Richmond, a primary proponent of the charity organization movement and a significant force in the early definition of social work.

Focus on American Indians: Attempts at Assimilation

Earlier we discussed how treaty formulation and tribal relocation characterized the early treatment of American Indians. From the 1870s to 1900, a new trend, *assimilation,* emerged, perhaps because the federal government was "developing a conscience" (Lewis, 1995, p. 219). In this context, *assimilation* is the process of incorporating another culture into the mainstream culture. The assimilated culture (i.e., that of First Nations Peoples) was thus expected to assume the dominant culture's values and practices while relinquishing its own. The "most devastating piece of Indian legislation in the United States" was the Indian General Allotment Act of 1887 (also known as the Dawes Act) (Lewis, 1995, p. 219). Its intent was to assimilate American Indians by giving them land and potential citizenship in return for their turning their backs on their culture and becoming "productive" citizens (Lewis, 1995, p. 219).

HIGHLIGHT 6.4
Jane Addams

Jane Addams "built her reputation as the country's most prominent woman through her writing, her settlement work, and her international efforts for world peace" (Jane Addams Hull-House Museum, 1997). She attained "worldwide recognition in the first third of the 20th century as a pioneer social worker in America, as a feminist, and as an internationalist" (Haberman, 1972).

Born in Cedarville, Illinois, on September 6, 1860, Jane was the youngest of six children in a well-to-do family. Her mother died when Jane was 2. Six years later, her father remarried and she gained two stepbrothers. Jane deeply respected her father, John Addams, a miller, who was "a shrewd and careful investor" and one of Cedarville's "leading citizens" (Stroup, 1986, p. 2). John "was a local political leader who served for 16 years as a state senator and fought as an officer in the Civil War; he was a friend of Abraham Lincoln, whose letters to him began 'My Dear Double D-'ed Addams'" (Haberman, 1972).

"Because of a congenital spinal defect, Jane was not physically vigorous when young nor truly robust even later in life," although the defect was corrected later by surgery (Haberman, 1972).

After graduating from the local school, Jane sought a college education at the Rockford Female Seminary (later called Rockford College) and graduated in 1881 as class valedictorian. Shortly afterward, her father died, which distressed her greatly as "she lost one of the most powerful influences in her life" (Stroup, 1986, p. 6).

Jane subsequently pursued further study in the field of medicine. "For seven months she worked at her medical studies with considerable zeal and secured high marks for her efforts. But the strain was too much, and her health broke down, forcing her to return to Cedarville" (Stroup, 1986, p. 6). Over the next few years, Jane "was

hospitalized intermittently, traveled and studied in Europe for 21 months, and then spent almost two years in reading and writing and in considering what her future objectives should be" (Haberman, 1972). Jane "wanted more in life" than marriage; if "her brothers could have careers in medicine and science, why couldn't she? Besides, she disliked household duties and the prospect of raising children held no appeal" (Women in History, 2005).

Stroup (1986) describes Jane's initial thoughts about the settlement house movement:

> [In the spring of 1887 at age 27], Jane went to Madrid along with four friends [including Ellen Starr]. Their tour included a bullfight, and when her friends left the arena because of the brutality, Jane stayed to see five bulls killed. She was drawn to the activity because of its callousness and at the same time repelled because of her idealism. This seems to have been a significant experience in her life because the very next morning she approached Ellen Starr with the idea of establishing a "big house" right in the middle of "horrid little houses" as a means of bringing help to the poor. Ellen was enthusiastic about the idea, and from this experience, Hull House was conceived. Its birth had to wait until Jane and Ellen discovered the work of Cannon Samuel Barnett in the East Side of London.
>
> Toynbee Hall had come into existence only four years prior to Jane Addams's visit. Barnett was its first warden, or "head resident," and it was the first settlement house. Its staff was composed of university men, mainly from Oxford, who lived in the slums of London . . . to learn conditions firsthand and to contribute to the improvement of life there with their own personal and financial resources. . . . It was this idea of the settlement house that Jane Addams also finally used. She believed that what Barnett had been able to do for the poor people of London she might attempt for the poor people of Chicago. She had found her mission, the purpose that she had struggled to find for so many years. (p. 9)

(continued)

HIGHLIGHT 6.4 *(continued)*

In 1889 with Ellen Gates Starr, an art teacher, Jane rented a house from "Charles J. Hull, an early resident of Chicago" who "had built his house when the neighborhood was young. It was a two-story brick house, set back from the street, and it seemed perfect as a settlement house" (Stroup, 1986, p. 10). "Programs at Hull House, which became models for other settlements, included children's clubs; nurseries; an art gallery; a circulating library; an employment bureau; a lunchroom; and classes in history, music, languages, painting, dancing, and mathematics. [Jane] . . . fought corrupt aldermen and was appointed neighborhood sanitation inspector, seeking to gain more services" for people in need (Quam, 1995, p. 2572).

"Hull House was a refuge for individuals who had no other place to turn in time of trouble. One child, for example, was lodged at the House until he could return to live with his parents. His mother didn't want him because he had been born with a cleft palate. On another occasion, a new bride took shelter in Hull House because her husband beat her during the first week of marriage" (Stroup, 1986, p. 12).

Jane "directed her efforts at the root causes of poverty" and continued living and working at Hull House until her death (Women in History, 2005). However, she was also actively involved in many other organizations and causes. She and her colleagues "forged a powerful reform movement" that initiated projects including "the Immigrants' Protective League, the Juvenile Protective Association, the first juvenile court in the nation, and a Juvenile Psychopathic Clinic (later called the Institute for Juvenile Research)" (Jane Addams Hull House Museum, 1997). Hull House workers advocated for and helped pass laws involving child labor

and mandatory education, which eventually spread to the national level. "They worked for legislation to protect immigrants from exploitation, limit the working hours of women, . . . recognize labor unions, and provide for industrial safety" (Women in History, 2005).

Jane, an exceptional speaker, often spoke publicly on the behalf of human welfare. She also wrote 11 books and published many articles. Her national efforts involving advocacy to improve social conditions included being the first female president of the National Conference of Charities and Corrections (an organization of social welfare agencies that changed its name to the National Conference of Social Work in 1917). Jane was involved in establishing the Chicago Federation of Settlements in 1894, and later helped found the National Federation of Settlements and Neighborhood Centers in 1911. Additionally, she was a member of national associations and committees too numerous to name here that were aimed at improving a wide range of social conditions and policies. She was a robust supporter of women's right to vote.

Jane was also a strong advocate for international peace. She initially helped form and later became president of the Women's Peace Party in 1915. She served as a delegate for a wide range of peace conferences around the world. Against opposition, she advocated for the United States to denounce war and join with other countries to form global organizations striving for international harmony. Because of her efforts, she was awarded the Nobel Peace Prize in 1931. Jane died in 1935 "three days after an operation revealed unsuspected cancer" (Haberman, 1972). She is remembered and revered as one of the most important advocates for human rights and well-being ever living in this country.

HIGHLIGHT 6.5
Mary Richmond

Born on August 5, 1861, in Belleville, Illinois, Mary Ellen Richmond, "a frail woman who spent most of her life overcoming chronic invalidism in order to help others," (Trattner, 1999, p. 255) "was the only surviving child of Henry and Lavinia Richmond" (Webster.edu, 2005). Tragedy struck Mary at the age of 3 when her mother became sick and died. She was then sent "to live with her grandmother and two aunts in Baltimore" (Webster.edu, 2005). "[F]requently ill, she spent a lonely, unhappy childhood in Baltimore" (Trattner, 1999, p. 255). There she attended high school, graduating in 1878. At that time one of her aunts became ill, so Mary assumed responsibility for her care until the aunt died 10 years later. Soon after her aunt's death Mary began working for the Baltimore Charity Organization as an assistant treasurer in 1989, becoming its general secretary two years later.

As early as 1897, Mary began to advocate for the development of professional schools of social casework (which emphasizes helping individuals and families) and structured social work education programming. In 1899 she wrote the first book that provided a thorough description of practical techniques used in doing charitable work with poor people called *Friendly Visiting Among the Poor*. Topics included suggestions for exploring health, child care, religious involvement, and financial management (Webster.edu, 2005). Her basic belief was that the poor could be helped and reformed by using structured, planned methods.

In 1900 Mary became general secretary of the Philadelphia Society for Organizing Charity, where she stressed the use of volunteers (Longres, 1995a, p. 2605). In 1909 she became the director of the Charity Organizational Department of the Russell Sage Foundation, where she conducted major social work research. The New York School of Philanthropy provided another setting where she taught and conducted research over the following years. One of Mary's major achievements was the development and

(continued)

One problem was that the European orientation of white Americans emphasized the importance of individuals owning their own property. The concept of sharing communal land, so integral to American Indians, was neither understood nor respected. Over the ensuing 35 years, the Dawes Act resulted in the loss of 75% of all American Indian lands, much of it being sold to non–American Indians or reverting back to federal control (Lewis, 1995; Morales & Sheafor, 2002).

At least three other thrusts were involved in assimilation (Lewis, 1995). First, the Bureau of Indian Affairs assumed responsibility for American Indian children's education, forcing them to abandon their own language, religion, and customs and to dress, speak, and act like whites. Second, government officials ignored the authority of tribal leaders when addressing legal and political issues. Third, missionaries were sent to reservations to "civilize" American Indians and purge them of their traditional spiritual beliefs and practices (Lewis, 1995, p. 220).

Assimilation attempts were finally mildly obstructed in 1934 with the Indian Reorganization Act. It "prohibited the further allotment of tribal lands to individuals," established a credit fund to provide tribes with loans, and gave American Indians preference for being hired in the Bureau of Indian Affairs (Lewis, 1995, p. 221).

HIGHLIGHT 6.5 *(continued)*

wide dissemination of educational materials training workers in the process and techniques of social casework.

Mary "wrote *Social Diagnosis,* the first book to address professional social work practice, in 1917. A guide for the beginning caseworker, the book outlined ways to diagnose and assess need, and it greatly influenced the new profession" (Segal, Gerdes, & Steiner, 2004, p. 50). Mary focused on defining typical tasks performed by early charity workers, especially those related to assessing the causes of families' poverty and dependence (Popple & Leighninger, 2005). She steadfastly investigated the process used by charity organization workers and established a process involving "diagnosis, prognosis, and treatment as entities in a chainlike series; the treatment of individuals, then, was an extended, logical process, the techniques of which could be ordered, described, analyzed, and transmitted from one generation of social workers to another" (Trattner, 1999, p. 255). Mary's work

established social casework as a cornerstone of social work by emphasizing individual functioning within the person's and family's environment. Although her primary focus was the individual and family, she did not disapprove of social reform involving larger systems; she simply felt that such reform efforts were generally unsuccessful and that work with individuals would always be necessary (Trattner, 1999). In essence, Mary provided the first articulate formulation of social work theories and techniques upon which the profession could be based.

Mary was a self-taught woman with no college background who read extensively and applied her knowledge in various avenues of social work research. It is interesting that despite her lack of formal training, she strongly advocated for professional social work education and the formal provision of necessary knowledge and techniques. Mary died in 1928 after a flourishing career in which she served as one of the founders of professional social work.

Even this restructuring met with resistance from many First Nations Peoples. As was typical, the act "did not incorporate any ideas or concepts of what the Indians culturally felt about authority or leadership or an American Indian concept of political structures" (Lewis, 1995, p. 221). Focus on Critical Thinking 6.1 raises some questions regarding the effects national policy can have on people's self-determination.

The Progressive Period: 1900 to 1930

The years from 1900 to 1930 were characterized by a progressive movement (Axinn & Stern, 2005; Karger & Stoesz, 2002; Leiby, 1987), although settlement houses and charity organization societies continued to characterize the early 20th century. Historical overlap and gradual transitions among trends occur as people's ideas change slowly over time.

The progressive period focused on "an active, morally responsible government" that addressed corruption in politics and business by establishing regulations (Reid, 1995, p. 2212). In this era of reform and activism, people felt that government was

FOCUS ON CRITICAL THINKING 6.1

Government Policy and Self-Determination for First Nations Peoples

Critical thinking involves *asking* questions, *assessing* facts, and *asserting* a conclusion. What are your answers to the following?

- To what extent did U.S. policy concerning American Indians reflect a racist orientation rather than appreciation for and nurturance of cultural differences?

- What types of policies might have been more sensitive to and supportive of American Indians' cultural differences and strengths?
- What policies do you think should have been instituted during this era?

responsible for their welfare. Many people, therefore, tackled major issues including "child labor, women's suffrage, immigration, and temperance" (Reid, 1995, p. 2213). The trend was to pursue cooperative goals for the good of society rather than focus on the interests of the individual; one result was the "expansion and improvement of local agencies" (Leiby, 1987, p. 765).

The following are some of the major events characterizing this era:

- The National Association for the Advancement of Colored People (NAACP), "the largest and oldest of the U.S. civil rights organizations," was created in 1909 (Barker, 2003, p. 286). Initially formed in outrage over the lynching of African Americans, and currently having over 1,500 chapters in all 50 states, the NAACP protects the rights of African Americans through legal proceedings, enforcement of civil rights laws, and provision of information to the public (Barker, 2003).
- The National Urban League was established in 1911 in response to "an extensive study of the social and economic conditions of African Americans in New York City. The league sought, as it does now, to pursue social and economic opportunities for African Americans in urban communities" (Leashore, 1995, p. 105).
- Between 1911 and 1920, 40 states initiated pension programs that provided assistance to single mothers (Barker, 1999; Jansson, 2005). These were the first financial assistance programs for mothers with dependent children.
- A major step forward in the development of protective services was the first White House Conference on Dependent Children in 1909. The "resulting strong recommendation in favor of family care strengthened the movement for home rather than institutional care for dependent and delinquent children" (Trattner, 1999, p. 216). The conference was such a success that it has been held every 10 years since, except for 1981 when the Reagan administration canceled it (Karger & Stoesz, 2002). Another important result of the initial conference was the formation of the U.S. Children's Bureau in 1912. One of its purposes was to collect systematic information on children. This marked the first time that children's

welfare had been considered significant enough to spur creation of a permanent federal agency to oversee it (Trattner, 1999).

- In 1920 the 19th Amendment to the U.S. Constitution granted women the right to vote.

Focus on Mental Health Policy

Mental health policy in the beginning of the 20th century reflected the *mental hygiene* movement, replacing the earlier focus on moral treatment. The mental hygiene movement, which lasted from about 1900 to about 1945, was characterized by three main ideas (Fellin, 1996; Lin, 1995; USDHHS, 1999). First, people were becoming disillusioned with mental hospitals and the substandard conditions in many. Second, although institutionalization was not abandoned, alternative types of care such as specialized psychiatric units in hospitals were being developed. This paved the way for the next mental health movement (community mental health), which focused on treatment within the community context. Finally, the concept of "mental illness" began to replace "insanity," and psychotherapy as a treatment method gained in popularity. Chapter 13 discusses psychotherapy and mental health issues generally in greater detail.

Focus on Asian Immigration

The "progressive period" label notwithstanding, this era was not so progressive for Asians and Hispanics trying to enter the United States. The first Asian people to immigrate to the United States during the mid-19th century were Chinese, who came to the United States like many others seeking a better life (Jansson, 2005). They often performed "manual labor for farmers, manufacturers, miners, and the railroads" (Jansson, 2005, p. 97). Chinese immigrants were easy to exploit. "They could be paid minimal wages (coercive tactics were used when they threatened to strike for higher wages) and used to depress the wages of white workers, and they did not constitute a political threat because as 'aliens' and people of color they were denied legal rights. (The California Supreme Court ruled in 1854 that Chinese people could not testify in court against whites, even if one of their number had been murdered by a white citizen.) They were disallowed from owning mines by tax levies, could not become citizens, were required to attend segregated schools, and could not vote" (Jansson, 2005, p. 97). Blatant racism and apprehension that Chinese immigrants were stealing jobs away from their white counterparts resulted in the Chinese Exclusion Act of 1882, which denied them further access to the country (Balgopal, 1995; Day, 2000; Jansson, 2005; Lum, 1995).

Japanese immigrants soon began to replace the Chinese in the U.S. labor market (Jansson, 2005). Like the Chinese, they were the victims of stereotypes and discrimination; for example, their children, too, attended segregated schools, they were prohibited from marrying interracially, laws banned the ownership of land, unions prohibited their entry into certain skilled trades, and instead they were diverted into manual labor jobs less appealing to white employees (Murase, 1995). Japanese immigration soon began to be politically discouraged, and finally the

Immigration Act of 1924 halted Asian immigration almost altogether, a state of affairs lasting until 1968 (Day, 2000). This act limited the number of immigrants allowed from any particular nationality to 2% of that nationality's population living in the United States in 1890. The effect was a greater percentage of people of Northern European heritage being admitted because a greater percentage already lived in the United States; because few Japanese lived in the United States during 1890, few were subsequently allowed admission (Jansson, 2005).

Focus on Chicano/a and Puerto Rican Immigration

Initiated by the Mexican Revolution of 1910, a "major wave" of Chicano/a "merchants, landowners, and professionals, as well as laborers" entered the United States as refugees (Curiel, 1995, p. 1234). As many as a million Chicanos/as migrated to the United States between 1910 and 1930 (Curiel, 1995; Meier, 1990). Substantial immigration continued across a 2,000-mile, relatively open boundary until 1924 when the U.S. Border Patrol was born; even then people continued to cross over to work on farms, orchards, and ranches and in food-processing plants (Jansson, 2005). White farmers and businessmen promoted Chicano/a immigration. Hiring migrant labor was much cheaper than employing other citizens at minimum wage. No legal consequences existed for employers who hired people without documentation even if these employers were fully aware of their status. Employers did not concern themselves with the workers' conditions and could readily discourage protests.

When the Great Depression (described next) shook the economy in the 1930s, many Americans, including Chicanos, lost their jobs and found themselves desperately competing for survival (Curiel, 1995). To decrease the economic pressure entire Chicano families were abruptly deported; shockingly, it is estimated that half of the deportees were U.S. citizens (Curiel, 1995).

Puerto Ricans migrated to the United States throughout the 20th century. (Highlight 6.6 provides a brief history of Puerto Rico.) Upon obtaining U.S. citizenship in 1917, Puerto Ricans gained the ability to readily travel back and forth without constraints.

The Great Depression and the 1930s

The Great Depression was initiated by the shocking stock market crash of 1929. The general trend over the next decade was an increasing reliance on the federal government to control and provide social services (Leiby, 1987). The Great Depression of the 1930s had a global impact, obliterating the idea that individuals control their own destiny. It became clear that the world contained various macro systems that worked together to profoundly affect individual lives. The United States was plagued by huge decreases in manufacturing productivity and wages, on the one hand, and skyrocketing unemployment, on the other. Banks closed, farmers lost everything, and urban poverty spread (Garvin & Tropman, 1998). Highlight 6.7 focuses on more of the Depression's consequences.

HIGHLIGHT 6.6
A Brief History of Puerto Rico

Campos (1995) presents a thumbnail sketch of Puerto Rico's history. The Taino Indians were the original inhabitants of Puerto Rico, which became a Spanish possession after Christopher Columbus "discovered" it in 1493. (Note how condescending the word *discovered* is when the island had probably been occupied for many centuries.) The Spanish conquerors believed that gold was plentiful on the island and coerced the Indians into working the mines. Poor treatment resulted in many Indian deaths, while others escaped the island entirely. When the available gold supply was exhausted, the Spaniards turned to agriculture, bringing in African slaves to work in the fields. Slavery was finally abolished in 1875.

The 19th century saw increased immigration to Puerto Rico from China, Spain, and other European countries, which together with the existing Spanish, Indian, and African residents resulted in a significantly diverse population (Campos, 1995). In 1898, after the Spanish-American War ended, Spain gave Puerto Rico to the United States under the Treaty of Paris of 1899. No Puerto Rican representatives were allowed to participate in this process or to influence what was to happen to their country. Puerto Rico then came under U.S. military rule until the U.S. president appointed an American governor two years later.

Many Puerto Ricans, who attained U.S. citizenship in 1917 under the Jones Act, expressed ambivalence about that new status. One faction felt it was an asset, while another preferred that Puerto Rico pursue independence. It wasn't until 1950 that Puerto Ricans were allowed to write their own constitution; in 1952 they could first elect their own governor and legislature.

Currently, a close relationship exists between Puerto Rico and the United States where both are committed to a common citizenship, legal tender, protection, and the value of democracy. Practically speaking, the United States retains control over specified arenas including "military defense," "foreign affairs, and federal agencies" (e.g., the U.S. Post Office) (Campos, 1995, p. 1246). Puerto Rico has primary control over its educational system, budget, governing laws, and correctional system.

President Franklin Delano Roosevelt (holding office from 1933 to 1945) aggressively addressed the crisis. In 1933 he initiated the *New Deal*, a vigorous plan that created a wide range of social programs and significantly extended federal control in social welfare matters. Reid (1995) contends that the New Deal established a new perspective on how a welfare state operates that still is in effect today.

Early Initiatives of the New Deal

In view of the social and economic crisis, Roosevelt initiated a range of programs to address people's dire needs. The New Deal's basic philosophy was "relief for the unemployed through provision of jobs. Direct relief was to be a temporary, necessary expedient until those who were employable could be employed" (Axinn & Stern, 2001, p. 185). Roosevelt pursued a three-pronged approach involving "cash relief, short-term work relief, and the expansion of employment" by hiring unemployed

HIGHLIGHT 6.7

Human Conditions During the Great Depression

Jansson (2005) lists some of the immediate consequences of the Depression:

- People from all levels of socioeconomic status were affected.
- Some families were forced to leave their homes and live in tents, and some had to share a small apartment with at least two other families.
- Single women clustered together in a single residence and often were compelled to depend on a single wage earner for sustenance.
- People raised crops in home gardens when they couldn't afford to buy food.

- Teenagers were booted from their homes to fend for themselves when families couldn't afford to support them.
- Middle-class citizens "feared foreclosure or evictions" and "had to pawn family possessions" to keep afloat.
- Starvation and malnutrition were rampant.
- Health care was often unavailable because people were denied care when they couldn't pay for it.
- Serious disturbances in family life and suicides were common occurrences. (pp. 172–173)

workers to undertake public works (Axinn & Stern, 2005, p. 190). The programs developed provide examples of what a government can do for its citizens during a national economic emergency.

The Federal Emergency Relief Act

In 1933 Roosevelt signed the Federal Emergency Relief Act (FERA), which provided federal grants to the states that would be administered by government units at the state and local levels to people in need. Although FERA's intent was to aid the unemployed, many working poor who could not earn enough to support their families also received aid. Additionally, it established camps for displaced persons, provided loans to college students, and purchased and sold 4 million acres of land to tenant farmers.

The Civilian Works Administration

Shortly after FERA was signed into law, Roosevelt assumed his presidential prerogative and created the Civilian Works Administration (CWA) in 1933. CWA channeled funds to finance various public works such as building roads, cataloging resources in libraries, digging drainage ditches, and renovating parks. The intent, of course, was to create jobs.

The Civilian Conservation Corps

Another program developed as part of the New Deal was the Civilian Conservation Corps (CCC), also created in 1933. This program initially recruited males between 18 and 25 who were receiving public assistance, and transported them to revitalize parks in the West and participate in reforestation, flood prevention, and fire control projects. Once again, the intent was to provide employment to a population that had an exceptionally high unemployment rate. Similarly, the National Youth Administration (NYA) provided part-time work for high school and college students to encourage them to remain in school.

The Public Works Administration

In 1935 Roosevelt established the Public Works Administration (PWA). PWA's intent was to "stimulate depressed industries" by contracting with private businesses to build public facilities, thereby increasing the number of available jobs (Barker, 2003, p. 351). Projects tended to be extensive and complex, such as "airports, dams, flood control projects, and military installations" (Jansson, 2005, p. 182).

The Works Progress Administration

Similarly, in 1935 Roosevelt established the Works Progress Administration (WPA) (renamed the Works Projects Administration in 1939). This was yet another program designed to provide work for unemployed people with various skills. One thrust was to support the "work of artists, musicians, writers, and scholars" (Barker, 2003, p. 468). WPA also provided jobs in a wide range of activities, from "heavy construction [of dams, bridges, parks, roads, and airports] to the painting of murals in local libraries and orchestral performances in the schools" (Axinn & Stern, 2005, p. 191; Jansson, 2005).

An End to the Programs

FERA, along with CWA, was terminated when the Social Security Act of 1935 was passed; CCC, NYA, PWA, and WPA saw their demise in the early 1940s at the beginning of World War II. Much of the legislation passed during the Depression was not intended to be permanent; rather, its purpose was to provide temporary jobs so people could support themselves during those hard times instead of being forced to accept charity (Ambrosino, Hefferman, Shuttlesworth, & Ambrosino, 2005).

The Social Security Act of 1935

The most notable piece of legislation shaping social welfare policy during this period was the Social Security Act of 1935. Consisting of 11 titles (or major parts, each of which addresses a specified issue and program), this legislation totally reconfigured the social welfare system and placed the burden on the federal government to provide a coordinated system of resources. It established a structure of benefits in three major categories: (1) social insurance, (2) public assistance, and (3) health services ("federal monies for state and local public health works") (Tice & Perkins, 2002, p. 156). (Note that, because of their significance, Chapter 8 elaborates upon current policies and programs in greater detail. Although the Social Security Act of 1935 forms the basis for current policies and programs, numerous modifications and additions to the social welfare system have been made since that time.)

Federal legislation affects service provision in two basic ways. First, it provides federal funding to states to help them pay for programs and services. Without federal help, states often wouldn't have the money for many resources and services.

Second, federal legislation imposes rules on the states that receive funding. If a state wants federal money, it must abide by the rules or forfeit the funding. All states want money. Therefore, federal legislation has set the stage for the types of programs that states must provide by making rules and establishing requirements to receive funding.

Social Insurance

Social insurance and public assistance both provide *financial benefits*—benefits in the form of cash or coupons that can be used in place of cash. *Social insurance* is a government program providing benefits related to certain designated risks working people assume; these include "old age, disability, death of a breadwinner, unemployment, and work-related injury and sickness" (Barker, 2003, p. 404). It's a type of insurance because workers and their employers pay premiums while they're working. They then receive benefits when encountering the specified conditions permitting benefits. The idea is that benefits are people's *right:* They worked and paid the premiums, and so deserve the benefits.

The Social Security Act established old age insurance (pensions) for the elderly, in addition to unemployment insurance and worker's compensation for the unemployed (Tice & Perkins, 2002). Unemployment insurance provides cash benefits to employees who lose their jobs. Workers' compensation gives cash benefits to employees who suffer work-related injuries or illness.

Public Assistance

In contrast to social insurance, *public assistance* programs are based on *need*. Public assistance is a government program providing financial resources to people who can't support themselves. The Social Security Act established public assistance for the elderly (Old Age Assistance), dependent children in single-parent families and children with disabilities (Aid to Dependent Children), and people who are blind (Aid to the Blind) (Tice & Perkins, 2002, pp. 154–156).

Often there is much greater stigma attached to people receiving public assistance than to those receiving social insurance. Many feel that it's their own fault that they're needy and that they should do something about it. Unlike people receiving social insurance, the argument goes, they never paid premiums for public assistance and so don't really deserve benefits. (Note that people receiving public assistance may also be eligible for social insurance benefits, depending on their work history and status.)

In reality, through no fault of their own, many people are in serious need of help—including many children. Although they are treated as a scourge primarily because of the costs, public assistance programs currently pay less than 25% of the total benefits paid by social insurance (U.S. Census Bureau, 2003, p. 357). Highlight 6.8 focuses on public assistance for children and families.

War and Wealth: The 1940s

The U. S. involvement in World War II (1941–1945) brought an end to the Depression as unemployment plummeted and incomes rose significantly (Axinn & Stern, 2005). Many people felt optimistic about the future and believed that the Social Security Act had adequately solved most of the problems related to poverty.

HIGHLIGHT 6.8

Public Assistance for Children and Families

The Social Security Act of 1935 expanded the government's responsibility for the well-being of children and their families. Title IV, Aid to Dependent Children (ADC) (later changed to Aid to Families with Dependent Children [AFDC] in 1962 to emphasize the importance of the family), "provided public relief to needy children through cash grants to their families"; another provision, Title V, broadened the role of the Children's Bureau to provide greater protection for children at risk of poverty, maltreatment, or delinquency (Karger & Stoesz, 2002, p. 419). The current public assistance program, which replaced AFDC in 1996, is Temporary Assistance for Needy Families (TANF), discussed further along with other public assistance programs in Chapter 8.

A significant piece of 1940s legislation was the Serviceman's Readjustment Act of 1944, commonly referred to as the G.I. Bill. Its purpose was to give veterans opportunities for "education and training, home and business loans, and employment services" to help them return to civilian life (Segal & Brzuzy, 1998, p. 33).

It is beyond the scope of this chapter to discuss the intricacies of World War II. However, the history of social welfare includes not only policies providing services that enhance people's welfare but also those depriving people of resources and even causing them harm. Unfair, racist treatment is of special concern to social workers. Highlight 6.9 addresses the atrocious and unjust treatment of Japanese Americans during World War II.

 ## Peace and Complacency: The 1950s

During the 1950s, the population exploded, resulting in the current huge bloc of aging baby boomers. (Chapter 10 addresses issues related to the elderly more thoroughly.) Many people think of the 1950s as a period of domestic complacency and relative conservatism. Criticisms of social welfare policy at the time focused on restricting eligibility for benefits and making it difficult to continue getting them (Axinn & Stern, 2001).

For example, one social worker employed in a county public assistance program during those years reflects on how policies urged workers to literally look under beds and in closets to determine if "there was a man in the house." Two somewhat conflicting assumptions were at work (Axinn & Stern, 2001). First, it was assumed that a legally unattached man living in the home of a family receiving benefits made the home morally unsuitable for raising children. Second, such a man should be able to provide support for the family so it would no longer require benefits. (Focus on Critical Thinking 6.2 poses some questions regarding the appropriateness of these policies.) A California Supreme Court decision in 1967 effectively ended such policies when the court determined that workers could not be fired for failing to comply with such

HIGHLIGHT 6.9

Japanese American Internment During World War II

On December 7, 1941, Japan bombed Pearl Harbor, and the United States entered the war the following day. Within days, Japanese Americans were placed under close and hostile public scrutiny. A few weeks later, California declared that Japanese Americans could no longer assume any civil service positions including holding public office. Japanese American citizens were fired from their jobs, forced to close their businesses, unlawfully confined, and even viciously assaulted (Day, 2000).

Although Roosevelt declared that all German, Italian, and Japanese aliens should leave the West Coast, only Japanese Americans were pressured to remain away more permanently (Day, 2000). Japanese American soldiers were identified and discharged or assigned menial labor like kitchen work.

By the fall of 1942, permanent detention (concentration) camps called "relocation centers" were established throughout the West, especially in California. With no trial or due process, over 112,000 Japanese Americans, two-thirds of whom were citizens, were forced to leave their homes and live in guarded camps until their release in 1944.

The secretary of the treasury charged the Federal Reserve Bank of San Francisco to look after Japanese American property, and the Farm Security Administration was supposed to do the same for Japanese farms and equipment. However, little, if anything, was done. The detainees lost $400 million worth of property, of which less than 10% was ever returned (Day, 2000).

rules (Axinn & Stern, 2002; *Benny Max Parrish v. the Civil Service Commission of the County of Alameda*, 1967). Later court decisions eliminated man-in-the-house rules altogether (*King v. King*, 1968; *Shapiro v. Thompson*, 1969).

Amendments to the Social Security Act

A major 1950 piece of social welfare legislation involved amendments to the Social Security Act. Public assistance coverage was broadened to include people who had temporary and permanent disabilities through a program entitled Aid to the Disabled (later called Aid to the Permanently and Totally Disabled) (Tice & Perkins, 2002). Additionally, the ADC program was expanded to provide benefits to primary caregivers of dependent children (Axinn & Stern, 2001).

The End of School Segregation

In a landmark ruling in 1954 in *Brown v. Board of Education*, the Supreme Court overturned the "separate but equal" doctrine and declared that racial segregation in public schools was unconstitutional—even when separate schools provided the same quality of education. Although this decision paved the way for stopping blatant racial discrimination in various other public settings such as train and bus stations, restaurants, and recreational facilities, it took many years of struggle to effectively put this principle into practice (Pollard, 1995).

FOCUS ON CRITICAL THINKING 6.2

Personal Rights of Assistance Recipients

Critical thinking involves the three-step, Triple-A process: (1) *ask* questions, (2) *assess* facts, and (3) *assert* a conclusion. How would you answer the following questions?

- To what extent should the government be allowed to intervene in the personal lives of people who receive financial assistance?
- To what extent should the government be allowed to intervene in the personal lives of its employees?

- To what extent should the government be allowed to intervene in your personal life?
- How should governmental intervention differ, if at all, concerning its involvement in the lives of people receiving assistance or people it employs, or in your own life?
- To what extent is the assumption true that a man romantically involved with a mother should be expected to provide her and her family financial support? To what extent, if any, does this reflect a sexist approach?

Focus on Mental Health: The Deinstitutionalization Movement

After World War II, the third mental health movement of the last century gained momentum, and it continues to characterize mental health service provision to this day (Fellin, 1996). The *deinstitutionalization* movement (following the mental hygiene movement) focuses on providing services and care for people within their own communities rather than in institutional settings (Fellin, 1996; Lin, 1995; USDHH, 1999). It stresses placing people back in the community and providing mental health treatment and services to them there. The deinstitutionalization movement resulted from the increasing belief that, with outpatient psychotherapeutic treatment and psychotropic drugs (i.e., drugs intended to affect mental or emotional functioning), people with mental illness could function in the community environment (Fellin, 1996; USDHHS, 1999). This effort has also been referred to as the *community mental health movement.*

 ## The 1960s and the War on Poverty

Any sense of optimism or complacency in the 1950s began to weaken as the 1960s began and poverty remained a large problem. Three dynamics shaped this view (Axinn & Stern, 2002). First, large pockets of poverty characterized various regions of the country, and attention was focused on what could be done to ameliorate this poverty. For example, "[i]f the people of Appalachia suffered from the decrease of jobs in coal mining, then the expansion of factory employment seemed appropriate" (Axinn & Stern, 2002, p. 238). Questions might be raised regarding what could be done to stimulate employment and industrial growth in that area.

A second dynamic shaping the nation's perspective on poverty involved the fact that the risk of poverty for people of color was significantly greater than for whites.

People of color clearly experienced regular discrimination in employment throughout the country.

The third dynamic concerning poverty involved the fact that public assistance rolls were escalating even as unemployment decreased. Prior to the 1960s, the two had a correlated relationship. That is, when unemployment was low, public assistance rolls declined because more people were working. But now this was no longer the case. Public assistance rolls were escalating regardless of whether employment was available.

The Public Welfare Amendments of 1962

Under the administration of President John F. Kennedy (serving from 1961 until his assassination in 1963), significant new amendments to the Social Security Act were passed. The Public Welfare Amendments of 1962 were rooted in the idea that supportive social services would enhance welfare recipients' ability to get back on their feet and eventually become self-supporting. Services included job training, job placement, and counseling, among others (Trattner, 1999).

The act directed the federal government to assume 75% of the cost of providing social services to people receiving public assistance. This was a tremendous incentive for states to provide services because they had to assume only 25% of the financial burden for doing so. The idea was to reduce welfare rolls. Unfortunately, this did not work, and welfare rolls continued to escalate.

The "Great Society"

During the 1960s, President Lyndon B. Johnson (whose administration lasted from 1963 to 1969) initiated the "War on Poverty" in an effort to fashion a "Great Society." The intent was to eliminate poverty and provide a high quality of life for all. The War on Poverty was founded on the idea that what poor families really needed was encouragement and training to acquire needed job skills, allowing them to achieve economic independence (Leiby, 1987). However, the poor faced not only economic hardship, but also psychological and sociological barriers (e.g., prejudice and discrimination) to living effective, successful lives (Leiby, 1987). Some theorists referred to the poor as living in a *culture of poverty*—the pattern of values, norms, and expectations conveyed from one generation to another that limits people to a life of poverty and discourages them from taking advantage of economic and social opportunities (Barker, 2003; Karger & Stoesz, 2002). The War on Poverty intended for poor families to be offered and have greater access to the resources and services they needed to pursue economic independence and a better quality of life.

As a result, numerous new programs were developed at the federal level, as the War on Poverty was entirely a federal initiative (Leiby, 1987). The Economic Opportunity Act of 1964 established a range of programs including Volunteers in Service to America (VISTA) and Operation Head Start, among many others. Highlight 6.10 describes some of these programs. Primary efforts were concentrated on fighting poverty in poor neighborhoods and communities by increasing jobs, resources, and opportunities for residents (Karger & Stoesz, 1998). Such programs encouraged

HIGHLIGHT 6.10

The Economic Opportunity Act of 1964

The following programs were established when the Economic Opportunity Act, also referred to as the "antipoverty bill," was passed in 1964 (Trattner, 1999, p. 322):

- *Volunteers in Service to America (VISTA):* A program designed to recruit volunteers to work in urban and rural neighborhoods experiencing economic and cultural problems, and to assist residents in enhancing their communities.
- *Job Corps:* A program that recruited impoverished youths ages 16–24 from disadvantaged urban and rural communities, and provided them with "residential training, employment, and work skills" (Barker, 2003, p. 232).

- *Upward Bound:* A program targeting school-age children and presenting them with special educational resources and incentives to prevent them from dropping out of school.
- *Neighborhood Youth Corps:* A program employing teenagers in local organizations.
- *Operation Head Start:* A program giving preschoolers resources designed to meet educational, health, and recreational needs throughout the year.
- *Community Action Program (CAP):* A program that developed and coordinated efforts by neighborhood organizations to fight poverty and improve social and economic conditions for community residents. (Operation Head Start was initially funded and coordinated under the CAP program.)

citizen participation. This was a time of activism for professional social workers on behalf of various populations in need, reflecting a renewed optimism that poverty could be eliminated and a good quality of life enjoyed by all.

Many other initiatives were undertaken during the War on Poverty. For instance, the Food Stamp Act of 1964 initiated a program in which eligible needy families could receive coupons that could be exchanged for food. Another initiative involved greatly expanded coverage by the Social Security Act in 1965 to include Medicare (a social insurance program of health care for the elderly) and Medicaid (a public assistance program of health care for needy children and families). The Housing and Urban Development (HUD) Act of 1968 provided new low-income housing opportunities for eligible families. Chapter 8 describes all four of these programs in greater detail.

Amendments to the Social Security Act in 1967 reorganized resource and service distribution. These changes

> divorced income maintenance functions from social services functions and split public welfare departments into two sections: social services, whose workers provide counseling services and services to neglected, abused, or dependent children and older people; and assistance payments, whose workers determine eligibility and set amounts of grants based on state levels of need, number in family, and their own discretion. (Day, 2000, p. 320)

The driving force behind this change was the idea that "services to the poor should not be connected to whether they receive financial aid" (Day, 2000, p. 320).

Focus on Mental Health: The Community Mental Health Centers Act

In 1963 the Community Mental Health Centers Act was passed, providing federal funding for community "mental health centers, training programs, and outpatient treatment programs" (Barker, 1999, p. 19). This, of course, was a manifestation of the deinstitutionalization movement. However, problems arose for three reasons (Lin, 1995, p. 1706). First, treating people in the community was much more complicated and difficult than anticipated. Second, many professionals preferred not to work with this population with its long-term problems. Third, communities either did not have or would not commit the resources necessary to sustain community care. As a result, many people with mental illness ended up on the streets or in jail, for lack of better placement and services. These problems continue to this day.

Note that during the 1960s a trend toward legal advocacy developed (Lin, 1995). As a consequence of the civil rights movement, it focused on emphasizing and clarifying the rights of mental patients. Two court cases are particularly significant (Lin, 1995). In *Wyatt v. Stickney* (1971) a federal court ruled that mental patients should not be exposed to extreme or possibly damaging types of treatment. And in *O'Connor v. Donaldson* (1975) "the Supreme Court ruled that mental illness and need for treatment are not sufficient justification for involuntary confinement" (Lin, 1995, p. 1706).

Focus on the Elderly: The Older Americans Act of 1965

Unlike the Social Security Act, the Older Americans Act (OAA) of 1965 is not a policy to provide programming and resources directly to people. Rather, it establishes an "administrative structure" for the coordination and delivery of social services to older people (Barusch, 2002, p. 289; Dobelstein, 2003). The OAA created an Administration on Aging (AOA) under the auspices of the Department of Health, Education, and Welfare to oversee state and area offices throughout the country. Support for resources and services is based on "partnerships between federal, state, and local authorities" (Barusch, 2002, p. 287).

Benefits coordinated by AOA offices include transportation; provision of hot meals delivered to people's homes or provided at senior centers ("focus points" where seniors can gather for a variety of purposes); preventive health care such as inoculations or health education; recreation; home care (in which various services involving health, daily living support, or other social services are provided in people's own homes); information; and resource referral (Barusch, 2000; Dobelstein, 2003, p. 258). Anyone age 60 or over is eligible for services, regardless of their economic status. Because the focus is on coordination of services, not prescriptions about what should be provided, services vary dramatically from one location to the next (Dobelstein, 2003). Chapter 10 discusses service provision to the elderly in detail.

Civil Rights in the 1960s

The concept of *civil rights* "refers primarily to claims by African Americans and other minorities of color, women, and people of different sexual orientations to be free to do the same kinds of things and have the same kinds of civil entitlements that everyone else in the society enjoyed" (Garvin & Tropman, 1998, p. 255).

During the early 1960s, "[p]overty was widespread in America, and nonwhite people were systematically discriminated against in all facets of American life" (Day, 2000, p. 308). It might be said that the civil rights movement actually began in 1955 when organizers selected a young African American minister named Martin Luther King, Jr., to spearhead a bus boycott in Montgomery, Alabama (Jansson, 2005). The protesters refused to comply with the public policy whereby African Americans were relegated to the backs of buses while whites got to sit in the front. After a long period of controversy and conflict, including violent acts of retribution against African Americans, the policy was withdrawn.

The Civil Rights Act of 1964 was the most important piece of civil rights legislation since the Civil War. Pollard (1995) summarizes its major features:

> The act strengthened voting rights and mandated equal access in a number of key areas. Any program receiving federal funding was forbidden to discriminate on the basis of race, color, religion, or national origin. . . . The U.S. Department of Education was authorized to desegregate public education. The Civil Rights Commission was given expanded investigative power. The Equal Employment Opportunity Commission [EEOC] was established to oversee civil rights in employment. (p. 499)

Establishment of the EEOC was important because it provided a mechanism to enforce the new regulations. The Civil Rights Act of 1964 made it illegal to deprive African Americans of the right to vote on the basis of minor technicalities or policies aimed at discriminating against them (Day, 2000). Such practices had deprived them of political clout since they had gained the right to vote. The act also prohibited discrimination in employment and segregation in public places such as hotels, restaurants, and theaters (Barker, 2003; Day, 2000). Focus on Critical Thinking 6.3 raises some key questions concerning the act and the issues it addresses.

Focus on Mexican Americans: The Chicano/a Movement

No clearly defined dates exist for the "Chicano movement" (Curiel, 1995). During the 1960s, various Chicano/a groups came together to address their social and economic plight. Common goals included "the maintenance of an ethnic identity, the assertion of the positive value of Chicano culture," and "the improvement of the socioeconomic status of the group as a whole" (Curiel, 1995, p. 1235). A key issue involved how Chicano/a income levels continued to lag significantly behind those of their white counterparts.

FOCUS ON CRITICAL THINKING 6.3
Civil Rights

Consider the following questions:

- Why did it take so long to establish equal rights for people of color?
- If you were denied certain rights held by others on the basis of some personal characteristic, how would you feel?

- If you were forced to sit in the back of a bus because of some personal characteristic, how would you feel?
- How might you react to such circumstances?

Because Chicano/a agricultural laborers were prevented from joining labor unions, they lacked power and were deprived of economic opportunities to get ahead (Day, 2000). A leading political figure and vigorous advocate for the rights of farmworkers was Cesar E. Chavez. Born in 1927 in Yuma, Arizona, on a farm homesteaded by his grandfather in the 1880s, he was to become one of the most famous activists of the 20th century.

Chavez's family became migrant agricultural workers when they lost their farm during the Great Depression. At age 25, Chavez was picking apricots on a farm near San Jose, California, when a community organizer for a Hispanic-based self-help group, the Community Service Organization, recruited him to work for the grassroots (i.e., sponsored directly by citizens) organization. He began working part-time, went on to work full-time, and eventually became the organization's director.

In 1962, when the Community Service Organization ignored his pleas to advocate more intensively on the behalf of farmworkers, Chavez quit and founded the National Farm Workers Association (NFWA). He then traveled from farm to farm and camp to camp, recruiting members and urging workers to strive for fair wages and improved health conditions. In addition to better wages, issues included providing rest breaks, making clean drinking water available, prohibiting dangerous pesticide use, and providing protection from agricultural hazards. In 1965 the NFWA initiated a successful five-year strike and boycott against grape growers. In 1966 it became affiliated with the American Federation of Labor–Congress of Industrial Organizations (AFL–CIO), the oldest and most extensive labor union in the United States.

Chavez continued leading vital advocacy efforts on the behalf of farmworkers until his death in 1993 at the age of 66. He was "the first Chicano leader to achieve nationwide recognition, and he became a national symbol of social justice for both Chicanos and non-Chicanos" (Curiel, 1995, p. 1235).

Focus on American Indians: Striving for Self-Determination

As with other population groups, the 1960s reflected the beginning of a more progressive era for Native Americans in their quest for self-determination. Despite the fact that policies enacted in the 1950s aimed at *terminating* the special status

Cesar Chavez was a powerful advocate for Chicano farm laborers.

of and benefits for certain tribes, and even breaking up reservations, these were eventually abandoned during the 1960s. The 1960s began a period of activism in which "Native American protest groups formed to assert their rights" (Tice & Perkins, 2002, p. 212).

Tice and Perkins (2002) indicate

> The most famous of these groups, the American Indian Movement (AIM), staged protests at Alcatraz in 1969, by then an unoccupied prison island, and in 1973 at Wounded Knee on Pine Ridge Reservation. In the former instance, AIM was trying to exercise its claimed treaty rights to unused federal lands. The protesters were removed in 1971. At Wounded Knee, they were armed and protesting the domination of the tribal government by whites. This action ended in violence as federal civilian and military forces took control of the reservation. Two Native Americans were killed and two federal officials wounded. (p. 212)

The struggle for self-determination continues today (Lewis, 1995). Morales and Sheafor (2002) state that current "federal policies are promoting self-determination and self-governance of Native American affairs by the Native peoples themselves. . . . American Indian professional organizations are working in collaborative efforts on behalf of many American Indian needs and causes" (p. 245).

Lewis (1995) is more skeptical, declaring that "[e]conomic, social, and political changes will not occur until there is a solid recognition among policymakers that American Indian people represent a departure from mainstream values and worldviews" (p. 224).

A Return to Conservatism in the 1970s

As the 1960s ended, so did the War on Poverty. The public was sick of the seemingly endless spending and questionable results. Johnson also had been battered by intense opposition to the Vietnam War and was increasingly unpopular in the polls. As a result, he withdrew from the presidential race, which was then won by Richard M. Nixon (who served from 1969 until his resignation in 1974). Nixon and subsequent presidents Gerald Ford (serving from 1974 to 1977) and Jimmy Carter (serving from 1977 to 1981) "were relatively conservative presidents who had little outward interest in major social reforms. Yet, social spending rose dramatically during this . . . [supposedly] conservative period" (Jansson, 2005, p. 273).

Old Age, Survivors, Disability, and Health Insurance

One notable change in social welfare benefit provision occurred in 1971 when it was proposed that the public assistance programs Old Age Assistance, Aid to the Blind, and Aid to the Permanently and Totally Disabled became social insurance programs. In 1972 these programs were replaced by the Supplementary Security Income (SSI) program. Because social insurance programs provide benefits to workers and their families based on their *right* to them rather than their *need*, recipient rolls soared. The changes obviously reflected a shift in public opinion regarding who was considered needy and who had the right to receive benefits without question. Elderly people and people with disabilities automatically received benefits without having to prove they were poor enough to need such resources.

Focus on Social Welfare Policies Concerning Child and Family Welfare

Despite conservative times, one emerging concern involved child abuse and neglect. LeVine and Sallee (1999) describe conditions from the 1950s to 1970s: "[T]he majority of services to children were financial in nature and not treatment oriented. Furthermore, what services and counseling children received were inconsistent and unorganized. Thus child abuse and neglect were 'rediscovered' in the late 1960s and early 1970s" (p. 31).

In 1974 the Child Abuse Prevention and Treatment Act was passed in response to increasing public concern about child maltreatment. To receive funding, states must establish a centralized reporting agency, collect systematic data about child maltreatment, and pass laws to protect children under age 18 from maltreatment (Liederman, 1995).

In 1975 Title XX of the Social Security Act was passed; it "provides federal funding to states to assist children and families in crisis" (Liederman, 1995, p. 428). One of its major goals was to prevent institutionalization of children (Barker, 2003; Levine & Sallee, 1999).

The Indian Child Welfare Act of 1978 addressed the importance of maintaining children's racial and cultural identity. It reflected a response to concerns that

American Indian children were being removed from their homes and placed in non–American Indian foster family and adoptive homes. The concern was that the linkage with their heritage, customs, and cultural identity was being severed. The act thus required that American Indian children be placed in homes that nurture the distinctive values, customs, and heritage of American Indian culture (Liederman, 1995).

The 1980 Adoption Assistance and Child Welfare Act had an impact on programs for children and families in two significant ways (Liederman, 1995). First, federal funding helped states assess, treat, and prevent child maltreatment. Second, funding was made available to states to help them pay for out-of-home care for children when necessary. This legislation also stressed the importance of *permanency planning* for children—that is, finding them a permanent home as soon as possible when return to their birth parents is not viable.

 # Conservative Extremes in the 1980s and Early 1990s

President Ronald Reagan (serving from 1981 to 1989) launched an overt return to conservative social welfare policies. Reagan "discounted the importance of racism and discrimination" and maintained that, "if they tried," African Americans, Hispanics, and American Indians could become just as successful as whites (Jansson, 2005, p. 308). He viewed American males as rugged individualists who could accomplish almost anything if they tried. Similarly, he ascribed to women "primarily domestic functions" and failed to appoint many women to significant positions of power during his presidency (or his California governorship in the 1960s and 1970s) (Barrett, 1983; Jansson, 2005, pp. 308–309). His primary accomplishments were (1) reducing taxes, (2) significantly increasing the defense budget, and (3) slashing social welfare spending (Haynes, 1991).

Reagan's frugal social welfare policies continued during President George H. W. Bush's term (from 1989 to 1993). Results included significant increases in the numbers of people living in poverty, in homelessness, in the numbers of public assistance recipients, and racial tension leading to various confrontations (Karger & Stoesz, 1998).

Focus on People with Disabilities: 1990s Legislation

Two positive pieces of legislation passed in the 1990s are of special significance for people with developmental or other disabilities in terms of improving access to resources (DeWeaver, 1995). The Americans with Disabilities Act of 1990 requires that public buildings, areas, and workplaces provide ready access to people with physical or mental disabilities. The intent is to let them actively involve themselves in everyday life as readily as possible.

The second important piece of legislation is the Developmental Disabilities Assistance and Bill of Rights Act of 1990. This law accomplishes several things—including establishing grant programs for, promoting advocacy on behalf of, and requiring adequate services for people with developmental disabilities (DeWeaver, 1995). Chapter 11 discusses both pieces of legislation more thoroughly.

Welfare Reform in the Clinton Era

When Bill Clinton was elected president in 1992 (his service ending in 2001), liberals hoped for positive changes in social welfare policy. However, he faced a Senate and House of Representatives dominated by Republicans as early as 1994, so most of his proposals were squelched. His overall performance was deemed middle-of-the-road instead of liberal, his achievements in domestic social welfare policy being "relatively modest" (Jansson, 2005, p. 398).

A major example of a conservative policy established during his presidency is the Personal Responsibility and Work Opportunities Act of 1996, which affects public assistance, SSI, immigrants' ability to receive benefits, child care, and nutritional and food programs. One of its facets, Temporary Assistance for Needy Families (TANF), described more thoroughly in Chapter 8, greatly restricts benefits compared to the program preceding it (Aid to Families with Dependent Children [AFDC]). TANF essentially changed "welfare as we know it" by placing time limits on benefits, allowing states great discretion in benefit distribution, and establishing stringent work requirements.

Additional significant pieces of legislation implemented during the Clinton era were the Family and Medical Leave Act of 1993 and the Crime Bill of 1994 (Jansson, 2005; Marx, 2004). The Family and Medical Leave Act requires that both public and private employers with 50 or more employees provide each employee up to 12 weeks of unpaid annual leave after a birth or child adoption, while caring for an ill family member, or during recuperation from illness (Axinn & Stern, 2005). Although health benefits must continue, the fact that the time is unpaid discourages many people from using this option. Leave only applies to caring for a spouse, child, or parent; others like a mother-in-law or a partner don't qualify (Axinn & Stern, 2005). The 1994 Crime Bill increased funding for hiring more police officers and building more prisons, in addition to enacting federal penalties and developing social services to decrease domestic violence (Jansson, 2005).

The Conservatism of George W. Bush

The election of George W. Bush in 2000 and his reelection in 2004 marks an era of what he terms "compassionate conservatism." This is the philosophy that although government should not interfere directly with people's lives, it should help people to help themselves. The compassionate part involves the fact that people should be helped. The conservative part concerns the idea that people should be responsible for their own actions and lives. Bush's presidency has been characterized by at least three major themes (Blau, 2004; Jansson, 2005).

First is the emphasis on homeland security. Domestic and foreign policy have been critically intertwined during his terms because of the costs involved. With a finite amount of money available, spending in one area limits funding available to finance other areas. After two airplanes slammed into the World Trade Center towers on September 11, 2001, Bush initiated a "war on terrorism" and established a Homeland Security Agency. Despite no solid evidence, Bush maintained that Iraqi leaders were concealing weapons of mass destruction and that there were relationships between Iraq and the Afghanistan terrorist organization Al Qaeda (which took responsibility for the September 11 attack) (Jansson, 2005). Bush demanded information about the alleged weapons, failed to get enough for his satisfaction, and declared war on Iraq in spring 2003, despite little international support. Although Bush declared victory on May 1, the costs involved to maintain control and to rebuild the social and political infrastructures have skyrocketed far beyond initial projections (Jansson, 2005). Money spent on the war and security issues takes potential funding away from many social programs in addition to escalating the national debt. Bush initiated huge increases in defense spending while concurrently slashing spending on domestic programs (Jansson, 2005).

A second theme characterizing Bush's presidency is the push to trim the federal government and give more decision-making capabilities to the states. Critics of this trend caution that this results in inconsistent access to resources and programs, in addition to greater inequities between the "haves" and "have nots."

A third theme involves shifting service provision from the public to the private sector. Bush maintains that private organizations and businesses are generally more efficient than government agencies and give people a wider range of choices (Jansson, 2005). Bush has also supported "faith-based initiatives" in which public funding would go to religious organizations. Although many religious organizations have a long history of providing effective social services, those receiving public funding have always carefully separated service provision from religious activities (Jansson, 2005). Bush proposed allowing such organizations greater freedom in terms of how they spend funding and combine these two facets. Critics of this view question the validity of using public funds to sponsor religious activities and wonder how such activities could be monitored for fairness and objectivity. A problem with financing religious activities with public funding involves a basic right to religious freedom. Which religious services should be supported? Those sponsored by Christians, Muslims, Roman Catholics, Jews, Buddhists, Episcopalians, Unitarians? To what extent should public taxes finance religious doctrines and projects in which not everyone believes?

Bush has also supported the *privatization* of Social Security, in which employees would be allowed to pursue their own investment plans instead of paying Social Security taxes. Critics of this plan raise the following questions (Ip, 2004): What proportion of traditional Social Security taxes should be made available for private investment? To what extent will most people be able to make sound investment decisions, especially in unpredictable markets? Would people face much greater risk of losing most or all of their benefits because of private investment strategies? Would traditional benefits be significantly cut because of less money being directed into the traditional Social Security system? Chapter 10 discusses these issues in greater depth.

One piece of legislation that has been quite controversial is the Medicare Modernization Act (MMA) of 2003, taking full effect in 2006, which includes the Medicare prescription drug benefit. As the name implies, the intent was to "modernize" the Medicare program, a highly debatable point. Chapter 8 discusses the MMA in greater detail, focusing on the controversial prescription drug program.

FOCUS ON CRITICAL THINKING 6.4

What Are Future Issues in Social Welfare?

Since the September 11, 2001, destruction of the World Trade Center, attention has been focused on the "war on terrorism" and on the aftermath of the war in Iraq. Many resources are being diverted to national and international security and to supporting troops. What effects will this have on domestic social welfare programs?

Specific issues include the following:

• Should Social Security be privatized, so that workers could invest funds however they saw fit, instead of the government holding funds and making investment and spending decisions, as is now the case?

• What should be done about rapidly escalating health care costs, especially for the huge number of citizens with no health insurance? To what extent is universal national health insurance coverage, available at little or no cost to everyone, an option?

• What is the future of Medicare in view of the increasing proportion of elderly people compared with working people, who support Medicare through taxes? What will happen when more people receive benefits from a much smaller contributing pool?

• What will happen to children and families currently receiving public assistance when their time-limited benefits end?

• To what extent should we continue to build new prisons to house an ever-increasing number of inmates at enormous public expense instead of focusing on treatment and rehabilitation?

• What should be done about the scarcity of low-cost housing and the large population of homeless people roaming the streets?

• Where should spending priorities be placed? On the "war on terrorism"? Supporting troops on an international level? Cutting the national deficit? Expanding social programs?

When Bush first took office he initiated and succeeded in getting a huge tax cut. The rationale was that giving money back to people would stimulate the economy because they would spend that money, which would in turn benefit business and the economy. However, critics maintained that the cut would have little effect on the economy because it primarily benefited the wealthy, who wouldn't spend the money anyway; in reality, 1% of the population received 40% of the tax benefits (Jansson, 2005). Giving money to the rich and taking programs and benefits away from the poor increases inequity and the chasm between the rich and the poor.

Focus on Critical Thinking 6.4 raises some issues to consider for the future of social welfare.

The Development of the Social Work Profession

The time line at the beginning of this chapter contained major events in the development of the social work profession, which is integrally involved with the progression of social welfare history. To some extent, social work's roots can be traced to the settlement house and charity organization movements.

Despite the different paths taken by the two movements, "social work pioneers were clear about the primary commitment owed to the poorest and most oppressed and disenfranchised members of our population" (Landon, 1995, p. 1101). Social work education actually began in 1898 "when the New York Charity Organization Society offered a summer training course for charity workers" (Beless, 1995, p. 635). In the early 20th century, social workers continued to seek a professional identity regarding what social work practice involved. The emphasis on scientific advances and the enticing new therapeutic approaches introduced during the first half of the century (e.g., psychodynamic and social learning theories) strengthened the profession's commitment to social casework (Landon, 1995). Social casework stressed therapeutically helping individuals and families solve their problems. Thus the target of change was the individual or family.

The divergence between the settlement orientation, emphasizing group and community work, and the individually oriented charity organization approach remained strong. Therefore, three method tracks—casework, group work, and community organization—characterized social work through the 1950s. Casework was further fortified by developing fields of practice or specializations that were generally incorporated under its umbrella. These included medical social work, psychiatric social work, child welfare, and school social work (Brieland, 1995).

Early Development of Social Work Education

Beless (1995, p. 635) describes the initial development of formal social work education in the United States. In 1919, 17 U.S. and Canadian schools of social work joined together to form the Association of Training Schools for Professional Social Work. This organization soon changed its name to the American Association of Schools of Social Work (AASSW) and by 1927 had "developed educational requirements for membership in the organization" (p. 635). The AASSW also began developing criteria for what was considered adequate preparation for professional social work practice. These formed the foundation for the initial accreditation standards for master's degrees in social work education.

Accreditation is the recognition and confirmation that an organization like a nursing home, mental health center, university, or other social service provider meets specific standards developed to make certain that the services provided are appropriate and effective. Accreditation with respect to social work education means that accredited programs must comply with a range of standards. These address curricular content and structure, staffing, adherence to nondiscrimination policies, adequate financial support from the college or university, and other variables.

Social Work During the Great Depression

During the Great Depression, the Social Security Act switched many aspects of service provision from the private to the public sector. Thus the type of social work jobs available and the characteristics of people getting them shifted.

HIGHLIGHT 6.11

Social Work Accreditation at the Baccalaureate and Master's Levels

By 1942 several undergraduate social work programs had formed their own separate organization, the National Association of Schools of Social Administration (NASSA). By 1943 NASSA "was recognized as the official accrediting body for baccalaureate programs" that developed and oversaw their curricular and program standards (Beless, 1995, p. 635).

Having two accrediting bodies for social work education was awkward and confusing. Therefore, in 1946 a coordinating body, the National Council on Social Work Education (NCSWE), was created to research the situation and make suggestions for achieving better coordination and consistency. The subsequent report and recommendations resulted in the birth of the Council on Social Work Education (CSWE) in

1952, representing the merger of AASSW and NASSA (Beless, 1995). At this time, the first Curriculum Policy Statement and accreditation standards were issued that reflected new guidelines for master's education concerning curricular content and structure (Brieland, 1995). Additionally, students were required to "develop a social philosophy rooted in an appreciation of the essential dignity of human beings" (Brieland, 1995, p. 2255). Such a broad goal inferred that social work should be more than merely casework. Rather, social work should seek to benefit society in general and oppressed populations in particular. Although the CSWE's objective was to oversee social work education, at this time it viewed undergraduate education as "preprofessional" and declined to offer these programs accreditation.

Popple (1995) describes the change. Prior to the Depression, social work was close to becoming a profession of graduate degrees only. Popple (1995) explains: "The nature of the social worker's task was coming to be defined as . . . providing skilled casework services based on a thorough understanding of psychotherapy" (p. 2286). Many clients were not poor but suffered from other problems such as mental health. Efforts to change communities and social policies were most often overlooked.

The Depression changed all this, however. The Social Security Act spurred a massive increase in the number of social work jobs, the majority of which "involved helping basically well-adjusted people deal with problems brought about by unemployment" (Popple, 1995, p. 2287). Essentially, these jobs required different skills than the ability to perform therapy, as many master's degree social workers (MSWs) were doing. The need became evident for practitioners to work in the public sector assisting people in solving their problems, meeting their needs, and obtaining necessary resources—tasks unrelated to providing "therapy." Thus numerous bachelor's degree social workers (BSWs) were being employed in these jobs. However, MSWs refused to accept BSWs as professional colleagues, and AASSW would not acknowledge baccalaureate social work programs. Highlight 6.11 explores how accreditation for social work programs was established.

Social Work in the 1950s

We have established that the economy grew rapidly during and after World War II with the increased demand for production of goods. Despite the CSWE's call for social work to assume a broader role in seeking social justice (via its Curriculum Policy Statement and accreditation standards), the relative affluence of the 1950s once again encouraged social workers to turn to psychotherapy and casework (Popple, 1995). During this decade, 85% of social work students selected casework as their orientation of choice (Popple, 1995). MSWs dominated the scene, and BSW programs were not yet being accredited.

Formation of the National Association of Social Workers

In 1955 seven separate professional organizations came together to form the National Association of Social Workers (NASW) (Brieland, 1995). The intent was to provide "a major force to advance the profession" and look "toward a program that would be broader in scope and richer in content than any specialty organization could provide" (p. 1747). The following organizations participated in the merger (Brieland, 1995; Goldstein & Beebe, 1995).

- The American Association of Group Workers (founded in 1936).
- The American Association of Medical Social Workers (founded in 1918).
- The American Association of Psychiatric Social Workers (founded in 1926).
- The American Association of Social Workers (founded in 1921).
- The Association for the Study of Community Organization (founded in 1946).
- The National Association of School Social Workers (founded in 1919).
- The Social Work Research Group (founded in 1949).

The need for a unifying generalist approach was inherent in this merger. Many social work leaders and educators became increasingly concerned about the profession's commitment to rectifying social injustice and advocating on behalf of positive social change.

Social Work in the 1960s to the Early 1980s

The 1960s and the War on Poverty produced a new focus on social change versus individual pathology. Many came to realize that poverty and other vast social problems still existed in the United States. A series of federal administrations began implementing antipoverty programs. At first, these programs generally disregarded social workers because the intent was to empower the poor themselves (Popple, 1995). However, it soon became clear that expertise was needed "in community organization, administration, and direct service with clients" for programs to run effectively (Popple, 1995, p. 2288). As a result, most social work schools added "policy, planning, and administration specialties to their curricula" (Popple, 1995, p. 2289). This probably reflected the growing awareness of the importance of working with and within organizations as a major facet of generalist practice.

At this point, the social work profession faced a serious problem—namely, fewer than a quarter of all people holding social work jobs were identified as professional social workers because only they had MSW degrees (Popple, 1995). Needless to say, it did not enhance the profession's reputation or accountability that the vast majority of the people doing social work were not considered social workers. Thus a logical move was to emphasize the BSW as the viable entry-level qualification to the social work profession. People performing social work jobs should be social workers. CSWE began developing criteria for accrediting BSW programs in 1962 and finally offered accreditation to programs in 1974.

The prolific development of BSW programs in the late 1960s and early 1970s emphasized the need for a generalist foundation for social work practice (Landon, 1995). Many social work leaders began calling for a unified foundation for social work practice (Bartlett, 1970; Boehm, 1959) and referring to social work practice as occurring among various sized systems (Pincus & Minahan, 1973; Schwartz, 1961; Siporin, 1975). Social workers needed a broad base of skills to work with individuals, families, groups, organizations, and communities. Baccalaureate and master's programs required differentiation regarding purpose. The fact that CSWE made accreditation available to BSW programs in 1974 and required a generalist practice foundation for the BSW level of practice was a big forward step. Another important step occurred in 1984 when CSWE "declared that the required foundation material at both undergraduate and graduate levels should consist of the knowledge, values, and skills essential to generalist practice" (Landon, 1995, p. 1102).

Other important developments including the first NASW Code of Ethics in 1960, the establishment of Political Action for Candidate Election (PACE) in 1976, and increasing attention to BSW professionalism are illustrated by the time line introducing this chapter.

Social Work Today

Currently, the "profession has come to the more realistic position that the BSW is considered the entry-level degree and that the MSW provides advanced, specialized training" (Popple, 1995, p. 2290). (As later chapters will explain, BSWs can provide many services such as crisis intervention, case management, community organization, and the linking of clients with services while working with a wide range of populations. MSWs usually fulfill more specialized functions such as providing psychotherapy, working in supervision and administration, or assuming higher levels of decision-making responsibility.) Landon (1995) concludes that "generalist programming is embedded in the profession, both in practice and education" (p. 1106).

Looking Ahead

Social welfare and social work history pave the way for today's social welfare policy and programs. The time line in Figure 6.3 highlights some of the major events in social welfare history as discussed in this chapter. The next chapter will discuss policy development and the structural components of policies. It will also focus on

English History

1300s	Feudalistic societies in Europe
1348	Europe devastated by Black Death
1349	Statute of Laborers
1531	Able-bodied people forbidden from begging
1601	Elizabethan Poor Law
1662	Law of Settlement
1795	Establishment of Speenhamland system
1834	Poor Law Reforms

U.S. History

1770s	Beginning of moral treatment movement in mental health
1778	First treaty between federal government and Native American Delaware tribe
1824	Establishment of Bureau of Indian Affairs
1830	Indian Removal Act
1838–1839	Trail of Tears
1840s	Dorothea Dix advocates for people with mental illness
1846	Beginning of the Mexican-American War
1848	The Treaty of Guadalupe Hidalgo (where Mexico ceded more than half of its territory to the United States)
1861–1865	Civil War
1865	Establishment of Freedmen's Bureau
1874	Etta Wheeler initiates child protective services
1882	Chinese Exclusion Act of 1882
1880s	Growth of settlement houses and charity organization societies
1870s	Federal attempts at assimilation for Native Americans
1899	Treaty of Paris of 1899 (where Spain ceded Puerto Rico to the United States)
1900s	Beginning of mental hygiene movement in mental health
1909	Establishment of National Association for the Advancement of Colored People (NAACP)
	First White House Conference on Dependent Children
1910	Establishment of National Urban League
	First major wave of Mexican immigration in response to the Mexican Revolution of 1910
1911	States begin to establish mothers' pensions
1917	Jones Act granting U.S. citizenship to all people born in Puerto Rico from then on
1924	Immigration Act of 1924 (which imposed stringent requirements on immigrants entering the United States, especially from Asia)
1929	Stock market crash initiates the Great Depression
1933	Federal Emergency Relief Act (FERA)
	Establishment of Civilian Works Administration (CSW)
	Establishment of Civilian Conservation Corps (CCC)
1935	Establishment of Public Works Administration (PWA)
	Establishment of Works Progress Administration (WPA)
	Social Security Act of 1935

Figure 6.3 Major events in the history of social welfare (*continued*)

1941	U.S. enters World War II
	Japanese American internment in response to bombing of Pearl Harbor
1942	Permanent relocation centers for Japanese American internment
1944	Serviceman's Readjustment Act of 1944 (G.I. Bill)
1945	World War II ends
1950	Amendments to Social Security Act adding Aid to Disabled
Early 1950s	Beginning of deinstitutionalization movement in mental health
1954	*Brown v. Board of Education* ending school segregation
1962	Public Welfare Amendments of 1962
Early 1960s	Initiation of War on Poverty and Great Society
1962	Formation of National Farm Workers Association (NFWA) led by Cesar Chavez
1963	Community Mental Health Centers Act
1964	Economic Opportunity Act of 1964
	Food Stamp Act of 1964
	Civil Rights Act of 1964
1965	Older Americans Act of 1965
1967	Amendments to Social Security Act
1969	American Indian movement protests at Alcatraz
1971	*Wyatt v. Stickney*
	American Indian movement protests at Wounded Knee
	Establishment of Supplementary Security Income (SSI)
1974	Child Abuse Prevention and Treatment Act
1975	Passage of Title XX of Social Security Act
	O'Connor v. Donaldson
1978	Passage of Indian Child Welfare Act of 1978
1980	Passage of Adoption Assistance and Child Welfare Act
1990	Passage of Americans with Disabilities Act of 1990
	Passage of Developmental Disabilities Assistance and Bill of Rights Act of 1990
1993	Family and Medical Leave Act of 1993
1994	Crime Bill of 1994
1996	Personal Responsibility and Work Opportunities Act of 1996 (including Temporary Assistance for Needy Families [TANF])
2001	Terrorist attacks on the World Trade Center
2003	Beginning and end of the war on Iraq
	The Medicare Modernization Act of 2003

Figure 6.3   *(Continued)*

theoretical perspectives regarding personal values and social welfare policy and program development, thereby setting the stage for policy and program analysis in various practice contexts.

For Further Exploration on the Internet

See this text's Book Companion Website at **www.socialwork.wadsworth.com/ kirstashman_intro2e** for descriptors and hot links to URLs relevant to this chapter, selected InfoTrac articles and exercises, and tutorial quizzes.

CHAPTER SEVEN

POLICY, POLICY ANALYSIS, AND POLICY ADVOCACY: FOUNDATIONS FOR SERVICE PROVISION

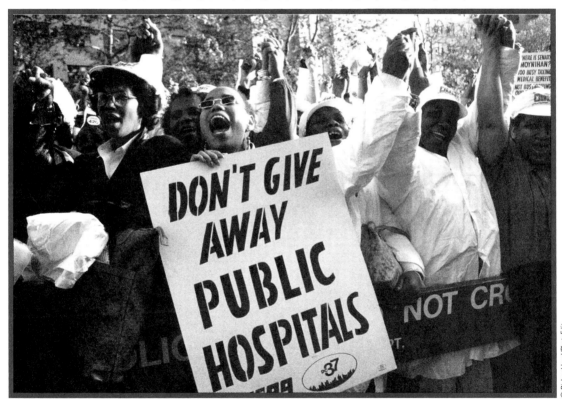

Policies have huge effects on citizens—including you. The following newspaper head-lines focus on controversial policies and their ramifications:[1]

"State Legislature May Slash Budget Across the Board: Local Officials Furious"
"County Executives Can Retire as Millionaires—A Retirement Policy Fluke?"
"Fetuses May Qualify for Federal Aid"[2]

The first headline concerns a northern state legislature's serious consideration not to share state tax revenues with communities (cities, towns, and villages). The intent is to address a huge state budget crunch resulting from a lagging economy. This decision will result in a 10% decrease in one small community's total budget—hence the headline. Elected community officials are irate because such decisions by the state have a direct impact on local service provision such as garbage pickup, health care services, fire and rescue emergency services, and law enforcement. They indicate that such a slash focused on one budget item could wipe out the entire roads department budget (including road repair and snow removal) or the whole fire department budget and half of the rescue squad budget.

Critical thinking about policy: Policy—in this case, state public policy—has a direct effect on people's quality of life. How would you like it if you had to take your own garbage to the dump every Saturday because there was no pickup? What if your defective electric toaster started a fire in your kitchen, and no fire department was available to respond to your emergency? What if an older relative suddenly collapsed from a heart attack, and there was no rescue squad to call for help?

The second headline concerns a county board (the elected group that oversees county responsibilities and staff) that has approved a change in retirement policy that was not well publicized to the voting public. The policy's alleged intent is to retain good employees (including the board members themselves) by providing generous retirement benefits, thus rewarding long-term employees for staying with the county. However, an investigation by the local media reveals that the new policy actually will grant well over a million dollars in retirement benefits to some highly paid, high-level, long-term county employees if they choose to receive their benefits in one lump sum. The retirement formula is based on long-term employment and salary level. Therefore, only those in high-level positions who receive high salaries will be eligible for these extraordinary benefits.

Critical thinking about policy: Amazingly, potential recipients include the board chair, other long-term board members, and additional county government leaders. Most board members claim that they had no idea of the ramifications of this policy because they had not done the requisite calculations. Much of the public feels that the board tried to "pull a fast one" but got caught. A citizen group is collecting signatures on a petition calling for a recall election in which they can vote current board members out. County government is in turmoil. Such huge retirement allocations will hike up county taxes, and citizens will be forced to bear the burden. This retirement policy has direct implications for the county's citizens who are financially responsible.

---

[1]Note that the ideas for the first two headlines were based on real events, but details in the ensuing discussion have been altered significantly.

[2]This headline was taken from the *Milwaukee Journal Sentinel,* Feb. 1, 2002, page A1, from an article by M. Johnson.

Another negative implication involves the impact on other county employees' morale and reputation. The policy is not their fault; they had no input into the decision to enact it. Yet the public is scrutinizing all county employees as if they are to blame for the problem. County employees say they work long, hard hours and are committed to contributing to a strong community that fosters residents' health and well-being. The vast majority of them will receive adequate, but certainly not exceptional, retirement benefits. It has already been established that the controversial retirement formula requires a high salary for the extraordinary benefits to kick in.

This example shows how policy—in this case, on the local level—has a major impact on various groups of citizens. Effects include county citizens' financial responsibility for huge outlays of cash, board members' potential receipt of large sums of money, and innocent county workers' diminished morale and reputation.

The third headline reflects a presidential policy decision "that developing human fetuses could be classified by states as unborn children so more low-income women would have access to prenatal care paid by the government" (Johnson, 2002, p. 1A). The result is that states can choose to provide health care to the fetuses via their mothers in programs designed to provide health care to children, not women.

Critical thinking about policy: This policy decision resulted in a heated debate between right-to-choose and anti-abortion proponents. People supporting the right to choose maintain that pregnant women have the right to decide what happens to their own bodies, including the right to have an abortion. People backing the anti-abortion perspective feel that abortions are wrong and so should be illegal.

Right-to-choose advocates "immediately labeled the move a blatant attempt to establish a fetus as a living person. They believe it lays the foundation . . . to make abortion a crime" (p. 1A). Rather, these proponents recommended extending "health care coverage to more women than designating a fetus an unborn child" (p. 12A). But anti-abortion advocates praised the decision, calling it a "compassionate" move to provide health care to pregnant women by expanding their access to prenatal care.

This policy has important current and potential implications for pregnant women. It paves the way for states to decide whether to pay for health care for unborn children—in essence, health care for pregnant women who were not eligible for services under child health care programs. It may also have implications for future judicial decisions concerning women's right to choose whether to have an abortion.

Regardless of where you stand on issues like these, the point is that policies significantly affect people. Sometimes they primarily affect only some category of people or segment of the population, such as pregnant women. Other times they may affect virtually everyone to one extent or another. For example, policy changes may result in cutbacks of essential community services or skyrocketing taxes for all citizens.

If you do not have any experience as a recipient of a social welfare program, you may not understand how important such programs can be to people who depend on their benefits. The examples given here illustrate how policies implemented through public services and programs can directly impact someone like you or those close to you. Policies regulate a wide range of social programs to provide many types of services for various groups of people (e.g., children, the elderly, people with disabilities, and those with health or mental health needs). Social welfare policies provide the basis for social welfare program implementation—what programs can and cannot do.

This chapter will

- Define social welfare policy and agency policy.
- Explore the process of policy development.
- Identify the primary structural components of social welfare programs.
- Explore the conservative–liberal–radical value continuum and examine how values affect policy development.
- Propose a model for analyzing a policy's appropriateness and adequacy.
- Describe policy practice and policy advocacy.
- Identify various methods social workers can use in policy practice, including involvement in politics.
- Encourage critical thinking about what kinds of policies should be formulated.

Social Welfare Policy

In a very broad sense, we have defined *policy* as rules that govern people's lives and dictate expectations for behavior. Policy determines how governments, communities, and organizations run in a predictable, coordinated fashion. We have also defined *social welfare policy* as the laws and regulations that govern which social welfare programs exist, what categories of clients are served, and who qualifies for a given program. Social welfare policy involves "decisions of various levels of the government, especially the federal government, as expressed in budgetary expenditures, congressional appropriations, and approved programs" (Morris, 1987, p. 664). For example, social welfare policy determines who is eligible for public assistance. In addition, social welfare policy sets standards regarding the types of services to be provided and the qualifications of service providers. For instance, social welfare policy specifies what social workers can do for physically abused children, in addition to what qualifications they must have to work in this practice area.

Note that throughout the rest of this book, for brevity's sake, when we use the term *policy* we will be referring to social welfare policy. Obviously this is the policy arena most relevant to a book about social work and social welfare.

Social workers must be well versed in social welfare policies. They must know what is available for a client and how to get it. For example, Enrique, a social worker for a county social services department, has a young female client, Daniela, with three small children, who has just been evicted from her apartment. Although the rent was relatively low and the apartment small (one bedroom), Daniela had been unable to pay the rent for the past three months. All her money had gone to clothing and feeding her children.

Enrique needs to know what other resources, if any, are available for Daniela and whether she is eligible to receive these resources. Policies determine the answers to a variety of questions: Does Daniela qualify for some temporary additional public assistance to help her relocate? Is there a local shelter for the homeless available whose policies allow Daniela and her children admission? If so, what is the shelter's policy for how long she can stay? Is there any low-rent housing available? If so, what does its policy designate as the criteria and procedure for admittance? Such questions may continue endlessly.

HIGHLIGHT 7.1
How Policies Structure and Coordinate Life

Einbinder (1995) maintains that policies serve to synchronize three primary arenas of life: "(1) the government; (2) the economy; and (3) private life" (p. 1850). All three are integrally intertwined. For example, consider the first headline cited at the beginning of the chapter, concerning a state slashing its budget. First, the national economy suffers a decline. As a result, unemployment increases, people reduce their spending, and less money circulates in the economy. Thus the state government gets less money in taxes (e.g., from personal earnings and sales) and must cut its spending. The economy affects government.

Government also affects the economy. Various governmental units make decisions about economic policy. For instance, a state might decide to decrease taxes levied on businesses within the state to encourage more firms to relocate there. The intent is for more companies to employ more people, who, in turn, pay more taxes. Additionally, because a larger number of businesses are contributing to the tax pool, the pool should be larger as well, even with a lower tax rate.

People's private lives are directly affected by both the government and the economy. What tax rates does the government levy on their earnings? Is the economy healthy enough for them to keep their jobs? As a result of these and other factors, do they have sufficient resources to purchase bare necessities or luxuries? Within this complicated system of policies and controls, are they able to maintain a good quality of life?

All citizens should be aware of what policies exist because of policies' direct effects on many aspects of life. They should also be alert to *changes* in policies for similar reasons.

Social workers must pay special attention to social welfare policies for two reasons. First, these policies dictate how programs are administered and how services are provided. Second, some policies are unfair, ineffective, or inefficient, and social workers must advocate for them to be changed.

Social welfare programs are simply the implementation (i.e., the putting into action) of social welfare policy. Sometimes the distinction between a social welfare policy and program is unclear. Some policies inherently provide detailed directions for how they should be implemented. In other words, they essentially *are* the program. Other policies are quite vague and require substantial elaboration regarding how they should be put into operation. In these instances, the social welfare program becomes more extensive than the policy on which it is based.

Consider the following fictitious policy: All publicly funded social service agencies have to provide child care for their employees. This policy simply mandates that agencies must provide this service; it does not elaborate upon details. A program must be developed that responds to the following questions, among others: Where will child care be provided (e.g., in the agency or in a separate day care center)? How will child care be funded? Who will run the child care center? What kind of environment will be available to the children (e.g., a stimulating, activity-centered milieu or basic overseeing with little interaction)?

Highlight 7.1 expands on how policies structure and coordinate people's lives.

Agency Policy

Chapter 1 established that a second type of policy directly affecting social workers' ability to practice is *agency policy*. This entails standards adopted by organizations and programs that provide services (e.g., a treatment center for troubled youths, a department of social services, or a sheltered workshop[3] for people with cognitive disabilities).

The terms *social services agency, human services agency,* and *social welfare agency* can be used interchangeably to refer to agencies or organizations that provide social welfare services. Similarly, for our purposes, the words *agency* and *organization* mean the same thing. A *social services agency* is a coordinated system of staff units and processes providing social services. Such agencies typically employ social workers, other professionals providing various social services, paraprofessionals (people with specific knowledge and skills who, under close supervision, carry out various duties previously undertaken only by professionals), clerical staff, and sometimes volunteers (Barker, 2003). Services are provided according to a prescribed set of social welfare and agency policies.

Agency policy may specify the agency's structure, the qualifications of supervisors and workers, the rules governing what workers may or may not do, and the proper procedures to follow for completing an assessment.

Agency policy may address in greater detail how agencies can implement social welfare policy. It can iron out the wrinkles and specify rules regarding how agency staff should work within their individual agency setting. Agency policy can also address questions about how the agency runs on a daily basis. What hours do staff work? How are staff evaluated for job performance and raises? Who is responsible for supervising whom throughout the organization structure? This involves everyone from the director or chief executive officer (CEO) running the entire agency down to practitioners working directly with clients.

Social Welfare Policy Development

How social welfare policies develop in government agencies is an extremely complex process due to the many opinions, people, and formal processes involved. However, to facilitate your basic understanding and emphasize the importance of policy for social work practice, Figure 7.1 depicts a basic six-phase process of how policy is developed and implemented. The process proposed here is quite simplistic, but it gives a general idea of how policies come into being.

Macarov (1995) provides an example that illustrates the policy development process—namely, the development of and change in policy governing the provision of financial aid to needy children and families. The value assumption upon which the policy was initially based was that it is most desirable for children to remain in their own homes, cared for by their own parents, rather than being institutionalized.

---

[3]A *sheltered workshop* is an organization that provides testing, counseling, social skills training, job training, sheltered employment, and job placement services for people with various disabilities or needs for rehabilitation (Barker, 2003).

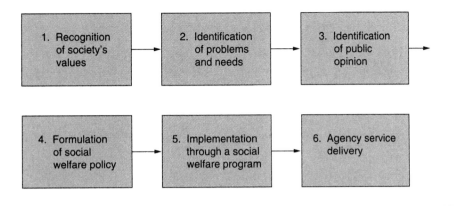

Figure 7.1 Social welfare policy development

Implications concern helping to keep a family together even when parents are poor and have trouble supporting children. This value is reflected in Aid to Families with Dependent Children (AFDC), a primary program that provided financial assistance to poor families with children until 1996, when new legislation was passed. (The next chapter discusses this and newer legislation more thoroughly.)

Phase 1

The *first phase* involves recognizing society's values about what is considered important or worthwhile. Absolute values are hard to pin down because of the tremendous number of people we're talking about.

Case Example For illustration, we will start with the value that children are generally best cared for within their own families. The task of identifying society's values becomes more complex because values also change over time. For instance, the value that children should remain in their own homes might be superseded by the value that all parents should work to support their families.

Phase 2

The *second phase* of the policy process concerns identifying problems and needs that require attention.

Case Example The problem related to our example is poverty and poor people's inability to provide adequate care for their families. Although the societal value is that children should remain in their own homes, a significant number of parents, mostly single mothers who are primary caregivers for children, lack resources to provide their children with adequate care. What should be done to address this problem?

Phase 3

The *third phase* of the policy process involves the identification of public opinion about an identified problem and people's related needs. Society's current values tend to guide public opinion concerning what should be done. Public opinion

© AFP/Getty Images

Policy development is a complex legislative process.

reflects values but involves more specific recommendations about what should be *done* to put these values into action. Values held by the majority sway public opinion in that direction. Dobelstein (2003) refers to such a prevailing public view as a *normative orientation* (p. 15). Highlight 7.2 discusses how the relationship between public opinion and policy development is often unclear.

Case Example   For several decades prior to 1996, general public opinion maintained that poor families should be given minimal assistance to keep children in their own homes.

Phase 4

In the *fourth phase* of the social policy process, legislators confronted with a problem or need and swamped with public opinion undertake the complicated formulation of social welfare policy to address the issue. It is beyond the scope of this text to elaborate on all the political processes involved. The following issues complicate the formulation of social policy (DiNitto, 2005; Meenaghan, Kilty, & McNutt, 2004; Popple & Leighninger, 2004):

- It is difficult to obtain a problem consensus because of the multiple perspectives and opinions involved. True public opinion is hard to pin down.
- Legislators' perceptions of the problem depend on the information and pressure they receive. Various factions and interest groups have varying degrees of access to legislators and wield varying degrees of influence.
- Because policy is formulated in such a political environment, the actual policy can change dramatically in focus while it is being debated. The policymaking

HIGHLIGHT 7.2

Public Opinion and Policy Development

Identification of public opinion is the third phase of the policy development process. Note, however, that the process may be more complicated than this. For one thing, majority public opinion is not always the deciding factor regarding what policy will be developed. Politicians usually pay attention to public opinion. Voters formulate public opinion, and they also vote politicians into or out of office. Thus it is usually in politicians' best interests to keep voters happy and to promote policies supported by voters.

However, many times such controversy exists over a policy issue that it is virtually impossible to satisfy the majority—or even to identify the majority. Sometimes many people will be dissatisfied no matter which side of the issue a politician supports. Consider the strong opposing opinions people hold over the death penalty or the right of women to get abortions.

Other times, it's difficult for legislators to get accurate information about public opinion on a particular issue. National Gallup polls aren't regularly done for every policy issue. Politicians must act on the basis of the information that is available. Sometimes this is biased because a small minority feels very strongly about an issue and regularly contacts politicians to voice their opinion. Consider people who have very strong feelings about the right to own guns. Hearing only from people supporting that side of the issue might leave legislators with the impression that most people hate gun control, when this may or may not be true.

Finally, even if legislators who formulate and vote on policy have fairly accurate data on public opinion, they may not pay much attention. Because the legislative decision-making process is so complex (as described in the fourth phase of the policy formulation process), public opinion about one issue may get lost. A politician may need to compromise significantly to get anything passed at all. Sometimes politicians will bargain by withdrawing support for one policy in order to pass another policy that is more important to them. Finally, politicians may receive extreme pressure from other party members or powerful leaders to support or not support a policy despite their own personal feelings to the contrary.

process is characterized by an ongoing struggle of give and take, conflict resolution, and compromise.

Consider a loosely analogous theoretical situation regarding how difficult it can be to come to a satisfactory consensus. Suppose during the first meeting of one of your classes your instructor indicates that it is the class's responsibility to determine how students will be graded. The only criterion given is that some configuration of exams and assignments must be specified and that they must not be too easy. Imagine the wide range of opinions students would probably voice. Some would want objective exams, and others would prefer essays. Some would want two exams, others four, and still others none. Some would prefer term papers, and others would opt for experiential assignments such as visits to relevant organizations or interviews with relevant people. Some would advocate for group projects, and others would express hatred for group projects and desire individual ones instead. It is difficult to establish a consensus: Controversy and differences of opinion tend to characterize decision making even in a relatively small group. Imagine magnifying this many times over in the complex legislative process.

Case Example After much legislative debate and struggle, Aid to Dependent Children (ADC), renamed AFDC in 1962, was initially formulated as part of the Social Security Act of 1935.

Phase 5

Following the initial formulation of social policy, the *fifth phase* of the social welfare policy process is implementation through a social welfare program. Popple and Leighninger (2001) comment:

> Many people think that once a policy is enacted, the process of alleviating a problem is well under way and implementation is simply a matter of carrying out a clearly specified program or initiative. This is far from the truth. Policies . . . are often broadly stated—long on mission and short on detail. The implementation phase is generally a time of filling in the detail through regulations, personnel procedures, program guidelines, and other specifications, all of which further shape the policy . . . the details of implementation constitute the closest part of the policy world for social work practitioners. Here are the memos, manuals, rules, and verbal directives to which workers must respond. It is also an important area for worker discretion[, input,] and influence. (pp. 129–130)

Case Example The ensuing implementation process of ADC required substantial effort and specification of detail to make the program clear and functional.

Phase 6

In the *sixth phase* of social welfare policy development and implementation, social services are delivered by social workers and other staff in the context of social service agencies.

Case Example Social service agency staff work directly with clients who apply for and receive benefits.

Highlight 7.3 explores how the six-phase process of policy development applies to this case example when society's values change.

Structural Components of Social Welfare Programs

Understanding a social welfare policy means investigating exactly what it says and what it does. Dolgoff and Feldstein (2003) cite five broad components to explore in order to understand any policy: (1) what people's needs and the program's goals are, (2) what kinds of benefits are provided, (3) what the eligibility criteria are to receive benefits, (4) how the program is financed, and (5) how the program is administered and run (pp. 137–139).

What Are People's Needs and Program Goals?

We have established that social welfare programs are the implementation of policies that are, in turn, the results of public values and opinion and the political process. Programs exist to meet certain goals related to addressing problems, fulfilling needs,

HIGHLIGHT 7.3

When Values Change

Society's values—namely, that it is most desirable for children to remain in their own homes and be cared for by their parents (primarily the mother) rather than being institutionalized—have gradually changed. New values stress how parents, including mothers, should work to support their families. In light of more and more mothers working outside the home, Macarov (1995) explains how new societal values came to characterize child care:

> As programs that require . . . parents [receiving financial assistance] to work became more popular, extensive child care facilities were needed. The desire of many mothers to take jobs outside the home also made such facilities a growth industry. As a result, providing child care outside the home has become not only accepted but prestigious. This social change led to a value change according to which contact with other children, even as early as age 2 or younger, is healthy, and professionally trained personnel provide better care than "amateur" mothers. This has reached the point to where working mothers are now postulated by some as more caring, and more capable of child care, than nonworking mothers. (p. 140)

This change in society's values led to a change in social policy, as illustrated by the following simplified process:

Phase 1—Recognition of society's (changing) values: Society's values changed from viewing parental child care as the optimum choice to viewing day care outside of the home as equally or even more valuable. (Note that you may or may not agree with Macarov's interpretation of how societal values have changed regarding this issue. That's not the point. The point is to provide an example of how policies can change in response to modifications in values.)

Phase 2—Identification of problems and needs: The problem remains generally the same: A significant number of parents, primarily single mothers who are primary caregivers for children, lack resources to provide their children with adequate care.

Phase 3—Recognition of public opinion: Society's new values were reflected in public opinion regarding this issue. Public opinion stressed the importance of parents, including single mothers, working to support themselves and their families. Requiring single parents, including mothers, to work outside the home means that someone must be responsible for caring for young children.

Phase 4—Development of social welfare policy: The Temporary Assistance to Needy Families (TANF) program was enacted in 1996 as part of significant legislation restructuring financial assistance eligibility and requirements. (Chapter 8 discusses this legislation more thoroughly.) This new legislation requires parents to receive job training and get jobs. It also places a five-year lifetime limit on recipients' ability to receive TANF payments; there had been no time limitation for the earlier AFDC.

Phase 5—Implementation through social welfare programs: The TANF program is being implemented throughout the United States. Because national policy gives states significant discretion in how to distribute benefits, each state has developed and is evaluating its own program.

Phase 6—Service provision by workers in agency settings: Social workers and other agency staff provide resources and services directly to clients according to the national policy and to state and local programs.

or improving people's lives (Dolgoff & Feldstein, 2003, p. 134; Gilbert & Terrell, 2005). Social welfare program goals address a wide range of problems including child maltreatment, "teen pregnancy, homelessness, and substance abuse." They attend to needs such as "economic security, child care, and health care." They enhance people's quality of life "through such means as education, socialization, and recreation" (p. 134).

Goals may be formal and clearly stated or implicit and unspoken. Dolgoff and Feldstein (2003) comment that "[t]he food stamp program, for example, has a stated objective to alleviate hunger and malnutrition by enabling low-income households to purchase a nutritionally adequate diet"; another stated goal is to enhance the market for food grown and distributed internally within the country (pp. 134–135). Low-income families using food stamps to "purchase" food results in profits for growers, producers, and distributors, thereby enhancing the economy. "But food stamps may not be used for the purchase of alcoholic beverages and tobacco, pet food, and cleaning and paper products, including toilet paper. Implicit in a portion of these restrictions is a moral objective to control the behavior of recipients" by regulating what they can and cannot buy (Dolgoff & Feldstein, 2003, p. 135).

What Kinds of Benefits Are Provided?

What does a particular social welfare program provide to recipients? Cash? Food? Housing? Counseling? In this context, a *benefit* is anything a client receives through a social welfare program. Because different programs serve people with different needs, the types of benefit also vary.

Benefits might be divided into two basic categories—cash and in-kind (Chambers & Wedel, 2005; Gilbert & Terrell, 2005; Marx, 2004). *Cash benefits* obviously involve providing eligible clients with prescribed amounts of money based on what the policies governing the program allow. *In-kind benefits* include virtually any benefit other than cash. Examples are food products (e.g., those available from agricultural surpluses), food stamps that can be exchanged for food, free school lunches, low-income housing, rent subsidies (e.g., whereby programs pay partial rent), day care, and personal social services. *Personal social services* are those intended to enhance people's quality of life by improving their ability to function within their environment. Such services (e.g., counseling) usually target specific groups (e.g., children or the elderly) or particular problems (e.g., family planning or counseling). Subsequent chapters will describe programs implementing policies designed to provide various benefits to a range of populations in a variety of contexts. Focus on Critical Thinking 7.1 raises some key issues related to cash versus in-kind benefits.

What Are the Eligibility Criteria for the Program?

Eligibility is the condition whereby people meet the designated criteria or requirements to receive benefits (Chambers & Wedel, 2005). For example, to be eligible for a particular public assistance program, an individual must fulfill the required criteria.

FOCUS ON CRITICAL THINKING 7.1

Which Benefits Are Most Beneficial to Poor People?

The next chapter discusses poverty and the programs implementing policies to help people who are poor. Some programs provide minimum cash benefits and allow people to determine for themselves how to budget the money and spend it. Other programs provide in-kind benefits, and the recipients have no choice in what they get.

Dobelstein (2003) questions the value of in-kind benefits versus cash. He indicates that "total federal government spending for all social programs, including cash and in-kind programs [including medical care], when added together is more than enough to raise the poor above the present poverty" line (p. 124). (The *poverty line* is the minimum amount of money the government believes a person needs to achieve the lowest acceptable standard of living [Orshansky, 1965].)

In other words, Dobelstein maintains that, if the government would divert the money it spends on in-kind benefits to providing cash directly, it would spend no more and possibly spend less. He continues that "[t]he share of cash expenditures as a portion of all income-maintenance expenditures has been decreasing over the past 25 years, while the share of in-kind benefits has been increasing" (p. 125). (*Income maintenance programs* are all those that provide people with enough money, goods, and services

to achieve an adequate standard of living and quality of life.)

Do you think it is better to provide poor people with all cash, all in-kind, or some combination of both benefits? What are the pros and cons of each choice? Consider the following questions:

- To what extent does provision of cash benefits allow for personal choice, thereby respecting an individual's right to self-determination and human dignity?
- To what extent does the provision of in-kind benefits ensure that individuals get their basic needs met?
- To what extent does the provision of in-kind benefits restrict individuals? For instance, people eligible for low-income housing (by having incomes under a designated level) must live in the housing provided; they have no choice about where to live. Similarly, people receiving food stamps must use them for food. Although such coupons allow people some choice in the food they obtain, recipients cannot choose to pay the electric or heating bill or to purchase toilet paper with them.
- What are the advantages and disadvantages of some mixture of cash and in-kind benefits?
- Where do your answers stand on the conservative–liberal continuum and why?

Public assistance is provision by the government of minimum monetary support to people who are unable to provide for themselves.

A common criterion used to determine eligibility is a *means test*—the evaluation of all the resources clients have at their disposal to determine if they have the *means* to pay for services or buy things for themselves. A means test might include assessment of people's "income, assets, debts and other obligations, number of dependents, and health factors" (Barker, 2003, p. 265). If people fail the means test, they are ineligible to receive benefits. Eligibility is an extremely important concept because it is the key to whether a person can obtain benefits.

Who Pays for the Program?

How the program is financed entails the fourth structural component for understanding a social welfare policy. There are several ways to finance social welfare programs (Dolgoff & Feldstein, 2003, pp. 136–138). National, state, and local taxes provide a primary avenue for getting funds. Sometimes funding is diverted from the general tax pool (referred to as *general revenues*); other times taxes are *earmarked* to provide specified services. For example, a county might increase its sales tax to help pay for a new stadium. Or funds from a state lottery might be earmarked to subsidize (partially pay for) citizens' property taxes. Finally, taxes might be collected specifically from employers and their employees to provide some benefit. Social Security, described more thoroughly in later chapters, is an example of such a program.

Sometimes benefits are not provided directly by government agencies. Rather, funds are collected by such agencies through taxes, and then specific services are purchased from another social service provider. Recall from Chapter 5 that this process is referred to as a *purchase-of-service agreement*. The purchasing agency and the provider agency agree in advance what types of services will be provided, for how long, and at what cost.

People who receive some benefit may also pay for it directly. Of course, many social welfare programs provide benefits to people with few resources. Therefore, a *sliding fee scale* might be used, with the amount paid based on the recipient's ability to pay rather than on fixed fees. The more income the person has, the more he or she is required to pay. Planned Parenthood, an agency providing family planning services and reproductive health care, including contraception, is an example of an agency that uses a sliding fee scale. Armstrong (1995) indicates that such family planning "clinics are particularly valuable sources of care for teenagers and low-income women" (p. 970).

Finally, some programs are financed in a combination of ways. For example, a private agency providing mental health counseling may receive funding from various sources. This includes some funding through sliding scale fees from clients, some through purchase of service by the state and county for clients unable to pay for the service themselves, some through grants furnished by private foundations, and some through charitable contributions from local citizens.

How Is the Program Administered and Run?

The fifth structural component involved in understanding a social welfare program is the level of government that actually oversees and runs the program. Is it national, state, or local? Many times this involves a combination. For example, consider Medicaid, a program that pays for medical and hospital services for eligible people in need. (Medicaid is discussed more thoroughly in the next chapter.) It is administered by state government but overseen at the federal level (Gilbert & Terrell, 2005).

Another example involves TANF, mentioned earlier, a primary program providing financial assistance to needy families. (The next chapter also describes TANF in greater detail.) TANF policy dictates that the federal government grant sums of money to states. States then have much discretion regarding how to administer the program and spend the money. They may channel more into cash benefits or provide more in-kind benefits like child care or nutritional programs for children.

A food bank located in a large city is an example of a locally administered program. Here food items such as canned goods and staples like flour and rice are provided to eligible poor people. This food bank may be financed by the city and county governments and by charitable contributions from private citizens.

There are other ways to look at how programs are administered and run. For example, you can explore program administration and service provision at the individual agency level. Chapter 5 reviewed the types of social agencies that implement social welfare programs, including public, private, nonprofit, for-profit, and proprietary.

 # Value Perspectives on Social Responsibility and Social Welfare Program Development

Chapter 1 introduced some basic value differences about whether social welfare is the primary responsibility of individuals or of society in general. It also discussed some related perspectives concerning how social welfare policy and programs should be developed. The concepts will be reviewed here, and some questions posed for assessing the values that characterize a range of specific social welfare programs discussed in later chapters. An additional issue to be addressed is whether social welfare benefits should be available to everyone or to only a select few.

Note that the following discussion simplifies highly complex and controversial concepts. The purpose is not to provide an absolute decree for how to think about these issues, but rather to offer a foundation for thinking about how values affect social welfare policy and program development.

The Conservative–Liberal Continuum

Conservatism is the philosophy that individuals are responsible for themselves, that government should provide minimal interference in people's lives, and that change is generally unnecessary (Jansson, 2003). It involves the idea that if people fail or have problems, except in extreme circumstances, it is generally their own fault. It assumes that people who are weak or lazy deserve what they get, which is often little or nothing. If people have access to free benefits, they will readily take them and "milk" the system. And if they don't have to work, they won't. Therefore, government should not interfere in people's lives unless it is absolutely necessary (e.g., for people who are extremely "worthy" poor, as described in Chapter 6, or who need help in an emergency like a flood or hurricane). Thus these primary principles are involved in conservatism:

- It is each individual's responsibility to work and succeed.
- Failure to succeed is generally the individual's fault.
- The government should not interfere unless absolutely necessary.

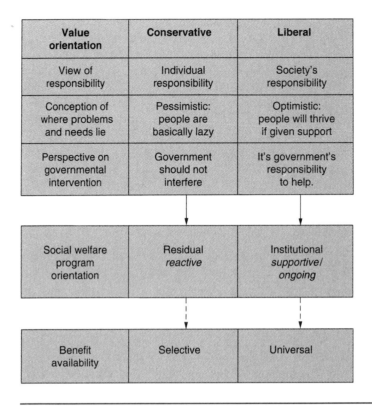

Value orientation	Conservative	Liberal
View of responsibility	Individual responsibility	Society's responsibility
Conception of where problems and needs lie	Pessimistic: people are basically lazy	Optimistic: people will thrive if given support
Perspective on governmental intervention	Government should not interfere	It's government's responsibility to help.
Social welfare program orientation	Residual *reactive*	Institutional *supportive/ongoing*
Benefit availability	Selective	Universal

Figure 7.2   Conservative versus liberal value orientations

Liberalism, in contrast, is the philosophy that supports government involvement in the social, political, and economic structure so that all people's rights and privileges are protected in the name of social justice (Jansson, 2003). Social welfare is the collective responsibility of society. It is society's obligation to assist people in adjusting to the turbulent and demanding contemporary environment. People will prosper only if given the chance to. Thus these major principles are involved in liberalism:

• It is society's responsibility to care for and support its members.
• Failure to succeed generally is due to complex, unfair stresses and problems in the environment.
• It is government's responsibility to support its citizens and help them cope with the stresses and problems in their environment.

The top portion of Figure 7.2 contrasts some of the basic principles of conservatism and liberalism. These include the view of responsibility, the conception of where problems and needs lie, and the divergent perspectives on government's responsibility.

Radicalism

Radicalism is the philosophy that the social and political system as it stands is not structurally capable of truly pursuing social justice (Marx, 2004). Rather, drastic, fundamental changes are necessary in the system to achieve true fair and equal treatment.

Radicalism involves extremes. It can reflect extreme conservatism or extreme liberalism. Essentially, the primary principle involved in radicalism is that the system requires a major overhaul to achieve more appropriate goals. Two questions may be asked:

- What goals should the system pursue?
- How should the system pursue these goals?

Chapter 1 established that a radical perspective requires the ability to propose a new social structure. It is beyond the scope of this introductory book to teach you how to plan new policies and promote major social changes. Therefore, critical thinking about social welfare policy in the remaining chapters will focus on the conservative–liberal continuum.

Residual and Institutional Perspectives on Social Welfare Policy and Program Development

We have established how policies and program implementation initially flow from society's values. Similarly, residual and institutional social welfare policy and program development, to some extent, are related to conservative and liberal values, respectively. Proposed here is one basic way to start thinking about social welfare policy and program development. The philosophical approaches and value systems involved are extremely complex.

The *residual* perspective conceives of social welfare as focusing on problems and gaps, with social welfare benefits and services supplied only when people fail to provide adequately for themselves and problems arise (Blau, 2004). The implication is that it's people's own fault if they require outside help. Basic concepts inherent in the residual view include these:

- Social welfare policies and programs should be *reactive*, solving problems only after they occur (McInnis-Dittrich, 1994, p. 7).
- Social welfare policies and programs generally respond to problems caused by individual personal failure.

The *institutional* perspective of social welfare, in contrast, views people's needs as a normal part of life (Blau, 2004). It is society's ongoing responsibility to support its members and provide needed benefits and services. It is not people's fault that they require such services, but rather an expected part of the human condition. Basic concepts inherent in the institutional view include these:

- Social welfare policies and programs should provide ongoing support to all people in need.
- Social welfare policies and programs relieve existing tensions and help solve problems distressing people in their environment.

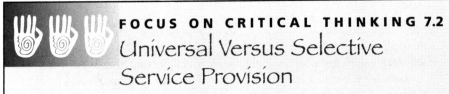

FOCUS ON CRITICAL THINKING 7.2
Universal Versus Selective Service Provision

Services available to all sounds like a great idea. Theoretically, everyone would have equal access to what they need. For example, national health insurance, through which everyone's health care needs would automatically and equally be covered, has been debated for decades. Health care costs are soaring. Wouldn't it be great not to have to worry about escalating health insurance premiums?

The problem with national health insurance, as with other universal programs, is cost. Who would foot the bill? Would taxpayers be willing to pay higher taxes so that all citizens would be covered equally? Thus far, apparently not. Congressional support has been consistently inadequate to pass national health insurance proposals. (Chapter 12 discusses national health care more thoroughly.)

When thinking about any social welfare policy, you might, then, ask two questions concerning the universality–selectivity issue:

- Should benefits be available to everyone or only to a select group?
- What would be the relative costs for each option?

The central portion of Figure 7.2 reflects how the residual perspective relates somewhat to the conservative value orientation and the institutional perspective to the liberal value orientation.

Universal Versus Selective Service Provision

One other perspective on social welfare policy and programming involves the concepts of universal versus selective benefits. *Universality* is the idea that social welfare benefits should be equally available "to all members of society, regardless of their income or means" (Segal & Brzuzy, 1998, p. 13). Public education through high school is a universal social welfare benefit available to all citizens regardless of status, class, or income level. This is despite the fact that the quality of education varies dramatically from one locale to another. Social Security is another universal program because it is available to all people who work (Dolgoff & Feldstein, 2003).

Universality contrasts sharply with *selectivity*—the idea that social welfare benefits should be "restricted to those who can demonstrate need through established eligibility criteria" (Segal & Brzuzy, 1998, p. 13). Any public assistance program requiring a means test that limits benefits to "the needy" reflects selective service provision. To some extent, the concept of universality coincides with the institutional perspective on social welfare, and the concept of selectivity with the residual (Dolgoff & Feldstein, 2003). Focus on Critical Thinking 7.2 raises some questions regarding the pros and cons of universal versus selective service provision.

Note that the bottom of Figure 7.2 shows how selective benefit availability coincides to some extent with a conservative value orientation and a residual perspective on social welfare policy and programming. Similarly, the figure shows how universal benefit availability corresponds somewhat with a liberal value orientation and an institutional perspective toward social welfare.

This connection, however, is not perfect. Therefore, the arrows leading from the residual and institutional social welfare program orientations to selective and universal benefit availability, respectively, are broken instead of solid lines. Actual policies may reflect a combination of selective, universal, residual, and institutional aspects. For example, student loans are universally available in that anyone can apply for them (Dolgoff & Feldstein, 2003). However, they are selective in that students must meet a financial needs test to actually receive them.

Another example of the complex and intertwining nature of these concepts involves disaster relief after the horrifying tsunami devastated the Indian Ocean coasts of Indonesia, Thailand, and Sri Lanka on December 26, 2004. Relief initially was residual: Its main goal was to fulfill temporary needs in reaction to the catastrophe (although the earthquake causing the tsunami, of course, was no one's fault). However, institutional relief was also needed over a longer term to help rebuild these countries' economic infrastructures. People who lost virtually everything required years of help in rebuilding their homes, work, communities, and lives. Disaster relief was also universal in that its availability was intended for everyone in need regardless of income level or social status. Universality was imperfect, however, because equitable distribution was initially difficult or impossible. Many areas were impenetrable because of destroyed roads, bridges, docks, and airstrips. Other communities, such as those on numerous remote islands, were difficult to reach because of their out-of-the-way locations.

Policy Analysis

We have discussed different value perspectives that shape social welfare policy. Examining a policy from a values perspective is one way of understanding it. Another approach involves evaluating the appropriateness and effectiveness of a social welfare policy, a form of policy analysis. However, *policy analysis* is a broad term that can have many specific meanings. Popple and Leighninger (2004) reflect:

> Some policy analyses look like literature, being composed mostly of stories. Some look like mathematics texts, with lengthy and complex formulas, tables, graphs, and so forth. Some look like stories in a newspaper or magazine (in fact, may *be* stories in newspapers and magazines). (p. 40)

Policy analysis can target how well a stated policy attains its goals, who should most likely benefit from the policy, whether the benefit type is appropriate, how efficiently the program that implements the policy is financed, or how the policy compares with alternative policies (Gilbert & Terrell, 2005; Haynes & Mickelson, 2003; Popple & Leighninger, 2004). Policy analysis is conducted by specialists who carefully scrutinize policies and make recommendations to legislators for future policy changes. Policy analysis is undertaken by social workers who evaluate a

Effectiveness

Efficiency

Ethical considerations

Evaluation of alternatives

Establishment of recommendations for positive change

Figure 7.3   The Five-E approach to policy analysis for social welfare policy

policy's effectiveness with respect to clients. Finally, policy analysis can and should be undertaken by all citizens who are affected by a range of policies and who, as voters, are responsible to provide input into policymaking.

For our purposes, *policy analysis* is a systematic evaluation of how effectively a policy addresses the targeted problem or issue, meets people's needs, and achieves its goals. Most of the remaining chapters in this book focus on programs that implement social welfare policy. The model of policy analysis proposed here provides one framework from which you can evaluate for yourself how appropriate a policy is and how well its program implementation works.

The Five-E Approach to Policy Analysis

The proposed Five-E model of basic policy analysis for social welfare policy is as follows:

- How *effective* is the policy?
- How *efficient* is the policy?
- Is the policy *ethically* sound?
- What does *evaluation* of potential alternative policies reveal?
- What recommendations can be *established* for positive changes?

Figure 7.3 summarizes the Five-E approach. Policy analysis involves scrutiny of both the policy and the program implementation resulting from the policy.

How Effective Is the Policy?

Effectiveness involves the extent to which a policy accomplishes its goals. What are the outcomes of the policy? How well does the policy's program implementation achieve its stated goals?

It is important to use critical thinking and ask questions to seek information. What are the program's strengths, on the one hand, and weaknesses, on the other (McInnis-Dittrich, 1994)? What empirical data are available to support program effectiveness? What do benefit recipients say about the policy and program implementation? Do workers administering the program support its effectiveness?

Case Example   Popple and Leighninger (2004) describe and analyze a policy concerning mandatory drug testing (e.g., a urine test) for people receiving public assistance.[4] The basic idea is that people receiving public money should not be wasting it on illegal drugs but should spend it on nurturing and supporting their children. An assumption is that people receiving assistance are likely to be irresponsible and do "bad" things like use drugs.

Several states have opted to require drug testing for welfare recipients. For example, Maryland became the first state to require such testing for all public assistance applicants. A state legislative committee approved a policy whereby anyone refusing the test would get no financial benefits. People testing positive for drug use would be forced to enter an expensive drug rehabilitation program. And failure to cooperate fully in the program would result in decreased benefits to the recipient's family.

How effective is the policy? What does *effectiveness* in this context mean? Does testing reduce drug use? Do welfare recipients who test positive and enter treatment stop using drugs? No clear evidence exists regarding the results of testing recipients for drugs.

Research focusing on required drug testing for workers in the general workplace reveals mixed findings. (Estimates are that 2–3% of all workers abuse legal and illegal drugs [Saunders, 1995].) One "study of 63 Silicon Valley companies" found "that urine testing reduces, rather than enhances, worker productivity" (Beaucar, 2000, p. 10).

Proponents of drug testing for welfare recipients argue that forcing abusers to get treatment improves their ability to be productive citizens, as well as enhancing their own and their family's well-being. Critics counter that such drug testing violates recipients' privacy and forces them to endure a humiliating experience. Estimates of recipients who abuse drugs range from 10% to 25%, depending on the source (Popple & Leighninger, 2004). (This compares with an estimated 6% in the general public.) However, a study in Louisiana, a state that also initiated drug testing for recipients, found that only 2% tested positive. Therefore, no hard evidence exists that most welfare recipients abuse drugs.

How Efficient Is the Policy?

Efficiency concerns whether a policy and its implementation through a program are economical. To what extent does the policy address the problem or issue it intends to with the least expenditure of time, effort, and money?

Case Example   Drug testing is very expensive, especially when conducted on a large population such as people receiving public assistance. Maryland determined that testing welfare recipients for drugs for one year would cost at least $1.2 million. Additionally, the state would have to pour significant additional funds into providing treatment for recipients who tested positive. Needless to say, the Maryland legislature determined that the policy was too expensive and dropped it after two months.

Is the Policy Ethically Sound?

To what extent do the policy and the program implementing it respect people's rights to dignity, confidentiality, and self-determination? Is the policy honest and straightforward

---

[4]The case example, the arguments posed, and many of the questions raised are adopted from a policy analysis of the issue discussed on pp. 269–271 from P. R. Popple and L. Leighninger, *The Policy-Based Profession*, 3e, © 2004 by Allyn & Bacon.

in its stated intent? Do people who might be affected by the policy clearly understand it and its implications? Does it concur with current legal requirements?

Case Example   We have already raised numerous ethical concerns, including violating individual rights and forcing innocent people to subject themselves to the demeaning process of drug testing. Additionally, some questions have been raised regarding whether drug testing in this context is legal and constitutional. How would you like it if drug testing was required for you to go to school?

What Does Evaluation of Potential Alternative Policies Reveal?

To what extent does the policy under examination propose the best way to address the issue or solve the problem? Are there other more effective, efficient, and ethical policy approaches?

Case Example   What other alternative policy approaches to the problem of possible drug abuse by public assistance recipients might be proposed? One alternative is to limit the focus on the potential drug abuse of welfare recipients and to concentrate on drug abuse prevention with respect to the general population. Saunders (1995) makes three recommendations among others. First, antidrug prevention programs could be conducted on a large-scale basis in the schools. Second, community coalitions could be established to explore problems, provide community outreach to targeted groups such as those at greatest risk of drug abuse, and undertake major media campaigns aimed at prevention. Third, policymakers could "adopt policies that reduce the harm caused by alcohol and drugs" and "eliminate policies that stress punishment to deter use. Such policies should emphasize the promotion and protection of health and the prevention of disease" (pp. 2345–2346).

Burke (1995) proposes diverting funds used to finance the War on Drugs to provide "treatment on demand" for people seeking to stop drug abuse (p. 2355). She indicates that, although huge amounts of public money have been poured into stopping illegal drug trafficking and use, "the availability of illicit substances remains virtually unchanged, . . . the potency and purity of drugs have increased, and prices in many cases have actually declined" (p. 2348). She maintains that making treatment accessible and affordable will be more cost-effective in the long run and will directly address the problem.

What Recommendations Can Be Established for Positive Changes?

How can the current policy be amended so that it becomes more effective, efficient, and ethically sound? Or should this policy be eradicated and a new one developed to take its place?

Case Example   We established that Maryland legislators withdrew their policy on drug testing. Instead, they decided to require all public assistance applicants to undergo an extensive interview process by trained substance abuse counselors in order to discover ongoing drug addiction. Apparently, the legislators felt that this was a positive change. However, this policy approach still is founded on the degrading assumption that people receiving public assistance should somehow be subjected to scrutiny for drug abuse.

Policy Practice and Policy Advocacy

It is the responsibility of social workers not only to analyze social welfare policies but also to strive to make changes when clients are inadequately served, treated unfairly, or could be better served. Schneider and Lester (2001) define *advocacy* as "the exclusive and mutual representation of a client(s) or cause in a forum, attempting to systematically influence decision making in an unjust or unresponsive system" (p. 65). Hepworth, Rooney, and Larsen (2002) elaborate a bit by defining *advocacy* as the process of

> working with and/or on behalf of clients (1) to obtain services or resources that would not otherwise be provided, (2) to modify or influence policies, procedures, or practices that adversely affect groups or communities, or (3) to promote legislation or policies that will result in the provision of much needed resources or services. (pp. 449–450)

Social workers advocate on their clients' behalf to obtain or improve service provision. This may or may not involve changing a policy. Rather, advocacy is an umbrella concept that includes a wide range of scenarios. Advocacy might involve assisting a client in urging a landlord to make needed rental unit repairs. It can entail providing an argument to an agency administrator to make an exception to some rule on a client's behalf. It also might mean advocating to improve a public assistance policy to provide adequate benefits to clients or to expunge a policy that requires humiliating drug testing to receive benefits.

Advocacy in the policy arena, thus, is a more specific subset of advocacy. Jansson (2003) defines *policy practice* as "efforts to change policies in legislative, agency, and community settings, whether by establishing new policies, improving existing ones, or defeating the policy initiatives of other people" (p. 13). Policy practice may also involve advocacy on behalf of "relatively powerless groups, such as women, children, poor people, African Americans, Asian Americans, Latinos, gay men and lesbians, and people with disabilities, [to] improve their resources and opportunities" (Jansson, 2003, p. 13). Highlight 7.4 profiles several people who pursued advocacy through policy practice at various times in history.

There are many ways that social workers and others can pursue policy practice and advocacy. Segal and Brzuzy (1998) explain:

> Policy practice is within the reach of all social workers. It can be as basic as registering to vote and voting, or as involved as running a political campaign or even running for office. The most important policy practice role is to become involved in one's community. Active participation in community affairs can open the way for involvement in local policy decision making, which may in turn lead to a national role. When greater numbers of social workers and social service agency clients become involved in the policymaking process, social welfare policies will become more responsive to people's needs. (p. 261)

Advocating for policy or program implementation change—whether at the national, state, local, or agency level—can involve a number of approaches. At least 10 methods exist that social workers can use to conduct policy practice and advocacy (Hepworth et al., 2002; Kirst-Ashman & Hull, 2002):

HIGHLIGHT 7.4
Figures Pursuing Policy Practice and Advocacy in a Historical Context

Jansson (2005) reflects on three cases in which social workers and other community advocates conducted policy practice and advocacy to improve social conditions and service provision. In 1966 George Wiley led various social workers, clients receiving public assistance, "civil rights workers," and assorted other welfare rights groups to take a stand against unfairness and inequity in public assistance policy and program implementation. Together, in 1967 they formed the National Welfare Rights Organization (NWRO), which planned and executed major welfare rights demonstrations (Day, 2000, p. 324). Jansson (2001) describes how, "[w]ith the help of community workers hired by settlement houses and other agencies, local chapters of welfare recipients were organized, not only to pressure local offices to be more responsive but to initiate lawsuits to force compliance with federal organizations" (p. 452). Additionally, the NWRO "challenged welfare laws[, and] . . . appeared on the behalf of the poor before congressional committees . . . to promote welfare reform. . . . The NWRO's efforts were augmented by the volunteered legal services of lawyers who shared the organization's convictions and supported the welfare reform movement. Many cases were argued and won before the Supreme Court, resulting in the expansion" of welfare recipients' rights (Jansson, 2005, p. 279). The organization "demanded publicity about welfare rights and benefits, information heretofore kept classified, and after extended struggles prepared and distributed handbooks on client rights to welfare mothers" (Day, 2000, p. 324).

Marian Wright Edelman provides another excellent example of policy practice and advocacy. She gave up other career aspirations to become a much needed civil rights lawyer in the 1960s. She

handled many civil rights cases, especially helping students "get out of jail" (Jansson, 2005, p. 284). Driven by her strong beliefs in positive change and hard work, she endured many hardships including being intimidated by dogs and even being thrown in jail herself. One of her greatest accomplishments was the establishment of the Children's Defense Fund (CDF) in 1973. This advocacy organization's purpose was "to provide systematic and long-term assistance to children and adolescents and to ensure that their needs are an important matter of public policy" (Jansson, 2005, p. 284). By soliciting "grants from foundations and private donors, . . . [Edelman and the CDF] developed research and lobbying capabilities that she used to document a variety of problems encountered by the nations' children" (Jansson, 2001, p. 452). Issues included teen pregnancy, mental health, family support, and child care. This paved the way for further attention to the necessity of providing adequate child care for the nation's children. In May 1996, over 3,000 organizations, along with the Children's Defense Fund, sponsored a "Stand for Children Rally" in Washington, D.C. Then, in 1997, President Bill Clinton and his wife, Hillary, sponsored another major event, the White House Conference on Child Care (Trattner, 1999, p. 133).

A final example of policy practice and advocacy involves the establishment of the Political Action Committee for Candidate Election (PACE) by the National Association of Social Workers (NASW) in 1976. PACE solicits information from political candidates to establish their positions on social welfare issues and determine the extent to which their stances comply with social work values and goals. It organizes NASW members throughout the country to support appropriate candidates, solicits funds, and provides significant campaign donations (Weismiller & Rome, 1995).

1. *Persuade:* In the policy practice context, *persuasion* is the act of providing decision makers "with additional information that may allow them to make a different decision" (Kirst-Ashman & Hull, 2002, p. 365). What information might a worker give decision makers so that they might view the issue or problem from a different perspective that coincides more with social work values?

2. *Use complaint or grievance processes:* These are "administrative procedures designed to ensure that clients or client groups who have been denied benefits or rights to which they are entitled get equitable treatment" (Kirst-Ashman & Hull, 2002, p. 366). Usually this involves an outside objective person or group making a decision regarding whether rights or policies have been violated. Initiating a complaint or grievance process draws attention to an issue and forces an agency or governmental unit to publicly make a determination regarding the complaint's validity.

3. *Initiate legal action:* This involves filing a lawsuit. As with following a formal complaint or grievance process, pursuing this alternative brings an issue to public attention and forces a decision to be made. A downside of legal action, however, is that it's expensive.

4. *Form coalitions with other social workers and agencies:* These can enhance political pressure (Hepworth et al., 2002). Greater numbers working together can wield greater political clout.

5. *Provide expert testimony in formal settings:* Doing this in courtrooms or community forums or before a legislature can help persuade decision makers. Hepworth and colleagues (2002) explain that "[s]ocial workers may exert a powerful force in influencing the development of public policies or developing resources by speaking forcefully about clients' problems and needs in the political and public arenas" (p. 453).

6. *Gather information and supportive data to bolster claims about issues and recommendations for change* (Hepworth et al., 2002): Conducting surveys and researching facts can provide persuasive information.

7. *Educate pertinent community groups:* This can be helpful in initiating policy change. Hepworth and colleagues (2002) suggest that "all forms of the media should be considered, including press campaigns; telephone contacts; local television programs concerned with public issues; panel discussions at local, state, and national conventions; exhibits and speeches at meetings of influential civic organizations" (p. 453). Relevant groups can also be educated by letter-writing and e-mail campaigns concerning issues.

8. *Provide decision makers with relevant information* (Hepworth et al., 2002; Kirst-Ashman, 2002): Sometimes collecting signatures on a petition can emphasize that substantial numbers of people feel as you do.

9. *Organize groups of clients affected by the policy:* This can help to convey to decision makers the strength of a policy change appeal (Hepworth et al., 2002).

10. *Practice legislative advocacy:* This is the process of influencing legislators to benefit some category of clients (Kirst-Ashman & Hull, 2001). Some of the approaches mentioned here (e.g., writing letters and working with other agencies and client groups) can be used to address issues in the political arena. The more people come together to raise issues and suggest policy changes, the greater the potential impact on politicians. NASW's PACE, described in Highlight 7.4, is an

HIGHLIGHT 7.5
Focus on Another Policy Practice Role: Social Workers in Politics

Note that some social workers have also assumed political roles. One social worker ran for the U.S. Senate and five for the U.S. House of Representatives in the November 2004 elections (Fred, 2004). Four of these workers have been in politics for years. NASW Government Relations Manager Dave Dempsey indicated that these people "have not forgotten their roots as social workers"; he continued that "[s]ocial workers who become politicians can bring their principles, values, ethics, knowledge, and skills to bear on social problems in a larger context than individual practice. . . . Virtually all the social worker politicians that I've had a chance to talk to personally have made the point that social work skills fit the political process and environment beautifully" (Fred, 2004, p. 11).

Sen. Barbara Mikulski (D-MD), for example, has served as a long-term advocate for "seniors, women, and poor people"; she has composed legislation protecting elderly couples from bankruptcy when one spouse has to enter a nursing home, pressed for "a prescription drug benefit under Medicare," written legislation requiring national "standards for mammograms," and advocated for "legislation that gives uninsured women access to screenings and treatment for breast and cervical cancer" (Fred, 2004, p. 11).

Rep. Susan Davis (DCA) provides another example of how a social worker can strive to affect national policy. She has "fought to regulate the dietary supplement industry and pushed for legislation requiring that health plans provide coverage for second medical opinions," in addition to advocating for increased benefits for veterans (Fred, 2004, p. 11).

example of how an organization might undertake legislative advocacy. *Lobbying*—that is, hiring individuals (called *lobbyists*) who attempt to influence legislators' decisions and votes through direct communication—is another means of conducting legislative advocacy. Highlight 7.5 introduces one other potential policy practice role for social workers—becoming a politician.

Looking Ahead

This chapter provided a basic perspective on social welfare policy and the ways in which programs are implemented based on their policy foundation. The next chapter will discuss policies regulating the primary financial programs in the United States. Subsequent chapters will discuss various contexts in which workers practice, the populations with whom they work, and the policies and programs that govern what they do.

For Further Exploration on the Internet

See this text's Book Companion Website at **www.socialwork.wadsworth.com/ kirstashman_intro2e** for descriptors and hot links to URLs relevant to this chapter, selected InfoTrac articles and exercises, and tutorial quizzes.

POLICIES AND PROGRAMS TO COMBAT POVERTY

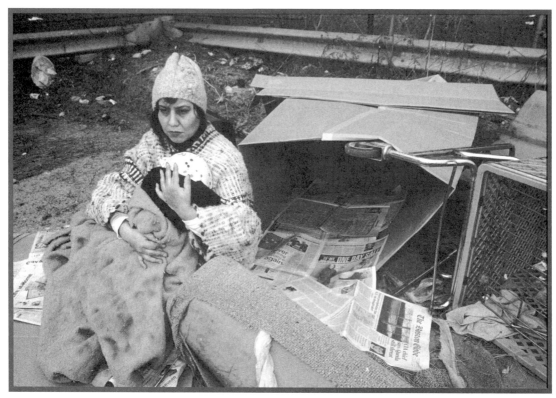

Think about these questions:

- Do you know people who are poor?
- What does poverty mean to you?
- Where would you place yourself on the continuum ranging from poor to middle class to wealthy?
- Who is to blame for people being poor? Is it their own fault, or are they victims of unfair social conditions?

Now consider the following facts:

- In the United States, a little over 9% of whites, almost 25% of African Americans, almost 26% of American Indians and Alaskan Natives, almost 13% of Asian Americans, and almost 23% of Hispanics live in families with incomes below the poverty line; over 12% of the total population or 33.9 million people are poor (U.S. Census Bureau, 2003, No. 697). (We have established that the *poverty line* is the annual cash income level, according to family size, that the federal government determines is necessary to maintain each individual or family at a minimal subsistence level.)
- Almost 16% of all U.S. children under age 18 and over 10% of people age 65 or older are poor (U.S. Census Bureau, 2003, Nos. 701, 703).
- When considering race as a factor, 30% of African American children and over 27% of Hispanic children under age 18 live in poverty, whereas only about 13% of white children do (U.S. Census Bureau, 2003, No. 701).
- The quality of living for the majority of Americans has been decreasing in recent years (Kornblum & Julian, 2004).
- The median (midpoint) household income in the United States is $41,994; over 29% of all households have incomes of less than $25,000, and almost 25% have incomes of $75,000 or more (U.S. Census Bureau, 2003, Nos. 680, 683).
- The median income for African American households is about 66% and for Hispanic households about 75% of the median income for white households (U.S. Census Bureau, 2003, No. 684).
- About 1% of all households in the United States have more than one-third of the wealth (Kornblum & Julian, 2004).

A huge and widening chasm exists between the wealthy and the impoverished, the "haves" and the "have-nots" (Kornblum & Julian, 2004, p. 179). This is true not only in the United States but also around the world, as Highlight 8.1 explains. This chapter explores the policies and programs designed to combat poverty in the United States.

Interestingly, although this chapter addresses policies formulating programs to *combat* poverty, there are many questions about their effectiveness. Do they really combat poverty, or do they simply alleviate some of people's most desperate needs? Specifically, this chapter will

- Recognize poverty as a global problem.
- Examine poverty in the United States.
- Address race, gender, and single parenthood as variables related to poverty and the feminization of poverty.
- Describe special assessment issues concerning women.

HIGHLIGHT 8.1

International Perspectives: Poverty Is a Global Problem

The gap between rich and poor is dramatically increasing not only in the United States but also all over the world. Kornblum and Julian (2004) report that 1.2 billion of the almost 6.5 billion people on Earth are so poverty-stricken that they must survive on $1 per day or less. They continue,

> One-fifth of the world's people live in the richest nations (including the United States), and their average incomes are 15 times higher than those of the one-fifth who live in the poorest nations. In the world today there are about 157 billionaires and about 2 million millionaires, but there are approximately 100 million homeless people. (p. 222)

Johannesen (1997) emphasizes how individual nations are no longer isolated and able to function independently from each other:

> Today we are more dependent on each other than ever before. Globalization is a consequence of increased human mobility, enhanced communications, greatly increased trade and capital flows, and technological developments. In turn it has created opportunities for growth and development and permitted countries to share experiences and learn from each other. It also promotes a cross-fertilization of ideals, cultural values, and aspirations. (p. 147)

Because of their growing interdependence, U.S. citizens can no longer remain isolated and "safe" from global crises. Bibus and Link (1999) explain:

With an international perspective, it becomes clear that the well-being, income distribution, and social security of people in one region are intimately related to worldwide economic, environmental, political, health, and other forces. No one government can enact social policies effectively without the cooperation of other governments. For example, both the United States and the United Kingdom have embarked on strategies for welfare reform. . . . However, neither country, despite their status as economically developed and recently prospering, can assure their citizens that jobs with living wages and decent benefits for health care, retirement, or disability compensation will be available. Job markets in both countries are predominantly dependent on global market forces such as the prevailing wages for skilled or unskilled labor, the availability of energy and fuel, and the movements of multinational corporations. (pp. 98–99)

Midgley (1997) emphasizes the importance of pursuing economic survival and social justice from an international perspective. Social justice, which involves equal treatment for all, is related to economic justice—the distribution of resources in a fair and equitable manner. He stresses "the urgent need" for the social work profession "to engage in political activism and to campaign more effectively on issues of social justice. . . . If social work is to fulfill its historic commitment to helping oppressed ethnic minorities, the poor, refugees, and the victims of HIV/AIDS, it must itself have the political potency to effect progressive social change" (p. 175).

- Examine empowerment of women through consciousness-raising and the use of a grassroots approach.
- Investigate what it is like to be poor.
- Explore the relationship between poverty and social class.
- Examine economic, political, and cultural explanations for poverty.
- Describe major social insurance and public assistance programs in the United States and address relevant policy issues concerning them.

- Review some aspects of the Canadian Child Tax Benefit program to reflect an international perspective.
- Appraise stereotypes about public assistance recipients.
- Encourage critical thinking about resource and service provision to combat poverty.

 # Poverty in the United States

People living in poverty obviously have less access to resources and, therefore, greater need. *Poverty* is the condition of having inadequate "money to buy things that are considered necessary and desirable" (Kornblum & Julian, 2004, p. 184). This concept is more complex than might be immediately apparent. What is considered "necessary and desirable" in Vietnam, Jamaica, or Morocco may be very different from what fulfills these criteria in the United States. Many people also expand the definition of poverty to include "not only the lack of money but also . . . a lifestyle composed of values, attitudes, and behaviors that are related to being poor" (Popple & Leighninger, 2005, p. 242).

When the U.S. government refers to *poverty*, it uses a designated formula focusing on the number of persons living in a family or household and the amount of income that family receives. Note the difference between income and wealth. *Income* is the amount of money earned by family members in a year. *Wealth* is the accumulated amount of money and other assets that makes up a person's total worth; this includes cars, property, stocks, and anything else of value the individual or family owns. The U.S. government gauges poverty by focusing on income because total wealth is too difficult to measure. It has established a *poverty line* intended to "specify the minimum amount required to support an average family of given composition at the lowest level consistent with standards of living prevailing in this country" (Orshansky, 1965, p. 214).

According to this measure, 33.9 million people live in poverty in the United States (U.S. Census Bureau, 2003, No. 697). White people, who have proportionately greater numbers, make up most of the poor population in the United States. However, as the U.S. Census Bureau data presented earlier suggest, people of color are much more likely to be poor.

Gender, Family Structure, and Race

Over 59% of all women age 16 and over work outside the home (U.S. Census Bureau, 2003, No. 588). In general, women earn about 77% of what men earn (Shaw & Lee, 2004). Discrepancies between men's and women's incomes exist regardless of educational level and profession (Renzetti & Curran, 2003; Sapiro, 2003). Women tend to be clustered in low-paying, supportive occupations such as clerical workers, teachers, and service workers, whereas men tend to be found in higher-paying occupations such as managers, skilled blue-collar workers, construction workers, and engineers; women are less likely than men to become doctors, dentists, or lawyers (U.S. Census Bureau, 2003, No. 615). With "equivalent work experience and skills, women are far less likely to get to the top of their professions or corporations. They are halted by unseen barriers, such as men's negative attitudes to senior women and low perceptions of their abilities, motivation, training, and skills. This barrier has been called a *glass ceiling*" (Kirk & Okazawa-Rey, 2004, p. 321).

Regarding family structure, almost 26% of households with children under age 18 are headed by single women (U.S. Census Bureau, 2003, No. 70). The median income of female-headed families is about 43% of the median for families with two parents present (U.S. Census Bureau, 2003, No. 689). Female-headed families are six times more likely to be poor than their married couple counterparts (Renzetti & Curran, 2003). Seventy-one percent of single women with children under age 6 and almost 82% single women with children aged 6 to 17 work outside the home (U.S. Census Bureau, 2003, No. 597).

Upon further examination racial differences emerge. The median income for all African American families is a bit over 62% and for Hispanic families almost 64% of the median income for all white families (U.S. Census Bureau, 2003, No. 689). Women of color are significantly more likely to be poor than white women (Renzetti & Curran, 2003). Almost 25% of white female-headed families are poor, while almost 41% of African American and almost 44% of Hispanic female-headed households live below the poverty line (Rawlings, 2000; Renzetti & Curran, 2003). As a result, children living in single-parent families headed by women, especially women of color, are at greater risk of poverty. All three of these variables—race, single parenthood, and female family head—increase risk.

Is this disturbing news for you? What do you think are the reasons for such discrepancies?

The Feminization of Poverty

An important concept, the *feminization of poverty* refers to the fact that women as a group are more likely to be poor than are men (Burn, 2005).

Case Example   Ginny, a divorced single mother of three, isn't making it. She doesn't earn enough at her waitress job, even with Saturday night tips, to pay the rent and put enough food on her table. Her baby-sitter has quit, and her sister-in-law says she can't help out anymore. Now what? Ginny surely has no money to pay a new baby-sitter even if she could find one. Ginny is frantic. Where will she go? What will she do?

Consider how the feminization of poverty may be involved here. We have established that women in general earn less than men, even with equivalent education and experience in the same field, although women tend to enter fields with lower pay. Additionally, single women with children are at increased risk of lower incomes and poverty. If Ginny is a non-Asian woman of color, her risk is even greater.

In what ways might Ginny be the victim of oppression? What aspects of her situation decrease her potential to maintain an adequate standard of living and provide for her family? What opportunities are unavailable to her? What support systems are lacking?

In addition to having a greater likelihood of being poor, women are more likely to be primary caregivers for children and the elderly than men, which can detract from their focus on career and making money. And they are victimized by specific kinds of violence, including sexual assault and domestic violence, rarely experienced by men.

As with other populations-at-risk and oppressed groups, social workers assess women's problems and issues within the context of their macro environments. Often problems are identified and goals defined with empowerment in mind. Sometimes planned changes focus on the individual; other times the focus is on the macro environment. Gutierrez and Lewis (1998) identify at least three approaches that assist in this assessment process: (1) using "a gender lens," (2) using "empowerment through consciousness-raising," and (3) thinking about a "grassroots, bottom-up approach" to changing communities (pp. 100–101). These principles help guide social workers' analysis of women's position within the macro social environment and provide clues for their empowerment.

A Gender Lens

Using a gender lens to view the plight of women in the macro social environment assumes that sexism is relevant to the experiences of many women and is the basis for many of women's difficulties. Such a gender lens emphasizes that women not only are part of the larger community but themselves make up a community of women within that larger community. In essence, this establishes a new way of looking at the world, with women and their issues becoming the focus (Bricker-Jenkins & Lockett, 1995).

Empowerment Through Consciousness-Raising and Critical Thinking

Consciousness-raising is the process of facilitating people's understanding of a social issue with personal implications when there was little grasp of that issue before. (Chapter 3 discussed consciousness-raising as a means of empowerment for women in groups.) In this case, it involves a serious examination by women of themselves and their feelings about a range of issues involving women. Using this approach, social workers can help women become aware of the issues engulfing them in their environment before these women take steps to address them.

Bricker-Jenkins and Lockett (1995) suggest that a basic approach for consciousness-raising entails helping women ask themselves a series of questions and think about potential answers. Such questions might include these:

> "Who am I?" What are my needs, my desires, my visions of a life that is safe, healthy, and fulfilling?
> "Who says?" What is the source of my self-definition and that of my reality? Does it conform to my experience of self and the world?
> "Who benefits from this definition?" Does it conform to my needs, my "truths"? Is it possible for me to live by these definitions? If not, . . .
> "What must change, and how?" (p. 2535)

A social worker can help a woman answer these questions by focusing on and helping her define her self-worth, her values, and her treatment by the world. If she determines that her treatment is unfair or inadequate because she is a woman, how can she make changes in her macro environment to receive better or fairer treatment? Consciousness-raising thus can become a foundation of empowerment. First, a woman explores herself. Next, she examines issues and appraises her status. Finally, she proposes plans to improve her life and her environment.

Case Example   Jazlyn is a single mother of two children, ages 2½ and 4. For the past few months, she's been receiving public assistance through Temporary Assistance to Needy Families (TANF). She is about to begin a job training program in food services. One of her problems is finding adequate and flexible day care. Another problem is receiving court-mandated child support payments from her ex-husband, who can't seem to hold down a job for very long. Still another problem is the high rent on her tiny apartment, given the shortage of adequate affordable housing. Other problems are lack of a social life and difficulties in obtaining credit to buy a sorely needed new car. Her "ex" ruined her credit rating while they were married.

Alone, Jazlyn feels stuck. She views her problems as personal and individual. She tends to blame herself after the fact for making the "wrong decisions." Jazlyn's social worker, Rochelle, in a *counselor* role, can help Jazlyn think through these issues, identify alternatives, evaluate their pros and cons, and develop a plan of action. Part of Jazlyn's consciousness-raising concerns her growing awareness that she is not alone, but rather shares the same plight with many other women. She can come to realize that many things in her world are not her fault, but rather result from basic social conditions working against her. As an *educator*, Rochelle can provide information about resources, services, and tactics for macro change.

Empowerment Through a Grassroots, Bottom-Up Approach

The final facet of empowerment involves proposing and working toward positive changes in the macro environment. A "grassroots, bottom-up approach" means that people at the bottom of the formal power structure, such as ordinary citizens, band together to establish a power base and pursue macro changes. Often the focus is on helping individual community residents strengthen relationships among themselves, develop shared goals, and establish coordinated plans to achieve these goals. The focus of change is usually an issue that directly affects the community residents involved.

The common theme of women's grassroots efforts is that women work together to initiate and implement change. Examples of established grassroots organizations include the National Organization of Women, the National Women's Political Caucus, the Women's Action Alliance, and the Older Women's League.

Another phrase often used for this approach is "the personal is political" (Gutierrez & Lewis, 1998, p. 101; Segal & Brzuzy, 1995, p. 150). In other words, some problems and issues that tend to affect women on the basis of their gender go beyond the personal or the individual. Rather, such problems are structurally based, affecting many women. The implication, then, is the need for macro-level social change to improve conditions and provide services.

Consider Jazlyn's plight and the ways in which a social worker like Rochelle might help women directly affected by circumstances and a lack of resources pursue macro changes. As a *mobilizer*, Rochelle can discuss with Jazlyn and other clients having similar concerns how to join together and confront community leaders and politicians about their various problems. Together they can raise issues and try to identify a plan of action to address them. Specific questions to ask include the following:

- Should they form a social action group?
- Can community funds be directed to help subsidize child care centers? Can Jazlyn and other local women establish their own center, pooling resources to pay for staff and volunteering their free time to help cut costs?
- How can Jazlyn and other women not receiving child support from itinerant ex-husbands or partners obtain their fair share? Is there some community agency available to help them locate missing fathers and force payment? If not, why not? Can such a service be developed?
- What about the lack of adequate, reasonable housing? How can the community address this problem? Can community leaders help? Can private developers be encouraged or subsidized to build the housing community mothers need?
- Might community events be organized to fulfill the social needs of single mothers and decrease their isolation? Can interested women form clubs or socialization groups to help them "get out" regularly? In a *facilitator* role, could Rochelle assist in establishing and coordinating such a group?
- How can Jazlyn and other community women work together to find ways to establish credit? As a group, might they approach local banks and businesses to discuss the issue? Can processes be established to determine when credit problems are not their fault, but rather the fault of ex-spouses?

Poverty and Social Class

Sociologists, who study how societies are structured, tend to divide the population into categories of social position based on the extent to which people have access to the goods and services the society values. Another term for this categorization is *social stratification*. The population, then, is divided into *social classes*—"categories of people who have similar access to resources and opportunities" (Macionis, 2005, p. 473). People in the same social class share things in common such as educational and employment opportunities, access to health care, and ability to acquire material possessions.

Nineteenth-century philosophers did much to shape the way we think about people and social class. Karl Marx, for example, viewed social class primarily as an economic phenomenon related to a person's wealth. Max Weber expanded on this idea, claiming that a person's social class is determined by status and power in addition to wealth. *Status* is one's social standing and prestige in comparison to others. *Power* is the ability to move people on a chosen course to produce an effect or achieve some goal (Homan, 2004; Martinez-Brawley, 1995). For example, a homeless person who has a mental illness and who lives under the lowest-level steps in a five-story parking garage is in quite a different class from the physician who is also the administrator of a large, prestigious research hospital next door.

We might think of our society as having several basic classes (Kendall, 2004). *Upper-class* people include "investors, heirs, and executives" who have extensive wealth, power, and status; this includes the billionaire creators of a computer company, powerful politicians from wealthy families, "sports or entertainment celebrities," chief executive officers (CEOs) of big corporations, and "top-level professionals" earning millions of dollars a year (Kendall, 2004, p. 30).

Upper middle-class people include "professionals (for example, physicians and attorneys), business analysts, owners of small businesses, stockbrokers, and corporate managers. These individuals generally do not own the means of production but have substantial control over production and other workers" (Kendall, 2004, p. 30).

Middle-class people include "white-collar office workers, middle-management personnel, and people in support positions (for example, medical technologists, nurses, and legal and medical secretaries), semiprofessionals, and nonretail sales-workers" (Kendall, 2004, p. 30).

Working-class people include blue-collar workers who perform manual and semiskilled jobs in industrial settings or occupy lower-level service positions "(for example, day care workers, checkout clerks, cashiers, and counter help in fast-food restaurants)" (Kendall, 2004, pp. 30–31). On the whole, they receive less prestige and have less access to resources than the classes above them.

The *working poor* are those who assume unskilled positions that might be seasonal, like migrant agricultural workers, or work in jobs that receive the lowest pay; despite the fact that they're employed, they often live paycheck to paycheck, just barely getting by (Kendall, 2004, p. 31).

Finally, the *chronically poor,* about 20% of the U.S. population who have only 3.6% of the total U.S. wealth, have very few resources and have difficulty finding adequate employment to support their families; these people live below the poverty level and often have more debts than assets (Kendall, 2004).

Focus on Critical Thinking 8.1 explores what it is like to be poor and what limitations are placed on options.

Reasons People Are Poor

Reasons offered to explain why poverty continues to exist tend to fall in three general categories: (1) economic, (2) political, and (3) cultural.

Economic Explanations

Economic explanations for poverty focus on the structure of the economy (Coleman & Cressey, 1999). Poverty occurs when wages are too low and not enough adequately paying jobs exist for people to earn what they need to survive. Another structural concern related to poverty involves the escalating number of technical jobs requiring specialized training. People without such training can be left behind. Still another factor contributing to poverty is the increasing trend for industries to move from North America to other parts of the world where production costs are cheaper because people are willing to work for less. The result, of course, is decreased availability of jobs here. The plight of many U.S. farmers poses yet an additional structural worry. If farming costs soar here and imported food is cheaper, farmers are put out of business because they can't compete. Where, then, do they turn to make a living?

Political Explanations

Political explanations for poverty emphasize that politicians shape social policies that can decrease, maintain, or increase poverty (Coleman & Cressey, 1999). For example, decreasing levels of financial assistance to poor people likely increase the number of poor and the depths of their poverty. Similarly, increasing the tax rate for people in the working and lower classes while decreasing the rate for people in the middle and upper classes will have comparable results.

FOCUS ON CRITICAL THINKING 8.1
What Is It Like to Be Poor?[1]

What kind of background do you come from? How would you describe it in terms of having adequate resources to grow, develop, and thrive? Do you come from a middle- or upper-class family in which resources were plentiful and you had lots of "stuff"? Or did your family have difficulty scraping by and paying essential bills on time?

Poor people must make hard choices regarding what things they can possess. There's little room for luxury. Of the following items, which do you feel are absolute necessities for your daily life? Which could you live without? How would you prioritize them in order of importance? What would it be like to be poor and forced to make hard choices? What would it be like to have to live without?

- A home that you or your family own
- A room of your own
- A home or apartment that your family rents
- A single room where you and your family can stay
- A working kitchen along with a range of utensils
- A plug-in electric frying pan
- Electricity
- Heat
- Air conditioning

- Three meals a day that are nutritionally well balanced
- Three meals a day of macaroni and artificial cheese
- A private shower with hot water
- Running water
- Access to a communal water supply
- A washer and dryer
- A good job that pays adequately or well
- A minimum-wage job
- Health insurance
- Dental insurance
- Nice clothes
- Two changes of old clothes
- A telephone
- A new car
- An old broken-down car
- A digital plasma surround sound home theater system
- A 13" TV
- A PC-based TIVO with DVD burner
- A plain old VCR
- A hyper transport 4.0 GHz Gamer PC with GeForce Ultra Graphics, 400 GB drive, 2,000 MHz system bus, and 16x dual layer DVD
- A Walmart discount special PC

[1]This idea for this is derived from Burger and Youkeles (2000, p. 313).

Gans (1971) proposes that the wealthy find that having a social class of poor people is useful. First, poor people can do the "dirty work" for rich people that the latter don't want to do. Poor people are more willing to take service jobs, jobs requiring hard labor, or those posing danger than their richer counterparts. Second, having a poor social class emphasizes that the wealthy are higher in the social structure. It reinforces their higher status and allows them to look down on classes below them.

Cultural Explanations: The Need for Empowerment

A third rationale for poverty's existence involves a cultural explanation (Coleman & Cressey, 1999; Kornblum & Julian, 2001; Popple & Leighninger, 2005). According to this view, a *culture of poverty* exists whereby people learn to live in poverty, accept its values and low expectations, and fail to see any way out of it (Lewis, 1965). Unfortunately, this is a negative view that places the blame on individuals. It assumes that poverty is their own and their families' fault. It implies that if these families would only pull themselves up by their bootstraps they could beat the poverty trap. In reality, it's much more complicated. Without financial resources, family support, and positive role models, it's much more difficult to "get ahead." Following are several case examples of children trapped in poverty.

Case Example   When thinking about children ensnared in poverty, three home visits come to mind. At the time, I was working as a social work counselor in a day treatment center for children and adolescents experiencing emotional, behavioral, and academic problems. The center provided counseling and special education for young people requiring special treatment but living in their own homes.

The first case involved a home visit with a 16-year-old client, Danielle, at the two-room apartment where she, her mother, and her little brother lived. I knocked, and Danielle invited me in. I noticed that the door into the apartment from the dark, dingy hallway didn't quite shut tightly. The walls inside the tiny apartment looked grimy, with peeling yellowed wallpaper. I stood there for a moment until Danielle asked me if I'd like to sit down. This was perplexing because the only furniture in the room was a shabby table and a twin bed. For lack of other options, I sat down on the bed, as did Danielle. There we discussed the business for which I had come, involving Danielle's progress and future plans. I noticed the only other items in the two rooms were an old 18-inch television on the table, two mattresses on the floor with some bedding on top in the other room, and eight brown paper bags filled with what looked like clothes or rags. They apparently shared a bathroom down the hall with some other tenants. Her mother and brother were nowhere to be seen; in fact, her mother, a cocaine addict, was rarely around.

Danielle had a dream of marrying one of the many men 10 to 20 years her senior with whom she was having sex. Her vision included living in a neatly painted white house surrounded by a white picket fence in a well-to-do neighborhood and living happily ever after. She balked when I gently questioned how realistic that picture was. I presented to her other potential alternatives such as finishing school and getting a job. (A higher level of education is clearly related to higher income later in life.) But Danielle was several years behind her grade in school and was not much motivated to achieve in that area. She didn't understand what purpose academic achievement had. No one in her family, or her neighborhood for that matter, had ever thought much of school. It hadn't seemed to do any of them any good. Instead, she was hoping to find some Prince Charming to save her and care for her. The adult boyfriends she described didn't sound much like Prince Charming to me.

It was much more difficult for Danielle to climb out of poverty than it had been for the students I had known in my middle-class high school, which boasted a strong academic program and active parental involvement, to survive and prosper. There, the majority of students simply assumed they would go to college. The main concern for many was whether they would get into one of the exclusive eastern private schools.

Case Example   Another young person living in poverty was Mike, an exceptionally bright 14-year-old who attended the same day treatment center. Mike found life depressing and tried to escape through drugs. He simply withdrew, caused virtually no problems (except failure to perform in school), and hoped that those around him would forget he was there. Like Danielle, he lived with his mother, a single parent who busied herself with her own life and relationships, and so was rarely home. Mike treasured an old broken camera he said his father had given him long ago. Mike's dream was to travel from his midwestern home to Utah, where he thought his father lived with a new family. However, he had not had any contact with his father for over seven years.

Mike grasped ideas quickly and had a perceptive sensitivity concerning others' feelings. I felt that Mike was clearly "college material." When I approached him about the possibility, he chuckled and then quickly apologized because he didn't want to offend me. He explained, "Are you kidding? Me? Go to college? How could I ever go to college? I'm so far behind. Who would ever pay for it?" I couldn't respond, because I didn't know the answer. What options were realistically open to Mike? What real chances did he have to "get ahead"?

Case Example   Another example, from the same treatment center, was Rosalie, age 13 going on 23. Rosalie looked like an attractive grown woman. She wore lots of makeup and expensive clothes. Although she supposedly lived with her mother, who had a cognitive disability, she usually resided with other people. Rosalie's attendance at the treatment center was spotty at best. She was too busy at night in her job as a prostitute. At that she made very good money and could afford many more things than her peers. She returned on Monday with a noticeable increase in bust size. She said one of her friends had taken her to a special clinic for implants, but it probably was her pimp. Eventually, Rosalie quit the center and disappeared. Her perceptions of the future her teachers and social workers offered her could not compete with the concrete rewards she was getting from her life on the streets.

A Culture of Poverty?

The idea that a culture of poverty exists is highly controversial. The term implies that people come to feel comfortable in such a "culture" and even consider it desirable to remain in poverty rather than expend the effort to change. Perhaps a more realistic way of looking at poverty involves understanding how difficult it can be for people with few resources and little support to break through into a higher social class. Few or no role models may exist. People who experience frequent failure and deprivation may quit trying to achieve in the system. Why try if there's no hope?

This is the reason the concept of empowerment is so critical. People in poverty must be empowered to see that change is possible. They must be provided viable options and credible hope.

 # Social Welfare Policies and Programs

Chapter 6 established that the Social Security Act of 1935 was one of the most significant pieces of legislation shaping social welfare policy during the last century. It established programs in three major categories:

1. *Health and welfare services*: Services provided to people including foster care, adoption, protective services, "activities for the aged, maternal and child health services, . . . public health activities," and a range of other public programs (U.S. Census Bureau, 2003, p. 355).
2. *Social insurance*: Financial benefits provided to people "to provide protection against wage loss resulting from retirement, prolonged disability, death, or unemployment, and protection against the cost of medical care during old age and disability" (U.S. Census Bureau, 2003, p. 353).
3. *Public assistance*: Financial and in-kind (services or goods versus cash) benefits provided to people who can't support themselves.

Chapter 6 also introduced divergent principles governing social insurance and public assistance, the two categories of programs discussed in this chapter. (The third category, health and welfare services, will be covered in subsequent chapters that address various fields of social work practice.) Social insurance is considered people's *right* because workers and their employers pay premiums while they work. Insurance protects people in the event of harm or loss. For example, you buy car insurance so that if you crash your car the insurance pays for repairs and any legal costs. Like other types of insurance, social insurance covers risks assumed while working, such as unemployment, injury, or illness, and inevitable conditions such as old age or death. Financial benefits are provided when such conditions occur. People receiving social insurance benefits work and pay premiums, so the benefits for them and their families are considered their right.

Public assistance, in contrast, is based on *need*. When people are unable to support themselves, the government provides financial benefits to help them do so. People receiving public assistance benefits never paid premiums, as did people collecting social insurance benefits. Therefore, many people believe that public assistance is not people's right and resent the fact that people need and get it. Public assistance is often derogatorily referred to as "welfare"—for example, TANF, which replaced Aid to Families with Dependent Children (AFDC) in 1996.

Note that terms can be confusing because they are used in different ways. Chapter 1 defined *social welfare* broadly as the general well-being of all people in a society. This is quite different from what most people mean when they refer to people "on welfare." Common negative conceptions about public assistance and its recipients are examined later in the chapter.

Both social insurance and public assistance are considered *income maintenance* programs. Such programs provide people with enough money, goods, and services to preserve an adequate standard of living and quality of life.

Figure 8.1 identifies some of the social programs under the U.S. social welfare system's social insurance and public assistance umbrellas. These reflect only a few examples of the many programs in the huge social welfare system.

 ## Social Work Roles

Social workers may or may not work in social service agencies implementing the programs this chapter discusses. However, they will most likely work with clients who are concerned about financial matters and who receive benefits

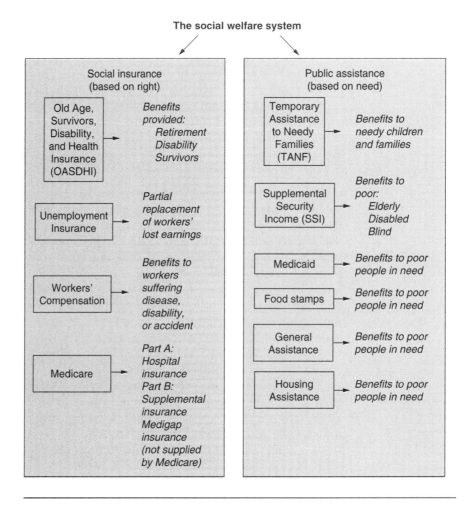

Figure 8.1 Social insurance and public assistance

from these programs. Therefore, brief overviews of major social insurance and public assistance programs are provided. Note that it's also important for you as an individual to understand these systems because, on a personal level, sooner or later they will probably impact you, your parents, and other older relatives.

 ## Social Insurance Policy

The primary social insurance programs in the United States include Old Age, Survivors, Disability, and Health Insurance (OASDHI); unemployment insurance; workers' compensation; and Medicare.

Old Age, Survivors, Disability, and Health Insurance

The term *Social Security*, commonly used in the United States, refers to "a group of social insurance programs developed by the federal government to provide economic security for people in their old age, disabled workers, and workers' survivors in cases of a worker's death" (Tracy & Ozawa, 1995, p. 2186). Social Security includes the financial benefits provided by Old Age, Survivors, Disability, and Health Insurance (OASDHI) and Medicare. Because these programs are types of social insurance, people are eligible to receive benefits only if they contributed an adequate part of their earnings according to established financial formulas. OASDHI, initially created by the Social Security Act of 1935, is the nation's most extensive social program, covering 90% of all workers; almost 45 million people receive Social Security checks each month (Social Security Administration, 2005). Benefits are administered by the Social Security Administration (SSA). Each major facet of OASDHI and Medicare is described briefly.

Retirement Benefits

People are eligible to receive retirement benefits if they are 62 or older, but they can receive full benefits only at age 65 or older. In the future, the minimum age to receive full benefits will increase to 67. Whiteman (2001) explains that "[a] complex set of factors including lifetime average earnings, age of retirement, and inflation factors determine the cash benefits that a person receives. . . . After a person begins receiving benefits, the Social Security Administration adjusts them each year to reflect changes in cost of living" (pp. 22–23). Because the eligibility requirements are highly complicated and complex, it's beyond the scope of this book to describe them in detail.

There has been much debate in recent years regarding the future of Social Security, especially with respect to retirement. Chapter 10 will review some of the issues as a major area of concern for people as they age.

Note that family members of retired or disabled Social Security beneficiaries may also receive benefits if they satisfy designated conditions. For example, family members including "an aged spouse, children, or a spouse taking care of a child under age 16 or disabled before age 22" may each receive some amount of benefits if they fulfill the required criteria (Tracy & Ozawa, 1995, p. 2188).

Disability Benefits

Tracy and Ozawa (1995) describe who can receive disability benefits:

> To receive disability benefits, a worker must be unable to engage in any substantial gainful activity . . . because of a severe physical or mental impairment that is expected to last for at least 12 months or to result in death. People with human immunodeficiency virus (HIV) infection or acquired immune deficiency syndrome (AIDS) may also qualify when they are no longer able to work or when they must severely limit their work. Education, work experience, and age are taken into account in determining disability. (p. 2188)

Survivors Benefits

Survivors of Social Security beneficiaries may also receive some portion of that recipient's benefits after his or her death if these survivors fulfill designated requirements. For example, widows and widowers "must be 60 years of age or older. They must be currently unmarried or have remarried after age 60 years to qualify" (Whiteman, 2001, p. 28). Similarly, "[u]nmarried children of an insured worker who are less than 18 years of age, or less than 19 years of age if they are attending elementary or high school full-time, are eligible for survivors benefits" (Whiteman, 2001, p. 29).

Unemployment Insurance and Workers' Compensation

Unemployment insurance and workers' compensation were also established by the Social Security Act of 1935. Although they are social insurance programs, they are usually not considered part of Social Security as such. The intent of these programs is to "provide cash benefits to workers as partial replacement of lost earnings. Unemployment compensation [insurance] covers workers who have lost their jobs, whereas workers' compensation covers individuals who are prevented from working as the result of a job-related disease, disability, or accident" (Jones, 1995, p. 2413).

Financing for unemployment insurance comes from a tax employers must pay based on a complicated formula involving their employees' wages. There are general federal mandates for how this is done, yet states also can dictate many specifics such as who is eligible and how long benefits are provided.

Funding for workers' compensation is totally different and varies from state to state. Most states require employers to purchase insurance to cover injured workers (Jones, 1995).

As with other forms of social insurance, establishing eligibility for benefits is complex. Social workers have little to do with these programs, which concentrate on providing some minimum income and ignore all other social, emotional, and physical needs. In any case, both programs are inadequate to meet actual needs, and their eligibility standards place extreme limitations on whom they cover (Jones, 1995).

Medicare

The Health Insurance for the Aged Act, passed in 1965, created Medicare and Medicaid (the latter will be discussed later as a public assistance program). *Medicare* is a form of social insurance financed by both employer and employee contributions based on earnings and other federal tax revenues. People who are eligible for Medicare include those who are 65 or older, are disabled, or have kidney disease.

Medicare comprises two main facets—Part A and Part B. Part A, Hospital Insurance, pays for four basic types of services. First, it covers services provided in and by hospitals (which is probably pretty obvious from the title). Second, it pays for limited stays in skilled nursing facilities such as nursing homes. Third, it covers some services (e.g., nursing care and speech, physical, and occupational therapy[2]) for people under a physician's care who are confined to their homes. Fourth, it provides *hospice* care, which involves health, homemaker, and other social services provided either at home or in a supportive, homelike facility for people suffering from a terminal illness. The idea is to make people as comfortable as possible during their final hours.

[2]*Physical therapy* is "the treatment or management of physical disability, malfunction, or pain by physical techniques, as exercise, massage, hydrotherapy, etc." (Nichols, 1999, p. 996). *Occupational therapy* is "therapy that utilizes useful and creative activities to facilitate psychological or physical rehabilitation" (Nichols, 1999, p. 914).

Too many children live in poverty. Almost 16% of all children in the United States live in poverty. When considering race as a factor, 30% of African American children and over 27% of Hispanic children under age 18 live in poverty here.

Note that all these services have designated time limits. Benefits are restricted based on certain criteria and also are limited in duration. People first must meet the requirements to receive treatment. Then treatment is administered according to complicated rules. Like OASDHI, the program is complex. Social workers accustomed to the programs and rules governing them often can help people navigate through the miles of red tape required to establish eligibility for benefits.

Medicare's Part B, Supplementary Medical Insurance, is designed to do just as its name implies—supplement benefits provided by Part A. It covers primarily physicians' fees regardless of where services are provided (e.g., their offices or hospitals). It also covers "diagnostic X-ray or laboratory tests, surgical dressing and devices, purchase or rental of durable medical equipment (such as wheelchairs and hospital beds), ambulance services, and prosthetic devices" (such as artificial limbs) (Tracy & Ozawa, 1995, p. 2190).

However, there are many things it does not cover including dental and vision care, routine physical examinations, and long-term nursing care (Whiteman, 2001).

It also is not free. Beneficiaries can enroll only during designated periods, have an initial deductible, and pay a monthly fee.

Because of its limited coverage, many elderly people opt to purchase additional insurance to make up for some of the gaps. Private insurance companies offer such policies, aptly called *Medigap* insurance (Whiteman, 2001). Like most other types of private insurance, the amount and type of coverage vary according to how much people are willing to pay for it.

Even Medigap insurance does not cover all the health care and services a person may need. Whiteman (2001) explains that "[c]overage for the costs of long-term care in nursing homes, adult family homes, assisted living, and adult day care must be covered by private means [such as additional personal insurance policies] or by welfare [public assistance] programs" (p. 36).

The Medicare Modernization Act

One of the problems with Medicare has been the lack of prescription drug coverage, especially in view of escalating drug costs. In December 2003 President George W. Bush signed into law the Medicare Modernization Act (MMA), which became effective on January 1, 2006. This is the greatest extension of Medicare since its birth in 1965 (Dickerson, 2003). A primary feature of the new law is the Medicare prescription drug benefit (U.S. Department of Health and Human Services [USDHHS], 2005). Participants can choose a prescription drug plan that costs approximately $35 each month. Highlight 8.2 summarizes the payment schedule. Participants must pay all of the first $250 (deductible) for prescriptions. As prescription drug costs add up, participants pay 25% of the total prescription costs from $250 to $2,250 (amounting to $500) and 100% of the amount they spend from $2,250 to $5,100, which brings them up to a total out-of-pocket cost of $3,600 ($250 deductible plus $500 plus $2,850) (Dickerson, 2003). This does not include their monthly fee to participate in the program (a suggested total of $420 annually). Participants pay 5% of costs after they have paid out a total of $3,600. Note that the "law is a good deal for seniors with very low incomes—less than $12,123 per year and not more than $6,000 in accessible assets" because they "will not have to pay premiums, deductibles, and gap costs" (Whitaker, 2003, p. 8).

HIGHLIGHT 8.2

The Medicare Prescription Drug Plan

Participants Pay	Of Total Paid for Drugs	Total Amount Paid by Participants
100%	$ 0–$250	$250
25%	$ 250–$2,250	$500
100%	$2,250–$5,100	$2,850 (subtotal $3,600)
5%	$5,100+	5% of amount

Critics of the legislation emphasize how drugs are still quite expensive for participants. First, there's the monthly fee of an estimated $35 (or $420 annually), which is "just a guess at this point" because private insurers will administer the program and determine the cost, which might vary depending on provider and location (Dickerson, 2003, p. 50). Second, the initial $250 deductible and the $500 on the next $2,000 seniors must pay, a total of $750, is not insignificant. This brings total costs up to $750 plus monthly fees. Third, a disturbing aspect of the bill is the gap in coverage where no drugs are covered as participants spend the next $2,850 on drugs, which brings their total outlay to $3,600. Only then will the program pick up 95% of the costs. It is estimated that, regardless of who pays for them, prescription drugs will cost $3,160 for the average senior in 2006 (Dickerson, 2003). Therefore, if their total drug cost falls within the gap where nothing is covered, seniors will have to pick up a significant percentage of the total costs themselves.

Another problem with the reform is that the Medicare bureaucracy is prohibited from bargaining to reduce prices charged by the pharmaceutical industry, which has imposed considerable political pressure (Dickerson, 2003; Whitaker, 2003). Importing cheaper drugs is also forbidden; they may be imported from Canada, but "only if the Department of Health and Human Services certifies their safety," which it may or may not do (Dickerson, 2003, p. 51). Critics also worry about the possibility that employers will use this legislation as an excuse to shed prescription drug coverage from their own health care plans that might be better than the Medicare plan (Whitaker, 2003). Numerous other criticisms of the bill are beyond the scope of this text.

The MMA does make some improvements in Medicare coverage. It provides for a "one-time initial wellness physical exam within six months of the day" when a participant first enrolls in Medicare Part B, in addition to paying for screening tests for early detection of heart disease and diabetes (USDHHS, 2005). Note that participation in the MMA program is voluntary and that participants "can choose to remain in the traditional Medicare plan" they already have (USDHHS, 2005).

Focus on Critical Thinking 8.2 questions what you think about the prescription drug policy for seniors. Focus on Critical Thinking 8.3 raises some key unresolved policy issues concerning social insurance in general.

FOCUS ON CRITICAL THINKING 8.2

Who Should Pay for Seniors' Prescription Drugs?

The issue of who pays for seniors' prescription drugs most likely would assume more prominence in your mind if it directly impacted you, your family, or your clients. Hopefully, thinking about it will help you develop empathy for people's situations and financial concerns. How would you answer the following questions?

- Should prescription drugs be free for seniors, where society assumes an institutional perspective and views this need as a normal part of life that should automatically be taken care of?
- Should seniors be required to pay for their own prescription drugs or get private

insurance for them as they have in the past?
- Should seniors be allowed to purchase cheaper drugs in other countries to curb costs?
- Should the Medicare system be allowed to bargain with the pharmaceutical industry to decrease costs?
- To what extent is the formula for purchasing prescription drugs effective and fair?
- What, if anything, should be done about the $2,850 gap?
- How would you change the prescription drug benefit formula if you could?

Public Assistance Policy

We have established that public assistance provides resources for people in *need* and that social insurance is based on people's *right* to receive benefits. Financing comes from general tax revenues—that is, taxes collected by federal, state, and local entities on personal income and property. Primary categories of public assistance include Temporary Assistance to Needy Families (TANF); Supplemental Security Income (SSI), which includes Old Age Assistance (OAA), Aid to the Blind (AB) and Aid to the Permanently and Totally Disabled (APTD); Medicaid; food stamps; general assistance; and housing assistance.

Historical Perspectives on Public Assistance to Families

Prior to August 22, 1996, a primary program providing minimal financial assistance to individuals and families in the United States was Aid to Families with Dependent Children (AFDC) (Dickinson, 1997). It was originally established as Aid to Dependent Children (ADC) by the Social Security Act of 1935. AFDC was a program providing payments funded by federal and state governments to children deprived of parental support because a parent was absent from the home, had died, or was incapable of managing the household for physical or mental reasons (Abramovitz, 1995; Barker, 2003). Most families receiving benefits were single mothers whose partners were not in the home.

FOCUS ON CRITICAL THINKING 8.3

Policy Issues in Social Insurance

Meyer (2001) identifies two as yet unanswered issues concerning problems in the U.S. social insurance system as it now stands. People eligible for benefits are those who have had "substantial recent employment in the regular employment sector" (p. 40). The problem is this does not cover people who have been able to get only part-time or temporary work on a sporadic basis. Many people, especially those with low skill levels, are primary family breadwinners yet can't find adequate employment to qualify them for social insurance. Meyer (2001) asks, "How should the social insurance system be adapted to fit this new economy and integrated with other benefits for children?" (p. 41).

The second issue concerns how supplementary benefits (including "health coverage to employees and their families, sick leave, pensions, and 'family-friendly' policies like on-site child care and flexible hours") are rarely offered for workers in minimum-wage or low-paying jobs (p. 41). These workers, many of whom have low skill levels, are left in the lurch when it comes to getting even rudimentary health care. Additionally, any crisis such as illness can result in devastation because, without sick leave, income can abruptly cease. What programs or policies do you think can or should be developed to remedy this situation?

AFDC established eligibility standards based on "family composition, income level, age of the children, and the applicant's willingness to participate in a welfare-to-work program and to cooperate with the welfare department to obtain paternity and child support" (Abramovitz, 1995, p. 184). Eligible families passed an *income test* (or *means test*)—that is, an eligibility guideline that established the maximum amount of income a family could earn without losing benefits. Those who made too much money were ineligible for benefits.

Eligible families could potentially receive financial assistance for many years in addition to Medicaid (provision of health care for qualified recipients), food stamps (coupons used like cash to purchase food), and partial financial support for housing "although a few states deduct[ed] the value of food stamps and housing grants from AFDC payments" (Abramovitz, 1995, p. 186). (Medicaid and food stamps are described later in the chapter.) Note that the duration of public assistance benefits (i.e., how long families remain eligible to receive benefits) is a matter of strong debate. A number of studies have determined that many families receive assistance for no more than two years, in stark contrast to the stereotype that once families get on welfare they never get off (Abramovitz, 1995).

Temporary Assistance to Needy Families

In 1996 Congress passed the Personal Responsibility and Work Opportunity Reconciliation Act that set up a new grant program, Temporary Assistance to Needy

Families (TANF). This "put a cap on federal funds provided to the states" and allowed states greater discretion in benefit distribution (Abramovitz, 1997, pp. 311–312).

As noted previously, TANF supplanted AFDC. Instead of providing cash payments directly to eligible poor families as AFDC did, TANF gives funds to states. These funds take the form of *block grants*—sums of money provided by the federal government that allow significant discretion in how the money should be spent. (This contrasts with *categorical grants* whereby specific amounts of funding are earmarked for specific objectives in designated programs.) These block grants replace "AFDC, food stamps, child care, child protection programs, school meals, and nutritional programs for low-income pregnant women and children" (Dickinson, 1997, p. 126). This also marks the first time that the federal government placed a limit on federal money provided to states for public assistance (Abramovitz, 1997).

TANF's stated goals are as follows:

1. Assisting needy families so that children can be cared for in their own homes.
2. Reducing the dependence of needy parents on government benefits by promoting job preparation, work, and marriage.
3. Preventing incidence of out-of-wedlock pregnancies.
4. Encouraging the formation and maintenance of two-parent families (U.S. Administration for Children and Families [ACF], 2005).

Issues concerning TANF include adequacy of funding, time limits, child care, equitable treatment by states, education and training, job quality and availability, and health insurance after TANF.

Adequacy of Funding

DiNitto (2005) describes some aspects of TANF spending. First, TANF requires states to spend at least 75% of what they spent on AFDC in 1994. States can choose to contribute more if they wish. However, most states have continued to fund TANF at the 1994 level; although some have increased benefits, five states and the District of Columbia essentially decreased benefit levels. After adjusting for inflation and looking at real dollars, only five states provided higher "real" benefits than those offered in 1994, most with very small percentage increases. With state budgets continuing to shrink, it's highly unlikely that states will divert proportionately more funding than they have in the past to address additional public assistance needs. Instead, they are likely to supply only the minimal funding required, which means fewer resources for potential recipients. TANF also permits states to impose tighter restrictions regarding who is eligible for benefits. Many social service agencies providing benefits have serious concerns about these restrictions and the negative effects on clients. Will TANF benefits be adequate during tough economic times?

Time Limits

TANF also establishes time limits for receipt of benefits (ACF, 2005). Clients must find work within two years of beginning the program (or sooner if the state so chooses) and can receive no more than five years of benefits in their lifetime. Beyond five years, states may opt to extend assistance to no more than 20% of their caseload or continue funding recipients through state funds alone. This is a huge change from AFDC, through which "people received assistance as long as they satisfied the program's

FOCUS ON CRITICAL THINKING 8.4

Working Mothers, Child Care, and the Quality of Family Life

The following questions can be raised concerning potential effects of TANF's restrictions:

- Who will provide all the additional child care services for newly working mothers?
- Will funding be adequate in view of the potential influx of children requiring care?
- What if no adequate day care is available?
- Will centers accept infants or toddlers who are not yet toilet trained—children many current child care facilities reject?

- How will these services be monitored for adequacy, safety, and quality?
- Is it fair to force women into assuming responsibility for both household caregiving and outside work when the same pressures do not generally apply to men?
- How will mothers adjust to separation from their children?
- How will children be affected by limited access to their single parent?
- How does this policy affect children's welfare?

eligibility rules, which were set by the individual states under federal guidelines" (Abramovitz, 1997, p. 312). "Seventeen states or jurisdictions have TANF time limits of less than five years," but nine other states have continued providing benefits funded solely by the state after the five years were up (DiNitto, 2005, p. 238). A concern is that agencies may have to turn away people in desperate need because these people have depleted their time allocation. What happens when time limits run out?

Child Care

TANF significantly increases the strictness of work requirements to make people eligible for financial assistance compared to AFDC. (Programs that discourage people from receiving public assistance benefits and that require recipients to earn part of their benefits through work are sometimes referred to as *workfare*.) Single parents must work at least 30 hours per week and two-parent families must total 35–55 weekly work hours, depending on their situation (ACF, 2005). This is increased from the 20 hours originally established in 1997 (Abramovitz, 1997). Questions concern how parents will cope with child care needs, work stress, homemaking responsibilities, and parenting.

TANF will not allow mothers with children age 6 or older to cite lack of adequate child care as their rationale for not working outside the home (Marx, 2004). Although states are not required to provide child care for working parents as AFDC did, states are allowed to transfer up to 30% of TANF funds for its provision; $2.6 billion was spent on child care in 1999, but this decreased to only $1.9 billion in 2002 (DiNitto, 2005, p. 243). Slashing child care expenditures has been connected to economic decline and resulting state budget deficits (DiNitto, 2005). When states need money to provide cash assistance and health care to recipients, child care may get a much lower priority. However, Focus on Critical Thinking 8.4 poses a number of questions regarding potential problems and issues.

Equitability Among States

TANF "eliminated the federal income test that previously determined eligibility for AFDC" (Abramovitz, 1997, p. 312). Instead, TANF lets states establish their own eligibility rules. However, with budget pressures, states could establish eligibility levels so low that only the very poorest of the poor would receive benefits. Additionally, benefit levels vary appreciably from state to state, which raises questions regarding the program's fairness (DiNitto, 2005; Waller, 2002). In 2003, maximum benefits for a family of three ranged from $170 per month in Mississippi to $923 per month in Alaska (DiNitto, 2005, p. 236).

Education and Training for Better Jobs

States spend comparatively small amounts on providing education and training for participants; "less than 2% ($462 million) [of the total TANF budget] was used to enhance skills in 2002. Similar amounts ($584 million) were spent on transportation and supportive services" (DiNitto, 2005, p. 243). How can former TANF recipients seek better jobs and experience upward mobility with little or no education and training? In contrast, pregnancy prevention programs received over a sevenfold increase from 1999 to 2002, amounting to 2.6% of total TANF funding (DiNitto, 2005, p. 243).

Job Quality and Availability

About 75% of TANF recipients are working when they leave welfare rolls (Waller, 2002). One-half to two-thirds of former recipients were still employed one to two years after leaving TANF (Loprest, 2003). The median hourly wage for former TANF recipients in 2002 was $8.02, up from $7.72 in 1999; "[a]bout a third of workers in each group work part-time" (Loprest, 2003). Realistically, how good are the benefits and potential for upward mobility offered by most low-paying jobs? Research also indicates that as the economy slowed between 1999 and 2002, TANF recipients had increasing difficulty finding jobs and also were more likely to return to TANF; a higher percentage of people became "disconnected leavers" who were neither employed nor recipients of assistance, possibly because of TANF's benefit time limits (Loprest, 2003).

Health Insurance After TANF

Only about a third of employed former TANF recipients had employer health insurance benefits in 2002 (Loprest, 2003). This is due to getting low-paying or minimum wage jobs that have poor or no benefits. After leaving TANF, families can continue receiving Medicaid for 12 months if their income does not surpass 185% of the poverty line (DiNitto, 2005, p. 235). For many families, what happens after that? To what extent does TANF force single mothers to deprive themselves of future health care by accepting low-paying jobs without benefits—the only jobs they can get?

Focus on Critical Thinking 8.5 asks some questions concerning your views about public assistance and where current policy stands on the conservative–liberal continuum.

Stereotypes About Public Assistance Recipients

Henley and Danziger (1997) reflect on the stereotypes often associated with public assistance recipients:

FOCUS ON CRITICAL THINKING 8.5
The Current State of Public Assistance

Where Do You Stand on the Conservative–Liberal Continuum?

Remember that *conservatism* generally reflects the view that individuals should be responsible for themselves, that people will take advantage of the system if allowed to, and that government should not interfere in people's lives. Thus government should react and provide benefits only when it absolutely has to. *Liberalism*, in contrast, generally espouses the view that it is society's responsibility to care for its people and that people will rise to the occasion and care for themselves if provided the support they need. Thus the government should be integrally involved in improving people's lives.

- Where do you stand on the conservative–liberal continuum with respect to what benefits should or should not be provided to needy families?
- Whose responsibility is it to provide for poor families and their young children—individual parents or society in general?
- Do you feel that people are basically lazy and are likely to abuse the system if they can? Or

do you feel that people will function much better if they receive adequate resources?
- To what extent do you feel that government should involve itself in caring for people in need? Or should people be given the responsibility to care completely for themselves and their families?

Residual Versus Institutional Social Welfare Programming

Do you believe that financial assistance programs to families in need should be *residual* in nature, reacting only to problems and serious needs? Or should programs provide ongoing *institutional* support to them?

Where Does TANF Policy Stand on the Conservative–Liberal Continuum?

To what extent does TANF policy reflect a conservative or liberal perspective concerning consistency in benefit provision from one state to another? Time limits for receiving benefits? Provision of medical care to current and past recipients? Requirements that single parents (primarily mothers) work outside the home?

According to the commonly held stereotype, poor people are poor because of individual character faults. In particular, welfare recipients are presumed to be lazy, able yet unwilling to work, and lacking appropriate family values. . . . The dominant American values of individualism and self-sufficiency . . . contribute to the unpopularity of welfare programs and support the popular opinion that welfare recipients are responsible for their impoverished condition and undeserving of assistance. (p. 125)

Who are the people receiving public assistance? To what extent is this portrayal accurate or false? Highlight 8.3 explores a number of these stereotypes.

Supplemental Security Income

Supplemental Security Income (SSI) is a federal public assistance program that provides a minimum income to poor people who are elderly, have a disability, or are blind. Most of it is administered by the federal government through the Social

HIGHLIGHT 8.3
What Are the Stereotypes About People "on Welfare"—and to What Extent Are They Accurate?

A number of popular negative ideas about public assistance and stereotypes about people who receive it exist.

Stereotype 1: The Public Assistance Caseload Has Been Expanding Relentlessly.

Popple and Leighninger (2004) reviewed the size of the population receiving TANF benefits. Although the public assistance caseload increased significantly between 1960 and 1975, its escalation rate dropped off noticeably after that until 1990. At that time, it increased once again until 1995, a year before TANF was approved. After TANF, the number of recipients decreased more radically, in 1998 reaching the lowest point since 1970. Since TANF began, 2 million families have departed from welfare rolls, representing a total decline of 54% (DiNitto, 2005).

Note also that not all people on welfare are parents. Many recipients are children.

Stereotype 2: Public Assistance Costs the Nation a Fortune.

Popple and Leighninger (2004) explain that, after adjusting for inflation, the actual cost of public assistance has decreased since 1976. They indicate that this is due to decreases in family size and benefit amounts. TANF costs less than 1% of the total federal budget; state contributions have decreased from $16.5 to $11.2 billion from 1996 to 2000. Although public assistance involves billions of dollars, it is meager compared, for example, to the hundreds of billions of dollars spent on national defense. Although expenditures for social programs in general have soared, the lion's share is attributed to massive increases in social insurance programs (Social Security and Medicare) and Medicaid.

Stereotype 3: People on Welfare Live "High on the Hog." (Abramovitz, 1997, p. 318)

Some maintain that people make more on welfare than they do working. DiNitto (2005) summarizes some facts. Some reports reflect "inflated estimates of benefits" because the assumption is that housing assistance is included in the total package, when it only rarely is (p. 227). We've established that most states maintained the 1994 benefit level when switching to TANF, but all states also have excluded benefits for people falling within certain categories, thereby limiting who can get assistance. One study indicated that TANF recipients received "from $2,400 to $3,200 per quarter, resulting in approximately 90% earning less than poverty wages" (Acs & Loprest, 2001; Dobelstein, 2003).

Follow this line of reasoning (Popple & Leighninger, 2004): Each state has the right to determine the monetary amount necessary to meet an individual's or family's minimal needs. The state then establishes what percentage of the minimum it will award in grants to recipients—usually 50%. How can a family live adequately on *half* of what it needs to barely stay alive?

Stereotype 4: Welfare Recipients Are Mainly African Americans.

Popple and Leighninger (2004) summarize the racial distribution of TANF recipients: 38% are African American, 25% white, 24% Hispanic, 3.6% Asian, and 1.5% Native American (pp. 158–159).

(continued)

H I G H L I G H T   8.3 *(continued)*

It is true that African American women are more likely to receive TANF benefits than white women. Whites make up 81% and African Americans about 12% of the total U.S. population. Seven percent of all white mothers get public assistance, whereas 25% of all African American mothers do. Indeed, poverty rates for most people of color are significantly higher than for whites, but it's important to remember that one-quarter of people receiving assistance are white.

Stereotype 5: Once People Get on Welfare, They Stay on It Forever.

Statistics can be framed very differently depending on what figures and variables are emphasized. Therefore, "facts" can be confusing. One way of looking at time spent on public assistance rolls involves the total number of people who have ever received public assistance. Almost 60% of these people received aid for less than two years (Popple & Leighninger, 2004). They usually turned to assistance after suffering some crisis such as a serious illness, divorce, job loss, or other unanticipated problem (Abramovitz, 1997). Most people, then, have received assistance only temporarily.

However, another way of looking at time spent on public assistance rolls involves "the onion metaphor" (Corbett, 1993; Popple & Leighninger, 2004, p. 161). The outer layer of the onion represents people who received benefits for two years or less in response to some crisis until they could get their lives back together. The middle layer of the onion reflects people who receive assistance for a longer period, perhaps two to eight years or more when it's available. They generally have some essential skills so that they can usually get work when it's available. However, their well-being directly correlates with the status of the economy. When jobs are available, they can make it; but when jobs aren't there, they need help. This group generally benefits from education and vocational training to improve opportunities.

The onion's core involves people who have fewer skills and more difficulty remaining independent. They require broader, more intensive support to become autonomous. Popple and Leighninger (2004) explain:

> In addition to low earning capacity brought on by lack of education, training, and job experience, this group also faces barriers to self-sufficiency such as drug abuse, psychological problems, health problems, abusive personal relationships, and so on. This group is also often suspected of lacking basic motivation and of possessing values that are not conducive to work. (p. 162)

The onion's nucleus represents people who have serious, ongoing issues and problems. They might have physical, mental, or psychological disabilities that prevent them from ever functioning in a totally autonomous manner. Popple and Leighninger (2004) urge that, first, we acknowledge that this group probably will never become totally independent and, second, that we "develop ways of providing nonstigmatizing support" for them (p. 162).

The issue of whether people remain on public assistance rolls for an extended time is probably now a moot point in most instances. As you know, TANF has a lifetime benefit limitation of five years with some exceptions. We're just beginning to find out what happens to these

(continued)

HIGHLIGHT 8.3 *(continued)*

people when they reach their benefit limit—and what will happen to their children.

Stereotype 6: Families on Welfare Only Breed Future Generations of Families on Welfare.

This idea stems from the concept of the *culture of poverty,* already discussed (Popple & Leighninger, 2004, p. 163). We have established that this means that children growing up under these conditions will learn values regarding and subsequently follow a lifestyle based on public assistance dependence. The facts concerning this issue are less clear. Some research has shown that only 19% of African American and 26% of white recipients who were deeply dependent on public assistance came from families that received welfare; there were no differences regarding welfare dependence for African Americans coming from welfare-dependent and nondependent families, whereas the difference for whites was little and inconsistent (Popple & Leighninger, 2004).

Stereotype 7: Families Receiving Welfare Are Huge.

Popple and Leighninger (2004) reflect on the facts: 42.3% of families receiving public assistance have one child, 29% two, 15.9% three, and only 11% four or more; the average number of children per family is two.

Security Administration. However, it is funded by general tax revenues, not employer and employee contributions as with social insurance. Eligibility is determined by a means test and proof of fitting into one of the three categories. Elderly people must be at least 65, and people who are blind or disabled must have "medical verification of their disability" (Meyer, 1995, p. 2381).

Monthly SSI payments in 2002 were $545 for individuals "(76% of the poverty line)" and $817 for couples "(91% of the poverty line)" (Blau, 2004, p. 291). Cost-of-living increases are made annually. To be eligible, applicants must adhere to stringent, complex guidelines regarding income and assets. The program orients itself more to people who have physical versus mental disabilities (e.g., people with mental illness who can work part-time are ineligible) and usually requires extensive "medical documentation" (Blau, 2004, p. 292). As a result, it is estimated that only 55–60% of people eligible for SSI actually receive benefits (Blau, 2004).

Medicaid

Medicaid is a public assistance program funded by federal and state governments that pays for medical and hospital services for eligible people who are unable to pay for these services themselves and are determined to be in need. It was established in 1965 along with Medicare by the Health Insurance for the Aged Act.

Under federal guidelines, states administer the Medicaid program either directly or "by contracting with private insurance agencies" to oversee the process (Dobelstein, 2003, p. 179). Recipients include people who are elderly, blind, or members of families with dependent children, or who have disabilities and meet the means test; "[s]tates must provide medical care for people who are recipients of aid in federally supported, means-tested income maintenance programs" (like TANF) (Dobelstein, 2003, p. 179). About 13% of the entire U.S. population receives Medicaid (Blau, 2004), half of whom are children under age 18 (Dobelstein, 2003). The program's cost of about $199 billion (Blau, 2004), 60% of which is paid by the federal government (Dobelstein, 2003), continues to escalate. Major questions are being raised across the country concerning where the money will come from to finance future health care costs in general and Medicaid costs in particular.

Note that Medicaid is a major player in financing long-term nursing home care for the elderly: 68% of nursing home residents rely partially on Medicaid to cover their care costs, which make up over a third of the total Medicaid budget (Blau, 2004). Medicaid covers some of the many gaps in Medicare for elderly people in poverty.

Food Stamps

Food stamps are credits distributed through a federal program to be used like cash to purchase primarily food, plants, and seeds (Barker, 2003). The program's intent is to fight hunger. Originally created in 1964, the food stamp program is administered through the U.S. Department of Agriculture and is paid for completely by the federal government.

Blau (2004) further explains the current situation. Although originally benefits were distributed in the form of coupons, now the majority of states have replaced this system with an electronic benefit transfer that resembles a credit card. "In 2002 the maximum benefit that can be drawn on this card is $356 a month for three people and $452 monthly for four" (p. 413). To be eligible, people must satisfy a means test, and benefits are determined by a formula involving income and assets. Special exemptions exist for the elderly and disabled people. "Most TANF, SSI, and general assistance recipients are automatically eligible" (p. 413).

The number of people receiving food stamps declined from 1994 to 2000, when it began to rise along with an increase in unemployment. The decline resulted primarily from fewer people being eligible, increased assets on the part of some recipients during a booming economy, changing eligibility guidelines, and a confusing application process (p. 414). Blau (2004) explains:

> An ever more burdensome application process is perhaps the best example of the rising barriers to food stamp eligibility. Although food stamps have often been targets of fraud and abuse charges, repeated studies have found, at most, very little real evidence of fraud. Nevertheless, the states keep erecting higher hurdles. Food stamp applications within the 50 states now average 12 pages in length. California, New York, and 27 other states ask applicants if they own a burial plot. Nevada and Nebraska want to know if applicants have sold their blood and for how much. Hawaii demands garage sale receipts, South Dakota totals bingo winnings, and on page 20 of a 36-page application, Minnesota checks to see if anyone earns money from a paper route. Such a daunting application process surely gives pause to even the most eligible applicant. (p. 414)

General Assistance

General assistance (GA) includes programs run by state and local agencies that provide basic cash and in-kind benefits to people who satisfy whatever means test has been established and are ineligible for other types of public assistance. It's usually the last resort for people who are desperately in need but are not eligible for benefits provided by other programs. GA recipients are often childless or under age 65. Hence they're ineligible for TANF or SSI, respectively. Some GA recipients suffer from a disability but haven't had it long enough to qualify for SSI benefits.

GA is the only public assistance program that is financed completely by state, county, or local governments. Guidelines for who can receive GA vary from location to location and from state to state. Most states restrict benefits to those who live below half of the poverty level, and almost all states require able-bodied recipients to work if they want to receive benefits (Karger & Stoesz, 2002). Many states and localities have severely cut back on GA benefits in recent years (Blau, 2004; Karger & Stoesz, 2002).

Housing Assistance

Adequate housing is a problem for vast numbers of Americans. Many find it to be the single most expensive item in their monthly budget. There's often little left over for food and clothing, let alone luxury items, after the rent is paid. And it must be paid, or families will be out on the street.

One of the problems is a serious lack of affordable, low-income housing. One reason is the recent extensive renovation of downtown urban areas into higher-rent districts, so that poor people can no longer afford to live in their old neighborhoods. Another reason is the mass abandonment of other dilapidated, aging, urban properties. Building owners and landlords often find such buildings too expensive to keep up. Unable to find anyone who wants to buy the properties, they simply abandon them.

Some housing assistance is available, primarily from the U.S. Department of Housing and Urban Development (HUD) in the form of rental subsidies or vouchers by which government programs assist with rent, mortgage payments, and low-rent public housing; block grants are also available to state and local governments "to increase the supply of affordable housing for low-income families" in the form of "rental assistance or the acquisition, rehabilitation, or, in limited circumstances, construction of both rental and ownership housing" (Dolgoff & Feldstein, 2003, p. 252). Although the stereotype persists that public housing involves huge, often dilapidated complexes of apartments for dozens or hundreds of low-income families, current trends involve placing recipients in smaller neighborhood units; funding is administered locally through public housing authorities that primarily offer rental assistance (DiNitto, 2005). Recent housing development has involved construction of smaller housing units using available funding because "HUD has not provided new funding for public housing development since . . . 1994" (HUD, 2004).

Means tests are used to determine eligibility. However, housing assistance has been cut back significantly in recent years and is not automatically available to everyone in need. Usually people must apply for rent subsidies, low-rent housing, or other assistance (considered an in-kind benefit). Because demand greatly exceeds supply,

HIGHLIGHT 8.4

International Perspectives: "Cash for Kids" in Canada[3]

There are many ways to make financial benefits available to families other than those provided by public assistance in the United States. These include *family allowances* (programs in which all eligible families receive designated sums of money regardless of their financial need) and *children's benefits* (programs in which families are given monetary allocations based on the fact that they have children). Canada has initiated a program that provides such children's benefits to families (Institute for Research on Poverty, 2001, Spring). The program's goals are to "help prevent and reduce the depth of child poverty; ensure that families will always be better off as a result of parents working; and reduce overlap and duplication of government programs and services" (Canada Revenue Agency, 2004).

Initiated during the 1980s and brought to fruition in 1993 (Institute for Research on Poverty, 2001), the Child Tax Benefit pays a maximum basic benefit of C$1,208 [C$ refers to Canadian dollars] per year for a child under age 18 (Canada Revenue Agency, 2004). There are small increments for families who have three or more children or have children under age seven. Maximum basic payments go to families with net incomes up to C$35,000. Families who have children with disabilities and lower-income families receive funding that is slightly higher than the maximum basic benefit. As income rises, benefits are reduced (Canada Revenue Agency, 2004).

All families without high incomes, therefore, receive cash benefits on the basis of how many children they have. The amount they receive decreases with the amount of income they earn until they surpass the upper limit, at which point benefits cease. Note that low-income families also receive financial support in addition to this basic benefit.

The Canadian Child Tax Benefit program contrasts sharply with the provision of financial benefits to families in the United States, which has the highest rate of child poverty among industrialized nations. Public assistance in the United States is limited to a maximum of five years regardless of the family's financial need and is subject to compliance with work requirements. Most families (with the exception of those considered well off) don't get financial benefits just because they have children. (Note that the United States does provide tax breaks such as deductions for families with children.)

How would you answer the following questions?

- Should all families receive financial benefits to supplement the additional costs they experience simply by having children? Why or why not?
- If you believe families should receive financial benefits, should these benefits be based on the family's income—namely, poorer families receive higher benefits and wealthier families lower? Or should all families receive the same amount of benefits per child regardless of family income? What is the fair thing to do?

[3]The term *cash for kids* and other information in this highlight (unless otherwise indicated) are taken from the Institute for Research on Poverty (2000, Spring).

they often remain on long waiting lists until benefits or residences become available, sometimes years later.

There are an infinite number of ways to provide financial assistance to families. Each country establishes its own priorities and policies. Highlight 8.4 discusses the

"Cash for Kids" policy in Canada, where financial assistance is provided to all families without high incomes.

Looking Ahead

This chapter addressed the problem of poverty and discussed programs implementing policies to help poor families and children. Families obviously need adequate financial resources to provide a protective, nurturing environment for their children. In addition to financial resources, many families need other *supportive services* to remain intact and thrive. Sometimes, for many reasons, children must be removed from their homes of origin, either temporarily or permanently, and be provided with *substitute care*. The next chapter explores a number of such supportive and substitute services. Chapter 9 is the first of several chapters in Part IV of this book that address various client populations and the contexts in which services are provided.

For Further Exploration on the Internet

See this text's Book Companion Website at **www.socialwork.wadsworth.com/ kirstashman_intro2e** for descriptors and hot links to URLs relevant to this chapter, selected InfoTrac articles and exercises, and tutorial quizzes.

Case Study for Critical Thinking: The WIC Program

The case presented here is an example of a social welfare policy, the Special Supplemental Food Program for Women, Infants, and Children (WIC).

Case study: WIC is a nutritional program designed to supplement the diets of low-income women and their young children up to age 5 who are determined by a health professional to be at nutritional risk according to federal guidelines (U.S. Department of Agriculture Food and Nutrition [FNS], 2003). Participants receive either food items or, more typically, coupons that can be exchanged for specific food that is high in important nutrients including "iron-fortified infant formula and infant cereal, iron-fortified adult cereal, vitamin C–rich fruit or vegetable juice, eggs, milk, cheese, peanut butter, dried beans/peas, tuna fish, and carrots" (FNS, 2003). Physicians may also prescribe special infant formulas or medical foods when needed. Additionally, eligible women receive nutritional counseling to educate them about their own and their children's nutritional needs.

WIC is administered through the U.S. Department of Agriculture with state agencies (e.g., a state health department) distributing benefits. Eligibility includes (1) being a pregnant woman, new mother, infant, or child up to age 5; (2) having an income level at or less than 185% of the poverty level "(currently $34,873 for a family of four)"; (3) fulfilling state residency requirements; (4) having been determined to be at "nutrition risk" by a health care professional; and (5) being a participant in other designated public assistance programs (FNS, 2003). "Nutrition risk" factors involve medical conditions such as having anemia or being underweight, having a history of problem pregnancies, or inadequate diet and nutrition (FNS, 2003). Over 7.5 million people, the majority of whom are children, currently receive WIC benefits (FNS, 2003). Note that eligibility is more lenient than TANF and other public assistance programs (Karger & Stoesz, 2002).

Critical thinking: You can apply critical thinking to evaluate the usefulness of this program by following the Five-E approach to policy analysis.

1. First, *ask* questions.
   a. How *effective* is the policy?
   b. How *efficient* is the policy?
   c. Is the policy *ethically* sound?
   d. What does *evaluation* of potential alternative policies reveal?
   e. What recommendations can be *established* for positive changes?

2. Second, *assess* the established facts and issues involved.

   a. How *effective* is the WIC policy and its resulting program implementation? WIC advocates cite research that program participation results in improved conditions at birth including "longer gestation periods, higher birthweights, and lower infant mortality" (DiNitto, 2005; FNS, 2003). Additionally, infants and young children generally prosper from good nutrition, which enhances normal development. More specifically, adequate iron in the diet has been found to reduce iron-deficiency anemia—a condition involving decreased hemoglobin levels in red blood cells and resulting in fatigue and lack of vitality (DiNitto, 2005; FNS, 2003). Other benefits not directly related to the program's stated goals include improved prenatal care and better immunization records (DiNitto, 2005).

Critics caution that although results sound good superficially, it is difficult to find comparable groups to establish that WIC is really the cause of positive results (DiNitto, 2005).

Others have raised questions regarding the effectiveness of nutritional counseling (DiNitto, 2005). What does such counseling involve? Is it really useful and worth the expense? Would providing information about other topics such as cooking be more effective?

From this discussion, how effective do you feel the WIC policy and program are? What other information would help make your decision easier?

b. How *efficient* is the WIC policy and program?

Participation in WIC is associated with significantly decreased Medicaid costs for newborns and new mothers during the first 60 days after birth; for every dollar spent on prenatal care, it is estimated that $1.77 to $3.13 is saved in Medicaid costs (Dolgoff & Feldstein, 2003; FNS, 2003). This implies that mothers and infants are generally healthier due to the WIC program so they don't have to seek as much help from Medicaid.

Critics of the program, including the Institute of Medicine, report that because there really is no valid classification system for "risk," conducting expensive assessments is a waste of time and money (Food and Nutrition Board, 2002). If anything, the entire population of low-income mothers and young children is at risk of nutritional deprivation. Money could better be spent providing more food or getting it to more people.

It is estimated that 90% of people eligible to receive WIC benefits do actually receive them (DiNitto, 2005). However, that is not 100%. Additionally, due to funding limitations, people may be placed on prioritized waiting lists (Dolgoff & Feldstein, 2003). Besides those who didn't apply to begin with, it was estimated that in 2002, 200,000 to 250,000 women, infants, and children did not receive benefits because of funding limitations (Dolgoff & Feldstein, 2003).

What does this mean to you in terms of efficiency? Do you think it's efficient because it saves public spending on Medicaid? Or do you think it's inefficient because it fails to reach a significant number of people who are eligible and sometimes makes potential recipients endure waiting lists?

c. To what extent is the policy *ethically* sound? We just established that some people who are eligible for WIC do not receive benefits. Is this fair? Or should nutritional support be provided to all pregnant women, new mothers, infants, and small children? What are our society's ethical values concerning the importance of healthy pregnancies, mothers, and children? What is society's responsibility for their care?

d. How does the *evaluation* of potential alternative policies compare with WIC? WIC's goals are to improve the nutritional intake of eligible mothers and children at risk of poor nutrition and to educate mothers about nutrition to prevent problems related to a poor diet. What other policies might be developed to achieve the same goals? Would they be able to better meet the established goals? Are there more efficient, less expensive ways to meet these goals?

e. What recommendations can be *established* for positive changes? How could the program be improved? How could benefits reach more eligible mothers? Would increased federal and state funding help? What changes in policy could facilitate program implementation?

3. The third step in critical thinking is to *assert* a concluding opinion. In summary, what do you think about WIC? Should it be continued, expanded, reduced, or discarded?

PART ✦ FOUR

CLIENT POPULATIONS AND CONTEXTS

Part IV includes seven chapters that focus on various fields of practice in social work, the client populations served, the social welfare policies governing that service, and the context in which benefits are provided. They include social work and services

1. For children and families.
2. For the elderly.
3. For persons with disabilities.
4. In health care.
5. In mental health.
6. In the schools.
7. In the criminal justice system.

CHAPTER ✾ NINE

SOCIAL WORK AND SERVICES FOR CHILDREN AND FAMILIES

Consider the following cases involving children and their families.

Case A: Burgundy, age 23, is a single mother desperately seeking day care for her children Sean and Shane, ages 1½ and 3. She has just found a clerical job at a law office not far from her home. Her sister can baby-sit for her in the mornings but has her own job to go to in the afternoons. Some of the available day care costs as much as she will make in her new job. Other day care centers won't take children who aren't toilet trained, which Sean definitely is not. Burgundy is at her wit's end!

Case B: Clark and Lois aren't doing well. They have three children to support, and not nearly enough money is coming in to pay the rent and buy groceries. Clark was laid off eight months ago from his job at the airplane factory. The economy's depressed, and he's been unable to find anything else. And then there are medical bills for Lois's breast cancer. She's had surgery and is only now finishing up radiation and chemotherapy treatments. Clark feels as if he's losing his grip on things. The least bit of aggravation makes him blow his stack. He finds himself more frequently slapping the kids around when they don't behave. The other day, he caught himself right before he hit one of them with a baseball bat.

Case C: Corazon is exhausted. Her daughter Juanita, age 9, is bedridden with a rare skin disease that makes any movement difficult and painful. Juanita requires almost constant care and attention. Corazon, a single parent, has no relatives or friends in the area willing to give her a break and help out even for a few hours by caring for Juanita. Corazon feels as if she's going crazy.

Case D: Tom, 15, is clinically depressed. He attends a school that focuses on fulfilling special education needs, addressing school behavior problems, and providing family counseling. He had been in five foster homes since his parents were killed in a car accident. The multiple placements were not Tom's fault but were simple results of fate. Two foster families moved out of the state when breadwinners got better jobs. One foster mother became pregnant and decided that having a foster child in addition to her own was simply too much. One foster father had a heart attack and died. The other foster family began having problems with their own teenage children, and so Tom was removed from the home. Tom and his older brother and sister have been separated for the past 10 years. For various reasons, "the system" has been unable to keep the three siblings together. Tom is doing poorly in school partly due to multiple school changes and partly due to his despair at the misfortune and loneliness that has characterized his life.

Case E: Ginny, age 18 months, has a severe cognitive disability (previously referred to as mental retardation) and so can do little more than lie in a prone position, suck on a bottle, and cry. She was removed from her home because her mother, a crack addict, did not provide adequate care. Shortly after Ginny arrived at her foster home, Ginny's foster mother took her to a diagnostic and treatment center for children with multiple disabilities. During a physical examination, the physician noticed that Ginny had odd-looking bruises around her vaginal area. They wondered what and who had caused them.

Cases A through C depict families that need *supportive* help to stay intact. For whatever reasons, families can become stressed or weakened and have trouble making it on their own. Causes may be economic, health related, or emotional. Sometimes a family is hit with an unexpected crisis like job loss or serious illness; other times, long-term problems wear a family down and undermine its ability to keep itself afloat.

Cases D and E portray children who can no longer stay with their families in their own homes. When families have such serious needs and problems that they can't care for their children, *substitute* services are necessary.

Because the family is the core of most people's lives, this chapter explores issues relevant to families. People who receive other types of social services (e.g., those concerning health, mental health, disabilities, or aging) are also members of families. Because of the complexity of people's needs and the services developed to meet them, the same individual or family may receive services or use resources from various fields of practice. Therefore, a thorough understanding of services for children and families is basic to understanding social welfare and social work.

This chapter will

- Explain the concept of child welfare.
- Describe the continuum of supportive and substitute services in the United States.
- Explain what child maltreatment is, whom it affects, and what the dynamics involved are.
- Discuss child protective services and the social work role.
- Emphasize the importance of risk assessment in protective services.
- Describe and examine family preservation, child day care, family life education, and respite care.
- Address the ongoing macro need to advocate for resources for children and families.
- Discuss some of the special issues experienced by gay and lesbian youths.
- Discuss foster family care—its uses and types, and the social work roles involved.
- Discuss and examine residential settings including group homes and residential treatment centers.
- Define independent living services.
- Explain the types of adoption available, the adoption process, social work roles, and controversial issues in adoption.
- Stress the importance of cultural competence when placing children in substitute care.
- Propose questions to stimulate critical thinking about advocacy to combat child maltreatment and controversial issues in adoption.
- Examine the issue of alcohol and other substance abuse, identify major terms, and discuss the family dynamics and treatment approaches involved in treating alcoholism.

 ## Major Thrusts of Services for Children and Families

One way of classifying services for children and families is to place them on a continuum, as shown in Figure 9.1. At one end of the continuum, families require basic financial and material resources to survive. Some families require additional supportive help (e.g., counseling) to continue functioning and remain intact. Some families need very little help to enhance their functioning and thrive. Others require comprehensive services and resources to solve problems and function as independent, healthy entities. The three middle boxes in Figure 9.1 reflect the continuum of need ranging from limited to moderate to extensive. Finally, at the other

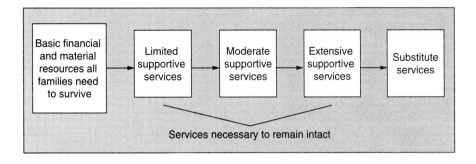

Figure 9.1 Continuum of need for families' survival

end of the continuum, some families are unable to function regardless of the resources and help they receive. In these cases, children must be removed from the home and substitute services provided.

Note that in the past treatment and services involving children were referred to as "child welfare." Highlight 9.1 describes this field and the current status of practice with children and families.

Supportive and Substitute Services

Supportive services "support, reinforce, and strengthen the ability of parents and children to meet the responsibilities of their respective statuses" (Kadushin & Martin, 1988, p. 83). The intent is simply to provide external support to enhance family functioning while children remain in the home. Services include basic financial and other resource assistance (discussed in Chapter 6); various types of mental health treatment such as family therapy, individual counseling, and group therapy (discussed more thoroughly in Chapter 13, which focuses on social work and mental health); child protective services; intensive family preservation services; day care; and family life education.

Case Example An example of supportive services involves Billy, a 13-year-old boy with moderate cognitive disabilities (Kadushin & Martin, 1988; Koch, 1979).[1] His parents, Norm and Norma Needing, had increasing difficulty controlling his behavior as he grew older and bigger. Billy was picking on his younger brother Benny and acting out uncontrollably in public settings such as grocery stores and restaurants. The Needings were at their wits' end and were considering placing Billy in an institutional setting.

Billy was referred by his school social worker to FACT (Family and Child Training), a program providing a range of services to persons with developmental disabilities and their families. FACT assigned the case to Emma Getic, a social worker

---

[1]This case example is loosely based on one provided in the sources cited. Various situational variables such as referral source have been changed.

HIGHLIGHT 9.1

Child Welfare: A Historical Social Work Field of Practice

Child welfare is the traditional term for the network of policies and programs designed to empower families, promote a healthy environment, protect children, and meet children's needs. Basic goals of child welfare include

- Meeting vulnerable children's unmet emotional, behavioral, and health needs.
- Providing adequate resources to address external conditions such as poverty and inadequate health care so children can develop and thrive in a healthy, nurturing social environment.
- Empowering families by building on strengths so parents can effectively provide for and protect their children.
- Improving internal family conditions involving interpersonal dynamics, communication, substance abuse, and conflict.
- Safeguarding children from various forms of neglect and abuse.
- When necessary, making permanent family living conditions available through adoption or transfer of guardianship.

Child welfare has always focused on children and families, with services traditionally provided by public agencies. Pecora, Whittaker, Maluccio, and Barth (2000) comment:

> [T]he historical areas of service [include] foster care and adoptions, in-home family-centered services, child protective services, and residential services—in which social work has a legitimate, long-standing, and important role and mission. . . . Readers also should be conscious of the many other fields of practice in which child and family services are provided or that involve substantial numbers of social work programs, such as services to adolescent parents, child mental health, and juvenile justice agencies. (p. xi)

In recent years the emphasis concerning children and families has shifted from a focus on the child to one on the family and social environments. Children are now viewed in the context of their families and other people around them. The idea is that this environment must be strengthened to provide a nurturant, supportive setting in which children can grow and thrive.

serving both as case coordinator and treatment provider. The first order of business was to assess the situation and develop a treatment plan. After spending substantial time observing Billy and his interactions both at school and at home, Emma worked with the Needings to develop goals and specify a plan for how to proceed.

Goals included improving Billy's interactions with peers and with Benny through supervised recreational activities, his ability to respond positively to parental guidance and directives, and his behavior in public places. The Needings attended parenting classes provided by FACT. Emma met weekly with the Needings to discuss what they had learned and help them apply the skills at home. Billy was enrolled in recreational activity groups sponsored and supervised by FACT staff. Initially, Billy was accompanied by a child care worker who modeled appropriate behavior for Billy and implemented the behavior modification program. Billy gradually learned how to relate much more positively with Benny, his peers, and his parents. Billy enjoyed his new levels of interaction and acceptance, so his overall quality of life was significantly enhanced. Because family life had stabilized, the Needings no longer considered residential placement.

Further along the continuum of family needs are *substitute services* (described later) whereby another family or environment is substituted for the child's own family. Here "someone else takes over all aspects of the parental role on a temporary or permanent basis" (Kadushin & Martin, 1988, p. 344). Substitute services include foster care; residential placement in a group home, treatment center, or institution; independent living; and adoption.

An example of substitute care in an institutional setting could have involved the Needing family. For instance, suppose the family had not been referred to FACT or FACT had failed to help the family improve its functioning. The Needings might then have pursued Billy's placement in a residential institution.

Child Maltreatment and Child Protective Services

Jaron, age 3, and Tomas, age 2, attended a day care center while their mother, Evita, worked during the day. Laura, the day care center social worker, and Sonja, Jaron's and Tomas's teacher, became increasingly concerned about the boys' health and hygiene. Their clothes were smeared with dirt, and their hair was filthy. They had an exceptionally strong, unappealing odor, apparently due to very infrequent bathing. Their teeth were dark with tartar. And they were ravenously hungry when they arrived at the center each day. The situation screamed neglect. Laura had the choice of sitting down with Evita and talking with her about the problems or referring the case to child protective services.

Consider another case. Peter, age 6, had been placed in foster care with Becca for the past year. Peter's mother, Mary, had visitation rights every Saturday afternoon. During their lives, Peter and his four siblings had periodically been removed from the home because of neglect and placed in foster care. Mary had a long history of drug use and abuse. She had started treatment programs on numerous occasions but was never able to complete them. After one of the Saturday visits with Mary, Becca noticed that Peter had a series of small circular burns on his left arm that looked as if they might be from a lighted cigarette. Was Peter actually being tortured on Saturday afternoons? Becca called Peter's social worker.

Another case involved Juanita, age 13, who was referred to Cheung, the school social worker, by Agate, Juanita's English teacher. Agate had given Juanita and the rest of her class an assignment to write a poem on any subject they wished. Juanita had written 18 poems. (How many times have you done 18 times the work a teacher assigned you?) Each of Juanita's poems involved explicitly sexual language and imagery. Juanita lived with her mother, sisters, and a stepfather. There was some concern about potential sexual abuse by the latter. Upon further investigation after referral to child protective services, it was determined that a maternal uncle, not the stepfather, was guilty of sexual abuse.

These three children are victims of various types of child maltreatment. Before we discuss the types of supportive services and treatment provided for this grave family problem, it's important to understand some of the reasons why it occurs and the ways it affects children.

What Are Child Maltreatment, Abuse, and Neglect?

Child maltreatment is the umbrella term for physical abuse, sexual abuse, emotional abuse, and neglect. *Physical abuse* occurs when "a child younger than 18 years of age has experienced an injury . . . or risk of an injury . . . as a result of having been hit with a hand or other object or having been kicked, shaken, thrown, burned, stabbed, or choked by a parent or parent-surrogate" (Kolko, 2002, p. 22). Physical indicators include bruises, lacerations, fractures, burns, head injuries, and internal injuries. Often the injuries don't make sense. For example, they might occur in odd patterns or places. A doughnut-shaped burn will appear on the buttocks if a child has been immersed in very hot water, or she may have bruises on the soles of her feet from being hit there with a stick. Explanations for injuries may not be logical. Consider a child who says he broke his leg when he tripped on a crack in the sidewalk, but there are no sidewalks in his neighborhood. Still another clue involves frequent or multiple injuries that are hard to explain.

Physically abused children can also exhibit behavioral indicators such as extreme passivity and submissiveness in order to avoid provoking an abusive parent or other caregiver. Other children will express themselves with marked aggression and hostility, modeling the behavior of a violent parent.

Sexual abuse is

> any sexual activity with a child where consent is not or cannot be given. . . . This includes sexual contact that is accomplished by force or threat of force, regardless of the age of the participants, and all sexual contact between an adult and a child, regardless of whether there is deception or the child understands the sexual nature of the activity. Sexual contact between an older and a younger child also can be abusive if there is a significant disparity in age, development, or size, rendering the younger child incapable of giving informed consent. The sexually abusive acts may include sexual penetration, sexual touching, or non-contact sexual acts such as exposure or voyeurism. (Berliner & Elliott, 2002, p. 55)

Incest, a form of sexual abuse, is "sexual intercourse between people too closely related to legally marry (usually interpreted to mean father–daughter, mother–son, or brother–sister combinations)" (Strong et al., 2005, pp. 639–640). Physical symptoms of sexual abuse include physical damage to or bleeding in the genital or anal areas. Emotional indicators are depression, low self-esteem, and thoughts of suicide. Other clues include compulsive masturbation and sexual behavior or knowledge inappropriate to a child's age.

Child neglect is "the failure of the child's parent or caretaker, who has the material resources to do so, to provide minimally adequate care in the areas of health, nutrition, shelter, education, supervision, affection, or attention" (Wolock & Horowitz, 1984, p. 15). For example, a child might lack appropriate winter clothing in a cold climate and, as a result, suffer frequent illness. Or a 6-year-old child might be left alone in charge of her two younger siblings. Constant hunger is yet another symptom.

Emotional or psychological neglect involves the "passive or passive/aggressive inattention to the child's emotional needs, nurturing, or emotional well-being" (Brassard, Germain, & Hart, 1987, p. 267). Parents may deprive an infant of physical contact and attention or simply ignore children who desperately need emotional involvement. *Emotional or psychological abuse* refers to "belittling, humiliating, rejecting [a child, to] undermining a child's self-esteem, and generally to not creating a positive atmosphere for a child" (Crosson-Tower, 1992, p. 175). Both emotional neglect and emotional abuse interfere with a child's psychological development and well-being. Emotional neglect involves withdrawal of support, attention, and encouragement. Emotional abuse concerns more active criticism, disapproval, and censure of children and their feelings and behavior.

Nine types of behavior illustrate parental emotional maltreatment (also referred to as *psychological maltreatment*) (Burnett, 1993; Downs et al., 1996):[2]

1. *Detaining children in a small space by tying or locking them up for long periods:* In one case, parents punished their 8-year-old son for misbehavior by locking him up in an abandoned outhouse out back. He experienced "severe emotional problems, with fears of being abandoned, hearing imaginary voices, and seeing things that are not there" (Burnett, 1993, p. 444).
2. *Extreme public embarrassment and disgrace:* For example, for years, parents reprimanded their 8-year-old daughter by listing her misdeeds on a sign and hanging it around her neck. They then forced her to stand out by the highway for several hours so passersby could gawk at her.
3. *"Cinderella syndrome"* (Burnett, 1993, p. 444): In one case, parents took three of their four children on a "fun" weekend trip while leaving the fourth, Donna, age 8, behind. Her parents told her that they were ashamed of her and that she would have to find someplace to stay while they were gone.
4. *Extreme verbal cruelty, whereby a child is sharply rejected, told she or he is useless, or made the recipient of scornful ridicule:* For example, when an 8-year-old boy's dog was accidentally killed by a car, his mother shrieked that it was all his fault because he was an evil seed of the devil.
5. *Urging or forcing a child into delinquent behavior:* For example, a parent might encourage petty theft or the use of alcoholic beverages or other drugs.
6. *Intimidating children by threatening serious injury, abandonment, or even death:* For example, parents of one 8-year-old boy discovered him playing outside when he was supposed to be inside. They told him that they could not trust him anymore and that if he ever did something like that again they would call the police or break his legs.
7. *Refusing to seek necessary psychological treatment:* In one case, a 9-year-old girl who had been depressed for a long time attempted suicide by slitting her wrists. Finally, after she sought help from a school nurse, her parents forbade her from getting treatment and told her to keep her feelings to herself.
8. *Restricting a child's emotional and social development:* For example, one mother never left her home and kept her 8-year-old son there with her. Although he displayed exceptionally immature behavior and lived in a make-believe world, she homeschooled him and forbade him from playing with other children.
9. *Depriving a child of love and emotional support:* For example, after his wife's death, a father ceased to take notice of his 9-year-old son. The boy was forced to spend much time alone while his father locked himself in his room and had to do his own cooking and wash his own clothes. His school performance declined as he started acting out aggressively and experimenting with drugs.

[2]These vignettes are based on those described in Burnett, 1993, pp. 441–454.

HIGHLIGHT 9.2

International Perspectives: The Child
Slave Trade in West Africa

Juliette Zinwue was thrilled! Although she lived in a small village in Benin, West Africa, she was actually going to travel somewhere in a car; some men said they would take her to work in Abidjan, a city in the Ivory Coast, and paid her parents to do so (Robinson & Palus, 2001). However, the journey soon turned into a horror story. Placed in a wealthy woman's home located in active, crowded Abidjan, Juliette "now rises at 6 AM to sweep the house and courtyard, wash dishes and clean out the garbage cans. She spends the rest of the day at a local market selling trinkets and hair accessories at her boss's stall" (Robinson & Palus, 2001, p. 40). She started three years ago. Today she's 10.

Robinson and Palus (2001) report on the experiences of the estimated 200,000 West and Central African children who are sold into slavery each year. The root of the problem is poverty. In the poorest countries, including Benin, where up to three-quarters of the population survives on less than $1 a day, children have no schools to attend and little hope for viable future employment. They are often sold, sometimes for the meager fee of

$15, because impoverished parents feel the children might be better off in a richer country—even as slaves. Most girls find themselves working as domestic help or prostitutes. Boys end up as field hands on plantations or as workers on fishing boats. Generally, "Africa has the highest rate of child labor in the world: 41% of 5-to-14-year-olds work" (p. 40).

The practice is bolstered by tradition. Historically, young children resided with wealthier urban extended family members or hired out as servants to newly married couples. However, the current practice of selling them to strangers in other countries is purely a matter of business. Somebody is making money in the process, and it surely is not the children. Although West African nations are attempting to halt the slavery process, it is difficult. Borders between nations are easily crossed, and police have few resources for enforcement.

Juliette resolutely states, "I don't care that I have not been to school . . . but I would like to go to church" (p. 41). She can't though, because she doesn't get Sundays off.

Note that some of these scenarios overlap with other forms of abuse and neglect. Indeed, Hart, Brassard, and Karlson (1996) maintain that emotional maltreatment "is embedded in all other forms of child maltreatment" (p. 77). Child maltreatment is a complex issue. What's important is not that a particular case fits neatly into a clearly defined category, but rather that children be protected and their needs addressed. Highlight 9.2 provides an international perspective on child abuse—small children being sold as slaves in West Africa.

How Many Children Are Maltreated?

The actual number of child maltreatment cases is difficult to determine. Specific definitions for who is included in specific categories vary dramatically from one state or locale to another. One thing, however, is certain—any figures that are reported reflect a minimal number of actual cases. All indications are that vast numbers of cases go unreported.

Millions of cases of child maltreatment are reported in the United States each year (Pecora et al., 2000). "Recent findings suggest that the incidence of child maltreatment is increasing dramatically"; one study found that the incidence had doubled over a decade (Petr, 2004, p. 20). According to a Children's Bureau report, 57.7% of child maltreatment results from neglect, 22.2% from physical abuse, 12.3% from sexual abuse, 5.9% from emotional maltreatment, and 14.5% from causes that don't fit well into the other categories (Winton & Mara, 2001; U.S. Department of Health and Human Services, Children's Bureau, 1998).[3]

What Causes Child Maltreatment?

People who physically abuse children tend to have the following needs (Crosson-Tower, 2005; Kolko, 1996, 2002):

- A need for personal support and nurturance.
- A need to overcome isolation and establish social contacts.
- A need to learn appropriate parenting skills.
- A need to improve self-esteem.

Parents who neglect their children appear to have characteristics similar to physically abusive parents, although poverty is also "highly correlated with neglect" (Lindsey, 1994; Mather & Lager, 2000, p. 102). A typical neglectful parent is "an isolated individual who has difficulty forming relationships or carrying out the routine tasks of everyday life. Burdened with the anger and sadness over unmet childhood needs, this parent finds it impossible to consistently recognize and meet the needs of her or his children" (Tower, 1989, p. 91). This description, in some ways, resembles the description of the physically abusive parent. However, an abuser lashes out, whereas a neglectful parent tends to withdraw and fails to provide adequately for children.

No clear-cut description characterizes people who sexually abuse children "other than that most are male and are known to the victim" (Crooks & Baur, 1999, p. 591; Gibbons & Vincent, 1994; Guidry, 1995). There is some evidence that they tend to be "shy, lonely, [and] poorly informed about sexuality" (Bauman, Kasper, & Alford, 1984; Crooks & Baur, 1999, p. 591). They also "are likely to have poor interpersonal and sexual relations with other adults, and may feel socially inadequate and inferior" (Crooks & Baur, 1999, p. 591; McKibben, Proulz, & Lusignan, 1994; Minor & Dwyer, 1997). Other possible characteristics include "[a]lcoholism, severe marital problems, sexual difficulties, and poor emotional adjustment" (Crooks & Baur, 1999, p. 591; Johnston, 1987; McKibben et al., 1994).

Miller-Perrin and Perrin (1999) describe some of the characteristics of parents who emotionally maltreat their children:

> Such parents exhibit more psychosocial problems, more difficulty coping with stress, more difficulty building relationships, and more social isolation compared to nonabusive parents. . . . [One study indicated that they] displayed deficits in child management

[3]Note that these figures add up to more than 100% due to inconsistencies in data collection and differences among states.

techniques. In addition, emotionally abusive mothers demonstrated a lack of support networks (both personal and community) as well as greater levels of perceived stress, marital discord, and alcohol and drug use. (p. 190)

Child Protective Services and the Social Work Role

Child protective services (CPS) are interventions aimed at protecting children at risk of maltreatment. CPS social workers are usually employed by state or county public agencies whose designated task is to protect children from harm. Liederman (1995) describes agency functioning:

> CPS agencies investigate reports of child abuse and neglect, assess the degree of harm and the ongoing risk of harm to the child, determine whether the child can remain safely in the home or should be placed in the custody of the state, and work closely with the family or juvenile court regarding appropriate plans for the child's safety and well-being. (p. 425)

Interventions in child maltreatment cases follow the same sequential steps used in other areas of social work intervention. These include receipt of the initial referral, gathering information about the case through a social study, assessment of the situation, case planning including goal setting, provision of treatment, evaluation of the effects of treatment, and termination of the case (Kadushin & Martin, 1988). Highlight 9.3 focuses on the importance of risk assessment in cases of child maltreatment.

Following assessment, a treatment *plan* is developed providing direction for how to proceed. According to Winton and Mara (2001), treatment goals for maltreatment victims "include increasing self-esteem, decreasing feelings of hopelessness and helplessness, decreasing aggressive behaviors, and decreasing negative behaviors such as lying, suicide attempts, running away, promiscuity, and drug or alcohol abuse" (p. 165). These can be achieved through individual counseling, group therapy, or family therapy.

Of course, basic aspects of treatment for physically abused children involve meeting their medical needs and keeping them safe. Sometimes removal from a dangerous situation is necessary, at least temporarily.

Treatment goals for parents focus on strengthening their "coping skills, parenting skills, and child management techniques" (Winton & Mara, 2001, p. 171). Intervention may involve individual counseling or family therapy. Many believe that group therapy, including self-help groups such as Parents Anonymous, is often the most effective (Winton & Mara, 2001). Through such groups, parents learn that they are not alone and can discover how others are experiencing stress and frustration. They can share coping ideas with each other, suggest new child management techniques, provide mutual support, and improve their communication skills.

Treatment for families experiencing abuse or neglect varies radically depending on the resources and services available, the level of risk to the children's well-being, the family dynamics, and motivation of the abusive or neglectful caregivers. An intensive family preservation approach (described in detail later in the chapter) involves a social worker spending concentrated time with a family, identifying specific treatment goals, emphasizing family strengths, and teaching other skills as needed.

HIGHLIGHT 9.3
The Assessment of Risk in Child Maltreatment Cases

A key word in the assessment of child maltreatment is *risk*. After a case involving suspected maltreatment is reported, it's the social worker's job to *assess* the extent to which children are at risk of maltreatment. Crosson-Tower (2005) urges that the following questions be answered during the assessment process:

- Is the child at risk from abuse or neglect and to what degree?
- What is causing the problem?
- Could services be offered to alleviate the problem?
- Is the home a safe environment or must the child be placed elsewhere? (p. 231)

Assessment focuses on many of the dynamics contributing to maltreatment discussed earlier. A number of variables have been found to affect a worker's decision that a case assumes a high level of risk and merits intensive agency intervention (Crosson-Tower, 2005; Kadushin & Martin, 1988; Meddin, 1985; Rosen, 1981). These include

- Clearly visible proof of abuse or environmental characteristics that obviously endanger a child.

- The degree of the child's helplessness and vulnerability (e.g., a child with a physical disability or an infant being extremely vulnerable).
- Self-destructive behavior on the part of the child.
- A history of severe abuse.
- Abusers who show no or little regret for their child's abuse and have difficulty accepting responsibility.
- Abusers who openly reject the child or blame the child for the problem.
- Serious emotional disturbances on the part of parents.
- Lack of cooperation by the parents.
- Families that are exposed to numerous and severe psychological and social pressures.
- Isolation of the family and lack of social support systems.

Assessment interviews involve both adults and children. Questions focus on the parents' history and current functioning; the way parents perceive their children; the way the family system functions as a whole; the condition of the home environment; the external support (e.g., friends or relatives) available to the family; and the children's condition, level of development, and overall functioning (Crosson-Tower, 2005).

Working with and Referring to Other Agencies

During the intervention process, CPS staff often work with the courts to declare that children require protection and to determine appropriate safe placement for them. CPS workers are frequently called on to testify in court to report assessment information and make recommendations (Gibelman, 1995). In the event that family problems cannot be resolved, CPS workers may work with the courts to develop alternative long-term or permanent placements.

Additionally, social workers may refer to a number of social services (Alexander, 2004). *Respite care* is the temporary provision of care so that the regular caregivers, in this case parents, have some time away from child care responsibilities (Murphy, 2004). This can ease stress and allow parents to take a break. *Day care* is the regular provision of care for children or others dependent on help when regular caregivers must work or be away from the home. This is another way of providing alternative child care for children so parents can attend to their own needs, go to work, and practice newly learned skills. *Support services* involve a wide range of assistance in helping parents undertake their daily tasks and assume their responsibilities; examples include "parent educational services, employment counseling and training services, budget management, legal services, homemaker services, . . . referrals to food banks, and transportation" (Alexander, 2004, p. 419). *Parental aides* are trained paraprofessionals, sometimes volunteers, who go into the home, serve as positive role models for behavior management and parent–child relationships, and provide someone for the parents to talk to. In effect, this is another way of taking the pressure off. Finally, *Big Brother/Big Sister* or *adopted grandparent programs* can let children form a special relationship with a supportive adult role model or mentor. Volunteers are paired with a child and, under supervision, offer that child guidance and friendship.

Referral opportunities are endless. It's up to the social worker to accurately assess family members' needs and creatively link them to available services.

Case Example   Cynthia, age 7, came to school one day with odd-looking bruises on her arm. Her teacher, Kari Meback, noticed them immediately and asked her where she got them. Cynthia, an aggressive, boisterous child who loved to get attention from her teachers, told Kari that she had tripped, fallen down the stairs, and hit her arm on some toys at the bottom. Kari thought that this seemed a bit peculiar but accepted Cynthia's answer and forgot about the incident.

Three days later, Kari again noticed some odd bruises on Cynthia's arm. She also observed that Cynthia was having difficulty writing, as if her fingers were sprained. Again she asked Cynthia what was wrong. The child answered that she had probably bumped her hand on something. But this time Kari did not leave the matter at that. That same day she talked to the school social worker, who, in turn, referred the matter to a protective services worker at the local social services agency.

The protective services worker assigned the case, Brian Bornthumper, immediately began a case assessment. He interviewed both Cynthia and her parents. He focused on the elements indicating that abuse was taking place and on the probable risk that Cynthia would come to further harm. He also examined the needs of the family as a whole and of its individual members.

Brian assumed as nonthreatening an approach as possible and maintained a focus on the family's and the child's welfare. He discovered that Cynthia's family had moved to the area from another state only a year before. Cynthia's mother, Amelia, was a shy, withdrawn woman who found it difficult to make new friends. She had no relatives in the area. Additionally, Cynthia's baby sister, Julie, had been born only three months after the move. Julie was a colicky baby who rarely slept more than two hours at a time and cried almost incessantly. Cynthia's father, George, was a mop salesman who was frequently out of town. And when he was home, he spent his time watching football and other sports on television or sleeping.

Social workers work with abused children and their familes.

Amelia obviously was under severe stress. She felt lonely, isolated, and worth-less. Even Julie didn't seem to love her. All the baby did was cry. George was hardly ever home, and when he was, he ignored the family. Amelia felt that her marital rela-tionship was deteriorating. As a result of all these stresses, she found herself vio-lently exploding at Cynthia. Whenever Cynthia did something the least bit wrong, Amelia found herself screaming at the girl and often physically assaulting her.

In fact, Amelia's relationship with her own family was quite poor. Her child-hood memories were filled with her father beating her with little provocation.

Cynthia's family exemplified the types of needs that are common in abusive families. Loneliness, isolation, lack of emotional support, marital problems, life crises, and lack of effective parenting skills were all apparent. Brian conducted an assessment by gathering relevant information regarding family relationships, his-tory, emotional status, and stress levels; child management approaches; and avail-able support systems. As a CPS worker, he sought to strengthen the family and enhance family members' interactions among themselves and with others in their environment.

Brian initially made several referrals to the appropriate services, after which he served as case manager, coordinating efforts and monitoring progress. He met with the family regularly to accomplish this. For instance, Brian referred Amelia to a Parents Anonymous group, in which she could experience mutual support, vent her frustrations, develop relationships, improve communication skills, and learn new coping methods. He referred both George and Amelia to a parent effectiveness training group to improve their ability to cope with and control their children's behavior. He also referred them to a local family services agency for marital counseling. The intent was to work on improving communication within the marriage and to address possible ways for George to spend more time with Amelia, provide her with greater support, and become more involved with the family.

In addition, Brian referred Cynthia to the family services agency for individual counseling. He also worked with her school social worker to involve her in a volleyball team and local Girl Scout troop.

Brian suggested that Amelia join a recreational group so she could develop some friendships and have some time to herself. Amelia decided to become a member of a bowling team and started attending an aerobics class. Finally, Brian helped Amelia find a day care center that would care for her children while she attended these activities.

In effect, Brian worked with this family to develop its members' strengths, improve communication and mutual support, utilize more effective behavior management techniques, stop abuse, maintain safety, and improve overall family functioning.

Sometimes it's necessary for social workers to do more than simply make referrals, as Brian's work with Cynthia and her family illustrates. Focus on Critical Thinking 9.1 addresses advocacy and child maltreatment in the macro arena.

Intensive Family Preservation: One Treatment Approach

Family preservation services are "intensive services generally delivered in the client's home over a brief, time-limited period. These services were developed to help prevent unnecessary out-of-home placements, keep families together, and preserve family bonds" (Tracy, 1995, p. 973). The concept of family preservation has become a major thrust in agencies throughout the country. It involves doing everything possible to keep the child in the home and provide treatment for the family. Family preservation services are also referred to as family-based services, "home-based services, or in-home treatment" (Alexander, 2004; Berg, 1994, p. 4).

Six goals of family preservation services are "(1) to protect children, (2) to maintain and strengthen family bonds, (3) to stabilize the crisis situation, (4) to increase the family's skills and competencies, (5) to facilitate the family's use of a variety of formal and informal helping resources, and (6) to prevent unnecessary out-of-home placement of children" (Tracy, 1995; Tracy, Haapala, Kinney, & Pecora, 1991, p. 1).

In past decades, working with families usually involved focusing on protecting the child. This, in turn, often meant removing the child from the home. Services were then provided in a segmented manner by a variety of workers. For example, consider an alleged case of child abuse. One protective services intake worker

FOCUS ON CRITICAL THINKING 9.1

Advocacy and Child Maltreatment in the Macro Arena

An ongoing part of the social worker's role is to evaluate the effectiveness of policy at the macro level and advocate for positive change where needed. Macro improvements are called for in at least five areas:

- More funding should be funneled to the *prevention* of child maltreatment (Chadwick, 2002; Daro & Donnelly, 2002). Until now "[s]ervices and interventions have developed as *responses* to the problems of abuse as the problems have been recognized" (Chadwick, 2002, p. 509). Preventing children from suffering from maltreatment in the first place is certainly much better for them than reacting after it has already occurred.
- A more supportive system geared toward improving resources and services for families in general is essential to maintain family strengths. Families need tangible resources including adequate shelter, food, clothing, and other necessities to thrive (Alexander, 2004).
- More community and neighborhood supports should be initiated and developed. Current availability of resources and services is significantly inconsistent (Chadwick, 2002). For

example, families in rural settings should have better access to child protective services (Chadwick, 2002).
- Public and private agencies should communicate and cooperate with each other more effectively concerning service provision (Chadwick, 2002). Sometimes "interventions are incompatible with others"; for example, an abusive parent may be imprisoned for a long period, conflicting with a treatment plan developed to reunite the family (Chadwick, 2002, p. 517).
- Organized continuing education plans should be developed to educate social workers and other social service providers about child maltreatment (Chadwick, 2002).

With the conservative—liberal and residual–institutional orientations in mind, answer these questions:

- To what extent do these suggestions reflect conservative or liberal values, and why?
- To what extent do they reflect a residual or institutional orientation to social welfare policy, and why?

would gather the intake data when the child was initially referred. Another outreach protective services worker would provide services to the family. Still another would work with the foster family if the child was placed there. And so it went.

Family preservation, in contrast, emphasizes service provision to the family unit in a more coordinated fashion. For instance, one worker might do the majority of the engagement, assessment, planning, intervention, evaluation, and termination. The child is likely to remain in the home during the entire process. All services are provided or coordinated by a designated worker with the intent of helping the intact family solve its range of problems. Service can be "provided by a treatment team" proceeding with a coordinated and unified effort, with the team "often made up of case manager, worker/therapist, and such support staff as the parent educator, homemaker, and so on" (Berg, 1994, p. 5).

Key Themes in Family Preservation

At least 11 themes tend to characterize family preservation programs (Downs et al., 2004; Maluccio, 1990, pp. 23–25). They include

1. *Crisis orientation:* Family preservation is based on intervention when a crisis is taking place within the home. Workers can then take advantage of the family's motivation to alleviate the stress it's experiencing.
2. *Focus on family:* The family is all-important; it is considered the optimum place for children to remain. All intervention emphasis is directed toward keeping the family together and strengthening its members.
3. *Home-based services:* Services are provided in the home whenever possible. The ongoing thrust is improving the home environment.
4. *Time limits:* Because family preservation workers intervene during times of crisis, they work quickly. The intervention process in most models ranges from 4 to 12 weeks, although some extend longer than that. Setting time limits helps workers and their clients evaluate progress regularly.
5. *Limited, focused objectives:* All intervention objectives are clearly specified. The primary goal is to alleviate the crisis situation and strengthen the family unit so that a crisis is less likely to erupt again.
6. *Intensive, comprehensive services:* Workers' time and attention are concentrated on the families and their progress. Workers may spend as much as 20–25 hours each week arranging for resources and providing services (e.g., problem solving, counseling, and parenting skills education).
7. *Emphasis on education and skill building:* The family preservation approach is a positive one. It assumes that people are capable of learning and can improve if they are given appropriate information and support.
8. *Coordination:* Because intervention is intensive and numerous resources may be involved, coordination is very important. Sometimes other service providers and specialists are involved with a case, requiring coordination of treatment efforts.
9. *Flexibility:* Each family is different, having varying problems and needs. Flexibility enables practitioners to match a wide range of services and resources with the individual family's needs.
10. *Accessibility:* Workers in family preservation must be readily accessible to families in crisis. Their work is intensive and time-limited. Workers' caseloads typically are small so they can concentrate their efforts.
11. *Accountability:* Accountability is the obligation of justifying one's work by accomplishing identified goals. The emphasis on focused objectives and time-limited interventions enhances workers' ability to evaluate their effectiveness.

The family preservation approach is expensive because workers have small caseloads; therefore, the ratio of worker salary to number of cases is high. For example, consider a worker being paid $32,000 per year who works with 12 families over the entire year. The cost of her salary is about $2,667 per family. Another worker serving in a more traditional child welfare capacity might have 90 cases in a year. The cost of her salary per case is only about $356. This is a bit oversimplified, but you probably get the idea.

Case Example   The following case illustrates how the themes just described might be employed in practice. (They are noted in italics.) Mary Jo, age 24, is the mother of three children—Ralphie, Sherry, and Jenna, ages 6, 4, and 3, respectively. Mary Jo has had a long, traumatic history of drug abuse and involvement with violent men. At her lowest point, high on crack, she was beaten bloody by her latest boyfriend and taken to the hospital emergency room. Her children, who had been removed from the home several times because of her neglect related to substance abuse, were taken from the home again. Mary Jo was told that unless she successfully underwent substance abuse treatment, she was not getting her children back.

It was a rough year, but she made it. She successfully completed a tough inpatient program and remained off crack. At the end of the year, she was desperate to get her children back. She was identified as a good potential recipient of family preservation services due to the *crisis* of trying to get her kids back and learning the skills she needed to do so. Edria was assigned as her social worker.

With a small caseload of two families, Edria was able to *focus on the family* and provide Mary Jo and her children with *intensive, comprehensive services.* Primary problems involved Mary Jo's homemaking abilities, child management skills, budgeting capability, and anger management. All three children were unruly and difficult to control, but only Ralphie was dangerous. He had set a number of fires and had threatened Mary Jo with a knife on three occasions.

Edria provided *home-based services* because she needed to help Mary Jo work out problems immediately when they occurred in her home environment. She also had to be *flexible* because of Mary Jo's unique set of needs. Edria focused on *education and skill building.* She helped Mary Jo work out a child behavior management program that identified negative behaviors requiring change and specified new, more appropriate behaviors to be established. Edria also worked with Mary Jo to teach her more effective responses to the children's behavior to enable her to regain control. One facet of this involved anger control, whereby Mary Jo developed a new awareness of her previously uncontrolled emotions and new, more appropriate responses to the children's behavior. For example, she replaced erratic physical punishment with a more methodical system involving positive and negative consequences. Edria also helped Mary Jo develop better household management and budgeting skills.

Edria established *limited, focused objectives* with Mary Jo concerning each area of skill development. The relatively high cost of treatment emphasized that Edria must be *accountable* for achieving these objectives. Because her time with Mary Jo was intensive, she also had to establish *time limits* within which objectives would be achieved. Edria's time was expensive, and she couldn't work with Mary Jo forever. But while she was working with Mary Jo, Edria had to be readily *accessible*. If a behavioral crisis occurred at 9:30 PM on a Saturday night, Edria needed to be available to help.

One other aspect of Edria's work with Mary Jo involved *coordination*. Remember that Ralphie had exhibited some fairly serious behavioral problems. In addition to the child behavior management program being implemented at home, he was also receiving individual therapy provided by another social worker specializing in child counseling. Edria needed to coordinate objectives and progress between this therapist and the home program.

This turned out to be a successful intervention. Mary Jo regained substantial control over her children's behavior, although they never became perfect angels. Ralphie no longer threatened her or exhibited dangerous behavior. Mary Jo had immensely improved control of her temper. Finally, Mary Jo was running the household more effectively, including paying her bills and balancing her checkbook. She still hated to dust and hoped to win the lottery, but she was maintaining a status quo. The family was together and relatively happy. Edria went on to another case. That was a hard part of the job—leaving a family after becoming so involved. However, she wished Mary Jo the best and knew that tomorrow would be just as action packed when she started out with a new family preservation case.

 # Child Day Care

Child day care is an agency or program that provides supervision and care for children while parents or guardians are at work or otherwise unavailable. It is critical for many families because the majority of women work outside the home (Renzetti & Curran, 2003). For instance, half of mothers with infants under 1 year of age are employed outside the home (Sapiro, 2003). Approximately 71% of single mothers and almost 61% of married mothers who have children under age 6 work outside the home (U.S. Census Bureau, 2003, No. 597).

Although not all day care centers employ social workers, practitioners often work with clients requiring day care and must help them with referrals. This is especially true because TANF requires parents receiving public assistance to get training and find work. Social workers may also have to help parents find high-quality day care.

Many types of day care are available. Downs and her colleagues (2004) describe the various types of day care that are most common and the advantages and disadvantages of each. In about half of all working families with preschoolers, family members provide day care. Each parent takes turns caring for children while the other is working outside the home, or relatives such as grandparents provide supervision.

Outside the family, day care is provided in three basic ways. First, parents can hire someone like a baby-sitter or a nanny to come into their home and provide care, which about 4% of working families with preschoolers do. Although most parents prefer this option, it's too expensive to be practical for many families. Second, parents can take their children to the care providers' homes for supervision. This is referred to as *family day care* and is used by 14% of families with preschoolers. Third, larger, organized day care centers can provide care. About a quarter of all preschoolers in working families attend these facilities.

Over three-quarters of all 5-year-olds are in some kind of day care arrangement. "[A]s children get older, they spend less time in child care settings outside of school. About half of children ages 6 to 12 with an employed primary caretaker were in some type of child care arrangement besides school, usually care by relatives (23%)" (Downs et al., 2004, p. 135). Another 15% of children this age attend before- or after-school programs, 7% are in family day care, and 10% look after themselves.

Advantages of family day care include a small caregiver-to-child ratio, proximity to the home, and opportunities to develop a closer relationship with the caregiver.

HIGHLIGHT 9.4
What Makes for High-Quality Day Care?

The quality of day care varies dramatically for each type (Burchinal, Roberts, Nabors, & Bryant, 1996; Santrock, 1999). The following variables are associated with high-quality day care (Clarke-Stewart, Gruber, & Fitzgerald, 1994; Lefrançois, 1999):

- Well-trained caregivers who can provide educational experiences to enhance social, emotional, and intellectual development.
- A well-structured program that provides multiple growth opportunities unavailable at home.
- A low caregiver-to-child ratio (e.g., 3 to 1) that allows for greater interaction and attention (Santrock, 2004).
- A positively oriented environment that does not focus on discipline. (One study revealed

that "children who received less discipline [in the sense of fewer demands, less control, less punishment, more choices, and more responsibility for responses] were more advanced cognitively, more obedient, and more likely to get along with peers" [Clarke-Stewart et al., 1994; Lefrançois, 1999, p. 240].)
- Sufficient chances to interact positively with other children.
- A physical environment that's interesting and thought-provoking.
- Strong agreement between the parents and the care providers regarding childrearing practices.

In contrast, the worst day care provides no more than custodial care that gives children only the bare necessities of supervision and physical care.

A chief disadvantage of family day care is that the vast majority of such care is unregulated and the caregiver unsupervised; another disadvantage is that the caregiver probably lacks formal training in how to provide educational opportunities for children.

Day care centers can serve from 15 to 300 children, although they average about 60. Advantages include being licensed under state supervision, usually having staff trained in child supervision and early education, and being able to provide a wider range of opportunities and activities than what's available in family day care. Disadvantages may include increased impersonality due to size, lack of parental knowledge of their children's individual caregivers, strict and inflexible hours, inconvenient locations, and restrictions regarding care for infants or sick children. Highlight 9.4 discusses variables involved generally in the quality of day care.

Other Supportive Services

A number of other supportive services are clustered under the child welfare umbrella. They are not necessarily jobs assumed by social workers. However, because the broker role in social work is so important, practitioners must be aware of and knowledgeable about these services to be able to provide clients with appropriate referrals. Examples of other supportive services include family life education and respite care.

Family Life Education

Family life education (FLE) is "a leader-directed group learning service . . . [seeking to increase people's] knowledge, develop skills, and examine their attitudes, with the goal of adjusting to, coping with, and growing during normal predictable life transitions" (Riley, 1995, p. 960). Several aspects of this definition are important. First, FLE is a group experience. The context usually involves a social worker or other professional providing information for 6–12 group members; weekly meetings last from 1½ to 2 hours and are held over a 1- to 8-week period (Barker, 2003).

A second aspect of the definition involves the purpose of these meetings. Because they may address either normal developmental or specific crisis issues, they may be appropriate for almost anyone, depending on people's learning needs. The four categories of FLE groups are (1) normal development, (2) crisis, (3) personal growth, and (4) life adjustment groups (Riley, 1995, p. 961).

Normal development groups provide information about various normal life stages. Examples are "parenting groups (for parents of newborns, preschool children, or adolescents), groups preparing for marriage, 'empty-nest' groups, and retirement groups" (Riley, 1995, p. 961).

Crisis groups are oriented toward people facing a serious life turning point or upheaval. Often these people are unprepared for the crisis and require information and help to cope. Examples of such crises are serious illness, divorce, recent death of a loved one, and loss of a job. Group leaders usually must give members emotional support in addition to information.

Personal growth groups help people develop specified social skills. They are unlike crisis groups because there's no sudden upheaval involved, and they differ from life adjustment groups because members are not striving to cope with a chronic problem. Rather, group members have in common the interest of improving themselves in some way. Examples are groups focusing on assertiveness training, time management, and communication skills.

Life adjustment groups help people who are dealing with some ongoing problematic issue. Most often, group members are coping with a crisis of their own or of someone close to them. This differs from a crisis group because it focuses on long-term issues instead of temporary crises. Examples are parents of children with a chronic illness or developmental disability, caregivers for elderly people with Alzheimer's disease, and adults with Parkinson's disease.[4]

Respite Care

Respite care is supervision of a child by another caregiver, allowing the parent an interval of relief from the responsibilities of child care. In essence, it gives the individual a break, a brief time during which the caregiver is free from stressful responsibilities. It allows an opportunity for parents to run errands or simply to relax. Some agencies use volunteers to provide respite care; others have programs in which parents can drop children off and have them be supervised for a few hours (Mather &

---

[4]*Parkinson's disease* is a neurological illness causing deterioration of brain cells and characterized by "tremors, especially of the fingers and hands, muscle rigidity, and a shuffling gait" (Nichols, 1999, p. 961).

Lager, 2000). One of this chapter's opening vignettes, involving Corazon and Juanita, provides an example of a situation in which respite care would be appropriate.

Note that respite care can apply not only to parents but also to other caregivers with primary responsibility for a dependent. For example, respite care might be provided to a person caring for a spouse dying of a rapidly debilitating disease. It might also apply to an adult child caring for an elderly parent who has limited mobility.

An Ongoing Macro Issue: Advocacy for Resources

Social workers live and struggle with many issues in providing supportive services to children and families. This book reflects only the tip of the iceberg. Children are indeed a population-at-risk, and social workers have a responsibility to advocate on their behalf. *Advocacy*, of course, involves taking an active, directive role on behalf of a client or client group in need of help. One important aspect of child advocacy is the acknowledgment and support of the basic rights of children. The concern for children's rights can be considered on a universal level; that is, every child should have certain specific rights such as the right to adequate food, clothing, shelter, and a decent home environment.

In an era of shrinking and competitive resources, ongoing advocacy is necessary for the following:

- Quality, accessible day care for children of working parents (Karger & Stoesz, 2002).
- Improved maternal and child health care in view of the high proportion of low-birth-weight babies (Karger & Stoesz, 2002).
- Better prevention and treatment programs to address the substance abuse epidemic and its contribution to child maltreatment (Liederman, 1995).
- Welfare reform to raise families' income levels above the poverty line (Liederman, 1995).

Substitute Services

Earlier we established that substitute services are those replacing

> another family for the child's own family, so that someone else takes over all aspects of the parental role on a temporary or permanent basis. Such a change is necessary when the home presents deficiencies so serious that even intensive home-based preventive services cannot assist the family in providing the child with minimally adequate social, emotional, or physical care. (Kadushin & Martin, 1988, p. 344)

When the best attempts at providing supportive services to maintain children in a healthy family environment do not work, alternative living arrangements for the children become necessary. These substitute family environments then give children the supervision, shelter, food, and clothing required to meet their daily needs. Figure 9.1 portrayed the continuum of care from supportive to substitute services.

Children are removed from their parents' care for a number of reasons. Parents may be unable to care for children because of their own serious illness, physical disability, emotional immaturity, cognitive disability, or substance abuse. They may neglect, abandon, or abuse their children. Children may have such serious developmental, emotional, or physical disabilities that parents are incapable of caring for them. Finally, there may not be sufficient community resources to provide the necessary supportive services to keep children in their own homes.

Length of removal depends on the severity of problems in the home environment and the extent to which it can be strengthened to allow the children's safe return. Changing a child's living environment often involves a change in *legal custody*—formal assumption of caregiving responsibilities for a child including meeting that child's daily needs.[5]

A guiding principle is to keep children in the *least restrictive* setting in which they can function with the greatest amount of independence. The overriding goal is to have children return to a normal family and community environment if at all possible.

Substitute care services can be placed on a continuum reflecting their intensity of supervision and restrictiveness. This continuum of care for children and adolescents ranges from supportive services for families with children remaining in their own homes to removal from the home and placement in a formal treatment setting. Proch and Taber (1987, pp. 9–10) rank children's placement from the least restrictive to most restrictive as follows (see Figure 9.2):

- Home of parent (rank 1).
- Home of relative (2).
- Foster family home (3).
- Specialized foster family home (4).
- Group home (5).
- Private child welfare institution (6).
- Shelter (7).
- Mental health facility (8).
- Correctional facility (9).

A theme characterizing substitute services is *permanency planning*—"a comprehensive care planning process directed toward the goal of a permanent, stable home for a child [placed in substitute care]" (Rycus, Hughes, & Ginther, 1988, p. 45). Children need a stable, healthy home environment. Being bounced from temporary home to temporary home does not contribute to emotional stability. Therefore, an ultimate goal of substitute care is to give children permanent homes.

Types of substitute services discussed here include kinship care, foster family care, residential placements, and adoption.

 ## Kinship Care

One type of out-of-home placement involves relatives or part of the child's family's supportive network, in what is referred to as *kinship care*. There are positive reasons for placing children with people who are already close to them:

[5]Note that legal custody may also involve granting responsibility to a caregiver for persons who are not children but who cannot function independently. Examples include people with severe cognitive disabilities and elderly people with serious mental incapacities.

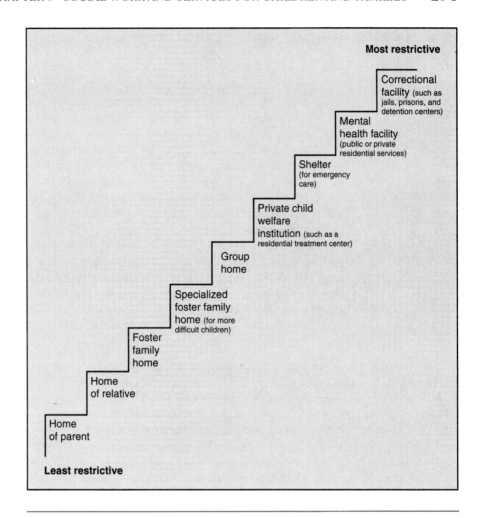

Figure 9.2 Continuum of care: Restrictiveness of setting

Family strengths often include a kinship network that functions as a support system. The kinship support system may be composed of nuclear family, extended family, blended family, foster family, or adoptive family members or members of tribes or clans. The involvement of kin may stabilize family situations, ensure the protection of children, and prevent the need to separate children from their families and place them in the formal child welfare system. (Child Welfare League of America, 1994, p. 1)

Informal kinship care involves families taking children in without intervention by social service agencies. In *formal* kinship care, a social services agency gains legal custody of a child and places that child in a kinship home, which it licenses. The agency pays the caregivers and is expected to monitor the home's compliance with standards to oversee the child's well-being.

Foster Family Care

Foster family care is the provision of substitute care with a family for a planned temporary or extended period when parents or legal guardians are unable to care for a child. Foster care involves a serious placement decision when a family is in such crisis that adequate care for children in their own home is impossible.

At least four basic principles underlie foster care (Downs et al., 2004; Pecora et al., 2000). First, the child's own family is important to the child, so that home environment should be maintained if at all possible. Therefore, supportive services should be provided to keep the child in the home. If the child still must be removed from the home, efforts should be made to maintain communication between children and parents to support and maintain the parent–child relationship. Second, when the child must be removed from the home, the foster care placement should provide a healthy, nurturing environment until the child is placed in a permanent family setting. Third, the child's own family should be viewed as the client system, with the child's return to a safe, healthy family environment a primary goal. Fourth, foster parents or child care staff in group homes are viewed as an important part of the treatment team working together toward the goal of reuniting children with their families. Highlight 9.5 discusses some reasons children require foster family care.

Types of Foster Family Homes

Depending on their circumstances, children should be placed in the type of foster family care that best serves their needs. At least four types of foster family care reflect special circumstances for children needing more specific types of care— shelter homes, long-term foster homes, specialized foster homes, and treatment foster care (Downs et al., 2004, pp. 346–347). *Shelter homes* provide a transitory haven for children during assessment and placement. *Long-term foster homes* offer an ongoing residence for children unable to return to their parents' home and unadoptable for various reasons. One is that parents refuse to give up guardianship, as in Devin's case in Highlight 9.5. (*Guardianship* is the legal responsibility to care for another person and oversee that person's affairs. A child's guardian assumes decision-making responsibilities such as giving consent for major surgery. This differs from custody, whereby the custodian is responsible only for daily care.) Other children aren't adopted because they have serious disabilities or health problems that adoptive parents couldn't afford. Additionally, there is often a shortage of people seeking to adopt children who are not infants.

Specialized foster homes serve children with special needs such as developmental disabilities or conditions such as fetal alcohol syndrome[6] or being infected with HIV. Other specialized homes prepare older children for living independently. Finally, *treatment foster care* provides specialized treatment for children with serious behavioral and emotional problems. The idea here is that a family setting offers a less restrictive environment than a group home or institution for children requiring

---

[6]Fetal alcohol syndrome (FAS) is "a condition in a fetus characterized by abnormal growth, neurological damage, and facial distortion caused by the mother's heavy alcohol consumption" (Kelly, 2001, p. 567).

HIGHLIGHT 9.5

Reasons for Foster Family Care

Children need foster family care for various reasons (Crosson-Tower, 2004). The family might have an emergency like a sudden illness or accident. Parents might be under such stress that they cannot care for their children adequately and desperately require relief. They may need time to address their problems and issues such as homelessness or substance abuse. Children may have to be temporarily removed from the home for their own safety because of abuse or neglect. Foster care may reflect a temporary placement to provide residence for the child before more permanent placement in an institution or adoption. The following are examples of reasons for placing children in foster care (Crosson-Tower, 2004):[7]

Example A: Cindy, a mother of five children, had heart disease. Although her physician told her to stop, she continued to have children because her religious beliefs prohibited her from using contraception. She had five more but died of a heart attack during the birth of her 10th child. Devin, her husband, was overwhelmed at being left alone with 10 children and began to drink. As an alcoholic, he relinquished his children to foster care but refused to give them up permanently for adoption.

Example B: Felicia, age 15, was a serious student who wanted to go to college. Unfortunately,

her mother, Mystique, who was quite unstable and into drugs, was vacillating emotionally between two men—her current boyfriend and her ex-husband. As a result, Mystique moved from one man to the other every six months or so, dragging Felicia with her. Because this forced Felicia to keep switching schools and school districts, her grades began to fall. Seriously depressed, she longed for some stability. Finally, at her wit's end, she slit her wrists in the girls' locker room at school. Her school social worker called protective services, and Felicia was placed in a foster home. Much relieved, Felicia was happy in her new environment, finished school, and applied to college. She still maintained regular contact with Mystique.

Example C: Mariko, a single mother, was shocked to find out she had colon cancer. The prognosis was fair to good if she had surgery immediately and underwent the subsequent radiation and chemotherapy. But what would she do with her two children April, age 2, and Mac, age 4, during recovery? Mariko's family lived in a different state, and she had no friends able to care for her children. She decided to place them in foster care until she recovered.

[7]These examples are loosely based on those provided by Crosson-Tower. Details and facts concerning the cases have been changed.

more structured behavioral management. Parents in such homes need specialized training to provide children with a therapeutic experience.

Social Work Roles in Foster Family Care

Social workers in foster care fulfill various functions. Before foster home placement, a worker must first carefully assess the risk in the child's own family to determine the necessity of removal from the home. The worker must conclude that supportive services will be unable to sustain the children and their family in the home environment.

Second, when a foster care placement is necessary, the worker must select the best available foster home. This should be "the least restrictive, most homelike environment possible," one that best meets the child's "particular physical, emotional and social needs" (Rycus et al., 1988, p. 55). For example, it's best to place children closer to their own homes to encourage involvement of the natural parents. Also, the fewer changes (e.g., a different school or lifestyle) the child is forced to experience, the better. The social worker also must assess the child's needs and "anticipated behavior problems" to place the child with a foster family that can best meet those needs (p. 55).

Throughout the foster care preplacement, placement, and postplacement process, the social worker fulfills a third function: case management. Coordinating services might require home visits, contacting schools regarding the child's performance, and dealing with crises such as children running away or natural and foster parents arguing.

The fourth function for foster care workers involves counseling and helping the children, natural parents, and foster parents prepare for changes, adjust to new circumstances, and work toward the children's return to the natural home. The worker should convey clear information about what's happening to all of them and encourage them to ask questions. The worker should also strive to develop "a supportive relationship" with children to help them deal with changes (Rycus et al., 1988, p. 58).

Children often are frightened of the unknown and worry about what will happen to them. They naturally experience a torrent of emotions including rejection, self-blame, anger, despair, depression, and apprehension. The worker may need to help a child verbalize such feelings to deal with them. For instance, a worker might say, "You look like you're about ready to cry. You probably feel really sad right now, and that's OK. You can cry if you like. I have lots of tissues," or, "I know how mad you are about having to move. It's a hard time, and it's OK to feel mad" (Rycus et al., 1988, p. 65). Regardless of how their parents treated them or what mistakes their parents made, children usually continue to care about their parents.

For example, one worker, Jannah, explained how difficult it was for her to work with Angel, a 9-year-old child in foster care (Crosson-Tower, 2004).[8] Before each of her mother's scheduled visits, Jannah would prepare Angel for her mother's visit by talking about how Angel felt toward her mother and what Angel might realistically expect during the visit. As the meeting time approached, Angel would eagerly await her mother by sitting at the front window, watching for her mother's car to pull in the driveway. Sometimes her mother would show up, but more frequently she wouldn't. Then Jannah had to watch Angel bite her lower lip and try to keep from crying in disappointment. Watching Angel's intense pain would infuriate Jannah. However, Jannah forced herself to remember that Angel deeply loved her mother and that their relationship was one of the most important things in Angel's life.

Foster care workers also counsel the birth parents. Sometimes goals involve teaching effective parenting skills and decreasing or controlling stressful life issues (e.g., poverty, substance abuse, social isolation, interpersonal conflict, mental illness). Other

[8]This example is loosely based on one provided by Crosson-Tower. Details and facts concerning the case have been changed.

times, workers focus on maintaining the parent–child relationship because, in many situations, it's easy for parents to "drift" away (Kadushin & Martin, 1988, p. 391). Here parents have less and less frequent contact with the child and may disappear altogether. Counseling and careful supervision are also required when children return to their birth parents.

Additionally, foster care workers counsel foster parents. This might involve preparing foster parents for a new foster child by providing information or helping foster parents integrate the child into their own family system. Foster care workers help foster parents develop effective ways of handling foster children and attending to their individual needs. These workers also must help foster parents deal with the grief they experience when foster children to whom they're especially attached return home. Finally, foster care workers can act as mediators between birth parents and foster parents.

Case Example   Jamie, age 13, had lived with his foster parents, Millie and Mert Muffin, since he was 6 months old. The Muffins, who had two other adult children of their own, dearly loved Jamie and considered him an integral member of their family. He also had an ongoing relationship with his birth parents, Jack and Jill Smith, whom he visited every other Sunday. The Smiths had five other children, all older than Jamie.

During his first few months of life, Jamie suffered from a condition called *failure to thrive*, in which "an apparently normal infant fails to gain weight" and falls to the lowest 3% on the normal weight chart for an infant his age (Lefrançois, 1999, p. 165). Despite intensive medical attention, Jamie didn't improve. The Smiths had been involved with their county social services before because of neglect concerning their other children. After a child protective services assessment, the court placed Jamie in foster care with the Muffins.

Jack Smith, who had a 10th-grade education, was a janitor at a local grade school; Jill didn't work outside the home. Along with her twin sister, she had been institutionalized throughout her childhood in a setting for persons with cognitive disabilities or mental illness. She had attended some high school classes but didn't graduate.

Over the years, the Smiths maintained an involvement with the social services system. All of their children had been in foster care at one time or another. Jamie's siblings all experienced difficulties in school, truancy, or skirmishes with the law. Because of the Smiths' limited ability to cope with raising their five other children, on the one hand, and the stability provided Jamie by the Muffins, on the other, Jamie remained in foster care. A pleasant, cooperative boy who loved both his families, Jamie had a cognitive disability, some congenital orthopedic problems, and poor coordination. He had always attended special education classes.

An ongoing problem was the huge discrepancy in lifestyle and values between the Smiths and the Muffins. Bill, Jamie's foster care worker, was constantly struggling to establish compromises that both families could live with. For example, Jack Smith and Millie Muffin could barely stand being in the same room with each other. Jack felt that Millie "mollycoddled" Jamie to the point of making him a "sissy." Millie thought Jack was a "macho man" who pushed Jamie into inappropriate, dangerous activities such as skateboarding and trampoline jumping—both difficult and dangerous for Jamie with his coordination problems.

Bill worked with the families to help them come to mutual agreements. One was that Jamie join a track team and a bowling league for children with cognitive disabilities. In the past, Millie wouldn't allow him to do so because she feared he'd hurt himself. Furthermore, she would not permit him to attend any activities with other children by himself, but rather stayed there with him. Reluctantly, she agreed to let him attend events alone. For his part, Jack agreed to stop encouraging Jamie to ride a skateboard and play on the trampoline. Instead, Jamie could play baseball or soccer with other children in the Smiths' neighborhood when he visited.

Another problem between the Smiths and the Muffins involved religious differences. The Muffins were Methodist, and the Smiths Roman Catholic. Each couple wanted Jamie to adopt their own faith. Bill helped both couples understand that constant bickering would do neither Jamie nor themselves any good. The reality was that, when Jamie was visiting the Smiths, he would attend the Catholic church with them regardless of what the Muffins requested. Similarly, when he was with the Muffins, he would attend the Methodist church with them regardless of what the Smiths said. Bill helped the couples agree that this arrangement should continue, given that it was what they would do anyway. When Jamie grew older, he could choose his own faith.

The Smiths and the Muffins would never be best friends. However, Bill helped them realize that both families had Jamie's best interests at heart, despite their radical differences. Bill stressed this as a strength. He also worked with both families to help them focus on Jamie's future. As Jamie entered adolescence, he needed to realize his own capabilities and make his own decisions to the fullest extent possible. Bill discussed with both families the value of vocational aptitude testing—another means of emphasizing Jamie's strengths to best prepare him for his future.

 ## Residential Settings: Group Homes, Treatment Centers, and Independent Living Arrangements

Residential settings reflect greater intensity and restrictiveness on the substitute care continuum than foster family care. They can be more beneficial for some troubled children than their own family environment in several ways. First, they can provide a treatment milieu (an all-encompassing environmental setting), in which rules for how to behave are more clearly specified than in most families, thus providing greater structure (Stein, 1995). This, in turn, allows for more consistency and predictability in the children's living environment. Many residents feel safer in this more controlled setting.

Second, in most settings children interact with multiple caregivers instead of one or two parents. This allows children to experience less intensive interactions in a more "diluted emotional atmosphere" (Cohen, 1992, p. 59).

Third, the treatment milieu provides a "[g]roup living experience, where children and youths learn to develop responsibility to the group and to develop and improve relational skills and behavior and where peer pressure can have a positive impact" (Cohen, 1992, p. 59).

Fourth, children in residential settings often come with unique histories reflecting wide ranges of behavior. Stein (1995) explains:

HIGHLIGHT 9.6

Who Is Placed in Residential Settings?

Three examples reflect the types of behavior typically leading to placement in a residential setting.

Example A: Robert, age 13, already has a long record of criminal offenses including theft, assault, and drug possession. He also has flunked several courses at school, having been truant most of the time. Robert lives with his parents, who are alcoholics and have a history of physically abusing him. Because he tends to fly into vicious rages at the least provocation, foster care is not a viable option. The juvenile court has ordered that Robert be placed in a residential facility.

Example B: Bree, age 15, constantly fights with her parents. She refuses to go to school, screaming that she hates it. When her parents try to force her to go by driving her there themselves, she leaves school anyway and runs away for several days. She smokes marijuana regularly and has started using crack cocaine. She likes to date men in their twenties and has been sexually active since age 12. Her parents are at a loss as to what to do. The school social worker suggests residential placement.

Example C: Jaron, age 9, stabbed his 6-year-old sister to death. He has a long history of torturing and killing small animals. He has also set several fires in the home that, fortunately, were discovered before major damage was done. He frequently threatens to kill his parents and schoolmates. People around him including his parents fear that he means it. He is referred to a residential treatment center for young children with serious emotional disturbance and behavioral problems.

Each child is unique, so each placement decision must be made based on the problems and needs involved in that particular case. On one hand, children should be placed in the least restrictive setting. On the other, children require placement that can respond to the severity of their problems and the intensity of the supervision required.

They come with histories of lying, stealing, fighting, truancy, breaking things, hurting people, and running away. They come with tales of sexual abuse by parents, stepparents, relatives, and live-ins. They come with tales of beatings and confinements in closets and being tied up. They come from parents who yell at them constantly but never discipline them, from homes in which they could do no wrong, and from homes in which they were barely noticed.

There are those who fight the program every step of the way, those who have to be pushed or dragged through the program, and those who are so proud of their accomplishments you think they're going to burst. There are those who seem to do everything right, but you wonder what's really going on in their heads. (p. 17)

The residential milieu is oriented to addressing a wide range of emotional and behavioral issues. Therefore, it is designed to tolerate and deal with a wider range of negative behaviors, individualize treatment plans, and attend to children's diverse needs. Conversely, in families, similar rules and expectations often apply to everyone, and more extreme forms of troublesome behavior are unacceptable.

Highlight 9.6 describes scenarios in which children require placement in a residential setting.

Residential settings discussed here include group homes, residential treatment centers, and independent living services. Because most group homes and residential treatment centers are oriented toward mental health, their therapeutic aspects will be discussed in Chapter 13. Correctional facilities for youths that involve incarceration are, of course, the most restrictive on the service continuum. Chapter 15 discusses these further.

Group Homes

Group homes provide greater structure and more intensive therapeutic care than that found in foster family homes. A group home provides a substitute setting and family environment for a group of children originating in different families. Each should include 5 to 12 children, with the most effective number of residents being 6 to 8 (Child Welfare League of America, 1978, p. 670). Too few children may deprive them of a group experience, whereas too many may not allow enough individual attention and treatment. The actual physical structure of a group home is usually a sizable single-family dwelling that blends into a residential neighborhood. Depending on the residents' needs, it can be staffed either by a live-in married couple or by counselors who work various shifts, "including overnight staff who are awake" (Stein, 1995, p. 357).

Group homes provide more structure than foster family homes but less than residential treatment centers. Thus they allow more "space" for adolescents seeking independence than for those living with their parents while providing consistent expectations and rules. Residents are expected to attend school, do assigned chores, and participate in counseling as specified in their treatment plans.

Residential Treatment Centers

Residential treatment centers are bigger agencies that are more structured and therefore more restrictive than smaller group home settings. They typically consist of either larger dormitory settings or a series of smaller units or cottages forming one center. Each has its own supervising staff and assigns juvenile residents according to such variables as age and type of problem. Structured expectations usually revolve around a behavior management system based on behavior modification approaches. Highlight 9.7 describes the staff working in residential treatment centers.

Independent Living Services

An alternative available to older adolescents fast approaching adulthood are independent living services. These serve as a transitional residence between out-of-home placement and entrance into adulthood with its onerous responsibilities. Independent living services aim to prepare young people to function independently in society. Services focus on helping them develop skills they can use in their personal and work worlds. These include decision-making, budgeting, and planning skills to organize their lives; educational, vocational, and job search skills to establish a career; and interpersonal skills to develop and maintain relationships.

HIGHLIGHT 9.7
Who Works in Residential Treatment Centers?

Residential treatment centers have various responsibilities concerning residents' care and treatment (Stein, 1995). Basic needs such as food and shelter must, of course, be met, so staff are employed to prepare food and to maintain the building and grounds. Supervisors and administrators oversee service provision, making certain that children are treated appropriately and that treatment plans are carried out. Designated medical staff must be available (although usually not on site) to meet health and dental needs.

Residential staff attend to the children's daily care and supervise them when they're not in school. Sometimes referred to as counselors or child care workers, residential staff oversee daily living activities, implement treatment plans, and monitor behavior.

Residents' educational needs must also be met. Most children in residential treatment centers are lagging academically. Either their problems have consumed their energy, leaving little or none for academics, or they have long histories of truancy. And once they fall behind in school, there is little incentive to work hard because, compared with their peers, they look and feel like academic failures. Although some residents may attend public school, many remain on-grounds for their education. The center's educational staff

assess children's abilities and develop individualized educational plans designed to maximize each student's ability to succeed.

Treatment staff attend to the children's emotional and behavioral needs. Stein (1995) explains:

> The behavior of children is a major concern in residential treatment and likely to consume considerable time and effort, regardless of the philosophical or treatment orientation of the program. No matter what their other problems may be, it is problems with their behavior that most often bring children into residential treatment. (p. 107)

Social workers, psychologists, and other therapists assess problems and strengths, develop treatment plans, provide individual and group counseling, and work with the other staff components to coordinate services and monitor children's progress. They may also make home visits and do family counseling. Group treatment is very important in residential treatment centers because peer pressure is so significant for children and adolescents. Additionally, most treatment plans involve improving interpersonal relationships. Groups can focus on managing anger, eliminating substance abuse, improving communication and social relationships, or dealing with issues resulting from victimization.

Adoption

Adoption is the legal act of taking in a child born to other parents and formally making that child a full member of the family. Adoptive parents take on all the rights and responsibilities given to birth parents or other former legal guardians, who relinquish all rights concerning that child.

HIGHLIGHT 9.8
Cultural Competence Issues

Gibbs and Huang (1998) explain that "[c]hildren and adolescents of color constitute the most rapidly growing segment of the youth population in the United States, yet relatively little literature is available to enlighten clinicians, educators, health professionals, and social workers about the problems and needs of these young people" (p. xi). Learning about clients' cultures and values is an ongoing process that social workers must continuously pursue. LeVine and Sallee (1999) emphasize that

the practitioner must possess specific detailed knowledge of the child's ethnic group. The greater the knowledge, the more effective the clinician can be. The practitioner should be competent in the culture's use of verbal and nonverbal messages, customs, and traditions. Finally, the culturally competent child counselor is aware of institutional barriers which inhibit minorities from using child welfare and social services. . . . Culturally competent child welfare workers view diversity as a strength and view the child within the cultural context. (p. 413)

Types of Adoption

Adoptions are undertaken either by people related to a child by blood or by unrelated adoptive parents. Examples of *blood-related adoptions* include a stepparent married to a birth parent adopting the birth parent's child, grandparents adopting their daughter's child, and other relatives adopting a child born into some branch of their own family.

Unrelated adoptions occur when the adoptive parents have no prior blood link to the child being adopted. *Agency* (or *relinquishment*) *adoptions* are conducted through a public or private social service organization, with the agency contracting with the adoptive parents, providing counseling, assessing the placement, and overseeing the entire adoption process. *Independent adoptions*, in contrast, are initiated and conducted independently by the adoptive and birth parents, without agency involvement. *International adoptions* are those in which parents adopt children from other countries. Federal regulations that require "a satisfactory home study" and proof of being orphaned govern these adoptions (Barth, 1995, p. 50).

Special needs adoptions involve children who have traditionally been more difficult to place in adoptive homes. These include children who have "a specific factor or condition (such as ethnic background; age; membership in a minority or sibling group; or the presence of factors such as medical conditions or physical, mental, or emotional handicaps)" such that adoptive placement is difficult without providing medical or other assistance (Barth, 1995, p. 50). Finally, *transracial adoptions* are those by parents of a different race than that of the child. For example, white parents might adopt an African American or Asian child. Highlight 9.8 stresses the importance of cultural competence for social workers in the adoption field or any other aspect of practice with children and families.

The Adoption Process

Several steps are involved in the adoption process. In step 1, a child is identified as being in need of adoption. For example, children may have been removed from an extremely abusive environment, or the parents may have abandoned them or died.

In step 2, the child must be legally freed so that adoption can take place. Assistance should be given children to ease the trauma of separation from birth parents or guardians. Similarly, they may require help in adjusting and becoming attached to the new adoptive parents. Guardianship rights of the birth parents must be formally terminated.

In step 3, adoptive parents are selected. Here the social worker conducts a home study in which potential adoptive parents are evaluated on a number of variables. These include

> age (usually below 45); physical health; marital status; infertility; religion; financial stability; emotional health; capacity for parenthood; adjustment to sterility; quality of marital relationship; motives for adoption; and attitudes toward illegitimacy. Some of these requirements can be assessed objectively. Others are determined by subjective perceptions on the part of professionally trained adoption workers (most possess the M.S.W. degree) often based on white, middle-class values and expectations of what constitutes "good" parents. (Cohen, 1992, p. 71)

There has been some liberalization, especially with respect to special needs children, whereby "[s]ingle parents, foster parents, parent(s) of below-average income, and in some instances gay or lesbian couples who demonstrate the ability to love, nurture, and provide care and security to a child are being considered as adoptive parents" (Cohen, 1992, p. 72; Mather & Lager, 2000).

In step 4, after the potential adoptive parents have been approved, the agency places the child with them. The agency social worker helps the adoptive family integrate the child into the family system.

In step 5, as Smith and Howard (1999) explain, "[a]doptive families undergo stresses and adjustments unique to the adoptive experience and lasting throughout the family life cycle whether the child is adopted in infancy or later" (p. 8). At least four types of agency services may be provided after placement. First, education on such issues as child behavior management can be helpful. Second, therapy may be necessary to deal with issues such as the child's grief at the loss of his or her family of origin or readjustment issues experienced by the entire adoptive family. Third, ongoing support groups may help both parents and adopted children handle emotional and relationship issues. Fourth, adoptive families may need help linking up with necessary resources (e.g., programs offering financial assistance, special education services, and therapy for children requiring special help).

Finally, in step 6, the adoption is formally legalized, and the birth parents' legal rights are terminated.

Social Work Roles in Adoption

Social workers assume various roles with respect to adoption. They always have the professional responsibility of advocating for children and serving children's best interests. They may help women with unwanted pregnancies evaluate their alternatives and determine the best course of action. Social workers may assess the readiness of a child for adoptive placement, especially if that child is older and has conflicting feelings about permanently leaving birth parents. Social workers may be in the position of helping children cope with their grief at bidding a final farewell to their birth family. One study revealed that adopted children often express strong

> feelings of loss and abandonment. . . . One 6-year-old boy expressed his fear that some-
> one would come and take him away, and talked about his nightmares, which reflected
> both strong anxiety and grief. . . . Although some children feared being kidnapped or
> abandoned again, others voiced their desire, expectation, or hope for a reunion with
> their birth family. (Smith & Howard, 1999, p. 48)

Downs and colleagues (1996) describe one moving incident: "One worker recalled two preschool age brothers who clung together and sobbed over a picture of their mother, trying to stroke her long hair in the photograph" (p. 331).

Social workers conduct extensive home studies of the appropriateness of potential adoptive families. Finally, social workers may help birth parents, adopted children, and adoptive parents evaluate their situations and choices realistically, make decisions, and cope with issues.

Several other issues characterize adoptive families that social workers can help these families address:

- *Lack of control:* Adoptive parents may experience feelings of inadequacy and lack of control because of their infertility. They may have been at the agency's mercy for years, patiently waiting for a child to become available. The integration of the child into the family system may be more difficult than they had anticipated.

  For example, one adoptive family, the Humperdinks, consisted of two parents, two teenage sons, and a 20-year-old daughter. The Humperdinks wanted to provide a needy child with a good home. The mother was a special education teacher, and the father a newspaper reporter. They adopted Katrine, age 11, whose parents had been killed in a car accident. She was a pleasant child with no history of problematic behavior, so they were totally taken aback by a problem they had never anticipated. The Humperdinks were a family of readers. Typically, one would find all five of them reading various newspapers and magazines and an endless assortment of novels. Katrine, in contrast, was an average student who simply did not enjoy reading. She read only when she had to. The family required fairly extensive counseling to work on such goals as appreciating each family member's unique strengths, including Katrine's, and identifying activities other than reading they could all do together.
- *Something wrong with the kid* (Hartman & Laird, 1990): Adoptive family members may worry that the adopted child has negative genetic traits or behavioral problems related to past treatment.
- *Strains on the adoptive mother and marriage:* Adopted children may manifest extreme needs that place pressure on the adoptive mother and, consequently, on the adoptive parents' marriage. Smith and Howard (1999) explain:

> The mother is typically the primary focus of the child's anger, extreme dependence, or
> rejection. Mothers are more likely to be in the child's presence, to discipline the child, and
> to represent the family to school, neighbors, and others in the community. Mothers are
> subjected to more of the talking back, noncompliance, and control struggles than fathers.
> . . . One mother reported her frustration with her child's unfillable need for reassurance.

This child, adopted at age 5, had experienced significant neglect. The child experienced panic when the mother was out of sight, even in the next room. When the mother would use the bathroom, the child would curl up against the door begging her to let him in. Consistent and very frequent reassurance and affection did nothing to alleviate his neediness. His incessant need to be near her, and her alone, left the mother feeling trapped and smothered. . . . The demanding child known by the mother is not the child known by the father. His wife's need to catalog the child's sins, her need for his sympathy, and her frustration and anger often appear exaggerated to the father. He sees a child pretty much being a child. She describes a monster. Tension in the marital pair emerges or is intensified by this very different understanding of the child. (pp. 61–62)

- *Quest for identity:* Adoptive children often ask themselves who they really are. Born to one set of parents and living with another, what does that make them? How should they think of themselves? How can they be positive about themselves and confident? Counseling is often needed to help them address these concerns.
- *Behavioral acting out:* It's logical that children who have been uprooted from their birth families experience various degrees of insecurity, apprehension about the future, and pressure to establish their own identities. As a result, as many other children do, some adopted children act out. They may be seeking to establish some control over their lives. They may find that acting out gets them the attention they crave. Or they may use negative actions as a means of keeping themselves emotionally isolated from other people because they're terrified of getting close. They may believe that maintaining emotional distance keeps them from being vulnerable to rejection. Acting-out behaviors may include lying, stealing, committing acts of vandalism, engaging in sexual activity, and stockpiling food (Smith & Howard, 1999).

Focus on Critical Thinking 9.2 addresses several other controversial issues in adoption.

 # Alcohol and Other Drug Abuse in Families

Because of the prevalence of alcohol and other drug abuse in families and its tragic effects on children, we will discuss this here. Social workers need background in substance abuse, also referred to as *alcohol and other drug abuse* (AODA), for three basic reasons. First, many social workers may work in agencies specializing in treatment for substance abuse and provide counseling to clients and their families.

Second, "graduate-level social workers also function as program or agency administrators, as analysts with local or state governmental bureaus responsible for drug abuse services, and as aides to legislative committees" (Roffman, 1987, p. 484). These positions require knowledge of substance use and abuse even when social workers are not providing direct service to clients.

The third reason for needing some background in AODA involves social workers' role as referral agents. Even if they don't work in such a specialized AODA setting, they will still probably have clients or family members of clients with alcohol and drug problems. Thus they must be capable of making appropriate referrals to relevant occupational, health, employment, and social services in addition to helping clients navigate these complex systems (Roffman, 1987).

FOCUS ON CRITICAL THINKING 9.2

Controversial Issues in Adoption

A number of controversial issues characterize adoption today. First, in recent decades, the number of children available for adoption has decreased. Reasons for this include increased use of birth control, the possibility of abortion, and social acceptance of single-parent families. The greatest demand is for healthy, young, white children, who are in the least supply; children of color, older children, and those with special needs are in the greatest supply.

This leads us to a second issue—transracial adoption. To what extent is it appropriate for parents of one race to adopt children from another? On one hand, adoptive parents are needed for children of color. On the other, to what extent is it in a child of color's best interests to be placed with, for example, white parents? To what extent will these children be deprived of the rich fabric of cultural heritage manifested by their own race? How can they develop a strong, confident identity as a person of color in a white environment? To what extent will that child experience

prejudice and discrimination in a social environment dominated by another race?

A third issue concerns special needs adoption. Unquestionably, children who have special needs are more difficult and often more expensive to care for. To what extent is it fair for agencies to encourage such adoptions when it's difficult for adoptive parents to fully comprehend the responsibilities involved in caring for a child with special needs? To what extent should financial burdens fall on such parents? To what degree should financial and medical assistance be provided to such adoptive parents?

A fourth issue involves open adoption. *Openness* is the extent to which, first, information about all parties involved (adopted child, adoptive parents, birth parents) is available, and second, the adoptive child and birth parents maintain contact with each other (Pecora et al., 2000). What can the adoptive parents know about the birth parents, and vice versa? What

(continued)

Raskin and Daley (1991) explain how alcohol and other drug abuse is often masked by and interrelated to many other problems:

> The addicted person may seek help in a medical setting, a crisis clinic, a mental health agency, a family service agency, or from a private practitioner or a public assistance agency. In the medical setting, the presenting problem may be pancreatitis, liver disease, traumatic injury, or broken bones. In the mental health setting, the person may present depression, suicidal feelings, self-destructive behavior, anxiety, psychotic symptoms, or problems associated with an organic brain syndrome. Each of these problems may be the result of alcoholism or drug addiction. (p. 25)

Thus, in almost any practice setting, a social worker may need to address AODA problems. The next section defines basic terms. Subsequent sections describe the dynamics of alcohol abuse, its effects on family relationships, and treatment approaches and resources.

Definitions in Alcohol and Other Drug Abuse

Language commonly used in substance abuse intervention tend to revolve around the terms *alcohol, drug,* and *substance* (often referred to as *psychoactive substance*).

can the adopted child find out about the birth parents? In the past, many people feared that openness concerning adoption might place children and parents in difficult or confusing positions. However, Grotevant and McRoy (1998) report that this really is not the case. In actuality, openness does not cause children to feel pulled between their family of origin and their adoptive family, or confused about which family is responsible for providing guidance and support.

Many questions can be raised about openness. Should children have ready access to their medical records and birth family history to identify hereditary diseases to which they might be prone? To what extent might adoptive parents feel threatened if their adopted children could readily contact the birth parents? Who should be allowed to make the decision about whether adoption records should be open? How open should they be—fully or only under some conditions and circumstances? This is a complex issue.

A fifth topic generating controversy involves independent versus agency adoptions. Register (1991) found that placement time for independent adoptions was much shorter than for agency-supervised adoptions. That's a plus. However, Crosson-Tower (2004) raises three major concerns about independent adoptions. First, there is no guaranteed protection of the child's rights. No extensive home study is conducted, and no evaluation of the appropriateness of the adoptive family is done. Second, once the child is placed, no follow-up is performed. No one monitors the extent to which the child is integrated into the family or whether the child is thriving. Third, there are no guarantees of confidentiality as there are in agency adoptions.

One other question about independent adoption involves the potential of black market adoptions, in which babies can be sold (Mather & Lager, 2000). To what extent does the flexibility inherent in independent adoption make this possible?

In everyday usage the term *alcohol* refers to any type of fermented or distilled liquor containing alcohol such as whiskey or beer. *Drug* refers to a wide range of materials that alter mood or consciousness when ingested, including amphetamines, cannabis, cocaine, and hallucinogens. *Substance* is commonly used to refer to mind-altering drugs, including alcohol (hence the term *alcohol and other substance abuse*). In the context of abuse described here, the terms *substance* and *drugs* are often used interchangeably (Gray, 1995). Several other terms used in conjunction with alcohol, drugs, and substances are *dependence, tolerance, withdrawal, abuse, intoxication, alcoholism, alcoholic,* and *addiction.*

The *Diagnostic and Statistical Manual of Mental Disorders* (DSM-IV-TR),[9] published by the American Psychiatric Association (APA, 2000), defines *substance dependence* as "a cluster of cognitive, behavioral, and physiological symptoms" resulting from continued use of a substance despite significant resulting problems (p. 192). It occurs when three or more of the following happen within one year:

[9]This manual is the official authority for defining and explaining mental disorders and their accompanying symptoms. It is used to enhance accurate communication among social workers and other professionals regarding clients' conditions. It is also used to provide diagnoses for eligibility to receive third-party payments (e.g., Medicare or private health insurance).

1. *Tolerance:* The user requires increasing doses of the substance to reach the same level of mood alteration, or the substance's effects diminish significantly with continued use.
2. *Withdrawal:* These are symptoms that develop as a result of discontinued use of the substance or the compulsion to absorb the substance to avert these symptoms. Despite discontinued use, the user still craves the substance. Withdrawal symptoms may include severe abdominal pain, convulsions, anxiety attacks, depression, and uncontrollable trembling.
3. The user takes greater amounts of the substance over a longer period than he or she meant to.
4. The user expresses an ongoing desire or failed attempts to decrease or control substance use.
5. The user spends large amounts of time participating in activities aimed at obtaining or using the substance and recuperating from its aftermath.
6. The user curtails or avoids significant social, work, or recreational involvement due to substance use.
7. The user continues to use the substance despite being aware that the substance is causing or intensifying physical or psychological difficulties.

The *DSM-IV-TR* defines *substance abuse* as "a maladaptive pattern of substance use manifested by recurrent and significant adverse consequences related to the repeated use of substances" (APA, 2000, pp. 198–199). This is reflected by one or more of the following criteria in any 12-month period:

1. Repeated failure to accomplish major work, educational, or social responsibilities due to substance use.
2. Repeated use of the substance at times when it could cause physical harm (such as when driving).
3. Repeated use of the substance that results in legal problems (such as tickets for driving under the substance's influence or arrests for disorderly conduct).
4. Continued use of the substance despite the fact that it causes frequent interpersonal problems.

The *DSM-IV-TR* adds one other criterion for abuse—namely, that it involves people who have never been diagnosed with substance dependence. Substance *abuse* might be regarded as "less problematic" than substance *dependence* because many of the physical and psychological symptoms associated with *dependence* are not yet evident (Barker, 2003, p. 422).

Intoxication, linked to drug abuse and dependence, is the development of a series of symptoms, often involving psychological or behavioral changes, directly related to intake of the substance and its influence on the central nervous system. Specific symptoms may include inability to think clearly, distorted perception, temporary euphoria, and impaired motor functioning.

Alcoholism is "a chronic disorder characterized by repeated excessive use of alcoholic beverages and decreased ability to function socially and vocationally" (Nichols, 1999, p. 31). *Alcoholics* are people who suffer from alcoholism. *Addiction* is a term referring to dependence on some substance, having the same consequences as those already described; the term *substance dependence* is now commonly replacing *addiction* (Barker, 2003).

Professionals working with alcohol and other substance abusers may be referred to as *substance abuse, AODA,* or *chemical dependence counselors.* Practitioners counseling people who abuse or are dependent on alcohol may be called *alcoholism* or *alcohol abuse counselors.*

With respect to substance use problems, in everyday usage the term *abuse* often is used to include symptoms evident in the technical definitions of both abuse and dependence. Similarly, the line between abuse and dependence is often not clearly distinct. Many of the dynamics are similar or identical. Therefore, in our ensuing discussion we will use the terms *abuse* and *dependence* interchangeably.

Note that people often have a substance of choice. That is, they prefer the type of mood alterations produced by one drug over that produced by another. For instance, one person may prefer beer over cocaine. Another person may feel just the opposite.

There are many similarities between alcohol abuse and other drug abuse in terms of the psychological and interpersonal dynamics (APA, 2000). It is beyond the scope of this book to elaborate on the effects of the numerous varieties of drugs readily available today. Therefore, we will focus here primarily on alcohol abuse and alcoholism.

People with Alcohol Problems

Historically, the concept of alcoholism was based on the medical model (i.e., it was considered a disease with the cure being abstinence). However, more current thought views such alcohol use as a more complex problem that can be analyzed from a range of theoretical perspectives having their respective treatment approaches (Doweiko, 2002; Johnson, 2004; Velleman, 2001; Wood & Dunn, 2000).

People who use and abuse alcohol can't be categorized at fixed "points on a substance use continuum. . . . Only the end points—total abstinence and active physical addiction to chemicals—remain relatively fixed" (Doweiko, 2002, p. 11). Velleman (2001) suggests that a better term for alcoholism is *alcohol problem,* defined as follows—"if someone's drinking causes problems for him or her, or for someone else, in any area of their lives, then that drinking is problematic"; this includes problems with "health, finances, the law, work, friends, or relationships" (p. 3).

Figure 9.3 reflects how people may fall anywhere on a continuum involving how much they drink and how many problems it causes them. Most people who drink alcohol do so on a social basis and consume socially acceptable amounts that do not result in drunkenness (Dunn, 2000). Problems arise for people who lose control of their consumption and become increasingly dependent on alcohol's effects. Kingery-McCabe and Frances (1991) stress that each individual responds differently to alcohol dependence in terms of severity of physical and psychological effects and the length of time it takes to become dependent.

People who abuse alcohol or other drugs typically adopt a series of defense mechanisms to protect themselves from having to deal with the problems caused by alcoholism. These include "minimization," "denial," and "rationalization" (Perkinson, 2002, pp. 60, 118–120). Each mechanism helps the person avoid taking responsibility for his or her behavior.

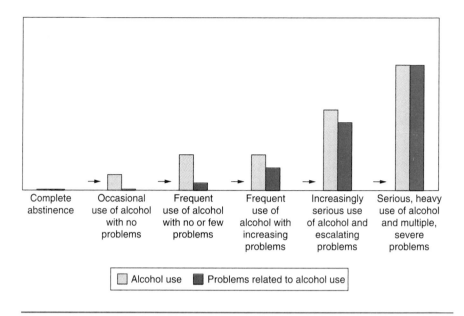

Figure 9.3 The continuum of alcohol use and resulting problems

Minimization means assigning little importance to drinking or its conse-quences. "Minimizing says, 'It's not so bad'" (Perkinson, 2002, p. 60). Here the alcoholic acknowledges that drinking is occurring, but admits to very little and tries to make it unimportant. An alcoholic might fill a 10-ounce glass halfway with whiskey instead of pouring it into a much smaller shot glass. This becomes "just one drink." Or an alcoholic might say, "I really don't drink that much," even though he drinks three six-packs of beer a night.

Rationalization involves making excuses for the problems caused by the depen-dence on alcohol. For example, an alcoholic might say to herself, "I really didn't flunk that exam because I had a hangover; the professor made the questions much harder than she said she would." Or "It's been a rotten day. I deserve a drink or two."

Denial, the most prevalent defense used by alcoholics, involves insisting to one-self that nothing's wrong. There's no problem. Denial distorts reality so you just don't see the truth. An alcoholic who drinks a fifth of cheap vodka or 12 cans of beer a day might say to himself, "I don't really have to drink." Or he might ignore his wife's com-plaints about spending money on booze or being verbally abusive to her when drunk. If you don't think about a problem, it doesn't exist: out of sight, out of mind.

Numerous social and relationship problems result from alcohol and other sub-stance abuse. They include marital and family difficulties, disruptions in friend-ships, trouble in work and school performance, accidents when operating vehicles, and being arrested for crimes committed while under the influence.

Alcohol or another substance of choice (i.e., the preferred substance) becomes the abuser's "best friend." It is something the abuser can always depend on. The effects are pleasantly predictable, and the abuser can escape from life's stresses whenever he or she wants. People can disappoint or place pressure on you, but a drug always acts the same.

Alcoholism Affects Family Relationships

Alcohol abuse and dependence are family system problems (Johnson, 2004; Paulus, 2000). That is, the problem affects the entire family; what happens to one family member affects all others.

People living in families of alcoholics "live in a whirlwind" of stress and crisis (Perkinson, 2002, p. 188). Their lives focus on the abuser's alcohol-related behavior, whether it's coming home drunk and throwing up or hitting them, losing jobs and money, failing to carry through with any range of responsibilities, breaking promises, or embarrassing them in front of friends and neighbors.

At least eight themes characterize the families of people dependent on alcohol. (Note that the family dynamics involved in families of other substance abusers resemble those with alcohol abuse.) First, the abuser's alcohol use becomes the "most important thing in the family's life" (Johnson, 2004; Wegscheider, 1981, p. 81). Because the abuser's top goal is getting enough alcohol, other family members must structure their own behavior around this.

Second, family members strive to keep the family together even when conditions are deteriorating due to the abuser's behavior (Johnson, 2004; Wegscheider, 1981). The unknown is scary. At least they know what the current conditions are, regardless of how bad.

Third, family members often act as *enablers* for the abuser's alcohol use (Perkinson, 2002; Wegscheider, 1981). Enablers assume increasing responsibility for maintaining family functioning and making excuses on the alcoholic's behalf (e.g., calling in sick for the abuser at work when the real problem is a terrible hangover). In essence, this role enables the alcoholic to continue drinking, yet assume less and less responsibility for the consequences of that behavior.

Fourth, "[f]amily members often feel incredible guilt. They think that they are at fault. The chemically dependent person keeps denying responsibility, and someone must be held accountable, so the family members often take the blame" (Perkinson, 2002, p. 189).

Fifth, family members often "do not know what they want. Their lives are centered around the chemically dependent individual. They only know what the addict wants. That is the focus of attention. Most family members are trying to hold onto their sanity and to keep themselves, and the family, from going under" (Perkinson, 2002, p. 190).

Sixth, "family members feel worthless. They feel as though no one cares for how they feel or for what they want. They feel profoundly inadequate and unlovable . . . and somehow they feel as though . . . it is all their fault anyway. This would not be happening to them if they were better persons. This is all they deserve. This is the best they can get" (Perkinson, 2002, p. 190).

Seventh, family members don't trust others (Perkinson, 2002). They have been disappointed so many times by the dependent person's behavior that they can't afford to dream about things getting better. They avoid discussing the problem with others inside or outside the family. They don't want to rock the boat.

Eighth, family members "have poor communication skills. They learned a long time ago the credo of the chemically dependent family: 'Don't talk, don't trust, and don't feel.' These individuals do not talk to their friends or other family members. They are cut off from everyone. They feel afraid of open communication. If they talked openly, then the truth might come out and the family would be destroyed" (Perkinson, 2002, p. 191).

Treatment for Alcoholics

There are numerous treatment approaches to chemical dependence (Connors, Donovan, & DiClemente, 2001). However, at least four principles are important regardless of the treatment approach or program (Johnson, 2004). First, engagement "with the social worker in a trusting and open relationship" is essential for successful treatment; practitioners should "engage clients as partners in treatment, eliciting responses and actions that enhance motivation and promote willingness to take action on their own behalf" (p. 291). Second, a multiple-system approach should be used. That is, an individualized treatment plan should be developed to address the "client's unique needs, issues, and strengths"; the practitioner might "provide individual, group, or family treatment, engage the client's local community if needed, and provide access to specialty services such as vocational, recreational, or spiritual counseling when appropriate" (pp. 291–292). Third, follow-up care after primary treatment has ceased is critical to maintain progress. Fourth, "clients need help in developing a social network" of "people or groups to call upon for support, guidance, and recreation" (p. 292). These might include "12-step meetings, church groups, sober friends, family members, and other sources" (p. 292). Such a network helps them maintain control of their gains by providing "social and recreational outlets that replace key elements" in a lifestyle sustaining abuse or dependence (p. 292). Highlight 9.9 identifies a range of community resources that are available for alcoholics and their families.

A Four-Stage Recovery Model

One approach to alcohol dependence treatment maintains that dependence involves an entire lifestyle; therefore, to recover, one must abstain from drinking alcohol entirely to establish a healthier, substance-free way of life. The following four steps are involved (Johnson, 2004, pp. 286–290):

Stage 1—Abstinence: During this stage, which can persist for as long as two years, clients strive to maintain sobriety. A major focus is on avoidance of mind-altering substances. In essence, "the individual learns to get through most days without experiencing or giving in to overwhelming cravings or urges to use" (p. 286). Relapses are common.

Stage 2—Confrontation: Lasting up to five years, this stage sees "clients begin confronting and changing the personal, family, and social issues that contributed to their chemically dependent lifestyle. . . . They learn how to conduct adult relationships, assume responsibility for their actions, and explore lifestyles that do not include drugs and the people associated with their chemically dependent past" (p. 287). Clients are often "obsessed" with their abstinence and recovery, confronting people and experiences in their past daily, often with shame and guilt about what happened. For example, a recovering client was with new friends who knew little about her past. She abruptly ran into old friends who unabashedly talked about the "good old days" when they got "really high" together and would do "wild and crazy things" like running through the city streets naked. The client felt extremely ashamed.

HIGHLIGHT 9.9

Resources for the Treatment of Alcoholism

The following are some of the resources that are available for alcoholics (Doweiko, 2002; Johnson, 2004; Lewis et al., 2002):

1. *Detoxification* "is short-term treatment designed to oversee the client's safe withdrawal from the substance to which he or she is addicted" (Lewis et al., 2002, p. 19). Clients may participate in an inpatient or outpatient program (both described here) overseen by medical personnel and professional counselors (Doweiko, 2002; Lewis et al., 2002). The severity of withdrawal symptoms is one factor to consider when choosing the appropriate program.

2. *Outpatient treatment* is received by clients who participate in a program without staying overnight at a treatment facility. People who are drug dependent can remain in their own homes and still have services available to them. Programs vary greatly regarding types of treatment involved (e.g., individual, group, or family therapy) and the extent of daily or weekly involvement.

3. *Inpatient treatment* is received by clients who remain at the facility all day and night. It provides a comprehensive, structured environment that maximizes control of the treatment process.

4. *Therapeutic communities* are residential programs where clients remain for one to three years, although some require only a six-month stay. Their intent is to immerse clients in an environment aimed at "a global change in lifestyle: abstinence from illicit substances, elimination of antisocial activity, development of employability, and prosocial attitudes" (DeLeon, 1994, p. 392).

5. *Halfway houses* are temporary residences to assist in the transition from an inpatient program to the real-life community. They provide support and supervision that is less extensive than that given on a 24-hour institutional basis. Emphasis is on gradually increasing each resident's ability to handle responsibility at his or her own pace.

6. *Pharmacological adjuncts* are prescribed medications (for example, Antabuse to combat alcoholism) that help addicts begin the recovery process. Such medication, of course, must be carefully monitored by medical staff.

7. *Mutual self-help groups* are composed of nonprofessional "people with a common problem or life predicament" who voluntarily gather to provide mutual support and share information aimed at improving their lives (Corey, 2000, p. 14). Specific programs include Alcoholics Anonymous (AA), Narcotics Anonymous (NA), and Cocaine Anonymous (CA). These groups provide exceptionally relevant treatment approaches in view of their established success. Support from peers in the process of recovery is especially critical.

Because of its prevalence, we will focus on AA here. This large, nationwide group provides support, information, and guidance necessary for many recovering alcoholics to maintain their recovery process. The organization's success seems to rest on several principles. First, other people who "really understand" are available to give the recovering dependent person friendship and warmth. Each new member is given a "sponsor" who can be called for support at any time during the day or night. Whenever the dependent person feels depressed or tempted, he or she can always turn to the sponsor.

Additionally, AA provides the recovering alcoholic a new social group with whom to talk and enjoy activities. Old friends with established

(continued)

HIGHLIGHT 9.9 *(continued)*

drinking patterns usually become difficult to associate with. The recovering alcoholic can no longer participate in the drinking activity, and social pressure is often applied to drink again. AA provides a respite from such pressure and the opportunity to meet new people.

AA also helps the recovering person to view alcoholism as a disease. This means that the alcoholic cannot cure himself or herself. She or he no longer needs to feel guilty about being an alcoholic. All that is required is to stop drinking.

Additionally, AA encourages introspection. Members are encouraged to look deeply inside themselves and face whatever they see. They are urged to acknowledge the fact that they have flaws and will never be perfect. This perspective often helps people to stop fleeing from the pain of reality and hiding in alcohol or drugs.

It helps them to redefine expectations for themselves and to gain control. Within the context of this honesty, people often can also acknowledge their strengths. They learn that they have some control over their own behavior and can accomplish things for themselves and for others.

Organizations are also available to provide support for other family members and to give them information and suggestions. For example, Al-Anon is an organization for the families of alcoholics, and Alateen is specifically for teenagers within these families.

Two contrasting treatment models are briefly described here. One is based on the traditional abstinence approach to recovery, and the other is a strengths-based model focused on achieving greater control of drinking behavior (which may not include total abstinence).

Stage 3—Growth: Usually occurring after at least five years of abstinence, this phase reflects beginning a new lifestyle not involving alcohol use. New social networks are established, and "daily life does not involve constant attention to maintaining abstinence and recovery" (p. 289).

Stage 4—Transformation: This stage marks a true change in life orientation from the former alcohol-using days. The client has established "social networks and personal skills" to live and thrive. Alcohol no longer has a place in this new existence.

Note that although these stages are presented as if they occur in a "smooth and recognizable manner," in many, perhaps most, cases they don't (p. 290). People can move back and forth between stages, and sometimes relapses occur. A relapse "signals the need to discover which parts of the client's recovery foundation need work" (p. 290).

The Strengths Perspective on Alcohol Abuse and Dependence Treatment

McCollum and Trepper (2001) stress that practitioners "should find ways to recognize the strengths and abilities that clients bring with them to treatment and not just focus on their liabilities" (p. 40). Identification of strengths provides clues to how clients can make positive changes occur.

Van Wormer and Davis (2003) propose a strengths-based approach to treating alcohol and other substance abuse and dependence based on *harm reduction,* a treatment approach emphasizing means to reduce the "harm caused by the addiction" (p. 70). They explain:

> [The idea is to] help people help themselves by moving from safer use, to managed use, to abstinence, if so desired. The labeling of clients, as is the custom in mental health circles ("He has an antisocial personality," "She is borderline") or in treatment circles ("He's an alcoholic," "She has an eating disorder") is avoided; clients provide the definition of the situation as they see it. Clients who wish it are given advice on how to reduce the harm in drug use such as, "Don't drink on an empty stomach," or "Always make sure to use a clean needle." Consistent with the strengths perspective, the counselor and client collaborate to consider a broad range of solutions to the client-defined problem; resources are gathered or located to meet the individual needs of the client. Above all, clients are viewed as amenable to change. (p. 27)

Van Wormer and Davis (2003) state that a more traditional disease model espoused by AA and described previously may experience success with "extroverted, severely addicted, structure seeking" people (p. 28). However, a harm reduction approach provides more flexibility in terms of treatment planning and goals. It also stresses how clients have the strength to assume responsibility for changing their behavior. The emphasis is on what people can *do,* not the problems they have. "Depending on their level of discomfort with their drug use and their desire to change, . . . people are empowered to move forward" (p. 28).

A key component of this approach is *choice* "about goals of the helping relationship (harm reduction, including abstinence); informed choice about a variety of treatment contexts (same gender, group, individual, day treatment, outpatient, inpatient, mutual-help groups); and informed choice about treatment methods" (p. 67).

"Harm reduction strategies for alcohol misuse are based on the premise that alcohol use ranges across a continuum, starting with no consequences for use and ending with devastating consequences for use, with lots of states in between" (Van Wormer & Davis, 2003, p. 76). A client may choose to establish a state of controlled consumption (e.g., limiting the amount drunk or times when drinking occurs) instead of seeking total abstinence. A plan might entail drinking only during weekends or special occasions and then limiting it to some designated amount. Drinking less is not as harmful as heavy, continuous, uncontrolled drinking.

The practitioner does not force clients to place labels on themselves. Rather, the practitioner helps clients understand the costs of drinking and explore what options they have to gain greater control of their lives if that is what they desire. In essence, the practitioner focuses on the client's motivation to make positive changes.

Highlight 9.10 cites a case example where a practitioner works with a client who changes his goal from total abstinence to decreased use of alcohol.

Looking Ahead

This chapter addressed the needs of families by focusing on children. Chapter 10 will shift the focus to the other end of the lifespan by talking about elderly people—their needs and the policies and programs that serve them.

HIGHLIGHT 9.10

A Case Example of an Alcoholic in Treatment

Velleman (2001) describes his therapeutic work with a client named Harry who changed his goal from attaining abstinence to gaining greater control over his drinking without stopping it altogether:

> Harry developed the goal that he wanted to abstain from drinking altogether. The two of us worked out a plan of action for the forthcoming week to enable him to do this, with the major thrust coming from Harry rather than from me: We identified possible at-risk situations, and we clarified the strategies and tactics he was going to employ so as to successfully overcome these.
>
> The next week, Harry returned saying he had failed: He had drunk four units of alcohol. He was out with one of his adult daughters, they went for a country walk, and ended up in a . . . [tavern] for lunch. He had two . . . [bottles of beer] with his meal, then continued with his walk, and had drunk nothing else throughout the week.
>
> This information was used in a variety of ways. It added more material which was useful for exploration—Harry can successfully control his intake under some circumstances, drinking four units did not precipitate a full-scale relapse, and so on. It also provided the possibility for reassessing the goal—perhaps some drinking, under controlled and monitored conditions, with certain people and in certain contexts might be a desired goal? This new material altered the plan of campaign for the next and subsequent weeks.
>
> If abstinence was still the goal, new at-risk situations had been identified, and new strategies had to be developed to overcome them—that is, do not go for walks, or take a packed lunch, or stop in a village with a café, or get his daughter to buy the [nonalcoholic] drinks, or get her to hold the money.
>
> Alternatively, if occasional controlled drinking was now the goal, the details of when, how much, with whom, where, and so on needed to be clarified; risky situations relating to these actions needed to be identified; and strategies to overcome them needed to be thought through—with, as always, the major thrust coming from Harry rather than me. (pp. 48–49)

For Further Exploration on the Internet

See this text's Book Companion Website at **www.socialwork.wadsworth.com/kirstashman_intro2e** for descriptors and hot links to URLs relevant to this chapter, selected InfoTrac articles and exercises, and tutorial quizzes.

CHAPTER ✸ TEN

SOCIAL WORK AND SERVICES
FOR THE ELDERLY

© David Young-Wolff/PhotoEdit

Consider the following facts:

- In 2002, 12.3% of U.S. residents were 65 and older (U.S. Census Bureau, 2003, No. 13).
- It is estimated that in 2010 that figure will increase to 20.7% (U.S. Census Bureau, 2003, No. 16).
- From 2010 to 2030 the number of persons age 65 and older will increase by over 57% (White House, 2005a).
- "The great advances in health and well-being of the 20th century will lead to significant increases in the average life span in the 21st century" (White House, 2005b). For example, it is projected that people born in 2000 will live almost six years longer than those born in 1970 (White House, 2005b).

People in the United States generally live longer than people in many other countries because of better nutrition and living conditions and significant advances in medicine and technology. On one hand, a higher proportion of older people means more people who are either retired or unable to work due to health reasons. On the other, it means a smaller proportion of younger workers who pay taxes on current earnings and support social programs. Lower birthrates have also contributed to fewer people entering the workforce. The *dependency ratio* is the number of people age 65 or over who are retired compared to the number of people age 18–64 who are working (Mooney, Knox, & Schacht, 2002).

Of course, this does not mean that all people work until age 65, their hair turns gray, and they abruptly retire. In reality, some people retire at age 65, others at 40, and still others at 80 or older. Consider the famous comedian and actor George Burns, who continued to tell stories and crack amazingly clever jokes until two years before his death at age 100. My own aunt Mabel worked as a maid at a motel until age 82, when she no longer had the strength to drag the heavy service carts up the outside stairways in the summer heat and winter snow. There were no elevators available. (She's still active and driving at age 92.) However, for various reasons, most people think of 65 as the general retirement age.

"As a result of declining birthrates and increasing life expectancy, the [dependency] ratio of workers to Social Security beneficiaries is expected to shrink from 5.1 in 1960 to 3.4 today to 2.1 in 2030" (White House, 2005a). In 1900 this ratio was 10 to 1 (Uhlenberg, 2000). In essence, this means significantly fewer workers will be paying taxes to support a growing number of elderly receiving Social Security benefits. Potential issues resulting from this trend include an increasing burden on future workers to support older generations, significantly less money collected from taxes on earnings for social services and programs, deteriorating pension programs because of inadequate support, and struggles among members of different age groups for scarce resources (Mooney et al., 2002).

There are various implications for social work and social workers in view of this changing world. (Note that Highlight 10.1 addresses a similar scenario on a global basis.) First, social workers will be called on to serve increasing numbers of aging people; indeed, social work with the elderly is a rapidly growing field. Second, developing policies and services to meet future needs is an important priority in social welfare. Third, advocacy on behalf of elderly people for essential resources

HIGHLIGHT 10.1

International Perspectives: "Global Graying"

George (1997) indicates that "global graying" is an international "phenomenon that affects the smallest Pacific islands as well as the most developed welfare states" (p. 57). Consider that throughout history, people age 65 or over never made up more than 2–3% of the total population; today they make up 14% of the population in "developed nations," which is expected to rise to 18% in 2023 and to as high as 25% of the total population in 30 years (Kornblum & Julian, 2004, p. 281).

Elderly people are treated very differently depending on their culture. Mooney and colleagues (2002) provide the following facts:

- Some tribal societies simply let elderly people die or actually kill them when these people are no longer "useful" and, instead, require care.
- Scandinavian nations pay for home care services for elderly people who remain in their homes but require assistance in daily tasks such as food preparation and cleaning.
- "Eastern cultures such as Japan revere the elderly, in part, because of their presumed proximity to honored ancestors" (p. 160).

George (1997) anticipates that the world will face at least three key issues as greater numbers of people age. First, "it is expected that graying will bring greater dependence as a result of greater longevity accompanied by chronic ill health" (p. 59). Second, "there will be an inadequate supply of caregivers because of smaller family sizes (for example, China's one-child policy and a resulting family structure of four grandparents, two parents, and one child), [and] women's increasing participation in paid employment

outside the home" (p. 60). Third, "state finances will be inadequate to support the increasing dependence of older people" (p. 60).

What can social workers do about this from a global perspective? George (1997) argues that social workers bring with them at least three strengths as they address the issues involved in aging. First, they emphasize self-determination and the achievement of maximum autonomy. Second, they focus on changing not only the individual but also the environments encompassing the individual including the political milieu. Finally, they build plans that stress existing strengths.

Social workers can advocate on behalf of elderly people around the world to establish policies and services that meet their vital needs for "health and autonomy" (George, 1997, p. 68). Initiatives can include

- Educating the public to see elderly people as a "resource" instead of a burden (Torres-Gil & Puccinelli, 1995, p. 164).
- Expanding community-based care to maintain people in their own homes as long as possible.
- Providing supportive measures (e.g., financial assistance, tax incentives, respite care) to family members who care for aging relatives.
- Emphasizing the significance of older people as having sufficient numbers to wield political clout and become important participants in the political process.
- Educating upcoming generations to prepare to care for an increasing proportion of elderly people, on the one hand, and for themselves as they age, on the other.

and services will surely be necessary. Fourth, social workers will be primary proponents of emphasizing and building on the strengths of elderly people to maximize their self-determination and quality of life.

This chapter will

- Explain the current and future demographics of the increasingly aged population.
- Introduce the issue of "global graying" (George, 1997, p. 57).
- Discuss problems elderly people commonly face including ageism, discrimination in employment, poverty, retirement, health care issues, elderly abuse, living conditions and family variables, and transitional issues.
- Examine various contexts for social work practice with the elderly including home- and community-based services, discharge planning in hospital settings, and service provision in nursing homes.
- Encourage critical thinking about financing Social Security, possibly through privatization, determining whether Social Security discriminates against women, and proposing how elderly people might be empowered through macro practice.
- Explore empowerment issues for diverse populations of elderly people, including African American grandparents who are primary caregivers for grandchildren and the culturally competent treatment of elderly Navajo people residing in a nursing home.

 ## Demographic Characteristics of the Elderly Population: Race, Gender, and Social Class

Three important variables in discussing the elderly population are race, gender, and social class (Mooney et al., 2002). People of color represented about 17% of the U.S. elderly in 2000 (Macionis, 2005). Projections suggest this will increase to 25% in 2035; the population of elderly people of color is expected to grow at a rate three times that of the white elderly between 1997 and 2030 (Mooney et al., 2002). This is partially due to higher fertility rates and increased immigration, especially on the part of Hispanics (AOA, 2000a). The fact that people of color tend to experience higher rates of heart disease, diabetes, and arthritis than whites has direct implications for social workers and other professionals working in health care (Mooney et al., 2002; Newman, 2000).

Although the overall U.S. population is approximately 49% male and 51% female, the population of people age 65 and over is 41% male and 59% female (U.S. Census Bureau, 2003, No. 11). The average life expectancy for women is almost age 80, and for men just over age 74 (U.S. National Center for Health Statistics, 2003). People in this age group are most likely to die from heart disease, cancer, and stroke in that order (U.S. Census Bureau, 2003, No. 129). Note, however, that women are more likely than men to suffer from "disabling diseases such as arthritis, Alzheimer's, diabetes, deafness, cataracts, broken bones, digestive conditions, and osteoporosis" (Doyal, 1995; Kirk & Okazawa-Rey, 2004, p. 179).

In previous chapters we established how women are more likely to be poor and to earn less than men, even for comparable work. Living longer means savings must be stretched out further, which means women are more likely to run out of money toward the end of their lives. In addition, earning less or not working outside the home means they are likely to receive lower Social Security benefits. Almost 75% of the elderly poor in the United States are women (AOA, 2000b). The social welfare system and social workers must, therefore, be prepared to address this population's needs.

Social class is the third important variable affecting the elderly. People populating the lower social classes tend to have shorter life expectancies, to experience more severe incapacitating illnesses, and generally to have a lower quality of life (Mooney et al., 2002). One study revealed that 26% of people age 65 or older who have annual incomes of at least $35,000 label their health as "excellent"; in contrast, only 10% of elderly people with incomes less than $10,000 could say the same thing (Mooney et al., 2002; Seeman & Adler, 1998). People of lower social classes generally are "chronically unemployed, underemployed, dependent on welfare, or working for a subsistence wage" (Longres, 2000, p. 239). Many barely survive, let alone have enough resources to save for old age.

Common Problems Facing Elderly People

I just told my father, age 73, who is a retired MSW social worker, that at this moment I'm writing about problems experienced by the elderly. (He happens to be at my home planting daffodil bulbs for next spring.) He replied, "The elderly don't have problems. Why are you writing about that?" The point is that it's easy to focus on all the negatives about growing older instead of the positives.

This chapter emphasizes how social work with the elderly is founded on clients' strengths and seeks to maximize their well-being. However, older people are more likely to experience some types of problems than are those who are younger. As people age, they eventually become weaker and more vulnerable to certain illnesses and diseases. *Primary aging* refers to the fact that physiological variables involving such decline will inevitably occur. However, there are huge variations among people concerning how fast this progresses. *Secondary aging*, then, concerns how the primary aging process can either be hastened or slowed by lifestyle and behavior. Factors that can slow aging include physical exercise, healthful diet, stress management, and ready access to adequate resources and medical treatment (Seeman & Adler, 1998).

The following section addresses some of the problematic issues affecting the elderly. The intent is to establish the context for how social workers strive to focus on their strengths and meet their needs. Such matters include ageism, discrimination in employment, poverty, retirement, health care, elderly abuse, and living conditions.

Ageism

Ageism involves harboring negative images of and attitudes toward people simply because they are older. Ageism is similar to sexism or racism in that it involves prejudice toward and discrimination against people who fit into a certain category. Ageism, like sexism and racism, also fails to identify individual strengths as means of empowerment. Focus on Critical Thinking 10.1 reviews some of the typical myths and stereotypes about older people that are grounded in ageism.

FOCUS ON CRITICAL THINKING 10.1
Confronting Myths About the Elderly

One dimension of critical thinking involves evaluating assumptions made by many people. A number of stereotypes about the elderly are cited here (Greene, 2000; Harrigan & Farmer, 2000). Confronting stereotypes involves *asking* questions, *assessing* facts, and *asserting* a conclusion. What are your conclusions about each of the following myths?

Myth A: All elderly people are burdened with multiple physical complaints and are riddled with disease.

Fact: Elderly people do experience increasing weakness and illness as they age. Of people age 65 or over, 80% experience at least one form of chronic illness such as arthritis, heart disease, or diabetes (Coleman & Cressey, 1999; Greene, 2000; Newman & Newman, 2003). However, as with the younger population, huge variation exists concerning individual health status. Regardless of age, some people are simply healthier and stronger than others, for many reasons. A healthful lifestyle in terms of diet and exercise correlates with better health. Of people age 85 and older who do not live in institutional settings, 80% manage their daily living tasks quite well (Harrigan & Farmer, 2000, p. 26).

Myth B: Old people are unattractive and smelly, have no teeth, and can barely see or hear.

Fact: Elderly people, like their younger cohorts, pay varying degrees of attention to their personal appearance, hygiene, and conformity with current, popular styles. Many older people take great pride in their appearance and their strong social skills. They actively strive to put forth a pleasant, attractive persona. Physical changes such as the tendency of skin to wrinkle and body fat to redistribute do occur. However, these are facts of life having little to do with a person's overall appearance and personality.

About half of today's elderly people have lost their teeth (Bee, 1996). However, think about what times were like when they were young. There was no preventive dental care or fluoride in the water supply (to combat cavities). They lived in an era in which they *expected* to lose their teeth and wear dentures. Everyone else did. My grandmother, born in 1890, told the story of how she never could stand pain very well. Whenever she got a toothache, she would get someone to pull the tooth out with the equivalent of pliers. Eventually she had no teeth left.

Sight and hearing tend to deteriorate with advancing age. However, having access to advanced medical services and techniques can slow the decline and even improve conditions. Hearing aids are now much more usable than in the past. Vision can be enhanced by glasses, contacts, laser surgery, and other new surgical techniques. One professor required cataract surgery at the relatively young age of 48. She had

(continued)

One example of ageism involves how government programs such as the Administration on Aging (which operates under the auspices of the Department of Health and Human Services) have both low status compared to other social programs and little influence with political leaders (Kornblum & Julian, 2004). Social programs for the elderly are frequently targeted for cutbacks before programs geared to help other populations. A second example of ageism concerns how the media typically

FOCUS ON CRITICAL THINKING 10.1 (*continued*)

been nearsighted since her early teens and could barely find her glasses when she put them down somewhere. As the cataracts developed, her vision became increasingly cloudy, and she viewed the world as if through a dense fog. Reading and driving became almost impossible. Cataract surgery involves removing the natural lens in your eye and replacing it with an artificial one. After the 15-minute outpatient surgery, her distance vision was better than it had been at age 14. She marveled at medical advances as she recalled the effects of her own grand-mother's cataract surgery years before. At that time, the natural lens could be removed but not be replaced internally. Her grandmother had to wear glasses almost three-quarters of an inch thick to replace the lenses she lost in order to restore only a portion of her vision.

Myth C: "Old people sleep all the time" (Harrigan & Farmer, 2000, p. 33).

Fact: Older people don't necessarily sleep less than younger people, but their sleeping patterns are somewhat different. They tend to have more difficulty sleeping through the night. They wake up more frequently and, by the time they reach age 80, remain awake about 20% of the night (Woodruff, 1985). However, they tend to compensate for this by taking short naps during the day. It should be emphasized that this is a strength: They adapt their daytime behavior to get the sleep they need.

Myth D: You can't teach an old dog new tricks; "old people are set in their ways" (Harrigan & Farmer, 2000, p. 35).

Fact: Greene (2000) reflects:

> Life span and life course theorists reject the view that growth ends with adulthood. They point out that, while there may be growth limits for attributes such as height, other qualities such as creativity and abstract reasoning do not fit this model. In this context, *growth* refers to differentiation, increased complexity, and greater organization, and can occur at every age. (p. 29)

Harrigan and Farmer (2000) add that

> [t]his growth and change vary from person to person and within each individual and are related to an individual's personality. . . . For example, a woman who is assertive, confident, and positive as she approaches new experiences will probably view old age as one more new and exciting adventure. Someone who approaches life from a pessimistic, complaining viewpoint no doubt will behave similarly as an aged person. (p. 36)

Myth E: All old people are senile.

Fact: Harrigan and Farmer (2000) indicate that "[t]his myth stems from the antiquated idea that confusion and loss of one's mental faculties are a natural part of the aging process. Only a small percentage of the aged develop an irreversible brain disorder" (p. 38). They go on to note that, of people age 65 and older, only about 5% experience such dementia that they can no longer look after themselves, and another 15% have mild dementia.[1]

[1]*Dementia* is a condition that involves numerous cognitive problems such as impaired memory, poor judgment, and inability to control emotions.

emphasize the importance of youth, beauty, strength, and physical prowess. For example, advertisers pitch expensive facial creams that minimize wrinkles and bring back youthful glow to aging skin. Still other reflections of ageism are discussed in the following sections.

Discrimination in Employment

Reio and Sanders-Reto (1999) conducted a national survey sponsored by the National Council on Aging. They found that "50 percent of employers surveyed believed that older workers cannot perform as well as younger workers" (p. 12). It's true that people in general will eventually experience increased weakness and slowness as they age. However, this occurs at vastly different rates depending on the individual. Additionally, the younger old—those closer to age 65—are much more likely to enjoy good health than the older old—those age 85 and over.

Congress passed the Age Discrimination in Employment Act (ADEA) in 1967 that prohibited discrimination against people age 40–65. This means that employers can no longer do things like advertise for employees "who are under 30." However, employers can still state that a job is "entry level" or "requires two to three years' experience" and then reject older people on the basis of being "overqualified" (Mooney et al., 2002, p. 170).

The ADEA also did little to help people age 65 and older. As the next section explains, many elderly people require additional income to keep afloat, and many want to work.

Poverty

Whereas until the early part of the 20th century elderly people were very likely poor, Social Security currently supports a large proportion of older people. Of the elderly living in the United States, 60% would fall below the poverty line if they were not receiving Social Security benefits (Coleman & Cressey, 1999). These benefits do not make people rich. In 2002 average monthly benefits for retired workers were $895 (U.S. Census Bureau, No. 543). However, lumped together with personal savings, other assets, and occasionally pensions, these benefits allow many people to make it.

Poverty rates for the elderly vary widely depending on "gender, race, ethnicity, marital status, and age"; people are more likely to be poor if they are female, a person of color, single, and age 85 or older (Mooney et al., 2002, p. 171). Poverty rates for elderly women reflect how women of color are especially at risk. Eleven percent of white, 25% of Hispanic, and 30% of African American elderly women are poor (AOA, 2000c).

Saving Social Security

We have established that Social Security is a primary means of keeping elderly people out of poverty. There has been much concern about the adequacy and ongoing solvency of the Social Security system. As Chapters 6 and 8 explained, workers automatically pay into Social Security, a type of social insurance, based on their earnings up to a specified annual maximum. It is tempting to think of Social Security as a savings account that automatically receives a percentage of each paycheck and lies there waiting for you to collect interest once you retire. But this is not the case. In reality, the money that workers contribute today is being spent to pay benefits to retired and other workers, as well as other government expenses. Tomorrow's beneficiaries—including you—must depend on tomorrow's workers.

The problem introduced at the beginning of the chapter is that "there are fewer and fewer workers for each person getting monthly checks. . . . In 1945, there were

42 payers for each recipient. In 1950, 17. Now, 3.4. In 15 years, 2.8" (Sloan, 2000, p. 22). So the disturbing question is, Who's going to pay for your Social Security when you retire? Note that some say that the Social Security system isn't really in that much trouble (Ip, 2004; Stelzer, 2005). The estimated amount to be spent in the future is only 1.2% of the gross domestic product (GDP: "the total monetary value of all goods and services produced in a country during one year" minus "payments on foreign investments" [Nichols, 1995, p. 577]), whereas "the administration's goal is to get the federal budget deficit below 2.2% of the GDP" during that same period (Ip, 2004, p. 3D). Additionally, some propose that "if the economy grows more rapidly and efficiently than some predictions suggest, the current system might well prove capable of meeting all of its obligations" (Stelzer, 2005).

Despite these more optimistic thinkers, it is predicted that Social Security will start going into the red as early as 2018 when baby boomers are retiring and the dependency ratio changes (i.e., more benefit recipients to fewer workers) (CBSMarketWatch, 2005). At that point, workers' contributions will be less than the benefits that must be paid out, and any benefits paid must come from reserves. By 2042 full benefits will no longer be available to retirees if no changes in the current formula are made (ABCNews, 2005; FOXNews, 2005). Many indicate that it's much better to plan far ahead "so that individuals and families have time to adjust their retirement plans, and so that changes can be phased in slowly over time" (White House, 2005a).

To address the problem, some suggest establishing a system based at least partially on *privatization*. This refers to a deduction system whereby workers have the option of investing part or all of their wages (depending on the proposed plan) currently deducted for Social Security into investments of their own choosing. The idea is that investing in the stock market can earn people significantly more money than funneling it through the current system. Various privatization plans propose investing varying percentages of Social Security contributions and specifying different investment options. Current proposals usually involve privatizing 16–32% of the total Social Security tax (versus most or all of it) (Bloomberg.com, 2005). Additionally, most recommend relatively secure investments such as mutual funds or bonds (Stelzer, 2005). Other questions concern how investments would be made (Would the government invest for you?), what investments would be considered appropriate, and the extent to which investors would be allowed to make their own decisions.

Supporters of privatization say that private investments would earn significantly more than traditional Social Security investment (Reuters, 2005; White House, 2005a). They suggest investors could actually become rich via stock market investment. However, opponents indicate that's not realistic: Investors "get rich" only when they invest in highly risky stocks that can provide extremely high returns—or extremely high losses (Bostick, 2005).

Privatization probably sounded like a better idea during the bull markets of the late 1990s when investors were receiving returns of up to 30% on investments. However, as the sobering stock market crash following the terrorist attacks on the World Trade Center and the Pentagon on September 11, 2001, made clear, stock market investments can be risky and can lose a lot of money.

Zuckerman (1999) expresses another concern:

[J]ust because people have money in the markets does not mean they have the investment savvy to handle their retirement funds. Our bedrock protections against destitution in old age should not be subject to market gyrations or the poor judgments of individual investors. We should not risk Social Security to save it. (p. 76)

One other worry concerning changing the system to one involving privatization is the estimated transition cost of $2 trillion or more (FOXNews, 2005; Reuters, 2005). Supporters of privatization say that this is only a better way of spending and using that money today to improve the system, instead of spending more tomorrow (FOXNews, 2005).

Others indicate that fixing and saving the system will require cutting benefits and/or increasing payroll taxes. Benefits can be decreased in several ways including

- Providing them at older ages (which has already been done to a limited degree).
- Decreasing the actual amount of benefits paid out to individuals.
- Increasing the maximum amount of income that can be taxed. As of this writing, the Social Security tax rate is 12.4%, shared equally by employees and employers (Blau, 2004) taxed up to a maximum of $87,900 [note that the maximum goes up every year] (CBSMarketWatch, 2005).[2]
- Cutting the increases in benefits regularly made to adjust for cost of living increases.
- More controversially, providing benefits only to those whose income or assets fall under some arbitrary line. This, of course, is quite radical because it violates the idea that all who pay into a social insurance system should benefit from returns.

Focus on Critical Thinking 10.2 urges you to think about how this problem should be solved.

Another controversial issue is whether Social Security discriminates against women. Focus on Critical Thinking 10.3 raises some key questions.

Retirement

Previously we established the concept of age 65 as the magic number for retirement. A hundred years ago, the notion of retirement was essentially unknown. Most people didn't live that long. Few had enough savings to support them without working. No programs such as Social Security or pension plans existed to pick up the slack when their work careers ended. As we know, the Social Security Act of 1935 established 65 as the age when people stop working and begin receiving maximum benefits. Current policy indicates that by 2022, people won't be able to receive Social Security benefits until age 67 (Whiteman, 2001).

In fact, most people retire before age 65; 60% stop working by age 62 (Goldberg, 2000). Retirement might sound good to many, but it often requires quite an adjustment. Retirees must cope with a new way of life. How does a retiree respond when someone asks, "And what do you do?" Many people's careers or jobs become a substantial part of their personal identities. What happens when they give up that significant part of their lives? How might the loss affect their self-concept and self-respect?

[2]Note that the 7.65% (which your employer matches) deducted from your paychecks is called FICA (the Federal Insurance Contributions Act); this includes 6.2% for Social Security (half of the 12.4% total) and 1.45% for Medicare (again, half of the 2.9% total) (Blau, 2004, p. 285).

FOCUS ON CRITICAL THINKING 10.2

How Would You Fix Social Security?

What are your own thoughts and values concerning the Social Security crisis? How would you answer the following questions?

Concerning privatizing the fund:

- Should Social Security be privatized?
- If so, what percentage should be privatized?
- Should privatization occur only on a voluntary basis?
- How safe do you think privatization is?
- Would most people be sophisticated enough to make sound investment decisions?
- Is privatizing the system at any level worth the potential cost of changing it?

Concerning raising the retirement age:

- Because people tend to live longer, should the retirement age be raised?
- If so, to what age?
- When would you like to be able to retire? If you haven't thought much about this, when would your parents (or grandparents) like to retire?

Concerning decreasing benefits:

- Should benefits be decreased?
- If so, for whom—current recipients? Note that two-thirds of retirees depend on Social Security as a major source of income; "34% rely on it for at least 90% of their income and 32% more for at least half of their income" (DiNitto, 2005, p. 138).
- Should benefits for future recipients be reduced? If so, when should this start? How much should they be reduced?
- Do you want reduced benefits?
- Would your parents and grandparents want reduced benefits?

Concerning increasing the maximum amount of income that can be taxed:

- Should the maximum amount of income that can be taxed be increased more than it regularly is now?
- If so, by how much?
- Should all income regardless of the amount be taxed?
- Should people who pay significantly more into the fund receive proportionally more benefits?
- To what extent is it fair to pay significantly more into a social insurance program and get the same benefits as those paying significantly less?
- Should richer people help support poorer people by sharing their wealth through the Social Security system?
- What is fair?

Concerning cutting increases in benefits:

- Should cost-of-living increases in benefits be decreased?
- If so, by how much?
- How would a decreasing standard of living affect the many people depending on Social Security?
- How severe would these effects be on recipients living 20 years after first receiving Social Security benefits in terms of their quality of life?

Concerning offering Social Security benefits only to those less well off:

- Should benefits be given only to retirees who are less well off?
- If so, how well off?
- To what extent is this fair to workers who paid significant taxes into the fund for decades and then don't qualify for benefits?
- To what extent would this transform a social insurance system into a public assistance system? To what extent is this right or wrong?

FOCUS ON CRITICAL THINKING 10.3
Does Social Security Discriminate Against Women?

One ongoing criticism of Social Security is that it discriminates against women. When a woman turns age 65, she is eligible to receive benefits equal to one-half of the benefits her husband receives. This is true whether she has ever worked outside the home or not. However, if she has worked outside the home, she may choose to take her own benefits instead. She cannot receive both.

How is this discriminatory? First, women who have been homemakers their entire lives are entitled to only half of what their husbands receive. Does this imply that their share of the marital partnership is worth only half of the husbands'? The system provides them with no way of making contributions based on their own labor within the home.

Many women work outside the home for years, build up their own benefits, but end up taking half of their husbands' anyway. Why? The husbands' benefits are worth more than twice as much as theirs, so they're better off taking half of the husbands'. We've established that men tend to enter higher-paid professions, earn significantly more than women in the same professions, and spend less time out of the workforce raising children and caring for a home. Thus women's

contributions, as structured by the current system, are often significantly less than their husbands'.

Barusch (2000) explains:

> Wives in dual-worker couples face a choice. They can receive benefits based on their earnings, or they can receive benefits as dependents. They cannot do both. Those who left the labor force to raise children or care for the sick, and those whose wages were lower than their spouses' receive more as dependents than on the basis of their own work histories. So they receive no benefit for the payroll taxes withheld from every one of their paychecks. (p. 570)

Note that a few positive changes have been made in the system. "For example, divorced spouses may begin collecting benefits at age 62 if their former spouses are eligible even if they have not yet claimed benefits, and payments to disabled widows and widowers aged 50–59 were increased. Other major gender inequities were not addressed and remain unresolved today" (DiNitto, 2005, p. 131).

Should the system be further reformed to make it more equitable? If so, how should the contributions of homemakers be measured? What about those who take time off to bear and raise children?

Another potential problem in retirement involves reduced income. How much adjustment is involved when retirees can no longer spend money and buy things as they used to? Still another aspect of retirement concerns losing daily work routines. Retirees must discover new ways to spend their time.

Health Care

Medicare, established in 1966, is not the total answer to health care for the elderly. Although it helps pay for medical expenses for 39 million people (Health Care Financing Administration, 2000), it pays only half for a visit to a physician and nothing for long-term care, hearing aids, glasses, or dental work. Chapter 8 discussed the partial supplementary coverage available in Medicare's Part B, medigap insurance (to fill in Medicare's gaps), and the Medicare Modernization Act's prescription drug benefit. However, these also cost the elderly more. And good coverage costs much more.

The older people get, the more likely they are to have long-term illnesses and to take more time to recuperate. The elderly spend three times as much on health care as younger population groups (Mooney et al., 2002).

Elderly Abuse

Physical and emotional abuse of elderly people is receiving increasing public attention. It includes not only inflicting physical or emotional harm but also taking advantage of elderly people financially or neglecting them (e.g., ignoring the fact that medical treatment is needed) (Hooyman & Kiyak, 1999). An estimated 1.5 million cases of physical abuse occur in the United States each year (Kornblum & Julian, 2004) in both private homes and residential facilities. Coleman and Cressey (1999) report shocking incidents of abuse involving family caregivers. One involved a man who sexually assaulted his 74-year-old mother-in-law. The victim's daughter refused to make a big deal of it or to allow her mother to report the incident to authorities. Another incident entailed an angry son chasing his 75-year-old father around with a hatchet.

In private homes, perpetrators of elderly abuse often are people who live with the victim such as a spouse or adult child; frequently alcohol abuse is involved (McInnis-Dittrich, 2005). Elderly people are also subject to abuse when living in residential settings. Abuse is more likely to occur when residents are isolated from family and friends who otherwise might look out for them.

Living Conditions and Family Variables

Many elderly people prefer to live on their own or with other family members. However, many older people's homes are located in older, deteriorating, inner-city neighborhoods with high crime rates. This puts them at greater risk of harm and also makes it increasingly difficult to maintain their homes.

Relatively few elderly people need the around-the-clock nursing and maintenance care of a nursing home. People are more likely to need this care when they suffer from debilitating chronic illnesses. Nursing homes vary markedly in cost and quality of service. Wealthy people can pay for private homes that have excellent facilities and attentive staff. People with fewer resources must often be satisfied with whatever care they can get.

Transitional Issues

As people get older, they are more likely to experience serious losses with which they must learn to cope. One issue already discussed concerns retirement and the accompanying drastic changes in productivity and routine. Other issues involve adjusting to more structured living situations. One spouse may die, leaving the other to adjust to a much more isolated life. Health may decline, requiring an elderly

HIGHLIGHT 10.2
"Gayging" and Invisibility

Elderly people can experience *invisibility*—the condition that others fail to acknowledge, attend to, or even notice their existence (Hooyman & Kiyak, 1999; Tully, 2000). The myths discussed in Focus on Critical Thinking 10.1 tend to reinforce the views often held by younger people that the elderly are inadequate, of lesser or little value, and unworthy of notice. Hence elderly people become invisible. Obviously such unfair, discriminatory attitudes and treatment fail to uphold human dignity and appreciate human diversity.

Lesbian, gay, and bisexual (LGB) people experience an additional dimension of invisibility. Tully (2000) establishes that *gayging* (gay aging) results in additional stresses and scenarios not experienced by heterosexuals (p. 197). LGB people do not enjoy the legal and social support systems taken for granted by heterosexuals. For example,

> [I]t is not uncommon for the surviving partner of a gay or lesbian couple to be the sole beneficiary of the partner's estate only to have the will legally

challenged. Too often, family of origin members, children, or other legal relatives will be seen as the lawful heirs. Dividing household items between an unacknowledged partner and "legal" heirs can be particularly devastating to the gay or lesbian surviving partner. (Tully, 2001, p. 601)

Additionally, health insurance policies often do not include nonheterosexual partners (who, of course, cannot legally marry). Hospitals, nursing homes, and other health facilities may not acknowledge LGB relationships. Family members who deny or fail to acknowledge a relationship may deny a longtime partner access to a dying partner.

LGB elderly people of color are at risk of experiencing discrimination because of race in addition to risks associated with age and sexual orientation. Social workers are trained to be sensitive to all these factors in empowering clients and providing help. Tully (2000) provides an example:

> Consider the older African-American gay man who, because of a stroke, has been confined to

(continued)

person to accept and adjust to increasing levels of assistance and dependence. Losses in ability such as sight, hearing, and mobility may also require the application of coping skills. There are many areas in which social workers can provide important assistance with respect to elderly people's adjustment.

Note that lesbian, gay, and bisexual (LGB) people not only face the same issues and transitions that heterosexual people do but also continue to suffer the consequences of homophobia. Highlight 10.2 describes one dimension of homophobia—invisibility.

Contexts for Social Work Practice with the Elderly

As in services for children and families, there exists a continuum of care for the elderly ranging from supplemental services for people in their own homes to intensive residential care. A primary value stressed when working with the elderly is

HIGHLIGHT 10.2 *(continued)*

the hospital's intensive care unit. The hospital, long known for its racist practices, began treating African Americans in the 1970s and has few doctors or nurses who are minorities of color. Most of the hospital support staff are Hispanic or African American. The patient's Puerto Rican lover, a 70-year-old retired artist, is kept from visiting because he is not considered a family member. Because he believes the true nature of the relationship to be a private matter, he remains quiet. The hospital social worker, being sensitive to the perceived needs of the patient and his friend, arranges for visitation. There are times when empowering individuals requires institutional flexibility. (p. 217)

The following provides another example of how a social worker must be sensitive to sexual orientation to empower a client (Tully, 2001):

Cecilia, a 54-year-old lesbian who was the guardian of her 90-year-old hospitalized terminally ill mother, was referred to the hospital social worker to assess the mother's pending death and the impact it might have on Cecilia. Her sexual orientation was not germane to the immediate problem, but it would be important to know that Cecilia's partner of 30 years was the primary care-

taker of Cecilia's mother and more likely to need the services. (pp. 608–609)

There are several ways social workers can address the issue of LGB people's invisibility for all clients including those who are elderly (Tully, 2001). First, practitioners can make their offices more "homosocial" or welcoming to people regardless of sexual orientation (p. 609). Including magazines and other reading material oriented to gay issues and interests can help. Second, using admissions or intake forms that feature more inclusive terms than *spouse* or *marital status* is constructive. When soliciting information, phrasing questions by using terms such as *significant other, partner, mate,* and *special friend* reflects more flexibility toward and acceptance of non-heterosexual orientations (p. 609). Third, careful listening can provide clues to sexual orientation. For example, clients who mention involvement in lesbian/gay activities or events may, in fact, be lesbian or gay. However, they also may not be, so social workers must be careful not to succumb to stereotypes or jump to conclusions.

autonomy. Social workers strive to keep elderly individuals as independent and autonomous as possible for as long as possible.

Because the elderly may have many needs, social workers practice in a wide range of agencies and settings. Three broader contexts for service provision are long-term care through home health and community services, discharge planning in hospitals, and service provision in nursing homes.

Long-Term Care Through Home-Based and Community Health Services

Long-term care is "health, personal care, and social services delivered over a sustained period of time to persons who have lost or never achieved some capacity for self-care. Long-term care may be continuous or intermittent and it strives to provide care in the least restrictive environment" (Kane, 1987). Long-term care implies that recipients

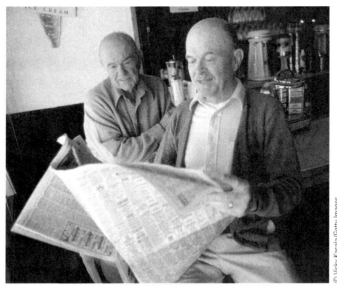

Elderly gay people suffer double "invisibility."

need either ongoing or periodic help over an extended period. Nursing homes, discussed more thoroughly later, provide one type of long-term care. A second type includes services provided to people living in their own homes. Finally, a third kind of long-term care includes services made readily available to people in their community.

Home-Based Services

As you know, social workers in the broker role link clients to services and in the case manager role oversee and coordinate service provision. *Home-based services* or *home care* are types of assistance provided to people in their own homes. They may involve either assistance to family members caring for an elderly relative or provision of services by formal social service agencies.

An *informal support network* is a system of individuals who provide emotional, social, and economic support to a person in need. The family is "the primary and preferred source of support for older people in the United States" (Kropf, 2000, p. 171). Informal support networks also include friends, neighbors, and fellow worshipers (Biegel, Shore, & Gordon, 1984; Kropf, 2000). For example, members of an informal support network might periodically chauffeur an elderly person who no longer can drive herself to the grocery store. Similarly, an elderly person with vision problems might need help paying bills and balancing his checkbook. Investigating the adequacy of an elderly person's informal support network is an important aspect of social work assessment.

"Because social workers are trained in understanding family dynamics, group processes, community organization, and volunteer management, they possess knowledge and skills to intervene in a variety of ways within an informal network" (Kropf, 2000, p. 175). For example, a social worker might help a family arrange for respite care while family members do other things such as "working, shopping, socializing, or relaxing" (Kropf, 2000, p. 177). *Respite care* is temporary care for an elderly person or other person in need, giving the primary caregivers (often family members) some time free of responsibility. (Note that Chapter 9 introduced the concept of respite care with respect to child care.) Another example involves a social worker arranging for telephone reassurance services (i.e., calling elderly people daily or periodically to make sure they're all right) when primary caregivers are unavailable.

In contrast, *formal support networks* include public and private agencies and their staffs, which provide services including health care (e.g., nursing), social services, and housekeeping help to elderly people in need. Home-based services provided by formal support networks may be necessary for two reasons. First, they address needs directly involving the home itself, such as cleaning or repair. Second, they more efficiently serve recipients who have difficulty transporting themselves outside the home to receive services elsewhere. Home-based services include any provided to people directly in their homes and those intended to facilitate people's ability to remain in their homes. They include homemaker and chore services (to assist in daily living tasks such as cooking, cleaning, home maintenance, and laundry), home health care (e.g., physical therapy or a visiting nurse), transportation, Meals on Wheels,[3] and respite care.

Community-Based Services

Community-based services—those provided outside the home in the community—form another dimension of the formal support network. They can fulfill a wide range of functions, from providing health care to meeting psychological and social needs. The following are examples of community-based services (Kropf, 2000):

- *Adult day care:* This service provides supervision outside the home for elderly people who live at home but whose primary caregivers are unavailable during the day, usually because they must work. It differs from respite care in that it is provided on a regular schedule and is generally provided in a day care center outside the home (respite care can be provided either inside or outside the home).
- *Hospices:* These programs provide end-of-life care to terminally ill people. The intent is to make people as comfortable as possible during their final days. Services may be provided either in a comfortable setting outside the home or in the individual's home.
- *Senior centers:* Here seniors can gather for social, recreational, and educational reasons. Senior centers often offer a wide range of activities including "drama, lectures, arts and crafts, physical fitness, . . . meal programs, health screenings, or day care" (Kropf, 2000, p. 179).
- *Congregate Meal Program:* Initially instituted by the 1973 Older Americans Act, this program provides hot meals for seniors at a variety of community locations. It offers seniors a source of good nutrition and an opportunity to socialize with their peers.
- *Senior home repair and maintenance programs:* These provide physical help in home upkeep. They may involve a handyperson service whereby volunteers make home repairs such as fixing pipes or repairing roofs as needed. They may also include seasonal services such as lawn mowing or snow removal.

Focus on Critical Thinking 10.4 gives you a framework to organize your thoughts as they relate to care for the elderly.

---

[3] *Meals on Wheels* is a program in which meals are delivered directly to the homes of people who need them. This service can be sponsored or cosponsored by public agencies such as human service departments or private organizations like senior centers.

FOCUS ON CRITICAL THINKING 10.4

Macro Practice Empowerment for the Elderly

Social workers have the responsibility to become politically involved in "protecting older people's autonomy, providing choices for care for older people and their families, and increasing the accessibility of services that are culturally competent for all groups of older people" (Bellos & Ruffolo, 1995, p.169).

Keeping a careful eye on proposed legislation addressing older people's health care and social service needs is critical (Cox & Parsons, 1994). For example, increasing the age at which older people can first begin receiving Social Security benefits significantly and negatively impacts elderly people's financial standing. Likewise, monitoring the availability of adequate health care for elderly people is paramount. Legislative advocacy involves efforts to change legislation to benefit some category of clients—in this case, the elderly. It includes such actions as contacting elected officials about some issue or policy under debate. It might also

entail communicating with other professionals and clients, encouraging them to contact officials concerning their views and recommendations. Public officials usually listen to their constituents when they want to get reelected.

Working to improve and develop community services for the elderly raises other important macro practice possibilities. For example, community-based adult day care services can be expanded (Bellos & Ruffolo, 1995). Day care programs can provide a wide range of "health, social, and related support services" for a community's elderly residents including "individual and family counseling, group work services, outreach and broker services, supportive services, and care planning services" (Bellos & Ruffolo, 1995, p. 170).

Another example of a community-based program is one directed at educating local clergy to enhance linkages "between organized and informal

(continued)

Discharge Planning in Hospital Settings

"Hospitals provide much of the acute health care of the elderly, and over a third of all nursing home admissions originate from hospitals" (Cummings & Jackson, 2000, p. 191). Social workers are integrally involved as leaders in interdisciplinary treatment planning[4] and in linking patients with necessary services. A common primary function of hospital social workers is *discharge planning*. This is the comprehensive assessment of a patient's abilities and needs, the development of a plan to facilitate that patient's transition out of the hospital and back into a community or agency setting, and the implementation of that plan. Discharge planning also involves identifying the appropriate resources available to meet needs and working closely with the patient, family members, and other health care providers to implement the plan as effectively as possible. Advocacy on the patient's behalf to make certain needs are met is frequently required.

Social workers must be prepared to deal with multiple potential problems when conducting discharge planning (Naleppa & Reid, 2003). The patient may be

---

[4]*Interdisciplinary treatment* involves teams composed of professionals from various disciplines such as doctors, nurses, social workers, psychologists, physical therapists, and occupational therapists who, in collaboration, share findings, make recommendations, and implement treatment plans.

FOCUS ON CRITICAL THINKING 10.4 *(continued)*

support systems" (Biegel et al., 1984, p. 99). A university school of social welfare provided training with the following goals: "to impart a foundation of knowledge of the aging process, to examine the specific needs and contributions of aged individuals, to impart knowledge of community resources available for the aged individuals, and to increase participants' awareness of creative ways to minister to the aged" (Biegel et al., 1984, p. 99).

With all this in mind, think about the following questions:

- To what extent do the preceding suggestions for empowerment reflect *residual* versus *institutional* policies and programming? (Recall that residual policies focus on reactions to problems, generally providing as few benefits as possible. Institutional policies view social services as people's right, providing ongoing benefits to enhance people's lives and well-being.)

- To what extent does current service provision for the elderly demonstrate *conservative* versus *liberal* values?

Now consider the three basic, divergent principles involved that relate to the following questions:

- Who should assume responsibility? Should the elderly be expected to provide for and take care of themselves? Or is it society's responsibility to help them when they need it?
- Who is to blame for elderly people's problems and needs? To what extent will the elderly take advantage of social welfare benefits when they really don't need them? Will providing ongoing services and benefits significantly enhance their health, welfare, and comfort?
- To what extent should the government interfere in people's lives? Is it the government's responsibility to improve older people's health and functioning?

confused, difficult to work with, or suffering from an unstable physical condition. Family members may be unavailable or may disagree with plans proposed by the patient or treatment team. Adequate financial resources for an appropriate placement or access to the placement itself may be unavailable.

Case Example[5]   Esra Tratnor, age 76, was admitted to the hospital after his two daughters, Vicki and Karen, suddenly noticed that he was having "spells" during which he would speak garbled nonsense or babble incessantly. This was quite unlike Esra, who was a quiet, withdrawn man of few words. Esra remained coherent the rest of the time.

The diagnosis was an inoperable brain tumor the size of a lemon. Upon hearing this, Esra insisted on returning to his farmhouse—the same house in which he was born. He wanted to live out his remaining days watching the birds and deer. He had been living alone since his wife of 49 years died 6 years ago.

Except for a liquid supplement, doctors prescribed no treatment except to make Esra as comfortable as possible. They anticipated ongoing mental and physical deterioration in the 6–12 months he had to live.

[5]Vicki Vogel creatively developed the idea and substance for this case example.

Esra gave Aiko, the hospital social worker, consent to contact Vicki and Karen regarding discharge plans. One or the other of them had visited him every day of his hospital stay. Aiko reviewed options with them. Although they were very concerned about their father, both were adamant about being unable to take him into their own homes. Both had full-time jobs, husbands and children, and no available room. Thus the only two alternatives for Esra were to return home and be provided with supportive home-based services or to enter a nursing home.

Aiko requested a psychiatric evaluation to assess Esra's mental competence. The psychiatrist's conclusion was that, although Esra manifested moderate depression, he was capable of making his own decisions. The psychiatrist prescribed an antidepressant.

Aiko consulted the hospital's attorney, who indicated that Esra had the right to return home because he had been pronounced mentally competent. Esra accepted Meals on Wheels (he confessed to being a pretty bad cook) but refused other home-based services including a visiting nurse and homemaker help. He insisted on remaining independent. Aiko asked Esra if he could afford the prescribed antidepressants and nutritional supplements. Esra replied that, although he had no medical insurance to cover them, Vicki and Karen would help him out. In reality, he had no intention of taking expensive drugs or of seeking financial help from his daughters.

Three weeks after his hospital discharge, Esra was readmitted with a broken hip. Apparently he had been climbing a stepladder to trim the branches of a tree in his front yard and had fallen. Luckily, neighbors noticed immediately and called an ambulance.

This time Esra was noticeably disoriented and confused. A psychiatric evaluation determined that he was mentally incompetent. Healing and rehabilitation for his hip would require extensive physical care for a long time, perhaps until his death. Vicki and Karen discussed with Aiko what they should do. Vicki couldn't bear the thought of placing her beloved dad in a nursing home, so she relented and said he could stay with her. Her own children would have to double up in a room. She would take an extended leave of absence from work to care for him. The court appointed Vicki legal guardian, and Esra moved in.

Two months later, Vicki called Aiko in desperation, saying that she just couldn't take it anymore. The friction between her and her husband over Esra's residence in their home was escalating precipitously, financial pressure from her loss of income was contributing to the tension between them, and her 17-year-old son had been busted for dealing drugs. Aiko provided Vicki with information about potential nursing home or hospice placement.

Service Provision in Nursing Homes

Nursing homes are residential centers that provide extended maintenance and personal nursing care for people who can't adequately take care of themselves. The vast majority of elderly people do not reside in nursing homes. However, a person's likelihood of spending time in a nursing home is fairly good. Approximately 1.4 million people over age 65 live in a nursing home (Newman & Newman, 2003).

The older you are, the more likely you are to have health problems that require extensive attention and help. You also become more likely to spend time in a structured environment that attends to such needs. Whereas only 13.3% of people age 65 to 74 live in a nursing home, 35.5% of those age 75 to 84, and 51.5% of those age 85 and over, live in nursing homes (U.S. Census Bureau, 2003, No. 185).

What are other characteristics of nursing home residents? In addition to being mostly age 75 and above, the nursing home population is characterized by four other characteristics: (1) 75% are female, (2) 66% are widowed, (3) 89% are white, and (4) the majority have serious illnesses or disabilities that interfere with their ability to care for themselves daily (Dey, 1997). Therefore, a typical profile of a nursing home resident is a very old, single, white woman who has extreme difficulty in providing adequate daily self-care.

In terms of staffing, nursing homes consist of seven categories (Stahlman & Kisor, 2000). These include the following:

- Dietary departments plan menus and focus on nutrition.
- Activities departments plan and operate a range of activities for residents, such as outings, crafts, games, and celebrations.
- Nursing services attend to the ongoing, daily care of residents and oversee their health care needs.
- Social services address the social and emotional needs of residents, work with their families, assist in financial planning, and link residents with services when necessary.
- Housekeeping and laundry staff perform basic daily maintenance tasks.
- Other medical staff including a medical director and various medical specialists (e.g., physical therapists, dermatologists) attend to residents' varying special needs.

Highlight 10.3 focuses on the roles of social workers in nursing homes.

Empowerment for Diverse Populations of Elderly People

Zuniga (1995) describes practice with the elderly as "complex and demanding, given the range of needs of this population, the various subgroups of at-risk elderly people, and the multiple roles social workers must undertake to address their needs" (p. 173). She adds that demographic trends indicate that practitioners will be working with increasing numbers of older people.

Cox and Parsons (1994) emphasize that an empowerment orientation to practice "can assist older people to utilize their strengths, abilities, and competencies in order to mobilize their resources toward problem solving and ultimately toward empowerment" (p. 19). They stress that empowerment rests on principles such as involving clients integrally in the problem definition and planned-change process, emphasizing and using clients' strengths, teaching needed skills, using support networks and collective action, and linking with necessary resources.

Elderly people often must deal with decreased power on several levels. First, physical health tends to decline as people age, so the elderly must rely increasingly on supportive help to survive. Second, although elderly people generally maintain good mental health (Dunkle & Norgard, 1995), many experience "a modest impairment of short-term memory, a decrease in speed of learning, a slowing of reaction

HIGHLIGHT 10.3
A Focus on Practice: Social Workers' Roles in Nursing Homes

Social workers help nursing home residents in many ways. First, they assess a resident's strengths and needs to develop and implement an appropriate treatment plan.

Second, they counsel residents when needed, helping them cope with illnesses and deteriorating functioning, deal with emotional problems, enhance social skills, and make decisions.

Third, social workers address issues concerning the residents' families. Sometimes communication difficulties must be ironed out. Other times social workers educate residents and their families about complicated medical conditions and treatments. Social workers also may assist residents and their families in making financial decisions such as applying for public assistance or a pension, contacting lawyers, or discussing end-of-life issues such as funeral arrangements.

Fourth, social workers link residents with outside services when needed. Perhaps a resident needs access to library holdings or wheelchair-capable transportation, or requires new glasses, a hearing aid, or a wheelchair.

Fifth, social workers assist other nursing home staff in understanding residents' needs and respecting their dignity. They can help residents maximize their autonomy by making their own choices whenever possible. This might involve how their room is decorated, what they wear, or what they can choose to eat. Because nursing homes are structured settings that provide such extensive care, maintaining residents' autonomy is an ongoing goal.

Finally social workers advocate for clients. Sometimes they advocate for improved quality of care or individualized attention within the nursing home setting. Other times they advocate for agency or social policies that provide more resources or better services for clients.

time, and some degree of mild forgetfulness" (Cox & Parsons, 1994, p. 23). Third, they often experience loss of support systems as their peers' health declines. Fourth, we have established that retirement may require adaptation on the elderly's part, requiring them to learn new ways to occupy their time. They may also experience feelings of uselessness when no longer employed. Fifth, the elderly may encounter age discrimination by younger people based on prejudicial stereotypes such as emphasis on physical, mental, and economic weakness.

Concepts and Strategies in Empowerment

Zuniga (1995) emphasizes four concepts essential to empowering elderly people—adaptation, competence, relatedness, and autonomy. First, social workers should focus on *adaptation* to new experiences, issues, and even losses. An empowering approach emphasizes how people use their strengths to survive, adapt to new experiences, and learn to appreciate the positive aspects of these new experiences. A second concept is *competence*. Social workers can help elderly people focus on and emphasize what they *can* do instead of what they *can't* do; each individual should appreciate her or his own level of competence. *Relatedness*, the third concept, involves the sense of belonging-ness and relating to other people. Hence practitioners should work to strengthen elderly people's relationships with others including friends, family members, and professional caregivers (e.g., visiting nurses, physical therapists). Support, activity, and educational groups are other mezzo options. Finally, *autonomy* involves helping people live as independently as possible. Zuniga (1995) comments:

> Adaptation for elderly people often is related directly to having to adjust to being less physically able, feeling weak because of an illness, having to rely on medication for the rest of their life, or having to rely on strangers for daily living needs. Thus, it appears that at every juncture, an elderly person's ability to maintain independence is threatened. Helping elderly clients accept their limitations while negotiating ways to support other areas of autonomy is a core practice need in working with this population. (p. 175)

Toseland (1995) suggests five strategies for social workers to increase their sensitivity to elderly people and thus enhance their effectiveness:

1. Identify and face any preconceived notions and stereotypes about the elderly. These must be identified before they can be eliminated or changed.
2. Appreciate the different life situations experienced by people from different age groups within the elderly population. For example, women seeking work in the 1930s will have experienced very different conditions from those employed in the 1940s (Toseland, 1995). Women in the 1930s probably had a very difficult time finding jobs during the Great Depression when unemployment was skyrocketing. However, women in the 1940s likely had a pick of many jobs when men were off fighting World War II and industry was begging women to come to work.
3. Understand that the elderly are individuals with unique characteristics, experiences, and personalities just like anybody else. Highlight 10.4 contrasts the personalities and life approaches of two women who were friends for many decades.
4. Learn about how both gender and cultural background influence the aging experience. Both elderly women and elderly people of color are much more likely to experience poor health, poverty, substandard housing conditions, and social isolation (Toseland, 1995). Long-term experiences with discrimination can affect attitudes and expectations. Worker sensitivity to cultural differences in terms of communication, family relationship, and gender roles is critical. (Chapter 12 discusses a range of cultural and ethnic differences more thoroughly.)
5. Understand the developmental aspects of later life including people's physical, mental, living, and socioeconomic conditions.

Cox and Parsons (1994) suggest six specific empowerment strategies for micro practice with elderly people. First, social workers can listen carefully to what clients are saying and work to understand what they mean. Cox and Parsons (1994) explain that "engaging and drawing out the emotions of elderly clients and helping them frame their situations in view of past experiences and events are effective listening techniques" (p. 112).

Second, social workers can help clients identify their coping skills and their abilities to implement planned change. Encouraging clients to talk about what's important to them, including their significant life experiences, is helpful. Exploring how they've coped with their difficulties in the past can also be valuable.

Third, social workers can show clients videotapes of other elderly people talking about how they've learned to cope with similar issues. As with support group

HIGHLIGHT 10.4
Diversity and Individual Differences Among the Elderly

Just like younger people, older people are unique individuals. Consider one woman, Myrtle, age 84, whose life was filled with difficulties including a decade of tuberculosis, the abrupt death from a heart attack of her husband at age 51 as he slept beside her, her caregiving responsibilities for her own aging and mentally ill mother for 15 years, and the need to pinch pennies her entire life. Nonetheless, Myrtle remained cheerful, optimistic, and interested in the world around her throughout her life. One of her nieces took her to China, Disney World, New Orleans, and Europe after she turned 78 (not all in one trip, of course).

Contrast Myrtle with Paula, also age 84, Myrtle's maid of honor 65 years earlier. Paula had a long, good life with a husband who adored her. He cooked and cleaned for her in addition to

holding a lucrative engineering job. He died when she was 78. At that time, Paula remained financially well off. Paula began experiencing health problems including hearing loss and diabetes at age 80. Complications from the diabetes forced her to enter a nursing home at age 83. Paula had always been persnickety. She demanded that she get her own way, and usually she did, thanks to her devoted spouse. She was never interested in the world around her, despite the many innovations developed during her lifetime (e.g., television, jetliners, computers). She was always a complainer; everything was always wrong.

Myrtle visited Paula faithfully every Sunday for years and endured her endless whining and complaining. There could hardly be two more different people.

involvement, this may help clients understand that they aren't isolated and alone in their concerns.

Fourth, workers can share newspaper articles, stories, and other informative materials with clients, especially those about elderly people who have initiated service activities and political action. The Gray Panthers, an advocacy organization for the rights and socioeconomic needs of elderly people, provides a good example of how people can work together for legislative and political change.

Fifth, practitioners can connect clients with other older people to provide "mutual support and education" (p. 112). Groups might include those experiencing similar life issues "such as retirement; illnesses such as Alzheimer's disease, and chronic health or mental health conditions; and families of older people who have a terminal illness" (Bellos & Ruffolo, 1995, p. 171).

Sixth, social workers can encourage clients to help others. For example, one social services agency organized a number of elderly clients and helped them assess their special competencies. They were then organized as volunteers to help each other. Those who could drive chauffeured others who couldn't for grocery shopping and medical appointments. People with good eyesight read to those who could not see as well. People with exceptional organizational skills organized and oversaw the volunteer activities. Many people put their strengths to use and became productive members of the community.

Empowerment of African American Grandparents Who Become Primary Child Caregivers

Multiple examples exist of how social workers and social welfare programs can empower the elderly. Various facets of the elderly population can be targeted and assisted in many creative ways.

Okazawa-Rey (1998) describes one approach to empowerment for African American grandparents who have become primary caregivers for their grandchildren. This reflects one type of programming social workers can initiate, develop, and provide. The problem addressed is one well established at the community and national levels. Many people have become addicted to crack cocaine or methamphetamine and are ignoring their responsibilities as parents and productive citizens to pursue drug use. An example of a program responding to this problem is the Grandparents Who Care Support Network of San Francisco. Most members are "poor and working class, middle-aged and elderly African-American women" (Okazawa-Rey, 1998, p. 54). They have gained custody of their grandchildren because of their own children's neglect. This is due to drug abuse, incarceration because of drug convictions, and an unwillingness to relinquish their grandchildren to strangers in the public foster care system.

These grandparents have found themselves in the strange and unusual circumstance of suddenly having responsibility for small children at a stage in life when they thought they were done with all that. This situation is compounded by the health problems many of these children suffer due to poor prenatal care, parental drug use during pregnancy, and child neglect. These grandparents "desperately need day care, special education services, transportation, respite care, and money" (Okazawa-Rey, 1998, p. 54). To get services, they find themselves trying to negotiate the confusing maze of bureaucracies governing service provision.

Two health care workers, Doriane Miller and Sue Trupin, identified the problems and needs and established Grandparents Who Care (Okazawa-Rey, 1998). The program is based on four principles. First, individual health problems transcend any assignment of individual blame; rather, they are related to problems in the environment. Second, cultural, legal, and organizational barriers often hinder access to needed services. Third, even if people can obtain needed services, these may be inadequate to meet their needs. Fourth, empowerment at the micro, mezzo, and macro levels is necessary for maintaining optimal health and well-being. The grandparents require not only support as individuals (a facet of micro practice) but also the development of an organization (an aspect of macro practice) to provide support group services (a dimension of mezzo practice).

Mezzo Practice Perspectives: Establishing Support Groups

Grandparents Who Care established a series of support groups to provide information, emotional support, and practical advice. Groups consist of 2–25 grandparents, are co-led by professional health care personnel including social workers and nurses, and meet weekly for 90 minutes. Grandparents Who Care has a board of directors made up of grandparents, citizens, and concerned health care professionals who advise the organization.

Group members support each other in addressing a range of issues. For example, "When one woman faces a particular problem with her grandchild in the school system, another one will describe her dealings with this system and offer suggestions concerning the most effective ways to intercede" (Okazawa-Rey, 1998, p. 58). In this way members can share their experiences and work through issues. The professional coleaders can assist the group by providing technical information about service availability, eligibility, and accessibility.

Macro Practice Perspectives: Expanding Influence

Grandparents Who Care expanded its work in several macro dimensions to further empower its members. First, grandparents were trained as group leaders to go out and form new groups, thereby extending support to grandparents elsewhere in the community.

Second, Grandparents Who Care undertook political advocacy and lobbying on its members' behalf. One problem advocates addressed involved the legal difficulties grandparents experienced in receiving foster care payments. As relatives, they did not technically qualify as foster parents. Other financial support available to them was not nearly as good as that provided to unrelated foster parents. Grandparents Who Care advocates lobbied with a state legislator to pass a bill allowing grandparents to receive increased benefits.

Appreciation of Spirituality and Empowerment for Navajo Elders in a Nursing Home

The Navajo community traditionally has maintained a rich fabric of cultural traditions, values, and spiritual beliefs. It is a nongeographical community because of its intricate interpersonal relationships, sense of identity, and recognition of members' belongingness regardless of where they reside. Members are tied to each other by much more than simple location. Of course, many Navajos live on the Navajo reservation, a large geographical community located in the south central Colorado Plateau, which includes parts of Arizona, New Mexico, and Utah. (Geographical communities have geographical boundaries and occupy a designated space.)

An ongoing theme in social work practice is the importance of responding to diverse ethnic and cultural values and needs. The following account portrays how the Navajo community and a nursing home it sponsors have responded to meet the needs of aging members in ways differing from commonly held Euro-American traditions.

A Focus on Traditional Navajo Values

Traditional Navajo elders, referred to here as "Grandparents," adhere to cultural values that differ from Euro-American traditions. For one thing, Mercer (1996) explains that

> traditional Navajo religion deals with controlling the many supernatural powers in the Navajo world. Earth Surface People (living and dead humans) and Holy People (supernatural beings) interact. . . . Navajos abide by prescriptions and proscriptions (taboos) given by the Holy People to maintain harmony with others, nature, and supernatural forces. . . . The goal of traditional Navajo life is to live in harmony and die of old age. If one indulges in excesses, has improper contacts with dangerous powers, or deliberately

or accidentally breaks other rules, then disharmony, conflict, evil, sickness of body and mind, misfortune, and disaster result. (pp. 182–183)[6]

Thus, when an imbalance occurs, a person may become sick, which can be attributed to "infection by animals, natural phenomena, or evil spirits such as ghosts (*chindi*) and witches" (p. 183). Preventive ceremonies can address the root of the illness, involve the appropriate Holy People, seek to restore harmony, and forestall ill fortune. "As major social and religious events involving entire communities, ceremonies are a major investment of time and resources for the afflicted person, extended family, and clan" (p. 183).

Another primary traditional value in Navajo life is the importance placed on the extended family. Referred to as a *clan*, such families include a much more extensive membership than that of grandparents, parents, and children. The Navajo community has "over 60 clan-based kinship groups." A related concept is the importance of the *hogan,* or home, as the center of Navajo family life.

Culturally Competent Treatment of Elderly Navajo People

Mercer (1996) explored the treatment of elderly Navajo people, the Grandparents, who reside in the Chinle Nursing Home, a nonprofit agency whose board of directors is composed solely of Navajos. She investigated how treatment for Grandparents in Chinle differs from typical treatment provided outside the reservation. She found that, essentially, Chinle emphasizes the importance of *cultural care*—"the learned and transmitted values and beliefs that enable people to maintain their well-being and health and to deal with illness, disability, and death" (Leininger, 1990, 1992; Mercer, 1996, p. 186).

Mercer (1996) found that culturally competent care is applied in at least six major areas (pp. 186–188):

1. *Communication:* Few Navajo Grandparents are fluent in English, so translators are used. Such translation is done with great sensitivity, because the Navajo language often has no word that means exactly what an English word does. Additionally, sensitivity is important while listening because interrupting a speaker is considered extremely rude.
2. *Clan associations and social structure:* Clan associations are very important to Navajo people. Upon introduction, Navajos traditionally announce their clan membership. Nursing home staff are sensitive to the fact that Grandparents often have many visitors from their clan who have traveled great distances at significant cost.
3. *Personal space, modesty, privacy, and cleanliness:* Grandparents value personal space. They often find it difficult and uncomfortable to sleep in the high nursing home beds, having been accustomed to mattresses or sheep skins on the floor. Staff comply with Grandparents' wishes to sleep where they want and usually find that Grandparents eventually adjust to sleeping in beds.

   Grandparents also value modesty and privacy. Therefore, communal showering is a problem. Rather, Grandparents often prefer sweat baths, which they feel

---

[6]This case example is taken from S. O. Mercer (1996, March). Navajo elderly people in a reservation nursing home: Admission predictors and culture care practices. *Social Work, 41* (2), 181–189. Copyright 1996, National Association of Social Workers, Inc., Social Work. Reprinted with permission.

cleanse them both physically and spiritually. The nursing home provides saunas to simulate these sweat baths and offers showers to residents twice each week.

Finally, Grandparents often prefer sleeping in their daytime clothes rather than changing into nightgowns or pajamas. Staff allow Grandparents to sleep in whatever they want. In time most choose night clothes.

4. *Traditional food:* Grandparents prefer "grilled mutton [meat of a mature sheep], mutton stew, fry bread, corn, fried potatoes, and coffee" (p. 187). In response, nursing home staff serve lamb three times a month and usually bake fresh bread. Staff also encourage family members to bring foods Grandparents prefer, as long as these comply with health-related dietary constraints.

5. *Dying and death:* "Traditional Navajo people have many restrictions regarding contact with the dead. They do not talk about death, believing that discussing death may 'bring it to you'" (p. 187). Navajo families will usually move a dying person to a nearby brush shelter to avoid having death occur in the hogan. In the event of a home death, that hogan is usually deserted and even demolished.

Traditionally, people touching a dead body followed specific rituals to avoid taboos. Similarly, most Grandparents and staff seek to avoid touching a dead person or his or her clothing. Usually a dying Grandparent is transferred to a hospital so that death will not occur in the nursing home. If a death does occur there, cleansing rituals are performed before other residents inhabit the room.

Because of their aversion to talking about death, no Grandparents will discuss such issues as living wills or power of attorney. Staff respect this value and do not pressure residents to do so.

6. *Cultural rituals:* To hold cultural rituals, a hogan was constructed near Chinle and is made available for ceremonies and prayers that remain important aspects of Grandparents' lives.

Examples of how diverse communities and social agencies may respond to members' values and needs are countless. The important thing for social workers is to respect and appreciate cultural differences and strive to help social services meet diverse members' needs.

Looking Ahead

This chapter addressed the needs of the elderly, a population-at-risk in terms of poverty, discrimination, and other problems associated with aging such as declines in health. It discussed service provision to the elderly and approaches to empowerment. Chapter 11 focuses on another population-at-risk that has special needs for policies and services—people with disabilities.

For Further Exploration on the Internet

See this text's Book Companion Website at **www.socialwork.wadsworth.com/ kirstashman_intro2e** for descriptors and hot links to URLs relevant to this chapter, selected InfoTrac articles and exercises, and tutorial quizzes.

CHAPTER ✸ ELEVEN

SOCIAL WORK AND SERVICES
FOR PEOPLE WITH DISABILITIES

© Tony Savino/The Image Works

Jane, age 20, was on a motorcycle outing with her fiancé, age 21, when he crashed head-on into a tree while trying to evade an oncoming car.[1] He was killed instantly. Jane's leg was so mangled she ultimately had to have it removed. "One year later she was seen by a social worker during her rehabilitation of the amputation. She was demonstrating signs of complicated grief and traumatic stress: continuing to live in her fiancé's room, refusing to let anyone remove his possessions from the room, delaying rehabilitation of her severed limb, and developing increasing fears and phobias. With the social worker she began to confront her anger toward her fiancé for losing control of the bike and causing her amputation, an emotion that seemed unacceptable to her since she had survived and he had not. Expressing and working through these feelings empowered her to become active in making more realistic plans for her life, including moving out of her fiancé's room" (Christ, Sormanti, & Francoeur, 2001, p. 126).

Jane provides an example of a person who has experienced a disability resulting from an accident happening when she was an adult. Of course, people can also be born with disabilities or gradually acquire them as a result of chronic debilitating illness. Regardless of the cause, social workers can fulfill at least the following roles when working with people who have disabilities:

- As counselors, social workers help people explore their feelings, confront issues, and make life plans. They can work with individuals, families, or groups to address various aspects of life with disability. For example, social workers may help families of people with disabilities discuss interpersonal issues, focus on strengths, cope with difficulties, and address needs. Similarly, working with groups of people with disabilities may involve exploring feelings, coping mechanisms, and potential resources in addition to providing mutual support.
- As educators, social workers provide information about disabilities and related issues.
- As brokers, social workers link people who have disabilities and their families with needed services.
- As rehabilitative team members, social workers consult with occupational therapists, physical therapists, speech therapists, psychologists, nurses, and other medical personnel to develop coordinated treatment plans for people with disabilities.
- As case coordinators, social workers synchronize and oversee service provision for people with disabilities who have multiple needs.
- As advocates, social workers seek to improve the treatment of people with disabilities through legislation and agency provision of service.

The U.S. Census Bureau indicates that almost 48 million people in the United States, or 23% of the population age 15 or older, have some type of disability; of these, almost 64% or some 30.5 million people have a "severe disability" (U.S. Census Bureau, 2000, No. 222).

Who are people with disabilities? They are anyone who has a permanent "physical or mental impairment [or ongoing health or mental health condition] that substantially limits

---

[1]This vignette was cited in Christ, Sormanti, and Francoeur (2001, pp. 124–162).

one or more major life activities"; these activities include "seeing, hearing, speaking, walking, breathing, performing manual tasks, learning, caring for oneself, and working" (Equal Employment Opportunity Commission, 1997, p. 1). Disabilities, which vary widely in severity and the extent to which they affect daily functioning, can commence at any point in life, from birth to old age.

To some extent, disabilities are related to both poverty and race. People who are poor are more likely to experience disability, and more severe disabilities, than people who are better off financially. And African Americans age 45–64 are four times as likely to experience disability as white Americans in that same age group (Christ et al., 2001).

How various people including experts categorize disabilities varies markedly, depending on what aspects of the disability they emphasize. For example, *developmental disabilities* involve early onset and a lifelong time span. This umbrella concept can include difficulties in cognitive ability such as mental retardation and physical disabilities such as orthopedic problems, affecting bones and joints, and hearing problems.

Mobility disabilities, in contrast, can occur at any time. Mobility disabilities reflect a lack of physical ability to get around and conduct life tasks.

However, different categories of disability may overlap. Some mobility disabilities can also be considered developmental. For instance, a person with cerebral palsy (a type of developmental disability involving problems in muscular control) who cannot walk without crutches also has a mobility disability.

Mobility disabilities are also a type of *physical disability* because they involve physical bodily performance, as opposed to cognitive or emotional functioning. Many developmental disabilities such as hearing loss or visual impairment are also physical disabilities because of their physical rather than mental nature. The matter is further complicated because many people have multiple disabilities.

The point of this discussion is not to confuse you but to clarify this chapter's overall approach to the wide range of disabilities. Arbitrary distinctions are made regarding how disabilities are sorted and discussed. It is far beyond the scope of this chapter to cover all disabilities. Thus the intent is to provide a general introduction to what disabilities might involve and how social work practitioners help empower people who have them.

On one hand, social workers practice directly with people who have disabilities and their families on the micro and mezzo levels. On the other, social workers have a responsibility to advocate on behalf of people with disabilities to make sure they get the resources and services they need.

A primary goal of social work education is "to formulate and implement social policies, services, and programs that meet basic human needs and support the development of human capacities" (Council on Social Work Education [CSWE], 2001, I.A). Social workers strive to enhance people's living conditions in their social environment to make them as comfortable and supportive as possible. To accomplish this, social workers should "pursue policies, services, and resources through advocacy and social or political actions that promote social and economic justice" (CSWE, 2001, I.A).

This chapter will

- Define mobility disabilities and developmental disabilities, and identify a range of specific disabilities clustered under each concept.

- Investigate the importance of self-determination for people with disabilities as an ethical aspect of social work practice.
- Examine the history of how people with developmental disabilities have been treated in the macro social environment.
- Describe generalist social work practice with people who have developmental disabilities.
- Discuss avenues of legislative, community, and worker empowerment.
- Examine the macro environment's potential for empowering people with visual impairment and cognitive disabilities.
- Encourage critical thinking about residual versus institutional approaches to service provision for people with disabilities, empowerment through language, deinstitutionalization, and the Americans with Disabilities Act.

People with Mobility Disabilities

People who have mobility disabilities "are those whose physical differences compel them to achieve physical activities in a variety of alternate ways" (Mackelprang & Salsgiver, 1999, p. 82). For example, a person with a spinal cord injury may require a wheelchair to move from place to place and achieve the mobility needed to conduct the business of life.

Mobility disorders may be *congenital*—that is, "acquired before, during, or immediately after birth"—or they may be *acquired* at some time later in life (Mackelprang & Salsgiver, 1999, p. 83). Many congenital mobility disabilities are also considered developmental disabilities (e.g., cerebral palsy, orthopedic problems) and will be discussed later in the chapter. A number of acquired mobility problems are described in Highlight 11.1.

Ethical Implications for Social Work Practice: The Importance of Self-Determination

It's easy to make false assumptions about people who have mobility and other physical disabilities. Myths about disabilities include the following:

Myth: The more severe a physical disability is, the less intelligent the person (Hallahan & Kauffman, 2000).
Fact: A person may have a severe physical disability and yet have a brilliant mind.
Myth: People with physical disabilities are unable to function normally in society.
Fact: People with physical disabilities can live productive, fruitful, happy lives when they receive the support they need.
Myth: People with one kind of disability also have other disabilities.
Fact: One disability may have nothing to do with other disabilities. A person with one disability can function as well as anyone else in other areas. This myth sometimes is referred to as the *spread of disability.*

HIGHLIGHT 11.1
Acquired Mobility Disabilities

The following are examples of *acquired* mobility disabilities (Mackelprang & Salsgiver, 1999). All may require the use of supportive equipment depending on the severity.

- *Stroke:* "[A] blockage or hemorrhage of a blood vessel leading to the brain, causing an inadequate oxygen supply and often long-term impairment of sensation, movement, or functioning" (Nichols, 1999, p. 1295). Brain cells die when they don't receive adequate oxygen, causing damage to the nervous system. Strokes can result in a wide range of symptoms including partial or total paralysis, memory loss, speech or language deficits, and inability to think clearly.
- *Muscular dystrophy:* "[A]ny of a group of hereditary diseases characterized by a progressive wasting of the muscles" (Mish, 1995, p. 766). Some forms progress so quickly that people require the use of wheelchairs by the time they reach adolescence. Symptoms include increasingly weakened muscles, an awkward gait, and increasing lack of coordination.
- *Rheumatoid arthritis (RA):* A chronic condition in which a person's immune system attacks the joints, causing pain, inflammation, stiffness, swelling, and deterioration. Joints tend to experience progressive deformity, often resulting in

the need for increased support through devices like canes, crutches, or wheelchairs. About 1% of the adult population in the United States has this disease, three-quarters of whom are women (Mackelprang & Salsgiver, 1999, p. 88).
- *Multiple sclerosis (MS):* A disease of the brain tissue in which the myelin sheath—the fatty material wrapped around and insulating the parts of nerve cells that conduct nerve impulses in the brain to other nerve cells—deteriorates, thereby causing varying degrees of muscular dysfunction, paralysis, and muscle tremors.
- *Myasthenia gravis (MG):* A disease affecting voluntary muscles (those controlled by one's will) in which nerve impulses are impaired, resulting in fatigue, weakness, and difficulties controlling muscles. Virtually any muscles can be affected, and symptoms range from weakness in the arms and legs to difficulties in swallowing, controlling eye movements, or breathing.
- *Spinal cord injury:* Damage to the spinal cord, often due to accidents or incidents of violence, resulting in the loss of muscular control and inability to experience sensation. Paraplegia is paralysis of the lower part of the body; quadriplegia is paralysis from the neck down. Severity of effects depends on the location and extent of damage to the spinal cord.

For example, Steve, age 19, has quadriplegia—the paralysis of all four limbs. He broke his neck in a swimming accident three years ago. He tells the story of how he went out to eat with his parents at a local family restaurant several months after the accident. The waitress approached the table and began to take orders. When it was Steve's turn to order, the waitress turned to his father and asked, "What would he like to order?"

Steve's father replied, "I don't know. Why don't you ask him?"

The waitress turned to Steve and shouted verrrrrry slowly, "WHAT . . . WOULD . . . YOU . . . LIKE . . . TO . . . ORDER?"

Steve, whose hearing was just fine, verrrrrry slowly shouted back, "A . . . QUARTER POUND . . . CHEESEBURGER . . . AND . . . FRIES . . . PLEASE!"

The waitress had made the assumption that because Steve couldn't walk and had limited use of his arms, he couldn't hear, either. She also took for granted that there was something wrong with his brain. She made the mistake of assuming a spread of disability—namely, that a person with one disability automatically has others.

People with disabilities have

> rights to participate fully and equitably in society. These rights include the freedom, to the fullest extent possible, of all people with disabilities to live independently, to enjoy the rights of full societal membership, to exercise self-determination, and to have full participation in issues related to education, housing, transportation, work, health care, social services, and other public accommodations. (NASW, 2000, p. 247)

The concept of self-determination has special ethical implications for adults with mobility and other physical disabilities. Major (2000) indicates that "[c]lient self-determination is closely linked with the concept of autonomy"—a person's ability to function independently (p. 9). Related to the type and degree of their disabilities, people with physical disabilities often experience greater difficulties maintaining autonomy than able-bodied people. For example, a person with a serious visual impairment may have great difficulty getting around in an unfamiliar neighborhood without assistance.

Gilson, Bricout, and Baskind (1998) interviewed six people with physical disabilities who felt that social workers tended to focus more on their health status and limitations than on themselves as unique individuals. Ethical concerns included stereotyping people based on the disability label and clearly visible disabilities, ignoring strengths, accessing personal information without receiving client permission, and not consulting with clients as expert resources for information about their disabilities and issues. Despite the small sample size, this study, with its implications of paternalism by practitioners, raises serious ethical questions regarding social workers' efforts to maximize self-determination. Apparently it is easy for social workers to make assumptions about people with disabilities that emphasize weakness instead of strength.

Social workers should follow three recommendations to maximize service provision and client self-determination. These include adopting a consumer-centered approach, learning about services and resources, and advocating for clients with disabilities whenever possible.

Adopting a Consumer-Oriented Approach

First, social workers should adopt a *consumer-centered approach* (Tower, 1994, p. 191). Treating people as consumers means accepting that they know their own needs and can make intelligent decisions about services. The term *consumer* implies greater power and choice than does the term *client*. This approach contrasts sharply with that of making decisions about what's best for clients without their input, recommendations, and consent. Adopting a consumer-centered approach, of course, is important in working with any client. However, because of stereotypes and misconceptions about disability, social workers must be particularly vigilant about this when working with clients who have disabilities.

Four facets are especially important. First, social workers must listen carefully to what the client is saying instead of jumping to conclusions based on the disability label.

Second, they must ask questions and seek clarification whenever they do not understand something. Third, they must scrutinize any possible assumptions they may be making about their client and his or her disability. In essence, they must confront their stereotypes and work to get rid of them. Fourth, they should obtain clients' *informed consent*. This is the condition in which clients grant permission for a social worker to undertake the intervention process after the worker clearly informs clients of all the facts, risks, and alternatives involved (National Association of Social Workers [NASW] 1996, 1.03).

Case Example Kachina is a case manager for people with severe physical disabilities. Earlier chapters established that case managers are practitioners who, on behalf of a specific client, assess needs; coordinate required services provided by any number of agencies, organizations, or facilities; and monitor service provision. Usually one individual is designated case manager for specific cases and coordinates a range of services, often provided by a variety of workers from different agencies. The intent is to make total service provision as effective and efficient as possible.

Kachina often coordinates services of group homes, in-home support services, Meals on Wheels, medical centers, physical therapists, speech therapists, occupational therapists, and others depending on individual client needs. Kachina always makes it a point to work the service plan out with individual clients, obtaining their permission to proceed. She reviews with clients the pros and cons of each prescribed service. She works hard to make certain clients understand what each service involves and what expectations they must fulfill. For example, physical therapy might involve a designated number of weekly sessions, physical work, and possible pain. Positive results may include significantly increased agility, flexibility, strength, and speed. Clients then can make informed decisions about whether to proceed with that service.

Learning About Services and Resources

A second way social workers can maximize service provision and self-determination for people with disabilities is to learn about services and resources (Major, 2000; NASW, 2000). People with physical disabilities have the same needs and wants as able-bodied people. They simply have more obstacles getting in the way of what they need. Services include those associated with rehabilitation, employment, health, place of residence, recreation, and personal care. Financial resources include various sources of public funding such as disability insurance, workers' compensation, Supplemental Security Income (SSI), and other forms of public assistance.

The Self-Determination Movement: Recommendations for Policy Change

Major (2000) urges that social workers familiarize themselves with various advocacy and resource groups. For example, the Self-Determination Movement, funded by grants from the Robert Wood Johnson Foundation, "is an attempt on the part of people with disabilities to guarantee client autonomy in their quest for services" (Major, 2000, p. 11). It provides an information network, advocacy, and a range of supportive services. Additionally, supporters encourage public policy changes that incorporate self-determination initiatives.

The Self-Determination Movement is founded on four primary principles (National Program Office on Self Determination [NPOSD], 1998). First, *freedom* concerns people with disabilities having the same rights as other citizens. They should be able to choose where they want to live and how to spend their time just like anybody else.

The second principle, *authority*, involves people with disabilities having control over their own finances, prioritizing how their money should be spent, and developing their own budgets. Major (2000) cites the following example:

> [A] married couple who had been previously receiving supports and services from two different agencies "frequently sought psychiatric hospitalizations to be together" (NPOSD, 1998). After implementing a self-determination program, the couple now lives together and is served by one agency. Because the couple can supply each other with many of the supports they need, they are much more comfortable and content with their situation. What is equally important to note here is that the overall cost of providing their services has decreased significantly. (p. 12)

Support, the third foundation principle for the Self-Determination Movement, involves having people with disabilities make decisions about where their support comes from. Instead of being given "supervision," people with disabilities should be able to seek their own support systems for companionship. Similarly, they should be able to determine what specific tasks necessitate formal assistance from paid staff and others.

The final principle, *responsibility*, involves the wise disbursement of public funding. Resources used by people with disabilities should be considered as investments in their quality of life, and not simply as lists specifying purchase of specific services. Just as all citizens should be responsible for the efficient and effective use of resources, so should they. Similarly, people with disabilities should be able to contribute to their communities' well-being in meaningful ways (e.g., volunteering, voting, running for public office).

Advocating for Clients with Disabilities Whenever Possible

A third suggestion for social workers to maximize service provision and client self-determination involves advocating for clients with disabilities whenever possible (NASW, 2000). Clients may need expanded services or additional resources. Social work practitioners work with their clients to determine their needs. Workers also strive to change agency policy and laws governing resources to benefit people with physical disabilities. Subsequent sections of the chapter discuss advocacy in more detail.

Sometimes political advocacy is necessary. The Americans with Disabilities Act of 1990 (ADA), discussed more thoroughly later in the chapter, is a good example of positive legislation on behalf of people with disabilities. Focus on Critical Thinking 11.1 raises questions concerning value orientations to working with people who have disabilities and social welfare policy perspectives.

 # Defining Developmental Disabilities

Five attributes characterize people with *developmental disabilities* (DeWeaver, 1995; Freedman, 1995; P.L. 101-496, 104 Stat. 1191, 1990). First, the disability is both severe and chronic, resulting from some mental or physical impairment.

FOCUS ON CRITICAL THINKING 11.1

Residual Versus Institutional Approaches to Service Provision for People with Disabilities

Think about the following questions:

- To what extent do the suggestions for empowerment through promoting self-determination for people with disabilities reflect *residual* versus *institutional* policies and programming? (Recall that residual policies focus on reactions to problems, generally providing as few benefits as possible. Institutional policies view social services as people's right and provide ongoing benefits to enhance people's lives and well-being.)
- To what extent does service provision for people with disabilities demonstrate *conservative* versus *liberal* values?

Now consider the three basic principles involved that relate to the following questions (these are similar to the questions posed concerning value orientations to service provision to the elderly):

- Who should assume responsibility? Should people with disabilities be expected to provide for and take care of themselves? Or is it society's responsibility to help them when they need it?
- Who is to blame for the problems and needs of people with disabilities? To what extent will people with disabilities take advantage of social welfare benefits when they really don't need them? Will providing ongoing services and benefits significantly enhance their health, welfare, and comfort?
- To what extent should the government interfere in people's lives? Is it the government's responsibility to improve the health and functioning of people with disabilities?

Second, the disability occurs before age 22. Third, the conditions are likely to be permanent. Fourth, the disability "results in substantial functional limitations in three or more of the following areas of major life activity: (i) self-care, (ii) receptive and expressive language, (iii) learning, (iv) mobility, (v) self-direction, (vi) capacity for independent living, and (vii) economic self-sufficiency" (P.L. 101-496, 104 Stat. 1191, 1990). Fifth, a developmental disability demonstrates the need for lifelong supplementary help and services.

Examples of developmental disabilities are cognitive disabilities, cerebral palsy, epilepsy, orthopedic problems, hearing impairment or deafness, visual impairment or blindness, and autism (DeWeaver, 1995). Each has serious implications for living in the macro social environment.

Cognitive Disabilities

Cognitive disabilities (also referred to as *mental retardation*) involve a condition manifested before age 18 such that an individual scores significantly below average on standard intelligence tests and has deficits in adaptive functioning (i.e., the ability to conduct daily living tasks) (American Psychiatric Association [APA], 2000).

FOCUS ON CRITICAL THINKING 11.2
Empowerment Through Language: People with Cognitive Disabilities

How do the words you use to describe people affect your opinions about them and the way you view them? To what extent can labels place people in a negative—or positive—light?

The following brief discussion focuses on the significance of words with respect to people who have cognitive disabilities. After reading it, think about what terms might be best to use when talking about this population. The *Encyclopedia of Social Work* notes that terms used to discuss these people continue to change:

> Today such terms as "retarded," "handicapped," and "disabled" people are no longer appropriate. The preferred terminology is "persons with" whatever condition, to emphasize the people, rather than the conditions. In addition, some agencies have been asked to change the term "client" to "consumer" and the term "problems" to "challenges." (DeWeaver, 1995, p. 714)

The term *mental retardation* clearly has negative connotations. One of the nastiest things children call other children when they're angry or making fun of others is "Retard!" or "Mental!" Social workers and others working with people who have this type of disability are trying to use less negative terms.

The term *cognitive disabilities* can be used to refer to people with *intellectual impairment*, a term that is less negative than *mental retardation*. However, note that even the term *cognitive disabilities* can be confusing because it may be used differently depending on the context. The American Psychiatric Association (2000) includes *delirium, dementia,* and *amnesia* among other cognitive disorders; it also still uses the term *mental retardation* as a diagnostic category. Others use the term *cognitive disability* to refer to such conditions as traumatic brain injury (Mackelprang & Salsgiver, 1999).

Also, note that, as indicated earlier, it is important to refer to people with disabilities as *people* before referring to any disability they might have (NASW, 2000). For example, referring to them simply as mentally or cognitively disabled people tends to emphasize the disability because the disability is stated first.

This book will use the term *people with cognitive disabilities* because it is currently one of the least negative, and thus most empowering, ways to refer to this population. It is interesting that Moreno (2001) suggests using the term disAbility (with a capital A) to replace *disability* (p. 205).

People with cognitive disabilities make up the largest group of people with developmental disabilities (Freedman, 1995). Focus on Critical Thinking 11.2 examines the language used to refer to people with such disabilities.

Cerebral Palsy

Cerebral palsy is a disability involving problems in muscular control and coordination resulting from damage to the brain before it has matured—that is, before or during birth. Problems include lack of balance, difficulty walking, weakness, and uncontrolled or restricted movements, depending on where in the brain the damage occurred. It should be emphasized that these people may experience only motor impairment, with intellectual ability being unaffected.

Epilepsy

Epilepsy (commonly referred to as *seizure disorder*) is an abrupt change in an individual's conscious state that may involve unconsciousness, convulsive motor activity, or sensory distortions. Seizures are caused by sudden bursts of electrical activity in some brain cells causing reactions in other brain cells. Epilepsy can result from virtually any type of injury to or condition in the brain including insufficient oxygen, chemical imbalances, infections, and physical damage (Hallahan & Kauffman, 2003).

Orthopedic Problems

Orthopedic problems "involve difficulties in the functioning of muscles, bones, and joints" (DeWeaver, 1995, p. 714). Although there is no neurological impairment, orthopedic problems result in an inability to move about normally. Usually difficulties involve "the legs, arms, joints, or spine, making it difficult or impossible for the child to walk, stand, sit, or use his or her hands" (Hallahan & Kauffman, 2003, p. 428). These problems can have genetic origins or can result from injury, disease, accidents, or other developmental disorders (Hallahan & Kauffman, 2003).

Hearing Impairment

Hearing impairment is a general concept indicating a hearing loss that can range from mild to extremely severe. At the extreme, a person who is deaf has no ability to hear sound or to process information through hearing. Depending on its severity, a hearing impairment can seriously influence an individual's ability to speak, communicate, and learn (DeWeaver, 1995).

Visual Impairment

Visual impairment is difficulty in perception compared to the norm that is experienced through sight. Many people have a mild visual impairment correctable by glasses or contact lenses. People of special concern here are those whose vision cannot be corrected and so experience significant functional limitations. Rothman (2003) explains:

> We are all familiar with the expression "20/20 vision." Having 20/20 vision means that one can see, at a distance of 20 feet, what a "normal" eye can see. As visual acuity decreases, the standard 20 that represent "20 feet" remains the same, but the second number changes. The higher the second number, the greater the visual impairment. To be *legally blind* [emphasis added] a person's vision must be 20/200, meaning that he or she can see at 20 feet what the "normal" eye can see at 200 feet. A measure of 20/80 in the best eye, with corrections, indicates a visual impairment. Using this model, there are about 500,000 people in the United States who are legally blind (Mackelprang & Salsgiver, 1999, p. 125) and a much larger number who are visually impaired. (p. 131)

Autism

Autism is an all-encompassing condition often characterized by four conditions (Hallahan & Kauffman, 2003). First, people with autism have an intense inner directedness and problems such as inability to participate in "normal" social interaction and relationships. Second, they tend to experience communication difficulties. They might have difficulties acquiring language in the first place, effectively expressing their thoughts and feelings, or accurately reading the meaning of nonverbal behavior and facial expressions. Third, they often demonstrate repetitive self-stimulating movements such as waving a hand in front of their eyes for a long time. Fourth, they may experience an intense obsession with objects, a limited range of interests that can capture their attention, and a compulsive need for predictability and sameness (e.g., they won't tolerate a piece of furniture being moved).

It should be emphasized that people differ markedly in the extent to which they experience each of these conditions. Additionally, similar or related conditions exist such as *Asperger syndrome* (AS), which is "much like mild autism [often with social and emotional deficiencies], but usually without significant delays in cognition and language" (Hallahan & Kauffman, 2003, p. 376). For example, a person with AS might do reasonably well in school and be fairly adept at communication. However, that person might also find it difficult establishing "normal" interpersonal relationships in addition to feeling the compulsive need to control his or her environment.

Multiple Disabilities

Any individual may experience several disabilities at the same time (Freedman, 1995; DeWeaver, 1995). For instance, a person with cognitive disabilities may also have an orthopedic problem or epilepsy (Freedman, 1995). A developmental disability may originate in some genetic disorder or from a problem occurring before, during, or after birth (DeWeaver, 1995). It may also result from problems derived from some combination of these conditions.

Treatment over Time of People with Developmental Disabilities: The Quest for Social and Economic Justice

Because of the difficulties experienced by people with developmental disabilities, community support systems and available agency resources are extremely important. How community residents and macro-level decision makers view people with developmental disabilities has tremendous implications for the latter's quality of life. To more fully understand the macro social environment's impacts, Mary (1998) describes how community attitudes and resulting social policies have changed in recent decades.

Prior to the Late 1960s: Individual Pathology

Until the late 1960s, community treatment and public policy emphasized individual pathology. The medical model formed the basis for conceptualizing developmental disabilities. People were considered "patients," with caregivers focusing on individual diagnoses and the resulting problems (Mary, 1998, p. 249; NASW, 2000). This "traditional model emphasized pathology, deficit, and malfunctioning . . . inappropriately viewing . . . [people with disabilities] as passive, dependent, and deficient" (NASW,

2000, p. 246). Many people with developmental disabilities were placed in large state or regional institutions, where they received custodial care and were kept clean and safe. These times obviously did not foster the current strong professional values of client self-determination and empowerment.

The 1970s and 1980s: A Community-Based Approach

The 1970s and early 1980s saw significant changes in how people with developmental disabilities were viewed. Principles becoming important, especially for people with cognitive disabilities, were "normalization," deinstitutionalization, "individual program planning," and "the developmental model" (Mary, 1998, p. 249).

Normalization

Normalization is the belief that every person, even those with the most severe disabilities, "should have an educational and living environment as close to normal as possible" (Hallahan & Kauffman, 2003, p. 40). Previously, people with developmental disabilities had been placed "out of sight and mind" in obscurely located institutions. During the 1970s and 1980s, however, communities and organizations started viewing such people as clients who had a right to live as normally as possible. This approach "shifted much of the problem from the individual to the environment" (Mary, 1998, p. 250). Instead of focusing on people's negative diagnoses, emphasis was placed on the importance of the social environment for an individual's quality of life.

Deinstitutionalization

A parallel concept to normalization is *deinstitutionalization*—the practice of moving people who require supportive care for physical or mental conditions from institutional settings into the community (DeWeaver, 1995; Mary, 1998; Mish, 1995). Community facilities vary in size and complexity, and include larger transitional settings, group homes, family homes, and individual residences. Placement depends on client needs and facility availability. Sometimes these facilities are referred to as *community-based residential facilities* (CBRFs). As explained earlier, deinstitutionalization assumes that the more people with developmental disabilities can be assimilated into the community and lead "normal" lives, the better their quality of life will be. Focus on Critical Thinking 11.3 addresses some of the problems with this approach.

Individual Program Planning

Social workers, often functioning as case managers, developed *individual programs*, a third principle espoused in the 1970s and 1980s. Such programs emphasized people's environments and intervention results that would enhance their functioning within those environments. With intervention, the focus was on helping people with disabilities "maximize independence and self-determination" (NASW, 2000) in the least restrictive environment possible (Garvin & Tropman, 1998; Mary, 1998; Suppes & Wells, 2003). The concept of *least restrictive environment* (discussed in Chapter 9) concerns the encouragement of clients to enjoy as much freedom and to make as many decisions for themselves as they can. This concept is related to normalization and deinstitutionalization. That is, people living in the community are more likely to lead normal lives and make their own decisions than those living under institutional care. Evaluating the effectiveness of entire programs was also stressed.

FOCUS ON CRITICAL THINKING 11.3
Deinstitutionalization: An Attempt at Empowerment

Think about people with cognitive disabilities who need some degree of support and care. Is it better to shelter and coddle them, to ensure that they're protected from life's perils—and many of its pleasures? Or is it worth the effort to encourage as much independence as possible? Consider the following issues concerning deinstitutionalization.

Although the proponents of deinstitutionalization had good intentions and many successes, there were also significant problems. For one thing, simply placing clients in the community did not necessarily mean integration or acceptance in that community (Mary, 1998). It did not mean automatic attitude readjustments on the part of community residents to alter their old stereotypes and unfounded fears about people with developmental disabilities.

Another problem with deinstitutionalization concerned inadequate community resources and services. Institutions were expensive, but so were community-based services. People could get lost and be severed from service provision altogether. Frequently community-based services were furnished "by a complex and often fragmented set of local and state agencies" providing an unevenly distributed conglomeration of public and private services (Freedman, 1995, p. 722). Service provision could be confusing to clients and their families because some services were available to the general public and others only to those with specific disabilities (DeWeaver, 1995). (Try calling the Social Security Office to get some specific information about a case. See how well you understand what's going on—and you're in college, at that.) Other criticisms of deinstitutionalization included people being discharged too quickly and sometimes inappropriately (e.g., without adequate planning for continued community service provision).

To what extent do you think the concept of deinstitutionalization is good or bad? What are your reasons? Under what circumstances might it be more likely to work?

The Developmental Model

The fourth important concept during the 1970s and 1980s was that treatment should be guided by a *developmental model* based on a continuum of service. People received services depending on the type and intensity of their needs. People with developmental disabilities were *clients* whom professionals assessed in terms of their needs. These professionals then determined necessary services depending on where the clients fell on the developmental continuum of service. You might picture a ruler. If a client was assessed as functioning at the 6¼-inch point, then that client would receive the services appropriate for that exact point. Likewise, a client at the 10-inch point would receive services designated for that level of assessment. Emphasis was placed not on the individual as a unique personality, but rather on the assessed level of need and the designated services available to address that need.

Often clients' needs change over time. One assumption was that many clients made progress toward greater independence in a step-by-step process. A client had to master one skill first before attempting a more difficult one. For example, a young woman with mild cognitive disabilities might start out living in a group home where she could learn basic housekeeping, cooking, and self-care skills including shopping and paying bills. She might then move to an apartment complex or boarding house for people with cognitive disabilities. Houseparents or residential caregivers would not be living with her, but would be available in another apartment to help her with problems or questions. Eventually the woman might achieve enough self-care mastery to live on her own or with a roommate.

Another assumption was that clients' needs changed over time, but they required increasing levels of help and assistance. A person with a deteriorating orthopedic problem involving his knees might require increasingly more intensive help as he lost mobility. Depending on his assessed state of need at any time, in the 1970s and 1980s he would have received a designated level of service.

The 1990s and Beyond: Consumer Empowerment

The 1990s brought with them a significantly greater emphasis on individual choice and personalized planning for people with developmental disabilities (DePoy & Gilson, 2004; Freedman, 1995; Mary, 1998). Previously, people with developmental disabilities had been viewed as clients whom professionals assessed and provided services based on their level of functioning. There was relatively little variation of service provision at the assessed level. Today's perspective reflects four new important concepts—individualization, choices, innovation, and family support.

Individualization

Today Mary (1998) stresses that practitioners should assume a much more *individualized* approach in that "services are driven by client needs, and clients are viewed as consumers with choices" (p. 253; Tower, 1994). We have established that the term *consumer* implies greater power and choice than does the term *client*. Each client has a unique set of needs. As consumers, clients should be able to choose their purchases or resource providers within a competitive market rather than having someone else do so for them.

Emphasis on Choice

A key word here is *choice*. The ruler concept explained earlier as characterizing the 1970s and 1980s no longer applies. Rather, clients are encouraged to make choices and decide what supports they want and what goals they wish to pursue. Earlier we discussed the importance of self-determination for people with disabilities.

Consider Dimitri, 44, a quadriplegic whose condition is the result of a congenital spinal cord malformation. Instead of professionals assessing his capabilities and designating where it is best for him to live, he can make those decisions himself. With practitioners and other caregiving professionals' input regarding what resources and services are available, Dimitri can determine the environment that will give him what he perceives as the highest quality of life. Of course, his choices are influenced by his own capabilities and the resources available. It is impossible for Dimitri to live in an apartment alone with no supportive help. His viable choices

HIGHLIGHT 11.2

A Word of Caution About Choice

Mackelprang and Salsgiver (1996) caution that practitioners "not be too quick to assume that consumers already have knowledge and abilities rather than recognizing that they may need assistance to develop their strengths" (p. 12). They present an example involving Jim, age 28, who had suffered traumatic brain injury. Although technically not a developmental disability because the injury occurred after age 22, it still illustrates concepts commonly addressed when working with people who have developmental disabilities.

While residing in an independent living center, Jim initially sought help with financial planning. As his counselor, an MSW student, helped him with budgeting issues, it became apparent that Jim was also experiencing difficulty in his marriage. However, because Jim did

not specifically seek help concerning his marriage, the student decided not to interfere with those issues. Because of his head injury, Jim lacked insight into the depths of his relationship problems. By the time he began to understand how far his marital situation had deteriorated, his wife had divorced him, retaining custody of their adolescent daughter.

Mackelprang and Salsgiver (1996) suggest,

This case illustrates the conflict between absolute self-determination and the need to sometimes impose professional intervention. Although some would argue against any change in Jim's intervention, a social work approach would have allowed for broader intervention and ultimately may have been more empowering to Jim and his family. (p. 13)

might include living in a nursing home or in a group home for people with severe physical disabilities, staying in an apartment with the necessary supportive attendants, or living with his family whose members would serve as primary caregivers (assuming, of course, that they were willing to do so).

Another example is Juanita, who has cerebral palsy resulting in major difficulties controlling her arm movements. With professional help and practice, she has learned to dress herself if her clothes have zippers and no buttons. However, it takes her over an hour each time and leaves her physically exhausted. A personal care attendant can do the job in about four minutes. Juanita might choose to have the attendant help her dress even though this option reflects less independence. This choice might be in her best interest to save herself substantial time and energy (Renz-Beaulaurier, 1998).

The concept of choice is important. However, social workers must also carefully evaluate a client's ability to make choices, as Highlight 11.2 explains.

Innovation

A key concept in today's approach toward working with people with developmental disabilities is *innovation*—the initiation, development, and application of new ideas. Innovative service provision may involve a unique combination of services depending on what an individual wishes to accomplish. In other words, "consumers define their own vision of the future—where they want to live, learn, work, and recreate—in a community that they define" (Mary, 1998, p. 253).

For example, Larisa, age 7, has spina bifida, a condition in which the spinal column has not fused shut and so some nerves remain exposed. Although she had surgery immediately after birth to close her spinal column, damage to the unprotected nerves resulted in paralysis and difficulties with bladder and bowel control. Larisa has an individualized service plan designed to meet her unique needs. She can live at home with an innovative combination of supports. A motorized wheelchair maximizes her mobility. Family counseling gives her parents information and help in responding to her special needs. A wheelchair-accessible van transports her to and from school. A teacher's aid assists her as needed in completing school assignments. Designated medical staff help Larisa and her family meet her special health and surgical needs.

Family Support

One other important concept in current service provision for people with developmental disabilities is *family support* (Freedman, 1995; Mary, 1998). Families often need special resources and help to respond to the extraordinary needs of members with developmental disabilities. For example, parents with a young child who has a developmental disability may experience stresses including "stigmatized social interactions, the prolonged burden of care, the lack of information about the disability and behavioral management issues, and grieving" (Freedman, 1995, p. 725).

Family members' strengths must be identified and fortified. Examples of strengths include good communication skills, sincere caring and consideration for each other, effective organizational and planning skills, a strong social network of friends and relatives, spiritual involvement with clergy and religious groups, and adequate financial resources.

Social workers and other professionals working with people who have developmental disabilities continuously strive to individualize plans, emphasize choice, initiate innovative treatment approaches, and maximize family support. Nonetheless, discrimination against them persists, as Highlight 11.3 shows.

Social Work with People Who Have Developmental Disabilities

Social workers often must use brokering, case management, and advocacy skills to provide effective services. We've established that *brokering* is the linkage of clients (consumers) to needed resources. *Case management* is the process of organizing, coordinating, and maintaining "a network of formal and informal supports and activities designed to optimize the functioning and well-being of people with multiple needs" (Moxley, 1989, p. 21). Obviously, many people with developmental disabilities require an innovative range of services to maximize self-determination and pursue an optimal quality of life. The key here is coordinating and monitoring services so clients with ongoing or changing needs get these needs met.

Advocacy is "the process of working with and/or on behalf of clients (1) to obtain services or resources for clients that would not otherwise be provided, (2) to modify or influence policies, procedures, or practices that adversely affect clients, or (3) to promote new legislation or policies that will result in the provision of much-needed resources or services" (Hepworth, Rooney, & Larsen, 2002, pp. 449–450). There is usually no problem when adequate resources and services are available. However, in reality, this is often not the case. When clients are not getting their needs met, the

HIGHLIGHT 11.3

Discrimination Against People with Developmental Disabilities

People with developmental disabilities continue to suffer discrimination. Shapiro (1995) cites the example of Sandra, a 35-year-old woman with Down syndrome who was denied a heart–lung transplant even though insurance covered the $250,000 necessary for the operation. Down syndrome is a congenital type of cognitive disability "characterized by moderate to severe mental retardation, slanting eyes, a broad short skull, broad hands with short fingers, and trisomy of the human chromosome numbered 21" (Mish, 1995, p. 349). The two hospitals granted approval to conduct this type of surgery "made issue of her intelligence and rejected her" (Shapiro, 1995, p. 59). One hospital administrator allegedly said, "We do not feel that patients with Down syndrome are appropriate candidates for heart–lung transplantation" (Shapiro, 1995, p. 59). Others at the hospitals indicated that they doubted she could maintain the rigorous medical requirements involved in taking medication and monitoring her health after the operations.

Sandra and her doctor strongly disagreed with these allegations. Sandra had bused tables in a public cafeteria, lived in her own apartment, and "testified eloquently before committees" on the behalf of people with developmental disabilities (Shapiro, 1995, p. 59). Sandra already had assumed responsibility for taking various medications and monitoring her blood pressure every day. Publicity compelled the hospitals to reconsider her plea. Without the surgery, Sandra had only a few years to live.

practitioner is obliged to advocate on their behalf. Resources may require redistribution. Policies may require change and improvement. New services may need development.

Case Example   One facet of advocacy is helping clients advocate for themselves when they can instead of doing it for them (Mackelprang & Salsgiver, 1996; NASW, 2000). This is another form of client empowerment. For example, it might be easy for Gamal, a social worker, to advocate for his client RyAnne, age 38, who has muscular dystrophy. We have established that this condition is "any of a group of hereditary diseases characterized by a progressive wasting of the muscles" (Mish, 1995, p. 766). RyAnne was diagnosed with the disease at age 12. Although RyAnne can take a few steps by herself, it is difficult for her, and she usually uses a motorized wheelchair. Balance is difficult because she has lost eight of her toes to the disease. She has little strength in her arms and hands, and so accomplishes tasks such as writing and eating very slowly. As her muscles deteriorate, her voice is weakening, so she tries to do most of her necessary talking earlier in the day when she is stronger. RyAnne is a strong-willed, independent-minded person who prides herself in accomplishing her goals. For example, she has earned a bachelor's degree in accounting and is able to work part-time at her own pace.

RyAnne lives with other people who have physical disabilities in a group home where Gamal is the social worker. RyAnne has several issues to address, such as some funding glitches and the need for some new medical equipment including a new wheelchair. Gamal talks to RyAnne about these needs and volunteers to make the calls, write the letters, and advocate on her behalf. He is taken aback when RyAnne responds with a dour look on her face and then avoids eye contact with him. He asks her what's wrong. She hesitantly responds that she would rather do it herself, although she admits she will probably need help negotiating the complicated bureaucratic maze. Gamal suddenly grasps the issue. He backs off and volunteers to help find out whom she needs to contact and what information she needs to present. Although it will be much slower for her to advocate for herself than for him to do it, the process will empower her. Gamal realizes that it's best to support her in her advocacy efforts instead of performing the primary advocacy role himself.

Empowerment Through Legislation: Seeking Social and Economic Justice

Two positive pieces of legislation passed in the 1990s are of special significance for people with developmental or other disabilities in terms of improving access to resources in the macro social environment (DeWeaver, 1995).

The Americans with Disabilities Act of 1990

The Americans with Disabilities Act of 1990 (ADA) intends to provide the millions of American "people [who have physical or mental disabilities] with access to public areas and workplaces" and to blast away barriers keeping these people isolated from "the mainstream of public life" (Smolowe, 1995, p. 54). The ADA defines people with disabilities as those who have substantial physical or mental difficulties that significantly hinder at least one primary life activity, who have an established record of such hindrances, or who are regarded by other people as demonstrating such difficulties (Asch & Mudrick, 1995; Kopels, 1995).

The ADA reflects one attempt by a national macro system to affect and improve the lives of a population-at-risk and provide greater social and economic justice (Kopels, 1995). The ADA consists of five major provisions. Title I forbids job and employment discrimination against people with disabilities. This includes discrimination concerning "job application procedures, hiring, advancement, compensation, job training, and other conditions and privileges of employment *simply because they have disabilities*" (Kopels, 1995, p. 399; emphasis added). Title II forbids public facilities, organizations, and transportation providers to discriminate against people with disabilities. Title III "prohibits discrimination in public accommodations and services operated by private entities" (Kopels, 1995, p. 338). Title IV requires that state and national telecommunication relay services accommodate people with hearing impairments and allow them communication access. Finally, Title V includes a number of miscellaneous provisions relating to more specific aspects of service provision and access.

The ADA "has legitimized the idea that the fundamental problems facing people are less medical than social and structural" (Renz-Beaulaurier, 1998, p. 81). It redefines problems as belonging to the *community,* and not to people with disabilities living in the community. For example, "the problem of how to get up the steps (problem within the individual) changes to how to get a ramp installed (problem outside the individual)" (Renz-Beaulaurier, 1998, p. 80).

This sounds wonderful in terms of providing people with fair access and service. The law requires "universal access to public buildings, transit systems, and communications networks" (Smolowe, 1995, p. 54). Significant gains have been made in terms of accessible curb ramps, wide bathroom stalls, and public vehicles with lifts for wheelchairs for persons with physical disabilities (Smolowe, 1995). Focus on Critical Thinking 11.4, however, poses some questions regarding the overall effectiveness of the ADA.

The Developmental Disabilities Assistance and Bill of Rights Act of 1990

The second major piece of 1990s legislation is the Developmental Disabilities Assistance and Bill of Rights Act of 1990, which accomplished several things (DeWeaver, 1995). First, it renewed funding for four major grant programs on behalf of people with developmental disabilities. Second, it increased the total estimated "number of people with developmental disabilities," thereby acknowledging that more resources are necessary. Third, it "indicated that a substantial portion of people with developmental disabilities remained unserved or underserved" (p. 716). Importantly, the law also called for advocacy on behalf of people with developmental disabilities. It requires provision of adequate services so people can attain their optimum potential, quality of life, and independence as integral members of the community.

Social Work and Community Empowerment for People with Disabilities

Social workers are concerned with how organizations, communities, and the government can offer resources and supports to people with disabilities. This is possible in at least two ways. First, federal and state legislation can make programs available to community residents with disabilities. (We just reviewed two pieces of federal legislation passed on behalf of this population.) Second, social workers can work with community residents to establish their own resources within the community.

Some examples of how to make progress through legislation, direct community support, and social work advocacy are presented next. The populations-at-risk addressed include people with visual impairment and those with cognitive disabilities.

Legislative Empowerment for People with Visual Impairment

Asch (1995) describes some of the legislation and services available for people with visual impairment. The Rehabilitation Act of 1973 and its 1992 amendments mandated reimbursement for some services provided by agencies specifically designated

FOCUS ON CRITICAL THINKING 11.4

Does the Americans with Disabilities Act (ADA) Actually Help People with Disabilities Attain Social and Economic Justice?

Although the ADA has helped people with disabilities in some areas, questions must be raised about its effectiveness in others. For one thing, employers and public agencies must make only "reasonable accommodation." In reality, they are not compelled to provide such access or encouragement if the ensuing costs would result in "undue hardship," often in the form of excessive financial burdens.

Because of the vagueness in terminology and lack of specification regarding how changes must be implemented, gains have been limited (Smolowe, 1995). For instance, what do the words *reasonable accommodation, undue hardship,* and *excessive financial burdens* mean? What kind of accommodation is reasonable? How much money is excessive? How can discrimination against capable people with mental retardation or other developmental disabilities be prohibited? How can the law be enforced? In fact, the hiring rate of people with disabilities by large corporations has made only a tiny gain over the past 10 years, and the percentage of people with disabilities hired by small businesses has decreased from 54 to 48% (Smolowe, 1995). This is despite the fact that office modification costs to increase accessibility appear to be relatively meager. One survey of corporate executives, about four-fifths of whom had altered their office space, indicated that it cost only about $223 per person with a disability to do so (Smolowe, 1995). A legislative representative for the National Federation of Independent Business reflected on the hiring decrease by small businesses: "They're fearful if it doesn't work out, they can't fire them [people with disabilities]" (Smolowe, 1995, p. 55).

Another striking finding is that the federal government now has 20% fewer employees with severe disabilities than it did 10 years ago; historically, it has had the reputation for being a model "haven of opportunity" (Government Hiring, 2004, p. 22A). If the federal government is supposed to be the leader, what does this say about the national momentum for hiring people with disabilities?

Only about one-third of people with disabilities are employed, which is about the same proportion as in 1990 before the ADA was passed (Smolowe, 1995). Therefore, the battle for equal access and opportunity for people with disabilities has not been won. Much of the public attention to the act has focused on people with physical disabilities, many of whom require wheelchairs for transportation. Where do people with mental retardation and other developmental disabilities fit in? Kopels (1995) states that the ADA "will be successful only to the extent that these individuals [with disabilities] and those who advocate on their behalf learn about the ADA and use it as a means to ensure employment opportunities" (p. 345). Mackelprang and Salsgiver (1996) call for the social work profession to ally itself with the movement to enhance access for people with either physical or mental disabilities. They encourage social workers to "become more involved in disability advocacy work in agencies with activist philosophies" and to work with the disability movement to "better empower oppressed and devalued groups, and understand the needs of people with disabilities" (p. 134).

to help people with visual impairment. One difficulty, however, is that individual states define *blindness* differently, which means that some states may limit service provision to those people with severe impairment or total blindness.

Other examples of supportive legislation are two 1930s laws that provide certain employment opportunities for people who are blind. The Wagner-O'Day Act (P.L. 75-739) "established a system of sheltered workshops," and the Randolph-Sheppard Act (P.L. 74-734) gave people who are blind "preference in obtaining employment as operators of vending facilities on federal properties" (Asch, 1995, p. 2465). Sheltered workshops offer a protective, supervised work environment for people who have trouble functioning more independently.

Additionally, people who are legally blind, who are unemployed, and who have assets falling below prescribed levels may receive Supplemental Security Income (SSI). SSI is a federal program that "provides uniform cash assistance to the needy, blind, aged, and disabled throughout the country. Average federal payments to SSI recipients in 2001 were $531 monthly for an individual and $796 monthly for a couple" (Gilbert & Terrell, 2002, p. 71). Benefits are provided on the basis of need instead of work history.

Several pieces of legislation make reading materials more accessible for people with visual impairment. For example, the 1931 Pratt-Smoot Act (P.L. 71-787) established a Library of Congress program that later formed the foundation for regional centers providing Braille and recorded materials to people with visual impairment.

Highlight 11.4 suggests how social workers can work with communities to further empower people with visual impairment.

Community Empowerment for People with Cognitive Disabilities

Considerable time will be spent here discussing people with cognitive disabilities for three reasons (Freedman, 1995). First, they constitute the largest proportion of people with developmental disabilities. Second, they are the most likely to use services provided by state agencies. Third, social workers are an integral part of service provision to this population (DeWeaver, 1995).

As for people with visual impairment, legislation provides support and programs for some people with cognitive disabilities. Funding for people with cognitive disabilities comes from a range of sources depending on whether individuals fulfill eligibility criteria, which often are related to their income level. For example, SSI may be available to people with cognitive disabilities who satisfy a means test (i.e., as Chapter 8 explained, a person or family must have an income less than a designated amount to be eligible for benefits).

Social workers can help communities and social service organizations develop resources and programs to integrate people with cognitive disabilities and enhance their quality of life. For instance, one state has a Community Options Program (COP), funded at the state level, that "provides assessments, case plans, and community services as an alternative to nursing home placements" (ARC Milwaukee, undated, b, p. 2).

HIGHLIGHT 11.4

Social Work and Community Empowerment for People with Visual Impairment

Laws and mandated programs make some resources available to people with visual impairment. However, social workers can serve as important advocates in their communities and agencies for additional needed services. One goal might be to disseminate information concerning the issues addressed by and strengths inherent in people with visual impairment. These people and their families "need accurate information about laws, services, and alternative techniques for performing household tasks, reading, writing, traveling, and the like that people customarily imagine cannot be handled without vision" (Asch, 1995, p. 2466). For example, social workers can help people realize that the long cane ("a mobility aid used by individuals with visual impairment who sweep it in a wide arc in front of them"), guide dogs, human guides, recorded information, adapted computers, and other technological devices (e.g., reading machines that convert print into spoken words) can help people organize home, work, and social lives in an effective and efficient, although different, manner (Asch, 1995; Hallahan & Kauffman, 2003, p. 357).

Another goal social workers might pursue with communities is sponsorship of self-help groups in which people with visual impairment can discuss issues, suggest ideas to each other, and offer mutual support. A third goal might be to work with schools that have students with visual impairment to educate parents about services, resources, and aids. Schools can encourage students with visual impairment to participate in sports, recreation, and other extracurricular and educational activities just as children with normal vision do.

Even such a basic thing as ensuring that public buildings use Braille next to the floor indicator buttons on elevators might be a community goal. Rosa, a student with a visual impairment, comes to mind. She attended a state university renowned for its support of and services for students with disabilities. Rosa felt that the campus focused its attention on serving people with physical disabilities involving mobility and viewed people with visual impairment as less significant. All buildings and classrooms had been readily accessible to people with physical disabilities for as long as anyone could remember. She advocated for years to have Braille information installed in elevators throughout the campus but got little response from university administration. Eventually, however, she was able to make her point, and all elevators were furnished with Braille directions.

ARCs and Related Resources

One excellent example of how a community can use a support system for people with cognitive disabilities is an organization called ARC. Historically known as the Association for Retarded Citizens, ARCs now are established in communities nationwide. The following discussion focuses specifically on ARCs. However, the types of services ARCs offer can certainly be sponsored by other organizations and community groups.

Typically funded through a variety of sources including donations by private citizens, corporations, local service clubs, and foundations, as well as government service contracts, ARCs provide a wide range of services that reflect a creative meld of public services, private contributions, and community resources. Social workers are often integrally involved with the provision of ARC services, which may include information and referral services, help lines, noninstitutional residential facilities, vocational and employment programs, support services, intervention advocacy, volunteer programs, and recreational activities.

Information and Referral Services and Help Lines

An information and referral service provides information about what services and resources are available in a community and assists people in accessing them. A help line is an information and referral system based on telephone contact. Persons requiring information about services, laws, or issues related to a specific problem or population—in this case, cognitive disabilities—call a trained professional (often a social worker), who connects them with the appropriate resource or gives them necessary information. Many ARCs develop an extensive computerized system that can quickly identify relevant linkages between questions, needs, information, and resources.

Noninstitutional Living Facilities

One type of resource that can help people with a disability maintain maximum independence and self-determination is a noninstitutional living facility. As discussed earlier in the context of deinstitutionalization, the intent is to place people in the least restrictive setting possible. Social workers often oversee or work in such settings. These include adult family care homes, where clients reside in the home of caregivers who supervise and care for them. Another setting is a group home or community-based residential care facility (CBRF). Residents often are selected on the basis of having similar needs such as required levels of supervision and support. For example, one CBRF might have residents capable of taking care of personal needs and working at a sheltered workshop.

Other, even more independent, supported living options include living with a roommate or by oneself in an apartment. Some limited supervision and assistance, such as help with paying bills or arranging transportation to work, is usually needed in these cases.

Vocational and Employment Programs

ARCs are also quite creative regarding vocational and employment opportunities. They can help clients gain employment by preparing them for the expectations of the workplace, assisting in placement, helping employers restructure jobs to maximize clients' ability to complete job tasks, and providing job coaching in basic work skills (e.g., getting to work on time, following a supervisor's instructions).

Individuals may also gain employment in more structured settings such as sheltered workshops. One ARC agency developed an employment program whereby clients made ceramic gifts for special occasions such as weddings and graduations. Another ARC organization created a work setting in which clients manufactured pillows for a national airline.

People who are unable to function in more demanding settings may receive "day services"; these aim to "maximize an individual's independent functional level in self-care, physical and emotional growth, mobility and community transportation, socialization, recreation, leisure time, and education and prevocational skills" (ARC Milwaukee, undated, a, p. 2).

HIGHLIGHT 11.5

Empowerment of Elderly Caregivers

Family services can support aging caregivers who find it increasingly difficult to maintain the same level of care as in the past. For example, because of decreasing strength, an aging caregiver might find it much more difficult to assist a person with a severe disability in dressing himself. Family services for elderly caregivers can help during crises such as a caregiver experiencing her own acute health problems. They can also assist caregivers in long-term planning for and with the person who has the disability. A common concern of aging caregivers is what will happen to the individual with a disability when the caregiver can no longer assume that function.

Other Support Services

Social workers and other human service professionals offer multifaceted support services. Organizations can provide outreach support services to clients in their own homes that involve instruction in daily living skills, budgeting and financial management, transportation, parenting skills, and personal issues such as interpersonal interaction, leisure activities, self-esteem, and assertiveness.

Respite care programs help parents and other caregivers for persons with cognitive disabilities, giving them a break from their responsibilities. Highlight 11.5 focuses on the special needs of aging caregivers.

Support groups can focus on many different issues. For instance, parent support groups "provide parents with an opportunity to get together and share stories, concerns, and achievements with other parents who are experiencing similar circumstances" (ARC, undated, a, p. 2). Support groups for seniors with disabilities give them opportunities to share concerns, discuss suggestions for prospering, and talk about how to maximize their quality of life.

Advocacy

Intervention advocacy "is designed to respond to the needs of persons with disabilities and their families when serious problems arise affecting legal rights, safety and health, financial security, or access to community resources" (ARC, undated, c, p. 2). The service system is complicated, and clients and their families may find it difficult to negotiate. As emphasized previously, social work advocacy is often necessary to get clients the resources and services they need.

Community Volunteers

Volunteers can help ARC programming in many ways. These include performing clerical duties and answering phones; caring for small children while parents attend support groups; serving as matched "friends" with persons who have disabilities to provide support and encouragement; giving support via telephone to persons needing intermittent help; participating in fund-raising activities; assisting at supervision of events such as group outings; and helping with household upkeep and maintenance (ARC, undated, c). Social workers often seek out, organize, and oversee volunteers performing such functions.

Aging caregivers often find it difficult to provide care.

Recreational Activities

Recreational activities and functions represent still another means of enhancing the quality of life for people with disabilities. Examples include athletic programs, Special Olympics, and summer camps at which groups of clients of any age can interact socially, work on crafts, play games, learn appreciation for nature, increase leisure skills, and gain confidence in expressing themselves (ARC, undated, c).

The past few sections have suggested means by which social workers and communities can empower people with cognitive disabilities. The following case example examines various dimensions of how a community both pursues and falls short of empowerment for one of its citizens.

Case Example   Consider Frank and how his community both succeeds and fails to support him. Frank, age 58, lives in a midwestern town of about 8,000 people in a rural farming community. Frank has mild cognitive disabilities. He graduated from high school, but only because in those days students like him were passed on whether they could perform the work or not. He is very proud of the high school ring he purchased at graduation. However, his community, especially the school system, did not serve him well. Instead of receiving special services and training that might now be available, the system basically ignored him and passed him on through.

A major problem for Frank is his speech. He has difficulty forming words and takes considerable time to structure his sentences. His comprehension of verbal communication is good, and he has an excellent sense of humor. His speech often fools people who don't know him well into thinking he is much less competent than he really is. Speech therapy might have helped if it had been available when he was young.

Frank works at a sheltered workshop in addition to working six hours per week as a janitor at Hilda's Happy Hot Dog Haven. Frank has a solid work history. For almost 20 years he worked at a local tanning factory hauling deer hides from one area to another as they proceeded through the leather-making process. It was gruesome, backbreaking work, and when Frank got home, he was exhausted. At the time, he was living with his father, who cooked for him, did his laundry, and helped him with other daily living tasks.

Work at the tanning factory was not without problems. Frank told his relatives about another "guy at work" who liked to pick on him. Frank had lots of experience being picked on. The guy would draw a knife and tease Frank, pretending to cut him and actually slitting his right hand one time. Frank also told how, one night after work, he slit all "the guy's" tires. The guy, who was fired shortly thereafter, never did find out who did it.

Frank was a saver. He would wear the same pair of polyester pants for years until the threads in the hem seams gave way. Although Frank made little more than minimum wage, he put almost all of it in savings while he lived with his dad. When the plant closed and he was laid off, he had accumulated over $40,000. Investing with the help of his brother Sharif and a slick financial planner brought his assets to almost $200,000 by the time he turned 58. Unfortunately, this prevented him from receiving public assistance and resources because he did not meet various programs' means tests.

When his father died, Frank was able, with Sharif 's help, to live in and pay rent for his own apartment. He preferred living alone to living with a roommate. One of Frank's strengths was his strong relationship with Sharif and his family, even though they lived 185 miles away. Frank didn't see his family as often as he liked since busing was deregulated and federal regulations no longer required companies to sponsor less popular runs. Sharif and his wife were periodically forced to endure a deadly dull four-hour trip through flat farmland to pick Frank up and spend another four hours to drive him home.

A major strength in Frank's life was his involvement with the local Center for People with Developmental Disabilities, an agency that did not have a means test. In its sheltered workshop, Frank felt productive and established many social contacts. As one of the highest-functioning clients, he achieved significant social status. At the center's periodic social dances, he was quite accomplished and admired. Frank also had a knack for taking pictures and videos, which he did regularly at the center's events. The center sponsored or cosponsored numerous events including Special Olympics, bowling tournaments, picnics, and outings to movies. Frank was extremely proud of a Volunteer's Award plaque he received from the center for all of the time he spent photographing and videotaping events.

At the center, he was assigned a social work case manager, Mandze, who helped to coordinate services and activities. To evaluate his daily living skills, she linked him with a trainer who tried to teach him how to cook. However, Frank didn't like to cook, so he ended up subsisting mostly on frozen dinners. (It might be noted that Sharif, who had superior intelligence, could barely boil water; he

HIGHLIGHT 11.6

Empowerment for People with Cognitive Disabilities: Creating Linkages with Community Life

Kretzmann and McKnight (1993) cite a number of situations in which adults with cognitive disabilities can be mainstreamed[2] and integrated as part of a large community. These are the types of scenarios social workers can actively seek out on their clients' behalf. The following three are adapted from Kretzmann and McKnight's ideas.

Example A: Reggie, age 28, thrives at playing games, so Reggie's social worker linked him with the local Boys Club. He now volunteers there regularly, teaching children games and supervising their activities.

Example B: Gina, age 22, spent most weekdays at a day program with other people who have cognitive disabilities. She passed much of her time coloring and watching other residents. She is an exceptionally warm person who lights up with a dazzling smile when spoken to or given any attention. Her social worker at the day program introduced her to a local day care center to see if she could help out there.

At first, her social worker or other day program staff always accompanied her to the day care center and provided some

supervision. Now she goes to the center by herself several times a week. The children love her and the attention she pays to them. She always has time to listen to what they have to say and give them a hug when needed. They realize she's different from their other teachers because sometimes they have to help her out in completing activities, but they don't care. They love her anyway.

Example C: Hugh, age 68, lives in a group home. He loves to bowl. Danyelle, his group home social worker, found out that a local church had a Thursday night bowling league. She talked to the team members and asked if they would consider including Hugh on their team. They were a bit hesitant because they take bowling very seriously and play to win. They were even more hesitant when they discovered that Hugh was not a very good bowler. However, Hugh obviously was ecstatic about being on the team. Team members worked out a rotation system whereby Hugh could periodically bowl but his score was omitted from the final total. Hugh beamed proudly as he wore his Beaver's Bowling Buddies T-shirt.

[2]*Mainstreaming* is "bringing people who have some exceptional characteristics into the living, working, or educational environments to which all others have access" (Barker, 1995, p. 221). Examples of such special groups include people with cognitive and other developmental disabilities.

didn't like to cook, either.) Mandze also helped coordinate any other supportive services Frank might need with Sharif and his family.

Although Mandze and Sharif tried to encourage Frank to manage his own finances and checkbook, this was too difficult for him. Frank didn't like doing computations or writing checks because he was afraid of making mistakes. When mail-ordering gifts for family members, he would always send cash despite the risk of losing it. Sharif finally gave up and determined that it was easier simply to keep track of Frank's finances himself than to keep after Frank.

Another major community strength was the spiritual and emotional support Frank received from his church. He attended services regularly and was involved in a group called the Sunday Evening Club, consisting of adult church members who met every other Sunday for a potluck dinner and a chance to socialize or hear speakers.

Frank's work at Hilda's was helpful in terms of making him feel useful and conserving his savings. However, the six-hour weekly work allocation was minimal. The management could have given him many more hours if they had not viewed him as an inadequate, "retarded" person. And the town provided no public transportation, so Frank had to walk to get anywhere, including two miles to work.

In summary, community strengths for Frank include the Center for People with Developmental Disabilities, its sheltered workshop, his social worker Mandze, public recognition via the Volunteer's Award, his spiritual involvement at church, his job at Hilda's, and strong connections with his family. Community weaknesses for Frank include the history of inattention to his special needs, local residents who made fun of him in a demeaning manner whenever they had the chance, inadequate involvement in his paid work environment, and lack of public transportation. Thus, in some ways, Frank's community environment supported and integrated him, thereby enhancing his quality of life. In other ways, the lack of community support hindered his ability to live the most useful, productive, and happiest life possible.

Highlight 11.6 reviews three other examples of how social workers might help people with cognitive disabilities become more integrally involved in community life.

Looking Ahead

Many people with disabilities require special health services. Another field of practice in which social practitioners serve clients is health care. Chapter 12 will explore social work roles, health care policy problems in the macro environment, and AIDS in an international context.

For Further Exploration on the Internet

See this text's Book Companion Website at **www.socialwork.wadsworth.com/ kirstashman_intro2e** for descriptors and hot links to URLs relevant to this chapter, selected InfoTrac articles and exercises, and tutorial quizzes.

CHAPTER TWELVE

SOCIAL WORK AND SERVICES
IN HEALTH CARE

© Jim McGuire/Index Stock Imagery

Consider the following headlines in national news magazines:

"Congress Seeks the Right Rx; But 44 Million Still Lack Health Coverage"[1]
"Is Your HMO [Health Maintenance Organization] Too Stingy?"[2]
"What Are They Hiding? HMOs Are Getting More Secretive About Quality"[3]
"Does Managed Care Work? HMOs Deliver Some of the Best Health Care Money Can Buy—and Some of the Worst"[4]
"No Time for the Poor; Physicians Dependent on Managed Care Provide Less Assistance to the Uninsured"[5]
"NASW Joins Fight for the uninsured"[6]
"Taking a Lead on HIV, Social Workers Manage Programs"[7]
"Death Stalks a Continent: In the Dry Timber of African Societies, AIDS Was a Spark. The Conflagration It Set Off Continues to Kill Millions"[8]

These headlines reflect some of the critical issues in health care provision in the United States and around the globe today. The World Health Organization (WHO) defines *health* as "a state of complete physical, mental, and social well-being and not merely the absence of disease and infirmity" (Ahmed & Kolker, 1979, p. 113). This definition goes beyond the conception of health as simply the lack of illness. Rather, it stresses the importance of strengthening and maximizing health, and not merely curing what's wrong.

Good health and health care involve every one of us. No one is immune to all the health problems encountered in life. People suffer maladies ranging from influenza, to chronic back pain, to cancer. Consider that 31 million people, excluding newborns, were discharged from U.S. hospitals in one recent year (Ginsberg, 2001, p. 130).

Social workers can play an important role in helping people live healthful lifestyles and seek the health services and resources they need. Practitioners can empower people by facilitating their pursuit of physical, mental, and social well-being.

A large proportion of social workers also practice in the arena of mental health. Note that sometimes *health care* is also used as an umbrella term to include mental *health care*. Although some of the issues involved in both mental health and physical health care are similar, this chapter will focus on the provision of physical health care and services. Chapter 13 will explore assessment issues and mental health services in greater detail. Specifically, this chapter will

- Identify the major types of health problems people encounter.
- Describe primary social work roles in health care provision.

[1]Shapiro, J. P. (1999, October 18). Congress seeks the right Rx. *U.S. News & World Report*, 32.

[2]Pederson, D. (1999, July 6). Is your HMO too stingy? *Newsweek*, 56.

[3]Spragins, E. E. (1999, March 1). What are they hiding? *Newsweek*, 74.

[4]Spragins, E. E. (1998, September 28). Does managed care work? *Newsweek*, 61–66.

[5]Shapiro, J. P. (1999, April 5). No time for the poor, *U.S. News & World Report*, 57.

[6]NASW joins fight for the uninsured. (2003, April). *NASW News*, 48 (4), 6.

[7]Beaucar, K. O. (1999, July). Taking a lead on HIV. *NASW News*, 44 (7), 1.

[8]McGeary, J. (2001, February 12). Death stalks a continent. *Time*, 36–45.

- Discuss major problems in the macro environment concerning health care, including escalating costs, unequal access, ethical dilemmas in managed care, and the need to enhance cultural competence in the health care system.
- Encourage critical thinking about universal health care coverage and overgeneralizations regarding various racial and ethnic groups.
- Explore some of the value discrepancies between Asian and Pacific Islander cultures and the U.S. health care system.
- Describe HIV/AIDS, social work roles, and empowerment for people living with AIDS.
- Examine the severity of AIDS as an international problem, particularly in sub-Saharan Africa.

 # Health Problems

Health problems include virtually any physical malfunction, injury, or disease you can imagine. They can affect anyone in the population, from an infant born 2½ months prematurely, to a 97-year-old suffering from arthritis and heart disease, to a young adult badly burned during the devastating September 11, 2001, terrorist attack on the World Trade Center in Manhattan or the Pentagon in Washington D.C.

Coleman and Cressey (1999, pp. 169–176) cite five key factors causing or contributing to health problems. First, people who pursue unhealthful lifestyles are more likely to experience health problems and die at a younger age. These include (Hatcher et al., 1998; Zastrow & Kirst-Ashman, 2004)

- Substance use and abuse.
- Cigarette smoking.
- An unhealthful diet high in fat and cholesterol.
- Being overweight.
- High levels of stress over long periods.

A second factor related to health problems is physical injuries. Sometimes these are related to mortality (i.e., death). For example, in a recent year, of young people age 10–24 in the United States who died, 31% did so as a result of motor vehicle accidents, 18% from homicide, 12% from suicide, and 11% from other accidental injuries (Kann et al., 2000).

A third factor contributing to health problems involves environmental factors. Air pollution is a serious threat, especially in larger cities such as Los Angeles, Beijing, Bangkok, and Mexico City. During the 1990s, simply breathing the air in Mexico City during one day was the equivalent of smoking two packs of cigarettes (Weiner, 2001). Other environmental dangers include water pollution, use of pesticides, and exposure to buried nuclear and other industrial wastes.

Poverty is the fourth variable related to health problems. It "is associated with unsanitary living conditions, hazardous working conditions, lack of access to medical care, and inadequate nutrition" (Mooney, Knox, & Schacht, 2002, p. 45).

Contagious disease poses the fifth serious health concern. On a global level, such diseases as cholera and typhoid still plague people in nonindustrialized nations; the industrialized countries have virtually eliminated them with improved sanitation. However, respiratory and intestinal diseases still afflict people in the United States regularly. Sexually transmitted diseases of various types also continue to infect millions of people annually (Strong et al., 2005). Human immunodeficiency virus (HIV), which causes acquired immune deficiency syndrome (AIDS), poses another major problem, one that will be discussed later in the chapter.

 # Social Work Roles in Health Care

Social workers who work in the health care field are often referred to as *medical social workers.* Social workers serve in both direct and macro practice capacities concerning health care.

Social Work Roles in Direct Health Care Practice

Dhooper (1997) explains social work's involvement in health care practice:

> Social work has been a part of the health care scene for more than 100 years. It has an impressive history of significant contributions to the field of health care in . . . [a wide range of settings]. . . . Social workers have been involved in health care at all levels: preventive care, primary care [ongoing care for patients prior to the onset of disease symptoms or care for those experiencing early symptoms], secondary care [treatment of full-blown illness], tertiary care [treatment of illness seriously endangering a person's health], restorative care [help during recovery from illness], and continuing care. Depending on the major purposes and functions of each health care setting, their roles have varied, requiring differential professional skills. (p. 1; Reynolds, 1975)

Health care settings in which social workers practice include hospitals, medical clinics, diagnostic and treatment centers,[9] public health settings, and managed care companies.

Hospitals, Medical Clinics, and Diagnostic and Treatment Centers

Social workers can fulfill many functions in hospitals, medical clinics, and diagnostic and treatment centers, including the following:

1. *Help patients understand and interpret technical medical jargon.* Physicians often receive little training in interpersonal and communication skills. Social workers can help define technical terms, explain physical and health implications of illnesses and injuries, and communicate with patients to make certain they understand what's happening to them.
2. *Offer emotional support.* Receiving a medical diagnosis can be a scary thing. Most patients are not experts on most illnesses, injuries, and health issues. Social workers can help patients look more objectively at health conditions and understand realistic potential consequences of various treatments.
3. *Help terminally ill people deal with their feelings and make end-of-life plans.* (This is discussed more thoroughly later in the chapter.) Social workers can also

[9]*Diagnostic and treatment centers* are facilities to which persons such as children with multiple disabilities are brought for assessment, diagnosis of various conditions, treatment planning, and specialized treatment by a range of therapists (e.g., speech, occupational, or physical therapists).

help people requiring more intensive care than that provided at home make the transition to a more supportive setting such as a group home, nursing home, or hospice.

4. *Help patients adjust their lives and lifestyles to accommodate to new conditions when they return home after medical treatment.* For example, persons diagnosed with heart disease or asthma, or those adjusting to an amputation or to blindness, may require help in adapting their behavior and habits to make life as healthy and efficient as possible.

5. *Help parents of children who have serious illnesses or disabilities cope with these conditions and respond to children's needs.*

6. *Serve as brokers who link patients with necessary supportive resources and services after leaving the medical facility.*

7. *Help patients make financial arrangements to pay hospital and other medical bills.* Social workers often assist patients in contacting insurance companies or applying for financial assistance, guiding them through the complex maze of rules and policies.

8. *Provide health education aimed at establishing a healthful lifestyle and preventing illness.*

Case Example   Donald, age 69, and Gerri, age 67, have been married for 50 years. At Donald's most recent annual physical examination, he was diagnosed with prostate cancer. (The prostate gland is a "partly muscular gland that surrounds the urethra of males at the base of the bladder and secretes an alkaline fluid that makes up part of the semen" [Nichols, 1999, p. 1060].) It is the second most common form of cancer in men, the first being skin cancer (Hyde & DeLamater, 2003). Prostate cancer is usually slow to spread and, when caught and treated early, generally has a good prognosis. Donald and Gerri, both retired, are avid health advocates who work out at their local health club four times a week and vigilantly eat food high in fiber and low in fat. They visibly tremble at the thought of not rinsing dishes after washing because of the possibility of ingesting soap residue. When Donald and Gerri found out about the cancer they were terrified. They wouldn't even tell any of their friends, whom they thought would immediately start discussing Donald's imminent death.

Bethany, the hospital social worker involved, sat down with them and discussed realistic expectations for and consequences of treatment. Donald's physician had recommended chemotherapy and radiation treatments instead of surgically removing the prostate gland. Bethany encouraged Donald and Gerri to express their feelings and fears. She provided them with statistics about the high success rates of treatment and facts about its effects. Donald and Gerri's terror subsided, and they began to develop a more realistic view of what lay ahead. Bethany encouraged them to turn to their three children and their families for support, which they did.

It's interesting to note that prior to this experience, neither Donald nor Gerri had a positive word to say about social work and social workers. They had run a successful hardware store business that Donald had inherited from his father. They had believed that people who turned to social workers or other such helpers were weak and lazy and didn't have the wherewithal to make it on their own. Now they changed their minds. They had developed sincere respect for Bethany, who helped them through an emotionally turbulent time.

Public Health Departments and Other Health Care Contexts

Public health is the complex system of health care programs and policies that address the following on the public's behalf (Dhooper, 1997; Hanlon & Pickett, 1984; Winslow, 1920, pp. 183–191):

(1) [P]reventing diseases, (2) prolonging life, and (3) promoting health and efficiency through organized community effort for
(a) the sanitation of the environment.
(b) the control of communicable infections.
(c) the education of the individual in personal hygiene.
(d) the organization of medical and nursing services for the prevention and treatment of diseases.
(e) the development of social machinery to ensure everyone a standard of living adequate for the maintenance of health . . . so organizing these benefits as to enable every citizen to realize his [or her] birthright of health and longevity.

Such broad goals relating to such a wide range of issues result in multiple facets of service provision. Facilities providing public health services include local, state, and federal health departments and agencies; private foundations and agencies focusing on specific health issues (e.g., the American Cancer Society, the March of Dimes); social service organizations; community health and mental health centers; family planning clinics; and virtually any other public agency providing services and benefits related to healthy living.

Specific services include any aiming to enhance health and mental health or prevent disease. These include crisis intervention, substance abuse treatment, health services for pregnant women, services to prevent and stop child maltreatment, health education, stress management training, and mental health counseling.

Managed Care Settings

An increasing number of social workers are also practicing in various facets of *managed care*—"a generic label for a broad and constantly changing mix of health insurance, assistance, and payment programs that seek to retain quality and access while controlling the cost of physical and mental health services" (Lohmann, 1997, p. 200). Social workers hold management positions in managed care. They also participate in assessment to determine whether patients are eligible for benefits and which are most appropriate. Managed care, discussed more thoroughly later in the chapter, involves work in health insurance companies, hospitals, and health maintenance organizations (HMOs). *HMOs* are organizations that provide a wide range of health care services for participants and employers, who typically pay an established monthly fee for services. These services generally must be provided by facilities and practitioners designated by the HMO.

Macro Practice in Health Care: Seeking Empowerment

As administrators and members of administrative committees in health care facilities, social workers work to develop agency policies that promote effective health care available to people who need it. Additionally, social workers can advocate for more comprehensive health coverage. Social workers and the National Association of Social Workers have historically served as significant forces in advocating for improved health care legislation, policies, and resources.

Health Care Policy and Problems in the Macro Environment

At least four main issues plague the U.S. health care system today. First, expenses are escalating dramatically. Second, people have unequal access to adequate health care, with poor people and people of color especially at risk of deprivation. Third, social workers and others working under the health care system's umbrella are plagued by a series of ethical dilemmas. Finally, many questions can be raised regarding the U.S. health care system's cultural competence in responding to the needs of various ethnic, racial, and cultural groups.

The Escalating Cost of Health Care

The U.S. health care system costs more than any other in the world (Coleman & Kerbo, 2002; Mooney et al., 2002). The United States spends 14% of its gross domestic product on health care, amounting to $4,270 per person; this is expected to escalate to 16.2% by 2008 (Mooney et al., 2002). Mooney and colleagues (2002) argue that health care costs are soaring for at least six reasons:

1. The rapid acceleration of technological advances has increased the types of services, drugs, and testing available.
2. The population is aging. Because of better medical treatment, more people are living longer. And the older people are, the more likely they are to suffer from more health problems that require more expensive treatment.
3. Administrative overhead for running health care organizations is the highest in the world (Health Care Financing Administration, 1998).
4. Fraud and abuse contribute to the high costs of Medicare and Medicaid (Brown, 2000; PNHP Data Update, 1997).
5. High-level executives in managed care and in pharmaceutical companies are paid exorbitant salaries. For example, "[i]n 1998 the chief executive officers (CEOs) of the top 10 drug companies averaged $290 million in annual compensation including stock options" (Mooney et al., 2002, p. 53; PNHP Data Update, 2000).
6. Public and private insurance premiums continue to rise.

Unequal Access to Health Care

Approximately 41.2 million Americans lack any health insurance (U.S. Census Bureau, 2003, No. 153), and millions more have strikingly insufficient coverage (Kornblum & Julian, 2004). What are the reasons for this? How can this occur in such a rich, industrialized, high-tech society? Highlight 12.1 describes how poor people and people of color are at special risk of receiving inadequate or no health care.

For decades U.S. politicians have been debating the issue of *national health insurance*—a publicly funded program that would expand the current system of health care provision to give some level of coverage to everyone regardless of their

HIGHLIGHT 12.1

Poor People and People of Color as Populations-at-Risk

Poor people are the least likely to have adequate health insurance; in one recent year, although 12.9 million people received Medicaid benefits, "10.4 million poor, or 32.4%, had no insurance of any kind during the year" (Mills, 2000; Mooney et al., 2002, p. 52). Another study found that people with private insurance were twice as likely to get the surgery they needed as people receiving Medicaid (Coleman & Kerbo, 2002). And these problems will likely get worse with the increased limitations on benefits established by 1996 legislation. Medicare beneficiaries also had inadequate benefits. The elderly must pay for as much as 25% of their health care (Mooney, Knox, & Schacht, 2005). As indicated earlier in the book, many seniors purchase supplemental insurance to cover some of the gaps. Although Congress passed a new prescription

drug plan effective in 2006 as part of Medicare, it has many critics. They "argue that the drug coverage is inadequate and complicated, denies beneficiaries the right to purchase supplemental coverage, and fails to lower the cost of prescription drugs" (Mooney et al., 2005, p. 49).

People of color, who are more likely to be poor, also are more likely to lack health insurance and adequate health care (Coleman & Kerbo, 2002; Kornblum & Julian, 2004). White seniors are 3½ times more likely to get lifesaving heart bypass surgery than African American seniors; similarly, whites are twice as likely to get a kidney transplant as African Americans (Coleman & Kerbo, 2002). The life expectancy for white males is six years greater than for African American males, and it is four years greater for white than African American females (Kornblum & Julian, 2004).

ability to pay. All industrialized countries except for the United States have established some kind of national system so that all citizens have access to some type of health care coverage (Coleman & Kerbo, 2002).

Much of the debate in the United States about establishing a national system has focused on two issues—cost and freedom of choice. Covering health care costs for everyone would require the government to expend huge amounts of money. Questions involve what types of coverage should be included and how coverage would be funded. Focus on Critical Thinking 12.1 addresses this policy issue.

The freedom-of-choice debate concerns the extent to which each citizen could choose his or her own health care provider. The United States has a strongly ingrained commitment to freedom of choice. How much would a government-sponsored system restrict people's ability to choose the care they want? However, with the advent of managed care and people's participation in HMOs (both discussed further shortly), this latter question may not be as relevant. Most people's choices for health care are already seriously restricted.

Problems in Managed Care

Managed care is now "an integral aspect of social work practice in many settings" including health, mental health, family and child welfare, and a wide range of other public social service settings (Corcoran, 1997, p. 191). Although there are various

FOCUS ON CRITICAL THINKING 12.1
Health Care Costs and Policy

Consider the following questions:

- Does U.S. health care policy require a major overhaul that would establish a national health insurance program providing *universal* coverage? Should the government fund a program available to all citizens, making private health insurance with its *selective* benefits obsolete?
- Do your views reflect a *conservative* or *liberal* perspective regarding this issue?

These value orientations involve the following variables:

- Is it each individual's responsibility to earn enough money to purchase his or her own health insurance or to find a job that provides such insurance? Or is it society's responsibility to provide health care services to its members?
- Should people be forced to earn enough to pay for their own health insurance so that they

don't take advantage of "the system"? Or would national health insurance significantly enhance people's quality of life, especially those who don't currently have health insurance?
- Is it individuals' responsibility to take care of themselves and their families with minimal governmental interference? Or is it the government's responsibility to provide health care services because they are so critically important to survival?

Consider two other questions:

- Because health care is increasingly expensive, who should bear the burden of paying for it? Workers? Employers? All citizens through increased taxes and subsequent government funding?
- What about the millions of poor people, including children, who currently have no health insurance or access to health services? Is that fair? What should be done about it?

definitions of managed care, a number of concepts tend to characterize it. We have established that, broadly stated, *managed care* is "a generic label for a broad and constantly changing mix of health insurance, assistance, and payment programs that seek to retain quality and access while controlling the cost of physical and mental health services" (Lohmann, 1997, p. 200). An identified group or range of health and mental health care providers contract with agencies to provide health care at a negotiated rate. Individual agencies thus avoid having to administer individual health insurance policies themselves. Managed care programs often provide services beyond those typically paid for by health insurance (e.g., prevention, family services).

Two primary principles promoted by managed care include retention of quality and access while controlling cost. That is, health and mental health services should be of high quality and readily accessible to clients. Yet they should also be cost-effective.

Managed care "fundamentally transformed" traditional relationships between clients and workers (Lohmann, 1997, p. 201). Historically, social workers in agency settings established treatment plans in conjunction with clients, in addition to stressing informed consent and confidentiality to comply with ethical standards. Managed care takes these decisions out of workers' and clients' hands and puts them into the hands of third-party decision makers. A managed care representative, often a utilization reviewer or case manager, then reviews documentation and regulates "the services that clients receive, especially what specific services will be provided and at what cost" (Corcoran, 1997, p. 194). To Lohmann (1997), managed care "represents the complete (and seemingly sudden) triumph of financial management concerns over virtually all other professional considerations" (p. 202).

Ethical Dilemmas in Managed Care

Spragins (1998) comments on the potential of managed care:

> Done right, managed care is not just a cheap imitation of fee-for-service medicine. It can work better. Its simplest contribution is to link hospitals, doctors and specialists so that they can administer care more efficiently. Besides saving money, shared electronic records and preset treatment protocols can improve the care that individual patients receive. (p. 62)

However, cost cutting and inappropriate decisions often hamper this potential effectiveness. The following are sad occurrences involving managed care that illustrate some of its potential problems:

- "A Medicare HMO threatened to take a 94-year-old's wheelchair."
- A woman experiencing a "life-threatening asthma attack" was taken to a more distant HMO-sponsored hospital instead of being rushed to the nearest medical facility.
- "A person with AIDS was denied approval by his managed care organization . . . of medications he had previously been on" (Vallianatos, 2001, January, p. 7).
- A man "suffered a stroke in 1993, after his HMO failed to treat his blood disorder. Clots have since cost him both legs. 'They treated my stroke like the flu,' he says."
- A 62-year-old woman "lost a kidney after her primary care doctor . . . [working under the auspices of a managed care system] refused her repeated requests to see a specialist for her constant abdominal pain." She noted that he prescribed "range-of-motion exercises" when she really "had an infected kidney" (Spragins, 1998, pp. 62, 66).

Social workers must work within their agency settings. However, they are also responsible for maintaining ethical practices and for making sure clients' needs are met. Several ethical issues may be raised concerning managed care.

The first involves the potential conflict between "the gatekeeping role of some managed care organizations and client self-determination" (Corcoran, 1997, p. 196). With managed care, clients no longer have the right to choose their service providers. Rather, the managed care utilization reviewer makes this determination.

Similarly, managed care may conflict with the ethical principle of informed consent. Corcoran (1997) remarks,

> Informed consent requires that the client know in advance the clinical procedures, the risk of those procedures, and the available alternative procedures. Managed care may destroy informed consent by restricting the available procedures to a limited number. For example, a managed care company may determine the preferred practice and the preferred providers, with little consideration or disclosure of alternative procedures. (p. 196)

Managed care also has the potential to violate client confidentiality (Corcoran, 1997). Social workers are bound by the National Association of Social Workers (NASW) Code of Ethics, which emphasizes how "social workers should respect clients' right to privacy" and "protect the confidentiality of all information obtained in the course of professional service" (NASW, 1999, 1.07a, 1.07c). (Chapter 2 reviewed

HIGHLIGHT 12.2
Responding to Ethical Dilemmas: Improving Health Care Provision

Managed care is here whether we like it or not. Social workers must respond to any ethical dilemmas it poses. Edinburg and Cottler (1995) suggest,

> Perhaps the most important role for social workers will be as advocates for patients and families in dealing with managed care delivery systems. Patients and families will need to know what their entitlement benefits are and how to obtain proper services. Social workers will also need to continue to advocate for improving the health care system by serving on advisory committees and lobbying their legislators. (p. 1641)

At least the following seven specific provisions could improve legislation to protect clients and their rights:

1. Guarantee patients the right to choose a doctor outside their health plans'

networks if they agree to share the cost of services.
2. Ensure patients' access to detailed information about coverage, treatment options . . .
3. Require companies to cover emergency care without prior authorization.
4. Make health plans comply with state and federal laws that protect the confidentiality of health information.
5. Require companies to set up procedures under which providers could appeal denials of coverage (Managed care, 1998, p. 1).
6. Allow physicians and patients to make decisions about treatment, instead of managed care bureaucrats.
7. Provide home care and continuity of care[10] when needed (Vallianatos, 2001, January).

[10]*Continuity of care* refers to the efficient ongoing provision of services by different or the same agencies to meet clients' needs as their circumstances and needs change.

major tenets of the NASW Code.) Additionally, it specifies that social workers "may disclose confidential information when appropriate with valid consent from a client" (NASW, 1999, 1.07b). However, the Code also provides an exception. It indicates that social workers should maintain confidentiality "except for compelling reasons. The general expectation that social workers will keep information confidential does not apply when disclosure is necessary to prevent serious, foreseeable, and imminent harm to a client or other identifiable person" (NASW, 1999, 1.07c). If a managed care organization demands information before providing services, what should the worker do? What if the worker does not agree with the organization's expressed need for information and believes that the regulations violate clients' right to privacy? Workers may be required to report confidential information whether or not they feel it's ethical in order for clients to receive necessary health care. Highlight 12.2 suggests what social workers can do to address some of these issues.

Cultural Competence and the U.S. Health Care System

Another important issue involves the U.S. health care system's responsiveness to the needs and values of the nation's various racial, ethnic, and cultural groups. Social workers have the ethical responsibility to examine, attend to, and advocate for positive change concerning these groups' health and welfare. It is beyond the scope of this book to examine the treatment of every cultural group, so we will explore one case example—the U.S. health care system's treatment of Americans with Asian and Pacific Islander roots in the context of their cultural values.

The U.S. health care system is a huge bureaucracy, with many of the characteristics of traditional bureaucracies. Although management approaches vary within its many organizational structures, strict regulations and decision-making hierarchies for health care provision tend to dominate. A problem commonly faced by such bureaucracies is the lack of cultural sensitivity. Rigid rules do not provide flexibility for adapting to culturally diverse values and needs. A major goal in social work is to enhance service provision for clients. Lack of responsiveness to clients' cultural values and belief systems can represent a major barrier to the provision of effective services.

The following discussion describes six general dimensions important in understanding Asian and Pacific Islander (API) cultures with respect to involvement in the health care system. (Note, however, that we should not overgeneralize. For example, we should not assume that all members of API groups adhere to traditional API values to the same extent. Focus on Critical Thinking 12.2 addresses this issue.) Subsequent content addresses five issues in U.S. health care policy—informed consent, advance directives, decisions about nursing home placement, disclosure of terminal illness, and making end-of-life decisions—and examines implications for improved health care provision.

Value Dimensions in API Cultures Relating to Health Care Provision

At least six concepts inherent in API cultures relate directly to U.S. health care provision. These include filial piety, collective versus individual decision making, emphasis on harmony versus conflict, nonverbal communication, fatalism, and a sense of shame at asking for help.

Filial Piety

An important value dimension in API cultures is *filial piety*—"a devotion to and compliance with parental and familial authority, to the point of sacrificing individual desires and ambitions" (Ho, 1992; Kirst-Ashman & Hull, 2002, p. 422; Kitano & Maki, 1996). Children are "expected to obey parents and elders" (Lum, 1995, p. 239). For example, "*Oya-KoKo*, a Japanese version of filial piety to parents, requires a child's sensitivity, obligation, and unquestionable loyalty to lineage and parents" (Ho, 1992, p. 37). Especially significant is the obligation of younger people to care for parents as they age.

Collective Versus Individual Decision Making

In contrast to the individualist orientation emphasized in U.S. health care, API values center on reliance on the family or larger group to make ultimate decisions about any individual member's care (Yeo & Hikoyeda, 2000). In the U.S. health care system the focus is on individuals making decisions about their own medical care.

Emphasis on Harmony Versus Conflict

API cultures emphasize the importance of members getting along and not causing trouble for the family, a concept that characterizes collectivist societies. The implication, then, is that individuals must "endure hardship and pain," especially if addressing issues that might disturb or cause discomfort for other family or group

FOCUS ON CRITICAL THINKING 12.2
The Hazards of Overgeneralizing

Note that when we speak about any racial, ethnic, or cultural group, it is important not to overgeneralize. Here we talk about general value dimensions evident in API cultures. However, individuals or families from any ethnic or racial group may embrace traditional cultural norms to various degrees. They may also experience *acculturation,* which we have established as "the adaptation of language, identity, behavior patterns, and preferences to those of the host/majority society" (Lum, 2004, p. 229). In other words, members of a diverse group may gradually blend into the larger society and adopt its values and customs.

Braun and Browne (2000) comment on other influential dynamics:

> Some of the factors, besides timing of immigration, that influence culturally linked health behaviors include socioeconomic status, language spoken at home, extent to which the community (and family) is ethnically homogeneous, educational attainment, and expectations about returning to one's ancestral home. (p. 186)

Therefore, when we think about a racial, ethnic, or cultural group, it's important not to assume that all members comply with all cultural values or conform to the same extent. Being of Chinese ethnic heritage does not automatically mean a person loves pan-fried dumplings, Szechuan shrimp, roast pork lo mein, kung pao chicken, or mushroom egg foo young simply because these are traditional ethnic foods. The trick is to view each person as a unique personality, yet be sensitive to the possible cultural values and beliefs that person may hold.

Another word of caution concerns differences among the many cultures included under the API umbrella. For example, "in contrast to other Asian cultures, the individual in Cambodian society is not necessarily subordinate to the family or social group. Although the extended family is acknowledged, family structure is based more on the couple relationship" (DuongTran & Matsuoka, 1995, p. 251).

Consider the following questions regarding your own ethnic and cultural heritage:

- What traditions and values characterize your heritage?
- To what extent do your own values comply with traditional ideas?
- What are the reasons for these discrepancies?

members (McLaughlin & Braun, 1999, p. 325). For example, in Vietnamese culture, "harmony in interpersonal relationships is accomplished through tact, delicacy, and politeness, sometimes at the cost of honesty and forthrightness" (DuongTran & Matsuoka, 1995, p. 251). In Hawaiian culture, "contributions to unity and harmony are more valued . . . than are competitive success or self-satisfaction" (Ewalt & Mokuau, 1996, p. 260). Many values in Hawaiian culture reflect the importance of harmony and affiliation, including "generosity, graciousness, keeping promises, intelligence, cleanliness, and helpfulness" (Mokuau, 1995, p. 1795).

There also tends to be respect for clearly defined family structures and hierarchies of authority, which clarifies expectations and encourages predictability of behavior. For instance, Samoan culture stresses "hierarchical systems with clearly defined roles. The highly structured organization of the family defines an individual's roles and responsibilities and guides the individual in interactions with others" (Ewalt & Mokuau, 1996, p. 261).

Nonverbal Communication

A fourth value inherent in API cultures involves silent or nonverbal communication. Yamashiro and Matsuoka (1997) explain that "in Asian and Pacific [Islander] cultures, language may not accommodate all that individuals think and feel—especially for those who are not socialized to use language as a primary means for expressing feelings" (Yamashiro & Matsuoka, 1997, p. 180). Diller (1999) remarks,

> Asians also tend to have a very different nonverbal communication system. Providers need to be aware of this, because unlike the Western therapeutic focus on speaking, much of the communication in Asian cultures is nonverbal. The meanings of facial expressions, gestures, eye contact, and various cultural symbols or metaphors are usually completely different from Western ones. Research has found Asians to have a "low-contact" culture—that is, more comfortable with little physical contact and larger interpersonal distances. (p. 202)

Much can be learned by carefully observing people's silent responses and subtle nonverbal gestures. For example, it is "improper" for children "to discuss issues of death and dying with parents, yet concern by either party may be expressed by nonverbal cues such as bowing of the head or eye contact" (McLaughlin & Braun, 1999, p. 324).

API cultures value both self-control and inconspicuousness, both of which discourage the sharing of information, especially about personal issues (Kitano & Maki, 1996). For example, "the traditional Japanese culture emphasizes the importance of inner discipline and encourages the concealing of frustrations and disappointments" (Murase, 1995, p. 246). Laotian culture stresses "the need to 'save face,' which means that an individual must stay cool or keep quiet in all circumstances"; furthermore, "it is considered humiliating to point out a person's errors directly" (DuongTran & Matsuoka, 1995, p. 250; Outsama, 1977).

Fatalism

Fatalism, a fifth value characterizing traditional API cultures, is the conception that "events are fixed in advance so that human beings are powerless to change them" (Ho, 1992; Kitano & Maki, 1996; Mish, 1995, p. 423). A "what will be will be" philosophy is contrary to both the medical and social work strategies of assessment, planning, intervention, and evaluation. The U.S. health care system is focused on change, stressing that illnesses and maladies should be treated and cured if at all possible. In contrast, a fatalistic perspective implies that medical treatment is useless because fate controls events. Therefore, why should one expend the effort to pursue it?

Shame at Asking for Help

API values include an emphasis on family, cooperation, and harmony, and an aversion to causing trouble. All these contribute to avoidance of the U.S. health care system. For Asian Americans and Pacific Islanders, "there is stigma about and shame in experiencing mental and emotional distress" (Balgopal, 1995, p. 236; McLaughlin & Braun, 1999). Thus family and group members strongly prefer to deal with issues and illnesses within the family, rather than expose problems to outsiders. For example, for Chinese Americans, "to share negative information outside the home is to bring disgrace on the family name; . . . mental illness and retardation, criminal behavior, job failure, and even poor school grades are kept in the family" (Lum, 1995, p. 239).

When it becomes obvious to family members that the family is incapable of resolving health problems, they hesitantly turn to health care providers. For example, for Japanese Americans, "any request for service" concerning mental health is of "an extraordinary nature . . . the presenting problem is likely to be a severe dysfunction beyond the coping capacity of the individual or his or her family" (Murase, 1995, p. 246). For physical illness, API families tend to pursue external health care services "only if emergency care is needed" (McLaughlin & Braun, 1999, p. 325). Once that step is taken, health care professionals are expected to make collectivist decisions—that is, those "in the best interest of the greatest number of people involved with the patient" (McLaughlin & Braun, 1999, p. 325).

Conflicts Between API Cultural Values and the U.S. Health Care System

Conflicts between API cultures and U.S. health care system policies and practice revolve around at least five areas: informed consent, advance directives, decisions about nursing home placement (McLaughlin & Braun, 1999), disclosure of terminal illness, and end-of-life decisions (Yeo & Hikoyeda, 2000). Given these conflicts, the U.S. health care system can either detract from the health and well-being of Asian Americans and Pacific Islanders or empower them.

Informed Consent

In the U.S. health care system, individual patients are subject to *informed consent*, which involves a person's right to receive adequate information about "the consequences and risks of a medical procedure" or treatment process, evaluate alternatives, and give permission for a procedure before it's begun (Pietsch & Braun, 2000, p. 38). In many API cultures, this presumed right does not comply with prevailing values and norms (McLaughlin & Braun, 1999). For instance, "unlike the custom among white people, for whom the individual patient is the decision maker, many Japanese and Chinese families assign decision-making duties to the eldest son. In Pacific Islander families, it may be less obvious who the decision maker is" (McLaughlin & Braun, 1999, pp. 323–324). The entire family may share duties and assume designated responsibilities like getting food. Because of the collective nature of decision making in API cultures, it is customary for "all family members" to "receive the same level of detail about the patient's diagnosis, prognosis, and treatment options" (Braun, Mokuau, & Tsark, 1997; McLaughlin & Braun, 1999, p. 324).

Three problematic issues relate to informed consent (McLaughlin & Braun, 1999). First, consider Asian Americans' and Pacific Islanders' emphasis on harmony and conformity to group wishes. Given the API cultural orientation toward cooperation, patients may feel obligated to sign consent papers presented to them when they don't really want to. Second, cultural norms emphasizing silence and inconspicuousness may prevent patients from voicing contrary opinions, asking questions about illnesses, and declining to sign papers. Third, health care personnel are often unaware of how API cultural values can affect the consent process and interfere with its integrity.

Advance Directives

A second problematic issue concerning API cultures and the health care system involves *advance directives*—written, witnessed, signed instructions regarding what individuals wish to have done in the event that they are unable to make decisions (McLaughlin & Braun, 1999; Yeo & Hikoyeda, 2000). They can either describe what should be done under certain medical circumstances or identify some other individual to make these decisions. For example, what should be done for a person who is brain-dead and living on a respirator? Should that person be kept alive as long as possible, or should someone "pull the plug"?

Two issues tend to surface here with respect to API cultures (McLaughlin & Braun, 1999). First, health care practitioners are legally required to "approach patients for copies of advance directives" (McLaughlin & Braun, 1999, p. 331). However, in Chinese, Japanese, and Hawaiian cultures, people avoid discussing death for fear of inviting it or suffering negative consequences. Second, it is pointless for Asian Americans and Pacific Islanders to discuss such issues because of their collectivist approach. They assume that family members will address those issues when the appropriate time comes.

Decisions About Nursing Home Placement

Many Asian Americans and Pacific Islanders embrace the concept of filial piety and believe that children should care for elderly parents (Balgopal, 1995; DuongTran & Matsuoka, 1995; Lum, 1995; McLaughlin & Braun, 1999; Murase, 1995). For them, nursing home placements are to be avoided at all costs. Thus API families tend to wait until situations reach crisis proportions before investigating possible nursing home placement (McLaughlin & Braun, 1999; Murase, 1995). Stress may escalate due to pressure to maintain two incomes, care for both children and elderly parents, and deal with the physical and cognitive health problems experienced by aging parents.

Interestingly, in contrast to Western culture, "many traditional API cultures expect death to occur at home and have mourning traditions that involve keeping the body at home for a number of days before burial" (McLaughlin & Braun, 1999, p. 331; Nichols & Braun, 1996). Thus imminent death may not spur API families to remove the dying member to a nursing or hospital facility.

Disclosure of Terminal Illness

Although physicians generally tell family members about a terminal illness, informing the patient about ensuing death is taboo in many API cultures (Yeo & Hikoyeda, 2000). It may be "that the family does not want the patient to become disheartened and give up on living, that the family feels it is disrespectful to speak of such things to an elder, or that talking about death is 'polluting' or will cause bad luck" (McLaughlin & Braun, 1999, p. 330). People in Japan, for example, believe that "a patient should not be informed of a terminal illness because he or she would lose the strength and hope needed to cope with the illness" (Yeo & Hikoyeda, 2000, p. 114).

Health care personnel thus face an ethical dilemma. Policy and professional ethics may require that a patient be informed of a terminal diagnosis so that practitioner and patient can discuss and weigh treatment options. However, culturally, the patient may not want to know and may well choose ignorance if given that option.

End-of-Life Decisions

A related issue to disclosure of terminal illness is whether to continue life support for individuals who cannot make decisions and have no hope of recovery (e.g., those who are brain-dead) (Yeo & Hikoyeda, 2000). We have established that traditional API cultures tend to rebuff advance directives. Yeo and Hikoyeda (2000) explain:

> Cultural values might emphasize longevity over quality of life, especially for one's parent. Some families do not want to make decisions that would preclude the possibility of a miracle from either God or the American medical system, of which they might have unrealistically high expectations. (p. 104)

Highlight 12.3 proposes five recommendations to address the five value conflicts discussed here—informed consent, advance directives, placement decisions, disclosure of terminal illness, and end-of-life decisions.

International Perspectives: AIDS—A Global Crisis

Consider these international scenarios.

In Africa "unscrupulous entrepreneurs" are "hustling for corpses" as thousands die from AIDS and funeral parlors are swamped with bodies. Masland (2001) describes the scene:

> So fast are AIDS victims piling up that . . . [m]orgues and cemeteries are out of space. A lively black market has grown up in stolen burial equipment. Crooked morgue workers sell corpses to favored undertakers, or to the highest bidder, sometimes even before bereaved families arrive to claim a body—leaving the relatives no choice but to pay the undertaker who collected the remains. (p. 45)

In China AIDS has become an "epidemic that races across the country" following a "route [from Burma] of drug smugglers, of truck drivers, of migrant workers and the prostitutes that wait for them." Fang (2001) paints this picture:

> Chen Ah-Yan usually gets up after midnight. She lounges on an L-shaped couch with three other girls in a tiny room open to the sticky air of the street, watching music videos halfheartedly and calling out to passers-by. Occasionally . . . [she] catches the attention of a man in one of the fancy cars with blackened windows cruising the streets—"drug smuggler," she comments casually—and brings him upstairs to the makeshift room not much larger than a twin mattress. The slim 18-year-old wearing dark-red lipstick and platform shoes came to this town [from the country] a few months ago [seeking excitement]. . . . "Sure, we know about AIDS," Chen giggles. "But we're just here to have fun." (pp. 22–23)

Worldwide 40 million people are infected with HIV (Marchione, 2003). It is estimated that 3 million people will be killed by HIV and 5 million people will contract it each year (Cowley, 2003). In the United States 900,000 people are currently infected, and it is estimated that another 40,000 will be infected annually (Cowley, 2003). Race and gender are also variables involved in the problem. Whereas African Americans embody 12% of the U.S. population, they "account for more than half of all new HIV infections" (Brink, 2004, p. 132). Another frightening fact is that women "now account for 26% of newly diagnosed AIDS cases in the United States—nearly four times the proportion they made up in 1986—and girls account for the *majority* of new HIV infections among teens" (Cowley & Murr, 2004, pp. 76–77). Because of

HIGHLIGHT 12.3
Recommendations for a More Culturally Competent Health Care System

Large service provision systems are never perfect. There are always quirks and problems because such a broad range of people are involved. Bureaucracies have established rules to assist in their functioning. A large health care system cannot adapt itself perfectly to all its beneficiaries' needs. However, an ongoing concern for social workers is the need to assess large systems' functioning, recommend improvements, and work to achieve positive changes. This is especially true in view of the U.S. population's cultural diversity.

How can the U.S. health care system become more sensitive to API (and other) cultures? And how can social workers address this issue? Five recommendations are proposed here:

1. Provide training for health care personnel that sensitizes them to API cultural values and issues (Braun & Browne, 2000; McLaughlin & Braun, 1999; Yamashiro & Matsuoka, 1997). Staff should be taught to carefully observe periods of silence, nonverbal behavior, and family or group interaction for clues to understanding such behavior. They should pay careful attention to "the language used to discuss the patient's disease, . . . whether decisions are made by the patient or by the larger family unit, . . . the relevance of religious beliefs, . . . [and] the patient's and family's degree of fatalism versus an active desire for control of events" (Braun & Browne, 2000, p. 186).

2. Encourage personnel in the health care system to "begin addressing end-of-life planning issues with whole families (not just individual patients) earlier in the life course (rather than waiting until the end) and in nonhospital venues" (McLaughlin & Braun, 1999, p. 333). Agency policy should encourage staff to tune in to cultural values regarding collectivist versus individual perspectives on decision making and to work with families accordingly.

3. Urge the health care system to begin investigating the adoption of family-centered rather than individual-centered decision-making models for virtually all health-related decisions (McLaughlin & Braun, 1999; Mokuau, 1995). Health care personnel should seek to understand individuals' and family's values and to work within those value systems to the greatest extent possible. The health care system should respect both the individual's and the family's right to self-determination (Ewalt & Mokuau, 1996).

4. Establish "parallel services" whereby attention and treatment are tailored to meet the cultural needs and expectations of API people. For example, some "successful programs in San Francisco and Los Angeles" use "language, signs, food and drinks, and [service] providers" representing "the culture being served" (Braun & Browne, 2000, p. 186). The downside of this approach, of course, is that it's expensive to duplicate services. In the event that it's financially unfeasible to develop parallel services, programs could at least employ bilingual staff to assist in the assessment and treatment process (Braun & Browne, 2000).

5. Encourage social workers to advocate for policy and practice changes in the health care system. The system should respect and appreciate cultural diversity and self-determination, not pretend they don't exist.

its significance on a national and global level, this section will devote considerable attention to AIDS and health care.

HIV and AIDS

Acquired immune deficiency syndrome (AIDS), caused by human immunodeficiency virus (HIV), is a disease that destroys the body's immune system. Infected people thus gradually become increasingly vulnerable to *opportunistic diseases*—conditions and infections that themselves are usually not life threatening but that take advantage of a weakened immune system and use this opportunity to invade it.

HIV is a type of virus called a *retrovirus*. A *virus* is a submicroscopic, infectious parcel of genetic material, resembling in some ways a tiny living organism and in other ways inert (lifeless) material, that can grow and multiply only within the living cells of bacteria, plants, and animals. There is no cure for a virus. Note that viruses also cause the common cold and influenza; available medications may alleviate symptoms but will not cure them.

A *retrovirus* is a special kind of virus that invades normal cells and causes them to reproduce more of the virus rather than reproduce themselves like other normal cells. HIV attacks normal white blood cells (called *T cells*) that fight off diseases invading the body (Rathus, Nevid, & Fichner-Rathus, 2002). The specific type of T cell that's vulnerable has *CD4 molecules* on its surface that help coordinate the body's resistance "to certain microorganisms such as viruses" (Aidsmap, 2005). Hereafter, we will refer to these cells as *CD4 T-cells.*

After invading the CD4 T-cell, HIV immediately begins destroying this host cell and injecting its own genetic material into the cell. The transformed CD4 T-cell then begins producing more HIV instead of reproducing its former self. As the invaded CD4 T-cells produce more of the virus and fewer disease-attacking white blood cells, the body's immune system deteriorates. As a result, the body is left defenseless and becomes easy prey to other infections. In short, HIV destroys the body's immune or defense system so that other diseases invade and eventually cause death. HIV is a frightening agent that has continued to mutate into various strains, making it difficult to find a cure.

People may have contracted HIV and be HIV-positive but not yet be diagnosed with AIDS. HIV gradually destroys the immune system, so it may take a while to develop the serious conditions characterizing AIDS. According to the CDC, an AIDS diagnosis applies when a person has a positive HIV blood test and a CD4 T-cell count below 200 per cubic millimeter of blood (normal people have about 1,000). (AllRefer.com, 2005). Among the numerous illnesses that may develop as the immune system plummets are blood and other serious viral infections; brain infections and deterioration; Pneumocystis carinii pneumonia (a rare form of pneumonia from which people with normal immune systems are protected); yeast infection of the esophagus, mouth, or genitals; cancer of the lymph glands; tuberculosis;[11] and exacerbated herpes simplex conditions (resulting in ulcers in the mouth or on the genitals that occur more frequently and severely than usual) (AllRefer.com, 2005). People who have not contracted HIV are generally immune to these ailments.

[11]*Tuberculosis* is a disease usually affecting the lungs that is characterized by the development of tubercules ("small, firm, rounded nodule[s] or swelling[s]") (Nichols, 1999, p. 1402).

HIGHLIGHT 12.4
How Is HIV Transmitted?

Documented means of HIV transmission include having sexual intercourse with an HIV-positive partner, using hypodermic needles that were also used by an HIV-positive person, and receiving transfusions of contaminated blood or other products derived from contaminated blood. Babies can contract AIDS before birth from their infected mothers and after birth through breast milk.

HIV has been isolated in semen, blood, vaginal secretions, saliva, tears, breast milk, and urine. Only blood, semen, vaginal secretions, and, to a much lesser extent, breast milk have been identified as capable of transmitting HIV. Many experts doubt whether there is enough of the virus present in tears and saliva for it to be transmitted in these fluids. Experts rule out casual kissing and swimming in pools as a means

of contracting HIV. Only the exchange of bodily fluids (e.g., through anal, oral, or genital intercourse) permits infection. The virus is very fragile and cannot survive long without a suitable environment, and it cannot penetrate the skin.

In summary, evidence has not shown that AIDS can be spread through any type of casual contact. Individuals can't contract HIV by shaking hands or sitting on a toilet seat unless some exchange of bodily fluids occurs. Although a very small percentage of all HIV-positive people have detectable HIV in their saliva, levels are small, and saliva provides a "hostile" environment for the virus; there are no documented cases of HIV transmission by saliva (Strong et al., 2005, p. 581). Research has also established that HIV cannot be transmitted by mosquitoes or other insects.

HIV affects each individual differently. Some people go for years before experiencing negative effects; others exhibit symptoms much earlier. Initial indications include a dry cough, abdominal discomfort, headaches, oral thrush, loss of appetite, fever, night sweats, weight loss, diarrhea, skin rashes, fatigue, swollen lymph nodes, and lack of resistance to infection. Unfortunately, other illnesses have similar symptoms, so it's easy for people to overlook the possibility that they are HIV-positive. As AIDS progresses, the immune system becomes less capable of fighting off opportunistic diseases, making the infected person vulnerable to a variety of cancers, nervous system degeneration, and infections caused by other viruses, bacteria, parasites, and fungi. AIDS is currently "the fourth leading cause of death globally and the leading cause of death in Africa" (Begley, 2001, p. 36). Highlight 12.4 reviews methods of HIV transmission.

Measurement of the CD4 T-Cell Count

Several tests have been developed to determine if a person has been exposed to the AIDS virus. These tests directly detect not the virus but the antibodies a person's immune system develops to fight the virus. Two of the most widely used tests are the ELISA (short for enzyme-linked immunosorbent assay) and the Western blot. The ELISA can be used in two important ways. First, donated blood can be screened to prevent the AIDS virus from being transmitted by blood transfusions. Second, individuals who fear they may be carriers of the virus can be tested. For a person who has been infected with HIV, it generally takes two to three months before enough antibodies are produced to be detected by the test.

The ELISA is an extremely sensitive test and therefore is highly accurate in detecting the presence of antibodies. It rarely gives a negative result when antibodies are present. However, it has a much higher rate of false positive results; that is, it indicates that antibodies are present when in reality they are not. Therefore, it is recommended that positive results on the ELISA be confirmed by another test called the Western blot or immunoblot. This test is much more specific and less likely to give a false positive. Because the Western blot is expensive and difficult to administer, it can't be used for mass blood screening as can the ELISA. Neither test can determine if a person already has AIDS or will actually develop it. The tests only establish the presence of antibodies that indicate exposure to the virus.

A new blood test for HIV screening has also been developed called the OraQuick Rapid HIV-1 Antibody Test; results have been 99.6% accurate and can be obtained within 20 minutes (Food and Drug Administration [FDA], 2003). Note that, as with the ELISA test, results must be confirmed with another more specific test to avoid false positives. A home testing kit, the Home Access Express HIV-1 Test System, is also available for about $50 where blood samples are collected at home and mailed to the lab; results then may be received within a week. Manufacturers indicate that such testing is 99.0% accurate (Aids.com., 2005). The Federal Trade Commission warns against the use of other HIV home testing kits where results are analyzed by users at home, not in a laboratory. Tests have indicated that such kits likely reveal false negatives—that is, that the individual is HIV-free when he or she is really infected (Federal Trade Commission, 1999).

Treatment for AIDS

No cure exists for HIV or AIDS. However, new drug treatments have significantly enhanced the health of people infected with HIV and lengthened their life spans (Strong et al., 2005). Treatment goals include decreasing the amount of HIV present in the body, improving the functioning of CD4 T-cells, preventing other infections from happening, and enhancing infected people's quality of life (Lexi-Comp, 2004). Generally a drug "cocktail" (a combination of three or more drugs) is used because such a combination decreases HIV's resistance to treatment (AIDSinfo, 2004; Carroll, 2005). This multiple-drug treatment approach is called *highly active antiretroviral therapy* or *HAART*. Many of the drugs help prevent HIV from making copies of itself; for example, AZT has been approved for use since 1987 (AIDSinfo, 2004; Lexi-Com, 2004). A new class of drug called a *fusion inhibitor,* which helps prevent HIV from entering cells, just received FDA approval in 2003 (AIDSinfo, 2004). However, despite early hopes of controlling AIDS with these drugs, the following problems have emerged:

- Cocktail drugs don't destroy HIV. At best, they inhibit it.
- People taking such drugs, which must be toxic to fight HIV, can experience agonizing side effects, especially after taking the drugs over time. Effects may include "lipodystrophy, which redistributes body fat in bizarre configurations, or osteonecrosis, a crippling bone disease, diabetes, or disorienting side effects; one patient described his experience, 'I felt like I wasn't in my body. My heart rate felt like it was in slow motion. I would touch my skin and it would feel like it wasn't mine. I'd be taking a shower and it would feel like the shower floor dropped 6 feet. It was very, very bizarre'" (Brink, 2001, pp. 45–46).

- Drug effectiveness depends on a relatively complicated schedule and routine that some people find difficult or impossible to follow. AIDS is the only disease requiring such meticulous "compliance"; if a patient misses "even a pill or two a month, the virus can mutate, figuring out how to resist the drug and forcing patients to switch regimens" (Brink, 2001, pp. 45–46).
- The annual cost of cocktail drugs is prohibitive at about $20,000 per person (Strong et al., 2005).

Another treatment approach simply involves healthful living. Good nutrition, regular exercise, stress management, and other practices consistent with good health can contribute to staying healthier longer (Strong et al., 2005).

Note that clinical research is also being conducted on vaccines for HIV, although none have been found as yet (AIDSinfo, 2005). Scientists have been working on vaccine development for two decades and have made progress (USDHHS, 2004). However, hope for success has resembled a roller-coaster ride in terms of highs and lows. "Even when a promising vaccine is discovered, it will take time to test and evaluate its safety and effectiveness" (USDHHS, 2004). Two avenues of research are being pursued. *Preventive vaccines* are being investigated to prevent HIV infection in HIV-negative people. *Therapeutic vaccines* are being explored to help improve the immune system in HIV-positive individuals.

Empowerment for People Living with AIDS

Empowerment is a key concept for social workers helping persons with AIDS. Empowerment involves feeling good about ourselves and feeling that we have some control and direction over our lives. Empowerment is clearly related to hope.

Empowerment is vital to people living with AIDS.

Because of the prevalence of AIDS in the United States, social workers will likely work directly or indirectly with persons having the disease. The essence of social work practice with people who are HIV-positive involves providing support, focusing on strengths, and seeking empowerment. People need to develop positive feelings about themselves and maximize the control they have over their lives. Social workers can help HIV-positive people seriously consider alternatives and make their best choices. It's important to remain as active in normal life activities as possible.

With the advent of cocktail drugs and significantly longer life expectancies for people with AIDS, the concept of empowerment becomes especially important. Persons with AIDS should never be referred to as *victims*. Rather, they should be referred to as *people living with AIDS,* with an emphasis on *living*. The word *victim* implies helplessness, powerlessness, and lack of control. People living with AIDS need to be viewed as individuals capable of empowerment, not as helpless victims. Hope should be maintained because many people living with AIDS have years of fruitful living ahead of them. Much research and effort are being directed at combating the disease. Highlight 12.5 explores the importance of critically evaluating both the positive and negative sides of life experiences.

Haney (1988) emphasizes that positives can come from any negative experience. Working through difficulties makes people stronger and wiser. He lists some of the positives that he has experienced since contracting AIDS. These include

> learning to accept [his] limitations; learning to cope by getting in touch with [his] strengths; experiencing a clarity of purpose; learning to live one day at a time; learning to focus on the good in [his] life here and now; and the incredibly moving experience of having complete support from [his] family, friends, lover, people [he] hardly know[s], and sometimes even complete strangers. (p. 252)

Social Work Roles and Empowerment for People Living with AIDS

Social workers assume many roles when working with people living with AIDS. First, a social worker can provide counseling, in which a client's issues are addressed, feelings and emotions are expressed and discussed, and plans are made. A social worker may help a client work out issues and objectively evaluate life situations. The worker may also assist the client in focusing on positives, even when the client is coping with the negative aspects of HIV/AIDS.

Social workers may help HIV-positive people deal with feelings of fear, guilt, anger, depression, hopelessness, abandonment, and any other emotions they may experience. Regardless of how clients feel, it is crucial to bring these feelings out in the open so clients can deal with them. Emotional repression and isolation should be avoided. If health significantly deteriorates, social workers may also help people with AIDS cope with disfigurement and loss of function. Highlight 12.6 discusses the importance of dealing with all life issues, including death.

As an educator, a social worker can provide information about the progression of the disease, drug treatments, stress management, positive lifestyle choices, and safe sex practices. Social workers may also provide *crisis intervention*, a brief and

HIGHLIGHT 12.5

Evaluating the Consequences of Life Experiences

Maintaining a meaningful quality of life involves focusing on the positive instead of the negative aspects of life. Each moment of each day, we can choose how to look at the exact same situation in either a positive or a negative light. For example, many of us dream of winning the lottery. When one man won $21 million, he was thrilled. He had spent many happy hours over the years with his pals at a local bar, watching the televised announcements of lottery winners and hoping that he would be one of them. Finally, it happened. Ecstatic, he said he would "take care of" all of his bar buddies. Although envious, they were also happy that he had won and were enthusiastically looking forward to their "cut."

However, the story does not have the happiest of endings. It seems the man forgot to give his friends the share they felt they had coming. Hard feelings emerged as former friends bandied about threats of lawsuits for unfair treatment. The winning man found that he no longer had friends at the bar. For that matter, he no longer had friends in his neighborhood, so he decided to move to a "better" neighborhood where he knew no one. He had lost most of his friends.

Additionally, he had to get an unlisted telephone number because he and his wife couldn't stand the barrage of solicitations. The man was approached by almost everyone he knew, including relatives. They either not so subtly hinted that they could use a few extra bucks or asked him point-blank for loans they felt they would never have to repay. Taxes eradicated a third of his winnings almost immediately. Still wealthy, he bought a red Porsche. But the man's life had changed. He no longer experienced the same sense of belongingness, peace, and happiness that he had in his poorer days.

There are numerous other examples of positive and negative sides to any event. The birth of a long-awaited baby may mark a couple's most joyous occasion. However, the hospital and other medical costs not covered by insurance may place a heavy financial burden on them. Finding reasonable yet high-quality day care so that the mother can return to work may be difficult. A colicky baby may keep them both up much of the night, making the thought of getting up the next day a nightmare.

The moral of this story is the importance of focusing on the positive aspects of any particular situation. People with AIDS need to work hard at identifying, concentrating on, and enjoying the positive elements in their daily lives.

---

time-limited therapeutic intervention through which a social worker helps a client learn to cope with or adjust to extreme external pressures. Examples of crises experienced by people with AIDS include sudden bouts of illness, job loss due to illness, and escalating expenses for medical treatments.

Empowerment can come from reconnections (Haney, 1988). Having AIDS often makes people feel isolated from family, friends, and others, and disconnected from their old lives. Social workers can help people with AIDS reconnect with other people. Support systems are essential and can include family members, friends, intimate others, and coworkers. Lines of communication need to be maintained. Significant others must also express and face their feelings in order to deal with

HIGHLIGHT 12.6
Empowerment by Dealing with Life and Death

It is important for people with AIDS to deal not only with life but also with death. Social workers can help people with AIDS address any spiritual issues that may concern them. Helping people with AIDS discuss plans for what will happen after their death can be useful. In a way, this may help them gain greater control. They may need to write a will or make funeral arrangements. They may want to finish unsettled business

or resolve disputes with significant others. A useful concept in working with people who are facing their own death is the idea of making them "the star of their own death." In other words, instead of avoiding issues concerning death because this can make people feel uncomfortable, emphasize that people approaching death have the right to make decisions and settle their affairs.

them and support people living with AIDS. Otherwise they might shun negative feelings by avoiding and withdrawing from people with AIDS.

Social workers may also provide *family counseling*, in which they help the person with AIDS discuss issues with other family members. Just as clients themselves must learn to cope, so must significant others and family members. Their feelings and fears must also be elicited so that they can be addressed.

Social workers, as brokers, may help link clients to needed resources and services. People with AIDS may need services concerning health, income maintenance, housing, mental health care, and legal assistance.

Social workers may refer clients with AIDS to support groups, in which they can talk with others who also have AIDS and are experiencing similar problems and issues. HIV-positive people need not feel isolated and alone. They can see that there are other people who understand their issues and feelings. Additionally, such groups provide excellent channels for gaining information on how others have worked out similar problems. Social workers can also facilitate support or educational groups by serving as leader and keeping the group on track.

In addition, social workers can provide case management services to people living with AIDS. Earlier chapters established that case management involves assessing a client's needs, developing plans to meet these needs, linking the client with the appropriate services, monitoring service delivery, and advocating for the client when necessary (Taylor-Brown, 1995).

Note that part of case management involves *advocacy*—the act of stepping forward and speaking out on the behalf of clients to promote fair and equitable treatment or gain needed resources. Social workers may advocate for clients with AIDS whether those workers are case managers or not.

Advocacy may be necessary for several reasons. Advocacy can target unfair treatment when HIV-positive people are discriminated against, denied services, fired from jobs, or evicted from housing. Advocacy can also be used to seek necessary resources such as health care or financial assistance when it's not readily available.

International Perspectives: AIDS in Sub-Saharan Africa

Sub-Saharan Africa is the region on the globe most severely ravaged by AIDS, as demonstrated by the following facts:

- Currently, 27 million people are HIV-positive in sub-Saharan Africa (Marchione, 2003). This is over two-thirds of the 40 million people infected globally.
- Another 14 million people have already died there from the disease (Rathus et al., 2002).
- In 2002, when 2.4 million people died of AIDS in sub-Saharan Africa, "only about 50,000 people [or 2%] were getting treatment" (Marchione, 2003, p. 26A).
- Almost two-thirds of those receiving needed treatment for HIV come from the United States and other industrialized nations (Marchione, 2003).
- The sub-Saharan population is 10% of the world's total, but the region has only 1% of the world's wealth (Rathus et al., 2002).
- Life expectancy for 2005–2010 has declined from 59 to 45 years in the entire region and, worse yet, from 61 to 33 years in Zimbabwe (Rathus et al., 2002).

Highlight 12.7 provides several scenarios describing what it might be like to have AIDS and live in sub-Saharan Africa.

HIV infection rates continue to escalate. (This is true especially among women, who are significantly more likely to catch HIV through sexual intercourse [Masland, 2000].) Because of the stigma associated with AIDS, people cling to denial, often resulting in lack of treatment and death. The migrant worker lifestyle contributes to the commonplace acceptance of casual sex. Women are taught early on that "the man is always in charge" and so feel "powerless to change sexual behavior" (p. 42). It's not uncommon for women who deny their partners sex or request that they use condoms to suffer severe beatings or even desertion. Men typically loathe condoms, about which the following myths run rampant:

- Condoms inhibit erections and detract from pleasurable sensations.
- One is not a real man if he has to use a condom.
- When condoms fill up with semen, they spread HIV.
- Condoms manufactured by foreigners come to Africa already infected with HIV.

What can be done to tackle this mammoth problem of rampant HIV infection in sub-Saharan Africa?

1. Launch serious and extensive preventive programs to educate people about HIV/AIDS and its transmission. The stigma associated with HIV/AIDS should be eliminated (Cowley, 2000, p. 38).
2. Publicize the potential consequences of unprotected casual sex with programs stressing safer sex (Cowley, 2000, p. 38). For example, Uganda has taken steps to promote sex education since 1986. "Primary schools and health centers tout the ABCs (abstinence, be faithful, and use condoms). The taboos have eroded so much that personal ads in . . . [one] steamy *Red Pepper* tabloid list HIV status along with age, height, and interests. Correspondingly, infection rates among the most vulnerable age groups dropped from 30% in 1992 to 6% today" (Whitelaw, 2003, p. 19). Similarly, Senegal has developed educational programming in addition to having "cut

HIGHLIGHT 12.7

What Would Your Life Be Like If You Had AIDS and Lived in Sub-Saharan Africa?

McGeary (2001) suggests that you consider what your life would be like if you lived in sub-Saharan Africa. She describes several scenarios.

Scenario A: Fundisi Khumao, age 22, has AIDS and tuberculosis (TB). He knows he has TB but does not acknowledge that he has AIDS. AIDS is something not to be talked about. Breathing is tremendously difficult for him and often characterized by violent coughing spasms. He is poor, cold, and alone. Vomiting, constipation, and extreme weakness are common occurrences. Before he got sick, he worked as a hairdresser in a large city. There he had several girlfriends, from one of whom he likely caught HIV. When he couldn't work anymore, he retreated to his rural village. No medicine is available for AIDS, and he has no money anyway. Fundisi won't go to a hospital because he feels people go there only to die.

Scenario B: Laetitia Hambahlane, age 51, has AIDS and admits it. She worked as a domestic servant for wealthy people in a large city before she became too sick. It was very difficult for her to accept the fact that she had AIDS. She told her four children, who were "ashamed and frightened" (p. 38). The worst part for her is the total rejection by her mother. Having AIDS is shameful, and having almost anything else would be better. Laetitia's children are sick of hearing about her problems and will no longer help her (e.g., by bringing her food when she's too weak to get it herself). "One day local youths barged into her room, cursed her as a witch and a whore, and beat her. When she told the police, the youths returned, threatening to burn down the house" (p. 40).

Scenario C: Louis Chikoka, age 39, is a married truck driver with three children. Because work close to home is rarely available, it is common in Africa to have work elsewhere and spend the majority of time away from home. When Louis is away from home for long periods, he has sex with other women. He knows this places him at great risk of contracting HIV, but he says he has needs and sees no other way to meet them. His life situation reflects a typical picture. The region is economically dependent on migrant laborers who often find themselves far from home, so having multiple sexual partners is common practice. Unfortunately, this frequently results in bringing the disease home to wives and girlfriends.

Scenario D: A tiny 3-year-old child whom we will arbitrarily call Adwowa lies dying of AIDS in the hospital. "Now her skin wrinkles around her body like an oversize suit, and her twig-size bones can barely hold her vertical as nurses search for a vein to take blood. In the frail arms hooked up to transfusion tubes, her veins have collapsed. . . . She mews like a wounded animal" while the nurses struggle to raise a vein to obtain a minuscule sample of her blood (p. 44). Her mother, age 25, does not know the little girl has AIDS. She has heard of AIDS but knows little else about it. For example, she does not know that it can be contracted through sexual intercourse or passed on to an infant at birth. She doesn't even know if she or her husband has it. Adwowa's father works far away in a large city and can return home only a couple of times each year. He probably often seeks sexual solace from strangers.

taxes on condoms and got[ten] religious leaders to participate in AIDS education"; this also has sharply reduced infection rates (Cowley, 2000; Lemonick, 2000, p. 39).

3. Empower women to have greater control over their sex lives. One option is the development of low-cost contraception over which they have more influence (Cowley, 2000).

4. Very importantly, have developed countries provide significant financial contributions and aid in the form of subsidized drug costs so that African nations can better afford to provide drug treatment. Despite prohibitive drug costs in the United States, it is estimated that "cocktail" drugs to fight HIV in Africa cost about $360 annually (Whitelaw, 2003) and are expected to drop to less than $140 a year (Brink, 2003). (A question for critical thinking is, Why does treatment for HIV in Africa cost potentially 1% to 2% of its cost in the United States?)

5. Develop a vaccine to prevent AIDS (Cowley, 2000).

 # International Perspectives: HIV in Thailand

Although sub-Saharan Africa faces the most extreme crisis, AIDS is a global problem. Asia generally has a very low rate of HIV infection. However, "Cambodia, Thailand, and Burma have infection rates above 1%" (Begley, 2001, p. 36). As one of the scenarios introducing this section on HIV/AIDS indicated, infection is spreading from these areas at accelerating rates.

Hyde and DeLamater (2003) explain the situation in Thailand. An estimated 40–50% of intravenous drug users and 20–45% of prostitutes are infected with HIV. Thailand is renowned for its booming "sex industry" and its swelling tourist trade (p. 534). Thailand also has a vast discrepancy between rich and poor. Young impoverished rural women are drawn to prostitution in the cities, where they can make up to 25 times more doing that than working at the other jobs available to them. Many enter prostitution to help out their families or assist in paying family debts.

Many tourists are well aware of the thriving sex trade and actively seek out prostitutes. The result is not only the spread of AIDS in Thailand but also international contamination when participating tourists return to their own countries. The Thai government has attempted to address the issue by initiating sex education in the schools and providing easy access to condoms. This strategy has resulted in some positive change. There has been a decreased incidence of sex with prostitutes and fewer HIV-positive new military recruits. However, HIV/AIDS remains a significant problem.

Looking Ahead

Health care and mental health care are related. Each has important issues involving managed care, health care access, and culturally competent service provision. Chapter 13 explores employment settings in mental health for social workers, as well as social work roles, policy issues, and cultural competence in mental health settings.

For Further Exploration on the Internet

See this text's Book Companion Website at **www.socialwork.wadsworth.com/ kirstashman_intro2e** for descriptors and hot links to URLs relevant to this chapter, selected InfoTrac articles and exercises, and tutorial quizzes.

CHAPTER THIRTEEN

SOCIAL WORK AND SERVICES
IN MENTAL HEALTH

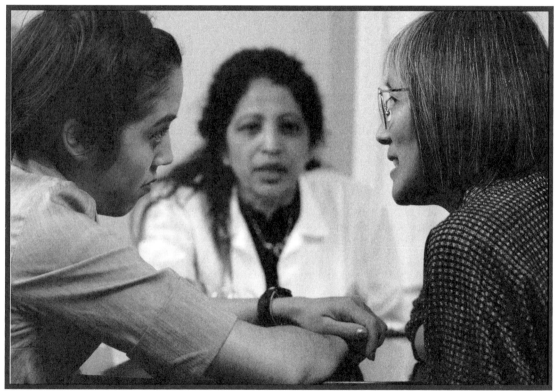

© Brand X Pictures/Alamy

Jennifer, age 18, is an extremely tall, thin young woman with olive skin and waist-length black hair. She is receiving psychotherapy for anorexia nervosa[1] and depression. She regularly found herself drinking a few shots of cheap whiskey prior to any social event she attended. Actually, she felt compelled to do so to avoid the inevitable panic attack she would abruptly experience. Each attack was characterized by extreme anxiety, dread, shortness of breath, sweaty palms, racing heart, and fears of going crazy. (Note that panic attacks had never been part of her diagnosis.) She always knew she'd get an attack at a party or a dance if she didn't come "prepared," but she never could predict exactly when it would happen. She was terrified of behaving "like a crazy woman" in front of everybody. She has even started to avoid social situations altogether if she can't figure out a way to drink discreetly first.[2]

Larry, a college sophomore, can't seem to get out of bed in the morning. He hasn't been to class in a week and a half. Nothing seems to matter to him anymore. Everything seems dark and murky. He feels his grades are terrible, his parents are disappointed in him, and people don't really like him. No one seems to care whether he lives or dies. Life is futile. What does anything matter? Larry is depressed.

Aquinnah, age 38, has murdered her 71-year-old mother. She responded to voices in her head commanding her to take the large kitchen knife and do so. Diagnosed with schizophrenia at age 18, she had a history of hearing voices and of getting into fights. She also compulsively collected hundreds of empty shampoo bottles and the shoelaces from discarded running shoes, which she kept in her mother's basement. Sometimes, when the voices told her to leave her mother's home, where she usually stayed, she would camp out behind dumpsters in parking lots of discount department stores. She was arrested for murder when found roaming around aimlessly in her mother's yard carrying the bloodied knife. At the time, she had her 11-year-old son with her; he was wearing girls' clothing and brilliantly colored makeup.

Roger, age 55, is a Vietnam War veteran. "Since he was discharged, he has worked erratically in construction, a pattern that has contributed to marital problems. Roger reports having flashbacks of his war experiences, difficulty sleeping, and angry outbursts against others. Occasionally he has gotten into fistfights with men at work, and on a few occasions he has beaten his wife. He has been going to the VA [Veterans Affairs][3] clinic on and off for 10 years, has been on medication, but has never been hospitalized. The mental health staff at the VA clinic suspect that he has minimal brain dysfunction, an organic condition, which is not war related, as well as posttraumatic stress disorder, which is war related. He has been turned down for disability" (Sands, 1991, pp. 186–187).

These vignettes illustrate various facets of emotional, psychological, and behavioral problems, also referred to as mental illness, a serious social problem. The first reflects a panic attack (a type of anxiety disorder), the second a case of depression, the third

---

[1]*Anorexia nervosa,* mainly afflicting girls and young women, is a condition whereby a person refuses to maintain a normal minimal body weight and has an extreme dread of gaining weight.

[2]This vignette is loosely adapted from one described in Hayward and Collier (1996).

[3]The U.S. Department of Veterans' Affairs, formerly the Veterans' Administration, provides a wide range of services to veterans including health and mental health care, long-term care such as nursing homes, educational benefits, and housing (Becerra & Damron-Rodriquez, 1995).

schizophrenia, and the fourth posttraumatic stress disorder. These represent the types of problems and issues social workers confront every day in mental health practice.

Note the following facts:

- Approximately 28% of the U.S. population suffers from some form of mental illness or substance abuse disorder every year (U.S. Department of Health & Human Services [USDHHS], 1999).
- At least 40% of people with mental illness receive no treatment for their condition (Kornblum & Julian, 2004).
- Approximately 3.5 million people experience extreme forms of mental illness such as schizophrenia and manic-depressive disorder every year (Kornblum & Julian, 2004).

Almost half of all members of the National Association of Social Workers (NASW) are employed in the health or mental health fields (Ginsberg, 2001). Of social workers with master's degrees, 33% work in the mental health field (O'Neill, 2003). The *Encyclopedia of Social Work* affirms that "[t]he social work profession has assumed a key role in the provision of mental health services" (Lin, 1995, p. 1705). Therefore, significant time will be spent discussing what social workers do in mental health and where.

This chapter will

- Review the wide range of mental health settings in which social workers practice.
- Identify some of the functions social workers perform in mental health settings.
- Examine managed care and stress the need for advocacy and empowerment.
- Encourage critical thinking about the effectiveness of the *Diagnostic and Statistical Manual-IV-TR* as the primary assessment system for mental illness, the pros and cons of electroconvulsive therapy, the real intent of managed care concerning mental illness, and national mental health policy issues.
- Address the issue of cultural competence in mental health settings, identify barriers many people of color face in accessing services, and suggest ways of improving access and enhancing cultural competence.

Mental Health, Mental Illness, and Social Work Roles

The concept of mental health has many dimensions. *Mental health* is the state of relative psychological and emotional well-being in which an individual can make acceptably rational decisions, cope adequately with personal and external stresses, and maintain satisfactory adjustment to society. *Mental illness* is any of a wide range of psychological, emotional, or cognitive disorders that impair a person's ability to function effectively. Causes may be "biological, chemical, physiological, genetic, psychological, or social"; mental illness is "extremely variable in duration, severity, and prognosis" (Barker, 2003, p. 269). Primary symptoms of mental illness include extreme anxiety, disturbed thinking processes, perceptual distortions, extreme mood variations, and other difficulties in thinking (USDHHS, 1999). Another common term for mental illness is *mental disorder*. A later section of this chapter will describe some of the conditions clients face when they have a mental illness.

Employment Settings in Mental Health for Social Workers

Social workers practice in a broad range of settings and can assume many roles. Just as in other practice areas, advocacy for rights and services is a vital social work function here. Rising costs for mental health care and increasing numbers of people requiring treatment and resources will challenge social workers in the coming years. Mental health programs compete for limited funds just like other forms of social services. There is a constant struggle in the political environment to empower people by getting them the services they need.

Social workers are employed, along with professionals in other, related fields, in a wide range of mental health facilities. These include inpatient mental and psychiatric hospitals, psychiatric units in general hospitals, residential treatment centers for children and adolescents, outpatient treatment agencies, employee assistance programs, and community mental health centers. NASW indicates that "there are more clinically trained social workers than members of other core mental health professions [including psychiatrists, psychologists, and psychiatric nurses] combined" (O'Neill, 1999, p. 1). Highlight 13.1 addresses the differences between social workers with a BSW and those with a MSW.

The Least Restrictive Setting on a Continuum of Care: Empowering Clients

A critical concept in mental health treatment is client treatment in the *least restrictive setting* possible. Earlier chapters defined this as the setting that allows the client maximum self-determination while providing the intensity of treatment needed to be effective. This involves the idea that clients should be empowered to have maximum control over their own lives while having access to the treatment level needed. The restrictiveness of treatment setting is related to the concept of the *continuum of care*. The continuum of available services should provide a range of treatment alternatives ranging from the least restrictive to the most. Chapter 9 discussed similar concepts with respect to substitute placements for children in out-of-home care.

One of the most restrictive settings is placement in a locked ward of a mental hospital. Clients placed here have minimal control over their lives and, theoretically, maximum access to treatment 24 hours a day. One of the least restrictive settings involves individuals receiving treatment in an outpatient facility for an hour or two each week while residing in their own homes and going about their regular daily activities.

One problem with the idea of minimal restrictiveness of setting is that adequate, effective services must be readily available in less restrictive parts of the continuum. For example, if a client released from an institution into the community requires some level of service, that service must be readily available to that client. The process of providing services and care for people within their own communities rather than in institutional settings is called *deinstitutionalization*.

Mental health settings that employ social workers include inpatient mental and psychiatric hospitals; residential treatment centers for children and adolescents; psychiatric

HIGHLIGHT 13.1

Differences Between BSW and MSW Positions and Responsibilities

Both BSWs and MSWs can find employment in a wide range of mental health settings. Likewise, both can have field placements in mental health agencies. However, there are some differences in the types of jobs for which each is qualified. MSWs are considered more specialized than BSWs (Johnson, 1998b). The implication is that MSWs are competent to address more difficult psychological problems than BSWs and have the potential to assume greater responsibility. However, both can and do work in mental health settings. Suppes and Wells (2003) comment:

> Mental health crises or emergencies are not uncommon in generalist social work practice across all possible settings; therefore, BSWs do need to have confidence in their ability to work with people with a wide range of problems. BSWs in mental health settings such as hospitals often provide crisis intervention, work with the families of patients, and counsel patients individually and in groups. They serve as the hospital's link to the community, teaching its staff about the population while at the same time offering preventive mental health education within the community. (pp. 204–205)

A major difference between BSWs and MSWs is that providing psychotherapy is solely the domain of MSWs. *Psychotherapy* is a skilled treatment process whereby a therapist works with an individual, couple, family, or group to address a mental disorder or alleviate other problems the client(s) may be having in the social environment. Sometimes the term *therapy* is used, especially in reference to various psychotherapeutic approaches such as behavioral therapy, psychodynamic therapy, or cognitive therapy. The term *therapy*, however, can also refer to treatment of problems other than mental health and adjustment problems. Examples are speech therapy, occupational therapy, and physical therapy.

Often, as Chapter 1 noted, higher-level supervisory and administrative positions require an MSW or other master's level degree. Such positions usually offer higher salaries. Finally, MSWs generally earn significantly more than BSWs, although years of experience enhance salaries for both groups.

units in general hospitals; outpatient treatment agencies; employee assistance programs; and community mental health centers, which provide a wide range of services.

Inpatient Mental and Psychiatric Hospitals

Inpatient treatment facilities such as publicly funded state and county mental hospitals and private psychiatric clinics provide one employment setting for social workers. *Inpatient* means that clients reside in the facility for some period. They are among the most restrictive treatment settings available. Depending on the problem, this period might be as short as days or as long as a lifetime. Medicare or Medicaid usually pays for treatment in public institutions. Private psychiatric facilities, which are usually quite expensive, most frequently are funded directly by clients or by their private insurance. Both types fulfill the functions of assessment, planning, provision of medications, and therapeutic treatment for various severe mental disorders.

Note that other long-term care facilities are also used when people with deteriorating or acute mental conditions can no longer remain in their own homes; examples are nursing homes and foster care homes (Ginsberg, 2001).

Residential Treatment Centers for Children and Adolescents

An area in which child welfare and mental health overlap is *residential treatment centers* (RTCs) and group homes for children. An RTC is an agency that provides children who have serious emotional and behavioral problems with residential round-the-clock care, education (often with an emphasis on special education), interpersonal skills training, and individual, group, and sometimes family therapy. Although all RTCs, by definition, provide residential care, other aspects of their orientation and programming vary substantially. Treatment may involve any of a wide range of psychotherapeutic approaches (e.g., behavioral, cognitive, psychoanalytic). Some RTCs have a school right on the premises, and others use public schools. Some RTCs are located in rural settings; others are in urban metropolises. Some have only male residents, others have only females, and still others have both.

Residents spend most of their time with the residential staff (typically called something like child care workers or unit counselors) caring for them. Therefore, such staff can have a huge impact on the treatment process. Residents usually spend relatively little time with psychotherapists, who may be MSWs, psychiatrists, psychologists, or some combination of these.

Many settings emphasize behavioral programming and provide structured guidelines for how counselors should respond to various types of behavior on the part of residents. Techniques such as using positive reinforcement (e.g., praising), employing empathy, and giving feedback about behavior can be useful in changing behavior for the better (Stein, 1995). *Positive reinforcement* is a procedure or consequence that increases the frequency of the behavior immediately preceding it. For example, a staff member might say to a resident, "Hey, Billy, you really did a nice job completing your chores this week. Way to go!" This is positive reinforcement if the result is that Billy continues doing his assigned chores on time. *Empathy* is the act of not only understanding how another person feels but also conveying to that person an awareness of how he or she feels. For example, a staff member might say to a client, "I can see how frustrated you are with your homework. I know how difficult it is for you." *Feedback* is the process of giving people information, positive or negative, about their performance or behavior.

Often RTCs use token or point systems in which tokens (i.e., symbolic objects such as poker chips or artificial coins that reflect units of value) or points on a chart are used in a coordinated system to control poor behavior, develop good behavior, and monitor progress. Appropriate and inappropriate behaviors are clearly defined, as are expectations and consequences for various behaviors. Residents earn tokens or points for good behavior and lose them for bad conduct. Highlight 13.2 gives an example of how positive reinforcement (usually in the form of praise), empathy, and feedback are used by a staff member in an RTC (Stein, 1995, pp. 205–206).

Group Homes

As Chapter 9 explained, group homes are considered less extreme on the continuum of care in terms of restrictiveness of setting. Children and adolescents placed in group homes don't need the more extreme institutional placement in an RTC. However, group homes also vary dramatically in terms of restrictiveness and intensity. Some are run by married couples; others have staff available around the clock.

HIGHLIGHT 13.2

Using Positive Reinforcement, Empathy, and Feedback to Change Behavior

The scene: Pete, age 12, is a resident of the Earl E. Bird Residential Treatment Center for Boys. He is quite unhappy. He needs to earn a certain number of points to go on a field trip to a big basketball game, which he *really* wants to do. But he lost points for poking another guy in the ear on Monday. Then, on Wednesday, Jethro, another kid in his unit, picked a fight with him. Although Pete ended up with a bloody nose, he gave Jethro a black eye, which cost him more points. He was so angry the entire week that he refused to make his bed, which resulted in still more points lost. By Thursday, it was impossible for Pete to earn enough points to go to the game. Furious, he stomps out of the unit and down the long driveway, contemplating running away. Rashaun, one of the residential staff on Pete's unit, catches up to Pete and starts to talk with him. (Note that in the following dialogue nonverbal behavior is indicated by regular roman type within brackets, and positive reinforcement [usually in the form of praise], empathy, and feedback are indicated by boldface type within brackets.)

Rashaun: Pete, it's time to get back to the unit.

Pete: [Continues walking, trying to ignore Rashaun]

Rashaun: Pete, did you hear me?

Pete: F___ you, buzzard breath. I ain't goin' back and you can't make me!

Rashaun: You sound like you're upset about something **[expression of empathy]**. You'll only lose points if you don't get back **[feedback]**.

Pete: Shove your f___ing points up your a___!

Rashaun: Come on. Let's walk over to the basketball court and talk. [Turns and walks

toward the basketball court, which is empty right now]

Pete: [Pretends to ignore Rashaun at first, but eventually follows him, his eyes downcast]

Rashaun: It's been a bad week for you, hasn't it? **[empathy]**.

Pete: Yeah . . . [Said gloomily and without eye contact]

Rashaun: You haven't earned enough points to go to the game this weekend, have you?

Pete: Nope. Life's a b___. I'll never get to go anywhere.

Rashaun: Well, you know, getting points for the game next weekend starts tomorrow **[feedback]**. How about starting fresh? You usually do a good job of keeping yourself together and getting enough points to go along **[praise]**.

Pete: [Finally looking up] Maybe. But it's such a long time till then.

Rashaun: I know, it's really tough living up to all the rules around here **[empathy]**. But, come on now, you can do it. You need to start getting those points back so you can get to the game next weekend **[feedback]**.

Pete: [Saying nothing, starts walking toward the unit, while Rashaun walks along with him]

Rashaun: I give you a lot of credit for getting yourself under control **[praise]**. I know it was hard for you **[empathy]**. I think you deserve 10 extra points for going back to the unit so quickly **[positive reinforcement]**. That should help you toward next week's goal so you can go to the game **[feedback]**.

Pete: [Finally looking up at Rashaun and smiling just a little] OK, thanks.

Some provide intensive individual, group, and family psychotherapy; others provide little, if any, such treatment. Group homes are smaller than RTCs, usually limited by law to a maximum number of residents such as eight.

The reasons children are placed in group homes also vary. The courts determine that they cannot remain in their own homes for reasons ranging from abusive situations to their own emotional and behavioral problems. Some simply need a protective environment with emotional support, consistent treatment, and exposure to positive role models. Others demonstrate extremely aggressive, deviant, or uncontrollable behavior and require a treatment setting almost as structured as an RTC, but smaller and more personal.

Why, then, are some children and adolescents placed in RTCs and others in group homes when their behavior is similar? Placement decisions involve complex issues. The value system of the person determining the placement (e.g., a judge or a social worker making recommendations to a judge), types of RTCs and group homes available, openings within these settings, and cost can all contribute to decisions about where a young client is ultimately placed.

Psychiatric Units in General Hospitals

Psychiatric units in general hospitals offer emergency psychiatric care on a temporary inpatient basis for people in crisis. They usually work closely with other, longer-term inpatient and outpatient facilities to provide care at whatever level on the continuum of care a client needs.

Outpatient Treatment Agencies

Not all people, of course, need inpatient treatment. *Outpatient treatment* agencies and clinics provide individual, group, and family counseling for a wide range of mental health and substance abuse problems. Clients come in for their treatment and then leave when they're done.

Sometimes private practitioners, including social workers, psychologists, and psychiatrists, establish their own practice and serve their own clientele, working as individuals or with a small group of colleagues. Social workers who do this often call themselves *clinical social workers* (previously *psychiatric social workers*). This means that they provide psychotherapy to clients to address mental health issues and other life problems. Clinical social workers may also work for other types of mental health agencies.

A *family service association* is a type of outpatient treatment agency that offers various types of counseling, often in addition to child welfare services such as adoption and foster care. These agencies usually have multiple funding sources and are governed by a board of directors. Many are part of a national organization, such as Family Service America (FSA), Catholic Social Services, and Lutheran Social Services.

Employee Assistance Programs

Employee assistance programs (EAPs) are services provided by organizations that focus on workers' mental health and on adjustment problems that interfere with their work performance. An underlying principle is that impaired worker performance due to factors such as absenteeism and stress costs companies money and that EAPs can significantly reduce such costs (Van Den Bergh, 1995). Problems addressed include substance abuse, family conflicts, financial problems, job stress, difficulties with day care for children or dependent parents, and other personal issues interfering with workers' psychological ability to do their jobs.

Occupational social work (also referred to as *industrial social work*) is the provision of mental health treatment by social workers in the workplace under the auspices of employers. Services can be either delivered by an internal office or purchased by employers from external contractors. Van Den Bergh (1995) notes that internal EAPs will likely be affected by the recent growth in managed mental health care "because many managed health care firms offer EAPs as part of their services" (p. 848). The implication is that internal EAPs may decrease in number. (Managed care in mental health is discussed more thoroughly later in the chapter.)

Occupational social workers provide direct service involving "assessment-and-referral counseling sessions," usually offering "as many as three sessions per problem" (Van Den Bergh, 1995, p. 847). When problems can't be resolved quickly, workers typically make referrals to outside social services or "community-based support groups (for instance, 12-step programs [for alcoholics], Parents Without Partners, and Parents and Friends of Lesbians and Gays)" (Van Den Bergh, 1995, p. 847). Sometimes occupational social workers run "support groups for employees with similar problems" such as an ongoing group for HIV-positive workers or a short-term group for workers distressed by organizational downsizing (characterized by extensive layoffs unrelated to worker performance) (Gibelman, 1995; Van Den Bergh, 1995, p. 847). Occupational social workers also provide preventive services in the form of seminars and training sessions on topics such as combating sexual harassment and increasing racial sensitivity (Gibelman, 1995).

Community Mental Health Centers: A Macro Response to Individual Needs

Community mental health centers are versatile local organizations that provide a range of services, from mental health treatment to education about and prevention of mental illness. They fulfill a range of functions for which social workers may be employed. Ginsberg (2001, pp. 124–127) identifies and describes at least six functions community mental health centers perform:

1. *Case management:* This is the process of assessing clients' needs, linking clients to appropriate services, coordinating service provision, and monitoring its effectiveness. Whereas the broker role involves linking clients to resources, key concepts in the case manager role are coordinating and monitoring service provision. Kanter (1985) describes how case management can be used with clients having a serious mental illness:

   [Such people] require a wide range of treatment and rehabilitation approaches that include medication, psychotherapy, family involvement, day treatment, crisis intervention, and brief and extended hospitalizations. Simultaneously, they often need a variety of social services that include housing, financial assistance, vocational training and placement, and medical care. Although obtaining needed services is not easy for "healthy persons," these . . . [clients] have particular difficulty in locating and negotiating such assistance. (p. 78)

Case management is described more thoroughly in the discussion of what social workers do in the mental health context.

2. *Child and adolescent services:* These are aimed at enhancing the overall functioning of child and adolescent clients. Activities may include counseling, working with the schools on behalf of these young people, making referrals for services such as prescription drugs or family therapy, and involving clients in recreational activities.

3. *Information and education programs:* Staff including social workers educate community residents, family members of people with mental illness, and other professionals in the community about prevention, the problems involved, and the treatment of mental illness.

4. *Long-term community care programs:* These serve people with mental illness on an ongoing basis. Often case managers help such people remain in the community by regularly visiting their homes, monitoring medication, and coordinating other needed services.

5. *Day treatment programs:* These provide daily activities for people with mental illness, including recreational pursuits like games or crafts, health services, and educational programs.

6. *Alcohol and other drug treatment programs:* These provide treatment, including individual and group counseling. Often staff in such units work cooperatively with other inpatient facilities to give clients the type of care they need.

Highlight 13.3 addresses the fact that the titles of professionals working in community mental health settings can be confusing.

Clients with Mental Health Problems

Because of their significance to social work practice and to practitioners in the mental health field, a number of conditions affecting people's mental health will be described here. The most commonly used classification system for defining and diagnosing mental illness is the *Diagnostic and Statistical Manual of Mental Disorders Text Revision (DSM-IV-TR)* (2000), written by work groups composed of professional clinicians and published by the American Psychiatric Association. (Note that the "IV" indicates that this is the fourth edition, and "TR" refers to *Text Revision.*)

The *DSM-IV-TR* includes 17 major diagnostic categories and dozens of more specific diagnostic classifications. It describes each diagnosis in detail, providing a description of symptoms and diagnostic criteria to determine whether a person falls within that category.

Despite some serious concerns raised in Focus on Critical Thinking 13.1, the *DSM-IV-TR* serves as the primary guideline for classifying various types of mental illness. This, in turn, qualifies people to receive treatment paid for by the government (e.g., Medicaid or Medicare) or private health insurance. In other words, to be eligible for services and payment for these services, a person must first have the appropriate diagnosis. The *DSM-IV-TR* includes not only mental disorders but also

HIGHLIGHT 13.3
What's in a Title?

Mental health settings are often characterized by professionals from a variety of disciplines working together for the benefit of clients. Such groups are referred to as *interdisciplinary teams*. Each professional brings to the team his or her professional perspective and area of expertise.

As you know, social workers can assume many roles. *Clinical social workers* provide psychotherapy in mental health settings. *Psychiatrists* are medical doctors with additional training in psychiatry, which, of course, focuses on mental health treatment. They are the only professionals who can prescribe psychotropic drugs. Other professionals rely on psychiatrists to fulfill this function. *Psychologists* have a doctorate or master's degree in psychology. Depending on their area of expertise, they may do psychotherapy and/or psychological testing. *Psychiatric nurses* who work in mental health settings have a bachelor's or master's degree in nursing. They bring their medical background and patient care expertise to the mental health setting.

Teams also may include *paraprofessionals*—persons with specialized training in some area—who are supervised by a professional and assume some of the professional's tasks. For example, a *case aid* might assist a social worker by helping clients fill out necessary forms or transporting clients to a treatment center.

other conditions that may be the focus of clinical treatment. Note that psychiatrists usually must make the official diagnosis for clients to qualify for benefits.

To provide some insight into what mental illness is like, a number of conditions will be briefly described here. These include dementia, schizophrenia and other psychotic disorders, mood disorders, anxiety disorders, dissociative disorders, eating disorders, sexual disorders, impulse control disorders, and personality disorders.

Dementia

Dementia is a state in which people develop numerous cognitive problems due to some medical problem. *Alzheimer's disease* is a common type of dementia of unknown origin, characterized by mental decline and usually occurring in late middle age.

Case Example   Jose, age 59, has Alzheimer's disease, having been diagnosed five years ago. His wife Maria, age 56, first started noticing Jose gradually withdrawing from her and spending more time to himself. He began having more and more trouble accomplishing at first more complex and, later, simpler tasks. He had been a professional trumpet player. Now when he picks up his trumpet, he doesn't know what to do with it. Sometimes he bangs it against the clothes dryer. Other times he picks up his razor and tries to make music with it. He constantly asks Maria questions. By the time she answers, he forgets what he asked and why. He has difficulty completing a simple task like drying the dishes because he forgets what he's doing even as he does it. He might put the dish down and walk away or else notice it in his hand and start washing it again.

While administering psychological testing to determine the extent of Jose's cognitive deterioration, a psychologist placed a pencil, a piece of paper, and a fluorescent

FOCUS ON CRITICAL THINKING 13.1

Potential Shortcomings of the *DSM-IV-TR*

Critical thinking involves asking questions, assessing facts, and asserting a logical conclusion. The *DSM-IV-TR* serves as the primary guide in the United States for assessing mental health problems and placing labels on people so they can receive treatment. Just because the manual exists doesn't mean it provides the best way or even the right way to approach dealing with people who have mental illness. In fact, many social workers have questioned the importance placed upon this manual and its reliability (Lin, 1995; Sheafor & Horejsi, 2003). For one thing, it focuses on people's pathologies and virtually ignores their strengths. Additionally, it places little value on the importance of the environment. Rather, it reflects the medical model that focuses on how to *cure* individuals. It does not stress how individuals are integrally involved with other people and systems in their environment, which provides the crucial context for mental health problems.

Another problem involves labeling. Critics maintain that labeling according to specified criteria is arbitrary and based on cultural expectations. What is considered normal for one culture or class might be viewed very differently by another. For example, Popple and Leighninger (2002) note that "a wealthy older woman who sometimes thinks she is the reincarnation of Cleopatra may simply be regarded as 'eccentric.' A bag lady who talks to herself as she roams the streets of New York may well be called 'crazy'" (p. 458). A later section of the chapter stresses the importance of enhancing cultural competence through understanding the values and expectations of other cultural groups.

To what extent do you feel that the *DSM-IV-TR*'s assessment and labeling system is fair and adequate? What are the reasons for your answer? What do you see as the *DSM-IV-TR*'s strengths and weaknesses?

orange plastic scissors in front of him on a table. He then asked Jose to place the pen on the piece of paper. In response, Jose ignored the pen and paper, picking up the scissors and placing it back on the table upside down. His personality, what made Jose a special and unique individual, was gradually being drained from him. It was difficult for his family to cope.

Schizophrenia and Other Psychotic Disorders

Schizophrenia is a severe mental disturbance characterized by delusions; hallucinations; confused, incoherent speech; bizarre behavior; flattened emotional responses; short, empty verbal responses that lack attentiveness; and inability to participate in goal-directed activities.

Schizophrenia is one of the most common forms of *psychosis*—any of a number of serious mental disorders characterized by disturbed, inappropriate behavior and "loss of contact with reality" (Pickett, 2002, p. 1125). Psychosis is often contrasted with *neurosis*, a mental disorder characterized by "feelings of anxiety, obsessional thoughts, compulsive acts, and physical complaints without objective evidence of disease" that occur "in various degrees and patterns" (Nichols, 1999, p. 888). Psychosis is sometimes thought of as more severe than neurosis because psychotic people lose contact with reality. The key concepts involved in neurosis are anxiety and the behaviors resulting from its extreme forms.

Case Example   Frances, age 61, has been diagnosed with schizophrenia. She lives in a tiny 75-year-old house in a rural midwestern town 80 miles from the nearest city. Even in the heat of summer, she wears multiple layers of clothing to "keep the evil spirits away." She never turns her lights on at night because, she believes, hands reach out from the ceiling light fixtures and try to grab her. Although most of her neighbors shy away from her, she seeks them out whenever she sees them outdoors. A typical comment she makes to them is, "Sometimes Sylvester Stallone appears and I take over his body and fight the spirits. But they can't tell who it is and sometimes we're the same. The dark makes the squash purple." Needless to say, this makes no sense. She also puts her garbage in small lunch bags, sometimes as many as 40, and lines them up in a perfect row along the curb for pickup. Frances periodically is hospitalized, in which event medication helps to curb her bizarre thought processes and behaviors. However, when she returns home she ceases taking her medication and symptoms subsequently resume.

Mood Disorders

Although *mood* is a difficult word to define, most of us have a general idea of what it means. *Mood disorders* are mental disorders involving extreme disturbances in a person's mood—that is, his or her emotional state and attitude. As with many other mental disorders, those concerning mood involve extremes beyond what people normally experience. Such extremes, involving intensity, duration, or fluctuation of mood, cause problems in a person's ability to function normally. Specific diagnostic classifications include depressive disorders and bipolar disorders.

Depressive disorders (often referred to as *depression* in common conversation) are characterized by low spirits, unhappiness, lack of interest in daily activities, inability to experience pleasure, pessimism, significant weight loss not related to dieting (or significant weight gain), insomnia, extremely low energy levels, feelings of hopelessness and worthlessness, decreased capacity to focus and make decisions, and preoccupation with thoughts of suicide and death. It's depressing even reading that list of symptoms.

Case Example   Sharissa, age 31, is an example of a depressed person. She has been married for eight years to Jarell, age 34, who labors full-time as a welder in addition to working overtime whenever he can. Sharissa does not work outside the home. The couple has two sons, ages 3 and 5, both of whom have cognitive disabilities.

Sharissa consistently dwells on the negative aspects of her life, usually speaking to others in a high-pitched, whining tone. She complains that Jarell "never pays any attention" to her or the boys and doesn't "know the meaning of housework." When together, she criticizes him nonstop, to the point at which he simply "tunes her out." This only escalates her whining. In addition to complaining about Jarell, she grumbles about how difficult it is caring for the two boys with their special needs. She complains that all she does is work, and she gets no joy out of her life. She has no time for friends, and she and Jarell never go out anywhere together. Each night, she

Depression has negative effects on one's emotional state.

lies awake dwelling on all the supposedly horrible things that happened to her that day. She frequently says she is much too fat (although she is 5 feet 5 inches and weighs 125 pounds), but she has no time or money to go to a health club. She also claims that she is really "ugly" (although she is really quite attractive) and that she has a "shy, bad personality." A common lament is, "What is the point of living anymore when everything is so terrible?" Sharissa spews forth one negative statement after another whenever given the opportunity to talk to someone else, so it's difficult to get a word in edgewise. It's depressing and draining talking to Sharissa.

Bipolar Disorders

Bipolar disorders (formerly referred to as *manic-depressive illness*) involve extreme mood swings. With some bipolar disorders, people experience primarily *manic* episodes characterized by abnormally elevated affect, feelings of euphoria, a grandiose sense of self, excessive movement or talkativeness, and poor judgment. With other bipolar disorders, people experience primarily periods of depression and at least one *hypomanic* episode (i.e., being extremely irritable). Finally, bipolar disorders may involve mixed mood swings resulting in abrupt changes from manic to depressive episodes.

Anxiety Disorders

Anxiety disorders are persistent or periodic states of extreme anxiety characterized by excessive fear, worry, apprehensiveness, and dread of the future. Physical symptoms include a rapid pulse, dizziness, perspiration, cold hands or feet, and rapid breathing (USDHHS, 1999). Examples of anxiety disorders are panic attacks and posttraumatic stress disorder.

Panic attacks are distinct episodes of extreme anxiety and excessive dread of the future. They are often accompanied by physical symptoms such as shortness of breath, sweaty palms, chest pains, racing heart, and fears of going crazy or dying.

Posttraumatic stress disorder (PTSD) is a condition in which a person continues to reexperience some traumatic event like a bloody battle or a sexual assault. Symptoms include extreme anxiety, nightmares, an inability to sleep or stay awake, an inability to concentrate, and explosive emotional outbursts. Examples of people who may experience PTSD are victims of sexual assault, and soldiers returning from war who have witnessed horrifying violence and death.

Dissociative Disorders

Dissociative disorders involve "a disruption in the usually integrated functions of consciousness, memory, identity, or perception" (American Psychiatric Association [APA], 2000, p. 519). An example of a dissociative disorder is *dissociative identity disorder* (formerly referred to as *multiple personality disorder*). This occurs when parts of a person's personality "split off " from the rest of that person's personality, resulting in at least two totally different identities existing within the same person.

I once had a student who confided in me that she had this disorder. She said that through therapy she was now down from several personalities to only two. The one who was speaking to me at that moment was 35 years old; there was also Joey, age 7. She said Joey might come out at any time during class, so I should be prepared. I thought, "Prepared for what?" Luckily, Joey never emerged in class.

Highlight 13.4 describes the world's most famous anonymous person with a multiple personality, who was finally identified right before she died.

Sexual Disorders

Sexual disorders are those involving sexual responses and behavior. Examples are sexual dysfunctions and paraphilias.

A *sexual disorder* is "a problem with a sexual response that causes a person mental distress" (Hyde & DeLamater, 2003, p. 492). For example, a *male erectile disorder* is the "persistent difficulty in achieving or maintaining an erection sufficient to allow the completion of sexual activity" (Rathus, Nevid, & Fichner-Rathus, 2002, p. 491). A *female orgasmic disorder* is "a recurrent problem with reaching orgasm despite adequate erotic stimulation" (McAnulty & Burnette, 2001, p. 612).

Paraphilias are "sexual disorders that occur primarily in males, are characterized by recurrent fantasies, urges, or acts involving objects, nonconsenting partners, or physical pain or humiliation, and are distressing to the person or cause problems in his or her life" (McAnulty & Burnette, 2001, p. 615). One type of paraphila, *exhibitionism,* "involves recurrent and intense sexual fantasies and urges to expose one's genitals to an unsuspecting stranger" (McAnulty & Burnette, 2001, p. 502).

Eating Disorders

Eating disorders involve extreme difficulties with eating behavior. They include anorexia nervosa and bulimia nervosa.

HIGHLIGHT 13.4

Who Was Sybil? The Most Famous Case of Multiple Personalities

The condition of dissociative identity disorder gained the public's attention in 1973 when Flora Rheta Schreiber wrote her best-seller *Sybil*. The book concerned an anonymous woman identified as "Sybil" who suffered from having 16 different personalities as a result of severe childhood abuse. The book suggested that, with each major trauma Sybil experienced, a new personality split off from her initial identity.

Sybil has been identified as Shirley Ardell Mason[4] (To avoid confusion, we will continue referring to Shirley as Sybil.) Sybil, a retired teacher and artist, died on February 26, 1998, in Lexington, Kentucky, only a few weeks after confessing that she was indeed the real Sybil. Before *Sybil*'s publication, only about 75 cases of dissociative identity disorder had been diagnosed; since then there have been about 40,000 (Miller & Kantrowitz, 1999).

Many people who knew Sybil, as well as psychiatrists and others, have questioned whether she was diagnosed correctly. Sybil remained a patient of Cornelia Wilbur, the psychiatrist who provided the book's story, beginning in 1954 and continuing for 11 years, during which time she participated in over 2,300 psychotherapy sessions. Sybil, described as "a very fragile and sensitive person," began treatment as an undergraduate at Mankato State Teacher's College after she "was questioned by an English teacher as to the originality of one of her poems"; this, in conjunction with financial pressures from home, caused Sybil to experience "anxiety attacks and even blackouts in the middle of class" (Romsdahl, 1997).

Sybil stayed in close contact with Wilbur in the years after her therapy. In 1991, when Wilbur developed Parkinson's disease, Sybil acted as her nurse and companion until Wilbur's death in 1992 (Miller & Kantrowitz, 1999).

Another psychiatrist who treated Sybil described her as "a brilliant hysteric" who was "highly hypnotizable" and subject to suggestion (Miller & Kantrowitz, 1999, p. 67). He indicated that Wilbur may well have helped create various characters during the therapeutic process, which involved frequent hypnosis and doses of sodium pentothal ("truth serum").

Sybil's parents were Mattie and Walter Mason, whom Miller and Kantrowitz (1999) describe as "strictly observant Seventh-Day Adventists" (p. 67). People from Sybil's hometown of Dodge Center, Minnesota, described Mattie, the supposed perpetrator of the abuse, as "bizarre" and having a "witchlike laugh" the few times she did see humor in things; some remember Mattie "as walking around after dark, looking in neighbors' windows" and at one time "apparently being diagnosed as schizophrenic" (Miller & Kantrowitz, 1999, p. 67). According to the book, alleged "tortures primarily featured enemas that she [Sybil] was forced to hold while her mother played piano concertos, but the sadistic parent also enjoyed pushing spoons and other items up her child's vagina, making Sybil watch sexual intercourse, and hoisting her up to hang helplessly from a pulley." Some neighbors report Mattie as being exceptionally strict with Sybil. However, no one seems to remember any physical or sexual abuse taking place, especially any resembling the horrors described in the book.

No one questions that Sybil had a serious mental illness, but the truth of her story and her diagnosis remains in doubt. In any case, Sybil

(continued)

[4]Facts presented here were retrieved from the following sources: Aestraea's Web (1998), Borch-Jacobsen (1997), Hewlett (1998), Romsdahl (2002), Quiet's Corner (2002a, b), Romsdahl (1997), and Van Arsdale (2002).

HIGHLIGHT 13.4 *(continued)*

never married or had children. During the last years of her life, apparently "happy," she primarily cared for her pets, gardened, and painted until arthritis prevented her from doing so (Miller & Kantrowitz, 1999, p. 68; Van Arsdale, 2002).

Among the 16 personalities attributed to Sybil in the book were the following (Van Arsdale, 2002):

- Peggy Lou, "an assertive, enthusiastic, and often angry pixie with a pug nose."
- Marcia, "a writer and painter" who was "extremely emotional" and had a British accent (Miller & Kantrowitz, 1999).

- Mike, a self-important, olive-skinned carpenter who hoped to get a woman pregnant (Miller & Kantrowitz, 1999.)
- Sybil Ann, a pale, shy, fearful person with almost no energy.
- Mary, a heavyset, "thoughtful, contemplative, maternal, home-loving person."
- Vanessa, a tall, slim, attractive redhead.
- Ruthie, a toddler with an undeveloped and childlike personality.
- The Blonde, a playful, high-spirited, happy-go-lucky teenager.

Anorexia Nervosa

Anorexia nervosa, usually afflicting girls and young women, is a condition in which a person refuses to maintain a weight level of at least 85% of normal minimal body weight and dreads gaining weight. Essentially, the person starves herself because she never sees herself as "thin enough."

Bulimia Nervosa

Bulimia nervosa, also primarily involving females, is characterized by binging (i.e., consuming huge amounts of food), experiencing a severe lack of control over eating behavior, and using methods to get rid of calories (e.g., forcing oneself to vomit [purging], using laxatives or enemas, and undergoing extreme exercising).

Bulimia nervosa afflicts from 1 to 3% of females in the United States and one-tenth as many males (APA, 2000). Several factors tend to characterize people suffering from bulimia nervosa (Lefrançois, 1999). First, they are obsessed with being thin. Our culture places a high value on thinness and its clear-cut positive correlation with attractiveness. Most bulimics remain at or near normal weight. Second, bulimics tend to have a distorted perception of their physical appearance. A young woman within a normal weight range might look into the mirror and "see" a fat person with a double chin and bulging stomach. Third, bulimics tend to experience depression (Ledoux, Choquet, & Manfredi, 1993). However, it is unclear whether depression, along with its accompanying shame and loss of control, is a result of or a trigger for bulimia nervosa.

Bulimia's Pattern A pattern typically characterizes people developing bulimia nervosa. First, a person concerned with being thin and attractive begins dieting. Second, dieting and the resulting deprivation become extremely difficult to maintain. Third, the craving for food results in overeating; this phase is usually initiated by some crisis or stress, and eating provides comfort that leads to contentment. Fourth, the person gains weight because of the overeating and so feels guilty, ashamed, and out of control. Fifth, the person discovers that weight can be somewhat controlled through methods such as purging, using laxatives or enemas, and exercising excessively. Sixth, the binge/purge cycle becomes an established way of coping with life's stresses, and the person comes to depend upon it. Seventh, as guilt and shame continue to build, the person expends increasingly greater energy to conceal the binge/purge behavior from those around her (or him).

Case Example   Elena, age 17, was an active high school junior—she was an attractive, popular cross-country runner and cheerleader. She also did some professional modeling on the side. Her cross-country coach and her modeling supervisor stressed the need for her to remain thin, and indicated that losing a few pounds couldn't hurt. (This demonstrates phase 1 of the bulimia nervosa pattern.)

Elena dieted to lose those few extra pounds and began to crave carbohydrates and sweets (phase 2). She had always adored Little Debbie Snack Cakes, doughnut holes, and potato chips. Finally, struggling to find time for cheerleading, running, modeling, and studying for exams, she broke down and ate two dozen snack cakes and two large bags of potato chips (phase 3). This happened more than once. A few days later, she discovered that she had gained a couple of pounds. She was ashamed of her gluttonous behavior and horrified at getting "fat" (phase 4). When she looked in the mirror, she saw every ounce of the added weight. She even thought she could see cellulite on her thighs that had never been there before.

Elena remembered hearing that girls could "get rid of" the food they've eaten by throwing up. She tried it after a binge (phase 5). She also discovered that laxatives and enemas helped. She continued to find comfort in binging and strove for control by purging, popping pills, and taking enemas. The binge/purge cycle was established (phase 6).

Elena continued to feel ashamed and guilty about her compulsive behavior. She expended great amounts of energy to hide it from her parents, siblings, and friends (phase 7). Usually she threw up in jars, which she hid in small brown paper bags in the back of her closet until she could get rid of them. She would also borrow her parents' car, tell them she was going out with friends, find a solitary place to park, and binge on junk food. The cycle continued.

Treatment Approaches for Bulimia   Bulimia nervosa is very difficult to treat because so many variables are involved including emotional needs, established behavioral patterns, and external social stresses (Lefrançois, 1999). Generally treatment has three aspects, all aimed at reestablishing physical and emotional health and normal eating patterns. First, medical attention may be necessary to treat any physical symptoms resulting from purging and nutritional deficits. For example, bulimics might suffer loss of dental enamel or damage to their esophagus or mouth from frequent contact with stomach acids. Or they might "experience malnutrition-related problems ([that] might include cardiovascular, kidney, gastrointestinal, or blood problems as well as insomnia)" (Lefrançois, 1999, p. 322).

Second, psychotherapy can help bulimics explore their emotional needs and their reasons for pursuing this destructive cycle of behavior (Lefrançois, 1999). Third, psychotherapy may include "behavioral counseling" such as "self-monitoring of food intake"; another approach "focuses on changing the thinking patterns and beliefs about weight and body shape that perpetuate eating disorders" (Coon, 2001, p. 413; Whittal, Agras, & Gould, 1999).

Impulse Control Disorders

Impulse control disorders are conditions in which people are unable to resist the temptation to participate in some activity that causes them or others harm or regret. Usually people with such disorders follow a cycle of succumbing to extreme temptation, participating in the activity, getting a real "high" during the activity, and suffering extreme remorse and guilt afterward.

Examples of impulse control disorders include kleptomania, pathological gambling, and trichotillomania. *Kleptomania* is characterized by a compulsive desire to steal things, not for personal need or gain, but simply for the sake of stealing them. *Pathological gambling* involves being driven irresistibly to gamble despite suffering extremely negative effects such as huge debt, considerable difficulties with significant others, and other life disruptions. *Trichotillomania* involves compulsively pulling out one's own hair, primarily from "the scalp, eyebrows, and eyelashes," to the extent that the loss is readily apparent to others (Barker, 2003, p. 442).

Personality Disorders

Personality disorders reflect long-term patterns of behavior, emotions, and views of self and the world that strikingly diverge from cultural expectations, cause considerable stress, and result in problematic social interactions. The following are the most common personality disorders and the persistent patterns characterizing each:

- *Schizoid:* Disconnection from interpersonal relationships and an extremely limited ability to express emotions.
- *Paranoid:* Extreme distrust of others, in addition to expectations that others have evil motives and, essentially, "are out to get you."
- *Schizotypal:* Social deficits characterized by difficulties forming close relationships and distorted views of appropriate behavior.
- *Antisocial:* Disrespect for and infringement on other people's rights.
- *Borderline:* Instability in interpersonal relationships, view of self, and emotional makeup, in addition to striking impulsivity.
- *Histrionic:* Excessive emotional expression and attention-seeking behavior.
- *Narcissistic:* Pompous and pretentious behavior, constant search for admiration, and lack of empathy.
- *Avoidant:* Uncomfortableness in social situations, feelings of inadequacy, and oversensitivity to negative feedback.
- *Dependent:* Needy, clinging, submissive behavior resulting from the "pervasive need to be taken care of" (APA, 2000, p. 725).
- *Obsessive–compulsive:* Preoccupation with organization and neatness, perfectionism, and control.

A recent major study indicated that 30.8 million or 14.8% of all Americans have experienced at least one personality disorder according to *DSM-IV-TR* criteria (Personality Disorders, 2004). Most common were obsessive–compulsive disorders (7.9%

of all adults), followed by paranoid (4.4%), antisocial (3.6%), schizoid (3.1%), avoidant (2.4%), histrionic (1.8%), and dependent (0.5%). The research found that women were more likely to experience avoidant, dependent, or paranoid personality disorders, whereas men more commonly had antisocial disorders. Except for histrionic disorders, all other personality disorders were "associated with considerable emotional disability and impairment in social and occupational functioning" (p. 10).

 # What Social Workers Do in Mental Health

Generalist social workers can address mental illness at all three practice levels. At the micro level, social workers provide case management, counseling (e.g., crisis intervention or substance abuse counseling), and intensive psychotherapy for chronically (long-term) mentally ill people. At the mezzo level, they conduct group therapy and provide various kinds of family treatment. Finally, at the macro level, they initiate changes in organizational and public policy to improve service provision to large groups of clients. Social workers may also assume administrative or supervisory responsibilities in agencies providing any level of service.

Case Management in Micro Practice

We have established that case management is a micro-level method of service provision whereby a social worker coordinates ongoing multiple services for a client. Specific tasks include assessing client needs and strengths, linking clients to services, planning treatment strategies, monitoring the appropriateness and effectiveness of these services, and advocating for improved service provision when necessary. Earlier we established that coordination and monitoring of services are key concepts. Case management is the treatment of choice for clients with chronic mental illness who have many ongoing needs that can be met only through services from a range of sources. The idea is that somebody has to take responsibility for making sure service provision makes sense and is effective.

Case managers may also provide direct services to clients that are related to the need for coordinated service provision. These include "crisis intervention (e.g., locating temporary housing for desperate, homeless people), supporting clients making difficult decisions, helping to modify clients' environments (e.g., arranging for transportation within the community), and helping clients overcome emotional reactions to their crisis situations" (Kirst-Ashman & Hull, 2002, p. 588; Moxley, 1989). Case management is an important role for social workers in mental health at both the BSW and the MSW levels.

Case Example   Amos, a case manager at a community mental health center, provides an example of what a case manager does. One of his clients, Beth, age 28, has schizophrenia. When taking her medication, she can function in the community, living in an efficiency apartment. Amos conducted her original assessment and developed a plan with her. After helping link her to the appropriate resources, he now coordinates and monitors a number of services she receives. Amos regularly talks to Beth about how she's doing and what new goals she wants to set.

Amos keeps in touch with Beth's psychiatrist, making certain she keeps her appointments and continues taking her psychotropic medication. He also makes sure she keeps appointments with her general physician (she has diabetes). Amos helped her get a part-time job at Betty's Best Butter Burger Bistro, and he maintains contact with Betty, Beth's boss, to monitor Beth's performance at work.

Amos referred her to a support group at the community health center for people who have schizophrenia and are coping with independent life in the community. He periodically contacts the group's facilitator to monitor her progress and participation there.

Beth has a sister living within a couple miles of her apartment who helps Beth with shopping and getting to the doctor. Amos checks with her regularly to make sure no problems are surfacing. Several times, Beth has stopped taking her medication when she felt she had recovered and didn't need it. Each time, she relapsed and was eventually found wandering half-naked through a park in her neighborhood. Once Amos advocated fervently on Beth's behalf when her benefits were mistakenly slashed. In summary, Amos watches over Beth, monitors the resources she receives, and helps her get new ones when she needs them.

Micro Practice: Psychotherapy

Chapter 4 discussed the process of generalist social work practice that reflects the foundation of social work skills. Building on this foundation, there is an infinite array of specific approaches to social work intervention.

Specialized psychotherapy is often used to treat people with mental illness. Highlight 13.5 identifies a case in which a psychotherapist who has an MSW practices cognitive therapy with a depressed adult male. This does not imply that cognitive therapy is necessarily any better or worse than other psychotherapeutic approaches. It merely represents an example of one type of therapy applied to one type of problem. Practitioners must do some research to determine what psychotherapeutic approaches are most effective with what mental disorders and other problems.

The Use of Psychotropic Drugs to Treat Mental Disorders

We have established that psychotropic drugs are employed by psychiatrists and other physicians to alter thinking, mood, and behavior. Walsh and Bentley (2002) identify five classes of psychotropic medication: antipsychotic, antidepressant, mood-stabilizing, anti-anxiety, and psychostimulant (pp. 646–649). These are frequently used to treat various mental disorders, often very effectively. Their uses, in addition to examples of generic drugs in each category and their brand names (in parentheses), are given here (Walsh & Bentley, 2002):

- Antipsychotic drugs are used to treat schizrenia. An example is chlorpromizine (Thorazine).
- Antidepressant drugs are employed in the treatment of major depression and anxiety disorders, particularly panic disorders. Examples are amitriptyline (Amitril) and fluoxetine (Prozac).
- Mood-stabilizing drugs are used to treat bipolar disorder. An example is lithium carbonate (Lithium).

HIGHLIGHT 13.5

Cognitive Therapy with a Depressed Adult Male

In the following case a therapist successfully uses cognitive therapy with Ed, a divorced 38-year-old male (Geary, 1992).

Basic Principles of Cognitive Therapy

Cognitive therapy, originated by Aaron T. Beck, "stresses the importance of belief systems and thinking in determining behavior and feelings. The focus of cognitive therapy is on understanding distorted beliefs and using techniques to change maladaptive thinking" (Sharf, 2000, p. 371).[5] Three major concepts are involved: cognitions, schemata, and cognitive distortion (Beck & Weishaar, 2000; Geary, 1992). *Cognitions* are thoughts and perceptions about someone or something. *Schemata* are thought patterns that sustain a person's convictions and notions about how the world works. *Cognitive distortion* occurs when a person experiences consistently flawed and inaccurate perceptions of reality. The aim of cognitive therapy is to help clients identify their unproductive and negative thoughts (cognitions), evaluate their thought patterns (schemata), and alleviate inaccurate perceptions about self, others, or circumstances (cognitive distortion).

For example, therapists using this approach help depressed clients evaluate their thinking and eventually change their perceptions and behavior by using the following process (Beck, Rush, Shaw, & Emery, 1979; Beck & Weishaar, 2000). First, under a psychotherapist's direction, a client identifies and monitors negative thoughts about himself. Second, the client examines his schemata—that is, his typical reactions to his negative thoughts. Third, the client assesses the extent to which such negative thoughts are valid and realistic. To what extent has he been exaggerating or even fabricating all the negative things he's been thinking about himself? To what extent is he

experiencing cognitive distortion? Fourth, the client begins to develop more realistic ways of viewing himself and the world. What are his actual weaknesses, and, more importantly, what are his genuine strengths? Fifth, the client develops new beliefs and ways of thinking about himself that are more realistic and productive. Typically a cognitive therapist sees a client with depression for 15–25 sessions (Beck & Weishaar, 2000; Geary, 1992).

The Client

Ed, age 38, was a soft-spoken, composed man of medium height, with a pale complexion and slightly receding light brown hair. He came to Juana Dance, a psychotherapist with an MSW, for help with his depression. Ed had been unemployed for over a year and, because he had nowhere else to go, was living with his parents.

He described his childhood as stable, living with both parents and two older brothers. He mentioned that his family was neither very demonstrative in showing affection nor very talkative with each other. Ed did well in school and graduated from college with a business degree. He married Anna, his college sweetheart, got a managerial job in sales, and had three daughters.

Everything seemed to be going fine until he turned 30. Suddenly his world started to crumble. His job was going nowhere—with no promotions or significant raises in sight. Ed told Juana that Anna, bored with the marriage, "dumped" him for Hank, a singer in a country-western band. She ran off with Hank, taking Ed's three daughters and moving to another state 1,000 miles away. This devastated Ed.

Ed subsequently quit his job and started several new ones, trying to make something go right

(continued)

---

[5]Sometimes cognitive therapy is referred to as *cognitive-behavioral therapy* because of its significant behavioral component (e.g., homework assignments) (Trower, Casey, & Dryden, 1988).

HIGHLIGHT 13.5 *(continued)*

in his life. Failing miserably, he had been forced to accept his parents' invitation to live with them.

Ed was at an all-time low. He felt listless, useless, and inadequate. Whenever he talked about anything, self-degrading comments peppered his conversation. For example, he'd say things like "It seems as if I can't do anything right," "I don't have a future so I don't have much to live for," and "What a flop I turned out to be."

Application of Cognitive Therapy

During the first several sessions, Juana spent time easing Ed into the therapeutic relationship and learning about his history and current status. Ed described his typical day as sitting around a lot, watching soaps, and bothering his parents. He rarely went out and had virtually no social life. He broke off relationships with old friends, who he felt were getting sick of all his misery and whining. He told Juana that he felt like he was carrying a picket sign that read "I'm a useless, no good piece of crap." In better, happier days, he might have said that people generally treated him as if he'd just eaten a clove of garlic and forgotten his breath mints.

Juana administered test instruments that measured Ed's level of depression and the type and incidence of his negative self-statements. Results indicated moderate to severe depression and a significant frequency of negative thoughts about himself.

With Juana's help, Ed began identifying and monitoring his negative self-thoughts. Whenever he criticized himself, Juana would discuss with him the implications of what he said and what he really meant. Juana continued to explore with Ed his schemata—how he automatically experienced self-critical thoughts and how they were directly related to feeling badly about himself. Periodically Juana administered the instruments measuring depression and incidence of negative self-statements to monitor progress.

Additionally, Juana assigned Ed graded homework assignments that he completed between sessions and subsequently discussed with her. *Graded assignments* refer to tasks of increasing difficulty and complexity that expand a client's repertoire of behavior. For example, at first Ed was to talk with a friend for 10 minutes each day to start opening his social world. Later he started attending a weekly support group for divorced men. Still later, he began a job search.

When reporting his progress, Ed continued to demean himself with comments like "Aw, that's nothin'" or "Anybody could do that." Juana praised his accomplishments and emphasized how so many small steps, taken together, eventually added up to real progress. She discussed with him the extent to which his perception of himself was realistic. Where was he being exceptionally and unfairly critical about

(continued)

- Anti-anxiety drugs are used to control anxiety disorders and insomnia. Examples are zolpidem (Ambien) and diazepam (Valium).
- Psychostimulant drugs are used to treat attention deficit hyperactivity disorder (ADHD). (ADHD is a syndrome of learning and behavioral problems beginning in childhood that is characterized by a persistent pattern of inattention, excessive physical movement, and impulsivity that appear in at least two settings [including home, school, work, or social contexts].) An example is methylphenidate (Ritalin).

HIGHLIGHT 13.5 *(continued)*

himself? What strengths was he trying to ignore instead of giving himself realistic credit for solid accomplishments?

One way Ed began to demonstrate increased awareness of self-criticism was to verbalize more frequently how Juana would respond before she said it (Geary, 1992). In other words, he would give himself the same kind of feedback she had given him many times before. For example, he'd say, "I know what you're thinking—I should appreciate how I am improving. I guess it beats being poked in the eye with a sharp stick."

Juana initiated a treatment method during therapy called the "triple column technique" to help Ed recognize cognitive distortion concerning his self-concept (Burns, 1980, p. 60; Geary, 1992). In the first column he would identify his automatic negative self-thought (e.g., "I never do anything right"). In the second column he'd identify his cognitive distortion (e.g., "Of course, I do some things right, although certainly not everything"). In the third column he'd write logical, more realistic reactions to the automatic negative self-thought (e.g., "Although I sometimes feel that my progress is as lively as a turtle's, I know that I am gradually doing better").

Although Ed suffered several setbacks when he panicked thinking about returning to work, he generally made steady progress. His activity level markedly increased, although he experienced a few ups and downs. His scores on the instruments measuring depression and incidence of negative self-statements also continued to improve.

Treatment began to focus on additional behavioral means Ed could use to validate his self-worth and improve how he thought about himself. Homework assignments included talking to other people such as family members about his insights in therapy and seeking their perspective (Geary, 1992). He even contacted old friends he hadn't seen in years. What he found out was that a lot of people really cared about him. They appreciated him for being the pleasant, thoughtful, kind person with a good sense of humor that he was. This bolstered his self-confidence.

He got a cat, found a full-time job, and even started dating. Life still wasn't perfect, and dating was a lot harder than he remembered it in college. However, he was generally much happier and more self-confident, and emotionally stronger than he had been prior to therapy.

During his last session, Ed reverted to some imagery he had used during an earlier meeting, which can be a useful therapeutic technique (Geary, 1992). He indicated his new picket sign read, "I'm okay and proud of it." He said he was amazed at how much better other people responded to him now. He added that he responded to himself a lot better, too. He also told Juana that he felt he could look at himself, the world, and others more realistically now. Jokingly, he added, "And Hank really can't sing."

There has been significant controversy over the use of many psychotropic drugs (Bentley & Walsh, 1998). Are they used too frequently when other means of treatment would suffice? Are drugs prescribed too freely for children with ADHD? Why does the "dramatic increase" in their use "have some claiming that such use hides the 'true' origins of problems and leads to stunted growth and underuse of effective psychosocial interventions?" Do some antidepressants "alter personality" so that people are no longer really themselves (Bower, 1994, p. 359)?

These issues notwithstanding, psychotropic drugs have become a mainstay in mental health treatment. Thus it's critical for mental health professionals to review current research carefully and use them carefully.

Note that psychotropic drugs are not used for all disorders and that many other methods of treatment exist and are being developed. Focus on Critical Thinking 13.2 examines the comeback of electroshock therapy.

Mezzo Practice: Running Treatment Groups

As discussed in Chapter 5, *treatment groups* help individuals solve personal problems, change unwanted behaviors, cope with stress, and improve their quality of life. Types of treatment groups include therapy, support, education, growth, and socialization; here are some examples:

- *Therapy:* A group of people diagnosed with schizophrenia who live in the community and meet at a local community health center.
- *Support:* A group of adults caring for their parents who have Alzheimer's disease.
- *Education:* A group of parents learning about effective child management techniques.
- *Growth:* A group of gay men focusing on gay pride issues (Toseland & Rivas, 2005).
- *Socialization:* A current events group at a nursing home that gets together to discuss their opinions.

Mezzo Practice: Treating Families

Collins, Jordan, and Coleman (1999) state that the major purpose of social work with families is "to help families learn to function more competently while meeting the developmental and emotional needs of *all* members" (p. 2). They continue that it "targets the following objectives: (1) reinforce family strengths to get families ready for change (or intervention); (2) provide additional support following family therapy so families maintain effective family functioning; [and] (3) create concrete changes in family functioning to sustain effective and satisfying daily routines" (p. 2).

Family counseling can involve virtually any aspect of family communication and dynamics. Chapter 9 discussed family preservation and social work with families at high risk of child maltreatment. Other issues for which families may need treatment include members' inability to get along, parental inability to control children's behavior, divorce, stepfamily issues, or crises (e.g., a death in the family, an unwanted pregnancy, unemployment, a natural disaster).

At this point, are you considering a career in mental health? Highlight 13.6 poses some suggestions for helping you think about a possible career in mental health.

Macro Practice and Policy Practice in Mental Health

Social workers practice in the mental health macro arena in at least three ways. First, they can advocate for positive change on behalf of large groups of clients. (The following section on managed care discusses some issues of concern and calls for advocacy to address these issues.) Second, social workers who function as administrators in mental health agencies can strive to improve policies and service provision.

FOCUS ON CRITICAL THINKING 13.2
Is Electroshock Therapy Back?[6]

What do you picture when you think about electroshock therapy (now referred to as *electroconvulsive therapy*)? Is it a group of physicians and nurses gathered around a patient lying on a gurney with electrodes protruding from his head? Do you picture his body convulsing violently and then him drooling like an imbecile? Perhaps you remember the scene from the movie *One Flew over the Cuckoo's Nest* in which the formerly spunky and rebellious mental patient Randle Patrick McMurphy (played by Jack Nicholson) lies mindlessly on his hospital bed, bereft of any remaining personality after receiving electroconvulsive therapy. (If you're going to be a social work major, this is a good movie to see because it portrays some of the dimensions of institutional life [Downey & Jackson, 2000].)

Electroconvulsive therapy (ECT) is the most controversial technique in modern psychiatry (Henderson, 2002; National Mental Health Association [NMHA], 2005a). It is used to treat mental health problems such as depression or schizophrenia, usually when drug therapies fail or patients are acutely suicidal (Familydoctor.org, 2003; NMHA, 2005a). Apparently at least 100,000 Americans are treated with electroconvulsive therapy each year, although the actual number is hard to pinpoint because reporting is not formally required (Electroshock Therapy, 2000; NMHA, 2005a). The controversy focuses on the fact that for some it works wonderfully to temporarily control depressive and bipolar disorders. For others it represents a nightmare of memory loss, brain malfunction, and continued mood disorder. Cloud (2001) suggests that "it works a little bit like banging the side of a fuzzy TV—it just works, except when it doesn't" (p. 60).

So how does ECT work? No one really knows. Electrodes are placed on a patient's head, and an electrical burst powerful enough to light a 40-watt bulb is sent through the patient's brain for 30–60 seconds. Currently, prior to the procedure, patients are given a muscle relaxant and anesthesia to eliminate pain and prevent the violent flailing of limbs that caused broken bones in the past. During ECT, a mouth guard is inserted to protect tongue and teeth, and an oxygen mask is put in place to sustain breathing. ECT usually involves 6–12 sessions administered three times per week. Theories about how ECT works focus on chemical interactions in the brain. It is thought that the electrical current either enhances the transmission of neurological impulses or releases hormones that influence (and thus improve) mood.

ECT technically dates back to the 16th century when torpedo fish (also known as electric rays), which transmit electrical impulses, were used to treat headaches. During the 1930s, insulin and camphor were used to induce seizures and temporarily improve some mental health conditions. "In the Oscar-winning film *A Beautiful Mind,* math scholar John Nash undergoes such insulin shock treatment for schizophrenia" (Griner, 2002). In 1938 two Italians, Ugo Cerletti and Lucio Bini, were the first to actually use an electrical current to treat a schizophrenic man experiencing severe hallucinations.

Curtis Hartmann, age 47, a lawyer in Westfield, Massachusetts, who indicates that he's had 100 treatments altogether, remains an avid advocate of ECT (Cloud, 2001). He says it's the only treatment that's been consistently able to control his bipolar disorder since 1976. He feels infinitely better after a treatment, stating that "[d]epression is like being a corpse with a pulse" (Cloud, 2001, p. 62).

(continued)

---

[6]Facts for this highlight are from Electroshock Therapy (2000); Familydoctor.org (2003); Griner (2002); Henderson (2002); Marcotty (1999); National Library of Medicine (2002); National Mental Health Association, 2005a; Papolos et al. (2002); Sabbatini (2002); Sackheim, Devanand, and Nobler (2002); and U.S. Office of the Surgeon General (2001).

FOCUS ON CRITICAL THINKING 13.2 *(continued)*

Similarly, Diane (no last name) notes that "[a]fter numerous hospital visits over a two-year period, ECT treatments were presented as my last chance at controlling depression. Medications were unable to control the illness." Although she did experience some temporary memory loss, she concludes, "In retrospect, the ECT treatments allowed the depression to improve significantly to be treatable by medications alone" (Voices of Experience, 2002).

Opponents of the approach vehemently protest its use. For example, Liz McGillicuddy, "once a decorated Marine Lt. Colonel with several college degrees to her name," underwent ECT when suffering from severe depression (The Horror, 2000). McGillicuddy claims that the "results were devastating." She can't remember her childhood or "anything" about her past; she also lost "her future" as she is "unable to form new memories" (The Horror, 2000).

Juli Lawrence provides another example of a negative experience. Prior to her undergoing ECT, her attending physician told her family that "it was an absolute cure for depression." However, he did not caution her and her family about the potential side effects such as memory loss, "which can range from forgetting where you parked your car to forgetting that you own a car at all" (Cloud, 2001, p. 60). She attempted suicide a week later and now claims that she can't remember a thing from two years prior to the treatment to several months following it.

In 2000 the U.S. surgeon general issued a report stating the following:

- Of persons receiving ECT, 60–70% improve. These rates resemble those for psychotropic drugs, but remember that most people receiving ECT have not responded to drug treatments.

- ECT is not considered long-term protection against suicide, but rather a short-term treatment for acute illness.
- The major risk of ECT involves anesthesia, the same risk occurring any time anesthesia is administered.
- "The most common adverse effects of this treatment are confusion and memory loss for events surrounding the period of ECT treatment. The confusion and disorientation seen upon awakening after ECT typically clear within an hour. More persistent memory problems are variable."
- "Although most patients return to full functioning following successful ECT, the degree of posttreatment memory impairment and resulting impact on functioning are highly variable across individuals. . . . Fears that ECT causes gross structural brain pathology have not been supported by decades of methodologically sound research in both humans and animals."
- "The decision to use ECT must be evaluated for each individual, weighing the potential benefits and known risks of all available and appropriate treatments in the context of informed consent."

Despite the furor over ECT, its use probably will continue. It does provide short-term relief for some people experiencing some types of severe mental disorders who don't respond to other treatment modalities or who are acutely suicidal. But ECT is not a cure-all. Its effects are usually only temporary; effects can vary radically from one recipient to the next; and it may cause brain damage. In any event, apparently ECT, for better or worse, is back.

What are your opinions about ECT? Do you think the advantages outweigh the disadvantages, or vice versa? Would you ever consider ECT for yourself or for someone close to you? What are the reasons for your answer?

HIGHLIGHT 13.6

Are You Thinking About Working in the Mental Health Field?

If you're considering a social work major, choosing a field of practice is not necessarily easy. A number of issues, problem areas, or populations may sound interesting to you. Kelly (2002) provides at least eight suggestions for exploring the mental health field before you commit to a professional job. Any of these suggestions can offer excellent opportunities for networking with mental health professionals. They may be effective ways of talking with practitioners about what they do and how they do it, in addition to finding out what jobs are available.

1. Check out job possibilities and mental health issues through the National Mental Health Association (NMHA) at http://www.nmha.org. Its goal is "to improve the mental health of all Americans, especially the 54 million people with mental disorders, through advocacy, education, research, and service" (National Mental Health Association, 2005b).

2. Become a member of the U.S. Psychiatric Rehabilitation Association (USPRA) (formerly the International Association of Psychosocial Rehabilitation Services [IAPSRS]) at http://www.iapsrs.org. This is "an organization of psychosocial rehabilitation agencies, practitioners, and interested organizations and individuals dedicated to promoting, supporting and strengthening community-oriented rehabilitation services and resources for persons with psychiatric disabilities" (USPRA, 2004).

3. Become a member of the National Association of Social Workers (NASW), an organization with chapters in all 50 states, Washington, D.C., Puerto Rico, the Virgin Islands, and Guam, that has almost 153,000 members (NASW, 2005) (http://www.socialworkers.org/). NASW also provides an excellent resource for networking

with social workers practicing in mental health. Members receive 10 issues annually of *NASW News,* containing updates on both issues and jobs in mental health and other social work fields of practice, in addition to the quarterly professional journal *Social Work.* "NASW membership connects you with cutting-edge ideas, current information, practice expertise, and quality resources" (NASW, 2005). Numerous continuing education programs are offered in specific aspects of mental health and other areas in which social workers practice.

4. Volunteer at a local crisis intervention program. Such programs usually offer excellent training to prepare volunteers for answering crisis hotlines. This may offer experience in addressing a wide range of crises (for example, suicide threats, drug overdoses, loneliness, and depression). You never know what the next phone call may bring.

5. Work as a paraprofessional or volunteer in an inpatient mental health clinic or in other facilities with clients who are dealing with mental health issues. If inpatient hospitals are unavailable due to deinstitutionalization, seek out opportunities "in community-based mental health centers, group homes for . . . [people with mental health issues], or day treatment programs" for people with chronic problems (Kelly, 2002, p. 5).

6. Work or volunteer at a homeless shelter. Although being homeless by no means indicates that a person has a mental disorder, many people who were living in inpatient facilities have been discharged into the community. Sometimes the community lacks funding and an adequate support network to sustain these people. The result may be

(continued)

HIGHLIGHT 13.6 *(continued)*

that they stop taking their medication and suffer a significantly decreased ability to function—involving work, socializing with others, and maintaining a place to live. One result may be homelessness. Homeless shelters may let you learn about community resources and link people with supportive services and benefits so they can maintain themselves in the community.

7. "Attend open meetings of support groups related to mental health" (Kelly, 2002, p. 5). Groups may be available for people with specific types of disorders (for example, schizophrenia, anxiety disorders, or eating disorders) or for family members of people with disorders. Support groups can teach you about the mental health issues people must address and provide suggestions for how to cope. However, make sure the meetings are "open" (i.e., anyone who is interested may attend). Always honestly identify your purpose for being there.

8. Use continuing education opportunities to explore your interests. NASW is only one of the numerous organizations addressing mental health issues that provide chances to learn about specific mental health disorders and treatment approaches. The following are examples of continuing education topics from one brochure: "Eating Disorders"; "Sex Matters for Women"; "Master Your Panic"; "The Ethics of Professional Practice"; "Anxiety and Depression"; "Child and Adolescent Counseling"; "Overcoming Binge Eating"; and "Anger Management" (Homestead Schools, 2004).

Note that after graduation your state might have certification or licensing requirements for a designated number of continuing education hours (CEHs) or units (CEUs). You can take these classes before you graduate, too, if there's an area in which you're exceptionally interested and are willing to pay the fee to attend.

(A later section discusses the need to improve cultural competence in the mental health macro system.) Third, social workers can strive to develop innovative programs to meet mental health needs.

For example, Johnson, Noe, Collins, Strader, and Bucholtz (2000) describe a project in which members of local church communities were recruited "to implement and evaluate alcohol and other drug (AOD) abuse prevention programs" (p. 1). "Community advocate teams" were created, made up of significant church leaders, usually pastors (p. 7). These teams subsequently recruited families with children at high risk of AOD abuse. Families and children were then given "comprehensive training" consisting of 25 weeks of $2^{1}/_{2}$-hour sessions along with case management services (pp. 10–11). Incentives were offered to keep families in the program including "the provision of food for participants, day care assistance, family portraits, transportation provisions, social activities, and nominal payments for the research interviews ($5.00 per interview)" (p. 12). Evaluation research revealed that the program was "highly successful in white American rural and suburban church communities" although "only partially successful in urban African American church communities" (p. 21).

It's just as important for social workers to attend to issues in the broad mental health arena as it is to acquire skills for working with individuals, families, and small groups. Problems involving policy and general provision of services (i.e., who gets services, who doesn't, and what they cost) affect huge numbers of people. These issues directly influence what social workers and other mental health professionals can do in their own practice. Issues addressed next include managed care in mental health and cultural competence in mental health settings.

Managed Care Policies and Programs in Mental Health

Most of the same issues apply to managed care in mental health as in other health care settings, as discussed in Chapter 12. There *managed care* was defined as "a generic label for a broad and constantly changing mix of health insurance, assistance, and payment programs that seek to retain quality and access while controlling the cost of physical and mental health services" (Lohmann, 1997, p. 200). An identified group or range of providers of health and mental health care contract with agencies to provide health care at a negotiated rate. Two primary principles promoted by managed care involve retaining quality and access while controlling costs. In other words, care should be readily accessible and of high quality, and yet be as inexpensive as possible. This is a hard row to hoe.

There is much pressure on physicians and clinicians to find the least expensive treatment modalities possible for any particular client in order to minimize costs. For example, because psychiatric hospitalization is very expensive, there is pressure to keep clients in that setting for as brief a time as possible. This pressure exists even when the client needs that kind of intensive treatment for a longer period. Less intensive settings, of course, include group homes and outpatient treatment facilities. Focus on Critical Thinking 13.3 questions the real intent of managed care.

Social workers are responsible for advocating for their clients. Vandivort-Warren (1998) urges social workers to advocate on the behalf of people with mental illness. She maintains that "[a]dvocacy forms the root of this profession and is needed now more than ever to infuse social work values into insurance-dominated interests" (p. 263). She makes three specific suggestions. First, social workers can fight for more adequate funding for mental health services. Second, states should "be actively involved in evaluating the services provided under managed care rather than delegating quality concerns to managed care firms" (p. 264). The latter resembles asking you to decide what grade you deserve for this course. Third, social workers can advocate for services that go beyond mere "medical necessity" and help empower people to improve their psychosocial functioning and quality of life.

Focus on Critical Thinking 13.4 addresses issues about mental health policy and programming.

Cultural Competence in Mental Health Settings

Cultural competence has been defined as "the set of knowledge and skills that a social worker must develop in order to be effective with multicultural clients" (Lum, 1999, p. 3). The National Institute of Mental Health (NIMH) indicates that

FOCUS ON CRITICAL THINKING 13.3

What Is the Real Intent of Managed Care?

Mechanic (1999) cites at least three concepts important in understanding the impact of managed care on mental health service provision: "capitation," "gatekeeping," and "utilization management" (p. 152). *Capitation* is

> a payment system through which a provider receives a set, predetermined dollar amount per participant or potential participant in a . . . targeted population of the managed care system. Capitation is based on a formula that pays a certain rate of dollars per person regardless of the individual's utilization of services. . . . The formula employs a smoothing philosophy for spreading costs and risks across the entire target population. (Wernet, 1999, p. 7)

A difference between mental health and other health care often involves the intensity of services needed (Mechanic, 1999). With general health problems, managed care providers assume that patient claims will vary greatly in any one year, with some people getting very sick unpredictably. However, they also assume that most people will not get sick, so "expenses are spread among a large population" (Mechanic, 1999, p. 159). Thus insurance premiums from the many who don't get that sick and their employers support health care services for the few who do. People with mental illness, however, often require

much more intensive care over long periods, and sometimes forever. This can be very expensive for managed care organizations. Hence managed care programs usually distinguish between mental health and general health benefits, placing more stringent limitations on those available for mental health (Mechanic, 1999).

Note that many people with mental illness don't have their own insurance, but receive benefits through government programs like Medicare or Medicaid. Most states are assertively moving to have these benefits administered through managed care organizations (Essock & Goldman, 1995). Figuring out how to fund treatment for the mentally ill population with its intensive need for service is a complex process.

A second issue concerning managed care and mental health involves the *gatekeeping* function of a person's primary care physician. Generally, patients in a managed care program pick their own doctor from a limited list. They then must go through this doctor to get referrals to any specialists they may need (e.g., psychotherapists, neurologists, ophthalmologists, proctologists). The main purpose of gatekeeping is to make certain patients see specialists only when necessary, essentially to cut down on costs. One problem is

(continued)

people of color underutilize the U.S. mental health system (USDHHS, 1999). It identifies the four major groups as (1) African American, (2) Asian and Pacific Islander [API], (3) Hispanic/Latino, and (4) Native American/Alaskan Native/Hawaiian Native.

Several characteristics of these groups differentiate them to various degrees from the white mainstream (USDHHS, 1999). First, their cultural orientation in terms of values, traditions, and beliefs often conflicts with the existing mental health system. Second, for many reasons, these groups generally have lower income levels and higher levels of poverty. Third, their generally lower socioeconomic status

FOCUS ON CRITICAL THINKING 13.3 *(continued)*

that a primary care physician may not be highly knowledgeable about a particular client's type of mental health problem—especially more severe, more chronic, or rarer disorders. Wells et al. (1989) report three interesting findings regarding primary care physicians. First, primary care physicians fail to identify even such common problems as depression about half the time. Second, even when they accurately recognize the problem, they often prescribe inappropriate drugs or administer the wrong dosage. Third, primary care physicians in managed care organizations fare worse in identifying depression than their counterparts working outside such organizations.

Utilization management means that certain medical and mental health services must be authorized ahead of time; otherwise the managed care organization won't pay for them. This involves a clinician or physician contacting the managed care organization and explaining the problem in sufficient detail to get permission for the service or procedure. A managed care representative, often a utilization reviewer or case manager, then reviews the documentation and, using a structured set of rules and steps, determines whether the symptoms and diagnosis warrant the requested procedure (Corcoran, 1997; Mechanic, 1999). "Clinical decisions are now

routinely challenged" (Matorin, 1998, p. 161). In this process, clinicians have lost a huge amount of decision-making power regarding what should and can be done to help clients.

Most mental health professionals have little trust in managed care and generally don't like it (Matorin, 1998; Mechanic, 1999). Matorin (1998) highlights several concerns. First, clinicians must often defensively justify their treatment recommendations to a managed care staff member who may or may not be familiar with the client's type of condition. Second, clinicians are often pressured "to discharge clients from the hospital prematurely, knowing full well the limited availability of adequate aftercare resources" (Matorin, 1998, p. 161). Third, "fragile patients are often shifted to lesser levels of care over the course of a week. Such 'treatment' plans subject them to multiple separations and changes in treatment team at the point when they most need continuity" (Matorin, 1998, p. 161).

Managed care in mental health practice is in place. Its proponents maintain that it's an effective way to provide mental health care, which is very expensive, while controlling costs. What do you think are the strengths and weaknesses of managed care in mental health? To what extent do you support or fail to support it? What are your reasons?

(as measured by such variables as income, education, and occupation) is clearly related to mental illness.

Barriers to Receiving Mental Health Services

Many people of color find the mental health system to be threatening, unresponsive, and noncompliant with many of their beliefs. Five barriers to these groups' access to services are lack of help-seeking behavior, mistrust, stigma, cost, and clinician bias (USDHHS, 1999).

FOCUS ON CRITICAL THINKING 13.4

Mental Health Care and Policy

Some mental health policy issues resemble those in other types of health care provision. Who is covered and who has access are major concerns. Should U.S. policy in mental health care be over-hauled to establish a national health insurance program providing *universal* coverage? Should the government fund a program made available to all citizens, making private health insurance with its *selective* mental health benefits obsolete?

Consider other, more specific questions:

• Should limits be placed on the type of treatment and number of sessions with a professional?
• Should all people who need them have ready access to expensive psychotropic drugs?
• As with other types of health care, who should pay for it? Workers? Employers? The government?

Lack of Help-Seeking Behavior

To receive services, people must acknowledge that a problem exists and seek help to address it. We have established that for various reasons people of color don't seek out and receive mental health services to the extent that white people do.

Yamashiro and Matsuoka (1999) explain some of the reasons people of Asian and Pacific Islander (API) cultural heritage fail to utilize the mental health system adequately. They resemble some of the reasons API people fail to seek formal services for other health problems, discussed in Chapter 12. Reasons include an emphasis on "collective identities," "fatalism," use of language, and the fear of trans-mission to offspring (Yamashiro & Matsuoka, 1999, p. 458).

As earlier chapters explained, the worldview of Asian Americans and Pacific Islanders involves a greater sense of collective identity than dominant Euro-American culture, which stresses the importance of individualism. Dependence on the family, extended family, and cultural community are emphasized. The implication is that API people will first turn to their families and others in their cultural community to address problems, including mental health issues, before turning to strangers, whether professionals or not.

A second reason for API underutilization of mental health services involves a sense of *fatalism*. This is the idea that everything happens as a result of predeter-mined fate, with individuals having little control over their general life course.

A third reason for underutilization of mental health services involves language. Not only might API people speak a different language or at least use a different lan-guage as their primary one, they also might use language differently in general. The Western world emphasizes the importance of people talking about emotions and feelings to improve how they feel. A clear connection between emotions and lan-guage is assumed. In Eastern psychology, no such clear connection exists. Yamashiro and Matsuoka (1999) explain that in API cultures "language may not accommodate all that individuals think and feel—especially for those who are not socialized to use language as a primary means for expressing feelings" (p. 463). Par-ticipating in some form of therapy that emphasizes talking about feelings and behavior may make no sense in the context of traditional API culture.

A fourth reason involves the fact that

[a]n ancient tradition in Asian and Pacific Islander cultures is arranging marriages to ensure that one's offspring is united with an appropriate partner for the primary purpose of procreation. . . . Because mental illness is believed to be genetically inherited, evidence of mental illness in a family's lineage could render their offspring unsuitable for marriage. (Yamashiro & Matsuoka, 1999, p. 465)

In other words, if the word got out that mental illness ran in the family, potential marriage partners would run in the opposite direction.

Herring (1999) reflects on reasons Native American people often fail to seek and receive formal mental health services. They tend to use such services only when help is unavailable in their own cultural communities (Weinbach & Kuehner, 1985). First, older Native Americans avoid services because of past bad experiences with the system. Second, many think that "mental illness is a justifiable outcome of human weakness or the result of avoiding the discipline necessary to maintain cultural values and community respect" (Harras, 1987; Herring, 1999, p. 52). Thus they believe that they do not need the system, that they should be able to take care of such problems themselves. Other Native Americans who have had experiences with the mental health system note how biased it is concerning Western beliefs, which often clash with traditional cultural values (LaFromboise & Bigfoot, 1988).

Mistrust

Mistrust is a second barrier to people of color receiving mental health treatment (USDHHS, 1999). For example, African Americans' reasons for avoiding the system include not having enough time and being apprehensive about what treatment involves (Sussman, Robins, & Earls, 1987). Many have also experienced racism and discrimination (Primm, Lima, & Rowe, 1996).

Central and South American immigrants and many from Southeast Asia who have experienced oppression and imprisonment, and have even had family members murdered in their countries of origin, fear involvement with any system including that of mental health services (USDHHS, 1999). Illegal immigrants from Mexico also fear involvement because they dread being deported.

Native Americans have a long history of negative experiences with white mainstream culture. These include facing recurring attempts to squelch their traditional culture and absorb them into the mainstream; being denied U.S. citizenship until 1924; and not having a constitutional right to pursue traditional religious practices until the American Indian Religious Freedom Act of 1978 was passed (Herring, 1999).

Stigma

A *stigma* is a smear of shame and reproach upon one's reputation. People of color often don't want to suffer the stigma of being labeled mentally ill (USDHHS, 1999). Uba (1994) found this to be true of Asian Americans; Sussman and colleagues (1987) did the same for both whites and African Americans. African Americans generally make every effort to combat mental illness themselves, without having to rely on external formal resources (USDHHS, 1999).

Yamashiro and Matsuoka (1999) report that there is a strong tradition of shame regarding mental illness in many API families; because of their collective identity, what one family member does "reflects on the entire family" (p. 466). The mental illness of one family member makes the others feel ashamed, so it makes sense to keep it a secret instead of seeking help.

Cost

Cost is yet another barrier to people of color using mental health services (USDHHS, 1999). We have established that people of color generally have lower incomes than their white counterparts. Not only are they more unlikely than whites to be covered by private health insurance, but even those who have such benefits underutilize services (USDHHS, 1999).

Clinician Bias

Clinician bias is the fifth barrier to people of color utilizing mental health services (USDHHS, 1999). How the assessing clinician perceives a person's emotional state and behavioral symptoms directly relates to the diagnosis. Clinicians who are unfamiliar with the cultural customs of people having different beliefs, values, and behaviors may well misdiagnose the problem. Behaviors considered appropriate for other cultures might be considered quite inappropriate in Western eyes. For example,

> Latino families seem to be more tolerant of unusual behavior, such as hearing voices or having delusions of grandeur, because of the way Latino cultures view religion. . . . [I]n the Latino culture, people often talk to Jesus and the saints and feel close to spirits, so family members are not as concerned about a patient hearing voices as they are by disruptive or disrespectful behavior. (Schram & Mandell, 2000, pp. 176–177)

Similarly, Earle (1999) indicates that for Seneca Indians "such attributes as having visions and guiding one's life according to spirits may incorrectly appear to be symptoms of a serious mental disorder such as schizophrenia" when they are really expressions of traditional religious practices (p. 434).

Several studies report significant bias on the part of clinicians diagnosing African Americans for schizophrenia and depression; African Americans are much more likely than whites to be diagnosed with schizophrenia and less likely to be diagnosed with depression (Hu, Snowden, Jerrell, & Nguyen, 1991; Lawson, Hepler, Holladay, & Cuffel, 1994; Snowden & Cheung, 1990; USDHHS, 1999).

Highlight 13.7 focuses on what can be done to improve mental health services to people of color.

Macro Perspectives on Cultural Competence

From a macro perspective, say Sue and colleagues (1998), not only do mental health agencies need to "employ individuals with multicultural counseling skills, but the agency itself needs to have a 'multicultural culture'" (p. 103). This involves establishing an organizational environment that celebrates diversity. Administrators should empower staff members by helping them develop and employ culturally competent skills. Agencies should be sensitive to the cultural perspectives of their clients and responsive to their needs.

Cross, Bazron, Dennis, and Isaacs (1989) describe culturally competent and culturally proficient organizations. *Culturally competent* mental health organizations display "continuing self-assessment regarding culture, careful attention to the

HIGHLIGHT 13.7
What Can Be Done to Improve Mental Health Services to People of Color?

An obvious suggestion for improving services for people of color involves all social workers continuously striving to enhance their own cultural competence. Developing guidelines to assist individual social workers in their practice is also helpful (Snowden, 2000). Lum (2003), for example, describes a cultural competence framework for social work that emphasizes four primary dimensions of competence. The first is *cultural awareness*—consciousness of one's own cultural values and "of ethnicity and racism and its impact on professional attitude, perception, and behavior" (p. 31). Second, *knowledge acquisition* is the process of gaining and organizing knowledge to critically think about ethnicity and to better understand its significance. Third, *skill development* involves learning effective ways to communicate with people of other cultures and applying culturally sensitive techniques to improve interventions. Finally, *inductive learning* is the creative quest for new information and the sharing of new ideas with others to enhance practice effectiveness.

dynamics of difference, continuous expansion of cultural knowledge and resources, and a variety of adaptations to service models to better meet the needs of culturally diverse populations" (p. 17). Such agencies have a diverse staff reflecting a range of racial and cultural backgrounds. Administrators and staff have clear ideas about what cultural competence involves. Staff members have frequent opportunities to enhance their level of cultural competence. Any services delivered to specific cultural groups are viewed as a vital part of an agency's total package of programs.

Culturally proficient agencies strive to expand knowledge about cultural competence by "conducting research, developing new therapeutic approaches based on culture, and disseminating the results of demonstration projects" (Cross et al., 1989, p. 17). Few organizations ever reach this level of proficiency. Such organizations serve as dynamic models for creative program development focusing on cultural competence in other programs.

Looking Ahead

Mental health issues and concerns overlap with many other areas of social work practice. For example, social work in schools and with youths often concerns emotional, behavioral, and family problems. Chapter 14 explores social work with youths, focusing on teenage sexual activity, pregnancy, and parenting issues.

For Further Exploration on the Internet

See this text's Book Companion Website at **www.socialwork.wadsworth.com/ kirstashman_intro2e** for descriptors and hot links to URLs relevant to this chapter, selected InfoTrac articles and exercises, and tutorial quizzes.

CHAPTER FOURTEEN

SOCIAL WORK AND SERVICES
FOR YOUTHS AND IN THE SCHOOLS

© Alon Reininger/Contact Press Images/PictureQuest

Penny, a ninth-grader, tells Ms. Bijou, the school social worker, that Levina, her best friend, has been awfully moody lately. Levina has even said that she doesn't care much about living anymore, that every day gets gloomier, and that it just isn't worth it. Penny is worried that Levina might do something to hurt herself.

Jorge and Jeremy, both juniors in a multiracial high school, are concerned about the racial tensions and even fights in school. They're glad when Mr. Reinheich, the school social worker, announces that he's organizing some encounter discussion groups in which students can talk about racial issues, share things about their own cultures, and try to work out their conflicts.

Marinda, age 15, is terrified that she's pregnant. She hasn't had her period for almost 2½ months now. She hasn't told her boyfriend Teddy, age 16, the bad news yet, because she's afraid he'll break up with her. And she hasn't told her parents, either. What is she going to do?

These examples reflect slices carved from adolescent life. Emotions run high, and a social crisis can erupt at any moment. Things are critically important *right now*—not tomorrow, next week, or next year.

Social work practitioners work with youths in a wide range of settings and fields of practice—school social work, corrections, mental health, child welfare, runaway shelters, and family planning clinics. This chapter will focus on three dimensions of social work with youths: (1) school social work; (2) macro programs servicing youths; and (3) teenage sexual activity, pregnancy, and parenting will be explored. Specifically, this chapter will

- Describe school social work and define the various roles of school social workers.
- Identify the types of groups school social workers run.
- Suggest ways multiculturalism can be enhanced and racism reduced in schools.
- Discuss lesbian, gay, and bisexual (LGB) youths as populations-at-risk, focusing on issues involved in the "coming out" process.
- Identify and refute various myths about LGB people.
- Describe two community programs for youths—one that empowers Latino/a youths through a community assets assessment and one that explores how an African American spiritual community empowers its youths.
- Examine the issues of teenage sexual activity, pregnancy, and parenting issues, and describe social work roles concerning them.
- Encourage critical thinking about the provision of sex education.

 School Social Work

School social work takes place in school settings, where practitioners work with students, families, other school personnel, and communities to provide the best education possible for today's youths. Constable (2002) explains:

> The educational process is dynamic and wide ranging. Involving children, their families, and an institution called school, it is the context for school social work. School is no longer a building, or simply a collection of classrooms in which teachers and pupils

work together. School is conceptualized as *a community of families and school personnel engaged in the educational process.* (p. 19)

School social workers, then, strive to improve the overall functioning of students, teachers, school systems, and communities. They address "[c]onditions that interfere with the pupil's ability to connect with the educational system" (Constable, 1999, p. 209). School social workers must be skilled and flexible because they assume a wide range of roles and usually must define their key functions within their own school setting (Constable, 2002). School social work involves not only providing clinical services such as counseling for students who have behavioral problems, are depressed, or are experiencing family difficulties. It also entails working with the multiple systems with which students are involved to strengthen them and make it easier for them to perform in the school environment.

As students in colleges and universities, you know it takes substantial concentration, work, and stamina to succeed in a school environment. This is also true for students in earlier phases of the educational process. One of the first things to suffer when a child experiences social and emotional problems is school performance and attendance. Such children simply do not have the strength and endurance to expend the emotional energy required to cope with serious personal problems and still have enough energy left over to perform well in school. School becomes a lower priority.

School social workers, then, may become major players in helping such children, along with their families, teachers, school administration, and social service agencies within the community, develop a plan to empower them. The following case example illustrates how a school social worker collaborated with various systems in a child's environment to improve it and empower her.

Case Example   Minnie Series, age 8, started having problems in school shortly after she entered third grade. She had transferred during the middle of the year when her family moved to the area. By that time the other third-graders had already formed friendships and cliques, so Minnie had a hard time fitting in. A shy, withdrawn child, she usually found herself on the fringes of class and recess activities. She also was having a hard time with her reading, spelling, and writing, in addition to having a terrible time concentrating on her lessons.

Minnie's teacher, Sybil Servant, noticed these difficulties and referred Minnie to the school's Pupil Services team for evaluation and planning. Part of the evaluation process involved the school social worker, Alan Aladdin, making a home visit and conducting a family assessment. Alan called Minnie's mother, Sue Series, and requested permission to make a home visit during which he gathered the following information.

Minnie had two siblings, Buffy and Brutus, both preschoolers, who also lived in the home. Minnie's father had abruptly left the family two years earlier and had not been heard from since. Sue appeared to be depressed: She expressed little affect and emphasized how overwhelmed and alone she felt. She worked full-time as a dental assistant and was having difficulty finding adequate day care for her preschool children.

At school, Alan met with Minnie, who seemed to lack self-confidence and made a number of derogatory remarks about herself. She also mentioned how she really missed her "Daddy" and wondered if he was OK. Sybil had told Alan that during their class art time, Minnie had drawn pictures of black daggers dripping red blood. Alan was concerned that Minnie was depressed.

Specialized testing revealed that Minnie had a mild learning disability, a disorder whereby a child has marked difficulty learning in some particular area (e.g., reading or working with numbers) while learning and functioning in other areas are normal or above average. Although there was a special learning disabilities class at the school, it was currently jam-packed. Alan advocated with the school principal to open up another section of the class. At first, the principal balked, saying that Minnie's disability was not that severe and that she would be placed on a waiting list. After doing his homework, Alan argued that another section of the class could be taught by a special education teacher from another school who was willing to help out on a part-time basis. Minnie was finally enrolled in the second section of the learning disabilities class; she spent the rest of the school day with her regular third-grade class.

At a subsequent meeting with Sue, Alan discussed resources in the community that could potentially meet the family's needs. He suggested that Minnie become involved with recreational programming at a nearby community center and that she be signed up for the Big Sister program, which would pair Minnie with a young adult who would spend time regularly with her, provide support, and serve as a positive role model. Alan also helped Sue look into some day care options for Buffy and Brutus. He suggested that Sue attend a Parents Without Partners meeting for companionship, support, and social activities.

Alan also recommended that Sue consider individual counseling for herself to address her feelings of being overwhelmed and isolated, and for Minnie to deal with personal issues, lack of self-confidence, feelings about her father, and social skills development. Although Sue was responsive to Alan's other suggestions, she was not at all interested in counseling. She maintained that she and Minnie were not "mentally ill" and so did not need it.

At school, Alan decided to provide Minnie with weekly counseling, which he had time to do with a select few students. Alan also urged Minnie to join a support group he ran for children of single parents. Minnie did so and began to develop a circle of friends she met there and in her learning disabilities class. As she became more outgoing, her relationships with children in her regular classes continued to improve.

Alan worked with Sybil to structure activities within the educational context so that Minnie could feel important and gain confidence. For example, at Alan's suggestion, Sybil gave Minnie the "special" responsibility of pinning up student artwork on the bulletin board and assigned Minnie to work in peer groups made up of children who were the most receptive to her.

This is not the end of Minnie's story. Alan, Minnie's teachers, and the Pupil Services team continued to monitor her progress and provide special services and attention. She persisted in making academic progress, developing social skills, and joining various social groups. As a sixth-grader, she was a socially and emotionally well-adjusted girl who could keep up with her classmates academically.

This case example illustrates how a school social worker can work with various individuals and aspects of systems to help students and their families get what they need. Alan worked with Minnie (providing individual and group counseling) and her family (linking her mother with needed services). He also provided consultation to Sybil and, in subsequent years, to other teachers to maximize Minnie's adjustment. He served as case manager to coordinate and oversee all aspects of service provision for Minnie. Additionally, he advocated with the school system's decision maker (i.e., the school principal) to get Minnie the special education services she needed when she needed them.

School Social Work Roles

Franklin (2004) cites at least nine roles that school social workers may assume. These include consultant, counselor, facilitator, educator, advocate, broker, case manager, community intervention collaborator, and policy initiator and developer.

Consultant

First, a school social worker may be a *consultant*—a person with specialized knowledge and expertise to whom others turn for information, help, and advice. Consultation may entail providing information about behavior management techniques or emotional problems to teachers as Alan did in the case example involving Minnie, or helping a school administration develop a new program.

Counselor

A second school social work role is that of *counselor*—a person who provides clinical intervention concerning social, emotional, or behavioral issues to individuals, families, groups, and communities. Clinical activities might include recognizing feelings, identifying issues and alternatives, offering information, and providing assistance to establish a plan of action. Problems that bring students to school social workers' attention may include behavioral difficulties in the classroom, controlled substance use and abuse, fighting and other acts of violence, truancy, and threats of suicide. In the earlier example, Alan counseled Minnie regarding her lack of self-confidence, depression, feelings about her father, and relationships with peers.

Facilitator

A third role for school social workers is *facilitator*—a person who "suggests, guides, eases, or expedites the way for others during a group experience" (Kirst-Ashman & Hull, 2002, p. 87). This role can involve groups of students, parents, teachers, administrators, and community leaders. Highlight 14.1 reviews 10 types of groups school social workers run.

Educator

A fourth role for school social workers is that of *educator*—a person who gives information and teaches relevant skills. School social workers can offer workshops or training sessions for students, parents, teachers, administrators, and community leaders and residents. Such educational input might involve a wide range of topics. An example of education for students involves family life education and information about sexuality (discussed later in the chapter). Other educational thrusts might include stress, time, or anger management; problem solving; and social skills. Workshops for parents and teachers might cover such issues as "parenting, values clarification, and communication skills" (Franklin, 2004, p. 305). Workshops for

Social workers counsel troubled young people.

HIGHLIGHT 14.1
Focus on Mezzo Practice: Types of Groups School Social Workers Run

Pawlak, Wozniak, and McGowen (1999) reviewed a decade's worth of articles published in the journal *Social Work in Education*. They identified the following 10 types of groups that school social workers run:

1. *Groups for parents of students:* School social workers may run such groups for any number of reasons, including dealing with children who have behavioral problems or eating disorders, helping parents who are recent immigrants cope with differences in language or customs, or discussing neighborhood issues such as crime.

2. *Groups for students who are parents:* Young single parents can face difficult issues including maintaining good health during pregnancy, balancing school and parenthood, caring for infants, and obtaining support from fathers.

3. *Groups for students whose families are experiencing divorce:* Divorce can have serious consequences for children's emotional well-being. Children might tackle many questions. (Was I to blame for my parents'

breakup? How could Mom and Dad do this to me? What will happen to me now? Will I ever see Daddy [or Mommy] again? Why doesn't Dad [or Mom] talk to me much anymore? Will Daddy [or Mommy] like their new family better than me?) Groups for children of divorce can "address children's feelings of isolation, loss, anger, guilt, and helplessness" (Pawlak et al., 1999, pp. 357–358).

4. *Groups for students dealing with substance abuse issues:* Such groups might deal with students' own or parental substance abuse, providing coping strategies in potentially abusive situations or peer support for abstinence.

5. *Groups for students with attention deficit hyperactivity disorder:* Recall that attention deficit hyperactivity disorder (ADHD) is a syndrome of learning and behavioral problems beginning in childhood that is characterized by a persistent pattern of inattention, excessive physical movement, and impulsivity that appears in at least two settings (including home, school, work, and social contexts).

(continued)

administrators or community leaders and residents might focus on current issues facing students or newly proposed school programs.

Advocate

A fifth role assumed by school social workers is that of *advocate*—a person who steps forward, intervenes or represents, or defends, supports, or recommends a course of action on behalf of one or more others. Franklin (2004) provides an example of a case requiring advocacy. A young boy kept getting in trouble for acting out in school. His mother felt that he might have a learning disability or ADHD and requested that he be tested and placed appropriately. The school social worker agreed with and supported the mother's request. However, the child's teacher emphatically maintained that no learning disability was involved and that the child was simply a "bad kid." Initially, abiding by the teacher's judgment, school administrators refused to test the child. The school social worker advocated on the child's behalf, explaining specific

HIGHLIGHT 14.1 *(continued)*

Such groups can focus on "self-esteem, feelings, behavior change, communication, conflict, friendship, anger, and problem solving" (Pawlak et al., 1999, p. 358).

6. *Groups for trauma-related recovery:* These groups can provide crisis intervention for students recovering from virtually any trauma, from a school bus accident, to a tornado in a small rural town, to a murderous assault by fellow students, as Dylan Klebold, age 17, and Eric Harris, age 18, did at Columbine High in Littleton, Colorado, in 1999. Traumas can result in posttraumatic stress disorder (described in Chapter 13). Groups can help students confront their fears, deal with anxiety, and provide mutual support.

7. *Groups for students at risk of dropping out:* Groups for these students may address how to handle their personal or behavioral problems, confront their anger at "the system," improve study habits, deal with family problems, and plan positively for the future.

8. *Groups addressing stress, grief, and loss issues:* These groups can focus on any type of grief or loss issues including the death of a loved one, the closing of a manufacturing plant that was a town's primary employer, or a recent miscarriage. School social workers can also run stress management groups that might focus on stress related to family issues or academic pressures.

9. *Groups addressing socialization and peer interaction skills:* Peer pressure in childhood and adolescence is awesome. Children want to fit in; they want to be popular; they want to feel important. These groups can address peer pressure issues, teach children more effective ways to communicate and interact with peers, and enhance self-confidence and self-esteem.

10. *Groups addressing racial and cultural issues:* Such groups can address issues concerning stereotypes and prejudice, with students expressing their opinions and confronting inaccurate perceptions. Groups also can enhance cultural awareness, with students discussing their own cultural values and issues and educating each other to increase their appreciation of diversity.

reasons the child should be tested. Additionally, the social worker used this opportunity to "educate the school district on their legal obligations to act and to provide an appropriate educational placement for this child" (p. 306). Because of the social worker's advocacy efforts, the school administrators determined that the child required testing. They discovered that the child did indeed have a learning disability in addition to another psychiatric condition that eventually led to the child's placement in a special education class.

Broker

A sixth role for school social workers is that of *broker*—a person who helps link clients with community resources and services. In Alan's case, he attempted to link Minnie and her mother with a therapist in an outside social services agency. Linkages or referrals might involve any type of resource (e.g., recreational programs, financial resources).

Case Manager

Related to the role of broker is that of *case manager*—a person who coordinates services from a variety of sources. Alan also functioned as case manager in Minnie's case, coordinating services provided by Minnie's teachers, other school personnel, and outside resources.

Community Intervention Collaborator

Another role assumed by school social workers is that of *community intervention collaborator*—a person who works with others in the community to initiate change or develop needed programs. Social workers can use their communication and organizational skills to educate and mobilize community groups. Potential goals include developing a shelter for runaways, crisis hot lines, bilingual education programs, or preschool day care programs for student parents.

Policy Initiator and Developer

The final role that school social workers might assume is that of *policy initiator and developer*—a person who works to "influence, initiate, and develop policy, which affects the social and emotional development of children and youth within the school and community. Through participating in policymaking committees, writing grants, and as members of professional organizations, they are active in creating programs that benefit the education process" (Franklin, 2004, p. 308). An example is writing letters to or e-mailing legislators to support social welfare policies that benefit students and their families.

Highlight 14.2 addresses the importance of multiculturalism in education. It suggests how social workers might enhance appreciation of cultural differences while assuming educator, advocate, community intervention collaborator, and policy initiator and developer roles.

Gay and Lesbian Youths: A Population-at-Risk

Social workers must respond to the special issues and needs of all children with whom they work. This is the case for not only school social workers but any practitioners serving children and families. Just as social workers must attend to a child's cultural heritage and racial identity, so must they be competent to deal with the issues of an adolescent's sexual orientation.

Generally, lesbian, gay, and bisexual (LGB) people have some "personal awareness of same-sex erotic feelings before puberty and that awareness becomes crystallized at puberty" (Hershberger & D'Augelli, 2000, p. 226). Laird (1995) explains that "adolescents, coming to terms with their own sexual identities at a time when peer relationships are so important, are often particularly vulnerable to peer cruelty and may need some special help in the form of groups or other kinds of supportive counseling" (p. 1611). Adolescence is a critical time of identity development including sexual identity; it is also a period when people are exceptionally vulnerable to peer pressure and criticism (Zastrow & Kirst-Ashman, 2004). Adolescents can be mercilessly cruel. This means that LGB youths must deal not only with whatever family problems involved them with the social service system in the first place but also with

HIGHLIGHT 14.2

Enhancing Multiculturalism and Reducing Racism in Schools

School populations are becoming more diverse. It is estimated that "nearly one in four school-aged children will be of Hispanic origin by 2030 and that the number of non-Hispanic white students in the United States will fall below 40 percent for the first time in history between 2030 and 2040" (Dupper, 2000, p. 256). It is time to broaden children's perspectives and appreciation of multiple cultures.

Spencer (1999) explains the nature of multicultural education:

> Multicultural education incorporates the study of racial and ethnic differences, as well as issues related to gender, age, socioeconomic status, and physical disabilities. . . . [Its aims] are to foster a sense of understanding and respect for differences, to overcome prejudice and discrimination and provide an understanding of the dynamics of racism, to replace historical and cultural misnomers [using wrong names] with accurate information, and to ensure that all students receive equitable benefits from the education system. (p. 155)

Note that an "outgrowth" of the multicultural education movement is "global education" (Drum & Howard, 1989; Spencer, 1999, p. 158). Spencer (1999) explains:

> Global education deals with diversity at the global level and focuses on the interrelated systems that affect the entire planet. The primary goal is to build understanding and respect for peoples and nations outside the United States. A global effort goes beyond the "Western-centric" curriculum pervasive in schools by providing an understanding of the dynamics of imperialism [nations extending their own power and authority over other nations and areas] and oppression and creating an awareness of the earth as an interrelated holistic system. (p. 158)

Social workers can pursue at least six approaches to enhancing the appreciation of multiculturalism and reducing racism in schools:

1. Initiate and encourage open discussions and dialogues among various ethnic, racial, and cultural groups (Dupper, 2000; Spencer, 1999). Sciarra (2001) explains: "Both small group counseling and classroom guidance units are excellent modalities for developing multicultural awareness. Small groups that are racially and culturally diverse give students the opportunity to share their heritage with the other members" (p. 721). Such interaction gives students a forum for discovering commonalities, appreciating differences, and working out conflicts.

2. Seek and adopt curricula that emphasize multiculturalism (and non-Western perspectives) (Dupper, 2000; Spencer, 1999).

3. Empower children by focusing on and appreciating their racial, ethnic, and cultural identities, and by teaching them strategies to stop racism (Dupper, 2000; Spencer, 1999).

4. Give teachers and other school staff training and consultation regarding multiculturalism (Kiselica, Changizi, Cureton, & Gridley, 1995; Spencer, 1999).

5. Involve parents in efforts to promote multiculturalism by encouraging their participation in and understanding of their children's education (Kiselica et al., 1995). Factors discouraging the parental involvement of people of color include "cultural value conflicts," "racism and alienation," and "poverty" (Kiselica et al., 1995, pp. 519–520). Social workers can

> work toward preventing and mediating cultural values conflicts and misunderstanding, taking measures to reduce feelings of alienation, and assisting parents in overcoming socioeconomic hardships. . . . [E]thnic minority parents benefit from community awareness workshops and parent

(continued)

HIGHLIGHT 14.2 *(continued)*

training programs designed to familiarize them with school policies, procedures, and goals. . . . Sending letters to parents . . . and making home visits . . . are other tactics that have been recommended for keeping racial/ethnic minority parents informed about school activities and for promoting parental participation in those activities. . . . Other strategies for reducing alienation from the school system include genuinely showing an interest in how the parents feel about the educational system and working to empower parents. (Kiselica et al., 1995, pp. 521–522)

6. Conduct research that monitors racial attitudes and other facets of the student and staff population (Sohng & Weatherley, 1999; Spencer, 1999). Sohng and Weatherley (1999) provide the following suggestions to school social workers:

School-based research can offer a promising vehicle for assessing cultural diversity in curriculum, classroom, and school practices and improving the campus climate for a diverse student body. You might, for example, take a look at how the composition of the student population at your school has changed over the years. . . . [Y]ou should also familiarize yourself with both official and informal institutional policies and procedures, academic programs, and instructional support. Have these policies kept pace with the changing student population? Another approach is to conduct a student survey on demographic and cultural backgrounds, financial status, living and working conditions, and curricular progress and problems. This can be an effective way to engage students and teachers in examining the implications of diversity. (p. 525)

their own sexual identity and related issues. Individual and group counseling in which they are offered support and provided an arena to address feelings and discuss issues can help LGB youths through this difficult period.

One such issue is *coming out*—the process of a person acknowledging that he or she is lesbian, gay, or bisexual. Becoming aware of one's identity as a gay or lesbian person takes time. It's not like a 250-watt lightbulb suddenly being turned on in a pitch-dark room. Rather, it's a gradual, frequently difficult process in view of the homophobia[1] and stereotypes saturating our society (Swigonski, 1995).

Note that, although we are discussing coming out in the context of adolescence, this process can occur during various stages of life (Tully, 2000). We examine it here because of sexual orientation's significance beginning very early in life and extending across the life span.

Coming out tends to occur in four stages (Boston Women's Health Book Collective, 1984): (1) coming out to oneself, (2) getting to know other people within the gay and lesbian community, (3) sharing with family and friends that one is lesbian or gay, and (4) coming out of the closet—that is, openly and publicly acknowledging one's sexual orientation.

Step 1, coming out to oneself, is difficult because of the negativity associated with being gay. The logic might go something like this: "Society says gay and lesbian people are bad. I am gay. Therefore, I am bad."

[1]We have established that *homophobia* is irrational obsessive fear and hatred of LGB people.

Social workers can help adolescents work through the experience of coming out. Practitioners must avoid minimizing or denying the young person's developing identity and sexual orientation. Rather, they can empower gay and lesbian adolescents by taking their expressed thoughts and feelings seriously and providing them with the information and support they need. Hershberger and D'Augelli (2000) maintain that "the fundamental approach" of professionals working with youths "who are questioning and exploring their sexual identity should be one of acceptance" (p. 237).

Step 2 in the coming-out process involves seeking other gay or lesbian people and learning about what it means to be gay. Social workers should strive to increase their own awareness, and that of their agency, regarding how to provide accessible services to gay and lesbian youths (Woodman, 1995). Such services may include "special advocacy efforts, peer support groups, recreational programs, and other resources to counter the isolation and despair that are all too common among gay and lesbian adolescents" (Laird, 1995, p. 1611).

Step 3 concerns youths taking the risk of sharing this self-identity with people who are close to them. This is scary because they might be rejected purely on the basis of being gay or lesbian. Hershberger and D'Augelli (2000) suggest that practitioners help adolescents "proceed with caution" and "discuss the risks involved"; they continue that "[u]nless youths are certain of support from family members who matter, they should not be encouraged to disclose" (p. 239). This can be a complicated issue for young people in substitute placements (e.g., foster family or group home care, discussed in Chapter 9) because they may be involved with a wide range of people. Whom should they tell?

Finally, step 4 involves being open to the world about being gay or lesbian. This is also risky for a number of reasons, including the potential for victimization and violence simply because they are gay or lesbian (Hershberger & D'Augelli, 2000; Shernoff, 1995).

One college freshman attended a campus "Speak Out," in which students gathered to share their opinions about the topic of sexual orientation. She stood up and said, "Why not let people do what they want to, as long as they're not hurting anybody? It's really nobody else's business." Note that this was simply a neutral comment about minding one's own business, not a statement promoting different sexual orientations. Ironically, she was heterosexual. In the ensuing weeks, she was brutally attacked twice, but she was unable to identify her attackers. Additionally, four different times, she found notes under the windshield wiper blades on her car saying, "Die, dike! Go to hell!" Eventually the harassment stopped, although she remained terrified for a long time. Another sad aspect of the story is that the school chancellor refused to issue a statement saying that violence against gay and lesbian people would not be tolerated on campus. That was too controversial.

Social workers must also be aware of the increased risks for gay and lesbian youths of substance abuse and suicide (Hershberger & D'Augelli, 2000; Hunter & Schaecher, 1995). Because they feel different and out of place in a heterosexual world, gay and lesbian youths may isolate themselves. They may turn to substance abuse or suicide as a means of escaping what they may see as a hostile and impossible world.

Highlight 14.3 focuses on some of the myths and stereotypes about LGB people that contribute to homophobia, discrimination, and potential emotional turmoil.

HIGHLIGHT 14.3
Myths and Facts About LGB People

Myth: Lesbians and gay men are obviously homosexual based on how they look and dress.

Fact: You can't identify lesbian, gay, bisexual, or heterosexual by physical appearance alone. "In reality, the gay population is as diverse as the heterosexual population not only in appearance, but also in social class, educational achievement, occupational status, race, ethnicity, and personality" (McCammon, Knox, & Schacht, 2004, p. 194; Tully, 2001).

Myth: Gay men are child molesters.

Fact: Heterosexual child molesters outnumber LGB child molesters 11 to 1 (McCammon et al., 2004).

Myth: Lesbian and gay people really want to be the opposite gender.

Fact: Being lesbian or gay has nothing to do with wanting to be the opposite gender (Tully, 2001). Gender identity and sexual orientation are two totally distinct concepts. *Gender identity* is a person's internal psychological self-concept of being either a male or a female. *Sexual orientation* is sexual and romantic attraction to persons of one or both genders.

Myth: Lesbian and gay people in couples like to assume traditional gender role stereotypes.

Fact: Lesbian and gay people in couples have their own identities and personalities that have nothing to do with traditional gender role stereotypes (Berger & Kelly, 1995). Rathus, Nevid, and Fichner-Rathus (2002) explain: "Many gay people claim that labels of masculine and feminine only represent the 'straight community's' efforts to pigeonhole them in terms that 'straights' can understand" (p. 307).

Myth: All LGB people are promiscuous and incapable of sustaining long-term relationships.

Fact: Just like heterosexuals, some LGB people have long-term relationships and some do not; just like heterosexuals, some have multiple partners and some do not (Tully, 2001).

Myth: Children growing up in LGB families become psychologically damaged.

Fact: All indications are that children growing up in LGB families do just as well as those raised in heterosexual families (Laird, 1995; McCammon et al., 2004; Woodman, 1995).

Creative Empowerment for Youths Through Macro Practice

A consistent theme throughout this book is how social workers address issues not only at the individual, family, and small group level but also at the macro level of organizations and communities. If a policy hurts clients, it is the social worker's responsibility to do something about it. If an absolutely necessary program for clients does not exist, it is also the worker's responsibility to initiate one to get clients the resources they need.

Social workers must be flexible and creative. Sometimes they need to explore new ways to accomplish goals, new avenues to empower clients. This is despite the fact that thinking of new ways to help clients is probably not part of their formal job description. The two case examples presented in this section detail creative approaches to helping youths by using strengths and resources already existing in their communities. One involves conducting a community assets assessment, and the other mobilizing a spiritual community to help its youths in the academic realm. Both programs relate to education. The first was implemented through the schools because they provide relatively easy access to the at-risk Latino/a youths involved. The second concerns building on preexisting resources to help African American students improve their computer skills. Although the two case examples involve the schools, such intervention is not necessarily limited to initiation by school social workers. Programs like this could be developed by any social workers working with youths.

Empowering Latino/a Youths by Conducting a Community Assets Assessment[2]

We have emphasized the importance of using community strengths to empower communities. Delgado (1998) describes a project conducted by New Bridges (*Nuevo Puente*), an agency established by a Center on Substance Abuse Prevention grant. The grant targeted at-risk youths who were considered vulnerable to a variety of negative circumstances including gang pressure, delinquency, emotional problems, substance abuse, and difficulties in school. New Bridges' purpose is to identify and recruit community resources for substance abuse prevention activities. Other facets of New Bridges include provision of "cultural and educational activities"; opportunities to learn about "the effect of substance abuse on individuals, families, and communities"; and training "to carry out school and community education on alcohol, tobacco, and other drugs" (Delgado, 1998, pp. 204–205).

The Plan

New Bridges hired six girls and four boys to conduct a community strengths assessment of a 40-block urban community. The interviewers asked local business owners and operators about the type of business, the availability of contact people, the social services provided (if a social services agency), and their "willingness to collaborate with schools and agencies on community projects" (Delgado, 1998, p. 205). Goals were to "provide youths with an appreciation of community strengths, raise school and human services agency awareness of community assets, and develop an assets directory" (Delgado, 1998, p. 205).

Results and Recommendations

Results indicate that "the use of Latino adolescents in community asset assessments offers much promise" for social work (Delgado, 1998, p. 210). Although this assessment was conducted via a grant-created community agency, Delgado (1998) offers a number of suggestions for implementation of community assets assessments. This is accomplished mainly through the schools because they give easy access to youths, including those at risk.

First, school social workers can recruit youths to identify "potential student leaders, candidates for peer education programs, and possible projects involving

[2] From "Community asset assessments by Latino youth" by M. Delgado. In P. L. Ewalt, E. M. Freeman, and D. L. Poole (Eds.), *Community building: Renewal, well-being, and shared responsibility,* pp. 202–212. ©1998, National Association of Social Workers.

natural support systems" (Delgado, 1998, p. 209). For example, the young people involved in the New Bridges project decided that they wanted to go on a trip and financed it by holding a car wash. They asked Latino/a businesses to contribute a small amount of money (e.g., a nickel or a quarter) for each car washed. In return, the youths listed the sponsors' names on a billboard to provide publicity for them. This is a good example of how community members can work together to enhance relationships among various facets (i.e., this group of young people and local businesses) to reach mutually positive goals (i.e., financial backing for the youths' trip and publicity for the businesses).

A second idea for using the community assets assessment is for schools to invite business owners from the community in to talk about how they started their businesses. In this way owners can provide positive role models for young people and sow some seeds related to career possibilities and goals.

A third idea is to use the information gathered in special school projects. Students might earn extra credit in a social studies course by investigating community strengths. They could videotape interviews with interested residents or community service representatives. They might then share these tapes with other students or even social service agencies to provide education about social issues and information about cultural strengths.

Helping a Spiritual Community Empower Its African American Youths[3]

The following is an example of how social workers helped to empower African American youths by mobilizing a spiritual community in Utah. First, a study was conducted to identify the values and opinions of community members. Subsequently, a program was implemented that demonstrates how social workers can creatively work with a spiritual community to help meet the needs of its youths.

The Study

Haight (1998) conducted an *ethnographic study*—that is, the scientific description of a culture—targeting African American youths belonging to the First Baptist Church in Salt Lake City, Utah. The church was established over a hundred years ago by " 'a Baptist Prayer Band,' a group of African Americans who, excluded from worshiping in the white churches, met in one another's homes" (p. 215). Haight (1998) notes that "African American Utahns, like African Americans in other parts of the country, experience racial discrimination in employment, housing, education, and everyday social interactions" (p. 216). African Americans are a tiny minority in Utah. Additionally, most of the Utah population belongs to the Church of Jesus Christ of Latter-Day Saints, a tightly knit spiritual community that sponsors an array of social and cultural activities for its members.

Extensive interviews with First Baptist Church members revealed an environmental context for children that was "negligent at best and virulently racist at worst" (p. 216). Of special concern were the perceived "negative expectations" of white

[3]This study is from " 'Gathering the Spirit' at First Baptist Church: Spirituality as a protective factor in the lives of African American children," by W. L. Haight. *Social Work, 43* (3), 123–221. © May 1998, National Association of Social Workers.

educators in the public school system (p. 216). First Baptist Church members felt that the church's spiritual community provided a safe, supportive environment in which children could learn about their cultural heritage. Emphasis was placed on "helping children understand the relevance of, and then apply, biblical concepts to their own lives" (p. 218). Additionally, children were strongly encouraged to participate in ongoing learning activities and were expected to respond to a series of "call-and-response sequences. For example, when the teacher said that they would no longer be fishermen, but that they would be fishers of _____?, the class responded that they would be fishers of men" (p. 217). The nurturing spiritual community gave children an environment in which they could develop the resilience to cope with any rejection, isolation, or discrimination they experienced in the outside world. Church members also placed great importance on positive, supportive relationships between adults and children.

The Intervention

Along with First Baptist Church leaders, social workers initiated and developed "an intervention, informed by knowledge generated through the ethnographic study, to support the development of children's resilience" (Haight, 1998, p. 219). This intervention strategy was the establishment of a "Computer Club" (p. 219). First Baptist Church members "both prioritized educational achievement and identified school as problematic for African American children" (p. 219). Furthermore, children's computer literacy was identified as "a specific area of need, and learning more about computers as an opportunity that children and families would embrace" (p. 219). Thus members viewed enhancing children's competence with computers as a valuable goal. Although the Computer Club's primary focus was educational computer games, student volunteers from a local university also participated with children in a range of activities including field trips, parties, picnics, "several computer-generated art shows," African dance groups, and a gospel choir (p. 219). The activities enabled students and children to enjoy mutual experiences, share ideas, and develop positive relationships.

The workers portrayed in this example first explored the values and strengths of the community, and then worked with community members toward a mutually desirable goal. Haight (1998) concludes that

> the ability of social workers to develop knowledge of cultural beliefs and practices relevant both to African American communities in general and to the unique African American communities in which they are practicing is critical to the development of ethnic-sensitive social work interventions such as the Computer Club. (p. 220)

 # School Social Workers' Role in the Prevention of School Violence

It was a phone call that will stay with Denver Police Officer John Lietz for the rest of his life. Shortly after 11 . . . [on a] Tuesday morning, he picked up the line to hear the voice of Matthew Depew, the son of a fellow cop: Depew and 17 other Columbine High School students were trapped in a storage room off the school cafeteria, hiding from kids with guns. Lietz himself had a daughter in the school, and he could hear bursts of gunfire in the background. Lietz told the kids to barricade the door with chairs and sacks of food, and to be ready to attack the gunmen if they got in. Several times Lietz heard the shooters trying to break into the room; they were so close that he could hear them reloading cartridges. At one point, as they pounded on the door, Depew calmly told Lietz that he was sure he was going to die. "Please tell my father I love him," he said. (Mai, 1999, p. 25)

Several hours later on April 20, 1999, 12 students, two gunmen, and a teacher at Columbine High in Littleton, Colorado were dead; 23 more students were wounded (Mai, 1999). The shooters were high school students Eric Harris, 18, and Dennis Klebold, 17. Isolated and filled with hatred, they shot themselves as part of the carnage. Harris allegedly explained his actions in an unnerving note: "Your children who have ridiculed me, who have chosen not to accept me, who have treated me like I am not worth their time are dead. THEY ARE (expletive) DEAD" (Williams, 1999, p. 18A). The two teens couldn't "manage their emotions. They feel rejected, enraged, jealous. They are kids who never learned how to solve problems. Combine that with easy access to guns, parents who may have too little time, as well as movies, video games, and music that toast violence, and the result can be lethal" (Cannon, Streisand, & McGraw, 1999, p. 19).

The tragedy in Colorado shook the nation and brought the issue of school violence to the forefront. However, this was not an isolated incident. Consider the following:

- Luke Woodham, 16, who "[f]irst killed his mother, [and] then . . . went to his high school and opened fire, killing three and wounding seven."
- Michael Carneal, 14, who "shot three students to death at an early-morning high school prayer meeting."
- Mitchell Johnson, 13, and Andrew Golden, 11, who "set off a fire alarm to draw their schoolmates outside and then started shooting, killing four students and a teacher."
- Kip Kinkel, 15, who "[a]fter killing his parents, . . . shot 24 students at school. Two died. Wrestled to the ground, he yelled, 'Shoot me!' " (Begley, 1999, pp. 32–33).

Fiske (2002, September 16) reports on a violence assessment tool developed by Donald. A. Shulman, a crisis specialist at Crestwood Children's Center in Rochester, New Jersey, and explains the dynamics of youth violence:

Children most likely to explode in violence are those who feel that nobody cares about them, who believe they have no support, and who feel truly alienated, according to Shulman. Therefore, what can be done to help potential perpetrators of violence and their possible victims? The answer, he states, is simple, inexpensive, and can be done by anyone, regardless of training or background. "When you, myself, or anyone—whether you are a social worker, teacher, or friend—look a child in the eye and say, 'You count. I care about you. You are important,' you can prevent a murder," Shulman offers. "It is when we feel meaningless and purposeless that we prey on others through violence." (p. 15)

Recent research indicates that the following risk factors may predict youth violence:

- Hyperactivity or attention deficits.
- Parent criminality.

- Poor family management practice.
- Low bonding to school [which is related to disinterest in school, truancy, and academic failure].
- Having delinquent friends.
- Gang membership (Sciarra, 2004, p. 346).

Similarly, the following provide early warning signs for violence potential:

- Social withdrawal.
- Excessive feelings of isolation and loneliness.
- Excessive feelings of rejection.
- Being a victim of violence.
- A feeling of being picked on or persecuted.
- Low interest in school and poor academic performance.
- Expressions of violence in writings and drawings.
- Uncontrolled anger.
- Patterns of impulsive and chronic hitting, intimidating, and bullying.
- A history of discipline problems.
- A history of violence and aggressive behaviors.
- Intolerance and prejudice.
- Drug and alcohol use.
- Gang membership.
- Inappropriate access to, possession of, and use of firearms.
- Serious threats of violence (Sciarra, 2004, p. 347).

What can school social workers do to prevent school violence? "Violence prevention in schools is becoming a major focus of practice for school social workers"; "school social workers play an increasingly important role in shaping and implementing policy, interventions, and procedures that make U.S. schools safer" (Astor, Benbenishty, & Marachi, 2004, p. 149). Regardless of how they proceed, school social workers must work closely with teachers, school administration, students, their families, and the community to effectively address school violence. Practitioners can assist "in the formulation of school policies and programs. In the context of these school policies, which expect safe, nonthreatening, nonharmful behavior in the school, school social workers work with victims and perpetrators of interpersonal violence and their families" (McDonald, Fineran, Constable, and Moriarty, 2002, p. 459). Other specific suggestions practitioners might follow to prevent school violence include conducting needs assessments, establishing conflict resolution strategies and teams, and developing violence prevention programs.

Needs Assessments

Social workers can work with teachers and school administrators to conduct *needs assessments*—systematic analyses of client problems and issues to determine clients' needs and develop problem-solving strategies. "A needs assessment can be as simple as examining existing data. It can be as complex as a multiyear, multiphase study involving the design of questionnaires to collect new data" (Bleyer & Joiner, 2002, p. 195). Another way of gaining such information is through the use of *focus groups,* where members gather to discuss and explore designated subjects; such groups generate ideas, describe issues, and potentially propose recommendations to address problems (Toseland & Rivas, 2005). In the context of school violence, students representing various social factions might be selected for group membership and asked to describe their perceptions of student hostility and the potential for violence. Regardless of how a needs assessment is done, the important thing is to gain an understanding of the school climate and to identify potential hot spots where violence might be brewing.

Conflict Resolution

Conflict resolution programs provide another means of addressing school violence (McDonald et al., 2002). *Conflict resolution* is the process of resolving disputes to come to some sort of agreement or compromise between opposing parties. McDonald and Moriarty (2002) explain:

> Students become increasingly vulnerable to a variety of problems, such as anxiety, stress, a sense of personal inadequacy, and low self-esteem when they are blocked from developing autonomy and self-determination. Such alienated students are at risk of becoming involved in conflict and can be disruptive to the educational process. Social workers can counter this alienation with strategies that reconnect and empower students in a positive manner. Conflict resolution skills are such a tool. (pp. 501–502)
>
> The actual process of conflict resolution has several components: (1) identification of the problem in specific language, (2) brainstorming possible solutions, (3) agreeing on a solution, and (4) confirming intent to make the resolution work. (p. 505)

Whereas the process of conflict resolution is usually the same, the way programs are implemented can differ. McDonald and Moriarty (2002) explain that

> [s]ome school districts have instituted systemwide training in conflict resolution skills but have no formal program, such as a trained team of mediators. [*Mediators* are neutral referees or peacemakers who help resolve disputes between opposing parties.] Other districts do some training with all students but also train a . . . [team] of students who are available in more difficult situations. This is especially important when emotions are running high, or when there seems to be an imbalance in power. In these situations care is required to ensure that each party to the dispute is respectful to the other. These specially trained students are often identified as a team and have regular meetings. . . . Other schools have students identified in each classroom who are the designated conflict resolvers and who may hold such dispute resolution sessions in the classroom, ideally in an area somewhat removed from the rest of the class. Other schools do not train all students but rely on a . . . team of conflict resolvers or mediators to deal with identified problems. In such schools there is likely to be a set policy regarding which types of problems are appropriate for referral to such specially trained teams. In all cases, the school must have a means to oversee the referral process so that conflict resolvers and mediators are at all times protected from serious problems or risks. (pp. 507–508)

Violence Prevention Programs

Astor and colleagues (2004) maintain that successful violence prevention programs must be organized endeavors with the following characteristics:

- They raise the awareness and responsibility of students, teachers, and parents regarding the types of violence in their schools (e.g., sexual harassment, fighting, weapon use).
- They create clear guidelines and rules for the entire school [that reinforce appropriate positive behavior and stress penalties for aggressive behavior].
- They target the various social systems in the school and clearly communicate to the entire school community what procedures should be followed before, during, and after violent events.
- They focus on getting the school staff, students, and parents involved in the program.
- The interventions often fit easily into the normal flow and mission of the school setting.
- They utilize faculty, staff, and parents in the school setting in order to plan, implement, and sustain the program.
- They increase monitoring and supervision in nonclassroom areas. (p. 158)

An example is the Positive Adolescents Choices Training (PACT) program "designed to teach African-American youth social skills to aid in prevention of violence" (Hammond & Yung, 1991, 1993; Yung & Hammond, 1998). A unique aspect of PACT is that it is culturally relevant and aimed at reducing aggression and victimization in high-risk youth. The program components include anger management, prosocial skills training, and violence risk education. The sessions are built around videotapes that demonstrate culturally sensitive social situations. Participants learn specific skills needed to solve the situation peacefully. Participants in the programs [improved their behavior] . . . in the areas of giving feedback, problem-solving, and resisting peer pressure [in addition to demonstrating a significant decrease in] physical aggression at school. (Astor et al., 2004, p. 169)

Teenage Sexual Activity, Pregnancy, and Parenting Issues

Sexual activity and teenage pregnancy are important issues for young people today. Any social worker working with youths will likely address the decisions concerning and the consequences of early sexual activity. Social work settings overlap. Work with youths occurs in various settings and fields of practice including school social work, corrections, mental health, child welfare, runaway shelters, and Planned Parenthood clinics.[4]

Of young women age 15–19, 10% become pregnant each year (Centers for Disease Control and Prevention [CDC], 2000; Westheimer & Lopater, 2005). Although there was a slight decline in the pregnancy rate over the past decade, there still are a million such births each year (Crooks & Baur, 2002; Westheimer & Lopater, 2005), representing 13% of all births in the United States (Alan Guttmacher Institute, 1999; Davtyan, 2000; Thomas, 2000). Of births to women in the 15–19 age group, 90% are not planned (CDC, 2000; Rathus et al., 2002). About "50 percent of these pregnancies result in live births, 30 percent are aborted, and 20 percent end in spontaneous abortions or stillbirths" (Alan Guttmacher Institute, 1999; Crooks & Baur, 2002, p. 387; Davtyan, 2000).

---

[4]Planned Parenthood is a national organization created in 1921 to promote research and disseminate information about contraception and family planning.

HIGHLIGHT 14.4
Global Perspectives on Adolescent Pregnancy and Birthrates

Crooks and Baur (2002) propose four factors affecting adolescent pregnancy rates and birthrates[5] around the world today, in contrast to a few decades ago. First, unmarried women of any age are more likely to have children. Second, births and childrearing outside marriage are much more accepted socially than in the past. Third, most industrialized nations have made contraception and abortion more readily available to women. Fourth, more people have better access to information about sexuality from various sources including improved sex education programs, the media, and the Internet.

Interestingly, both pregnancy rates and birthrates for teens have decreased in the industrialized world in the past few decades (Crooks & Baur, 2002). Singh and Darroch (2000) propose at least two reasons for this. First, education has

assumed greater importance in young people's life plans; they see it as a means to attain adequate economic and social standing and so are motivated to pursue it. Second, young women have more options than they did in the past, when roles as wives and mothers were stressed more pointedly.

Singh and Darroch (2000) explored the pregnancy rates and birthrates for 33 industrialized nations. Pregnancy rates were the lowest in Japan (10.1 per 1,000), Italy (12.0), the Netherlands (12.2), and Spain (12.3). In contrast, they were the highest in the Russian Federation (101.7 per 1,000), the United States (83.6), Bulgaria (83.3), and Romania (74.0). Birthrates were the lowest in Japan (3.9 per 1,000), Italy (6.9), Sweden (7.7), and Spain (7.8). The highest birthrates occurred in the United States (54.4 per 1,000), Moldova (53.2), Georgia (53.0), and Bulgaria (49.6).

[5]*Pregnancy rates* refer to the number of women per 1,000 who get pregnant in a particular age group; *birthrates* are the actual number of births per 1,000 occurring in that age group.

These data reflect the highest rate of teenage pregnancy in the West and the second highest rate among industrialized nations, with the Russian Federation having the highest (Alan Guttmacher Institute [AGI], 2004b). Highlight 14.4 reviews the global picture.

Reasons for Concern

What happens to these babies after birth? Teenage pregnancy is a serious social welfare concern for at least four reasons.

Children Begetting Children

First, teen mothers are children themselves. The vast majority of babies born to single teens remain at home with their young mothers. Westheimer and Lopater (2005) indicate that "87 percent of teenagers who have their baby will keep it. Only 8 percent give it up for formal, legally binding adoption, and 5 percent place their child informally with someone in their extended family: a parent, a grandparent, or even an older sibling" (p. 453).

Keeping their babies places these young women in a situation very different from that of most of their peers. Adolescence and young adulthood are the usual times of life for finding a mate, obtaining an education, and making a career choice. The additional responsibility of motherhood places serious restrictions on the amount of freedom and time available for these activities. Additionally, such young women are often ill prepared for motherhood. They are usually in the midst of establishing their own identities and learning to care for themselves.

Negative Physical Consequences

A second reason teenage pregnancy is a social welfare concern involves the likely negative physical consequences for mother and baby. Young mothers are more likely than more mature women to experience difficulties (Kail & Cavanaugh, 2004; Papalia, Olds, & Feldman, 2004). Young mothers' problems include prolonged labor, hemorrhaging, and miscarriage. The infant is more likely to have a low birth weight, to be born prematurely, and to have neurological difficulties than infants born to adult mothers (AGI, 2004a; McCammon et al., 2004; Papalia et al., 2004). Many of these problems are due to poor or nonexistent prenatal care and to poor nutrition.

Long-Term Negative Effects for Mothers

Research indicates that negative effects on the young mother continue long after the baby's birth. Teenage mothers are much less likely to finish high school than their peers who are not mothers (Kelly, 2004; Papalia et al., 2004). Subsequently, they're less likely to go to college (Strong et al., 2005). They are also more likely to be poor, receive public assistance, and have subsequent pregnancies (Papalia et al., 2004; Strong et al., 2005).

Compared to more mature mothers, teenage mothers tend to have poorer parenting skills and are more likely to abuse their children (Newman & Newman, 2003). Thus the added stress and responsibility of motherhood tend to take a heavy toll on teen mothers. Raising a child demands time, energy, and attention. Time taken to care for a baby must be subtracted from the time available for school and recreational activities.

All this sounds quite negative. Santrock (2004) cautions, "Keep in mind that not every adolescent female who bears a child lives a life of poverty and low achievement. Thus, while adolescent pregnancy is a high-risk circumstance and in general adolescents who do not become pregnant fare better than those who do, some adolescent mothers do well in school and have positive outcomes" (p. 380). Adolescent motherhood puts adolescents at risk of hardship. It does not necessarily doom them to a bad life.

Long-Term Negative Effects for Children

Studies also reveal negative effects on the children themselves. As the children of teenage mothers mature, they tend to have more emotional, intellectual, and physical problems than their counterparts born to adult mothers (Carroll, 2005; Papalia et al., 2004; Rathus et al., 2002). Specifically, these children tend to perform more poorly in school and, "in turn, are likely to drop out of school, to be depressed, to get in trouble with the law, and to become adolescent parents themselves" (Papalia et al., 2004, p. 439).

What does all this mean for social workers? It means that children having children is a serious issue. Social work practitioners working with youths may need to provide these young people with information about contraception, sexually transmitted diseases, and the responsibilities of parenthood. Social workers may also be in the position to help adolescents undertake a decision-making process whereby they make educated, responsible choices.

Reasons Teens Get Pregnant

To determine what resources and services are needed, we must understand the dynamics behind a problem. Why does the problem exist? What are teenagers' needs? What can social services and social workers do to meet them?

Although female adolescents are more likely to use contraception than they've been in past decades, they often don't use it conscientiously, and frequently don't use it at all (AGI, 2004a; Crooks & Baur, 2002). About 22% of young women do not use contraception the first time they have sexual intercourse (AGI, 2004a). Teens who are not in stable relationships, have sexual intercourse only infrequently, or begin having intercourse at an early age are more likely not to use contraception (Crooks & Baur, 2002).

Failure to Use Birth Control

There are a number of reasons for imperfect contraceptive use. Adolescents often have a deep sense of privacy about sexual behavior and feel embarrassed discussing it with partners, friends, or parents (Hyde & DeLamater, 2003). Thus a young woman may feel extremely uncomfortable talking to a partner about such intimate issues as putting a condom on his penis or placing a diaphragm in her vagina.

Many adolescents may have inadequate knowledge about birth control methods and inadequate access to contraception (Hyde & DeLamater, 2003). Other adolescents adhere to myths about sex (Crooks & Baur, 2002). For instance, many teens inaccurately believe that they are not old enough to conceive, that "the first time" doesn't count, that they must have intercourse much more frequently than they do in order to conceive, that it is perfectly safe to have sex during certain times of the month, and that withdrawal before ejaculation is an effective birth control method.

Focus on Critical Thinking 14.1 discusses conservative and liberal views concerning whose responsibility it is to provide young people with adequate sex education and information.

Case Example   Once I gave a one-time sex education program (as an invited guest social work professor) to about 200 teenagers in which I responded to their questions, written anonymously. After the program, two teenagers sheepishly approached me. Apparently they had been too embarrassed to ask their questions even anonymously. The first young woman, age 16, said that she had had sex with her boyfriend and used vaginal foam as a contraceptive. Unfortunately, afterward she had noticed that the

FOCUS ON CRITICAL THINKING 14.1

Conservative and Liberal Views on Policy Regarding the Provision of Sex Education

A *conservative* value orientation might emphasize that it is parents' responsibility to provide information about sex to their children and that schools should not interfere with parental prerogative. A *liberal* perspective, in contrast, might stress that children need information about sex regardless of who provides it. The important thing is that they get information so they can make responsible decisions.

How would you answer the following questions?

- Should parents have primary responsibility for providing sex education to their children?
- Should schools ask parents permission to provide sex information to their children?
- In the event that parents refuse permission, should their children be denied information about sex?
- What type of content about sex should be provided to young people? Information about contraception? Moral values? Abortion?
- Do your answers to these questions reflect more of a conservative or a liberal perspective?

container had an expiration date of six months before. She asked if I thought that she would be all right, that she would not be pregnant. This was a difficult situation, and there was not much I could do. Even when they have not expired, spermicides (sperm killers) such as contraceptive foam used without other forms of contraception such as a condom have a failure rate as high as 26% (Hyde & DeLamater, 2003). I responded by encouraging the young woman to get a home pregnancy test or go to a Planned Parenthood clinic for one. Even if she chose the home test, I suggested going to Planned Parenthood anyway. In the event that she was pregnant, a counselor could help her make a decision about what to do. And if she was not pregnant, a counselor could assist her in determining what type of contraception would be most effective for her in the future. I made certain she knew the nearest Planned Parenthood clinic's location and that she had a means of getting there.

The second teen, a thin, gangly young woman with braces who looked like she was 12, hesitantly approached me. She bluntly asked, "If someone gives a guy oral sex and swallows it, can she get pregnant?" I had to keep myself from smiling and explained to her that someone could not get pregnant under those circumstances. I did caution her, however, about the potential for contracting sexually transmitted diseases, including HIV.

Other Psychological Reasons

Other reasons for not using birth control involve psychologically wanting to have a baby. Strong and colleagues (2005) comment, "The idea of having someone to love them exclusively and unconditionally is a strong incentive for some teenage girls" (pp. 402–403). In essence, they feel a baby will fulfill their own emotional needs.

Unfortunately, they don't understand that it's supposed to be the other way around. The last person you should expect to meet all of your needs for nurturance is a help-less infant. Strong and colleagues (2005) continue:

> Others see having a baby as a way to escape from an oppressive home environment. Both teen males and females may see parenthood as a way to enhance their status, to give them an aura of maturity, or to enhance their masculinity or femininity. Some believe a baby will cement a shaky relationship. (p. 403)

There are yet other reasons teens may not use birth control (Harris et al., 1986). They might not want to bother with contraception. They might believe that sexual activity is more pleasurable without it. They may worry that their parents will find out. Finally, they may feel invulnerable to pregnancy, viewing it as something that happens only to other people.

Social Work Roles

No consistent national policy exists for addressing teen pregnancies and parenting services; however, federal funding is available to develop programs through "block grants to states for direct services" (Mather & Lager, 2000, p. 204). Social workers may assume many roles and pursue various goals when providing services to adolescents concerning pregnancy and parenting. Goals include prevention of pregnancy, identification of pregnancy, counseling concerning alternatives, help during pregnancy, help for teenage fathers, and help after the pregnancy.

Prevention of Pregnancy

Primary prevention of pregnancy involves preventing the problem altogether, assuming that the pregnancy is a problem (Weatherley & Cartoof, 1988). Adolescents need both information and ready access to contraception so they can make responsible decisions.

Some people may wonder whether sex education programs in schools teach youths everything they need to know. The answer is, Not necessarily. Although almost all states require some type of sex education, fewer than 10% of all students receive "comprehensive sex education in school" (Bronner, 1998; Rathus et al., 2002, p. 426). Also, program content and methods vary radically (Hyde & DeLamater, 2003; Rathus et al., 2002). They range from showing a couple of videos and handing out brochures to offering "well-developed curricula which include lectures, books, videos, and class-room discussion" (Hyde & DeLamater, 2003, p. 618). Rathus and colleagues (2002) comment:

> Today, nearly all states mandate or recommend sex education, although its content and length vary widely. Most programs emphasize biological aspects of puberty and reproduction . . . Few deal with abortion, masturbation, sexual orientation, or sexual pleasure. (p. 426)

Research indicates that good sex education programs can delay first intercourse, reduce the frequency of intercourse, decrease the number of partners, and increase condom use (Hyde & DeLamater, 2003). In effect, such programs "make students less permissive about premarital sex than students who do not take these courses" (Carroll & Wolpe, 1996, p. 641). Effective sex education programs

> focus on reducing risk-taking behavior, . . . are based on theories of social learning, . . . teach through experiential activities that personalize the messages, . . . address media and other social influences that encourage sexual risk-taking behaviors, . . . reinforce clear and appropriate values, . . . [and] enhance communication skills. (Hyde & DeLamater, 2003, p. 626)

Social workers working in social service agencies or schools may see the need to advocate for and develop sex education programs for adolescent clients. They may also provide information during counseling to individuals or groups. Highlight 14.5 offers some suggestions about how to provide straightforward information about sex.

Access to methods of birth control also is important in preventing pregnancy. Components that seem to increase adolescents' use of clinics include "free services, an absence of parental notification, convenient hours for students, walk-in service, a diversity of locations, and warm and caring staff" (Weatherley & Cartoof, 1988, p. 39).

Identification of Pregnancy

It's important for social workers to help young clients identify a pregnancy as early as possible for two basic reasons. First, good nutrition, prenatal medical care, and avoidance of harmful substances are essential for healthy fetal development. A fetus is at greatest risk of harm early in the pregnancy. Second, adolescents have more options potentially available to them early in the pregnancy (e.g., a first-trimester abortion).

Social workers who work with teenagers should encourage them to confront the fact that pregnancy might result from sexual activity. As discussed previously, workers can give adolescent information about potential consequences of their behavior so they can make more responsible decisions. Workers can also help adolescents face the fact that they might be pregnant instead of ignoring the possibility as long as possible. Many pregnant teenagers adopt an "out of sight, out of mind" attitude: If they don't think about the pregnancy, it doesn't exist. Unfortunately, their options decrease as time goes on. Unless there's a miscarriage, pregnancy usually doesn't go away by itself.

Counseling Concerning Alternatives

Once the pregnancy has been established as fact, decisions must be made. Social workers apply the basic approach of helping the adolescent identify her alternatives, and then evaluate the pros and cons of each. Options include having an abortion, going through with the pregnancy and keeping the baby, or continuing with the pregnancy and giving the baby up for adoption.

For each individual, options will have different pros and cons. One individual may have strong religious beliefs that affect her decision; another will not have such convictions. States also have large variations regarding the legal circumstances under which abortions may be obtained. It's a social worker's job to help the client evaluate the situation from her unique perspective and make the choice that's best for her.

HIGHLIGHT 14.5

Providing Straightforward Information About Sex

Effectively conveying sensitive information about sexuality can be difficult. Social workers and other professionals in the position of supplying sexual information to teenagers (and adults, for that matter) ideally should do the following (Hyde & DeLamater, 2003):

1. *Have accurate information about sexuality.* To convey information about sex and answer explicit questions, accurate information is essential. Workers don't need a degree in sexology to convey such information. Rather, they can learn via taking courses, attending seminars, or reading sexuality textbooks. No one knows the answer to every question. Instead of being defensive about gaps in their knowledge, workers should feel comfortable enough to admit ignorance and simply look up the answer.

2. *Feel comfortable talking about sexuality.* Providing accurate information is only one part of teaching about sex. Teenagers should feel as comfortable as possible approaching a worker and asking questions. They should not fear that the worker will criticize them or make fun of them.

3. *Be a good listener.* No matter how much knowledge workers have or how warm and caring they are, if they don't connect with the teenager, they won't convey the information needed. Listening means striving to understand what the person making a statement or asking a question really means. What does she or he really want and need to know?

The following are actual questions asked anonymously by teenagers age 13–18. They are straightforward and may be considered vulgar by some. However, they reflect the serious need for specific, practical information concerning topics usually not addressed in school. They are cited as they were written, spelling errors and all (actually, these are some of the tamer questions asked).

(continued)

Mather and Lager (2000) also suggest that the father "needs to be given every opportunity to take part in this decision, if possible, and his legal rights need to be clearly laid out for him" (p. 205).

Help During Pregnancy

Social workers can provide important help and support during pregnancy (Weatherley & Cartoof, 1988). It's easy for teenagers to become depressed and isolated during that time. Physical changes may have an impact, especially in view of the great emphasis placed on physical appearance, attractiveness, and popularity during adolescence. One junior high teacher once said that talking about the responsibility of pregnancy and teen parenthood had absolutely no effect on her students. However, the young women sat up with serious faces and widened eyes when told that once they have a baby women often have stretch marks on their abdomens for the rest of their lives. To these young women, stretch marks were serious consequences.

HIGHLIGHT 14.5 (*continued*)

As you read the questions, think about how you might answer them.

- What is the average age a woman has an organism?
- What happens if a girl is too tight?
- When a girl gives a guy "head" can she get any STDs?
- How big is the average penis?
- What are the girls erotic zones?
- Do women always bleed when the hymen is broken?
- What are the risks of having an abortion?
- How does it feel when you get devirginized?
- What can you do if your boyfriends is too big and it hurts every time you have sex?
- What can you do if the guy tries something and you say no but he keep going?
- Should you have sex if you're ashamed of your body?
- What is the percentage of boys that masturbate? Girls?

- When you're making love with a guy, does he honestly think of the emotional aspect or does he just want a piece?
- What is group sex?
- Why do males and females hide their feelings about each other?
- How do you have better orgasm?
- How do you know if you've had an orgasm? For female, what does it feel like inside?
- What is the next best contraceptive other than the pill for girls and guys?
- Can a man sperm and urine at the same time?

Note that professionals must be aware of the controversial nature of talk about sex. They must also be attuned to the attitudes and expectations of agencies, administrators, communities, and parents. This can pose a dilemma for workers. On the one hand, they may know what information teens require to make responsible decisions. On the other, they may face negative reactions by parents and others.[6]

[6]SIECUS (Sexuality Information and Education Council of the United States) is an excellent source of information concerning sex education programming, and how to work with agencies and communities to provide young people with information concerning sexuality. It is located at 130 West 42nd Street, Suite 350, New York, NY 10036-7802. Phone: 212/819-9770. Fax: 212/819-9776. E-mail: SIECUS@siecus.org.

Pregnant adolescents may also need help relating to friends and family members. This involves maintaining good communication with and receiving emotional support from others around them. Many times a social worker may need to do active outreach to the pregnant teen. Home visits may be especially useful. Counseling can be provided either individually or on a group basis.

Pregnant teens most often need counseling about good nutrition and the effects of lifestyle on the fetus. For instance, they need to be well informed about the results of alcohol and drug use during pregnancy. Teens also may need help in determining what to do about the pregnancy and making other plans involving living conditions, day care, education, and employment.

Case Example Prenatal care is critically important for mothers and infants. Some good news is that the use of prenatal care during the first three months of pregnancy rose from 74.2% to 83.4% during the 1990s (U.S. Census Bureau, 2003). However, "in 2000, nearly 1 in 6 expectant mothers got no care until after the first trimester, and 1 in 25 received no care until the last trimester or no care at all (Martin et al., 2002)" (Papalia et al., 2004, p. 102). Women who are "young, poor, unmarried, relatively uneducated, uninsured, or living in inner cities or rural areas" are likely to receive the poorest prenatal care (Balsanek, 1998, p. 411). These women are thus at risk of problems and complications. Women who receive less than adequate prenatal care are significantly more likely to have infants with low birth weights and a range of disabilities (Papalia et al., 2004).

Shared Beginnings, a Denver program, provides a good example of how various facets of a community came together to address the issue of at-risk young pregnant women and provide resources (Balsanek, 1998).[7] Initial consciousness-raising occurred through extensive media coverage of the problem, alerting the public to the fact that increasing numbers of poor, single, and young mothers were failing to seek or receive prenatal care. Although the program was spearheaded by a concerned volunteer philanthropist, it illustrates how social workers can start up a program to meet clients' needs. The initiator brought citizens, social services representatives, health care personnel, and potential financial backers together to launch the project. Fund-raising efforts included a luncheon program supported by influential community members and solicitation of financial donations.

Participants involved in the project established five basic program goals. The first was to educate the community concerning the importance of prenatal health care and to alter attitudes on health care's behalf. The second goal was the initiation of a "Sharing Partners" program that sent volunteer paraprofessionals out into the community to educate residents about prenatal care and to encourage them to use services. The third goal was to establish an agency complete with director, administrative assistant, and volunteer coordinator to monitor progress. The fourth was the creation of a "Baby Store" located in a local hospital where "coupons could be redeemed for new baby care items to reinforce health care appointment attendance before the baby is born and immunizations after the baby is born" (Balsanek, 1998, p. 414). The final goal was to integrate a research component to evaluate the program's effectiveness and provide suggestions for improvement. In summary, "Shared Beginnings represents a grassroots [developed and supported by citizens at lower levels of the power structure] approach to providing the community support that poor and at-risk families need to raise healthy children" (p. 418).

Helping Adolescent Fathers

It's important not to forget that babies born to adolescent mothers also have fathers (Weatherley & Cartoof, 1988). Despite myths to the contrary, most teen fathers are significantly affected by their child's birth and are involved to various degrees in the child's early life (Strong et al., 2005; Weatherley & Cartoof, 1988).

[7] From "Addressing at-risk pregnant women's issues through community, individual, and corporate grass-roots efforts" by J. Balsanek. In P. L. Ewalt, E. M. Freeman, and D. L. Poole (Eds.), *Community building: Renewal, well-being, and shared responsibility*, pp. 411–419. ©1998, National Association of Social Workers, Inc.

An adolescent father may need help in expressing his feelings, defining his role, and contributing where he can in caring for his child. Many adolescent fathers have psychological repercussions as a result of the pregnancy (Carroll & Wolpe, 1996; Strong et al., 2005). Additionally, they may need help and encouragement in pursuing educational and vocational goals.

Helping Mothers After the Pregnancy

It's important to keep in mind the continuum of service that social workers may provide. The young mother's needs do not suddenly stop after the baby is born; the case is not automatically closed. Weatherley and Cartoof (1988) cite three major areas where adolescent mothers may need ongoing help.

First, they may need help in learning about positive parenting and child management skills. Several features have been found to enhance this training. For one thing, training should be "flexible, informal, and individualized" (Weatherley & Cartoof, 1988, p. 49). For another, training is more beneficial when provided after the baby is born rather than during the pregnancy (McGee, 1982). Finally, all involved family members and caregivers, including the child's father, should be included in the training (Furstenberg & Crawford, 1978).

Second, adolescent mothers often need help in avoiding more pregnancies. Pregnancy is no guarantee that they have an adequate knowledge of conception or of birth control methodology. Both information and ready access to contraception are necessary.

Third, young mothers often need assistance in life planning. Issues include continuing their education, gaining employment, finding day care for their child, and determining where and how they will live.

Looking Ahead

Chapter 15 explores the final field of social work practice in this book—social work and services in criminal justice. As with health care and mental health, there is some overlap between social work with youths and criminal justice—specifically, juvenile corrections and young people's involvement with gangs. Chapter 15 will introduce crime and criminal justice, describe social work roles, and explore primary criminal justice settings.

For Further Exploration on the Internet

See this text's Book Companion Website at **www.socialwork.wadsworth.com/ kirstashman_intro2e** for descriptors and hot links to URLs relevant to this chapter, selected InfoTrac articles and exercises, and tutorial quizzes.

CHAPTER FIFTEEN

SOCIAL WORK AND SERVICES
IN THE CRIMINAL JUSTICE SYSTEM

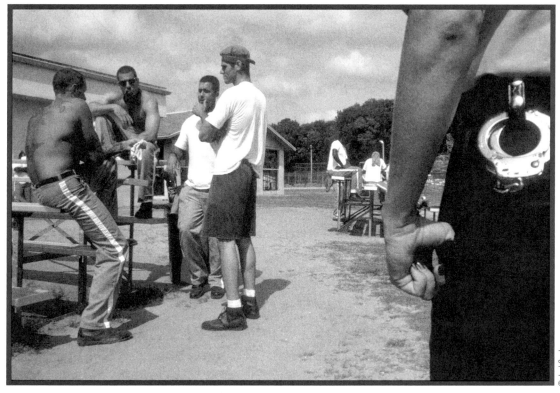

© Joel Gordon

Consider the following facts about crime and the criminal justice system:

- Approximately 6.9 million people were jailed, imprisoned, or on probation or parole in 2003; this amounts to 3.2% of the total U.S. adult population or 1 in 32 adults (U.S. Department of Justice, 2005).
- About 5.1% of all citizens will serve some time in prison during their lifetimes (McNeece & Roberts, 2001).
- African Americans are responsible for 38% of all violent crimes and 30% of all property crimes (e.g., theft), although they represent only 12% of the total U.S. population (Macionis, 2005).
- Although women historically have been less likely to commit crimes than men, the "number of women arrested and incarcerated is growing faster than that for men" (Eitzen & Zinn, 2003, p. 339).
- According to data collected by the *Uniform Crime Reports* issued by the Federal Bureau of Investigation (FBI), about 12% of reported crimes are violent, with the remaining 88% being property crimes (Macionis, 2005). Of violent crimes, most are aggravated assault (62%) followed by robbery (30%), forcible rape (7%), and murder (1%); most property crimes involve larceny–theft (67%), followed by burglary (21%) and motor vehicle theft (12%) (FBI, 2005).

As these figures suggest, crime is a serious social problem in the United States. Social workers practice in a range of settings characterized by people who have committed or are accused of committing crimes.

This chapter will

- Introduce the criminal justice system and define some of the key concepts involved.
- Describe the types of crime.
- Examine who commits crime.
- Explore whether crime rates are rising or falling.
- Examine and encourage critical thinking about the ethical dilemma of punishment versus empowerment and the issue of providing expensive health care for prisoners.
- Review the wide range of criminal justice settings in which social workers practice.
- Describe the cycle of domestic violence, its dynamics, and treatment.
- Describe a program focusing on the empowerment of African American youths involved in the juvenile justice system.
- Discuss youth membership in gangs, types of gangs, and gang prevention and treatment.

Introducing Crime and Criminal Justice

Social workers are among the many people who work in the *criminal justice system*—the complex, integrated system of programs, policies, laws, and agencies devoted to preventing and controlling crime. The system's functions include *adjudication* (passing legal judgment), *incarceration* (confining by putting in prison or jail), and *rehabilitation* (restoring to a state of productive, noncriminal functioning in society).

HIGHLIGHT 15.1
Main Types of Crime

Crimes are either felonies or misdemeanors. *Felonies* are grave offenses punishable by at least a year in prison and possibly even death; *misdemeanors* are less severe offenses, with punishments ranging from incarceration of less than a year to monetary fines (FindLaw, 2002; Macionis, 2005).

Crimes fall within three categories. *Violent crime* (or crime against persons) is the act of using "force or the threat of force against others"; *property crime* (or crime against property) is "the taking of money or property from another without force, the threat of force, or the destruction of property" (Kendall, 2004, pp. 186, 191). These two categories involve eight more specific crimes identified by the *Uniform Crime Reports* (compiled by the FBI) that are "most likely to be reported to the police by victims, that occur frequently, and that are serious by nature or as a result of their frequency of occurrence" (Abadinsky, 2000, p. 5).

Violent crimes include

- *Homicide:* The act of "causing the death of another person without legal justification or excuse" (Abadinsky, 2000, p. 5).
- *Aggravated assault:* The act of attacking another person with the intent to inflict serious harm or kill that person.

- *Rape:* "Sexual penetration against a person's will through the use or threat of force" (Strong et al., 2005, p. G-10). (Note *that statutory rape* is "a legal term used to indicate sexual activity when one partner is under the age of consent; in most states that age is 18" [Kelly, 2004, p. G-8].)
- *Robbery:* The act of stealing property in the hands of another person by using force or the threat of force. (Note that because of the force involved this is considered a violent crime even though it involves property.)

Property crimes include

- *Larceny (simple theft):* The act of stealing property.
- *Burglary:* The act of breaking into a house or other building with the intent to steal.
- *Motor vehicle theft:* The act of stealing a "self-propelled road vehicle" from another person with the goal of keeping it "permanently or temporarily" (Abadinsky, 2000, p. 6).
- *Arson:* The "malicious burning of another's property or, sometimes, one's own property, as in an attempt to collect insurance" (Nichols, 1999, p. 75).

(continued)

Crime is the commission of a harmful offense or act that is legally prohibited. *Criminals* include anyone whom the courts convict of a crime. *Law* is the body of formal principles and decisions established by government that determine what behavior is appropriate and allowed and what is not. Laws essentially guide social behavior. Highlight 15.1 describes the main types of crime committed in the United States.

Who Commits Crimes? Race, Social Class, and Gender Issues

Although people with virtually any characteristics can commit crimes, some people are simply more likely than others to do so. People who are young men of color, have a lower-class standing, and live in an urban area fit the most likely profile

HIGHLIGHT 15.1 *(continued)*

A third umbrella category of crime involves those offenses not considered violent or property crimes. Examples include the following:

• *White-collar crime:* Offenses "committed by middle-class and upper-middle-class people in their business and social activities, such as theft of company goods, embezzlement, bankruptcy fraud, swindles, tax evasion, forgery, theft of property by computer, passing bad checks, illicit copying of computer software, movies, and music, and fraudulent use of credit cards, automatic teller machines, and telephones" (Eitzen & Zinn, 2003, p. 347).

• *Corporate crime:* Illegal acts committed by large organizations to enhance profits. For example, consider the utility conglomerate Enron's fall into bankruptcy, the largest in U.S. history (CNN.com, 2001). Corporate leaders were accused of "fraudulent trading schemes" and devious "financial moves to hide debt and inflate profits that fueled Enron's downfall in 2001" (FindLaw, 2005). The bankruptcy resulted in thousands of Enron "employees losing their life savings in 401(k) plans" linked with Enron stock (CNN.com, 2001).

• *Victimless (vice) crimes:* Illegal acts that technically have no victim or complainant (e.g., prostitution, selling illegal drugs, unlawful gambling). These are also referred to as "crimes against the moral order" (Eitzen & Zinn, 2003, p. 344) or "public-order crimes" (Kornblum & Julian, 2004, p. 141).

• *Organized (syndicated) crime:* Illegal acts committed by an organized, hierarchical network of professional criminals working together to make money "by supplying illegal goods and services such as drugs, prostitution, pornography, gambling, loan sharking, the sale of stolen goods, money laundering, cigarette bootlegging, and even disposal of hazardous wastes" (Eitzen & Zinn, 2003, p. 346).

• *Hate crime:* The "violence of intolerance and bigotry, intended to hurt and intimidate someone because of their race, ethnicity, national origin, religion, sexual orientation, or disability. The purveyors of hate use explosives, arson, weapons, vandalism, physical violence, and verbal threats of violence to instill fear in their victims, leaving them vulnerable to more attacks and feeling alienated, helpless, suspicious, and fearful" (U.S. Department of Justice, 2001).

(Coleman & Kerbo, 2002; Mooney et al., 2002). Thus crime is related to race, age, gender, social class, and place of residence.

In the United States, Jews and Japanese Americans have crime rates below the average, while African Americans, Latinos, and Native Americans have crime rates above the average (Coleman & Kerbo, 2002). Young people under age 21 are more likely to commit crimes, and these crimes are more likely to involve property. Almost one-third of all arrests in 2001 involved people in this age group, and 58.3% of arrests of individuals under age 25 involved property, as opposed to violent, crimes (Kornblum & Julian, 2004). Women are much less likely to be arrested for crimes and tend to commit less serious and violent crimes than men. However, as noted previously, their crime rate is increasing proportionally with respect to men (Eitzen & Zinn, 2003).

Crime is also related to social class and the context in which people live. More than two-thirds of men and almost 90% of women currently in prison have poverty-stricken or working-class backgrounds (Coleman & Kerbo, 2002). The book titled *The Rich Get Richer and the Poor Get Prison* by Jeffrey Reiman (1998) provides food for critical thought about economic conditions and prison. Geographical location provides yet another influence on crime rates, which are highest in urban areas, followed by suburban locations and, finally, by rural areas (Mooney et al., 2002).

Note that some of these variables also relate to each other. People of color are more likely to be poor and to live in urban areas. They are also more likely to be arrested and incarcerated than their wealthier white counterparts (Mooney et al., 2002). A controversial issue regarding potentially unfair treatment based on race is *racial profiling*—the greater likelihood of suspecting and apprehending people of color based on their racial status. Another serious issue involves *police brutality*—the unnecessary infliction of pain on suspects under the guise of controlling their behavior.

Are Crime Rates Rising or Falling?

It is not altogether clear whether crime rates are rising or falling. Crime rates are recorded in three basic ways: official statistics of crimes reported to police (i.e., the *Uniform Crime Reports*), surveys administered to population samples regarding victimization rates, and offenders' self-reports (Mooney et al., 2002). Crime statistics indicate that crime rates have been decreasing since the late 1980s until a 2% increase in serious crime occurred between 2000 and 2001 (Kornblum & Julian, 2004). It makes sense that crime decreased during the economic boom times of the 1990s and could potentially escalate again when economic hardships increase. "While violent crimes have not increased significantly, property crimes have, providing further evidence that economic factors (rather than drugs or gangs, for example) account for the increases in crime rates" (Kornblum & Julian, 2004, p. 129). Questions remain unanswered concerning the incidence of organized, white-collar, and occupational crime (Kornblum & Julian, 2004).

In any event, crime statistics may be misleading. For one thing, victimization surveys indicate that many crimes are not reported (Kornblum & Julian, 2004). Some surveys suggest that only a third of all serious crimes (Macionis, 2005) and half of all violent crimes are actually reported to the police (Bureau of Justice Statistics, 1996; Kornblum & Julian, 2004). Why do victims fail to report crimes? People may believe that nothing can be done about the crime anyway or that the crime was too insignificant to report. They might also fear negative repercussions.

For example, Florence, age 78, was sideswiped by a young man as he was trying to pass her car. She had been driving along a familiar neighborhood road, being careful not to exceed the speed limit. The man, who looked to be about 20, stopped to see if she was all right but then jumped in his car and sped away. The accident was his fault. However, Florence's insurance agent suggested that filing a formal police report of the incident would almost certainly *not* result in the man's apprehension. But it *would* result in a significant increase in her own car insurance simply because the accident happened to a person of her age. Needless to say, Florence did not report the incident and paid for the repairs herself.

Focus on Critical Thinking 15.1 addresses a controversial issue concerning the purposes of imprisonment.

FOCUS ON CRITICAL THINKING 15.1
An Ethical Dilemma: Punishment Versus Empowerment

Disparity in Goals

A great debate rages regarding the purpose of imprisonment (or incarceration). Prisons exist to achieve four primary purposes (Coleman & Kerbo, 2002; Kendall, 2004). First, prisons punish people who commit crimes by denying them freedom for some designated period. Second, prisons discourage people who have committed crimes from committing them again and deter others from committing them in the first place—at least theoretically. Third, prisons protect potential victims from dangerous offenders by putting them behind bars. These first three goals basically focus on the rights of society. They might be clustered under the umbrella of *incapacitation*—namely, using various means to inhibit offenders from committing more crimes, thereby protecting other members of society (Mooney et al., 2002, p. 112).

The fourth goal, established much more recently in the 1940s and 1950s, involves inmate *rehabilitation* through programs involving therapy, education, and job training. The intent is to help criminals become productive members of society who do not commit crimes. The concept of *corrections* implies that people who break the law should be treated in ways that attempt to make them correct their inappropriate behavior and stop breaking the law. Rehabilitation ideally involves empowering offenders so they have viable alternatives to pursue other than a life of crime.

The wide disparity in goals poses a serious question for social workers: To what extent can offenders be empowered at the same time that they are incapacitated as a means of control and punishment? Prison life allows for few choices, and most prisoners definitely do not want to be there.

To make it worse, the public has increasingly supported stricter, more incapacitating policies. Tactics include longer mandatory sentences, less use of probation and parole, policies requiring lifetime imprisonment after committing three serious crimes (sometimes referred to as the *three strikes and you're out* approach), mandated sentences that reflect the seriousness of the crime, accelerated prison construction, and increased use of the death penalty (Dilulio, 1999; Human Rights Watch, 2000; Karger & Stoesz, 2002).

Kenyon (1999) reflects:

> [F]inding a compromise between what seems ethically appropriate and what is legally mandated can be a source of professional burnout. Feeling forced to make decisions and to take actions that cause internal conflict leads to feelings of helplessness and hopelessness and a belief that one is ineffective. (p. 162)

Issues and Potential Solutions

The following are examples of potential issues:

- Mandatory sentencing results in prisons accommodating over double the number of prisoners for which they were built. Cells built to house two inmates now must house four. Prison conditions are almost unbearable.
- A prisoner made a mistake at age 19 and accidentally killed another teenager in a fight. The court sentenced him to several decades of time with no possibility of parole. Now, at age 21, he has expressed serious remorse for his crime and a willingness to shape up his life. A prison social worker sees great potential for rehabilitation. But what can be done when there is no hope of freedom for many years?

(continued)

FOCUS ON CRITICAL THINKING 15.1 *(continued)*

- A 25-year-old inmate has been sentenced to life imprisonment in a state requiring such punishment after the commission of three serious crimes—in his case, armed robberies. What kind of treatment and rehabilitation can help him?

To what extent does incapacitation as a means of control and punishment conflict with the basic social work values of self-determination and empowerment? How can social workers who are empowerment oriented function in such a constricted and controlled setting? Should offenders be forced to participate in treatment activities against their will?

Garvin and Tropman (1998) make five suggestions for working with offenders:

1. When possible, help offenders identify alternative behaviors to solve problems and address their needs. This is especially useful for inmates returning to their communities.
2. Advocate for inmates when prison conditions work against their best interests. In the community, social workers can advocate for prisoner's rights as they try to reintegrate themselves. For example, neighborhood residents might resent a former inmate living in their neighborhood. Or a parolee might be fired from her job when her employer finds out about her prison history.

3. Provide opportunities for individual and group treatment for inmates to work on personal issues (e.g., substance abuse treatment groups).
4. Seek positions in prison administration so as to improve prison policies concerning humane rehabilitation approaches.
5. Advocate in the macro arena for less punitive legislation that provides greater opportunity for rehabilitation.

Conservative Versus Liberal Value Orientations Toward Crime and Criminals

How do you respond to these questions?

- What are your personal values concerning the issues just described? To what extent do your values reflect a *conservative* perspective that emphasizes individuals' responsibility for their own behavior and that people who do bad things deserve to be punished?
- To what extent do you support a *liberal* approach that focuses on rehabilitating offenders and emphasizes the idea that people will thrive and do well when given enough support?
- To what extent should resources be used to build more prisons and keep offenders in prison longer? Or to what extent should resources be diverted to rehabilitation and the goal of reintegrating offenders into communities?

Criminal Justice Settings and Forensic Social Work

Forensic social work is social work involving the law—both criminal and civil (i.e., concerning private personal rights)—and the legal system. Forensic social work tasks include conducting assessments regarding suspects' mental competence to understand their behavior and stand trial; making recommendations concerning child custody, divorce, and the placement of emotionally disturbed or delinquent

What provides greater hope—punishment or empowerment?

juveniles; preparing for court presentations as expert witnesses; and advocating for welfare rights.

Ginsberg (2001) cites six broad criminal justice settings in which social workers can serve important functions. These include adult correctional institutions, administrative planning centers, probation and parole services, victim assistance programs, domestic violence services, and juvenile corrections.

Adult Correctional Institutions

Social workers in adult correctional institutions perform at least five functions (Ginsberg, 2001). First, they can provide either individual or group counseling to inmates when needed or requested. Treatment might focus on such issues as anger management, preparation for release, and coping with substance abuse.

The second social work function involves helping prison administrators make determinations regarding job placement within the institution. Inmates often seek prison jobs to combat the boredom of prison life, to earn extra privileges, or to establish credit for doing "good time," thereby increasing the possibility of parole (McNeece, 1995, p. 65).

The third function for social workers in correctional facilities involves assisting prison personnel in determining how individual inmates are treated. Fourth, social workers can help develop and organize prison activities. Finally, practitioners can "assist in planning modifications in prison procedures" and advocate for improved conditions (Ginsberg, 2001, p. 148).

Focus on Critical Thinking 15.2 addresses the question of providing expensive health care for prison inmates.

FOCUS ON CRITICAL THINKING 15.2

Should Prisoners Get Expensive Health Care?

The costs of keeping more people in prison longer are huge. The average annual cost for supervising a person on probation is approximately $1,200; on parole, it's $1,500; and in prison, it's between $12,000 and $30,000 (Abadinsky, 2000).

Levine (2002) explains how health care for aging and ill prisoners is also an expensive issue. It already eats up 17% of many prison budgets, and current estimates indicate that 20% of prison inmates will "be over age 55 by 2010" (Levine, 2002, p. 44). Money spent on prison populations detracts from the total financial pool available for other benefits and services including schools, police, the environment, and domestic security. Levine (2002) raises the following additional ethical questions: "Should a killer in a Minnesota prison have received a life-saving, $900,000 bone marrow transplant? Should a California robber have received a new heart" costing approximately $1 million? (p. 44). Both states provided these treatments because

they determined it would be "cruel and unusual punishment" not to (p. 44).

How would you answer the following questions?

- To what health care standards should prisons adhere in providing treatment to prisoners?
- Should prisoners receive extremely expensive health care treatment?
- How would you define "extremely expensive"?
- To what extent is it fair that prisoners are "the only people in America guaranteed medical treatment" when about 40 million U.S. residents have no health insurance (p. 44)?
- Should all U.S. residents receive the same health care benefits as prisoners? If so, who should pay for these benefits?
- Should more time, money, and effort be expended to rehabilitate prisoners instead of imprisoning them so they will become responsible for their own health care needs "on the outside"?

Administrative Planning Centers

As in other fields of practice, social workers can take on administrative and planning roles for correctional systems. These might involve planning new programs and procedures, developing more humane policies, and supervising lower-level administrators and other employees.

Community-Based Corrections: Probation and Parole Services

The criminal justice system may give people who have been convicted of crimes alternatives to serving a full sentence of incarceration. Two primary options are probation and parole. These are considered *community-based corrections*—programs that supervise or monitor offenders' behavior while they reside in the community.

Probation

Morgan (2000) describes *probation*:

> Probation takes place when a person is convicted but the judge determines that confinement is not warranted. Instead, that person is placed on probation and is allowed to live in society but under the court's supervision. Terms of probation often include psychological or chemical-dependence treatment and mandatory community service. People who receive probation are generally considered low risk, and the goal of probation officers is to involve them in community service and steer them away from criminal behavior. (pp. 142–143)

Probation officers conduct assessments prior to when clients begin probation in order to provide recommendations to the court. They help clients establish work and other living plans and subsequently see them regularly, overseeing their activities and often making home and work visits. Probation officers also link clients with needed resources.

To avoid incarceration, probationers must abide by whatever restrictions and terms the judge establishes. Typically these include obeying the law, getting and keeping a job, staying within a prescribed geographical location, avoiding relationships with other identified felons, and shunning firearms (Morgan, 2000). Individualized restrictions may also apply, such as getting substance abuse treatment or attending anger management groups.

Parole

Parole is the early release of inmates from prison based on the "promise and likelihood of good behavior" (Morgan, 2000, p. 139). Parole officers must initially assess the amount of supervision necessary. Some parolees require extensive supervision to stay out of trouble; others require very little. Parolees must abide by the general restrictions and requirements established by their parole officer. These include avoiding illegal activity, possession of firearms, involvement with identified felons, and use of alcohol or other drugs. They must also remain gainfully employed and attend regularly scheduled meetings with their parole officer.

Both probation and parole officer positions usually require a bachelor's degree in social work, psychology, criminal justice, or a related field in addition to "strong interpersonal skills" (Morgan, 2000, pp. 142, 144).

There are other community-based corrections programs in addition to probation and parole. For example, *victim/offender mediation programs* are face-to-face confrontations between victims and offenders in which an impartial third party serves as a mediator. The intent is to give victims an opportunity to confront offenders with the emotional and other consequences of their behavior, address emotional issues, and arrange compensation of losses. Similarly, *restitution programs* involve arranging cash reimbursement from offenders to victims (typically of property crimes) to compensate for losses.

Victim Assistance Programs

Included under the victim assistance umbrella are both victim/witness assistance programs and crisis intervention programs. *Victim/witness assistance programs* include various facets intended to assist victims and witnesses in the stressful and potentially traumatic process of testifying in court against offenders, thereby enhancing their ability to testify effectively. Specific services include ongoing notification to witnesses of the case's legal status as it progresses through the courts; provision of separate, comfortable waiting rooms for witnesses; transportation to court; and support staff who accompany witnesses throughout the court process, helping them understand what's happening.

Crisis intervention programs, although not as common, provide wide-ranging services for crime victims, frequently within the first 24 hours after the crime occurs. Services can include crisis counseling, provision of transportation, assistance in making a legal complaint, linkage to needed resources such as support groups for survivors of violence, and temporary financial help. Agencies providing services include rape crisis centers and domestic violence shelters.

Jobs include counselor/advocate and administrator. Volunteers are also often used. Most counselor/advocates have a bachelor's degree, and most program directors have a master's degree in social work or a related discipline (Roberts, 1995).

Domestic Violence Services

Domestic violence services and shelters for battered women have sprung up across the country. Often they have been initiated and are staffed and run by social workers. Women who have been battered by their male partners frequently need temporary shelter for themselves and their children, usually having nowhere else to go. Additional services include providing counseling and linking women with necessary resources. Battered women eventually need a permanent place to stay. They might require additional education or job training so they can support themselves and their families. They may need help finding employment and getting legal assistance.

Of course, females can batter their male partners, or one partner may batter the other of the same gender. However, "[w]omen are much more likely to be victims of both lethal and nonlethal intimate partner violence, and men are much more likely than women to commit that violence" (Sapiro, 2003, p. 389). Therefore, Highlight 15.2 focuses on domestic violence as a women's issue.

Juvenile Corrections

Juvenile corrections is the "broad term denoting a range of interventions for young people whose actual or alleged behavior has brought them to the attention of law enforcement personnel or the courts" (Barton, 1995, p. 1563). Juveniles—people under age 18—are generally treated differently than adults who commit crimes. *Juvenile delinquent offenses* are acts that are considered crimes if committed by adults. (Highlight 15.1 reviewed common crimes.) *Status offenses* are acts that are considered inappropriate when done by juveniles but are not crimes if committed by adults. These include running away, being truant, being out of parental control, having sexual intercourse, and drinking alcohol. Considered together, juvenile delinquent and status offenses are regarded as *antisocial behavior*—acts that are hostile, detrimental to others, and contrary to social expectations. *Juvenile courts* are those having jurisdiction over proceedings involving delinquent, dependent, or maltreated children and their parents or guardians.

HIGHLIGHT 15.2

The Cycle of Domestic Violence: Empowering Women as Survivors

The dynamics of domestic violence usually revolve around the male partner's need to control the victim. Over time, the perpetrator gradually cuts off his female partner from her family, friends, church, workplace, and other sources of support. He typically criticizes her on as many grounds as possible. Without support and validation from others, the victim often comes to believe what the perpetrator is saying—to see herself as no good, stupid, and worthless, as a whore and a tramp. In some ways this process resembles brainwashing. Prior rational thinking is gradually erased and replaced with a barrage of criticism.

Phase 1: Buildup of Tension

The cycle of violence typically occurs in three phases. First, tension builds as the perpetrator becomes increasingly controlling, demanding, and annoyed with the victim. He might place impossible demands on her such as ordering her to have dinner ready at 5:30 sharp when he arrives home. Then he might show up at 7:00 and blame her for the food being cold and dried up. Or he might chastise her for making the wrong kind of food or not cooking it the way he likes it. He often plays a game with her, making demands and then changing them after she complies with his original instructions.

Phase 2: The Explosion

The second phase in the cycle involves the explosion—the abusive incident in which he beats her to teach her a lesson. He then usually tells her it's all her fault. If she had cooked better or not yelled back or done what she was told, he wouldn't have *had* to hit her. She *made* him try to keep her in line.

Phase 3: The Honeymoon

The third phase is the honeymoon period. The perpetrator has released his tension. The victim is

frightened, hurt, emotionally beaten, downtrodden, and depressed. She might be so damaged that she considers leaving him, but he will never allow her to do this. He makes up with her, says loving things, and perhaps brings her flowers or candy. He often tells her that he loves her and that he can't live without her. For that matter, he might also tell her that she could never survive without him. The pain is gone—temporarily—so she stays. And the cycle begins all over again.

Reasons Women Stay

Women continue to stay with abusive partners for a number of reasons (Zastrow & Kirst-Ashman, 2004). These include economic dependence, lack of self-confidence, lack of power, fear of the abuser, guilt about what they did wrong or how they failed to nurture their relationship with the abuser, fear of isolation, fear for their children's safety, hope that things will somehow improve, and the fact they still feel they love their partners despite it all.

Treatment Strategies

Social work treatment strategies involve empowering the victim and helping her survive. Strategies include the following:

1. Offer support.
2. Identify and focus on her strengths.
3. Provide information regarding resources and services.
4. Help her establish a plan of action.
5. Advocate on her behalf with legal, medical, and social services when necessary.

The goal is to help the domestic violence survivor gain confidence and get back on her feet. It takes a brave and strong person to break the cycle of violence.

We have already established that young people (particularly males of African American and, to a lesser extent, Hispanic heritage) are more likely than older people to commit crimes (Jenson & Howard, 1999). Remember, however, that juveniles from virtually any racial, ethnic, and socioeconomic background can and do participate in antisocial behavior.

A Special Perspective on Juveniles

Juveniles require a special perspective because they are minors whose parents (or guardians) are supposed to care for, supervise, and protect them. One ongoing question concerns the extent to which juveniles, on the one hand, and their parents, on the other, are responsible for juveniles' antisocial behavior. It is beyond the scope of this book to review all the potential causes of such behavior. However, the following are a few of the family factors that research suggests may contribute to violent behavior (Howard & Jenson, 1999):

- *Child maltreatment:* Some research identifies an existing, if weak, relationship between child abuse and subsequent violent behavior. But child neglect appears to be more strongly correlated with subsequent violent acts.
- *Family bonding and support:* Children raised in families characterized by more positive interaction among and higher levels of involvement with and support from members are less likely to commit violent acts.
- *Management of children's behavior and discipline:* Extremes in child management approaches contribute to the potential for subsequent violent behavior. One extreme entails extremely authoritarian, punitive parenting, which may teach children violent behavior and make them angrier. The other extreme involves lax, inconsistent, uncaring approaches to child management, which may cause children to feel unwanted and develop serious hostility.
- *Early departure from home:* Children who leave home before age 16 are more likely to participate in violent activity later.
- *Parental separation:* Children who are separated from one or both parents early are more likely to exhibit subsequent violent behavior.

As with adult offenders, the current trend is an emphasis on punishment rather than treatment and rehabilitation for delinquent youths (Coleman & Kerbo, 2002). One development involves passing laws that require more juvenile offenders who commit serious violent crimes to be treated as adults. Another concerns the imposition of stricter sentences on juvenile offenders who in the past might have been given a warning or probation.

We have established that social work values generally comply more directly with rehabilitation and treatment approaches than with punishment. Highlight 15.3 describes a more positive, empowerment-oriented approach to youths in the juvenile justice system.

Overlaps Among Juvenile Corrections, Mental Health Services, and Child Welfare

Note that substantial overlap exists among juvenile corrections, mental health services, and, to some extent, child welfare. Chapters 9 and 13 address issues concerning child

HIGHLIGHT 15.3

Mezzo Practice and Empowerment for African American Youths in the Juvenile Justice System

Harvey (1997) describes the development and implementation of a program for groups of African American juvenile offenders that uses an Afrocentric approach. The groups' purpose is to enhance members' self-respect, establish a stronger identity with African heritage and culture, create ties with a positive peer group, develop vocational aspirations, and strengthen members' ability to make socially responsible decisions. Although in some ways these might be considered treatment groups, they address and help members cope with broader social issues.

Common Themes

Young African American offenders are viewed within their macro context. Poverty, marital and family dissolution, white oppression and discrimination, the strong antisocial pressure of peer groups and gangs, and a lack of career prospects all contribute to an environment in which crime becomes a logical means of survival. These young men typically express a number of themes (Harvey, 1997):

- Adults around here do it, so why shouldn't I?
- Violence is a way of life. If you don't stand up for yourself, you're history.
- How can I be moral and still survive the horrendous peer pressure to be bad?
- You have to be "cool" (i.e., strong and not expressing emotion) to get any respect and protect yourself (p. 166).
- Women should be treated as inferior and handled with violent behavior.
- Police are the bad guys.
- How can I deal with whites' racist treatment?
- I don't know that much about African culture.

An Afrocentric Approach

An Afrocentric approach emphasizes both spirituality and connectedness with others in the environment, including family members and community residents. The goal is to engender self-understanding, self-respect, and "a strong sense of responsibility for the well-being and harmonious interconnection between self and others" (Harvey, 1997, p. 163; Nobles, 1976). The Afrocentric approach rests on seven basic principles called the *Nguzo Saba*, described in Chapter 3 (Karenga, 1965; Karenga, 2000, pp. 58–59). These include "unity among families, neighborhoods, and nations," (2) "self-determination," (3) "collective work and responsibility," (4) "cooperation economics" to establish a strong economic base, (5) "purpose" to gain respect as a world community, (6) "creativity," and (7) "faith" in themselves and their capabilities.

Group Formation and Progress

Groups, then, are designed to provide members with "a positive perspective on African and African American culture, assist them in developing their own African American group identity, and provide them with tools to deal with the oppressiveness of white supremacy" (Harvey, 1997, p. 164). The group is viewed as part of a program rather than a treatment group. To many potential group members, treatment implies mental illness and turns them off. Groups consist of 15 boys age 14–18 who are on probation. Offenses include drug dealing, sexual assault, car theft, armed robbery, and burglary.

Group coleaders include social workers and people with other types of expertise such as in

(continued)

H I G H L I G H T   15.3 *(continued)*

African studies, music, or theater. Group process involves the acquisition of positive interpersonal, relationship-building, communication, and introspective skills. Groups stress enhancing members' self-concepts, developing "constructive lifestyles and positive solutions to life problems," and appreciating their cultural heritage and personal strengths (Harvey, 1997, p. 167).

The initial group phase takes eight weeks, during which time coleaders teach members about the group process, the Afrocentric perspective, and the important formalized rites of passage involved in group membership. Group members then participate in a weekend retreat in which coleaders and older adult men decide which 15 young men will be included in the group. Chosen members then undergo an initiation ritual in which they pledge to uphold the Nguzo Saba's principles, are given an African name, and are presented a "special identifying symbol" they are expected to wear at all group meetings. No new members are admitted after this point (Harvey, 1997, p. 167).

Groups then meet weekly for 90 minutes as members develop their group identity and learn skills. Group activities may include videos and music depending on the topics addressed. Guests are invited to speak on various topics, called "modules," that stress the importance of African and African American culture (Harvey, 1997, p. 168). Modules, which last from four to six group sessions, address any number of topics ranging from African American culture, to relationships between men and women, to racism.

Upon completion of all modules, group members participate in another weekend retreat in which they demonstrate their newly learned skills and prepare for the final recognition ceremony. This ceremony is the culmination of the group experience as members demonstrate before their families and community what they have achieved. They proclaim their sacred name and "receive a symbol and a certificate of sacred transformation" (Harvey, 1997, p. 168).

Intent and Results

We have established that this process seeks to enhance group members' self-respect, sense of African American identity, and sense of responsibility for and belonging to the African American community. Other anticipated effects include crime reduction, improved school attendance, better grades, and increased employment. Initial results are promising (Harvey, 1997). Family members report improved behavior at home, and group members express enhanced self-respect and appreciation of their African heritage.

welfare and mental health. Decisions about the needs and placement of each individual depend on a number of conditions. Statutes, policies, and agency practices may vary from state to state and from locality to locality. Available resources for placement also differ dramatically. Finally, juvenile court judges often have great discretion regarding the appropriate placement of juveniles.

Youth Gangs

An additional concern related to violent behavior by youths involves escalating gang membership. It is estimated that over 770,000 gang members belong to almost

25,000 gangs throughout the United States (Egley & Arjunan, 2002; McWhirter, McWhirter, McWhirter, & McWhirter, 2004). Most gang members are male, although female membership appears to be increasing, as is their participation in violent crimes (Jenson & Howard, 1999; Potter, 1999).

McWhirter and his colleagues (2004) provide a further overview of gang activity and composition:

> Youths in these gangs were responsible for a wide variety of offenses including street crime, drug trafficking, and witness intimidation, and they are highly likely to use firearms in an assault crime (Esbensen, 2000). A high percentage (95%) of gang activity occurred within one or more high schools, with as nearly as high of a percentage (91%) of gang activity occurring within one or more intermediate schools. Involvement with gangs remains one of the most powerful predictors of violence (Office of the Surgeon General, 2001).
>
> When one gang gains power and control in an area, rival gangs sometimes relocate to other areas of the city or even to other cities. These divisions of power and region are frequently related to ethnicity, although there is some evidence to suggest that a new type of gang, *hybrid gangs,* is emerging. Hybrid gang culture is characterized by mixed racial and ethnic participation within a single gang (Starbuck, Howell, & Linquist, 2001). Economic opportunities, such as the availability of new markets for drug profits, may also play a part in a gang's decision to relocate. Many communities and neighborhoods once untouched by organized violence now find themselves threatened by gang activity. The proliferation of youth gangs in recent decades is of concern, and of particular concern is the spread of homegrown youth gangs to rural communities (Esbensen, 2000). (pp. 160–161)

Defining Gangs

There is no consensus regarding an accurate definition for the concept of *gang*. Morales and Sheafor (2002) reflect on how a "popular criterion [for identifying a gang member] is 'if it looks like a duck, walks like a duck, and quacks like a duck, it is a duck'" (p. 174). However, they continue by noting that

> not all ducks are the same, and even among ducks, some are more passive and some are more aggressive than others. Even with many years of experience in working with gang members, . . . [it is difficult to] tell if an 8- to 25-year-old person 10 feet in front of . . . [you] is in fact a gang member with a violent criminal past or simply one who has knowingly or unknowingly adopted some of the gang culture (e.g., clothing, hairstyle, or speech). (p. 174)

Williams and Van Dorn (1999) identify some common themes evident in gangs:

> Some consensus about the nature of juvenile gangs has emerged in recent literature. First, gangs cannot be stereotyped. Some gangs are simply a source of social support and entertainment for members, others serve as drug distribution organizations, and still others do both. Gang members may commit a significant number of crimes, but crime is often not their primary, and certainly not their only, focus. Second, youths often join gangs to achieve goals that they perceive as difficult or impossible to achieve without gang support. However, members differ in their motivations for joining and their degree of commitment to gang life. Third, it is rare for entire gangs to organize their activities exclusively around the sale of drugs. Finally, communities with gangs differ in some respects, but generally all are struggling with social problems such as poverty, racism, mobility, and demographic changes. (p. 200)

HIGHLIGHT 15.4
International Perspectives: Gangs Around the World

Huff (1993) emphasizes that gangs as a group experience are a typically occurring pattern often characterizing the "adolescent subculture" that "represent an extreme manifestation of that age-typical emphasis on being together and belonging to something." He continues,

Gangs are certainly not unique to the United States. In fact, most societies seem to have a term that corresponds, at least loosely, to our own term *gang*. Whether it is the *chimpira* of Japan, the *raggare* of Sweden, the Dutch *nozem*, the Italian *vitelloni*, the *stilyagi* of the USSR, the Yugoslavian *tapkaroschi*, or their counterparts in many other nations, there is usually some way of designating youth gangs. (p. 6)

Huff (1993) arbitrarily defines a *youth gang* as a group of people composed mainly

of adolescents and young adults who (a) interact frequently with one another; (b) are frequently and deliberately involved in illegal activities; (c) share a common collective identity that is usually, but not always, expressed through a gang name; and (d) typically express that identity by adopting certain symbols and/or claiming control over certain "turf" (persons, places, things, and/or economic markets). (p. 4)

Highlight 15.4 offers a global perspective on gangs.

Types of Gangs

Morales and Sheafor (2001, pp. 404–405) categorize juvenile gangs into three basic types. First, *criminal gangs* have as their "primary goal material gain through criminal activities" that include "theft of property from premises or persons, extortion, fencing, and obtaining and selling illegal substances such as drugs." Second, *conflict gangs* are extremely "turf oriented and will engage in violent battle with individuals or rival groups that invade their neighborhood or commit acts they consider insulting or degrading. Respect is highly valued or defended." *Retreatist gangs'* primary aim is to get "loaded" or "high" on various mind-altering substances and thereby withdraw from the stresses of real life. Retreatist gangs differ from criminal gangs despite the fact that they both may be involved in illegal drug activity. Retreatist gangs emphasize escape from reality, whereas criminal gangs focus on financial gain.

Prevention and Intervention Involving Gangs

Young people often become gang members to meet personal needs and gain power. In a way, gang membership is a means for youths to empower themselves. Young people should be empowered in other ways so they don't have to turn to gangs for support, belongingness, financial gain, or social status.

Combating gangs can assume three primary thrusts: prevention, intervention, and suppression (Regulus, 1995; Williams & Van Dorn, 1999). *Prevention* involves providing enough resources and services to communities and individuals that young people don't need to seek out gang membership in the first place. Prevention requires communities to offer adequate social programs for reducing poverty, educating parents about children's needs and child management, enhancing policing resources, developing high-quality educational systems that respond to young people's needs, and diminishing accessibility to handguns (Williams & Van Dorn, 1999).

Prevention can also be geared to individual youths' needs. For example, the Peace Power program in New York City was developed by several social work graduate students in conjunction with some "local social service agencies and high schools." This empowerment approach emphasizes

> four essential steps: recognizing contributions and successes [e.g., even simple things such as offering feedback notes recognizing specific positive actions on the part of young people]; acting with respect [e.g., initiating a "respect day" during which young people interview each other and share their own definitions of respect]; sharing power to build community [e.g., "working collectively and sharing responsibility"]; and making peace [e.g., teaching conflict resolution strategies]. (Vallianatos, 2001, July, p. 3)

An *intervention* approach to combating gangs and reducing gang membership includes "opportunity provision" and "social interventions" (Regulus, 1995, p. 1052). "*Opportunity provision* provides gang youths access to training and status-enhancing resources and services such as jobs, job training, mentoring, better schooling, and advocacy within conventional social systems" (Regulus, 1995, p. 1052, emphasis added). *Social interventions* involve therapeutic strategies aimed at developing both positive attitudes toward others and social skills. "Strategies include assistance with schooling, counseling and therapy, and drug treatment" (Regulus, 1995, p. 1052).

A *suppression* approach to gangs focuses on control "through law enforcement and legal statutes emphasizing crime detection, apprehension, and prosecution tactics targeting gang offenders" (Regulus, 1995, p. 1051). The focus, of course, is on punishment, not rehabilitation and treatment.

Looking Ahead

This book concludes by stressing the importance of critical thinking in evaluating social welfare policy issues in various fields of practice. It also encourages you to explore your personal values and ideas about your future career.

For Further Exploration on the Internet

See this text's Book Companion Website at **www.socialwork.wadsworth.com/ kirstashman_intro2e** for descriptors and hot links to URLs relevant to this chapter, selected InfoTrac articles and exercises, and tutorial quizzes.

Case Study for Critical Thinking: A Client with a Serious Hereditary Disease

The case presented here represents an application of this entire section of the book on client populations and contexts, not specifically on criminal justice. This case involves a hospital social worker talking with a client who just discovered she has a serious hereditary disease involving mental and physical deterioration and eventual death.[1] Subsequent questions are posed to promote critical thinking.

Case study: A hospital social worker is counseling Myla, age 24, a patient who has just been informed that she has a genetic marker for Huntington's chorea, a hereditary disease commencing in middle age that causes gradual deterioration of the brain and voluntary muscular movement. No cure currently exists for the disease. Myla enthusiastically desires to have children, but they could all potentially be infected with the disease.

Myla states she does not want her husband, Richard, or her family to know about this. Myla fears that if Richard finds out he will refuse to have children with her and possibly leave her because he, too, desires children. Myla is reeling over the shocking news.

Critical thinking: The first step in the critical thinking process involves *asking* questions about problems, needs, and issues. A number of basic ethical questions can be raised:

- What are the issues involving confidentiality in this case? Does Richard have the right to know that Myla has the disease and that their future children might also have it? Does he have the right to know that within the next 20 or 30 years Myla will likely begin experiencing serious mental and physical deterioration?
- "What is the best interest of the as-yet-unborn child?"
- "[W]ho is the person or are the persons entitled to make such decisions?"
- "What are the religious implications for all concerned (if any) of playing God?"
- "Who speaks for the fetus?"
- "What are statistical relationships between a genetic marker and the actual occurrence of the genetic defect, and what bearing do they have on making a decision?"
- "What is society's best interest in this situation?" (Loewenberg, Dolgoff, & Harrington, 2000, p. 218).

Additionally, what specific questions might be asked concerning Myla's responsibility to herself and others in addition to planning for the future?

Consider the following:

- If Myla does not tell Richard, how will he react when he inevitably does find out about her condition? If she doesn't tell him beforehand, how will he feel toward her after having children who potentially harbor the disease?

[1]This case study is based on one presented in Loewenberg, Dolgoff, and Harrington (2000, p. 218).

- Might Myla consider the alternative of not having children or of adopting them?
- How can Myla plan her life over the next few decades to maximize her appreciation and enjoyment of it?
- How might she plan for the more distant future when she begins to experience symptoms of the disease?

Note that these latter questions are very solemn and would not be ones a social worker would pose to Myla flippantly. Rather, the practitioner would help Myla address them over time when she was emotionally ready. First Myla would have to work through her grief concerning the diagnosis and begin coping with her reality. Only then could she begin to make more objective decisions about and plans for her future.

The second step in critical thinking entails *assessing* the established facts and issues involved. What are the answers to the questions posed? Some require facts such as more information about Huntington's chorea. Others involve serious thinking about values and ethics.

The final step in critical thinking is the *assertion* of a concluding opinion. The social worker would assist Myla in *asking* questions about her situation and options and then in *assessing* her answers. The worker would also be forced to address the ethical questions posed and determine what was the right thing to do. For example, should Richard be told? There are no easy answers. If you were Myla, what would you do?

YOUR VALUES AND YOUR FUTURE: APPLYING CRITICAL THINKING SKILLS

© Stockdisc/ PictureQuest

This book has discussed a wide range of social welfare policy and programming issues. The emphasis has been on critical thinking about these issues using the Triple-A approach:

1. *Ask* questions.
2. *Assess* the established facts and issues involved.
3. *Assert* a concluding opinion.

At this point, what are your opinions and values concerning the following issues?

- What policies should the government adopt concerning the treatment of poor children and families?
- Can poverty be eliminated? If so, how? What policies and programs need to be developed? To what extent do you feel this is possible?
- What supportive and supplementary services best serve children and families? What are the most important concepts involved in developing policies and services?
- To what extent should society support the elderly by providing services and benefits? What services and benefits are most critical? What new policies could improve their quality of life?
- To what extent should society promote self-determination on the part of people with disabilities by providing services and benefits? What policies could improve this population's quality of life? What important concepts are involved in policy development and service provision?
- What are the major issues involved in the provision of health care in the United States? What are the pros and cons of managed care? Should changes in health care policy be pursued? If so, what changes? Should a universal national health insurance policy initiative be advanced? If so, who would pay for it?
- What are the primary issues involved in mental health policy and service provision? What policy initiatives might be advanced to address these concerns?
- What are the principal issues and concerns in providing services to youths and in the schools? What methods of empowerment can be proposed?
- What are the main issues and concerns involved in criminal justice and service provision? To what extent does criminal justice policy reflect a punitive versus rehabilitative perspective? Can policy be improved, and if so, how?

Do these values and opinions tend to reflect a conservative or a liberal perspective? Do you tend to support a residual or an institutional orientation to service provision?

 # The Importance of Values in Career Decision Making

This book has stressed the significance of professional values in social work practice. It has also emphasized the importance of social workers pursuing policy practice when advocacy is called for to improve social welfare policies and programming. It is important that professional values be acceptable to people who choose to become social workers. Of course, we all have personal opinions about an extensive range of topics. However, social workers' personal values must be in adequate compliance with professional values for individuals to be comfortable and productive professionals.

Assessing Your Own Capabilities and Interests

The following sections encourage you to think about your personal capabilities, potential job preferences, and initial career goals. They are intended to give you some insight into whether social work might be the field for you.

What Are Your Competencies?

Competencies are your skills and abilities. What are you good at? What skills have you mastered that would enhance your performance in a professional social

---

Box A Assessing Your Capabilities

The following are areas that may reflect your professional knowledge, skills, and values. Place a check mark next to each item that you consider a strength:

_____ Assessment of individual, family, group, community, and organizational problems and functioning
_____ Communication
_____ Understanding people
_____ Problem solving
_____ Decision making
_____ Planning
_____ Organizing
_____ Recording
_____ Clear thinking
_____ Acceptance of responsibility
_____ Dependability
_____ Pacing efforts
_____ Coordination
_____ Case management
_____ Conducting meetings
_____ Advocacy
_____ Creativity
_____ Initiating ideas
_____ Undertaking action

These concepts simply reflect the beginning of your capability assessment. The potential list is unlimited. These are merely intended to give you some initial ideas.

After giving your capabilities serious thought, write out several paragraphs summarizing and prioritizing your greatest strengths. This can help you articulate for yourself (and later for potential employers) the reasons you are or will be a capable professional.

work setting? Think about the social work knowledge and values that you have acquired and the skills that you have mastered. Box A identifies some potential competencies.

What Are Your Employment Goals?

This question concerns the context of employment. What aspects of work are important to you other than the type of social work skills you use or population you serve? In other words, what aspects of your working environment motivate you to perform and encourage you to like your job? Box B portrays a range of work dimensions that may be of varying importance to you. To what extent do you think that these would characterize a career as a social worker?

What Are Your Job Preferences?

If you are considering a career in social work, what would the ideal job be? Think in terms of four areas: (1) the types of professional activities you would most like to pursue, (2) your preferred client population, (3) the problems you are interested

---

Box B   Employment Goals and Work Context

What aspects of the work environment are the most important to you? Prioritize the following:

____	Salary	____	Challenging environment
____	Sick leave	____	Low stress levels
____	Hours of work	____	Realistic recording requirements
____	Effective supervision	____	Being rewarded for achievement
____	Geographic location	____	Little travel
____	Potential for advancement	____	Potential for new skill development
____	Substantial discretion in decision making	____	Competent colleagues
		____	Good office
____	Vacation time	____	Good relationships with colleagues
____	Health care benefits	____	Working as part of a team
____	Not being "on call"	____	Potential for travel
____	In-service training opportunities	____	Respect from other staff
____	Clear job description	____	Clear rules and regulations
____	Opportunity to function independently	____	Responsive administration
		____	Time flexibility

(Is there anything else that would be motivating to you? If so, specify.)

____ _____

____ _____

Box C   Job Preferences

1. What types of professional activities are you most interested in pursuing? Prioritize the following:

____	Counseling	____	Budgeting
____	Brokering resources	____	Administrative activities in general
____	Supervising volunteers	____	Case management
____	Writing grants	____	Supervising staff
____	Running groups	____	Lobbying
____	Management	____	Research
____	Community organizing	____	Fund-raising
____	Program evaluation	____	Training staff
____	Public relations	____	Policy development
____	Running meetings	____	Advocacy

(What else?) _____

_____

_____

2. Ideally, what client population would you prefer to work with? Prioritize the following:

____	Children	____	Teenagers
____	Young adults	____	Middle-aged adults
____	Elderly people	____	Married couples
____	Women	____	Men
____	Intact families	____	Single parents

____ Minority groups (If so, specify which) _____

____ Other client populations (If so, specify which) _____

3. What problems and issues are you interested in addressing? Prioritize the following:

____	Community development	____	Child maltreatment
____	Alcohol and other drugs		*(continued)*

in addressing, and (4) the type of agency setting in which you would like to work. The questions posed in Box C illustrate examples in each area.

Note that simple identification of your preferred job characteristics does not mean that you will get that exact job or even one very similar. The intent here is to help you seriously consider your own goals and career objectives. The better you know yourself, the more capable you will be of both presenting yourself to others (like potential employers) and making decisions about what job to pursue and accept.

Box C (*continued*)

____	Battered women	____	Unemployment
____	Probation and parole	____	Vocational rehabilitation
____	Mental illness	____	Developmental disability
____	Family problems	____	Health
____	Crime in communities	____	Eating disorders
____	Teen pregnancy	____	Suicide prevention
____	School problems (e.g., truancy)	____	Physical challenge
____	Financial resources acquisition	____	HIV/AIDS
____	Prison	____	Homelessness
____	Couples conflict		

(What else?) _____

____ _____

____ _____

4. In what type of agency setting would you prefer to work? Prioritize the following:

____	Private *or*	____	Close, directive supervision *or*
____	Public	____	Supervision primarily on a consultation basis
____	Large bureaucracy *or*		
____	Smaller agency	____	Hospital
____	County social services	____	School
____	Institution	____	Community organization
____	Group home	____	Prison
____	Primary social work setting	____	Family planning agency
____	Primary medical setting	____	Mental health center or counseling agency
____	Primary educational setting		
____	Serving clients with a wide range of problems *or*	____	Hospice
____	Focusing on specialized problems	____	Shelter (e.g., for homeless people or survivors of domestic violence)

Looking Ahead

These exercises and this book only scratch the surface of what social work is all about. It's just the beginning if you're thinking about some area of social work as the career for you.

REFERENCES

Abadinsky, H. (2000). *Probation and parole* (7th ed.). Upper Saddle River, NJ: Prentice-Hall.

ABCNews. (2005, January 8). *Democrat disputes Social Security "crisis."* Retrieved January 8, 2005. http://abcnews.go.com/Politics/print?is=395503

Abdelkarim, R. Z. (2002, September-October). American Muslims and 9/11: A community looks back…and to the future. *Washington Report on Middle East Affairs, 21* (7), 82–85. Retrieved July 9, 2004. http://infotrac-college.thomsonlearning.com

Abramovitz, M. (1995). Aid to families with dependent children. References In R. L. Edwards (Ed.), *Encyclopedia of social work* (19th ed., Vol. 1, pp. 183–194). Washington, DC: NASW Press.

Abramovitz, M. (1997). Temporary assistance to needy families. In R. L. Edwards (Ed.), *Encyclopedia of social work supplement* (pp. 311–330). Washington, DC: NASW Press.

Acs, G., & Loprest, P. (2001, January). *Initial synthesis report of the findings from ASPE's "leavers' grant."* Washington, DC: Urban Institute.

Administration for Children and Families (ACF), U. S. (n.d.). *Fact Sheet: Office of Families Assistance (TANF).* Retrieved January 7, 2005. http://www.acf.hhs.gov/opa/fact_sheets/tanf_printable.html

Administration on Aging (AOA). (2000a). *Demographic changes.* www.aoa.gov/stats/aging21/demography.html

Administration on Aging (AOA). (2000b). *Older women.* www.zoz.dhhs.gov/may2000/factsheets/olderwomen.html

Administration on Aging (AOA). (2000c). *AOA annual profile of older Americans shows drop in poverty rate.* www.aoa.dhhs.gov/pr/pr2000/Oaprofile.html

Aestraea's Web. (1998). *Was "Sybil" really a multiple personality?* Retrieved April 27, 2002. www.aestraeaweb.net/plural/sybilbogus.html

Ahearn, F. L., Jr. (1995). Displaced people. In R. L. Edwards (Ed.), *Encyclopedia of social work* (19th ed., Vol.1, pp. 771–780). Washington, DC: NASW Press.

Ahmed, P. I., & Kolker, A. (1979). The role of indigenous medicine in WHO's definition of health. In P. I. Ahmed & G. V. Coelhi (Eds.), *Toward a new definition of health.* New York: Plenum.

Aids.com. (2005). *Home access standard HIV test kit.* Retrieved January 23, 2005. http://www.aids.com/product/homekit1_info.htm

AIDSinfo. (2004, October). *Approved medications to treat HIV infection.* Retrieved January 28, 2005. http://aidsinfo.nih.gov/other/cbrochure/english/05_en.html

Aidsmap. (2005). *CD4 T-cell counts.* Retrieved January 29, 2005. http://www.aidsmap.com/en/docs

Alan Guttmacher Institute. (1999). *Teenage pregnancy: Overall trends and state-by-state information.* New York: Author.

Alan Guttmacher Institute (AGI). (2004a). *Facts in brief: Teen sex and pregnancy.* Retrieved January 30, 2005. http://www.agi-usa.org/pubs/fb_teens.html

Alan Guttmacher Institute. (2004b). *Facts in brief: Teenagers' sexual and reproductive health: Developed countries.* Retrieved January 30, 2005. http://www.agi-usa.org/pubs/fb_teens.html

Alavi, K. (2001, October). At risk of prejudice: Teaching tolerance about Muslim Americans. *Social Education, 65* (6), 344–349. Retrieved July 13, 2004. http://infotrac-college.thomsonlearning.com/itw/infomark/145/808/51630275w5/22!ar_fmt .

Alexander, S. (2004). Intervention with families. In C. R. Brittain & D. E. Hunt (Eds.), *Helping in child protective services: A competency-based casework handbook* (pp. 393–446). New York: Oxford.

Allen, J. A. (1995). African Americans: Caribbean. In R. L. Edwards (Ed.), *Encyclopedia of social work* (19th ed., Vol.1, pp. 121–129). Washington, DC: NASW Press.

AllRefer.com. (2005). *AIDS.* Retrieved January 29, 2005. http://health.allrefer.com/health/aids-diagnosis-tests.html

Ambrosino, R., Heffernan, J., Shuttlesworth, G., & Ambrosino, R. (2005). *Social work & social welfare: An introduction* (5th ed.). Belmont, CA: Brooks/Cole.

American Association of Sex Educators, Counselors, and Therapists (AASECT). (2000, April). Quick hits: Sex in the news. *Contemporary Sexuality, 34* (4), 6–9.

American Association of Sex Educators, Counselors, and Therapists. (2004, June 6). Marital bliss or legal chaos facing gay newlyweds? *Contemporary Sexuality, 38* (6), 7.

American Psychiatric Association (APA). (2000). *Diagnostic and statistical manual of mental disorders text revision* (4th ed.). Washington, DC: Author.

American Psychological Association. (2001). *Publication manual of the American Psychological Association.* Washington, DC: Author.

ARC Milwaukee. (Undated, a). *Employment programs.* Milwaukee, WI: Author.

ARC Milwaukee. (Undated, b). *Figuring out funding.* Milwaukee, WI: Author.

ARC Milwaukee. (Undated, c). *Services profile.* Milwaukee, WI: Author.

Armstrong, B. (1995). Family planning. In R. L. Edwards (Ed.), *Encyclopedia of social work* (19th ed., Vol. 2, pp. 965–973). Washington, DC: NASW Press.

Arredondo, P., Topper, R., Brown, S., Jones, J., Locke, D. C., Sanchez, J., & Stadler, H. (1996). *Operationalization of the multicultural counseling competencies*. Washington, DC: Association for Multicultural Counseling and Development.

Asch, A. (1995). Visual impairment and blindness. In R. L. Edwards (Ed.), *Encyclopedia of social work* (19th ed., Vol. 3, pp. 2461–2468). Washington, DC: NASW Press.

Asch, A., & Mudrick, N. R. (1995). Disability. In R. L. Edwards (Ed.), *Encyclopedia of social work* (19th ed., Vol. 1, pp. 752–761). Washington, DC: NASW Press.

Association of Social Work Boards. (2002). *Social work laws & regulations: A comparison guide*. Culpeper, VA: Author.

Association of Social Work Boards [ASWB]. (2004a). *Licensing examinations*. Retrieved July 24, 2004. http://www.aswb.org/exam_info.shtml

Association of Social Work Boards. (2004b). *School pass/fail summary*. Culpeper, VA: Author.

Astor, R. A., Benbenishty, R., & Marachi, R. (2004). Violence in school. In P. Allen-Meares (Ed.), *Social work services in schools* (4th ed., pp. 149–182). Boston: Allyn & Bacon.

Axinn, J., & Stern, M. J. (2001). *Social welfare: A history of the American response to need* (5th ed.). Boston: Allyn & Bacon.

Axinn, J., & Stern, M. J. (2005). *Social welfare: A history of the American response to need* (6th ed.). Boston: Allyn & Bacon.

Baccalaureate Educational Assessment Package (BEAP). (2004, November 22).

Bai, M. (1999, May 3). Anatomy of a massacre. *Newsweek*, 25–31.

Balgopal, P. R. (1995). Asian Americans overview. In R. L. Edwards (Ed.), *Encyclopedia of social work* (19th ed., Vol. 1, pp. 231–238). Washington, DC: NASW Press.

Ballman, P. K. (2004, July 18). Civil unions might solve gay marriage debate. *Milwaukee Journal Sentinel*, J1–2.

Balsanek, J. (1998). Addressing at-risk pregnant women's issues through community, individual, and corporate grassroots efforts. In P. L. Ewalt, E. M. Freeman, & D. L. Poole (Eds.), *Community building: Renewal, well-being, and shared responsibility* (pp. 411–419). Washington, DC: NASW Press.

Barker, R. L. (1995). *The social work dictionary* (3rd ed.). Washington, DC: NASW Press.

Barker, R. L. (1999). *Milestones*. Washington, DC: NASW Press.

Barker, R. L. (2003). *The social work dictionary* (5th ed.). Washington, DC: NASW Press.

Barrett, L. (1983). *Gambling with history: Reagan in the White House*. New York: Penguin Books.

Barringer, F. (1993, April 15). Sex survey of American men finds 1 percent are gay. *The New York Times*, 1A.

Barth, M. C. (2001, February). *The labor market for social workers: A first look*. Prepared for The John A. Hartford Foundation, Inc.

Barth, M. C. (2003). Social work labor market: A first look. *Social Work*, 48 (1), 9–19.

Barth, R. P. (1995). Adoption. In R. L. Edwards (Ed.), *Encyclopedia of social work* (19th ed., Vol.1, pp. 48–59). Washington, DC: NASW Press.

Bartlett, H. (1970). *The common base of social work practice*. New York: National Association of Social Workers.

Barton, W. H. (1995). Juvenile corrections. In R. L. Edwards (Ed.), *Encyclopedia of social work* (19th ed., Vol. 2, pp. 1563–1577). Washington, DC: NASW Press.

Barusch, A. S. (2000). Social Security is not for babies: Trends and policies affecting older women in the United States. *Families in Society*, 81 (6), 568–575.

Barusch, A. S. (2002). *Foundations of social policy: Social justice, public programs, and the social work profession*. Itasca, IL: Peacock.

Baruth, L. G., & Manning, M. L. (1999). *Multicultural counseling and psychotherapy: A lifespan perspective* (2nd ed.). Upper Saddle River, NJ: Prentice-Hall.

Bauman, R., Kasper, C., & Alford, J. (1984). The child sex abusers. *Corrective and Social Psychiatry*, 30, 76–81.

Beaucar, K. O. (1999, July). Taking a lead on HIV. *NASW News*, 44 (7), 1.

Beaucar, K. O. (2000, January). Federal study profiles substance abuse: Chamber of Commerce notes value of employee assistance programs. *NASW News*, 45 (1), 10.

Becerra, R. M., & Damron-Rodriguez, J. (1995). Veterans and veterans services. In R. L. Edwards (Ed.), *Encyclopedia of social work* (19th ed., Vol. 3, pp. 2431–2439). Washington, DC: NASW Press.

Beck, A. T., & Weishaar, M. E. (2000). Cognitive therapy. In R. J. Corsini & D. Wedding (Eds.), *Current psychotherapies* (6th ed.). Itasca, IL: Peacock.

Beckett, J. O., & Johnson, H. C. (1995). Human development. In R. L. Edwards (Ed.), *Encyclopedia of social work* (19th ed., Vol. 2, pp. 1385–1405). Washington, DC: NASW Press.

Bee, H. L. (1996). *The journey of adulthood* (3rd ed.). Upper Saddle River, NJ: Prentice-Hall.

Begley, S. (1999, May 3). Why the young kill. *Newsweek*, 32–35.

Begley, S. (2001, June 11). AIDS at 20. *Time*, pp. 34–37.

Beless, D. W. (1995). Council on Social Work Education. In R. L. Edwards (Ed.), *Encyclopedia of social work* (19th ed., Vol. 1, pp. 632–637). Washington, DC: NASW Press.

Bellos, N. S., & Ruffolo, M. C. (1995). Aging: Services. In R. L. Edwards (Ed.), *Encyclopedia of social work* (19th ed., Vol. 1, pp. 165–173). Washington, DC: NASW Press.

Benny Max Parrish v. The Civil Service Commission of the County of Alameda, S. F. 22429, Supreme Court of California in Bank, March 27, 1967.

Bentley, K. J., & Walsh, J. (1998). Advances in psychopharmacology and psychosocial aspects of medication management: A review for social workers. In J. B. W. Williams & K. Ell (Eds.), *Advances in mental health research: Implications for practice* (pp. 309–342). Washington, DC: NASW Press.

Berg, I. K. (1994). *Family based services: A solution-focused approach*. New York: Norton.

Berg, I. K., & Jaya, K. P. (1993). Different and same: Family therapy with Asian-American families. *Journal of Marital and Family Therapy*, 19 (1), 31–38.

Berg-Cross, L., Craig, K., & Wessel, T. (2001). Multi-culturalism at historically black colleges and universities: A case study of Howard University. In J. G. Ponterotto, J. M. Casas, L. A. Suzuki, & C. M. Alexander (Eds.), *Handbook of multicultural counseling* (2nd ed., pp. 849–870). Thousand Oaks, CA: Sage.

Berger, R. M., & Kelly, J. J. (1995). Gay men overview. In R. L. Edwards (Ed.), *Encyclopedia of social work* (19th ed., Vol. 2, pp. 1064–1075). Washington, DC: NASW Press.

Berliner, L., & Elliott, D. M. (2002). Sexual abuse of children. In J. E. B. Myers, L. Berliner, J. Briere, C. T. Hendrix, C. Jenny, & T. A. Reid (Eds.), *The APSAC handbook on child maltreatment.* (2nd ed., pp. 55–78). Thousand Oaks, CA: Sage.

Bibus, A., & Link, R. J. (199). Global approaches to learning social welfare policy. In C. S. Ramanathan & R. J. Link (Eds.), *All our futures: Principles and resources for social work practice in a global era.* Pacific Grove, CA: Brooks/Cole.

Biegel, D. E., Shore, B. K., & Gordon, E. (1984). *Building support networks for the elderly: Theory and application.* Thousand Oaks, CA: Sage.

Black, L. (1996). Families of African origin: An overview. In M. McGoldrick, J. Giordan, & J. K. Pearce (Eds.), *Ethnicity and family therapy* (2nd ed., pp. 57–65). New York: Guilford.

Blackless, E., et al. (2000). How sexually dimorphic are we? Review and synthesis. *American Journal of Human Biology, 12,* 151–166.

Blau, J. (2004). *The dynamics of social welfare policy.* New York: Oxford.

Bleyer, L. R., & Joiner, K. (2002). Conducting a needs assessment in a school setting. In R. Constable, S. McDonald, & J. P. Flynn (Eds.), *School social work: Practice, policy, and research perspectives* (5th ed., pp. 194–207). Chicago: Lyceum.

Bloomberg.com. (2005, January 6). *Bush budget may omit Social Security, underscoring changes.* Retrieved January 6, 2005. http://www.bloomberg.com/apps/news?pid=10000103&sid=ajYQx.LcUF9g& refer=us

Blythe, B., & Reighoffer, A. (2000). Assessment and measurement issues in direct practice in social work. In P. Allen-Meares & C. Garvin (Eds.), *The handbook of social work practice* (pp. 551–564). Thousand Oaks, CA: Sage.

Bocchi, S. (2005). *The meaning of marianismo in Mexico.* Retrieved June 14, 2005. http://www.lclark.edu/~woodrich/Bocchi_marianismo.html

Boehm, W. W. (1959). *Objectives of the social work curriculum of the future.* New York: Council on Social Work Education.

Borch-Jacobsen, M. (1997, April 24). Sybil: The making of a disease? *New York Review of Books.* Retrieved April 28, 2002. www.aestraeasweb.net/plural/spiegel.html

Bostick, B. (2005, January 6). How secure is your retirement? Social Security privatization scams young and old. *People's Weekly World Newspaper Online.* Retrieved January 8, 2005. http://host9.cupusa.org/article/articlepring/6280

Boston Women's Health Book Collective. (1984). *The new our bodies, ourselves.* New York: Simon & Schuster.

Bower, B. (1994, June 4). Antidepressants may alter personality. *Science News, 145,* 359.

Brammer, R. (2004). *Diversity in counseling.* Pacific Grove, CA: Brooks/Cole.

Brassard, M., Germain, R., & Hart, S. (1987). *Psychological maltreatment of children and youth.* Elmsford, NY: Pergamon.

Braun, K. I., & Browne, C. V. (2000). Perceptions of dementia, caregiving, and help seeking among Asian and Pacific Islander Americans. In S. M. Keigher, A. E. Fortune, & S. L. Witkin (Eds.), *Aging and social work: The changing landscapes* (pp. 175–191). Washington, DC: NASW Press.

Braun, K. I., Mokuau, N., & Tsark, J. (1997). Cultural themes in health, illness, and rehabilitation for Native Hawaiians: Observations of rehabilitation staff and physicians. *Topics in Geriatric Rehabilitation, 12,* 19–37.

Brave Heart, M. Y. H., & Chase, J. (2005). Social work practice with First Nations Peoples. In D. Lum (Ed.), *Cultural competence, practice stages, and client systems: A case study approach* (pp. 32–58). Pacific Grove, CA: Brooks/Cole.

Breton, M., & Nosko, A. (1997). Group work with women who have experienced abuse. In G. L. Greif & P. H. Ephross (Eds.), *Group work with population at risk.* New York: Oxford University Press, 134–146.

Bricker-Jenkins, M., & Lockett, P. W. (1995). Women: Direct practice. In R. L. Edwards (Ed.), *Encyclopedia of social work* (19th ed., Vol. 3, pp. 2529–2539). Washington, DC: NASW Press.

Brieland, D. (1995). Social work practice: History and evolution. In R. L. Edwards (Ed.), *Encyclopedia of social work* (19th ed., Vol. 3, pp. 2247–2258). Washington, DC: NASW Press.

Brink, S. (2001, January 29). Improved AIDS treatments bring life and hope—at a cost. *Time,* 44–46.

Brink, S. (2003, December 13). Dancing in the dark. *U.S. New & World Report,* 45–56.

Brink, S. (2004, July 12). AIDS: Darkening in America. *U.S. News & World Report,* 132–134.

Brody, R., & Nair, M. D. (2003). *Macro practice: A generalist approach* (6th ed.). Wheaton, IL: Gregory.

Bronner, E. (1998, February 1). Just say maybe. No sexology, please. We're Americans. *The New York Times,* p. WK6.

Brown, J. G. (2000, June). *Annual report: State Medicaid fraud control units.* Washington, DC: Department of Health and Human Services. www.hhs.gov.oig/oi/mcfu /index.htm

Buchan, V., Hull, G., Rogers, J., Rodenhiser, R., & Smith, M. (2004, November). *BEAP use and outcome trend summary.* Paper presented at the meeting of the Baccalaureate Association of (Social Work) Program Directors, Detroit, MI.

Burchinal, M. R., Roberts, J. E., Nabors, L. A., & Bryant, D. M. (1996). Quality of center child care and infant cognitive and language development. *Child Development, 67,* 606–620.

Bureau of Justice Statistics. (1996). *National crime victimization survey, 1995: Preliminary findings.* Washington, DC: U.S. Department of Justice.

Burger, W. R., & Youkeles, M. (2000). *Human services in contemporary America* (5th ed.). Pacific Grove, CA: Brooks/Cole.

Burke, A. C. (1995). Substance abuse: Legal issues. In R. L. Edwards (Ed.), *Encyclopedia of social work* (19th ed., Vol. 3, pp. 2347–2357). Washington, DC: NASW Press.

Burn, S. M. (2005). *Women across cultures: A global perspective* (2nd ed.). New York: McGraw-Hill.

Burnett, B. (1993). The psychological abuse of latency age children: A survey. *Child Abuse and Neglect, 17,* 441–454.

Burns, D. (1980). *Feeling good: The new mood therapy.* New York: Morrow.

Campos, A. P. (1995). Hispanics: Puerto Ricans. In R. L. Edwards (Ed.), *Encyclopedia of social work* (19th ed., Vol. 2, pp. 1245–1252). Washington, DC: NASW Press.

Canada Revenue Agency. (2004, May 20). *Your Canada child tax benefit.* Retrieved January 10, 2005. http://www.cra-arc.gc.ca/E/pub/tg/t4114/t4114-e.html

Canby, W. (1981). *American Indian law in a nutshell.* St. Paul, MN: West.

Cannon, A., Streisand, B., & McGraw, D. (1999, May 3). Why? There were plenty of warnings, but no one stopped two twisted teens. *U.S. News & World Report,* 16–19.

Carlton-LaNey, B., Edwards, R. L., & Reid, P. N. (1999). Small towns and rural communities: From romantic notions to harsh realities. In I. B. Carlton-LaNey, R. L. Edwards, & P. N. Reid (Eds.), *Preserving and strengthening small towns and rural communities* (pp. 5–12). Washington, DC: NASW Press.

Carroll, J. L. (2005). *Sexuality now.* Pacific Grove, CA: Brooks/Cole.

Carroll, J. L., & Wolpe, P. R. (1996). *Sexuality and gender in society.* New York: HarperCollins.

Carton, B. (1994, January 27). Growing up in a gay household. *Boston Globe,* 45.

CBSMarketWatch. (2005, January 6). *Bush sees Social Security fix support.* Retrieved January 8, 2005. http://cbs.marketwatch.com/news/story.asp?guid=%7B60501BB1-7078-4D43-9518-544FC . . .

Centers for Disease Control and Prevention (CDC). (2000). Youth risk behavior surveillance—United States, 1999. *Morbidity and Mortality Weekly Report, 49* (SS05), 1–96.

Chadwick, D. L. (2002). Community organization of services to deal with and end child abuse. In J. E. B. Myers, L. Berliner, J. Briere, C. T. Hendrix, C. Jenny, & T. A. Reid (Eds.), *The APSAC handbook on child maltreatment* (2nd ed., pp. 509–523). Thousand Oaks, CA: Sage.

Chambers, D. E., & Wedel, K. R. (2005). *Social policy and social programs: A method for the practical public policy analyst* (4th ed.). Boston: Allyn & Bacon.

Cherokee Messenger (1995). *Brief history of the trail of tears.* Retrieved November 20, 2004. http://www.powersource.com/cherokee/history.html

Child Welfare League of America. (1978). *Standards for group home service for children.* New York: Author.

Child Welfare League of America. (1994). *Kinship care: A natural bridge.* Washington, DC: Author.

Chilman, C. S. (1993). Hispanic families in the United States: Research perspectives. In H. P. McAdoo (Ed.), *Family ethnicity: Strength in diversity.* Newbury Park, CA: Sage.

Christ, G. H., Sormanti, M., & Francoeur, R. B. (2001). Chronic physical illness and disability. In A. Gitterman (Ed.), *Handbook of social work practice with vulnerable and resilient populations* (2nd ed., pp. 124–162). New York: Columbia University Press.

Clarke-Stewart, K. A., Gruber, C. P., & Fitzgerald, L. M. (1994). *Children at home and in day care.* Hillsdale, NJ: Erlbaum.

Cloud, J. (2001, Feb. 26). New sparks over electroshock. *Time,* 60–62.

CNN.com. (2001). *The end of Enron?* Retrieved February 5, 2005. http://cnn.com/SPECIALS/2002/enron/

Cohen, N. A. (1992). The continuum of child welfare services. In N. A. Cohen (Ed.), *Child welfare: A multicultural approach* (pp. 39–83). Needham Heights, MA: Allyn & Bacon.

Coleman, J. W., & Cressey, D. R. (1999). *Social problems* (7th ed.). New York: Longman.

Coleman, J. W., & Kerbo, H. R. (2002). *Social problems* (8th ed.). Upper Saddle River, NJ: Prentice-Hall.

Collins, D., Jordan, C., & Coleman, H. (1999). *An introduction to family social work.* Itasca, IL: Peacock.

Connaway, R. S., & Gentry, M. E. (1988). *Social work practice.* Englewood Cliffs, NJ: Prentice-Hall.

Connors, G. J., Donovan, D. M., & DiClemente, C. C. (2001). *Selecting and planning interventions: Substance abuse treatment and the stages of change.* New York: Guilford Press.

Constable, R. (1999). Developing and defining the school social worker's role. In R. Constable, S. McDonald, & J. P. Flynn (Eds.), *School social work: Practice, policy, and research perspectives* (4th ed., pp. 207–225). Chicago: Lyceum.

Constable, R. (2002). The role of the school social worker: History and theory. In R. Constable, S. McDonald, & J. P. Flynn (Eds.), *School social work: Practice, policy, and research perspectives* (5th ed., pp. 3–24). Chicago: Lyceum.

Coon, D. (2001). *Introduction to psychology: Gateways to mind and behavior* (9th ed.). Belmont, CA: Wadsworth.

Corbet, T. (1993, Spring). Child poverty and welfare reform: Progress or paralysis? *Focus, 15,* 4–5.

Corcoran, K. (1997). Managed care: Implications for social work practice. In *Encyclopedia of social work 1997 supplement.* Washington, DC: NASW Press.

Corey, G. (2000). *Theory and practice of group counseling* (5th ed.). Pacific Grove, CA: Brooks/Cole.

Corey, G., Corey, M. S., & Callanan, P. (1998). *Issues and ethics in the helping professions.* Pacific Grove, CA: Brooks/Cole.

Corey, G., Corey, M. S., & Callanan, P. (2003). *Issues & ethics in the helping professions* (6th ed.). Pacific Grove, CA: Brooks/Cole.

Corey, M. S., & Corey, G. (1997). *Groups process and practice* (5th ed.). Pacific Grove, CA: Brooks/Cole.

Corey, M. S., & Corey, G. (1998). *Becoming a helper* (3rd ed.). Pacific Grove, CA: Brooks/Cole.

Corey, M. S., & Corey, G. (2002). *Groups: Process and practice* (6th ed.). Pacific Grove, CA: Brooks/Cole.

Corey, M. S., & Corey, G. (2003). *Becoming a helper* (4th ed.). Pacific Grove, CA: Brooks/Cole.

Council on Social Work Education. (2001). *Educational policy and accreditation standards.* Alexandria, VA: Author.

Council on Social Work Education. (2002). Glossary to *Educational policy and accreditation standards* developed by commission of the Council on Social Work Education. Alexandria, VA: Author.

Cournoyer, B. R. (2005). *The social work skills workbook* (4th ed.). Pacific Grove, CA: Brooks/Cole.

Coven, M. (2002, October 3). *An introduction to TANF*. Washington, DC: Center on Budget and Policy Priorities.

Cowger, C. D. (1994). Assessing client strengths: Clinical assessment for client empowerment. *Social Work, 39* (3), 262–268.

Cowley, G. (2003, December 8). New inroads against AIDS. *Newsweek,* 84–85.

Cowley, G. (2000, January 17). Fighting the disease: What can be done. *Newsweek,* 38.

Cowley, G., & Murr, A. (2004, December 6). The new face of AIDS. *Newsweek,* 76–79.

Cox, E. O., & Parsons, R. J. (1994). *Empowerment-oriented social work practice with the elderly*. Pacific Grove, CA: Brooks/Cole.

Crooks, R., & Baur, K. (1999). *Our sexuality* (7th ed.). Pacific Grove, CA: Brooks/Cole.

Crooks, R., & Baur, K. (2002). *Our sexuality* (8th ed.). Belmont, CA: Wadsworth.

Crooks, R., & Baur, K. (2005). *Our sexuality* (9th ed.). Belmont, CA: Wadsworth.

Cross, T. L., Bazron, B. J., Dennis, K. W., & Isaacs, M. R. (1989). *Toward a culturally competent system of care*. Washington, DC: Child and Adolescent Service System Program Technical Assistance Center.

Crosson-Tower, C. (1992). Child abuse and neglect. In N. A. Cohen (Ed.), *Child welfare: A multicultural focus* (pp. 157–191). Boston: Allyn & Bacon.

Crosson-Tower, C. (2004). *Exploring child welfare: A practice perspective* (3rd ed.). Boston: Allyn & Bacon.

Crosson-Tower, C. (2005). *Understanding child abuse and neglect* (6th ed.). Boston: Allyn & Bacon.

Cummerton, J. M. (1986). A feminist perspective on research: What does it help us see? In N. Van Den Bergh & L. B. Cooper (Eds.), *Feminist visions for social work* (pp. 80–100). Washington, DC: NASW Press.

Cummings, S. M., & Jackson, D. R. (2000). Hospital discharge planning. In R. L. Schneider, N. P. Kropf, & A. J. Kisor (Eds.), *Gerontological social work: Knowledge, service settings, and special populations* (2nd ed., pp. 191–224). Pacific Grove, CA: Brooks/Cole.

Curiel, H. (1995). Hispanics: Mexican Americans. In R. L. Edwards (Ed.), *Encyclopedia of social work* (19th ed., Vol. 2, pp. 1233–1244). Washington, DC: NASW Press.

Daley, M. R., & Avant, F. L. (2004). Rural social work: Reconceptualizing the framework for practice. In T. L. Scales & C. L. Streeter (Eds.), *Rural social work: Building and sustaining community assets* (pp. 34–41). Belmont, CA: Brooks/Cole.

Daro, D., & Donnelly, A. C. (2002). Child abuse prevention: Accomplishments and challenges. In J. E. B. Myers, L. Berliner, J. Briere, C. T. Hendrix, C. Jenny, & T. A. Reid (Eds.), *The APSAC handbook on child maltreatment* (2nd ed., pp. 431–448). Thousand Oaks, CA: Sage.

Davenport, J. A., & Davenport, III, J. (1995). Rural social work overview. In R. L. Edwards (Ed.), *Encyclopedia of social work* (19th ed., Vol. 3, pp. 2076–2085). Washington, DC: NASW Press.

Davtyan, C. (2000). Contraception for adolescents. *Western Journal of Medicine, 172,* 166–171.

Day, P. (2000). *A new history of social welfare* (3rd ed.). Boston: Allyn & Bacon.

DeCesare, D. (1993, March). El Salvador: War, poverty and migration: A photo essay. *Fellowship, 59,* 3.

DeLeon, G. (1994). Therapeutic communities. In M. Galanter & H. D. Kleber (Eds.), *Textbook of substance abuse treatment*. Washington, DC: American Psychiatric Press.

Delgado, M. (1998). Community asset assessments by Latino youth. In P. L. Ewalt, E. M. Freeman, & D. L. Poole (Eds.), *Community building: Renewal, well-being, and shared responsibility* (pp. 202–212). Washington, DC: NASW Press.

Delgado, M., & Barton, K. (1999). Murals in Latino communities: Social indicators of community strengths. In P. L. Ewalt, E. M. Freeman, A. E. Fortune, D. L. Poole, & S. L. Witkin (Eds.), *Multicultural issues in social work: Practice and research* (pp. 229–244). Washington, DC: NASW Press.

Dembling, B. (1995). Colonial family care. *Psychiatric Services, 46* (2).

Department of Veterans Affairs. (1994). *Annual report of the Secretary of Veterans Affairs: Fiscal year 1993*. Washington, DC: Author.

DePoy, E., & Gilson, S. F. (2004). *Rethinking disability: Principles for professional and social change*. Belmont, CA: Brooks/Cole.

Devore, W. (2001). "Whence came these people?": An exploration of the values and ethics of African American individuals, families, and communities. In R. Fong & S. Furuto (Eds.), *Culturally competent practice: Skills, interventions, and evaluations* (pp. 33–46, 132–146). Boston: Allyn & Bacon.

Dewar, H. (2004, July 15). Senate blocks amendment on gay marriage. *Milwaukee Journal Sentinel,* 1A, 17A.

DeWeaver, K. L. (1995). Developmental disabilities: Definitions and policies. In R. L. Edwards (Ed.), *Encyclopedia of social work* (19th ed., Vol. 1, pp. 712–720). Washington, DC: NASW Press.

Dey, A. M. (1997). *Characteristics of elderly nursing home residents: Data from the 1995 National Nursing Home Survey. Advance data from vital and health statistics,* no. 289. Hyattsville, MD: National Center for Health Statistics.

Dhooper, S. S. (1997). *Social work in health care in the 21st century*. Thousand Oaks, CA: Sage.

Dhooper, S. S., & Moore, S. E. (2001). *Social work practice with culturally diverse people*. Thousand Oaks, CA: Sage.

Dickerson, J. F. (2003, December 1). Can we afford all this? *Time,* 48–51.

Dickinson, N. S. (1997). Federal social legislation from 1994–1997. In R. L. Edwards (Ed.), *Encyclopedia of social work:* Supplement 1997. (19th ed., pp. 125–131). Washington, DC: NASW Press.

DiIulio, J. (1999, Winter). Federal crime policy: Time for a moratorium. *Brookings Review, 17* (1), 17.

Diller, J. V. (1999). *Cultural diversity: A primer for the human services*. Pacific Grove, CA: Brooks/Cole.

Diller, J. V. (2004). *Cultural diversity: A primer for the human services* (2nd ed.). Pacific Grove, CA: Brooks/Cole.

DiNitto, D. M. (2005). *Social welfare: Politics and public policy* (6th ed.). Boston: Allyn & Bacon.

Dobelstein, A. W. (2003). *Social welfare policy and analysis* (3rd ed.). Pacific Grove, CA: Brooks/Cole.

Docter, R. F. (1988). *Transvestites and transsexuals: Mixed views*. Los Angeles, CA: Delacorte.

Dolgoff, R., & Feldstein, D. (2003). *Understanding social welfare* (6th ed.). Boston: Allyn & Bacon.

Dolgoff, R., Feldstein, D., & Skolnik, L. (1997). *Understanding social welfare* (4th ed.). New York: Longman.

Dolgoff, R., Loewenberg, F. M., & Harrington, D. (2005). *Ethical decisions for social work practice* (7th ed.). Pacific Grove, CA: Brooks/Cole.

Doweiko, H. E. (2002). *Concepts of chemical dependency*. Pacific Grove, CA: Brooks/Cole.

Downey, E. P., & Jackson, R. L. (2000). *Contemporary film applications in social work education: Bridging classroom and practice*. Paper presented at the Meeting of the Association of Baccalaureate Program Directors, Dallas, TX.

Downs, S. W., Costin, L. B., & McFadden, E. J. (1996). *Child welfare and family services: Policies and practice* (5th ed.). White Plains, NY: Longman.

Downs, S. W., Moore, E., McFadden, E. J., Michaud, S. M., & Costin, L. B. (2004). *Child welfare and family services: Policies and practice* (7th ed.). Boston: Allyn & Bacon.

Doyal, L. (1995). *What makes women sick: Gender and the political economy of health*. New Brunswick, NJ: Rutgers University Press.

Drum, J., & Howard, G. (1989, January). *Multicultural and global education: Seeking common ground* (Summary). Paper presented at a conference cosponsored by Las Palomas de Taos, REACH Center for Multicultural and Global Education, and the Stanley Foundation, Taos, NM.

Dunkle, R. E., & Norgard, T. (1995). Aging overview. In R. L. Edwards (Ed.), *Encyclopedia of social work* (19th ed., Vol. 1, pp. 142–153). Washington, DC: NASW Press.

Dunn, P. C. (2000). In A. A. Abbott (Ed.), *Alcohol, tobacco, and other drugs: Challenging myths, assessing theories, individualizing interventions* (pp. 74–110). Washington, DC: NASW Press.

DuongTran, Q., & Matsuoka, J. K. (1995). Asian-Americans: Southeast Asians. In R. L. Edwards (Ed.), *Encyclopedia of social work* (19th ed., Vol. 1, pp. 249–255). Washington, DC: NASW Press.

Dupper, D. R. (2000). The design of social work services. In P. Allen-Meares, R. O. Washington, & B. L. Welsh (Eds.), *Social work services in schools* (3rd ed., pp. 243–272). Boston: Allyn & Bacon.

Dworkin, S. H. (2000). Individual therapy with lesbian, gay, and bisexual clients. In R. M. Perez, K. A. DeBord, & K. J. Bieschke (Eds.), *Handbook of counseling and psychotherapy with lesbian, gay, and bisexual clients* (pp. 157–181). Washington, DC: American Psychological Association.

Earle, K. A. (1999). Cultural diversity and mental health: The Haudenosaunee of New York State. In P. L. Ewalt, E. M. Freeman, A. E. Fortune, D. L. Poole, & S. L. Witkin (Eds.), *Multicultural issues in social work: Practice and research* (pp. 423–438). Washington, DC: NASW Press.

Edinburg, G. M., & Cottler, J. M. (1995). Managed care. In R. L. Edwards (Ed.), *Encyclopedia of social work* (19th ed., Vol. 2, pp. 1635–1642). Washington, DC: NASW Press.

Edwards, E. D., & Edwards, M. E. (2002). Social work practice with American Indians and Alaskan Natives. In A. T. Morales & B. W. Sheafor (Eds.), *The many faces of social work clients* (pp. 239–265). Boston: Allyn & Bacon.

Egley, A., Jr., & Arjunan, M. (2002). *Highlights of the 2000 national youth gang survey: Facts sheet*. U.S. Department of Justice, Office of Justice Programs, Office of Juvenile Justice and Delinquency Prevention. Washington, DC: Department of Justice.

Einbinder, S. D. (1995). Policy analysis. In R. L. Edwards (Ed.), *Encyclopedia of social work* (19th ed., Vol. 3, pp. 1849–1855). Washington, DC: NASW Press.

Eitzen, D. S., & Zinn, M. B. (2003). *Social problems* (9th ed.). Boston: Allyn & Bacon.

Electroshock therapy slowly gains greater use in the treatment of mental illness. (2000, March–April). *American Scientist*. Retrieved April 27, 2002. www.signaxi.org/news&events/ArchivesAmsci/0003summary.htm

Epstein, L. (1981). Advocates on advocacy: An exploratory study. *Social work research and abstracts, 17* (2), 5–12.

Equal Employment Opportunity Commission, U.S. Department of Justice Civil Rights Division. (1997, May). *The Americans with Disabilities Act: Questions and answers*. Washington, DC: Author.

Esbensen, F. (2000). *Preventing adolescent gang involvement*. Youth Gang Series Bulletin. Bulletin of the Office of Justice Programs. Washington, DC: U.S. Department of Justice, Office of Juvenile Justice and Delinquency Prevention.

Essock, S. M., & Goldman, H. H. (1995). Embrace of managed mental health care. *Health Affairs, 14,* 34–44.

Ewalt, P. L., & Mokuau, N. (1996). Self-determination from a Pacific perspective. In P. L. Ewalt, M. Freeman, A. E. Fortune, D. L. Poole, & S. L. Witkin (Eds.), *Multicultural issues in social work: Practice and research* (pp. 225–268). Washington, DC: NASW Press.

Facts about upcoming new benefits in Medicare (n.d.). Retrieved January 9, 2005. http://medicare.gov

Familydoctor.org. (2003, March). *Depression: Electroconvulsive therapy*. Retrieved January 30, 2005. http://familydoctor.org/058.sml?printxml

Fang, B. (2001, September 3). On the trail of a killer. *U.S. News & World Report*, 22–26.

Fatout, M., & Rose, S. R. (1995). *Task groups in the social services*. Thousand Oaks, CA: Sage.

Federal Bureau of Investigation (FBI). (2005, February 5). *Uniform crime reports: Table 1: Crime in the United States*. Retrieved February 5, 2005. www.fbi.gov.ucr/cius_03/xl/03bt/01.x/s

Federal Trade Commission. (1999, June). *Home-use tests for HIV can be inaccurate, FTC warns*. Retrieved January 29, 2005. http://www.ftc.gov/bcp/conline/pubs/alerts/hivalrt.htm

Fellin, P. (1995). *The community and the social worker*. Itasca, IL: Peacock.

Fellin, P. (1996). *Mental health and mental illness: Policies, programs, and services.* Itasca, IL: Peacock.

FindLaw for the Public. (2002). *What is the difference between a felony and a misdemeanor?* Retrieved February 5, 2005. http://criminal.findlaw.com/articles/1382.html

FindLaw Legal News and Commentary. (2005). *Evidence shows longstanding Enron scams.* Retrieved February 5, 2005. http://news.findlaw.com/ap_stories/f/1310/2-3-2005/20050203151127_17.html

Finn, J., & Smith, M. (1997). The use of the world wide web by undergraduate social work education programs. *The Journal of Baccalaureate Social Work, 3* (1), 71–84.

Fiske, H. (2002, September 16). A youth violence assessment tool: Can we predict problems? *Social Work Today,* 13–15.

Fiske, H. (2002, November 11). Adolescent group therapy: Not just hearing, listening, too. *Social Work Today, 2* (23), 16–18.

Food and Drug Administration. (2003, April 4). *Frequently asked questions about the OraQuick Rapid HIV-1 Antibody Test.* Retrieved January 23, 2005. http://www.fda.gov/cber/faq/oraqckfaq.htm

Food and Nutrition Board. (2002). *Dietary assessment in the WIC program.* Washington, DC: Institute of Medicine.

Food & Nutrition Service (FNS), U. S. Department of Agriculture. (2003, September 29). *About WIC.* Retrieved January 7, 2005. http://www.fns.usda.gov/wic/aboutwic/default.htm

FOXNews. (2005, January 7). *Time for Social Security reform.* Retrieved January 8, 2005. http://www.foxnews.com/printer_friendly_story/0,3566,143733,00.html

Frame, M. W. (2003). *Integrating religion and spirituality into counseling: A comprehensive approach.* Pacific Grove, CA: Brooks/Cole.

Franklin, C. (2004). The delivery of school social work services. In P. Allen-Meares (Ed.), *Social work services in schools* (4th ed., pp. 295–325). Boston: Allyn & Bacon.

Fred, S. (2004, October 24). Social workers vie for federal office. *NASW News,* 11.

Freedman, R. I. (1995). Developmental disabilities: Direct practice. In R. L. Edwards (Ed.), *Encyclopedia of social work* (19th ed., Vol. 1, pp. 721–729). Washington, DC: NASW Press.

Fung, M. T. (2001, October 4). The effect of war on American soil: Reports of anti-Muslim prejudice echo an earlier tragedy. *The Christian Science Monitor,* 21. Retrieved July 9, 2004. http://infotrac-college.thomsonlearning.com

Furstenberg, F., & Crawford, A. (1978). Family support: Helping teenage mothers to cope. *Family Planning Perspectives, 10,* 322–333.

Gambrill, E. (2000). The role of critical thinking in evidence-based social work. In P. Allen-Meares & C. Garvin (Eds.), *The handbook of social work direct practice* (pp. 43–64). Thousand Oaks, CA: Sage.

Gans, H. J. (1971). The uses of poverty: The poor pay all. *Social Policy, 2,* 21–23.

Garvin, C. D., & Cox, F. M. (1995). A history of community organizing since the Civil War with special reference to oppressed communities. In J. Rothman, J. L. Erlich, & J. E. Tropman (Eds.), *Strategies of community intervention* (pp. 64–69). Itasca, IL: Peacock.

Garvin, C. D., & Tropman, J. E. (1998). *Social work in contemporary society* (2nd ed.). Boston: Allyn & Bacon.

Geary, B. B. (1992). Individual treatment of depression using cognitive therapy. In C. W. Lecroy (Ed.), *Case studies in social work practice.* Belmont, CA: Wadsworth.

George, J. (1997). Global graying. In M. C. Hokenstad & J. Midgley (Eds.), *Issues in international social work: Global challenges in a new century* (pp. 57–73). Washington, DC: NASW Press.

Gibbons, M., & Vincent, C. (1994). Childhood sexual abuse. *American Family Physican, 49,* 125–137.

Gibbs, J. T., & Huang, L. N. (1998). *Children of color: Psychological interventions with culturally diverse youth.* San Francisco: Jossey-Bass.

Gibbs, L., & Gambrill, E. (1999). *Critical thinking for social workers: Exercises for the helping profession* (rev. ed.). Thousand Oaks, CA: Pine Forge.

Gibbs, L., Gambrill, E., Blakemore, J., Begun, A., Keniston, A., Peden, B., & Lefcowitz, J. (1994). *A measure of critical thinking about practice.* Unpublished paper presented at the Fall Conference of the Wisconsin Council on Social Work Education, Stevens Point, WI.

Gibelman, M. (1995). *What social workers do.* Washington, DC: NASW Press.

Gibelman, M. (2003). So how far have we come? Pestilent and persistent gender gap in pay. *Social Work, 48* (1), 22–32.

Gil, R. M., & Vazquez, C. I. (1996). *The Maria paradox.* New York: Perigee.

Gilbert, N., & Terrell, P. (2002). *Dimensions of social welfare policy* (5th ed.). Boston: Allyn & Bacon.

Gilbert, N., & Terrell, P. (2005). *Dimensions of social welfare policy* (6th ed.). Boston: Allyn & Bacon.

Gilson, S. F., Bricout, J. C., & Baskind, F. R. (1998). Listening to the voices of people with disabilities. *Families in Society: The Journal of Contemporary Human Services, 79* (2), 188–202.

Ginsberg, L. H. (2001). *Careers in social work* (2nd ed.). Boston: Allyn & Bacon.

Glenmaye, L. (1998). Empowerment of women. In L. M. Gutierrez, R. J. Parsons, & E. O. Cox (Eds.), *Empowerment in social work practice: A sourcebook* (pp. 29–51). Pacific Grove, CA: Brooks/Cole.

Goldberg, B. (2000). Age works. In R. L. Edwards (Ed.), *Encyclopedia of social work* (19th ed., Vol. 2, pp. 1747–1764). Washington, DC: NASW Press.

Golden Ink. (1997). *The trail of tears.* Retrieved November 20, 2004. http://ngeorgia.com/history/nghisttt.html.

Goldenberg, H., & Goldenberg, I. (2002). *Counseling today's families* (4th ed.). Pacific Grove, CA: Brooks/Cole.

Goldstein, S. R., & Beebe, L. (1995). National Association of Social Workers. In R. L. Edwards (Editor-in-Chief), *Encyclopedia of social work* (19th ed., Vol. 1, pp. 1747–1764). Washington, DC: NASW Press.

Gomory, T. (1997). Mental health services. In M. Reisch & E. Gambrill (Eds.), *Social work in the 21st century* (pp. 163–174). Thousand Oaks, CA: Pine Forge.

Gotterer, R. (2001). The spiritual dimension in clinical social work practice: A client perspective. *Families in Society, 82* (20), 187–193.

Government hiring fewer disabled than a decade ago. (2004, July 11). *Milwaukee Journal Sentinel,* 22A.

Gray, M. (1995). African Americans. In J. Philleo & F. L. Brisbane (Eds.), *Cultural competence for social workers: A guide for alcohol and other drug abuse prevention professionals working with ethnic/racial communities.* Washington, DC: U.S. Department of Health and Human Services, 69–101.

Graybeal, C. (2001). Strengths-based social work assessment: Transforming the dominant paradigm. *Families in Society,* 82 (3), 233–242.

Green, J. W. (1999). *Cultural awareness in the human services: A multi-ethnic approach* (3rd ed.). Boston: Allyn & Bacon.

Greene, R. R. (2000). *Social work with the aged and their families* (2nd ed.). New York: Aldine de Gruyter.

Greene, R. R., & Livingston, N. C. (2002). A social construct. In R. R. Green (Ed.), *Resiliency: An integrated approach to practice, policy, and research* (pp. 63–93). Washington, DC: NASW Press.

Griner, D. (2002, April 7). Electroshock therapy emerges from disrepute. *The Journal Gazette.* Retrieved April 27, 2002. www.fortwayne.com/mld/journalgazette/3017094.htm

Grotevant, H., & McRoy, R. G. (1998). *Openness in adoption: Exploring family connections.* Thousand Oaks, CA: Sage.

Guidry, H. (1995). Childhood sexual abuse: Role of the family physician. *American Family Physician, 51,* 407–414.

Gushue, G. V., & Sciarra, D. T. (1995). Culture and families: A multidimensional approach. In J. G. Ponterotto, J. M. Casas, L. A. Suzuki, & C. M. Alexander (Eds.), *Handbook of multicultural counseling* (2nd ed., pp. 586–606). Thousand Oaks, CA: Sage.

Gutierrez, L. M. (1990). Working with women of color: An empowerment perspective. *Social Work, 35* (2), 149–153.

Gutierrez, L. M. (2001). Working with women of color: An empowerment perspective. In J. Rothman, J. L. Erlich, & J. E. Tropman (Eds.), *Strategies of community intervention* (6th ed., pp. 209–217). Itasca, IL: Peacock.

Gutierrez, L. M., & Lewis, E. A. (1998). A feminist perspective on organizing women of color. In F. G. Rivera & J. L. Erlich (Eds.), *Community organizing in a diverse society* (3rd ed., pp. 97–116). Needham Heights, MA: Allyn & Bacon.

Haberman, F. W. (Ed.). (1972). Jane Addams—Biography. In F. W. Haberman (Ed.), *Nobel Lecture, Peace 1926–1950.* Amsterdam: Elsevier. Retrieved June 14, 2005. http://nobelprize.org/peace/laureates/1931/addams-bio.html

Haight, W. L. (1998, May). "Gathering the spirit" at First Baptist Church: Spirituality as a protective factor in the lives of African American children. *Social Work, 43* (3), 123–221.

Hallahan, D. P., & Kauffman, J. M. (2000). *Exceptional children: Introduction to special education* (2nd ed.). Boston: Allyn & Bacon.

Hallahan, D. P., & Kauffman, J. M. (2003). *Exceptional learners: Introduction to special education* (9th ed.). Boston: Allyn & Bacon.

Halley, A. A., Kopp, J., & Austin, M. J. (1992). *Delivering human services: A learning approach to practice* (4th ed.). New York: Longman.

Halley, A. A., Kopp, J., & Austin, M. J. (1998). *Delivering human services: A learning approach to practice* (5th ed.). New York: Longman.

Hamilton College. (2002, May 20). Hamilton College Muslim America poll: Accounts of anti-Muslim discrimination not exaggerated. *Ascribe Higher Education New Service,* p. NA. Retrieved July 13, 2004. http://infotrac-college.thomsonlearning.com

Hammond, W., & Yung, B. (1991). Preventing violence in at-risk African American youth. *Journal of Health Care for the Poor and Underserved, 2,* 358–372.

Hammond, W., & Yung, B. (1993). Psychology's role in the public health response to assaultive violence among young African-American men. *American Psychologist, 48,* 142–154.

Hancock, M. R., & Millar, K. I. (1993). *Cases for intervention planning: A source book.* Chicago: Nelson-Hall.

Haney, P. (1988, May–June). Comments on currents: Providing empowerment to persons with AIDS. *Social Work, 33* (3), 251–253.

Hanlon, J., & Pickett, G. (1984). *Public health administration and practice.* St. Louis, MO: Times Mirror/Mosby.

Harjo, S. S. (1993). The American Indian experience. In H. P. McAdoo (Ed.), *Family ethnicity: Strength in diversity.* Newbury Park, CA: Sage.

Harras, A. (1987). *Issues in adolescent Indian health: Suicide* (Division of Medical Systems Research and Development Monograph Series). Washington, DC: U.S. Department of Health and Human Services.

Harrigan, M. P., & Farmer, R. L. (2000). The myths and facts about aging. In R. L. Schneider, N. P. Kropf, & A. J. Kisor (Eds.), *Gerontological social work: Knowledge, service settings, and special populations* (2nd ed., pp. 26–64). Pacific Grove, CA: Brooks/Cole.

Harris, H., et al. (1986). *American teens speak: Sex, myths, TV and birth control: The Planned Parenthood poll.* New York: Planned Parenthood Federation of America.

Harrison, W. D. (1995). Community development. In R. L. Edwards (Ed.), *Encyclopedia of social work* (19th ed., Vol. 1, pp. 555–562). Washington, DC: NASW Press.

Hart, S. N., Brassard, M. R., Karlson, H. C. (1996). Psychological maltreatment. In J. Briere, L. Berliner, J. A. Bulkley, J. Carole, & T. Reid (Eds.), *The APSAC handbook on child maltreatment* (pp. 72–89). Thousand Oaks, CA: Sage.

Hartman, A., & Laird, I. (1990). Family treatment after adoption: Common themes. In D. M. Brodzinsky & M. D. Schechter (Eds.), *The psychology of adoption* (pp. 221–239). New York: Oxford University Press.

Harvey, A. R. (1997). Group work with African American youth in the criminal justice system: A culturally competent model. In G. L. Greif & P. H. Ephross (Eds.), *Group work with populations at risk* (pp. 160–174). New York: Oxford University Press.

Hatcher, R. A., Trussel, J., Stewart, F., Cates, W., Jr., Stewart, G. K., Guest, F., & Kowal, D. (1998). *Contraceptive technology* (17th ed.). New York: Ardent Media.

Haynes, J. (1991). *Sleepwalking through history: America in the Reagan years.* New York: Norton.

Haynes, K. S., & Mickelson, J. S. (2003). *Affecting change: Social workers in the political arena* (5th ed.). Boston: Allyn & Bacon.

Hayward, C., & Collier, J. A. (1996). Anxiety disorders. In H. Steiner (Ed.), *Treating adolescents* (pp. 187–221). San Francisco: Jossey-Bass.

Health Care Financing Administration. (1998). *The Clinton administration's comprehensive strategy to fight health care fraud, waste, and abuse.* www.hcfa.gov/facts/ f980316.htm

Health Care Financing Administration. (2000). *Medicare.* www.hcfa.gov/medicare/medicare/htm

Hellenbrand, S. (1987). Termination in direct practice. In A. Minahan (Ed.), *Encyclopedia of social work* (Vol. 2, pp. 765–770). Silver Spring, MD: NASW Press.

Henderson, C. (2002). *What is electroshock therapy?* Retrieved April 27, 2002. ky.essortment.com/whatiselec troc_riek.htm

Henley, J. R., & Danziger, S. K. (1997). Confronting welfare stereotypes: Characteristics of general assistance recipients and postassistance employment. In P. W. Ewalt, E. M. Freeman, S. A. Kirk, & D. L. Poole (Eds.), *Social policy reform research and practice* (pp. 124–139). Washington, DC: NASW Press.

Hepworth, D. H., Rooney, R. H., & Larsen, J. A. (2002). *Direct social work practice: Theory and skills* (6th ed.). Pacific Grove, CA: Brooks/Cole.

Herring, R. D. (1999). *Counseling with Native American Indians and Alaska natives: Strategies for helping professionals.* Thousand Oaks, CA: Sage.

Hershberger, S. L., & D'Augelli, A. R. (2000). Issues in counseling lesbian, gay, and bisexual adolescents. In R. M. Perez, K. A. DeBord, & K. J. Bieschke (Eds.), *Handbook of counseling and psychotherapy with lesbian, gay, and bisexual clients* (pp. 225–247). Washington, DC: American Psychological Association.

Hewlett, J. (1998, December 23). Kentucky art teacher was "Sybil," scholar confirms. *Detroit Free Press.* Retrieved April 27, 2002. www.asarian.org/~quiet/sybildfp.html

Ho, M. K. (1987). *Family therapy with ethnic minorities.* Newbury Park, CA: Sage.

Ho, M. K. (1992). *Minority children and adolescents in therapy.* Thousand Oaks, CA: Sage.

Hodge, J. L., Struckmann, D. K., & Trost, L. D. (1975). *Cultural bases of racism and group oppression.* Berkeley, CA: Two Riders Press.

Hoffman, K., & Sallee, A. (1993). *Social work practice: Bridges to change.* Needham Heights, MA; Allyn & Bacon.

Hokenstad, M. C., & Midgley, J. (1997). Realities of global interdependence: Challenges for social work in a new century. In M. B. Hokenstad & J. Midgley (Eds.), *Issues in international social work: Global challenges for a new century* (pp. 1–10). Washington, DC: NASW Press.

Homan, M. S. (2004). *Promoting community change: Making it happen in the real world* (3rd ed.). Pacific Grove, CA: Brooks/Cole.

Homestead Schools, Inc. (2004, September). *Continuing education courses for social workers, counselors, and marriage family therapists.* Torrance, CA: Author.

Hooyman, N. R., & Kiyak, H. A. (1999). *Social gerontology: A multidisciplinary perspective* (2nd ed.). Boston: Allyn & Bacon.

Housing and Urban Development (HUD), U.S. Department of. (2004, April 8). *Public housing development.* Retrieved January 14, 2005. http://www.hud.gov/progdesc/pdev.cfm

Howard, M. O., & Jenson, J. M. (1999). Causes of youth violence. In J. M. Jenson & M. O. Howard (Eds.), *Youth violence: Current research and recent practice innovations* (pp. 19–42). Washington, DC: NASW Press.

Hu, T. W., Snowden, L. R., Jerrell, J. M., & Nguyen, T. D. (1991). Ethnic populations in public mental health: Services choice and level of use. *American Journal of Public Health, 81,* 1429–1434.

Huber, R., & Orlando, B. P. (1995). Persisting gender differences in social workers' incomes: Does the profession really care? *Social Work, 40* (5), 585–591.

Huff, C. R. (1993). Gangs in the United States. In A. P. Goldstein & C. R. Huff (Eds.), *The gang intervention handbook* (pp. 3–20). Champaign, IL: Research Press.

Human Rights Watch. 2000. *Human rights watch world report 2000: United States.* www.hrw.org/wr2k/us.html

Hunter, J., & Schaecher, R. (1995). Gay and lesbian adolescents. In R. L. Edwards (Ed.), *Encyclopedia of social work* (19th ed., Vol. 2, pp. 1055–1063). Washington, DC: NASW Press.

Hyde, J. S., & DeLamater, J. D. (2003). *Understanding human sexuality* (8th ed.). Boston: McGraw-Hill.

Iatridis, D. S. (1995). Policy practice. In R. L. Edwards (Ed.), *Encyclopedia of social work* (19th ed., Vol. 3, pp. 1855–1866). Washington, DC: NASW Press.

Info-Prod (Middle East) Ltd. (2003, July 17). USA: CAIR report sees sharp rise in anti-Muslim discrimination. *IPR Strategic Business Information Database,* P. NA. Retrieved July 13, 2004. http://infotrac-college.thomsonlearning.com

Institute for Research on Poverty. (2001, Spring). Cash for kids in four countries: Child benefits in Australia, Canada, the United Kingdom, and the United States. *Focus, 21* (3), 44–49.

Ip, G. (2004, December 19). Social Security: Five burning questions. *The Milwaukee Journal Sentinel,* 3D.

Ivey, A. E., & Ivey, M. B. (2003). *Intentional interviewing and counseling: Facilitating client development in a multicultural society* (5th ed.). Pacific Grove, CA: Brooks/Cole.

Jane Addams Hull House Museum. (1997, February). *Biographical sketch of Jane Addams.* Retrieved June 14, 2005. http://www.uic.edu/jaddams/hull/ja_bio.html

Jansson, B. S. (2001). *The reluctant welfare state.* Belmont, CA: Wadsworth.

Jansson, B. S. (2003). *Becoming an effective policy advocate: From policy practice to social justice* (4th ed.). Pacific Grove, CA: Brooks/Cole.

Jansson, B. S. (2005). *The reluctant welfare state: American social welfare policies: Past, present, and future* (5th ed.). Belmont, CA: Brooks/Cole.

Jenson, J. M., & Howard, M. O. (1999). Prevalence and patterns of youth violence. In J. M. Jenson & M. O. Howard (Eds.), *Youth violence: Current research and recent practice innovations* (pp. 3–18). Washington, DC: NASW Press.

Johannesen, T. (1997). Social work as an international profession. In M. C. Hokenstad & J. Midgley (Eds.), *Issues in international social work: Global challenges for a new century.* Washington, DC: NASW Press.

Johnson, H. W. (1998a). Basic concepts: Social welfare, social work, and social services. In H. W. Johnson, *The social services: An introduction* (5th ed., pp. 13–30). Itasca, IL: Peacock.

Johnson, H. W. (1998b). Professionalization, education, and personnel in the social services. In H. W. Johnson, *The Social services: An introduction* (5th ed., pp. 451–465). Itasca, IL: Peacock.

Johnson, J. L. (2004). *Fundamentals of substance abuse practice.* Pacific Grove, CA: Brooks/Cole.

Johnson, K., Noe, T., Collins, D., Strader, T., & Bucholtz, G. (2000). Mobilizing church communities to prevent alcohol and other drug abuse: A model strategy and its evaluation. *Journal of Community Practice, 7* (2), 1–27.

Johnson, M. (2002, February 1). Fetuses may qualify for federal aid. *Milwaukee Journal Sentinel,* A1.

Johnston, S. (1987, February). The mind of the molester. *Psychology Today,* 60–63.

Jones, L. R. W. (1995). Unemployment Compensation and Workers' Compensation. In R. L. Edwards (Ed.), *Encyclopedia of social work* (19th ed., Vol. 3, pp. 2413–2417). Washington, DC: NASW Press.

Kadushin, A., & Martin, J. A. (1988). *Child welfare services* (4th ed.). New York: Macmillan.

Kail, R. V., & Cavanaugh, J. C. (2004). *Human development: A life-span view* (3rd ed.). Belmont, CA: Wadsworth.

Kamya, H. A. (1999). African immigrants in the United States: The challenge for research and practice. In P. L. Ewalt, M. Freeman, A. E. Fortune, D. L. Poole, & S. L. Witkin (Eds.), *Multicultural issues in social work: Practice and research* (pp. 605–621). Washington, DC: NASW Press.

Kane, R. A. (1987). Long-term care. In A. Minahan (Ed.), *Encyclopedia of social work* (Vol. 2, pp. 59–72). Silver Spring, MD: NASW Press.

Kann, L., Kinchen, S. A., Williams, B. I., Ross, J. G., Lowry, R., Grunbaum, J. A., Kolbe, L. J., & State and Local YRBSS Coordinators. (2000). Youth risk behavior surveillance—United States, 1999. *Journal of School Health, 70* (7), 271–285.

Kanter, J. S. (1985). Case management of the young adult chronic patient: A clinical perspective. In J. S. Kanter (Ed.), *Clinical issues in treating the chronic mentally ill.* San Francisco: Jossey-Bass.

Karenga, M. (1965). *Kwanzaa: Origin, concepts and practice.* Los Angeles: Kawaida Publications.

Karenga, M. (2000). Making the past meaningful: Kwanzaa and the concept of sankofa. In S. L. Abels (Ed.), *Spirituality in social work practice: Narratives for professional helping* (pp. 51–67). Denver, CO: Love.

Karger, H. J., & Stoesz, D. (1998). *American social welfare policy: A pluralist approach* (3rd ed.). New York: Longman.

Karger, H. J., & Stoesz, D. (2002). *American social welfare policy: A pluralist approach* (4th ed.). Boston: Allyn & Bacon.

Kasee, C. R. (1995). Identity, recovery and religious imperialism: Native American women and the New Age. In J. Ochshorn & Cole (Eds.), *Women's spirituality, women's lives* (pp. 83–93). Binghamton, NY: Haworth.

Kelly, G. F. (2001). *Sexuality today: The human perspective* (7th ed.). Boston: McGraw-Hill.

Kelly, G. F. (2004). *Sexuality today: The human perspective* (7th ed.). Boston: McGraw-Hill.

Kelly, L. W. (2002, Summer). So you want to practice in mental health! *The New Social Worker,* 4–6.

Kendall, D. (2004). *Social problems in a diverse society* (3rd ed.). Boston: Allyn & Bacon.

Kenyon, P. (1999). *What would you do? An ethical case workbook for human service professionals.* Pacific Grove, CA: Brooks/Cole.

King v. King, 392 U.S. 309 (1968).

Kingery-McCabe, L. B., & Frances, A. C. (1991). Effects of addiction on the addict. In D. C. Daley & M. S. Raskin (Eds.), *Treating the chemically dependent and their families* (pp. 57–78). Newbury Park, CA: Sage.

Kirk, G., & Okazawa-Rey, M. (2004). *Women's lives: Multicultural perspectives* (2nd ed.). Boston: McGraw-Hill.

Kirst-Ashman, K. K. (1992, Summer). Feminist values and social work: A model for educating nonfeminists. *Arete, 17* (1), 13–25.

Kirst-Ashman, K. K., & Hull, G. H., Jr. (1999). *Understanding generalist practice* (2nd ed.). Pacific Grove, CA: Brooks/Cole.

Kirst-Ashman, K. K., & Hull, G. H., Jr. (2001). *Generalist practice with organizations and communities* (2nd ed.). Pacific Grove, CA: Brooks/Cole.

Kirst-Ashman, K. K., & Hull, G. H., Jr. (2002). *Understanding generalist practice* (3rd ed.). Pacific Grove, CA: Brooks/Cole.

Kirst-Ashman, K. K., & Hull, G. H., Jr. (2002). *Understanding generalist practice* (3rd ed.). Pacific Grove, CA: Brooks/Cole.

Kirst-Ashman, K. K., & Hull, G. H., Jr. (2006). *Understanding generalist practice* (4th ed.). Pacific Grove, CA: Brooks/Cole.

Kiselica, M. S., Changizi, J. C., Cureton, V. L. L., & Gridley, B. E. (1995). Counseling children and adolescents in schools: Salient multicultural issues. In J. G. Ponterotto, J. M. Cases, L. A. Suzuki, & C. M. Alexander (Eds.), *Handbook of multicultural counseling* (pp. 516–532). Thousand Oaks, CA: Sage.

Kitano, H. H. L., & Maki, M. T. (1996). Continuity, change, and diversity: Counseling Asian Americans. In P. B. Pederson, J. G. Draguns, W. J. Lonner, & J. E. Trimble (Eds.), *Counseling across cultures* (4th ed., pp. 124–145). Thousand Oaks, CA: Sage.

Koch, G. (1979). Home-based support services: An alternative to residential placement for the developmentally disabled. In S. Maybanks & M. Bruce (Eds.), *Home-based services for children and families: Policy, practice, and research* (pp. 157–164). Springfield, IL: Thomas.

Kolb, P. J. (1999). A stage of migration approach to understanding nursing home placement in Latino families. *Journal of Multicultural Social Work, 7* (3/4), 95–112.

Kolko, D. J. (1996). Child physical abuse. In J. Briere, L. Berliner, J. A. Bulkly, J. Carole, & T. Reid (Eds.), *The APSAC handbook on child maltreatment* (pp. 21–50). Thousand Oaks, CA: Sage.

Kolko, D. J. (2002). Child physical abuse. In J. E. B. Myers, L. Berliner, J. Briere, C. T. Hendrix, C. Jenny, & T. A. Reid (Eds.), *The APSAC handbook on child maltreatment* (2nd ed., pp. 21–54). Thousand Oaks, CA: Sage.

Kopels, S. (1995). The Americans with Disabilities Act: A tool to combat poverty. *Journal of Social Work Education, 31* (3), 337–346.

Kornblum, W., & Julian, J. (2004). *Social problems* (11th ed.). Upper Saddle River, NJ: Prentice-Hall.

Kornblum, W., & Julian, J. (2001). *Social problems* (10th ed.). Upper Saddle River, NJ: Prentice-Hall.

Kretzmann, J. P., & McKnight, J. L. (1993). *Building communities from the inside out: A path toward finding and mobilizing a community's assets.* Chicago: ACTA Publications.

Kropf, N. P. (2000). Home health and community services. In R. L. Schneider, N. P. Kropf, & A. J. Kisor (Eds.), *Gerontological social work: Knowledge, service settings, and special populations* (pp. 167–190). Pacific Grove, CA: Brooks/Cole.

Kropf, N. P., & Hutchinson, E. D. (2000). Effective practice with elderly clients. In R. L. Schneider, N. P. Kropf, & A. J. Kisor (Eds.), *Gerontological social work: Knowledge, service settings, and special populations* (pp. 3–25). Pacific Grove, CA: Brooks/Cole.

Krout, J. (1994). Community size differences in senior center resources, programming, and participation. *Research on Aging, 16,* 440–462.

Kurtz, L. F. (2004). Support and self-help groups. In C. D. Garvin, L. M. Gutierrez, & M. J. Galinsky (Eds.), *Handbook of social work with groups* (pp. 139–159). New York: Guilford.

Lacayo, R. (2003, December 1). Popping the question. *Time, 46.*

LaFromboise, T. D., & Bigfoot, D. (1988). Cultural and cognitive considerations in the prevention of American Indian adolescent suicide. *Journal of Adolescence, 11,* 139–153.

Laird, J. (1995). Lesbians: Parenting. In R. L. Edwards (Ed.), *Encyclopedia of social work* (19th ed., Vol. 2, pp. 1604–1616). Washington, DC: NASW Press.

Land, H. (1995). Feminist clinical social work in the 21st century. In N. Van Den Bergh (Ed.), *Feminist practice in the 21st century* (pp. 3–19). Washington, DC: NASW Press.

Landon, P. S. (1995). Generalist and advanced generalist practice. In R. L. Edwards (Ed.), *Encyclopedia of social work* (19th ed., Vol. 2, pp. 1101–1108). Washington, DC: NASW Press.

Lawson, W. B., Hepler, N., Holladay, J., & Cuffel, B. (1994). Race as a factor in inpatient and outpatient admissions and diagnosis. *Hospital and Community Psychiatry, 45,* 72–74.

Leashore, B. R. (1995). African Americans overview. In R. L. Edwards (Ed.), *Encyclopedia of social work* (19th ed., Vol. 1, pp. 101–115). Washington, DC: NASW Press.

Ledoux, S., Choquet, M., & Manfredi, R. (1993). Associated factors for self-reported binge eating among male and female adolescents. *Journal of Adolescence, 16,* 75–91.

LeFrançois, G. R. (1999). *The lifespan* (6th ed.). Belmont, CA: Wadsworth.

Leiby, J. (1987). History of social welfare. In A. Minahan (Ed.), *Encyclopedia of social work* (Vol. 1, pp. 755–777). Silver Spring, MD: National Association of Social Workers.

Leininger, M. M. (1990). Historic and epistemologic dimensions of care and caring with future directions. In J. Stevenson (Ed.), *American academy of nursing* (pp. 19–31). Kansas City, MO: American Nurses Association Press.

Leininger, M. M. (1992). *Cultural care diversity and universality: A theory of nursing* (Pub. No. 15–2401). New York: National League for Nursing Press.

Lemonick, M. D. (2000, July 24). Little hope, less help. *Time,* 38–39.

Leon-Guerrero, A. (2005). *Social problems: Community, policy, and social action.* Thousand Oaks, CA: Pine Forge.

LeVine, E. S., & Sallee, A. L. (1999). *Child welfare: Clinical theory and practice.* Dubuque, IA: Eddie Bowers.

Levine, S. (2002, August 5). Criminal care at a high price. *U.S. News & World Report,* 44–45.

Lewis, E. A., & Suarez, Z. E. (1995). Natural helping networks. In R. L. Edwards (Ed.), *Encyclopedia of social work* (19th ed., Vol. 2, pp. 1765–1772). Washington, DC: NASW Press.

Lewis, J. A., Dana, R. Q., & Blevins, G. A. (2002). *Substance abuse counseling* (3rd ed.). Pacific Grove, CA: Brooks/Cole.

Lewis, O. (1965). *La vida.* New York: Random House.

Lewis, R. G. (1995). American Indians. In R. L. Edwards (Ed.), *Encyclopedia of social work* (19th ed., Vol. 1, pp. 216–225). Washington, DC: NASW Press.

Lexi-Comp, Inc. (2004). *HIV and AIDS treatment.* Retrieved January 29, 2005. http://www.diseases-explained.com/HIVandAIDS/hisaidstreatment.html

Library of Congress. (2004, May 14). *The Treaty of Guadalupe Hidalgo.* Retrieved November 20, 2004. http://www.loc.gov/exhibits/ghtreaty/

Licensure boosts profession, protects public. (2004, October). *NASW News,* p. 12.

Liederman, D. S. (1995). Child welfare overview. In R. L. Edwards (Ed.), *Encyclopedia of social work* (19th ed., Vol. 1, pp. 424–433). Washington, DC: NASW Press.

Lin, A. M. P. (1995). Mental health overview. In R. L. Edwards (Ed.), *Encyclopedia of social work* (19th ed., Vol. 2, pp. 1705–1711). Washington, DC: NASW Press.

Lindsey, D. (1994). *The welfare of children.* New York. Oxford University Press.

Link, R. J., Ramanathan, C. S., & Asamoah, Y. (1999). Understanding the human condition and human behavior in a global era. In C. S. Ramanathan & R. J. Link (Eds.). *All our futures: Principles and resources for social work practice in a global era* (pp. 30–51). Pacific Grove, CA: Brooks/Cole.

Linsley, J. (2003, Winter). Social work salaries: Keeping up with the times? *The New Social Worker, 10* (1), 7–8.

Local lady took Natex year ago—had good health ever since. (1935, May 27). *Morning Call* (Allentown, PA), p. 7.

Locke, D. C. (1998). *Increasing multicultural understanding: A comprehensive mode.* Thousand Oaks, CA: Sage.

Loewenberg, F. M., Dolgoff, R., & Harrington, D. (2000). *Ethical decisions for social work practice* (6th ed.). Itasca, IL: Peacock.

Lohmann, R. A. (1997). Managed care: A review of recent research. In R. L. Edwards (Ed.), *Encyclopedia of social work:* Supplement 1997 (19th ed., pp. 200–213). Washington, DC: NASW Press.

Longres, J. F. (1995a). Biographies: Richmond, Mary Ellen (1861–1928). In R. L. Edwards (Ed.), *Encyclopedia of social work* (19th ed., Vol. 3, p. 2605). Washington, DC: NASW Press.

Longres, J. F. (1995b). Hispanics overview. In R. L. Edwards (Ed.), *Encyclopedia of social work* (19th ed., Vol. 2, pp. 1214–1222). Washington, DC: NASW Press.

Longres, J. F. (2000). *Human behavior in the social environment* (3rd ed.). Itasca, IL: Peacock.

Loprest, P. J. (2003, August 21). *Fewer welfare leavers employed in weak economy.* Urban Institute. Retrieved January 12, 2005. http://www.urban.org/urlprint.cfm?ID=8550

Lorber, J. (2005). *Gender inequality: Feminist theories and politics* (3rd ed.). Los Angeles: Roxbury.

Lott, B. (1994). *Women's lives: Themes and variations in gender learning* (2nd ed.). pacific Grove, CA: Brooks/Cole.

Lowe, G. R. (1995). Social development. In R. L. Edwards (Ed.), *Encyclopedia of social work* (19th ed., Vol. 3, pp. 2168–2173). Washington, DC: NASW Press.

Lowe, S. M., & Mascher, J. (2001). The role of sexual orientation in multicultural counseling: Integrating bodies of knowledge. In J. G. Ponterotto, J. M. Casas, L. A. Suzuki, & C. M. Alexander (Eds.), *Handbook of multicultural counseling* (2nd ed., pp. 755–778). Thousand Oaks, CA: Sage.

Lum, D. (1995). Asian Americans: Chinese. In R. L. Edwards (Ed.), *Encyclopedia of social work* (19th ed., Vol. 1, pp. 238–241). Washington, DC: NASW Press.

Lum, D. (1999). *Culturally competent practice: A framework for growth and action.* Pacific Grove, CA: Brooks/Cole.

Lum, D. (2000). *Social work practice and people of color: A process-stage approach* (4th ed.). Pacific Grove, CA: Brooks/Cole.

Lum, D. (2003). *Culturally competent practice: A framework for understanding diverse groups and justice issues* (2nd ed.). Pacific Grove, CA: brooks/Cole.

Lum, D. (2004). *Social work practice and people of color: A process-stage approach* (5th ed.). Belmont, CA: Brooks/Cole.

Macarov, D. (1995). *Social welfare structure and practice.* Thousand Oaks, CA: Sage.

Macionis, J. J. (2005). *Social problems* (2nd ed.). Upper Saddle River, NJ: Prentice-Hall.

Mackelprang, R., & Salsgiver, R. (1996). *People with disabilities and social work: Historical and contemporary issues.* Social Work, 41 (1), 7–14.

Mackelprang, R., & Salsgiver, R. (1999). *Disability: A diversity model approach in human service practice.* Pacific Grove, CA: Brooks/Cole.

Mai, M. (1999, May 3). Anatomy of a massacre. *Newsweek,* 25–31.

Major, E. (2000, Winter). Self-determination and the disabled adult. *The New Social Worker,* 7 (1), 9–16.

Maluccio, A. N. (1990). Family preservation: An overview. In A. L. Sallee & J. C. Lloyd (Eds.), *Family preservation: Papers from the Institute for Social Work Educators 1990.* Riverdale, IL: National Association for Family-Based Services.

Maluccio, A. N., Pine, B. A., & Tracy, E. M. (2002). *Social work practice with families and children.* New York: Columbia.

Managed care. (1998, January). *NASW News,* 1.

Marchione, M. (2003, November 30). Mission aims to shed light on suffering abroad. *Milwaukee Journal Sentinel,* 1A, 26A.

Marcotty, J. (1999, November 11). Electroshock therapy revised. *Minnesota Star Tribune.* Retrieved April 27, 2002. www.ect.org/news/revised.htm

Marsella, A. J. (1998, June). Urbanization, mental health, and social deviancy. *American Psychologist,* 53 (6), 624–634.

Marson, S. M. (1998). Major uses of the Internet for social workers: A brief report for new users. *Arete,* 22 (2), 21–28.

Marson, S. M. (2000). Internet ethics for social workers. *The New Social Worker* 7 (3), 29–30.

Martin, J. A., Hamilton, B. E., Ventura, S. J., Menacker, F., & Park, M. M. (2002). Births: Final data for 2000. *National Vital Statistics Reports,* 50 (5). Hyattsville, MD: National Center for Health Statistics.

Martinez-Brawley, E. E. (1995). Community. In R. L. Edwards (Ed.), *Encyclopedia of social work* (19th ed., Vol. 1, pp. 539–548). Washington, DC: NASW Press.

Marx, J. D. (2004). *Social welfare: The American partnership.* Boston: Allyn & Bacon.

Mary Ellen Wilson. (1874, April 22). *New York Times,* p. 8.

Mary, N. L. (1998). Social work and the support model of services for people with developmental disabilities. *Journal of Social Work Education,* 34 (2), 247–260.

Masland, T. (2000, July 17). Breaking the silence. *Newsweek,* 30–31.

Masland, T. (2001, September 7). Hustling for corpses. *Newsweek,* 45–46.

Mather, J. H., & Lager, P. B. (2000). *Child welfare: A unifying model of practice.* Belmont, CA: Wadsworth.

Matorin, S. (1998). The corporatization of mental health services: The impact on service, training, and values. In G. Schamess & A. Lightburn (Eds.), *Human managed care?* (pp. 159–170).Washington, DC: NASW Press.

Matthews, C. R., & Lease, S. H. (2000). Focus on lesbian, gay, and bisexual families. In R. M. Perez, K. A.. DeBord, & K. J. Bieschke (Eds.), *Handbook of counseling and psychotherapy with lesbian, gay, and bisexual clients* (pp. 225–273). Washington, DC: American Psychological Association.

McAnulty, R. D., & Burnette, M. M. (2001). *Exploring human sexuality: Making healthy decisions.* Boston: Allyn & Bacon.

McAnulty, R. D., & Burnette, M. M. (2003). *Fundamentals of human sexuality: Making healthy decisions.* Boston: Allyn & Bacon.

McCammon, S. L., Know, D., & Schacht, C. (2004). *Choices in sexuality* (2nd ed.). Cincinnati, OH: Atomic Dog Publishing.

McCollum, E. E., & Trepper, T. S. (2001). *Family solutions for substance abuse.* Binghamton, NY: Haworth.

McDonald, S., & Moriarty, A. (2002). Mediation as a form of peer-based conflict resolution. In R. Constable, S. McDonald, & J. P. Flynn (Eds.), *School social work: Practice, policy, and research perspectives* (5th ed., pp. 501–514). Chicago: Lyceum.

McDonald, S., Fineran, S., Constable, R., & Moriarty, A. (2002). Creating safe and responsive schools: Bullying and peer sexual harassment. In R. Constable, S. McDonald, & J. P. Flynn (Eds.), *School social work: Practice, policy, and research perspectives* (5th ed., pp. 458–480). Chicago: Lyceum.

McGeary, J. (2001, February 12). Death stalks a continent. *Time*, 36–45.

McGee, E. (1982). *Too little, too late: Services for teenage parents.* New York: Ford Foundation.

McInnis-Dittrich, K. (1994). *Integrating social welfare policy and social work practice.* Pacific Grove, CA: Brooks/Cole.

McInnis-Dittrich, K. (2005). *Social work with elders: A biopsychosocial approach to assessment and intervention* (2nd ed.). Boston: Allyn & Bacon.

McKibben, A., Proulz, J., & Lusignan, R. (1994). Relationships between conflict, affect, and deviant sexual behaviors in rapists and pedophiles. *Behavior Research and Therapy, 32*, 571–575.

McLaughlin, L. A., & Braun, K. L. (1999). Asian and Pacific Islander cultural values: Considerations for health care decision-making. In P. L. Ewalt, E. M. Freeman, A. E. Fortune, D. l. Poole, & S. L. Witkin (Eds.), *Multicultural issues in social work: Practice and research* (pp. 321–336). Washington, DC: NASW Press.

McNeece, C. A. (1995). Adult corrections. In R. L. Edwards (Ed.), *Encyclopedia of social work* (19th ed., Vol. 1, pp. 60–68). Washington, DC: NASW Press.

McNeece, C. A., & Roberts, A. R. (2001). Adult corrections. In A. Gitterman (Ed.), *Handbook of social work practice with vulnerable and resilient populations* (2nd ed, pp. 342–366). New York: Columbia University Press.

McWhirter, J. J., McWhirter, B. T., McWhirter, E. H., & McWhirter, R. J. (2004). *At-risk youth: A comprehensive response* (3rd ed.). Belmont, CA: Brooks/Cole.

Mechanic, D. (1999). *Mental health and social policy: The emergence of managed care.* Boston: Allyn & Bacon.

Meddin, B. J. (1985). The assessment of risk in child abuse and neglect investigations. *Child Abuse and Neglect, 9*, 57–62.

Meenaghan, T. M., Kilty, K. M., & McNutt, J. G. (2004). *Social policy analysis and practice.* Chicago, IL: Lyceum.

Meier, M. S. (1990). Politics, educations, and culture. In C. McWilliams (Ed.), *North from Mexico* (rev. ed., pp. 285–308). Westport, CT: Greenwood Press.

Mercer, S. O. (1996, March). Navajo elderly people in a reservation nursing home: Admission predictors and culture care practices. *Social Work, 41* (2), 181–189.

Meyer, D. R. (1995). Supplemental Security Income. In R. L. Edwards (Ed.), *Encyclopedia of social work* (19th ed., Vol. 3, pp. 2379–2385). Washington, DC: NASW Press.

Meyer, D. R. (2001, Spring). Income support for children in the United States. *Focus, 21* (3), 38–41.

Midgley, J. (1997). *Social welfare in global context.* Thousand Oaks, CA: Sage.

Midgley, J., & Livermore, M. (1997). The developmental perspective in social work: Educational implications for a new century. *Social Work, 33* (3), 573–585.

Miller, D. W. (2001, May 18). Programs in social work embrace the teaching of spirituality. *The Chronicle of Higher Education*, A12.

Miller, M., & Katrowitz, B. (1999, January 25). Unmasking Sybil: A re-examination of the most famous psychiatric patient in history. *Newsweek*, 66–68.

Miller-Perrin, C. L., & Perrin, R. D. (1999). *Child maltreatment: An introduction.* Thousand Oaks, CA: Sage.

Mills, R. J. (2000, September). Health insurance coverage: 1999. *Current Population Reports.* Washington, DC: U.S. Government Printing Office.

Minor, M., & Dwyer, S. (1997). The psychosocial development of sex offenders: Differences between exhibitionists, child molesters, and incest offenders. *International Journal of Offenders Therapy and Comparative Criminology, 41*, 36–44.

Mish, F. C. (Ed.). (1995). *Merriam Webster's collegiate dictionary* (10th ed.). Springfield, MA: Merriam-Webster.

Mitchell, E. P., & Mitchell, H. H. (1989). Black spirituality: The values in that ol'time religion. *Journal of the Interdenominational Theological Center, 17* (1/2), 98–109.

Mokuau, N. (1995). Pacific Islanders. In R. L. Edwards (Ed.), *Encyclopedia of social work* (19th ed., Vol. 3, pp. 1795–1801). Washington, DC: NASW Press.

Money, J. (1987). Sin, sickness, or status: Homosexual gender identify and psychoneuroendocrinology. *American Psychologist, 42*, 384–399.

Mooney, L. A., Knox, D., & Schacht, C. (2002). *Understanding social problems* (3rd ed.). Belmont, CA: Wadsworth.

Mooney, L. A., Knox, D., & Schacht, C. (2005). *Understanding social problems* (4th ed.). Belmont, CA: Wadsworth.

Morales, A. T., & Sheafor, B. W. (2001). *Social work: A profession of many faces* (9th ed.). Boston: Allyn & Bacon.

Morales, A. T., & Sheafor, B. W. (2002). *The many faces of social work clients.* Boston: Allyn & Bacon.

Morales, J. (1995). Gay men: Parenting. In R. L. Edwards (Ed.), *Encyclopedia of social work* (19th ed., Vol. 2, pp. 1085–1095). Washington, DC: NASW Press.

Moreno, C. L. (2001). Developmental disabilities. In A. Gitterman (Ed.), *Handbook of social work practice with vulnerable and resilient populations* (2nd ed, pp. 205–223). New York: Columbia University Press.

Morgan, M. (2000). *Careers in criminology.* Los Angeles: Roxbury Park.

Morris, R. (1987). Social welfare policy: Trends and issues. In A. Monahan (Ed.), *Encyclopedia of social work* (Vol. 2, pp. 664–681). Silver Spring, MD: NASW Press.

Morrison, P. (2002, September 6). Loss of civil rights post-9/11 alarms Muslims, legal experts: Muslims worry about profiling, unjust detention; attorneys see link to troubling history of erosion of liberties. (September 11: a year later). *National Catholic Reporter, 38* (38), 8–9. Retrieved July 9, 2004. http://infotrac-college.thomsonlearning.com

Moxley, D. P. (1989). *The practice of case management.* Newbury Park, CA: Sage.

Murase, K. (1995). Asian Americans: Japanese. In R. L. Edwards (Ed.), *Encyclopedia of social work* (19th ed., Vol. 1, pp. 241–249). Washington, DC: NASW Press.

Mueller III., R. S. (2002, July 15). American Muslims: All Americans pulling together (Robert S. Mueller III address). *Vital Speeches of the Day, 68* (19), 480–484. Retrieved July 9, 2004. http://infotrac-college.thomsonlearning.com

Murphy, K. C. (2004). Child development. In C. R. Brittain & D. E. Hunt (Eds.), *Helping in child protective services: A competency-based casework handbook* (pp. 249–306). New York: Oxford.

Nadir, A., & Dziegielewski, S. F. (2001). Islam. In M. Van Hook, B. Hugen, & M. Aguilar (Eds.), *Spirituality within religious traditions in social work practice* (pp. 146-166). Belmont, CA: Brooks/Cole.

Naleppa, M. J., & Reid, W. J. (2003). *Gerontological social work: A task-centered approach.* New York: Columbia.

NASW joins fight for the uninsured. (2003, April). *NASW News, 48* (4), 6.

National Association of Social Workers (NASW). (1973). *Standards for social service manpower.* New York: Author.

National Association of Social Workers (NASW). (1996). *Code of ethics.* Alexandria, VA: Author.

National Association of Social Workers (NASW). (1999). *NASW code of ethics* (amended). Washington, DC: Author.

National Association of Social Workers (NASW). (2000). *Social work speaks: National Association of Social Workers Policy Statements 2000–2003* (5th ed.). Washington, DC: Author.

National Association of Social Workers. (2003). *Social work speaks: National Association of Social Workers policy statements 2003–2006.* Washington, DC: Author.

National Association of Social Workers. (2004). *Social work profession.* Retrieved July 24, 2004. http://www.socialworkers.org

National Association of Social Workers. (2005). *The power of social work.* Retrieved February 12, 2005. http://www.socialworkers.org/

National Committee for Pay Equity. (2003). Questions and answers on pay equity. In A. Kesselman, L. D. McNair, & N. Schniedewind (Eds.), *Women: Images and realities* (3rd ed., pp. 192–195). Boston: McGraw-Hill.

National Mental Health Association. (2005a). *Electroconvulsive therapy (ECT).* Retrieved January 30, 2005. http://www.nmha.org/infoctr/factsheets/ect.cfm

National Mental Health Association. (2005b). *NMHA welcomes you.* Retrieved February 12, 2005. http://www.nmha.org/

National Park Service. (n.d.). *A history of Mexican Americans in California: Introduction.* Retrieved November 20, 2004. http://www.cr.nps.gov/history/online_books/5views/5views5.htm

National Program Office on Self-Determination (NPOSD). (1998). *The Robert Wood Johnson Foundation initiative in self-determination for persons with developmental disabilities* [online]. Princeton, NJ: The Robert Wood Johnson Foundation. www.selfdetermination.org

Negroni-Rodriguez, L. K., & Morales, J. (2001). Individual and family assessment skills with Latino/Hispanic Americans. In R. Fong & S. Furuto (Eds.), *Culturally competent practice: Skills, interventions, and evaluations* (pp. 132–146). Boston: Allyn & Bacon.

Neukrug, E. (2000). *Theory, practice, and trends in human services* (2nd ed.). Pacific Grove, CA: Brooks/Cole.

Neukrug, E. (2004). *Theory, practice, and trends in human services: An introduction* (3rd ed.). Pacific Grove, CA: Brooks/Cole.

Newman, B. R., & Newman, P. R. (2003). *Development through life: A psychosocial approach* (8th ed.). Belmont, CA: Wadsworth.

Newman, C. (2000, August 10). Older, healthier and wealthier. *Washington Post,* A3.

Nichols, R., & Braun, K. L. (1996). *Death and dying in five Asian and Pacific Islander cultures: A preliminary study.* Honolulu: University of Hawaii, School of Public Health, Center on Aging.

Nichols, W. R. (Ed.). (1999). *Random House Webster's college dictionary* (2nd ed.). New York: Random House.

Nobles, W. W. (1976). African consciousness and black research: The consciousness of self. In L. M. King, V. Dixon, & W. Nobles (Eds.), *African philosophy: Assumptions and paradigms for research on black persons* (pp. 163–174). Los Angeles: Fanon Center.

Norman, E. (2000). Introduction: The strengths perspective and resiliency enhancement—A natural partnership. In E. Norman (Ed.), *Resiliency enhancement: Putting the strengths perspective into social work practice* (pp. 1–16). New York: Columbia.

O'Connor v. Donaldson, 422 U.S. 563 (1975).

Office of the Surgeon General. (2001). *Youth violence: A report of the surgeon general.* Retrieved February 6, 2005. http://www.surgeongeneral.gov/library/youthviolence/

Okazawa-Rey, M. (1998). Empowering poor communities of color: A self-help model. In L. M. Gutierrez, R. J. Parsons, & E. O. Cox (Eds.), *Empowerment in social work practice: A sourcebook.* Pacific Grove, CA: Brooks/Cole.

Okun, B. F., Fried, J., & Okun, M. L. (1999). *Understanding diversity: A learning-as-practice primer.* Pacific Grove, CA: Brooks/Cole.

O'Neill, J. V. (1999, June). Profession dominates in mental health. *NASW News,* 1, 8.

O'Neill, J. V. (1999, September). Social work turns back to the spiritual. *NASW News,* 3.

O'Neill, J. V. (2001, April). Social work labor market is a mystery. *NASW News,* 3, 4.

O'Neill, J. V. (2003, February). Private sector employs most members. *NASW News,* 8.

Orshansky, M. (1965). Measuring poverty. In *The social welfare forum: Proceedings of the 92nd annual forum of the national conference on social welfare.* New York: Columbia University Press.

Outsama, K. (1977). *Laotian themes.* New York: Center for Bilingual Education.

Pack-Brown, S. P., & Williams, C. B. (2003). *Ethics in a multicultural context.* Thousand Oaks, CA: Sage.

Padavic, I., & Reskin, B. (2004). Moving up and taking charge. In L. Richardson, V. Taylor, & N. Whittier (Eds.), *Feminist frontiers* (6th ed., pp. 209–225). Boston: McGraw-Hill.

Padilla, Y. C. (1999). Immigrant policy: Issues for social work practice. In P. L. Ewalt, E. M. Freeman, A. E. Fortune, D. L. Poole, & S. L. Witkin (Eds.), *Multicultural issues in social work: Practice and research* (pp. 589–604). Washington, DC: NASW Press.

Paniagua, F. A. (1998). *Assessing and treating culturally diverse clients: A practice guide* (2nd ed.). Thousand Oaks, CA: Sage.

Paniagua, F. A. (2005). *Assessing and treating culturally diverse clients: A practical guide* (3rd ed.). Thousand Oaks, CA: Sage.

Papalia, D. E., Olds, S. W., & Feldman, R. D. (2004). *Human development* (9th ed.). Boston: McGraw-Hill.

Paplos, D. (2002). *About ECT—Electroconvulsive therapy.* Retrieved April 27, 2002. www.medhelp.org/lib/ect.htm

Parham, T. A., & Brown, S. (2003). Therapeutic approaches with African American populations. In F. D. Harper & J. McFadden (Eds.), *Culture and counseling: New approaches* (pp. 81–98). Boston: Allyn & Bacon.

Parsons, R. D. (2001). *The ethics of professional practice.* Boston: Allyn & Bacon.

Patterson, C. J. (1995). Lesbian and gay parenthood. In M. H. Bornstein (Ed.), *Handbook of parenting: Vol. 4. Status and social conditions of parenting* (pp. 255–274). Mahwah. NJ: Erlbaum.

Patterson, L. E., & Welfel, E. R. (2000). *The counseling process* (5th ed.). Pacific Grove, CA: Brooks/Cole.

Paulus, M. D. (2000). Intervention with families. In A. A. Abbott (Ed.), *Alcohol, tobacco, and other drugs: Challenging myths, assessing theories, individualizing interventions* (pp. 305–340). Washington, DC: NASW Press.

Pawlak, E. J., Wozniak, D., & McGowen, M. (1999). Perspectives on groups for school social workers. In R. Constable, S. McDonald, & J. P. Flynn (Eds.), *School social work: Practice, policy, and research perspectives* (4th ed., pp. 356–375). Chicago: Lyceum.

Pecora, P. J., Whittaker, J. K., Maluccio, A. N., & Barth, R. P. (2000). *The child welfare challenge: Policy, practice, and research* (2nd ed.). New York: Aldine de Gruyter.

Pederson, D. (1999, July 6). Is your HMO too stingy? *Newsweek*, 56.

Perkinson, R. R. (2002). *Chemical dependency counseling: A practical guide* (2nd ed.). Thousand Oaks, CA: Sage.

Personality disorders said pervasive in U.S. (2004, November). *NASW News*, 10.

Petr, C. G. (2004). *Social work with children and their families: Pragmatic foundations* (2nd ed.). New York: Oxford.

Phillips, N. K., & Straussner, S. L. (2002). *Urban social work: An introduction to policy and practice in cities.* Boston: Allyn & Bacon.

Phillips, W. (1996). Culturally competent practice understanding Asian family values. *The Roundtable: Journal of the National Resource Center for Special Needs Adoption*, *10* (1), 1–3.

Pickett, J. P. (Ed.). (2002). *The American Heritage college dictionary* (4th ed.). Boston: Houghton Mifflin.

Pietsch, J. H., & Braun, K. L. (2000). Autonomy, advance directives, and the patient self-determination act. In K. L. Braun, J. H. Pietsch, & P. L. Blanchette (Eds.), *Cultural issues in end-of-life decision making* (pp. 37–54). Thousand Oaks, CA: Sage.

Pincus, A., & Minahan, A. (1973). *Social work practice: Model and method.* Itasca, IL: Peacock.

Pinderhughes, E. (1995). Direct practice overview. In R. L. Edwards (Ed.), *Encyclopedia of social work* (19th ed., Vol. 1, pp. 2282–2292). Washington, DC: NASW Press.

PNHP Data Update. (1997, December). *Physicians for a national health program newsletter.* www.pnhp.org.Data/dataD97.html

PNHP Data Update. (2000, September). *Physicians for a national health program newsletter.* www.pnhp.org/Press/2000/data_update0900.htm

Pollard, W. L. (1995). Civil rights. In R. L. Edwards (Ed.), *Encyclopedia of social work* (19th ed., Vol. 1, pp. 740–751). Washington, DC: NASW Press.

Popple, P. R. (1995). The social work profession: History. In R. L. Edwards (Ed.), *Encyclopedia of social work* (19th ed., Vol. 3, pp. 2282–2292). Washington, DC: NASW Press.

Popple, P. R., & Leighninger, L. (2001). *The policy-based profession: An introduction to social welfare policy analysis for social workers* (2nd ed.). Boston: Allyn & Bacon.

Popple, P. R., & Leighninger, L. (2002). *Social work, social welfare, and American society* (5th ed.). Boston: Allyn & Bacon.

Popple, P. R., & Leighninger, L. (2004). *The policy-based profession: An introduction to social welfare policy analysis for social workers* (3rd ed.). Boston: Allyn & Bacon.

Popple, P. R., & Leighninger, L. (2005). *Social work, social welfare, and American society* (6th ed.). Boston: Allyn & Bacon.

Potter, C. C. (1999). Violence and aggression in girls. In J. M. Jenson & M. O. Howard (Eds.), *Youth violence: Current research and recent practice innovations* (pp. 113–138). Washington, DC: NASW Press.

Power, C. (1998, March 16). The new Islam. *Newsweek*, 35–37.

PR Newswire. (2004, June 15). U.S. Muslims to launch national PSA campaign; Spots celebrate diversity, challenge anti-Muslim discrimination, p. NA. Retrieved July 13, 2004. http://infotrac-college.thomsonlearning.com

Practitioners surveyed: Incomes increase. (2003, February). *NASW News*, 1, 8.

Primm, A. B., Lima, B. R., & Rowe, C. L. (1996). Cultural and ethnic sensitivity. In W. R. Breakey (Ed.), *Integrated mental health services: Modern community psychiatry* (pp. 146–159). New York: Oxford University Press.

Proch, K., & Taber. M. A. (1987). Alienated adolescents in foster care. *Social Work Research & Abstracts*, 23 (2), 9–13.

Quam, J. K. (1995). Biographies: Addams, Jane (1860–1935). In R. L. Edwards (Ed.), *Encyclopedia of social work* (19th ed., Vol. 3, pp. 2571–2572). Washington, DC: NASW Press.

Quiet's Corner. (2002a). Shirley Ardell Mason's (Sybil's) obituary. Retrieved April 27, 2002. www.asarian.org/~quiet/sybilobit.html

Quiet's Corner. (2002b). Where multiple personal(ity) bodies are considered normal. Retrieved April 27, 2002. www.pooh.asarian.org/~quiet/

Quittner, J. (1997, July 7). Unshackling net speech. *Time*, pp. 28–29.

Raskin, M. S., & Daley, D. C. (1991). Assessment of addiction problems. In M. S. Raskin & D. C. Daley (Eds.), *Treating the chemically dependent and their families* (pp. 22–56). Newbury Park, CA: Sage.

Rathus, S. A., Nevid, J. S., & Fichner-Rathus, L. (2002). *Human sexuality in a world of diversity* (5th ed.). Boston: Allyn & Bacon.

Rathus, S. A., Nevid, J. S., & Fichner-Rathus, L. (2002). *Human sexuality in a world of diversity* (5th ed.). Needham Heights, MA: Allyn & Bacon.

Rawlings, L. (2000). *Poverty and income trends: 1998.* Washington, DC: Center on Budget and Policy Priorities.

Reamer, F. G. (1998). *Ethical standards in social work.* Washington, DC: NASW Press.

Reamer, F. G. (2001). *Tangled relationships: Managing boundary issues in the human services.* New York: Columbia.

Register, C. (1991). *Are those kids yours? American families with children adopted from other countries.* New York: Free Press.

Regulus, T. A. (1995). Gang violence. In R. L. Edwards (Ed.), *Encyclopedia of social work* (19th ed., Vol. 2, pp. 1045–1055). Washington, DC: NASW Press.

Reid, P. M. (1995). Social welfare history. In R. L. Edwards (Ed.), *Encyclopedia of social work* (19th ed., Vol. 3, pp. 2206–2225). Washington, DC: NASW Press.

Reiman, J. (1998). *The rich get richer and the poor get prison* (5th ed.). New York: Macmillan.

Reio, T. G., & Sanders-Reto, J. (1999). Combating workplace ageism. *Adult Learning, 11,* 10–13.

Renz-Beaulaurier, R. (1998). Empowering people with disabilities: The role of choice. In L. M. Gutierrez, R. J. Parsons, & E. O. Cox (Eds.), *Empowerment in social work practice: A sourcebook* (pp. 73–84). Pacific Grove, CA: Brooks/Cole.

Renzetti, C. M., & Curran, D. J. (2003). *Women, men, and society* (5th ed.). Boston: Allyn & Bacon.

Resnick, H. (1980a). Effecting internal change in human service organizations. In H. Resnick & R. J. Patti (Eds.), *Change from within: Humanizing social welfare organizations* (pp. 187–199). Philadelphia: Temple University Press.

Resnick, H. (1980b). Tasks in changing the organization from within. In H. Resnick & R. J. Patti (Eds.), *Change from within: Humanizing social welfare organizations* (pp. 200–216). Philadelphia: Temple University Press.

Reuters. (2005, January 8). *Democrats attack Bush's Social Security plan.* Retrieved January 8, 2005. http://www.reuters.com/printerFriendlyPopup.jhtml?type=domesticNews&storyID=7271952 .

Reynolds, R. E. (1975). Primary care, ambulatory care, and family medicine: Overlapping but not synonymous. *Journal of Medical Education, 50* (9), 893–895.

Riley, D. P. (1995). Family life education. In R. L. Edwards (Ed.), *Encyclopedia of social work* (19th ed., Vol. 2, pp. 960–965). Washington, DC: NASW Press.

Roberts, A. R. (1995). Victim services and victim/witness assistance programs. In R. L. Edwards (Ed.), *Encyclopedia of social work* (19th ed., Vol. 3, pp. 2440–2444). Washington, DC: NASW Press.

Robinson, S., & Palus, N. (2001, April 30). An awful human trade. *Time,* 40–41.

Robison, W., & Reeser, L. C. (2000). *Ethical decision making in social work.* Boston: Allyn & Bacon.

Rochefort, D. A. (1993). *From poor houses to homelessness: Policy analysis and mental health care.* Westport, CT: Auburn House.

Roffman, R. A. (1987). Drug use and abuse. In *Encyclopedia of social work* (18th ed., vol. 1, pp. 477–487). Silver Spring, MD: National Association of Social Workers.

Romsdahl, I. (1997, April 27). *Sybil: Multiple personalities manufactured.* Retrieved April 27, 2002. www.mankato.msus.edu/dept/reporter/reparchive/04_27_97/news3.html

Rosen, B. J. (1981). How workers use cues to determine child abuse. *Social Work Research and Abstracts, 17,* 27–33.

Rothman, J. (2001). Approaches to community intervention. In J. Rothman, J. L. Erlich, & J. E. Tropman (Eds.), *Strategies of community intervention* (6th ed., pp. 27–64). Pacific Grove, CA: Brooks/Cole.

Rothman, J. C. (2003). *Social work practice across disability.* Boston: Allyn & Bacon.

Rycus, J. S., Hughes R. C., & Ginther, N. (1988). *Separation and placement in child protective services: A training curriculum.* Washington, DC: Child Welfare League of America.

Sabbatini, R. M. E. (2002). *The history of shock therapy in psychiatry.* Retrieved April 28, 2002. www.epub.org.br/cm/n04/historia/shock_i/htm

Sackheim, H. A., Devanand, D. P., & Nobler, M. S. (2002). *Electroconvulsive therapy.* Retrieved April 28, 2002. www.acrip.org/g4/GN401000108 /CH106.html

Saleebey, D. (2002a). Introduction: Power in the people. In D. Saleebey (Ed.), *The strengths perspective in social work practice* (3rd ed., pp. 80–94). Boston: Allyn & Bacon.

Saleebey, D. (2002b). The strengths approach to practice. In D. Saleebey (Ed.), *The strengths perspective in social work practice* (3rd ed., pp. 80–94). Boston: Allyn & Bacon.

Sands, R. G. (1991). *Clinical social work practice in community mental health.* New York: Macmillan.

Santiago-Rivera, A. L., Arredondo, P., & Gallardo-Cooper, M. (2002). *Counseling Latinos and la familia: A practical guide.* Thousand Oaks, CA: Sage.

Santrock, J. W. (1999). *Life-span development* (7th ed.). Boston: McGraw-Hill.

Santrock, J. W. (2004). *Life-span development* (9th ed.). Boston: McGraw-Hill.

Sapiro, V. (2003). *Women in American society* (5th ed.). Boston: McGraw-Hill.

Saunders, D. N. (1995). Substance abuse: Federal, state, and local policies. In R. L. Edwards (Ed.), *Encyclopedia of social work* (19th ed., Vol. 3, pp. 2338–2347). Washington, DC: NASW Press.

Schneider, R. L., & Lester, L. (2001). *Social work advocacy.* Pacific Grove, CA: Brooks/Cole.

Schram, B., & Mandell, B. R. (2000). *An introduction to human services* (4th ed.). Boston: Allyn & Bacon.

Schwartz, W. (1961). The social worker in the group. In W. Schwartz (Ed.), *New perspectives on services to groups: Theory, organization, practice* (pp. 104–111). New York: National Association of Social Workers.

Sciarra, D. T. (2001). School counseling in a multicultural society. In J. G. Ponterotto, J. M. Casas, L. A. Suzuki, & C. M. Alexander (Eds.), *Handbook of multicultural counseling* (2nd ed., pp. 701–728). Thousand Oaks, CA: Sage.

Sciarra, D. T. (2004). *School counseling: Foundations and contemporary issues.* Belmont, CA: Brooks/Cole.

Seaward, B. L. (2004). *Managing stress: Principles and strategies for health and well-being* (4th ed.). Boston: Jones and Bartlett.

Seeman, T. E., & Adler, N. (1998, Spring). Older Americans: Who will they be? *National Forum,* 22–25.

Segal, E., & Brzuzy, S. (1995). Women actors for women's issues. In N. Van Den Bergh (Ed.), *Feminist practice in the 21st century* (pp. 143–157). Washington, DC: NASW Press.

Segal, E., & Brzuzy, S. (1998). *Social welfare, policy, programs, and practice.* Itasca, IL: Peacock.

Segal, E. A., Gerdes, K. E., & Steiner, S. (2004). *Social work: An introduction to the profession.* Belmont, CA: Brooks/Cole.

Shapiro, J. P. (1995, September 11). Who cares how high her IQ really is? *U.S. News & World Report,* 59.

Shapiro, J. P. (1999, April 5). No time for the poor. *U.S. News & World Report,* 57.

Shapiro, J. P. (1999, October 18). Congress seeks the right Rx. *U.S. News & World Report,* 32.

Shapiro v. Thompson, 364 U.S. 618 (1969).

Sharf, R. S. (2000). *Theories of psychotherapy and counseling: Concepts and cases* (2nd ed.). Belmont, CA: Wadsworth.

Shaw, S. M., & Lee, J. (2004). *Women's voices, feminist visions: Classic and contemporary readings* (2nd ed.). Boston: McGraw-Hill.

Sheafor, B. W., & Horejsi, C. R. (2003). *Techniques and guidelines for social work practice* (6th ed.). Boston: Allyn & Bacon.

Sheafor, B. W., & Landon, P. S. (1987). Generalist perspective. In R. L. Edwards (Ed.), *Encyclopedia of social work* (19th ed., Vol. 1, pp. 660–669). Washington, DC: NASW Press.

Sheler, J. L. (2001, October 29). Muslim in America. *U.S. News & World Report,* 50–52.

Shernoff, M. (1995). Gay men: Direct practice. In R. L. Edwards (Ed.), *Encyclopedia of social work* (19th ed., Vol. 2, pp. 1075–1085). Washington, DC: NASW Press.

Simpson, C., & Simpson, D. (1992). *Exploring careers in social work.* New York: Rosen.

Singh, S., & Darroch, J. E. (2000). Adolescent pregnancy and childbearing: Levels and trends in developing countries. *Family Planning Perspectives, 32* (1), 14–23.

Siporin, M. (1975). *Introduction to social work practice.* New York: Macmillan.

Slattery, J. M. (2004). *Counseling diverse clients: Bringing context into therapy.* Pacific Grove, CA: Brooks/Cole.

Sloan, A. (2000, July 3). The social security crackup. *Newsweek,* pp. 18–23.

Smith, R. F. (1995). Settlements and neighborhood centers. In R. L. Edwards (Ed.), *Encyclopedia of social work* (19th ed., Vol. 3, pp. 2129–2135). Washington, DC: NASW Press.

Smith, S. L., & Howard, J. A. (1999). *Promoting successful adoptions: Practice with troubled families.* Thousand Oaks, CA: Sage.

Smolowe, J. (1995, July 31). Noble aims, mixed results. *Time,* 54–55.

Snowden, L. R. (2000). The new world of practice in physical and mental health: Comorbidity, cultural competence, and managed care. In P. Allen-Meares & C. Garvin (Eds.), *The handbook of social work direct practice.* Thousand Oaks, CA: Sage.

Snowden, L. R., & Cheung, F. K. (1990). Use of inpatient mental health services by members of ethnic minority groups. *American Psychologist, 45,* 347–355.

Social Security Administration. (2005, January 7). *Monthly statistical snapshot.* Retrieved January 7, 2005. http://www.ssa.gov/policy/docs/quickfacts/stat_snapshot/index.html

Sohng, S. S. L., & Weatherley, R. (1999). Practical approaches to conducting and using research in the schools. In R. Constable, S. McDonald, & J. P. Flynn (Eds.), *School social work: Practice, policy, and research perspectives* (4th ed., pp. 521–537). Chicago: Lyceum.

Solomon, B. B. (2002). Social work practice with African Americans. In A. T. Morales & B. W. Sheafor (Eds.), *The many faces of social work clients* (pp. 295–315). Boston: Allyn & Bacon.

Spencer, M. S. (1999). Reducing racism in schools: Moving beyond the rhetoric. In P. L. Ewalt, E. M. Freeman, A. E. Fortune, D. L. Poole, & S. L. Witkin (Eds.), *Multicultural issues in social work: Practice and research* (pp. 151–163). Washington, DC: NASW Press.

Spragins, E. E. (1998, September 28). Does managed care work? *Newsweek,* 61–66.

Spragins, E. E. (1999, March 1). What are they hiding? *Newsweek,* 74.

Stahlman, S. D., & Kisor, A. J. (2000). Nursing homes. In R. L. Schneider, N. P. Kropf, & A. J. Kisor (Eds.), *Gerontological social work: Knowledge, service settings, and special populations* (2nd ed., pp. 225–254). Pacific Grove, CA: Brooks/Cole.

Staples, L. H. (2004). In C. D. Garvin, L. M. Gutierrez, & M. J. Galinsky (Eds.), *Handbook of social work with groups* (pp. 344–359). New York: Guilford.

Starbuck, D., Howell, J. C., & Lindquist, D. (2001, December). *Hybrid and other modern gangs.* Bulletin of the Office of Juvenile Justice and Delinquency Prevention. Washington, DC: U.S. Department of Justice, Office of Justice Programs.

Stein, J. A. (1995). *Residential treatment of adolescents & children: Issues, principles, and techniques.* Chicago: Nelson-Hall.

Stelzer, I. M. (2005, January 17). *Social Security snares and delusions.* Retrieved January 8, 2005. http://www.weeklystandard.com/Utilities/printer_preview.asp?idArticle=5112&R=C3BC1E . . .

Strong, B., DeVault, C., Sayad, B. W., & Yarber, W. L. (2005). *Human sexuality: Diversity in contemporary America* (5th ed.). Boston: McGraw-Hill.

Stroup, H. (1986). *Social welfare pioneers.* Chicago: Nelson-Hall.

Sue, D. W. (1992). The challenge of multiculturalism: The road less traveled. *American Counselor, 1* (1), 6–15.

Sue, D. W., Carter, R. T., Casas, J. M., Fouad, N. A., Ivey, A. E., Jensen, M., LaFromboise, T., Manese, J. E., Ponterotto, J. G., & Vazquez-Nutall, E. (1998). *Multicultural counseling competencies: Individual and organizational development.* Thousand Oaks, CA: Sage.

Sue, S. W., & Sue, D. (1999). *Counseling the culturally different: Theory and practice* (3rd ed.). New York: Wiley.

Suppes, M. A., & Wells, C. C. (2000). *The social work experience: An introduction to social work and social welfare* (3rd ed.). Boston: McGraw-Hill.

Suppes, M. A., & Wells, C. C. (2003). *The social work experience: An introduction to social work and social welfare* (4th ed.). Boston: McGraw-Hill.

Survey data show earnings increased. (2004, October). *NASW News,* 1, 8.

Sussman, L. K., Robins, L. N., & Earls, F. (1987). Treatment-seeking for depression by black and white Americans. *Social Science and Medicine, 24,* 187–196.

Swigonski, M. E. (1995, Winter). Claiming a lesbian identity as an act of empowerment. *Affilia, 10* (4).

Syme, G. (2003). *Dual relationships in counseling & psychotherapy.* Thousand Oaks, CA: Sage.

Taylor-Brown, S. (1995). HIV/AIDS: Direct practice. In R. L. Edwards (Ed.), *Encyclopedia of social work* (19th ed., Vol. 2, pp. 1291–1305). Washington, DC: NASW Press.

The horror of electroshock therapy. (2000, March 1). *Extra: Daily News.* Retrieved April 27, 2002. extratv. warnerbros.com.cmp/spotlight/2000/03_01b.htm

Thomas, M. (2000). Abstinence-based programs for prevention of adolescent pregnancies. *Journal of Adolescent Health, 26,* 5–17.

Tice, C. J., & Perkins, K. (2002). *The faces of social policy: A strengths perspective.* Pacific Grove, CA: Brooks/Cole.

Torres-Gil, F. M., & Puccinelli, M. A. (1995). Aging: Public policy issues and trends. In R. L. Edwards (Ed.), *Encyclopedia of social work* (19th ed., Vol. 1, pp. 159–164). Washington, DC: NASW Press.

Toseland, R. W. (1995). Aging: Direct practice. In R. L. Edwards (Ed.), *Encyclopedia of social work* (19th ed., Vol. 1, pp. 153–159). Washington, DC: NASW Press.

Toseland, R. W., & Rivas, R. F. (2005). *An introduction to group work practice* (5th ed.). Boston: Allyn & Bacon.

Tower, C. C. (1989). *Understanding child abuse and neglect.* Needham Heights, MA: Allyn & Bacon.

Tower, K. D. (1994, March). Consumer-centered social work practice: Restoring client self-determination. *Social Work 39* (2), 191–196.

Tracy, E. M. (1995). Family preservation and home-based services. In R. L. Edwards (Ed.), *Encyclopedia of social work* (19th ed., Vol. 2, pp. 973–983). Washington, DC: NASW Press.

Tracy, E. M. (2002). Working with and strengthening social networks. In A. R. Roberts & G. J. Greene (Eds.), *Social workers' desk reference* (pp. 402–405). New York: Oxford.

Tracy, E. M., Haapala, D. A., Kinney, J. M., & Pecora, P. J. (1991). Intensive family preservation services: A strategic response to families in crisis. In E. M. Tracy, D. A. Haapala, J. M. Kinney, & P. J. Pecora (Eds.), *Intensive family preservation services: An instructional sourcebook.* Cleveland, OH: Case Western Reserve University.

Tracy, M. B., & Ozawa, M. N. (1995). Social Security. In R. L. Edwards (Ed.), *Encyclopedia of social work* (19th ed., Vol. 3, pp. 2186–2195). Washington, DC: NASW Press.

Trattner, W. I. (1999). *From poor law to welfare state: A history of social welfare in America* (6th ed.). New York: Free Press.

Treguer, A. (1992). The Chicanos—Muralists with a message. *UNESCO Courier, 45,* 22–24.

Trower, P., Casey, A., & Dryden, W. (1988). *Cognitive-behavioral counseling in action.* Thousand Oaks, CA: Sage.

Tully, C. T. (2000). *Lesbians, gays, and the empowerment perspective.* New York: Columbia University Press.

Tully, C. T. (2001). Gay and lesbian persons. In A. Gitterman (Ed.), *Handbook of social work practice with vulnerable and resilient populations* (2nd ed, pp. 582–627). New York: Columbia University Press.

U.S. Census Bureau. (2003). *Statistical abstract of the United States: 2003* (123rd ed.). Washington, DC: Author.

U.S. Census Bureau. (2004). *Statistical abstract of the United States: 2003* (123rd ed.). Washington, DC: Author.

U.S. Department of Health & Human Services (USDHHS). (n.d.). *The facts about upcoming new benefits in Medicare.* Retrieved January 9, 2005. http://medicare.gov/

U.S. Department of Health & Human Services (USDHHS). (1999). *Mental health: A report of the Surgeon General—Executive summary.* Rockville, MD: Author. www.nimh.nih.gov

U.S. Department of Health & Human Services (USDHHS). (2004, February). *HIV vaccines explained.* Retrieved January 29, 2005. http://www.niaid.nih.gov/daids/vaccine/default.htm

U.S. Department of Health and Human Services, Children's Bureau. (1998). *Child maltreatment 1996: Reports from the states to the National Child Abuse and Neglect Data System.* Washington, DC: U.S. Government Printing Office.

U.S. Department of Justice Community Relations Service. (2001, December). *Hate crime: The violence of intolerance.* Retrieved February 5, 2005. http://www.usdoj.gov/crs/pubs/crs_pub_hate_crime_bulletin_1201.htm

U.S. Department of Justice Office of Justice Programs. (2005, February 3). *Corrections statistics.* Retrieved February 5, 2005. www.ojp.usdoj.gov/bjs/correct.htm

U.S. National Archives & Records Administration. (n.d.). Retrieved November 21, 2004. http://www.archives.gov/digital_classroom/lessons/treaty_of_guadalupe_hidalgo/treaty_of_guadalupe_hidalgo.html

U.S. National Center for Health Statistics. (2003). Deaths: Preliminary data for 2001. *National Vital Statistics Reports, 51* (4), 17.

U.S. Office of the Surgeon General, Report on Mental Health. (2001). *Adults and mental health treatment of mood disorders.* Retrieved April 28, 2002. www.loren.bennett.org/osgtreat.htm

U.S. Psychiatric Rehabilitation Association (USPRA). (2004). *Who we are.* Retrieved February 12, 2005. http://www.iapsrs.org/

Uba, L. (1994). *Asian Americans: Personality patterns, identity, and mental health.* New York: Guilford Press.

Uhlenberg, P. (2000). Integration of young and old. *The Gerontologist 40,* 276–279.

Vallianatos, C. (2001, January). Managed care is faulted. *NASW News, 46* (1), 7.

Vallianatos, C. (2001, May). Profession extolled on Hill. *NASW News, 46* (5), 1.

Vallianatos, C. (2001, July). Programs keep the peace among teens. *NASW News, 46* (7), 3.

Van Arsdale, S. (2002, January 8). Sybil: Famous multiple-personality case was stranger in our midst. *Ace Weekly.* Retrieved April 27, 2002. www.aceweekly.com/Backissues_ACEWeekly/010802/cover_story010802.html

Van Den Bergh, N. (1995). Employee assistance programs. In R. L. Edwards (Ed.), *Encyclopedia of social work* (19th ed., Vol. 1, pp. 842–849). Washington, DC: NASW Press.

Van Den Bergh, N., & Cooper, L. B. (1987). Feminist social work. In A. Monahan (Ed.), *Encyclopedia of social work* (Vol. 1, pp. 610–618). Washington, DC: NASW Press.

Van Wormer, K., & Davis, D. R. (2003). *Addiction treatment: A strengths perspective.* Pacific Grove, CA: Brooks/Cole.

Vandivort-Warren, R. (1998). How social workers can manage managed care. In G. Schamess & A. Lightburn (Eds.), *Human managed care?* (pp. 255–267). Washington, DC: NASW Press

Velleman, R. (2001). *Counseling for alcohol problems* (2nd ed.). Thousand Oaks, CA: Sage.

Voices of Experience. (2002). *Electroshock therapy: Firstperson stories from our community.* Retrieved April 27, 2002. bipolar.about.com/library/uc/uc-shock1.htm

Waller, M. (2002, June 15). *TANF reauthorization: Options and opportunities.* The Brookings Institution. Retrieved January 12, 2005. http://www.brook.edu/index.htm

Walsh, J., & Bentley, K. J. (2002). Psychopharmacology basics. In A. R. Roberts & G. J. Greene (Eds.), *Social workers' desk reference* (pp. 646–651). New York: Oxford.

Watkins, M. L. (2002). Listening to girls: A study in resilience. In R. R. Greene (Ed.), *Resiliency: An integrated approach to practice, policy, and research* (pp. 115–131). Washington, DC: NASW Press.

Watkins, S. A. (1990). The Mary Ellen myth: Correcting child welfare history. *Social Work, 35* (6), 500–503.

Watkins, T. R. (2004). Natural helping networks: Assets for rural communities. In T. L. Scales & C. L. Streeter (Eds.), *Rural social work: Building and sustaining community assets* (pp. 65–76). Belmont, CA: Brooks/Cole.

Weatherley, R. A., & Cartoof, V. G. (1988). Helping single adolescent parents. In C. Chilman, E. Nunnally, & F. Cox (Eds.), *Variant family forms.* Newbury Park, CA: Sage.

Weaver, H. N. (2003). Cultural competence with First Nations Peoples. In D. Lum (Ed.), *Culturally competent practice: A framework for understanding diverse groups and justice issues* (2nd ed., pp. 197–216). Pacific Grove, CA: Brooks/Cole.

Weaver, H. N. (2005). *Explorations in cultural competence: Journeys to the four directions.* Pacific Grove, CA: Brooks/Cole.

Webster.edu. (2005). *Mary Ellen Richmond.* Retrieved June 14, 2005. http://www.webster.edu/~woolflm/richmond.html

Wegscheider, S. (1981). *Another chance: Hope and health for the alcoholic family.* Palo Alto, CA: Science Behavior Books.

Weinbach, R. W., & Kuehner, K. M. (1985). Selecting the provider of continuing education for child welfare agencies. *Child Welfare, 64,* 477–488.

Weiner, T. (2001, January 5). Terrific news in Mexico City: Air is sometimes breathable. *The New York Times.* www.nytimes.com/2001/01/05/world/05MEXI.html

Weismiller, T., & Rome, S. H. (1995). Social workers in politics. In R. L. Edwards (Editor-in-Chief), *Encyclopedia of social work* (19th ed., vol. 3), 2305–2313.

Wernet, S. P. (1999). Introduction to managed care in human services. In S. P. Wernet (Ed.), *Managed care in human services.* Chicago: Lyceum.

Westheimer, R. K., & Lopater, S. (2005). *Human sexuality: A psychosocial perspective* (2nd ed.). Baltimore, MD: Lippincott, Williams & Wilkins.

Whitaker, J. K., & Garbarino, J. (1983). *Social support networks: Informal helping in the human services.* New York: Aldine de Gruyter.

Whitaker, W. H. S. (2003, Winter). Medicare prescription drug legislation is bad medicine for seniors. *Acosa, 17* (4), 8–9.

White House. (2005a). *4. Modernize and reform Social Security.* Retrieved January 8, 2005. http://www.whitehouse.gov/news/usbudget/blueprint/bud04.html

White House. (2005b). *5. Modernize and reform Medicare.* Retrieved January 8, 2005. http://www.whitehouse.gov/news/usbudget/blueprint/bud04.html

Whitelaw, K. (2003, July 21). In death's shadow. *U.S. News & World Report,* 17–20.

Whiteman, V. L. (2001). *Social Security: What every human services professional should know.* Boston: Allyn & Bacon.

Whittal, M. L., Agras, W. S., & Gould, R. A. (1999). Bulimia nervosa: A meta-analysis of psychosocial and pharmacological treatments. *Behavior Therapy, 30* (1), 117–135.

Wilensky, H. L., & Lebeaux, C. N. (1965). *Industrial society and social welfare.* New York: Free Press.

Williams, J. H., & Van Dorn, R. A. (1999). Delinquency, gangs, and youth violence. In J. M. Jenson & M. O. Howard (Eds.), *Youth violence: Current research and recent practice innovations* (pp. 199–225). Washington, DC: NASW Press.

Williams, M. (1999, April 25). Diary reveals school attack "timeline." *Milwaukee Journal Sentinel,* 1A, 18A.

Wilson, Mary Ellen (1874, April 22). *The New York Times,* 8.

Wimberly, E. P. (1991). *African American pastoral care.* Nashville, TN: Abingdon Press.

Winkelman, M. (1999). *Ethnic sensitivity in social work practice.* Dubuque, IA: Eddie Bowers.

Winslow, C. E. A. (1920, March). The untilled field of public health. *Modern Medicine 2,* 183–191.

Winton, M. A., & Mara, B. A. (2001). *Child abuse and neglect: Multidisciplinary approaches.* Boston: Allyn & Bacon.

Wirth, L. (1945). The problem of minority groups. In R. Linton (Ed.), *The science of man in the world crisis* (pp. 347–372). New York: Columbia University Press.

Wolock, I., & Horowitz, B. (1984). Child maltreatment as a social problem: The neglect of neglect. *American Journal of Orthopsychiatry, 54* (4), 530–543.

Women in History. (2005, June 14). *Jane Addams biography.* Lakewood Public Library. Retrieved June 14, 2005. http://www.lkwdpl.org/wihohio/adda-jan.htm

Wong, M. G. (1988). The Chinese American family. In C. H. Midel, R. W. Habenstein, & R. Wright, Jr. (Eds.), *Ethnic families in America: Patterns and variations.* New York: Elsevier.

Wood, K. M., & Dunn, P. C. (2000). Criteria for selecting theories and models for ATOD practice. In A. A. Abbott (Ed.), *Alcohol, tobacco, and other drugs: Challenging myths, assessing theories, individualizing interventions* (pp. 20–43). Washington, DC: NASW Press.

Woodman, N. J. (1995). Lesbians: Direct practice. In R. L. Edwards (Ed.), *Encyclopedia of social work* (19th ed., Vol. 2, pp. 1597–1604). Washington, DC: NASW Press.

Woodruff, D. S. (1985). Arousal, sleep, and aging. In J. E. Birren & K. W. Schaie (Eds.), *Handbook of the psychology of aging* (2nd ed., pp. 261–295). New York: Van Nostrand Reinhold.

Woodward, K. L., & Johnson, P. (1995, December 11). The advent of Kwanzaa: Will success spoil an African-American fest? *Newsweek,* 88.

Wyatt v. Stickney, 324 F. Supp. 781 (1971).

Yager, J. (1999). *Creative time management for the new millennium.* Stamford, CT: Hannacroix Creek Books.

Yamashiro, G., & Matsuoka, J. K. (1997). Help-seeking among Asian and Pacific Americans: A multiperspective analysis. *Social Work, 42* (2), 176–186.

Yamashiro, G., & Matsuoka, J. K. (1999). Help-seeking among Asian and Pacific Americans: A multiperspective analysis. In P. L. Ewalt, E. M. Freeman, A. E. Fortune, D. L. Poole, & S. L. Witkin (Eds), *Multicultural issues in social work: Practice and research* (pp. 458–472). Washington, DC: NASW Press.

Yeo, G., & Hikoyeda, N. (2000). Cultural issues in end-of-life decision making among Asians and Pacific Islanders in the United States. In K. L. Braun, J. H. Pietsch, & P. L. Blanchette (Eds.), *Cultural issues in end-of-life decision making* (pp. 101–125). Thousand Oaks, CA: Sage.

Yessian, M. R., & Broskowski, A. (1983). Generalists in human service systems: Their problems and prospects. In R. M. Kramer & H. Specht (Eds.), *Readings in community organization practice* (pp. 180–197). Englewood Cliffs, NJ: Prentice-Hall.

Yung, B., & Hammond, R. (1998). Breaking the cycle: A culturally sensitive violence prevention program for African-American children. In L. Lutzker (Ed.), *Handbook of child abuse research and treatments.* New York: Plenum Press.

Zastrow, C. (2004). *Introduction to social work and social welfare* (8th ed.). Pacific Grove, CA: Brooks/Cole.

Zastrow, C., & Kirst-Ashman, K. K. (2004). *Understanding human behavior and the social environment* (6th ed.). Pacific Grove, CA: Brooks/Cole.

Zhang, W. (2003). Use with care: Culturally incorrect attending can be rude. In A. E. Ivey & M. B. Ivey (Eds.), *Intentional interviewing and counseling: Facilitating client development in a multicultural society* (5th ed., p. 47). Pacific Grove, CA: Brooks/Cole.

Zuckerman, M. B. (1999, March 15). Don't go it alone. *U.S. News & World Report,* 76.

Zuniga, M. E. (1995). Aging: Social work practice. In R. L. Edwards (Ed.), *Encyclopedia of social work* (19th ed., Vol. 1, pp. 173–183). Washington, DC: NASW Press.

NAME INDEX

512

SUBJECT INDEX